ESSAYS ON WOMEN IN EARLIEST CHRISTIANITY

VOLUME TWO

Edited by

Carroll D. Osburn

ESSAYS ON WOMEN IN EARLIEST CHRISTIANITY

VOLUME TWO

Edited by

Carroll D. Osburn

COLLEGE PRESS
PUBLISHING COMPANY
Joplin, Missouri

Copyright © 1995 College Press Publishing Company

Printed and Bound in the United States

Library of Congress Catalog Card Number: 93-73234
International Standard Book Number: 0-89900-734-1

Contents

Editor's Preface xii

1. In the Beginning: Male and Female (Gen 1-3) 1
   Rick R. Marrs

2. Sarah—Her Life and Legacy 37
   Jack W. Vancil

3. Deborah—Judge, Prophetess, Military Leader, and
   Mother in Israel 69
   Charme E. Robarts

4. "Wise Women" in the Bible: Identifying a Trajectory . 87
   Michael S. Moore

5. Huldah and Other Biblical Prophetesses 105
   John T. Willis

6. Mate, Mother, and Metaphor: Gomer and Israel in
   Hosea 1-3 125
   Timothy M. Willis

7. The Capable Wife (Prov 31:10-31) 155
   Jack P. Lewis

8. A Note on Luke 18:29-30 181
   John McRay and Carroll D. Osburn

9. Women in the Gospel of John 197
   Frank Wheeler

10. ΥΠΑΝΔΡΟΣ—Subordination of Women
    in Rom 7:2 225
    James C. Walters

11. 1 Cor 7:4—Authority over the Body 239
    Robert F. Hull, Jr.

Contents

12. Priscilla and Aquila—Co-Workers in Christ 261
    Wendell Willis

13. Women and Prophecy in the Corinthian Church .. 277
    Gary Selby

14. 1 Cor 11:2-16—Public or Private? 307
    Carroll D. Osburn

15. Was Sarah a Believer? Reflections on
    Hebrews 11:11 317
    James Thompson

16. Tertullian—Against Women? 331
    Earl Lavender

17. Women Ministers in Constantinian Christianity ... 357
    Frederick W. Norris

18. Women in the European Middle Ages 375
    Dale Pauls

19. The Problem of Credulity of Women in the
    History of Christian Thought .... .401
    Gerald C. Tiffin

20. Gender Roles and Conservative Churches:
    1870-1930 443
    Kathy J. Pulley

21. The Cult of True Womanhood and the Disciple
    Path to Female Preaching 485
    Fred A. Bailey

22. The Role of Women in the New Testament
    Doctrine of Ministry 519
    Allan J. McNicol

23. Women in the Church: The Hermeneutical Problem 545
    Thomas H. Olbricht

Contents

Appendix 1: Practical Implications of a Change in the Role of Women 571
Bill Love

Appendix 2: Faith and Gender: Reflections on Discussions at the Stamford Church of Christ 579
Dale Pauls

Appendix 3: Reflections on the "Women's Issue" at Meadowbrook Church, Jackson, MS 587
David B. Jackson

Indexes 595

Participants

Fred A. Bailey, Ph.D., University of Tennessee; Professor of History, Abilene Christian University

Robert F. Hull, Jr., Ph.D., Princeton Theological Seminary; Professor of New Testament, Emmanuel School of Religion

David B. Jackson, D.Min., Abilene Christian University; Minister, Meadowbrook Church of Christ, Jackson, MS

Earl Lavender, Ph.D., Saint Louis University; Minister, Harpeth Hills Church of Christ, Nashville, TN

Jack P. Lewis, Ph.D., Harvard University; Ph.D., Hebrew Union College; Emeritus Professor of Bible, Harding University Graduate School of Religion

Bill Love, Ph.D., Louisiana State University; Minister, Bering Drive Church of Christ, Houston, TX

Rick R. Marrs, Ph.D., the Johns Hopkins University; Professor of Religion, Pepperdine University

Allan J. McNicol, Ph.D., Vanderbilt University; A. B. Cox Professor of New Testament and Biblical Theology, Institute for Christian Studies, Austin, TX

John McRay, Ph.D., University of Chicago; Professor of New Testament and Archaeology, Coordinator of Graduate Theological Studies, Wheaton Graduate School

Michael S. Moore, Ph.D., Drew University; Adjunct Assistant Professor of Old Testament, Fuller Theological Seminary in Arizona

Frederick W. Norris, Ph.D., Yale University; Dean E. Walker Professor of Church History and Professor of Christian Doctrine, Emmanuel School of Religion

Thomas H. Olbricht, Ph.D., University of Iowa; Distinguished Professor of Religion, Pepperdine University

Participants

Carroll D. Osburn, Ph.D., University of St. Andrews (Scot.), D.Min., Vanderbilt University; Carmichael-Walling Distinguished Professor of Greek and New Testament, Abilene Christian University

Dale Pauls, M.Th., Harding Graduate School of Religion; M.A., Ph.D. (cand.), New York University; Minister, Church of Christ, Stamford, CT

Kathy J. Pulley, Ph.D., Boston University; Associate Professor of Religious Studies, Southwest Missouri State University

Charme E. Robarts, M.A. (cand.), Abilene Christian University

Gary Selby, Ph.D. (cand.), University of Maryland; Minister, Church of Christ, Columbia, MD

James Thompson, Ph.D., Vanderbilt University, Professor of New Testament, Abilene Christian University

Gerald C. Tiffin, Ph.D., Stanford University; Dean and Professor of Social Sciences, Pacific Christian College

Jack W. Vancil, Ph.D., the Dropsie College for Hebrew and Cognate Learning; Minister, Church of Christ, Hammonton, NJ

James C. Walters, Ph.D., Boston University; Resident Research Fellow, *Heartbeat*

Frank Wheeler, Ph.D., Baylor University; Associate Professor of Bible, York College

John T. Willis, Ph.D., Vanderbilt University; Coffman Distinguished Professor of Old Testament, Abilene Christian University

Timothy M. Willis, Ph.D., Harvard University; Associate Professor of Religion, Pepperdine University

Wendell Willis, Ph.D., Southern Methodist University; Associate Professor of New Testament, Abilene Christian University

Abbreviations

AB	Anchor Bible
ABD	D. N. Freedman (ed.), *Anchor Bible Dictionary*
AcOr	*Acta Orientalia*
ACW	Ancient Christian Writers
ANET	Ancient Near-Eastern Texts
ANF	Ante-Nicene Fathers
ANRW	*Aufstieg und Niedergang der römischen Welt*
ATAT	Arbeiten zu Text und Sprache im Alten Testament
AUSS	*Andrews University Seminary Studies*
BA	*Biblical Archaeologist*
BAGD	W. Bauer, W. F. Arndt, F. W. Gingrich, and F. W. Danker, *Greek-English Lexicon of the NT*
BASOR	Bulletin of the American Schools of Oriental Research
BETL	Bibliotheca ephemeridum theologicarum lovaniensium
BHS	*Biblia Hebraica Stuttgartensia*
Bib	*Biblica*
BibRev	*Bible Review*
BJRL	*Bulletin of the John Rylands University Library of Manchester*
BJS	Brown Judaic Studies
BSac	*Bibliotheca Sacra*
BTB	*Biblical Theology Bulletin*
BWANT	Beiträge zur Wissenschaft vom Alten und Neuen Testament
BZ	*Biblische Zeitschrift*
BZAW	Beihefte zur ZAW
BZNW	Beihefte zur ZNW
CBQ	*Catholic Biblical Quarterly*
ConBNT	Coniectanea Neotestamentica, New Testament
DACL	*Dictionairre d'archéologie chrétienne et de liturgie*
Ebib	Etudes bibliques
EvQ	*Evangelical Quarterly*
EvT	*Evangelische Theologie*
ExpB	Expositor's Bible
FOTL	Forms of the Old Testament Literature
GKC	Gesenius' Hebrew Grammar

Abbreviations

GTJ	*Grace Theological Journal*
HAR	*Hebrew Annual Review*
HBT	*Horizons in Biblical Theology*
HKNT	Handkommentar zum Neuen Testament
HNT	Handbuch zum Neuen Testament
HSM	Harvard Semitic Monographs
HR	*History of Religions*
HTKNT	Herders theologischer Kommentar zum Neuen Testament
HTR	*Harvard Theological Review*
HUCA	Hebrew Union College Annual
ICC	International Critical Commentary
IDB	Interpreter's Dictionary of the Bible
Int	*Interpretation*
ISBE	G.W. Bromiley (ed.), *International Standard Bible Encyclopedia*, rev.
JAAR	*Journal of the American Academy of Religion*
JB	A. Jones (ed.), *Jerusalem Bible*
JBL	*Journal of Biblical Literature*
JBR	*Journal of Bible and Religion*
JETS	*Journal of the Evangelical Theological Society*
JJS	*Journal of Jewish Studies*
JNES	*Journal of Near Eastern Studies*
JNWSL	*Journal of Northwest Semitic Languages*
JPsychTh	*Journal of Psychology and Theology*
JQR	*Jewish Quarterly Review*
JSNT	*Journal for the Study of the New Testament*
JSNTSup	Journal for the Study of the New Testament Supplemental Series
JSOT	*Journal for the Study of the Old Testament*
JSOTSup	Journal for the Study of the Old Testament Supplemental Series
JTS	*Journal of Theological Studies*
KAT	Kommentar zum Alten Testament
KB	L. Koehler and W. Baumgartner, *Lexicon in Veteris Testamenti libros*
KEKNT	Kritischer-exegetiker Kommentar zum Neuen Testament
KJV	King James Version
KNT	Kommentar zum Neuen Testament

Abbreviations

LCL	Loeb Classical Library
LSJ	Liddell-Scott-Jones, *Greek-English Lexicon*
MNTC	Moffatt NT Commentary
NAB	New American Bible
NAC	New American Commentary
NASB	New American Standard Bible
NEB	New English Bible
NIBC	New International Biblical Commentary
NICNT	New International Commentary on the New Testament
NICOT	New International Commentary on the Old Testament
NIGTC	The New International Greek Testament Commentary
NIV	New International Version
NJB	H. Wansbrough, ed., *New Jerusalem Bible*
NJBC	New Jerusalem Biblical Commentary
NovT	*Novum Testamentum*
NovTSup	Novum Testamentum, Supplements
NPNF	Nicene and Post-Nicene Fathers
NRSV	New Revised Standard Version
NTAbh	Neutestamentliche Abhandlungen
NTD	Das Neue Testament Deutsch
NTS	*New Testament Studies*
OBO	*Orbis Biblicus et Orientalis*
OTL	Old Testament Library
PG	J. Migne, *Patrologia graeca*
PL	J. Migne, *Patrologia latina*
RAC	Reallexikon für Antike und Christentum
RB	*Revue biblique*
RefJ	*The Reformed Journal*
ResQ	*Restoration Quarterly*
RNT	Regensburger Neues Testament
RSV	Revised Standard Version
RV	Revised Version
SBLDS	SBL Dissertation Series
SBLMS	SBL Monograph Series
SBS	Stuttgarter Bibelstudien
SecCent	*Second Century*
SJOT	*Scandinavian Journal of the Old Testament*

Abbreviations

SJT	Scottish Journal of Theology
SNTSMS	Society for New Testament Studies Monograph Series
SP	Sacra Pagina
SVTP	Studia in Veteris Testamenti pseudepigrapha
StVladThQ	St. Vladimir's Theological Quarterly
TBT	The Bible Today
TDNT	Theological Dictionary of the New Testament
TDOT	Theological Dictionary of the Old Testament
TEV	Today's English Version
THKNT	Theologischer Handkommentar zum Neuen Testament
TNTC	Tyndale New Testament Commentaries
TRu	Theologische Rundschau
TS	Theological Studies
ThStud	Theologische Studien
TToday	Theology Today
TU	Texte und Untersuchungen
TynBul	Tyndale Bulletin
TZ	Theologische Zeitschrift
UBSGNT	United Bible Societies Greek New Testament
USQR	Union Seminary Quarterly Review
VT	Vetus Testamentum
VTSup	Vetus Testamentum, Supplements
WBC	Word Biblical Commentary
WC	Westminster Commentary
WMANT	Wissenschaftliche Monographien zum Alten und Neuen Testament
WTJ	Westminster Theological Journal
WUNT	Wissenschaftliche Untersuchungen zum Neuen Testament
ZAW	Zeitschrift für die alttestamentliche Wissenschaft
ZDMG	Zeitschrift der deutschen morgenländischen Gesellschaft
ZNW	Zeitschrift für die neutestamentliche Wissenschaft

Editor's Preface

In the closing years of the twentieth century, as Christians seek to understand what it means to be "in the world but not of the world," they are faced with changing roles of women in society. There is tremendous controversy among Christians today regarding womanhood in Christian practice and in society—even people who agree that Scripture must determine one's understanding of women in the church do not always agree on what the Bible teaches or on how to implement biblical understandings in church life.

Volume Two focuses on texts treating women in the OT and NT, as well as in the history of Christian thought, including Restoration history. With respect for biblical authority, the contributors ask hard questions on matters involving women in the church. Acknowledging that we must take the biblical text seriously, they also agree that limited and poor biblical exegesis has all too often obscured these questions rather than clarifying them. Consequently, these essays seek to engage contemporary thought with a careful and exacting approach to texts, utilizing a rigorous literary-historical method. Like Volume One, this collection of essays offers stimulating thought for discussion and for serious reevaluation of traditional assumptions. It is our hope that these wide-ranging essays will help readers to formulate their own views about this important topic with greater precision.

The contributors are some of the best-known scholars from the Churches of Christ and Independent Christian Churches, but also include a few younger scholars, both male and female, who are continuing the rich tradition of Restoration scholarship. The purpose of the essays is not to argue a traditional understanding, but to engage the texts and topics to see what results from controlled exegesis and responsible hermeneutic. Writing independently and free to draw their own conclusions, each writer attempts to follow a commonly-accepted method which places firm controls upon interpretation. The resultant textual studies do yield a rather uniform perspective that is neither fundamentalist nor radical feminist.

Editor's Preface

The problem of women in the church focuses, in my opinion, more pointedly than any other issue the complex aspects of hermeneutics. Two writers address the problem of hermeneutics regarding gender issues. One follows textual conclusions other than those in these volumes and, while accepting the "order of creation" argument, nevertheless calls for greater participation of women in all ministries except preaching and eldership. The other accepts the textual understandings presented in the various essays in these two volumes and calls for the full and responsible implementation in church life of the biblical principles which emerge.

Several responses to Volume One requested information on how this information "plays out" in church life. I am grateful to the publishers for permitting the inclusion of three appendixes in which ministers reflect on their experiences in treating this question in their congregations. As might be expected, their experiences are not at all similar in many respects. One congregation, with considerable frustration and hard work, has women active in all aspects of church life, except for preaching and eldership. Another has studied the problem extensively and is aggressively continuing the investigation, with hope for achieving some workable consensus before long. The third congregation has worked with the question on occasion, but faces the perennial hindrances of traditionalism in pursuing the matter. The minister has opted to keep the topic open, but not to push the question aggressively, placing a premium upon unity. As might be expected, though, these three agree in many respects. The search for truth must have priority. The biblical text must be the basis for any change, rather than traditionalism or societal pressure. The text must be approached in terms of a responsible literary and historical method. While not viewed as at the center of the gospel, the matter of women in the church should result in "the door to women today being opened at least as wide as it was to women in the earliest churches."

Editor's Preface

In an effort to assist those whose working knowledge of ancient languages may be "a little rusty" or even non-existent, each Greek and Hebrew term is defined afresh at its first occurrence in a paragraph or footnote.

I remain indebted to Mrs. Lucille Carmichael of Dallas, TX, for her continuing interest in biblical scholarship. To Ms. Jo Ann Walling Halbert of Carrollton, TX, I owe a special debt of gratitude for her lively interest in bringing scholarship in the Restoration tradition to bear on current religious and societal issues. Mrs. Paula Varner of Wichita, KS, has graciously funded much of the secretarial work done in preparation of this volume. For the diligence of my research assistant, Mrs. Charme Robarts, the careful and patient secretarial work of Ms. Paige Martin and Ms. Tiffany Touchstone, and the meticulous work of my graduate assistant, Mr. Darren Williamson, I am most grateful. As with the first volume, Mr. John M. Hunter of College Press has brought a degree of professionalism and competence to the project that is most appreciated.

Carroll D. Osburn

Abilene, Texas
1 June 1995

Chapter One

IN THE BEGINNING: MALE AND FEMALE (GEN 1-3)

Rick R. Marrs

Perhaps no section of Scripture has generated more attention and discussion than Gen 1-3. Its importance in the Judeo-Christian tradition can hardly be overestimated. Historically at the center of discussions regarding the relation of science and the Bible, theological reflection concerning the "Fall" (and the larger anthropological concerns of what it means to be human) and debate comparing the relation of ancient Israelite thought and literature with that of the ancient Near East, its message continues to attract us.

In recent years Gen 1-3 has played a central role in the socio-theological discussion regarding the relationship and roles of male and female. Of considerable interest has been the question of whether Gen 1-3 provides a definitive statement concerning the nature and roles of man and woman in the divine order of creation, and if so, what that message is. This essay focuses principally upon those aspects of Gen 1-3 which are most pertinent for understanding the theological and anthropological message of the material regarding the divine-human relationship and the male-female relationship.

1. The Larger Literary Context of Gen 1-3

A. *Gen 1-3 in Relation to Gen 1-50*

Genesis divides rather unevenly into two major sections: 1-11 (primeval history) and 12-50 (patriarchal history). Gen 12:1-3 serves as the centerpiece to the book, as God's call and promise to Abraham occupy center stage throughout the remainder of the book of Genesis as well as much of the Pentateuch. Consequently, the place and function of Gen 1-11 as a prelude to this pivotal theme of God's election and blessing of Abraham is of no small significance.[1] Gen 1 serves as a fitting preamble to Gen 12-50. Gen 1:26-28 commissions humanity to procreate and possess responsibly the land. Gen 12-50 is the dramatic account of the working out of that commission in the life of Abraham and his heirs. Gen 1:26 tells us that humans are created in the image of God. Throughout the remainder of Genesis (and the Pentateuch), Israel is called to be God's image to the nations.[2] So, Gen 1 presents the divine intent for creation; the remainder of Genesis recounts the multivalent responses of creation, especially the human element of creation, to that divine intent.

B. *Gen 1-3 in Relation to Gen 1-11*

In general, Gen 1-11 divides clearly into five major narrative units. Chap. 1 sets the stage for chaps. 1-11 as a panoramic overview of the creation of the world. This creative masterpiece serves as backdrop for four dramatic episodes, each replete with intrigue, tragedy, and an open future to be resolved: 1) Adam and Eve; 2) Cain and Abel; 3) Noah and the flood; 4) the Tower of Babel. Not insignificantly, extensive genealogies immediately precede and follow the flood, marking its central importance to humanity.[3] Although numerous themes and issues are

---

[1]The ties between Gen 1-11 and 12-50 are apparent, the former closing with a people striving unsuccessfully for fame (name) and security, through the building of a tower. The Patriarchal history opens with the call of Abraham, through whom God brings blessing and purpose to life, while making for him a "name."

[2]For a fuller discussion, see Richard Clifford, "The Hebrew Scriptures and the Theology of Creation," *ThStud* 46 (1985): 507-23. For an introductory overview of the theological structure of Genesis, see Rick Marrs, "Thinking Theologically on Genesis: How to get at the Theological Message of the Book," *Where Genesis Meets Life* (Searcy, AR: Harding Univ. Press, 1991): 165-75.

[3]The positioning of genealogies immediately preceding and following the flood reassures the reader that despite the propensity of

treated in this opening section, pivotal is the dramatic interplay between the reality of life in God's world (Gen 3-11) versus God's intent for life in his world (Gen 1-2). Repeatedly we see the failure of humanity to respond appropriately to God's promise and purpose. Such failure results in a world filled with strife, violence, deceit, and an unending struggle for power and preeminence.

Of considerable significance is the carefully crafted linkage between the account of creation and the account of the flood.[4] In many ways, the flood appears as creation revisited.[5] Because of the overwhelming level of social violence and chaos, Yahweh regretfully returns this creation which is "out of control" to its prior watery status. However, disorder and chaos was never the divine intent, and so out of this watery chaos God once again re-creates his world, centering it this time in Noah, one who understands and models the appropriate human response to the divine creator (Gen 6:9; 8:1).

2. *The Relationship of Gen 1 to Gen 2-3*

Since the Enlightenment, heated debate has raged regarding the literary relationship between chaps. 1 and 2-

---

humanity toward disobedience and *hubris*, God's grace and providence insures order and continuity to the creation.

[4] For various thematic analyses of Gen 1-11, highlighting the close relationship of creation and the flood, see Bernard Anderson, "From Analysis to Synthesis: The Interpretation of Genesis 1-11," *JBL* 97 (1978) 23-39; Gary Rendsburg, *The Redaction of Genesis* (Winona Lake, IN: Eisenbrauns, 1986): 8-12; George Coats, "Strife and Reconciliation: Themes of a Biblical Theology in the Book of Genesis," *HBT* 2 (1980): 15-37; Susan Niditch, *From Chaos to Cosmos: Studies in Biblical Patterns of Creation* (Chico, CA: Scholars Press, 1985).

[5] At one level, the literary structure of the flood account returns us to the watery mass world of days 2-3. Out of this watery mass, God once again surfaces dry land and its vegetation. Noah is commissioned (Gen 9:1-7) in a manner strikingly reminiscent of Adam (Gen 1:26-30). Though finite and fickle, humans retain the image of God and are called to live in a manner reflecting that image.

3.[6] Clearly the focus of attention differs in the presentation of creation in Gen 1 from that in Gen 2-3. Gen 1 paints the universe in broad strokes; each creative act of God marches inexorably toward the pinnacle of creation—the creation of humanity on day six. This depiction is thoroughly theocentric—God the Creator unfolds in regal fashion his creative design across the expanse of the universe. Remarkably, this all-powerful and transcendent cosmic Creator chooses to stamp his own image upon creation in the form of humanity. Gen 2-3 must be read against this panoramic backdrop. If Gen 1 presents humankind as the pinnacle of creation, Gen 2-3 presents humankind as its center. The thoroughly theocentric view of Gen 1 is somewhat moderated by anthropocentric concerns in Gen 2-3. If Gen 1 depicts creation in telescopic majesty, Gen 2-3 addresses the nature of humankind and its relation to the Creator in microscopic detail. In Gen 2-3 we learn that the Cosmic Creator of Gen 1 is also a caring covenant God (יְהוָה אֱלֹהִים) who attends to the needs and complexities of human life.

3. Analysis and Exegesis of Genesis 1

A. Structure and Literary Character

In Gen 1, creation spans six days, the watery mass (1:1-2) being transformed into an ordered universe. On the first three days, the Creator progressively induces separation in this watery mass—light from dark, water from sky, dry land from water. Over the next three days, God fills and enumerates these various arenas. Having created light on day one, God creates specific lights on day four (sun, moon, stars). Having separated air and water on day two, God places birds and aquatic creatures in those two realms on day five. Having made dry land with its vegetation on day three, God creates land animals and humans to inhabit that area on day six. With day seven, order is present throughout creation and the Creator rests (2:1-3).

---

[6] As our interest is in determining the meaning and message of chaps. 1-3 in its final form, the subtle linguistic nuances and various images depicted throughout the narrative are of vital importance.

In the Beginning: Male and Female (Gen 1-3)

Formulaic repetition typifies Gen 1. Each day is recounted in strikingly similar fashion. We are struck with the orderliness of creation and the ease with which God creates. He simply speaks (commands) and creation is executed. Creation is good; the Lord of the universe deems it so.[7] Throughout we never lose sight that there is purpose and direction in the plan of the Creator. This God who began with a formless void concludes creation with every element in its proper place. Having blessed and commissioned his latter creative acts, he affirms the goodness of his creation and rests over it.

B. *Specific Exegetical Issues Pertinent to an Understanding of Humankind*

1. *Creation of Humankind.* Prior to the creation of humankind, we have become familiar with the standard formula: "God said . . . and it was so." However, we now hear: "Let us make . . . and God created."[8] God's creative

---

[7]Although in general there is an apparent sameness to the presentation of each day, on closer reading we note minor variations in the account, variations which add to the beauty of the reading. Key terms repeatedly surface: "made" (days 2, 4, 5, 6); "created" (day 6), "rule" (days 4, 6); "bless" (days 5, 6, 7). God calls (names) only on days 1-3. Claus Westermann, *Genesis 1-11* (Minneapolis, MN: Augsburg, 1984): 87, considers God's "naming" (קָרָא) significant. God names only what he separates. God creates in such a way that after the creation of the earth through separation and naming, life can come forth, but only because the creative word of God is at its origin.

[8]The divine plural (let us . . .) has been variously interpreted: 1) as a reference to the Trinity; 2) as a plural reflecting the morphological plurality of the term אֱלֹהִים (god); 3) as a plural of majesty; 4) as God speaking to his royal (divine) court; 5) as a plural of deliberation. Although long a favorite in Christian circles, the irrelevancy of the Trinity to the original hearers of Gen 1 leads us to search elsewhere for a more suitable interpretation. However, Gerhard Hasel, "The Meaning of 'Let us' in Gn 1:26," *AUSS* 13 (1975): 65, while avoiding specific Trinitarian terminology, has a rather nuanced interpretation which he designates the "plural of fullness," i.e., here we have presented in germinal form the acknowledgment of the fullness of personality and person within the deity. Although it is true that the term אֱלֹהִים is a

actions on day six, particularly the creation of humankind, provide the pinnacle of creative activity in chapter one. This is evidenced not only by the inordinate detail with which this action is recounted, but also through the introduction of direct discourse. Humankind stands as the only creature God addresses directly. Here creation moves between direct discourse (vv. 26, 28-30) and narrated discourse (v. 27). Humans clearly share aspects with the rest of the created order; their essence as creature is never forgotten. However, their uniqueness from the rest of creation captures our attention. This uniqueness is expressed through receiving their commission directly from God,[9] and through their creation in the image of God.

2. Image of God. The issue of the nature and essence of humankind being in the image of God has occupied scholarship for generations. Numerous and creative theories

---

masculine plural noun, it regularly occurs with singular verbs elsewhere in Gen 1, rendering the second interpretation questionable. The third interpretation (plural of majesty) envisions God speaking in the manner of a king (the "royal *we*"). This interpretation argues that kings regularly issued royal decrees in first person plural. Although the plural of majesty *may* occur with nouns in the OT, there is no evidence for its use with verbs or pronouns in the OT. Assuming a similar backdrop, the fourth interpretation envisions God encircled by his divine court and announcing his intention to them. God's heavenly court is mentioned elsewhere in the OT (1 Kgs 22:19-22; Job 1:6-7; 2:1-2; 38:7; Isa 6:8; Ps 82:1); its presence in Gen 1 continues to be disputed. For the use of the plural ("of deliberation") as a literary device to underscore the importance or solemnity of the event, see Isa 6:8; 2 Sam 24:14; Gen 11:7. God speaks to himself about his most important creation; with its execution he returns to the singular (v. 27). Given the royal imagery of Gen 1, the latter two interpretations are most compelling.

[9]As Walter Brueggemann, *Genesis* (Atlanta: John Knox, 1982): 31, notes, the human is the "speech creature" par excellence. He continues, "This is the one to whom God has made a peculiarly intense commitment (by speaking) and to whom marvelous freedom has been granted (in responding)."

have been propounded regarding its meaning.¹⁰ Part of the difficulty in determining the meaning results from the text being more concerned to articulate the *result* of being in God's image (viz., dominion) than the *essence*. However, two issues are clear: 1) whatever the image entails, it was not lost with expulsion from the garden (Gen 9:6); 2) both male and female are created in the image of God.

"Image" (צֶלֶם) in the OT refers to any sculpture or plastic work, whether made of wood or stone. It is often used of idols (e.g., 1 Sam 6:5; Num 33:52; 2 Kgs 11:18; Ezek 23:14). Throughout the OT it signifies a concrete representation.¹¹ "Likeness" (דְּמוּת) is an abstract noun derived from the root דָּמָה (to be like).¹² This term connotes similarity and analogy rather than dissimilarity. Thus, צֶלֶם and דמות jointly describe a single idea.¹³

Thus, humankind in some way images God in the world. As Westermann¹⁴ notes, the uniqueness of humans consists in their being God's counterparts. The text describes an action, not the nature of human beings. God's image is not something added to humanity; rather, humans are created in such a way that their very existence is intended to be their relationship with God. The divine-human correspondence is not static, but dynamic—evidenced in God's call to humanity to procreate and have dominion. To be

---

¹⁰For a detailing of several such theories, see David Clines, The Image of God in Man," *TynBul* 19 (1968): 53-103; John Willis, *Genesis* (Austin: Sweet, 1979): 88; Westermann, *Genesis*, 147-55; Hans Wildberger, "Das Abbild Gottes," *TZ* 21 (1965): 245-59, 481-509; Werner H. Schmidt, *Die Schopfungsgeschichte der Priesterschrift* (WMANT 17; Neukirchen: Neukirchen-Vluyn, 1967).

¹¹This renders suspect attempts to import Western notions of the image of God involving our moral or spiritual nature.

¹²For examples, note Ezek 1:5, 10, 26, 28; 2 Kgs 16:10.

¹³No distinction seems intended in the variation of prepositions used in 1:26 (in our image, בְּצַלְמֵנוּ; according to our likeness, כִּדְמוּתֵנוּ). In Gen 5:3, Adam becomes "the father of a son, *in his image* (בִּדְמוּתוֹ) *according to his image* (כְּצַלְמוֹ).

¹⁴Westermann, *Genesis*, 157-158.

created in the image of God means that we are gifted by the Creator to be in personal relationship with Him. Remarkably, we are the only creatures with whom he has chosen to communicate directly.[15]

Finally, of utmost interest is the parallelistic statement of 1:27: "God created humankind (אָדָם) in his image, in the image of God he created him (אֹתוֹ); male (זָכָר) and female (נְקֵבָה) he created them (אֹתָם)." The shift from singular (אֹתוֹ) to plural (אֹתָם) shows clearly that אָדָם is not one single creature who is both male and female, but two creatures.[16] Further, no indication is given that these two creatures are created in opposition rather than in harmony. In Gen 1, male and female appear simultaneously, with no mention of superiority or subordination.[17]

3. *The Commissioning and Blessing of Humanity.* Just as the sun, moon, and stars were commissioned to rule the sky, separating night from day and delimiting time and season, so humans are now commissioned (1:28-30) to have dominion over the earth. Although the verbs "subdue" (כָּבַשׁ) and "have dominion" (רָדָה) often denote royal power and

---

[15]Gen 1:26-28 may also implicitly reflect ancient Israel's constant aversion to idols and graven images. Israel stood unique among her neighbors as an aniconic society. Her God could not be captured through the construction of any idol, for such images partook of creation itself. The Creator of the universe stands free from Israel and his world. However, inexplicably, this same Creator freely chooses to image himself in none other than his creation of humans! I.e., God cannot be imaged by any human construction, for he has already imaged himself in his own creation of humans (note especially Deut 4:12-18, where imaging is directly linked to creation).

[16]This disallows any androgynous interpretation.

[17]Phyllis Trible, *God and the Rhetoric of Sexuality* (Philadelphia: Fortress, 1978): 17-19, argues forcefully that what is left *unsaid* allows freedom in interpreting the contours of the male and female creatures. In this first appearance of male and female, no attention is given to delineating sexual relationships, roles, characteristics, attitudes, or emotions. Rather, the text identifies two human responsibilities: procreation and dominion (with both male and female being assigned these tasks).

domination, one should not conclude that coercion and wanton exploitation of the created order is justified. Sarna argues that such a conclusion is unwarranted for several reasons: 1) humankind is not inherently sovereign, but enjoys dominion solely by the grace of God; 2) the model of kingship in ancient Israel denied unrestrained power and authority to a sole monarch, who stood under carefully defined divine law; 3) humans have been given sovereignty in a "very good" world in which God intends harmony and acts that are beneficial to his creation (see Isa 11:1-9).[18]

Blessing occurs three times in this opening account of creation (1:22, 28; 2:3). In its first two occurrences, blessing evokes fertility and multiplication. The capacity for sexual reproduction is a divine blessing bestowed by the Creator upon his creatures. The third blessing bestows a sacredness upon the Sabbath.[19]

C. *Place of Gen 1 within the Larger Context of the Ancient Near East*

The metaphor that best captures the essence of God as Creator in Gen 1 is that of a royal monarch who simply

---

[18]Nahum Sarna, *Understanding Genesis* (New York: Jewish Theological Sem. of America, 1966): 13. Similarly, Brueggemann, *Genesis*, 32-33, links the nature of dominion and authority presented here with the NT concept of dominion, where the one who rules is the one who serves (Mk 10:43-44). Lordship means servanthood. Gen 1:26-28, he says, ". . . is revolutionary. It presents an inverted view of God, not as the one who reigns by fiat and remoteness, but as the one who governs by gracious self-giving. It also presents an inverted view of humanness. This man and woman are not the chattel and servants of God, but the agents of God to whom much is given and from whom much is expected."

[19]Sarna, *Genesis*, 10-11, 15: "Through his weekly suspension of normal activity, man imitates the divine pattern and reactualizes the original sacred time of God, thereby recovering the sacred dimension of existence. Paradoxically, he also thereby rediscovers his own very human dimension, his earthliness, for the Sabbath delimits man's autonomy, suspends for a while his creative freedom, and declares that on that one day each week nature is inviolable."

issues commands (and God said) which are then executed (and it was so). As noted above, the crowning achievement of his creative activity is the creation of humankind in his image. In ancient Mesopotamia,[20] when a monarch subdued another territory, he frequently erected a statue (image) of himself in that conquered country before returning to his homeland. That image was a constant reminder to the subjugated people of their Mesopotamian overlord, his "image" in effect reflecting his "presence."[21] Given this backdrop, we suggest that Gen 1 reflects just such imagery, but with a dramatic twist. God, the royal sovereign of the universe, has placed his own "images" *within* his created order. Man and woman are essentially accorded "royal status." It is no wonder that Ps 8:3-9 exclaims:

When I look at your heavens, the work of your fingers,
  the moon and the stars that you established;
What are humans that you are mindful of them,
  mortals that you care for them?
Yet you have made them a little lower than God,
  and crowned them with glory and honor.

---

[20]For an intriguing and provocative reading of Gen 1-11 against the backdrop of the Mesopotamian world, see Bernard Batto, *Slaying the Dragon* (Louisville: Westminster/John Knox, 1992).

[21]In Mesopotamia and Egypt the king is considered the image/likeness of his god. In Egypt, Tutankhamen is called "the living image of (the god) Amun"; Thutmose IV is designated "the likeness of Re." On Assyrian royal steles, the gods are often depicted by their symbols (e.g., Ashur by a winged disk; Shamash by the sun disk); these depictions were called "the image (*salam*) of the great gods." Not uncommon are statements such as: "The father of my lord the king is the very image of Bel (*salam bel*) and the king, my lord is the very image of Bel"; "the king, lord of the lands is the image of Shamash"; "O king of the inhabited world, you are the image of Marduk." At Tell-Fekheriyeh (Syria), a 9th-century bilingual (Assyrian-Aramaic) inscription contains the word pair צֶלֶם / דְמוּת (image/likeness) in parallelism on a statue. For a fuller discussion of this phenomenon, see Sarna, *Genesis*, 12; Alan Millard and Pierre Brodrueil, "A Statue from Syria with Assyrian and Aramaic Inscriptions," *BA* 45 (1982): 135-41.

You have given them dominion over the work of
 your hands;
 you have put all things under their feet,
all sheep and oxen,
 and also the beasts fo the field,
the birds of the air, and the fish of the sea,
 whatever passes along the paths of the seas.
O Lord, our Sovereign,
 how majestic is your name in all the earth!

Although much could be said in this context, three observations will suffice: 1) in Mesopotamia a frequent image of humanity is that of a slave (lackey) functioning primarily to serve the gods, whereas in Gen 1 humans are exalted creatures given responsibility for the rest of creation;[22] 2) in Mesopotamia only the king bears the image of God, whereas in Gen 1 this view is democratized (*all humankind* reflect God's image);[23] 3) (to my knowledge) no Mesopotamian material recounts the creation of woman and her relationship to the divine world and the rest of creation.

D. *Theological Significance of Gen 1*

Scripture opens with a powerful affirmation of what it means to be human in a God-centered and God-ordered world. Humankind, consisting of male and female, reflect the very image of God. The sovereign Lord of the universe has entrusted to his sovereign subjects direct responsibility for the rest of creation. Humankind as male and female stands neither in opposition (antonymous) to each other nor as indistinguishable (synonymous). Rather, they stand in community with a common commission and function.[24]

---

[22] In *Enuma elish*, Marduk creates humankind to take the place of the lesser gods who are tired of the demeaning service they must perform for the greater gods.

[23] For all humanity to be stamped in the image of God reflects the infinite worth of humanity and affirms the inviolability of humankind (Gen 9:6).

[24] Bernard Anderson, "'Subdue the Earth': What Does it Mean?" *BibRev* 8 (1992): 4, states: "Crowned as kings and queens, they are

Human sexuality partakes of the very blessing of God. God's creation is "good," a designation not simply denoting its aesthetic quality, but more importantly its functional nature. God has created each element suitable to its purpose. Divine creation is neither an afterthought nor without focus and direction. Rather, the world God has created has meaning and purpose; he has ordered it in such a manner that it can fulfill its purpose. Crucial to this realization is the place and role of humanity. Created in the image of God, these human creatures have the awesome task of providing maintenance and direction in such a way that creation fulfills its divine goal. Although transcendent, there is a closeness between the Creator and his creatures, reflected in his daily attentiveness to his creation. Inexplicably, it is humanity which benefits most dramatically from this awesome creative power and blessing. Humankind as male and female finds its meaning, direction, and purpose only in relation to its benevolent and gracious Creator.

4. *Analysis and Exegesis of Genesis 2-3*

In OT scholarship, the attention accorded the opening chapter of Genesis pales only in comparison to the attention given the creation of Adam and Eve and their expulsion from the garden (Gen 2-3). This latter narrative has been the breeding ground for countless discussions regarding the nature of man and woman and their relationship.[25] Having

---

commissioned to exercise their God-given role wisely and benevolently so that God's dominion over the earth may be manifested in their actions. When viewed in the light of Ps 8, the creation story of Gen 1 is a call to responsibility." For further discussion of this passage within the specific context of human sexuality, see Phyllis Bird, "'Male and Female He Created Them': Gen 1:27b in the Context of the Priestly Account of Creation," *HTR* 74 (1981): 129-60; *idem*, "Sexual Differentiation and Divine Image in the Genesis Creation Texts," *Image of God and Gender Models* (ed. K. Borresen; Solum Forlag, 1991): 10-31.

[25] A not infrequent reading of this text assumes that in its presentation of Adam and Eve, it proclaims male superiority and female inferiority as the will of God. Woman is portrayed as a "temptress" and troublemaker who is dependent upon and must be dominated by her

In the Beginning: Male and Female (Gen 1-3)   13

seen the lofty position the Sovereign God has accorded humankind (Gen 1), we now turn our attention to the human response to this exalted status. Gen 2-3 allows us to focus more closely upon the creation of the first couple and their response to the place accorded them in the created order by the Creator of the universe.[26]

A. *Structure and Literary Character*

Gen 2-3 is a carefully-crafted narrative. Readers for generations have been struck by the dramatic unfolding of the plot, the suspense, and the ensuing tragedy. The thrust of the material clearly revolves about the creation of the first

---

husband. This misogynous reading is often agreed upon both by those who applaud or deplore this narrative. Trible, *Sexuality,* 73, notes several reasons that are cited to justify this rendering: 1) a male God creates first man and last woman; first means superior and last means inferior/subordinate; 2) woman is created for the sake of man: a helpmate to cure his loneliness; 3) contrary to nature, woman comes out of man: she is denied even her natural function of birthing (that function being given to man); 4) woman is the rib of man, dependent upon him for life; 5) taken out of man, woman has a derivative, rather than autonomous, existence; 6) man names woman and thus has power over her; 7) man leaves his father's family in order to set up through his wife another patriarchal unit; 8) woman (being untrustworthy, gullible, and simpleminded), tempted man to disobey and thus is responsible for the entrance of sin into the world; 9) woman is cursed by pain in childbirth (pain in childbirth is a more severe punishment than man's struggle with the soil, signifying that woman's sin is greater than man's); 10) woman's desire for man is God's way of keeping her faithful and submissive to her husband; 11) God gives man the right to rule over the woman. She suggests that none of these premises are *altogether* accurate; most are simply not present in the story and violate the real purpose and thrust of the story! For her, the true focus of the story concerns life and death.

[26]From the cosmic sweep of Gen 1 we direct our attention to the creation and placement of humans—the glory and central problem of creation. As Brueggemann, *Genesis,* 51, notes, Gen 2-3 principally addresses how to live with creation in God's world on God's terms. This narrative probes the extent to which one may order one's life autonomously, without reference to any limit or prohibition (a problem which endures throughout the OT).

man and woman and their relationship to their Creator. However, brief interludes balance and enhance the overall movement of the story. In broad strokes, Gen 2-3 recounts a garden that is given to (2:8-17) and then lost by (3:1-24) the first human couple. More precisely, it narrates the coming to full life of this first couple (2:7-25) and the disintegration of that life (3:8-24) through disobedience (3:1-7). Repetition of key phrases at the beginning (2:4-9, 15) and end (3:22-24) provide *inclusio*, compelling the reader to read chapters 2-3 as a unified whole.[27]

The narrative of Gen 2-3, though rather straightforward with its three major scenes (2:7-25; 3:1-7, 8-24) and four major characters (God, Adam, Eve, the serpent), continues to intrigue us with unanswered questions, language with multiple meaning, and apparent ambiguity. Yahweh, the principal determiner of the nature of human existence in scenes one and three, is noticeably absent from scene two (the temptation). That middle scene is fraught with drama, for there the serpent, man, and woman turn God-the-subject into God-the-object.[28] It is often easy to overlook what the text does tell us in our search for answers to questions left unaddressed by this narrative.

---

[27]Gen 3 must be read against the backdrop of chap. 2. Throughout terminology and themes resurface which can only be properly understood against the whole of the narrative. Alan Hauser, "Genesis 2-3: the theme of intimacy and alienation," *Art and Meaning* (ed. D. Clines, *et al.*; Sheffield: JSOT, 1982): 20-33, utilizes the themes of intimacy and alienation to depict the thematic relation of chaps. 2-3. The world of harmony and intimacy (chap. 2) is shattered in chap. 3 and replaced by a world of disruption and alienation. For Brueggemann, *Genesis*, 51, the contrast concerns the faithful work of God (chap. 2) and the resultant human distrust (chap. 3). In God's garden, as God intends it, there is mutuality and equity (chap. 2); in God's garden, now permeated by distrust (chap. 3), there is struggle for control and distortion.

[28]So Trible, *Sexuality*, 75.

B. *Specific Exegetical Issues Pertinent to an Understanding of Humankind*

1. *Creation of Humankind.* Out of the earth (אֲדָמָה) created by God, an "earthling" (אָדָם) is fashioned.[29] We immediately are confronted with the strikingly complex nature of this creature[30]—formed from dust, yet infused with the very breath of God. The importance of these twin relationships (i.e., with the earth, with God) cannot be overemphasized. At one and the same time we encounter אָדָם in his frailty as mere dust and yet empowered for life through the gracious gift of God's breath.[31] The creation of אָדָם is set against the backdrop of the initial barrenness of the land. Two reasons are given for this barrenness: 1) God has not yet watered his earth (i.e., sent rain); 2) there is as yet no creature to care for (i.e., till) the earth. This initial tension is quickly erased.

a) *Relation of Man to the Earth.* Following quickly upon the heels of the creation of אָדָם (earthling), God's grace manifests itself in the planting of a beautiful garden for

---

[29]The verb יָצַר (formed) is often, though not exclusively, used of a potter / sculptor. Significantly, two-thirds of its occurrences have God as subject. The imagery of man originating from dust and being molded by God occurs elsewhere in the OT (Gen 3:19; Job 10:9; Pss 18:27; 90:3; 104:29; 119:73; 146:4; *et al.*). The image is shared with other ancient Near Eastern cultures. For a fuller discussion, see Sarna, *Genesis*, 17; Westermann, *Genesis*, 203-4.

[30]Contra Trible, *Sexuality*, 80, it seems to me that we are expected to understand אָדָם as a "man" from the beginning. However, she is surely correct in noting that his maleness is of no significance at the outset. Rather, it is his relationship to the earth אֲדָמָה that is of central importance. See Richard Davidson, "The Theology of Sexuality in the Beginning," *AUSS* 26 (1988): 121-31.

[31]As Sarna, *Genesis*, 17, notes, here we see humanity simultaneously in its glory and its utter insignificance. Adam enjoys exalted status through the nature of being God's creation in which the divine breath of life is present; at the same time he is mere dust taken from the earth.

the creature's dwelling.³² Already two clear anthropological themes are sounded: 1) אָדָם shares an intimate connection with the earth (אֲדָמָה); 2) אָדָם is created with meaning and purpose—to care for the earth.³³

Placed within this wondrous garden, the man's life finds meaning and purpose—he is to "till and keep" the garden (2:15). אָדָם and the garden stand in somewhat of a reciprocal relationship. As he serves and tends the garden, so it feeds and sustains him. However, this gracious provision of God is not without limitations, for in the midst of the garden stands the tree of knowledge of good and evil, from which the man must not eat. Although the tendency among readers is to concentrate almost exclusively upon the prohibition (2:17), in actuality the text makes a powerful threefold statement regarding the man's status: 1) he is given a vocation (v. 15);³⁴ 2) he is given permission (v. 16); 3) he is given a prohibition (v. 17). Human life before God is characterized by vocation, permission, and prohibition. If any is missing, human life is perverted.³⁵

---

³²So that we not miss the beauty and magnitude of this gift, the contours of this garden are depicted in some detail (2:8-14). Even the name of the garden conveys this message; Eden means "delight, enjoyment."

³³What Gen 1 expresses through the motif of the image of God, Gen 2 conveys through the medium of the very name of man (אָדָם/אֲדָמָה).

³⁴Trible, *Sexuality*, 85, rightly concludes that since the garden is a work of delight, caring for it should foster pleasure. The terms used for the human task are significant. עָבַד (serve [till]) connotes respect; indeed, in numerous OT texts it is used of reverence and worship of the Lord. שָׁמַר (keep) denotes protection rather than possession. Both terms intend care and attention rather than plunder and exploitation. Not insignificantly, work appears indigenous to creation; however, it may be of some significance that initially the man's commission envisions only care for the garden, whereas in chap. 3 he will receive the virtually impossible task of "tilling the earth" (3:23). Not unexpectedly, there the joy of work gives way to frustration and despair (3:17-19).

³⁵As Brueggemann, *Genesis*, 46, rightly notes, although the gift of the garden is an act of utter graciousness on God's part, the tree(s) in

In the Beginning: Male and Female (Gen 1-3)

b) *Relation of Man to the Animals.* Having been graciously placed in the garden and entrusted with a task, Yahweh's concern and care for Adam does not suddenly disappear. Rather, just as Gen 1 shows us that God intends humanity as community, so here he addresses the aloneness of אדם (earthling).[36] Like man, animals are formed from the earth (2:7, 19); unlike man, they are not inbreathed with the breath of God. Although similar to אדם, it is their difference which receives attention.[37] Having created the animals, Yahweh entrusts to אדם yet another task—that of naming the animals.

Although a rather common perception is that naming implies domination by a superior and subordination of an inferior, such a view is less than compelling in the present context. Although the naming of persons and places often occurs in contexts which also reflect hierarchical concerns, it more typically denotes the activity of providing identity, specifically identity with respect to the one naming. Naming allows one to determine the identity and placement of various elements.[38] In our present context, such an interpretation is cogent. In Gen 2, the animals appear initially to address the issue of man's loneliness. However, we quickly realize that, although they will have a place in אדם's (earthling)

---

the midst of the garden disclose the character of God's graciousness. There is no cheap grace here.

[36]In Gen 1 the creation of male and female results in God's assessment of creation as "very good"; in Gen 2 God assesses the man's solitariness as "not good."

[37]The ambiguous drama of this scene has been noted often. Are we to understand that Yahweh initially falters in his attempt to alleviate the man's aloneness? Are we to view Yahweh's creative activity as less than stellar? We would suggest that the present ambiguity is intentional and foreshadows the introduction and presentation of woman. Rather than intending to detract from the creation of animals, we are already made aware that the man's solitariness can only be resolved through a dramatic and direct intervention on God's part. Nothing less than an equal portion of God's attentive care will suffice to resolve the man's dilemma.

[38]So Westermann, *Genesis,* 228.

world, they are insufficient to meet his deepest need—human companionship.

c) *Relation of Man to Woman.* Strikingly, the creation of woman is presented in greater detail than that of man. Further, she is the only creature that does not derive directly from the earth (הָאֲדָמָה). Rather, אָדָם (earthling) functions as the אֲדָמָה did earlier.³⁹ Because of their importance in detailing the first interaction between man and woman, vv. 21-24 demand careful reading.

Although virtually impossible to read this material without importing concepts and materials from elsewhere, it is crucial that we initially struggle to hear what the immediate text says concerning this original man and woman. Several things are worthy of note: 1) while the creation of man is covered in one verse (2:7), the creation of woman is detailed in five verses; 2) unlike the animals, woman realizes fully God's provision for the man of a "helper fit for him" (עֵזֶר כְּנֶגְדּוֹ); 3) whereas the man simply names the animals when they are presented to him, with the introduction of the woman the naming is enveloped in exclamation; 4) just as man was given a vocation that should bring joy, so now he is given a companion that brings joy; 5) man's initial observation (and assessment?) regarding woman focuses entirely upon their commonality and mutuality (v. 23); 6) the solitary אָדָם (earthling) finds true "oneness" in union with the woman (they "become one flesh" [v. 24]).

Repeatedly, Gen 2:21-25 has been used to justify a hierarchical relationship of female subordination toward the male.⁴⁰ Arguments for a hierarchical interpretation include:

---

³⁹Trible, *Sexuality,* 96.

⁴⁰See, among others, Stephen B. Clark, *Man and Woman in Christ: An Examination of the Roles of Men and Women in the Light of Scripture and the Social Sciences* (Ann Arbor: Servant Books, 1980): 23-28; Susan Foh, *Women and the Word of God: A Response to Biblical Feminism* (Phillipsburg, NJ: Presbyterian and Reformed Pub. Co., 1979): 61-62; Michael Stitzinger, "Genesis 1-3 and the Male / Female Role Relationship," *GTJ* 2 (1981): 23-44.

1) man was created first and woman last; first connotes superiority while last denotes subordination (inferiority); 2) woman was created for the sake of man—to be his helpmate (assistant) to cure his loneliness; 3) woman comes out of man, implying a derivative or subordinate status; 4) woman was created from man's rib, indicating a dependence upon him for life; 5) man names woman, indicating his power/ authority over her. Each of these arguments is problematic. Literarily, Gen 2 reflects a "ring composition." That is, the order of creation (man first, woman last) intends not a move from superiority to inferiority, but through *inclusio* (man/ woman) a move from incompleteness to completeness. Literarily, one can more compellingly argue that woman is presented as the climax and culmination of the story—she is the crowning work of creation![41] Regarding the place of woman in creation, we should not too quickly assume that the designation "helper" necessarily connotes subordinate status and position (a point to which we will return). The suggestion that derivation implies subordination would force us to conclude that man is subordinate to the earth, from which he was derived![42] Finally, as noted above, naming does not necessarily imply dominion. In the immediate context, the man's naming of woman actually occurs within his joyous exclamation at God's marvelous creative act. Man is not so much "determining" woman as delighting in what God has done.[43] Thus, a hierarchical interpretation of

---

[41]If superiority derives from order of appearance, then animals take preeminence over humans in Gen 1! Willis, *Genesis,* 111-12, argues that although the creation of woman was in God's mind from the beginning, he withholds her appearance until man can appreciate her value in the fullest sense.

[42]The woman is *not* Adam's rib; rather, it is simply the raw material from which she is made, just as dust is the raw material from which man is formed. Woman is not molded from clay (dust), but "architecturally constructed" (*banah*). Conversely, one might argue that woman is superior, being created from animate (superior) matter rather than inanimate matter. More likely, the rib implies equality rather than inferiority—woman is created to stand side by side.

[43]For this discussion I have relied principally on the work of R. Davidson, *AUSS* 13.

Gen 2:21-25 is less than compelling. However, three aspects of this text merit further consideration: 1) the designation of woman as man's "helper"; 2) the naming of woman by man; 3) the designation of man and woman together as "one flesh."

The creation of woman occurs within the context of God's intent to provide man with a "helper fit for him" (עֵזֶר כְּנֶגְדּוֹ). The noun עֵזֶר occurs several times in the OT, primarily as a relational term describing an anticipated beneficial relationship. It can be used of humans, nations,[44] or God.[45] The latter is telling; throughout the OT God is designated and called upon as the helper of humankind. However, to suggest that in these contexts God functions as subordinate to humans is ludicrous. Rather, it is the relationship that is paramount; the hierarchical dynamics of that relationship are left unspecified by עֵזֶר.[46] For this reason the prepositional phrase כְּנֶגְדּוֹ is of paramount significance.[47] If עֵזֶר designates the relationship, כְּנֶגְדּוֹ designates the nature of the relationship. Woman is created as a companion (neither subordinate nor superior) who alleviates man's isolation through identity.[48]

---

[44]Isa 30:5; Hos 13:9.

[45]Exod 18:4; Deut 33:7, 26; Pss 20:3; 33:20; 70:5; 115:9-11; 121:1; 146:5.

[46]Just as importing a nuance of inferiority into the term עֵזֶר lacks cogency, so does the attempt of R. Freedman, "Woman, a Power Equal to Man: Translation of Woman as a 'fit helpmate' for Man in Question," *BibRev* 9 (1983): 56-68, to see here a nuance of superiority. Freedman argues that etymologically עֵזֶר is a combination of עָזַר (to save, rescue) and עָזַז (to be strong). Determining the precise nuance of terminology must derive principally from context rather than solely from etymological constructs.

[47]כְּנֶגְדּוֹ literally means: "like (כְ) his counterpart (נֶגֶד + object suffix)," i.e., "corresponding to him."

[48]In general, we would suggest that Gen 2-3 recounts three relationships in which אָדָם finds himself: that with God (superior/ subordinate); that with woman (equal); that with the rest of the created order (superior/subordinate).

This interpretation finds support in the naming of woman by man: 1) whereas man is asked to name the animals, with the arrival of woman this occurs spontaneously; 2) although the customary expression for naming consists of the verb קָרָא (to call) plus the noun שֵׁם (name), the noun is noticeably absent here;[49] 3) the designation "woman" (אִשָּׁה) is not in actuality a personal name, but simply a generic term; 4) in naming his counterpart "woman," אִשָּׁה, the man simultaneously names himself אִישׁ.[50] Thus, upon awakening, the man exultantly acknowledges God's marvelous accomplishment in creating a "partner suitable for him."

The realization of woman as man's "suitable partner" and his attendant response of jubilation culminates in the remarkable designation of their union as "one flesh." The language of 2:23-24 is most striking. Introducing another human into the creation scene to relieve the solitary situation of the man results not in a statement of differentiation regarding the man and woman, but in an affirmation of their solidarity and mutuality. Although the affirmation of "bone and flesh" may speak to the sexual union created between a husband and wife, we would suggest another focus. The terms "bone" (עֶצֶם) and "flesh" (בָּשָׂר) are a common word

---

[49]Trible, *Sexuality*, 100, concludes: "Hence, in calling the woman, man is not establishing power over her but rejoicing in their mutuality." Perhaps noteworthy also is that the verb קָרָא in v. 23 occurs in the passive (to / for this one it shall be called woman). For a detailed study of naming in the OT, see George Ramsey, "Is Name-Giving an Act of Domination in Genesis 2:23 and Elsewhere?" *CBQ* 50 (1988): 24-35. Ramsey argues that naming for the Hebrews was determined primarily by circumstances, rather than the naming determining the essence of an entity. Specifically regarding Gen 2, he argues that when Adam names the animals he is simply discerning their essence (already established by God). Adam's exclamation at 2:23 is a cry of discovery, or recognition, rather than a prescription of what woman shall be (i.e., an act of discernment rather than of domination).

[50]אִישׁ (man) occurs here for the first time. Sarna, *Genesis*, 23, suggests that אָדָם (earthling) discovers his own manhood and fulfillment only when he faces the woman.

pair used in the OT to express a close relationship between two parties.[51] However, it is worthy of note that this designation often occurs in decidedly covenantal contexts. That is, the language may underscore more covenantal loyalty than blood ties.[52] Thus, Gen 2:23-24, the first statement regarding the conjugal relationship between man and woman, makes a most powerful statement about the covenantal nature of marriage. Gen 2:24 affirms the divine intent of a man abandoning his familial identity to enter into a lasting covenantal relationship with a woman, a relationship typified by mutual concern, fidelity, and commitment.[53]

2. The Temptation. The temptation scene (3:1-7) both fascinates us and leaves us desiring more information. Several features of the narrative merit close attention: 1) the dialogue between the serpent and the woman; 2) the nature of the serpent and its relationship to the woman; 3) the nature

---

[51]Gen 29:14; Judg 9:2-3; 2 Sam 5:1; 19:13 (see also Job 2:5; Ps 102:5). Walter Brueggemann, "Of the Same Flesh and Bone, Gn 2, 23a," *CBQ* 32 (1970): 533, understands flesh and bone as merismus (i.e., flesh = weakness and absence of power; bone = strength and might).

[52]The verb "cleave" (דָּבַק) also occurs in covenantal contexts (Deut 10:20; 11:22; 13:4; Josh 22:5; 23:8; 2 Sam 20:3; 2 Kgs 18:6).

[53]Westermann, *Genesis 1-11*, 233. Trible, *Sexuality,* 104, captures well the radical message of the text: From one comes two; from wholeness comes differentiation. Now, at the conclusion of the episode, this differentiation returns to wholeness; from two come the one flesh of communion between female and male. Robert Lawton, "Genesis 2:24: Trite or Tragic?" *JBL* 105 (1986): 97-98, argues that the verb "leaves" (עָזַב) should not be read as a frequentive imperfect (i.e., as descriptive of that which typically occurs), but as a potential imperfect (i.e., as that which should occur). He translates v. 24: "a man *should* leave his father and mother . . . ." Since social custom reflected the reverse of this practice (i.e., the woman typically left her family for that of her husband), he interprets this verse as a statement of divine intent rather than a habitually observed reality. Reading v. 24 in this way places it within a series of reversals which occur between chaps. 2 and 3. Just as 2:25 is reversed by 3:7, so 2:24 is dramatically reversed in 3:12, 16 when the man fails to take responsibility for his own actions, blaming instead his wife.

In the Beginning: Male and Female (Gen 1-3)

of the woman and her response to the serpent; 4) the presence/absence of the man.

The surprising absence of God from the scene is heightened by the sudden presence and dominance of the serpent. The serpent initiates and concludes the dialogue, implicitly demonstrating that the woman has been "surrounded and captured."[54] The serpent's opening question is a "masterpiece of psychological shading."[55] Through subtle distortion, the question defies a simple "yes or no" response. In responding, the woman corrects the serpent's distortion, but in the process shades the command herself. Having been captured by the serpent's apparent knowledge and insight, she succumbs to the temptation. Remarkably, we are told that having eaten of the fruit, the "eyes of the woman and her husband were opened"; knowledge of some sort has in fact been gained. The scene concludes with a vignette of the man and woman acting somewhat self-sufficiently—unsatisfied with their nakedness, they make clothing for themselves.

The linguistic and thematic links between Gen 2 and 3 must not be missed. The introduction of the serpent, the most crafty (עָרוּם) of the animals, follows the note that the man and woman were both naked (עֲרוּמִּים) and unashamed. "Made" (עָשָׂה) by God (3:1), this most cunning representative of the animal kingdom threatens the harmony of the created order and challenges the intent of the Creator.[56] Incredibly, the serpent contends that the divine statement

---

[54]Trible, *Sexuality,* 108. God is consistently designated יְחוָה אֱלֹהִים in Gen 2-3, except by the serpent who simply calls him אֱלֹהִים.

[55]Gerhard Von Rad, *Genesis* (trans. J. Marks; rev. ed.; Philadelphia: Westminster, 1972): 88.

[56]A discussion of the nature and full identity of the serpent is beyond the scope of this essay. In the immediate context, the serpent is clearly identified as a wild animal. For extensive discussions regarding the use of this passage in other biblical contexts, and the motif of the serpent in the larger ancient Near Eastern world, see Westermann, *Genesis 1-11,* 237-38; Willis, *Genesis,* 120; Karen Joines, "The Serpent in Genesis 3," *ZAW* 87 (1975): 1-11.

concerning death is inaccurate and that the divine intent is rooted in jealousy rather than care and concern.[57]

In her initial response, the woman faithfully defends God, even to the point of utilizing his sentence structure. However, her response allows the serpent to assert his presumed superior insight and force the woman away from her position of believing obedience to a position of neutrality from which she might judge God and his command.[58] Herein lies the essence of the temptation—to become like God, living not under command to be responsible, but under the power to decide what responsible is.[59] However, it is important that we acknowledge the presentation of the woman in this temptation scene. As Trible notes, her response reveals her as intelligent, informed, and perceptive. She assumes responsibility for obedience (to a command delivered originally to the man), a responsibility the man will quickly abdicate (3:12).[60] To portray the woman as weak,

---

[57]Westermann, *Genesis 1-11,* 240. As Trible, *Sexuality,* 111, notes, the motivation of the serpent is unstated. We are not told whether his "quarrel" is with God or the human couple; neither are we told whether his primary desire is to expose God's deceptive jealousy or his own superior slyness (which can overcome even humans). Although the motives of the serpent may be obscure, the enormity of its claims are clear—knowledge of divine action and intent.

[58]Von Rad, *Genesis,* 88, noting that the serpent gives the woman opportunity first to be right and defend herself for God's sake, states, "In the form of a question, however, the serpent has already made a deadly attack on the artlessness of obedience."

[59]George Coats, *Genesis* (FOTL I; Grand Rapids: Eerdmans, 1983): 54; see also *idem,* "God of Death: Power and Obedience in the Primeval History," *Int* 29 (1975) 227-39. Westermann, *Genesis 1-11,* 249, states: "The narrator wants to point to the inscrutable riddle which is always part of human existence wherever and as long as it is lived, namely, that people have the urge to transcend themselves by overstepping the limits set for them."

[60]Trible, *Sexuality,* 110, somewhat overstating the situation, calls her a theologian, ethicist, hermeneut, and rabbi! The woman, in adding the prohibition against touching the tree, "builds a fence around the Torah." Her "addition" to the command should insure obedience!

feeble-minded, and an easy target for the serpent finds no warrant in the text.⁶¹

The serpent's challenge of the divine command brings tragic results. The word of the serpent supplants the word of God. The movement of the woman is dramatically drawn out: "So when the woman saw that the tree was good for food, and that it was a delight to the eyes, and that the tree was to be desired to make one wise, she took of its fruit and ate (3:6)."⁶²

To this point the man has received no mention. We are now told that the woman took some of the fruit and gave it to her husband, who also ate. Again, although it has long been popular to presume the man's absence from this scene, and thus to develop elaborate theories for the serpent's selection of the woman and her succumbing to the temptation, the text challenges such explanations. Though left explicitly unstated, several features of the text would suggest that the man is present throughout: 1) from the moment that God presents the woman to the man, no mention is made of their separation; 2) the serpent consistently uses a plural address; the woman answers in first person plural (we); 3) in 3:6b, we are told that she gives fruit also to her husband "with her" (עִמָּהּ).⁶³ Whether the man is absent or present from the

---

⁶¹The question of the serpent's selection of the woman rather than the man has fascinated readers for centuries. Since the text gives no reason, speculation abounds. Quite popular of course is that her "inferiority" makes her more vulnerable to temptation than the man. Conversely, Richard Hess, "The Roles of the Woman and the Man in Genesis 3," *Themelios* 18 (1993): 16, theorizes that since the woman was not present during the naming of the animals, she would be unaware of the serpent's shrewdness and thus more susceptible to its persuasive powers!

⁶²Ironically, the woman's assessment of the "goodness" of the tree results in tragedy; through disobedience to the divine command the "goodness" of God's creation (chap. 1) brings harm rather than benefit. Sarna, *Genesis,* 25, notes the reason for the contrast: no longer is the goodness rooted in God's verdict; now it is rooted in the appeal to the senses and utilitarian value.

⁶³This prepositional phrase is best taken as a nominal attribute

beginning, clearly absent is any nuance of the woman as a "temptress" of the man. Unlike the serpent, she makes no overtures toward him or in any way verbally entices him to partake; she simply hands him the fruit.[64]

The results are tragicomic. Knowledge does ensue; the couple become painfully aware of their nakedness. The "one flesh" find themselves exposed. Ironically, with their eyes opened, they realize the opposite of what the serpent promised: "They know their helplessness, insecurity, and defenselessness. What characterized their life in creation now threatens it in disobedience."[65]

This newly-acquired knowledge has failed to make them like God and completely autonomous. Although numerous interpretations have been given for the meaning of "knowledge of good and evil," in the present context it seems best understood as that knowledge which allows humankind to determine for itself what is beneficial or

---

(i.e., "to her husband [who was] with her" [so NRSV], rather than as an adverbial (i.e., "she took and ate, and also [besides feeding herself alone] gave it to her man along with herself"). For a full discussion arguing in favor of the man's presence throughout, see Jean M. Higgins, "Myth of Eve: the Temptress," *JAAR* 44 (1976): 645-46, who notes that 3:6b in some versions ends: "she gave to her husband and *they* ate" (perhaps presuming his presence from the outset).

[64]Westermann, *Genesis 1-11,* 250, sees here two temptations. The temptation of woman reflects the desire to rise above oneself; the temptation of man demonstrates the desire toward conformity.

[65]Trible, *Sexuality,* 114, further states: "The defenselessness that belongs to creation produces neither shame (2:25) nor fear (cf. 3:10). But the knowledge of defenselessness that is acquired through disobedience yields simultaneous affirmations and denials of itself: "and they sewed leaves together and made for themselves clothes" (3:7cd). What they conceal, they reveal. Having exceeded the limits set for Eros, this couple has destroyed its harmony. Instead of fulfillment, joy, and gift, they now experience life as problem that *they* must solve; as threat that *they* must eliminate; and as shame that *they* must cover up. God-given helplessness has become danger; existence has become burden."

detrimental.⁶⁶ The serpent has essentially challenged the necessity of humans living in relationship with God and under his command. With the acquisition of this knowledge, divine beneficence and protection will be irrelevant and unnecessary, since humans will have the capacity within themselves to address such matters.⁶⁷ It is to this situation that Yahweh responds.

3. *The Divine Response.* Strikingly, when Yahweh comes, he begins not with condemnation but with questions.⁶⁸ This final scene is somewhat cyclic, consisting of a trial (3:8-13), ensuing judgment (3:14-19), and its

---

⁶⁶For a thorough presentation of the various interpretations of this phrase, see Westermann, *Genesis 1-11*, 242-245; Howard Wallace, *The Eden Narrative* (HSM 32; Atlanta: Scholars Press, 1985): 115-128; H. Stern, "Knowledge of Good and Evil," *VT* 8 (1958): 405-18; W. Malcolm Clark, "Legal Background to the Yahwist's Use of 'good and evil'," *JBL* 88 (1969): 266-78.

⁶⁷Von Rad, *Genesis*, 89, states, "So the serpent holds out less the prospect of an extension of the capacity for knowledge than the independence that enables a man to decide for himself what will help or hinder him. This is something completely new in that as a result man leaves the protection of divine providence. God had provided what was good for man (2:18!), and had given him complete security. But now man will go beyond this, to decide for himself. The question in mind is probably whether the coveted autonomy might not be the greatest burden of man's life. But who thinks of that now? The step to be taken is such a small one! . . . What the serpent's insinuation means is the possibility of an extension of human existence beyond the limits set for it by God at creation, an increase of life not only in the sense of pure intellectual enrichment but also familiarity with, and power over, mysteries that lie beyond man. That the narrative see man's fall, his actual separation from God, occurring again and again in *this* area (and not, for example, as a plunge into moral evil, into the subhuman!), i.e., in what we call Titanism, man's *hubris*—this is truly one of its most significant affirmations."

⁶⁸In the OT, divine questions often allow the listener to realize the full implications of prior actions and affirmations (see Gen 4:6, 10; Job 38:2; 1 Kgs 19:9). In Gen 1, God "calls" (קָרָא) creation into orderly existence (1:5, 8, 10); in 3:9 he "calls" (קָרָא) אָדָם (earthling) into question.

aftermath (3:20-24).⁶⁹ To this point, the presence of God has consistently meant the presence of grace and beneficence. However, God's appearance creates fear and the disappearance ("hiding") of the humans. Through God's questioning, confession results. However, it is confession tinged with deniability. The man refuses complete responsibility for his actions, as does the woman. At one level the serpent is right, the human couple do not experience immediate death; at a deeper level they suffer a fate worse than death—they no longer stand together as one flesh.⁷⁰ The man, strangely silent throughout the temptation, becomes verbose, while the woman's response is brief.⁷¹ Paradoxically, the man cites his nakedness as cause for his fear and hiding, even though he has only recently clothed himself!

The trial concluded and verdict self-evident, judgment swiftly follows (3:14-19). The divine pronouncements upon the serpent, woman, and man, hauntingly echo the language of Gen 2. The serpent, unaddressed in vv. 8-13, is deemed guilty (without a trial). The "craftiest" (עָרוּם) of animals is cursed (אָרוּר).⁷² Having challenged humankind to forsake

---

⁶⁹Gen 3:8-24 is clearly set in contrast to 2:7-24. Harmony and intimacy disintegrate into disharmony and alienation.

⁷⁰Coats, *Genesis*, 55.

⁷¹Trible, *Sexuality*, 118-20, insightfully compares the responses of the man and the woman. The man, heaping up words in response, testifies to the damage of disobedience. Explanation, rationalization, and justification have entered life. "Defenselessness has become defensiveness; self-centeredness prevails . . . . Ironically, his opposition to her [the woman] speaks of his solidarity with her in transgression. Though he betrays her, he does not say that she tempted him . . . Neither God nor the woman has tempted the man, and yet he implicates them both in his guilt." Regarding the woman's response, Trible states: "By betraying the woman to God, the man opposed himself to her; by ignoring him in her reply to God, the woman separates herself from the man."

⁷²Trible, *Sexuality*, 123, captures it well: "The very animal who tempted the human creatures of dust to eat the forbidden fruit and assured them that death would not result (3:1, 4) eats dust himself all the days of his life."

In the Beginning: Male and Female (Gen 1-3)

believing trust for knowledge, this creature now will experience constant enmity with the human realm. The harmony of the created order has been shattered. Having presumptuously pitted his knowledge and skill against that of the divine order, he now suffers repeated defeat in his conflict with the human realm (3:15).[73]

The punishment pronounced upon the woman (3:16) bristles with difficulties and ambiguity which defy resolution. The difficulty of this verse is matched only by the important weight it has borne in studies treating the male/female relationship. Several aspects merit attention: 1) What is the precise syntax of v. 16? What is the relationship of 16a to 16b? 2) How should v. 16b be translated? 3) What is the intended nuance and meaning of "desire" (תְּשׁוּקָה)? 4) How is this statement related to Gen 2? 5) What is the hermeneutical significance of this statement?

It is worthy of note that the pronouncement upon the woman is the only pronouncement which contains no curse. Surrounded by curse (the serpent [v. 14], the ground [v. 17]), she remains uncursed.[74] Also, in contrast to the serpent and the man, no "reason" (because . . .) is given for the pronouncement.[75] However, it is unclear whether her punishment is singular (pain in childbearing) or dual (pain in childbearing; desire for husband)? A decisive answer to this question eludes us.[76]

---

[73]For an excellent treatment of this passage and its interpretation throughout history, see Jack P. Lewis, "The Woman's Seed (Gen 3:15)," *JETS* 34 (1991): 299-319; Westermann, *Genesis 1-11*, 259-61.

[74]As noted by Trible, *Sexuality*, 126, this should give us pause in claiming she is judged more severely than any other party.

[75]No reason is necessary; her earlier statement (3:13) acknowledges her guilt.

[76]The number of punishments in each of the addresses in vv. 14-19 continues to be disputed. Presently, the majority of scholars envision one punishment per party, with the remainder of the pronouncement explanation of the conditions under which the punishment will take place. For a detailed discussion of this aspect of the text, see Irvin A. Busenitz, "Woman's Desire for Man: Genesis 3:16 Reconsidered," *GTJ*

A valid translation of v. 16b must take into account two factors: 1) the meaning and precise nuance of תְּשׁוּקָה (desire); 2) the syntactical force of the preposition אֶל (to, for). The noun תְּשׁוּקָה occurs only twice elsewhere in biblical Hebrew: Gen 4:7 (its desire is for you, but you must master it [a most enigmatic passage]); Cant 7:10 (I am my beloved's, and his desire is for me). Three readings of v. 16b prevail: 1) the woman's desire, whatever it may be, will be subjected to that of her husband;[77] 2) the woman's desire specifically entails her drive to dominate her husband and the relationship;[78] 3) the woman's desire involves primarily her

---

7 (1986): 203-12. This lack of clarity is most unfortunate, since a comprehensive understanding of v. 16 necessitates an understanding of the relationship of v. 16a to 16b.

[77]So Edward Young, *Genesis 3* (London: Banner of Truth, 1966): 127, states: "Her desire, whatever it may be, will not be her own. She cannot do what she wishes, for her husband rules over her like a despot and whatever she wishes is subject to his will." Similarly, but less harshly, Willis, *Genesis,* 131, endorsing the rendering of the KJV and ASV ("thy desire shall be *to* [אֶל] thy husband"), states: "The previous context described what happened when the woman was left to follow freely her own desire. Her inability to cope with the situation made it necessary for God to impose a control upon her, which would be superior to her innermost wishes (viz., the decision of her husband). In matters of great importance and ultimate concern, it is his decision that must prevail, no matter how strong the woman's desire for a different route of action may be." Perhaps in support of this position, the LXX and Peshitta apparently emended or (mis)read תְּשׁוּקָה (desire) as תְּשׁוּבָה (your return), possibly implying that since the woman failed to act responsibly, she must return to the role originally intended for her (and her husband will make sure she discharges that role).

[78]This interpretation is most forcefully articulated by Susan Foh, "What is the Woman's Desire?" *WTJ* 37 (1975): 382; *idem, Women and the Word of God* (Grand Rapids: Baker, 1980): 69. Her argumentation is elaborate. She first argues that any notion of sexual desire is eliminated by an etymological tracking of the noun תְּשׁוּקָה. She derives תְּשׁוּקָה from Arabic *saqa* (to urge, drive on, impel), not *shaqa* (to desire, excite). For Foh, male headship was God-ordained from the beginning (see below); it is not a result of or punishment for sin. Utilizing the enigmatic line in Gen 4:7, she states that the woman's desire for her husband is of the same type as that of Cain—the desire to possess and control. Thus, what 3:16b affirms is that woman will

sexual desire[79] for her husband. Although difficult, the last interpretation seems least problematic. The first two interpretations necessitate a hierarchical reading of Gen 2 (which we have seen to be quite problematic) and a reading of the temptation scene for which there is no solid textual evidence.[80] A straightforward reading of Gen 2 seriously undermines attempts to read that chapter hierarchically. First, Eve's derivation from Adam does not presume subordination, else Adam, derived from the earth, would find himself inferior to it. Second, reading "helpmate" as implying subordination defies the lexical evidence for the term. Third, the grammatical evidence for Adam's naming of Eve reflects more the world of recognition and discovery than the world of dominion and subordination. In naming the woman, Adam is not determining her identity, but rejoicing in what God has done.[81] Finally, the language of 2:24 (leaves . . . cleaves) reverberates with covenantal significance.[82] In Gen 2, woman was created for meaningful and fulfilling companionship—companionship best reflected in a covenantal relationship of both partners giving fully of themselves to the other. Eve and Adam have shattered that wonderful covenantal relationship through their desire to become their own gods.[83] As noted earlier, there is no indication in Gen 3:1-7 that the woman's

---

constantly strive to control and master her husband; the husband will be forced to fight for his headship. The primary change from Gen 2 to 3 is that sin has corrupted the willing submission of the wife and the loving headship of the husband. The rule of love founded in Paradise is replaced by struggle, tyranny, and domination. Hess, *Themelios* (1993): 17, partly follows Foh, but in the final phrase Hess reads, "he *will* rule over you" (*not* "he *should* rule over you"). The difference is vital.

[79]Alternately, her desire for intimacy.

[80]Specifically, if the woman's sin involved usurping of the man's authority, we would expect some mention of his failure to control his wife enumerated in his punishment (3:17-19), but none occurs.

[81]In actuality, in naming the woman (אִשָּׁה) the man (אִישׁ) simultaneously names himself (so Sarna, *Genesis*, 23).

[82]See Deut 10:20; 11:22; 13:4; Josh 22:5; 23:8.

[83]"To love and to cherish" has given way to "desire and dominate."

succumbing to temptation was in any way related to her separation from her husband. In actuality, the woman's sin in 3:1-7 has nothing to do with usurping the man's authority; rather, it involves exalting herself above the Creator to determine for herself right and wrong.[84] If v. 16b has any relation to v. 16a, we would expect the woman's desire to have some connection to the pain that now accompanies her giving birth. It seems plausible that given the extreme pain that will now attend childbirth, the woman's desire for intimacy would be diminished.[85] V. 16b counters such an assumption. However, her desire will be met with rule.[86]

Davidson[87] notes the possibilities of the hermeneutical significance of this passage: 1) the subordination of woman was a creation ordinance (i.e., God's ideal from the beginning), but through sin this original form of hierarchy

---

[84]Busenitz, *GTJ* 7 (1986): 203-12, correctly notes that the immediate context speaks not of the woman's desire to rule, but of the continuation of life in the face of death. He states: "Woman may desire to dominate or rule over man, but it is not a part of the punishment pronounced upon woman; it is just the essence, character and result of all sin against God. Self-exaltation and pride always result in the desire to dominate and rule." However, he vacillates by concluding that "the contention that 'sin has corrupted both the willing submission of the wife and the loving headship of the husband' (Foh, *Women*, 69) is unquestionably true. But it is a natural consequence of sin and not the result of God's judgment upon woman in Genesis 3:16." Within the larger context, Gen 3:8-24 serves as a contrast to 2:7-24. The harmony and intimacy of covenantal togetherness has given way to disharmony and alienation.

[85]We should remember that in the ancient world technology to alleviate the pain of childbirth and greatly reduce the potentially fatal consequences of labor and delivery was not advanced. As the possibility of a mother's loss of life during pregnancy and especially delivery was staggering, it is remarkable that women would continued to put themselves in such life-threatening circumstances.

[86]Trible, *Sexuality*, 128, states: "The man will not reciprocate the woman's desire; instead, he will rule over her. Thus she lives in unresolved tension. Where once there was mutuality, now there is a hierarchy of division."

[87]Davidson, *AUSS* 26 (1988): 121-31.

was distorted and corrupted and must be restored by the gospel; 2) subordination was a creation ordinance; however, Gen 3:16 reflects not a distortion of subordination but a reaffirmation of subordination as a blessing and comfort to woman in her difficulties as mother;[88] 3) the subordination of 3:16b is a blessing rather than a curse; however, subordination was not a creation ordinance; 4) subordination did not exist prior to the sin; further, the statement of subordination of 3:16 intends only a *description* of the evil consequences of sin (to be removed by the gospel), not a *prescription* of God's will for subsequent husband-wife relationships; 5) subordination did not exist prior to the sin; however, 3:16 is *prescriptive*, not merely *descriptive*. Ultimately, our decision will be rooted in our larger understanding of the husband-wife relationship found throughout Scripture. Not unexpectedly, how this passage is utilized in subsequent portions of Scripture impacts greatly our reading of it in its original setting. Although not without difficulties, in its *original* setting, the fourth reading seems to reflect most closely the original intent of the passage.[89] Having desired to rule her own life, the woman finds herself in a situation in which subsequent life comes only through

---

[88]I.e., the woman in her labor will be eager for her husband and he will rule, not through domination and oppression, but through care and help.

[89]Establishing a sound exegetical method is crucial for understanding the larger hermeneutical ramifications of this passage. Sound exegetical procedure involves reading a passage first within its immediate context. Taking seriously the internal dynamics and nature of the text within its immediate context entails a close reading of the text *on its own terms* (i.e., initially without regard to its use elsewhere in Scripture), followed by close attention to the scriptural placement of the text (i.e., noting what immediately precedes and follows the text under discussion). To be specific, one must determine first the exegetical meaning and theological thrust of Gen 2-3—only then can one determine profitably Paul's use of this material in 1 Tim. To reverse the process seriously undermines the validity of the exegetical process. For example, were one to begin with Rom 5:12-21, one might come to Gen 2-3 assuming that Eve's actions were of no significance whatsoever, since she is not mentioned in Rom 5! The only sin of any consequence, then, would be that of Adam!

excruciating pain and in a relationship where mutuality and equality have been replaced by desire and control.

With the punishment of the man, curse returns (upon the earth, however, not the man), with the reason for the punishment.[90] The man's punishment is relatively clear. He receives the longest address, perhaps in response to his earlier lengthy assertions (3:10, 12) or as an indication of the extent of his culpability.[91] Just as his intimate relationship of mutuality with the woman has been shattered, so now his joyful working of the garden is replaced with burdensome and never-ending toil.

With the trial complete and judgment having been pronounced, expulsion from the garden remains. The final scene (3:20-24) is freighted with language that hauntingly echoes earlier sections. Irony dominates the scene. The man now names his wife, giving the reason.[92] This woman, who initially receives no mention of family (2:25), is now designated the "mother of all living" (3:20). However, we cannot help but remind ourselves that life will come through extreme pain and toil (3:16). Their inadequate attempt to address their vulnerability and exposure through the making

---

[90]In 3:17, the man "listened to the voice (לְקוֹל שָׁמַעְתָּ) of his wife." Although one might assume that this statement affirms the nature of the woman as "temptress," it seems preferable simply to understand here an acknowledgment of the man's decision to follow his wife's direction rather than God's command. The expression לְקוֹל שָׁמַעְתָּ regularly occurs in Hebrew with the nuance "to obey." Here, the man chose to "obey" his wife rather than God. Again, it is important to note that the man is faulted for failing to be a responsible creature, not for failing to control the woman.

[91]Sarna, *Genesis,* 28, regards the man as most culpable, since he received the prohibition directly from God.

[92]Whereas God articulates no reason for her punishment (3:16), the man provides reason through wordplay: "Eve" (חַוָּה)/"life" (חָי). Numerous scholars have suggested that, unlike the earlier acknowledgment of the woman (2:23), this act of naming implicitly carries a notion of control and authority.

of garments (3:7) is corrected by Yahweh through the gracious gift of leather garments (3:21).[93]

However, a most significant issue remains to be addressed. Through partaking of the knowledge of good and evil, the man and woman have dramatically altered the relationship between themselves and their Creator. Contrary to the serpent's arrogant assertions, their eating has not resulted in eliminating their need for relationship with God, but rather in bringing them to full awareness of their helplessness and vulnerability in the created order. The quest for power and self-sufficiency has ironically resulted in the eruption of conflict, tension, and struggle in God's harmonious creation. The resulting human creatures in no way are worthy candidates for participation in the tree of life.[94] Expulsion is necessary. Poignantly, as the man and woman are driven from the garden to "till the ground from which he was taken," cherubs are positioned "to guard" (לִשְׁמֹר) against their possible re-entry.[95]

---

[93]It may be appropriate to contrast the ambiguous stance between the man and the woman with the constant stance of God in grace toward his creatures. God the creator becomes God the sustainer. God, having "made" (עָשָׂה) the world and its inhabitants, now "makes" (עָשָׂה) clothing for his human creatures. These creatures, who began "naked and unashamed," are now given the clothing necessary to endure the shame and fear they have created, and the harsh conditions of life now theirs.

[94]Trible, *Sexuality,* 136, notes: "Perhaps irony, a device that has appeared often in scene three, best interprets this closing speech by God. Helpless creatures, their lives shattered by strife, discord, and enmity, are hardly candidates for divinity." Thus, Yahweh may be mocking the serpent's assertion. Sarna, *Genesis,* 30, suggests that through the desire to exceed the limits of creaturehood, the human has radically altered the perspective of human existence. The next temptation quite likely would entail the attempt to restore the previous condition through artificial means (viz., the quest for eternal life) rather than through restoring the ruptured relationship with the Creator.

[95]Originally, the man was entrusted with the task of "tilling and keeping (guard)" (שָׁמַר/עָבַד) the garden. Now, he is sent forth to "till" (עָבַד) the earth, a task which will tax him severely, while the cherubs "guard" (שָׁמַר) the garden. The man struggles to eke out sustenance from the very dust from which he was created (2:7; 3:19).

Conclusion

Gen 2-3 provides a powerful account of the nature of God, the relationship of God to his human creatures, and the relation of human creatures to one another. Whereas God is presented primarily through the metaphor of a sovereign monarch in Gen 1, in Gen 2-3 several images arise. As God creates, he is a potter sculpting the dust of the earth into a man. As gardener, he plants a luxurious garden to address the physical needs of this creature. As surgeon and architect, he crafts a woman from man. With the completion of creation in Gen 2, humankind have vocation (caring for the garden), permission (eating of the garden) and prohibition (refraining from that which will harm them). Perhaps most significantly, they have community (2:23-25).

However, in Gen 3 Yahweh's intent for creation is ruptured. In challenging the divine design for creation, the human couple tragically alter their vital relationships: 1) their relationship with their Creator; 2) their relationship with each other; 3) their relationship with the rest of the created order. Where once there was harmony, productivity, and meaning, there is now pain, struggle, and potential meaninglessness to life. The contrast could not be more poignantly drawn. In their desire to circumvent the need for a sovereign Lord, they achieve not fulfillment but become keenly aware of the weakness and vulnerability of their creatureliness. In their relationship to each other, equality, mutual concern, and care are replaced by struggle, conflict, and obsession with hierarchical order. Finally, the rest of creation, given to them for enjoyment and sustenance, now deals them endless toil and backbreaking labor. The joy and freedom of life under the protective wing of the Creator has given way to a constant awareness of struggle and the omnipresence of mortality and finitude. However, the story continues—for the God of Gen 1-3 is a God of infinite grace and mercy, a God who repeatedly calls his creation to realign with his purposes and intent. Most dramatically, he ultimately exhibits that posture himself in the gift of his own Son.

Chapter Two

SARAH—HER LIFE AND LEGACY

Jack W. Vancil

First mentioned in the early Genesis narratives, Sarah is relatively obscured by the male figures in the text and later by a religious interest centered on her husband, Abraham. Nevertheless the stories about both characters are so important that all later biblical history is understood to begin here. There are many questions concerning Sarah and diverse opinions are found among the students of Genesis. These pertain to uncertainties about her role in the narratives, her family background, her status in the ancient society, her relationship to Abraham, her beauty, her involvement in Pharaoh's harem, her power over Hagar, her being taken by Abimelech and, finally, an entire chapter devoted to her death.

The scarcity of direct information on Sarah should not, however, detract from her unique and crucial place in the total biblical story and as the principal matriarch in the history of faith. Beyond Genesis, she receives only brief mention in the rest of the Bible, but there developed an early and extensive interest in Sarah, as is indicated in extrabiblical Jewish sources and in the Koran and its exegetical commentators.

1. *Sarah's Name And Pagan Background*

The patriarchs and matriarchs bore names common to the West Semitic region of the ancient Near East.[1] Sarah appears first as the Hebrew שָׂרַי (*sarai*, Gen 11:29) and later,

---

[1] See Claus Westermann, *Genesis 12-36* (trans. J. Scullion; Minneapolis: Augsburg, 1985): 84-86, 137-139.

the name is changed to שָׂרָה (*sarah*, Gen 17:15). It is apparently derived from שַׂר (*sar*, prince, from the root שָׂרַר, *sarar*, to rule; see Judg 9:22; Isa 32:1; Prov 8:16; Esth 1:22). Sarah is cognate with the Akkadian name *sharru* (king).[2]

Sarah's world is set in ancient Mesopotamia, a society that archaeology shows was thoroughly polytheistic and idolatrous. The names in Terah's own family tree suggest, in fact, that his clan followed the common practice of naming the children after popular deities. One of Israel's earliest historical creeds remembers that Hebrew ancestry was once involved with pagan religion: "thus says the Lord, the God of Israel, 'Your fathers lived of old beyond the Euphrates, Terah, the father of Abraham and of Nahor; and they served other gods'" (Josh 24:2). We also know that the original cities of the patriarchs, Ur and Haran, were prominent cultic centers for the astronomical moon-god, Sin,[3] and that this

---

[2]Note Sargon=*sharru-ken*, "the king is legitimate," and *shar kishati*, "King of the universe." Sarah is more a title than a name, meaning "princess," or in Akkadian, "queen" (note the term in Judg 5:29; 1 Kgs 11:3; Isa 49:23; Lam 1:1; Esth 1:18). The title is attested in Ugaritic (2058 rev. frag. b:3; see also 69:2; 138:8, 12, 17; 1015.2; and 2009:2 is an epistle of the king to the Queen Mother, Shar-el-li). Some have derived the term from the Hebrew verb שָׂרָה (*sarah*), meaning "to strive, persevere" (see Hos 12:4; Gen 32:28). See *BDB*, 975a; S. J. De Vries, *IDB* (ed. G. Buttrick; Nashville: Abingdon, 1962): 4.219; J. Boyd, *ISBE* (ed. J. Orr; Grand Rapids: Eerdmans, 1957): 4.2691. A large number of official names such as Shara (god of Umma), Shar-kali-sharri of Agade, Sharrish-takal (minister and oracular priest) of Agade, Sharrum-bani (governor of Awak), Sharrum-bani (a Sumerian official), support the view that the name *Sarah* was, in fact, a title.

[3]Sin is also known as Nanna. In the "Hymn to the Moon-God" he is praised variously: "Father Nanna, lord Sin, hero of the gods, . . . lord of Ur, . . . lord of Egishshirgal (the moon-god temple in Ur)" (*ANET*, 385-386). Sin, Shamash, and Ishtar represented the three great astronomical bodies of the heavens: the moon, the sun, and Venus. On the travels of the patriarchs, see Umberto Cassuto, *Genesis* (trans. I. Abrahams; Jerusalem: Magnes Press, 1974): 2.275, who says, "The fact that Ur and Haran were the chief centres of the cult of the moon-god Sin, and consequently were linked together by firm and permanent ties, serves to explain the movements from one to the other."

cult was eminently important throughout the land from very early times, and even the crescent moon symbolized the boat carrying Sin across the night sky.[4] Thus the extensive influence of this cult has led to the speculation that Sarah's name, like the other names in Terah's family, honored the moon-god.[5] It would appear that the clan of Terah was deeply involved in Mesopotamian culture and religion, and, as is typical in many societies, honored the gods and goddesses of their homeland in their own family names.

One scholar, Savina Teubal,[6] has even seen in Sarah herself an involvement in the religion so extensive that she

---

[4]See H. W. F. Saggs, *The Greatness that was Babylon* (New York and Toronto: Mentor, 1962): 317-318. The crescent shape continued on into the later iconography of Islamic tradition.

[5]Cassuto, *Genesis* 2.276, notes that her name, like Terah's, was possibly connected "with the Mesopotamian worship of the hosts of heaven" and that *Sharrat* (queen) was one of the Akkadian designations of Ishtar, the goddess of the planet Venus. Also, the later Terahite name *Laban* (white, glorious; Gen 24ff.), is perhaps linked to the moon (see Isa 24:23; 30:26; Cant 6:10).

[6]Savina J. Teubal, *Sarah The Priestess The First Matriarch of Genesis* (Chicago and London: Swallow, 1984). Her thesis is that Sarah was a priestess who had "intimate relationship with the supernatural" and was "privy to the mysteries of religions" giving her great power. She suggests that "the particular office held by Sarah was the most elevated in rank and status, the most sacred and most revered— a position comparable to that of women known as *en* and *naditu* who belonged to religious orders in the ancient Mesopotamian region of Sumer" (xv). She bases her views on ancient Near Eastern society and practices and also on a literary analysis of the narratives (17). She follows Thorkild Jacobsen, "Mesopotamia: The Cosmos as a State" in *Before Philosophy* (Baltimore: Penguin, 1971): 141-142, that a "Primitive Democracy" existed very early in Sumer and was the "prevalent type of state." I refer to Teubal several times in this article since the topic of goddesses in various world traditions has emerged as an important question in contemporary feminist discussions, e. g., see Larry Hurtado, ed., *Goddesses in Religion and Modern Debate* (Atlanta: Scholars Press, 1990). The relation of this subject for biblical studies may be followed in the articles by Dawne McCance and Joan B. Townsend. The subject has become important in modern historical and theological debate; the biblical view of monotheism and the

has ascribed to her the status of a priestess. The evidence she uses is deductive. While her approach is thorough and interesting, these assumptions about Sarah are highly speculative and diverge radically from the views of most scholars. She suggests, for instance, that the early period of Mesopotamia was not patriarchal but matriarchal, and that it was only later, in Canaan and during the biblical period, that the role of women became obscured by patriarchal bias and authority. Teubal sees evidence, however, of matriarchy displayed even in the Genesis text. She says that it is "the interpretations of the commentators, not the texts themselves, which place the stories in patriarchal focus."[7] She rightly points out that the ancients were not as unsophisticated as is popularly believed and that:

> In particular, women have traditionally been depicted as primitive and childish in their aspirations and generally lacking in vision. Fresh study of our female forebears, however, invalidates this view and shows us that the matriarchs were learned, wise women who were highly developed spiritually.[8]

---

development of the Western religious outlook is being challenged along the lines of the assumed important position of goddesses, or, "The Goddess," in the ancient world. The time of early polytheism and the reign of "The Goddess" is presented as being a time when the world was peaceful and lacked warfare; the time of violence came only when the world became patriarchal and ruled by men. Though this subject is not researched well by many who write on the topic, Teubal's work on Sarah is an exception. Teubal is not the first to suggest Sarah's association with a pagan cult; see A. von Gall, *Altisraelitische Kultstatten* (Giessen: J. Ricker, 1898): 55-59; J. Boyd, *ISBE* 4.2691.

[7]Teubal, *Sarah the Priestess*, xii. An entire chapter, "Examining The Non-Patriarchal Social System and Genealogy in Genesis" (53-68), is devoted to the issue. Tikva Frymer-Kensky, *In the Wake of the Goddesses: Women, Culture, and the Biblical Transformation of Pagan Myth* (New York: Free Press, 1992): 118-143, esp. 120, points out that it is a false understanding to charge that ancient Israel was responsible for the beginning of patriarchy; it existed as a structure of ancient Near Eastern society long before Israel came on the scene.

[8]Teubal, *Sarah the Priestess*, xii.

Though Teubal's observations are grounded in an understanding of ancient Mesopotamian society, the assertion that Sarah occupied the high position of a priestess in the moon-cult of Ur and Haran remains an open question that continues unanswered. She does, however, remind us that the role of the matriarchs in Genesis, and especially Sarah, was active rather than passive and her effort to find in Sarah a positive female model has in some measure been realized.[9]

Sarah brings to the Genesis narratives a strong legacy from ancient Mesopotamia. Her residence in Ur and Haran and her later associations with the oak groves at Moreh and Mamre imply her pagan heritage. Her ancient Near-Eastern name, meaning "princess" or "queen," however, appropriately symbolizes how Sarah would be esteemed in the centuries to follow.

2. *Sarah's Tribal Background and Marriage*

Sarah was a member of the clan of Terahites, assumably by marriage, since she is said to be Terah's "daughter-in-law" (Gen 11:31). Later, however, Abraham identifies her as "the daughter of my father, but not of my mother" (Gen 20:12). According to the latter text, therefore, Sarah is Abraham's half-sister. But why is she not identified as Terah's daughter initially (Gen 11:31)? Is some prior social or legal custom assumed here, but later rejected? Teubal[10] deals with the question by maintaining that the matriarchal line of descent was highly important in early Mesopotamia, just as much as the patriarchal, and that we can deduce from the narratives that there was, in fact, a "matrilineal kinship system" where descent is traced through the female. She argues that in the world of Sarah the custom was matriliny, which meant that descent is more importantly traced through the mother. What Abraham did was to stress that they had

---

[9]See also Katheryn Pfisterer Darr, *Far More Precious Than Jewels* (Louisville: John Knox Press, 1991): 120-123, for comments about Teubal's ideas.

[10]Teubal, *Sarah the Priestess*, 14.

different mothers and this meant they were not considered relatives, and therefore were permitted to marry. Teubal[11] concludes that a sister-brother marriage is "quite understandable in a female-oriented society if the siblings have the same father, but not the same mother, as was the case with Sarah and Abram" and that even though incest taboos existed, "close relationships are defined differently than in our society because family relationships are traced through the mother alone."

The tension created by the relationship of Abraham and Sarah has a long history and can be noted among many Jewish interpreters. In Islam, it is interesting that in the Koran itself, with all of its stories of Abraham, there is no allusion or mention of Sarah as also his sister, but the question is extensively dealt with in a large amount of Islamic interpretive and exegetical literature.[12] Since the Torah forbids marriages between relatives (see Lev 18), the question for Jewish exegetes became whether this marriage was legitimate or not.

The vexing nature of the problem has caused some to conclude that the name Iscah (Gen 11:29) is another name for Sarah, therefore removing the difficulty of Abraham marrying his half-sister; instead, he marries his niece. The odd structure of Gen 11:29 opens the way for this identification. Because Iscah remains unidentified in the passage, the obvious question is raised, "Who is she?" She simply appears in the text and, like Sarah, is found in a genealogy including only males. Iscah is never again mentioned, and since one of the cardinal rules of mishnaic thinking is that Scripture is never redundant and wastes no words, Iscah must therefore be someone quite identifiable in Scripture. Thus the conclusion is reached that Iscah is an alternate name for Sarai, and further that Sarai is not actually the real name,

---

[11]*Ibid.*, 15.
[12]See Reuben Firestone, "Difficulties of Keeping a Beautiful Wife: The Legend of Abraham and Sarah in Jewish and Islamic Tradition," *JJS* 42 (1991): 198.

but rather Iscah. Both the Palestinian and Babylonian Targums make this Sarah=Iscah identification (Meg. 14a; Sanh. 69b). In the eleventh century, Rashi also makes the equation that Iscah is Sarai. He says that "one's childrens' children are considered as one's own children."[13] So the daughter of Abraham's brother would therefore still be considered Terah's daughter, as claimed in Gen 20:12. The arguments used to reach the conclusion that Sarah and Iscah are one and the same are quite pedantic.[14] Essentially, the identification is made because *Iscah* denotes "seeing" (in var. Aramaic dialects).

What does this have to do with Sarah? It is because Pharaoh's princes, in "seeing Sarai," admired her beauty; "hence the name Iscah becomes an elliptical reference to Sarah's great beauty."[15] So, the awkwardness and vagueness of 11:29, "And Abram and Nahor took to them wives there; Abram's wife was Sarai and the name of Nahor's wife was Milcah—daughter of Haran, father of Milcah and father of Iscah," is explained. Iscah is the daughter of Haran, Abraham's brother, and so, if Iscah is another name for Sarah, then Abraham marries his niece.

Others refer to the ancient Near Eastern precedent for endogamous relationships, a practice that was later forbidden in the Torah (see Lev 18:6, 9; cf. 2 Sam 13:13). Marriages between relatives were known especially in Egypt's royal families. The pharaohs sometimes married sisters, half-

---

[13]*Ibid.*, 202. See Rashi, *Pentateuch with Rashi's Commentary* (trans. M. Rosenbaum & A. Silbermann; London: Shapiro, Vallentine & Co., 1929): 47-48, 86. See also Ibn Ezra, *Ibn Ezra's Commentary on the Pentateuch* (trans. and annot. by H. N. Strickman & A. M. Silver; New York: Menorah, 1988): 147, 212-213.

[14]See assessment of the arguments in Eliezer Segal, "Sarah And Iscah: Method And Message In Midrashic Tradition," *JQR* 82 (1992): 417-429.

[15]*Ibid.*, 420. Rashi says she was called Iscah because she saw by inspiration what would happen; and another explanation that it was because everybody looked at her beauty, as it so happened with the princes of Pharaoh.

sisters, or cousins. In Egyptian mythology, we read of the pairing of brothers and sisters among divine beings, such as Geb and Nut, Osiris and Isis. These must have served as models for the practice in the royal family. In Mesopotamia, the prominent deities Kishar and Anshar, daughter and son of Tiamat and Apsu were married to each other. Canaanite myths tell about the close relationship between Baal and his sister, Anath.[16] We must, however, use great caution in our evaluation of ancient mythology.[17] Nevertheless, long before the time of Abraham and Sarah, there is evidence for the practice of marriage between persons closely related.[18]

Steinberg contends that the function of marriage, and the reason for endogamous marriages, specifically in Gen 11:27-36:43, is in order to establish descent. She says it is from the "vantage point of Israelite exclusivity," that the patrilineage of Terah is maintained; therefore, these "boundaries of endogamy are narrowly drawn."[19] She maintains that the marriages in Genesis were in order to establish rights of inheritance, holding that, "In Genesis, we find a pattern in which marriage is legitimate if it enables heirship. All the marriages described in Gen 11:27-36:43 are 'legitimate' because they lead to offspring."[20] She also argues that,

> The marriage pattern in Gen 11:27-36:43 is consistent with anthropological theory on kinship relationships: social contexts that emphasize inherit-

---

[16] See the various myths in *ANET*, 3, 4, 17, 61, 140-142.

[17] Henri Frankfort, *Kingship and the Gods* (Chicago: Univ. of Chicago Press, 1965): 283, warns that on the relation between gods and goddesses "we are misled if we take these terms too literally. They indicate that the relationship between god and goddess is extremely close and more comprehensive than any known to man."

[18] It is interesting to note that in the later Egyptian Empire (1300-1100 BC), in secular love songs lovers addressed each other as "my brother" and "my sister,"*ANET*, 467-469.

[19] Naomi Steinberg, "Alliance or Descent? The Function of Marriage in Genesis," *JSOT* 51 (1991): 45-46.

[20] *Ibid.*, 50.

ance maintain endogamy. Marriage to an agnate, an individual related by patrilineal descent, results in isolation of the lineage in order to uphold a certain social status determined by property.[21]

All this is relevant to the subject because, as she says, "The marriage rule of patrilineal endogamy may also shed light on the enigmatic statement by Abraham that his wife Sarah is his sister" (Gen 20:12).[22]

Speiser viewed Abraham's calling his wife his sister a reflection of a custom in ancient Hurrian society (which included the city of Haran), wherein a man could adopt his wife as his sister; this somehow gave him more authority over her, amounting to a legal advantage for both parties. Speiser noted that, "In Hurrian society the bonds of marriage were strongest and most solemn when the wife had simultaneously the juridical status of a sister, regardless of actual blood ties."[23] However, Speiser has been criticized in recent years from various directions, and not the least from Teubal, who says that his "explanation and interpretation of the sister-brother marriage theme is typical of much of biblical scholarship in its attitude toward women."[24] She criticizes the approach as making the woman only a kind of vessel by which an heir might be provided.[25] Needless to

---

[21]*Ibid.*

[22]*Ibid.*, 52-53. Steinberg, *ibid.*, 53, notes, "Although I am inclined to consider Abraham's statement that Sarah is his half-sister through his father as an example of fast-talking to get out of trouble, and to recognize that no independent evidence establishes a consaguineal link (related by blood and descent) between Abraham and Sarah, one must consider the possibility that he could be telling the 'truth,' namely, expressing the reality of her place in a system of patrilineal endogamy. Sarah, even though she is Abraham's wife, nonetheless falls within the patrilineage of Terah, and hence could also be called his sister."

[23]E. A. Speiser, *Genesis* (AB 1; Garden City: Doubleday, 1964): 92; see 91-94.

[24]Teubal, *Sarah the Priestess*, 12.

[25]*Ibid.*, 13; cf. Speiser, *Genesis*, 93-94.

say, Teubal goes counter to many other scholars, both male and female, on these points.

Teubal's explanation that matriarchy prevailed to the extent that a father could be excluded in the descent line is an interesting possibility, but such a conclusion—in spite of her incisive conjectures—still seems strained in the context of Genesis. The Iscah equation made in Jewish circles is tendentious and is inferred in order to protect the ancestors from an incestuous relation. The suggestion that the lives of royalty or the gods served as models for the marriage of Abraham and Sarah seems too far removed from the text of Genesis and commands little merit. Steinberg's suggestion is most attractive and comes closest to the overall concerns of the biblical material in Genesis and elsewhere. Speiser's historical and archaeological reconstructions rest on such meager information about the social structures of the second millennium BC that no firm analysis is possible at the present.

Abraham's marriage to Sarah is difficult and enigmatic. She is clearly called Terah's daughter-in-law in the introductory material and then later is represented as his daughter (20:12), which suggests an incestuous marriage. But it is quite possible they may not have been brother and sister, and that the arrangement is based on social mores and laws of the time which are unclear to us. If they were actually siblings, then the relationship may fall somewhere within the proposals made above. The initial identification of Sarah as Terah's "daughter-in-law" at the beginning of the narratives may suggest the real familial relationship. The statement in 20:12 could well be, as Steinberg[26] has suggested, the patriarch doing a bit of "fast talking" and trying to ease the tension with Abimelech. Abraham could, therefore, declare Sarah to be Terah's daughter because she belonged to his clan, but no endogamous relation existed at all. This would be a fitting inference based on the initial statement that refers to Sarah as Terah's "daughter-in-law" (11:31).

---

[26]See n. 22.

3. *Sarah in the Genesis Narratives*

The first mention of Sarah in Genesis identifies her as Abraham's wife (Gen 11:29), a reference immediately following the genealogy of ten male figures (11:10-26; cf. ch. 5). The new genealogy represents a dramatic shift from the primeval history spanning the period from Creation to Babel (Gen 1:1-11:9) and introduces the beginning of a patriarchal history. It is a much later history and one probably set sometime within the framework of the Middle Bronze Age (2100-1550 BC). The worldwide perspective has changed to the lineage of Terah, a specific descent group that occupies the rest of the Genesis narratives and becomes the basis of all later biblical history and theology.

Beginning in Gen 12, the focus is on Abraham. He continues as the central character in the narratives until just after the death and burial of Sarah. Sarah, as Abraham's wife, is encountered mostly as a background figure, a fact often pointed out by some feminist writers.[27]

On the other hand Sarah's introduction, though brief, stands at the very beginning of the patriarchal narrative: "Now Sarai was barren, she had no child" (11:30). This is

---

[27]See Sylvia Albrecht Aschliman, "A New Look at Women of Old," *TBT* 28 (1990): 353-357. Pheme Perkins, "Women in the Bible and Its World," *Int* 42 (1988): 33-44, surveys how the Bible generally has been interpreted by men. See also J. Cheryl Exum, "The Mothers of Israel: The Patriarchal Narratives from a Feminist Perspective," *BibRev* 2 (1986): 60-67, who notes, "In the patriarchal world males are the significant figures: Abraham follows the divine call to the Promised Land; Sarah, on the other hand, is 'taken' with him: 'Abraham took his wife Sarah . . . and they set out for Canaan' (Genesis 12:4, 5). Indeed, she is repeatedly 'taken' elsewhere in chapter 12 (verses 15, 19). Sarah is thus treated as an object or a possession" (63). Gale Yee, *ABD* (ed. D. N. Freedman; New York: Doubleday, 1992), 5.981, says this central plot is about "how this promise is passed on from father to son" and that "The narratives about the matriarchs, then, are not primarily about the women themselves as individuals, but rather about their roles as the legitimate or 'correct' wife and mother of the male successor."

significant when considered with the total narrative material down to the time of her death. Though the simple notation on Sarah's lack of offspring, which indeed follows a genealogy of only men, may sound depreciative, casting insignificance on Sarah, in fact it announces the basic theme that runs through all the following narratives. The subject of her barrenness evolves in the text as the major motif about the couple and anticipates the promises to Abraham that immediately follow (12:1-3, 7). With this subtle declaration, the reader is left with a question concerning the whole future—if Sarah is barren how can such promises ever be fulfilled?[28]

The first event in the narratives, following the promises to Abraham, is the episode in Egypt (Gen 12:10-20).[29] Because of Sarah's "beauty" (יְפַת־מַרְאֶה; fair to look at, 12:11), Abraham fears he would be killed if the Egyptians discover she is his wife, so he implores Sarah: "Pray, say (אִמְרִי־נָא) that you are my sister so that it may go well with me on your account בַּעֲבוּרֵךְ)" (12:13). His plea sounds apologetic. Instead of being a proud and overbearing patriarchal figure, Abraham begs Sarah to lie for him. This appears uncharacteristic for a totally dominant patriarchal society. Is Sarah a completely submissive wife, or does she retain some right and control? The text does suggest that she maintained some sort of authority and that Abraham was not

---

[28]The barrenness theme is found in other important junctures of biblical history. See Westermann, *Genesis 12-36*, 140-141; cf. 1 Sam 1:2; Luke 1:7. Gerhard Von Rad, *Genesis, A Commentary* (Philadelphia: Westminster, 1972): 158-159, notes, "Sarai's barrenness is mentioned in passing. The narrator had to do that not only to prepare the reader for the event that is conditioned by this fact, but, above all, to make him conscious of the paradox of God's initial speech to Abraham." Cassuto, *Genesis 12-36*, 277, says her barrenness is "to underline Abram's merit, to wit, that he believed in the Lord who had promised him (xii 2) . . . ." Note the promise and covenant passages in 12:1-3, 7; 13:14-17; 15; 17; 18; 21:12; 22:16-18.

[29]Westermann, *Genesis 12-36*, 159, calls this section "The Ancestral Mother in Danger." The basic story is found three times in Genesis, twice involving Sarah and once Rebekah (Gen 12; 20; 26).

the absolute master figure that might be assumed even though the story is set within the patriarchal period. The idea is conveyed also that Abraham is at fault in this scheme and is in debt to his wife.

Abraham had correctly guessed the course of events. When the courtiers of Pharaoh (שָׂרֵי פַרְעֹה) saw his wife, they did indeed praise her to the king, after which she was taken to his house (12:14-15). All this was based on the lie that she was Abraham's sister. It was "on her account" (עֲבוּר, 12:16; see v. 13) that things went well for him. He gained materially, receiving from Pharaoh many animals and servants. However, Abraham's actions raise serious questions about his faith and character. He saves his own life, but his wife Sarah was taken away and forced into Pharaoh's harem.[30] Berquist thinks that in the ancient world Abraham would have been considered exemplary in all this conniving since he had outwitted Pharaoh (and another king, later, ch. 20). However, Sarah was placed in danger, and "for her the ruse means rape and abuse, along with humiliation and isolation."[31] That everything went well with

---

[30]This material is interpreted variously. See e.g., Hugh C. White, *Narration and Discourse in the Book of Genesis* (New York: Cambridge Univ. Press, 1991): 174-186; Jon L. Berquist, *Reclaiming Her Story* (St. Louis: Chalice, 1993): 41-51; Carroll Stuhlmueller, "The Women of Genesis," *TBT* 28 (1990): 350-352; William E. Phipps, *Assertive Biblical Women* (*Contributions in Women's Studies* 128; Westport, CT: Greenwood Press, 1992): 9-17. Teubal, *Sarah the Priestess*, 6-18, 136, notes that "Sarah is symbolic of woman's struggle against a male culture that finally prevailed and eventually subordinated women."

[31]Berquist, *Reclaiming Her Story*, 43, who also notes that "Abraham is seen to be clever and tricky, which were characteristics that the ancient Israelites considered virtuous." He continues to stress that Abraham had sold "her sexual services for money and personal advantage" and that "Abraham is a pimp and he makes a whore out of his own wife, for his own financial benefit," *ibid*. These are strong words, but they do indeed strike at a truth in the narratives revealing something often overlooked about our earliest figures of faith. Phyllis Trible, *Texts of Terror: Literary-Feminist Readings of Biblical Narratives* (Philadelphia: Fortress, 1984): 9, says, "Abraham betrays

Abraham is stressed ("on her account," see vv. 13, 16), but the "matter concerning (עַל־דְּבַר) Sarai" (v. 17) brought great plagues to the king's house, as he became an unwitting victim in the deception.[32] While we must use caution when applying a modern value system upon the social world depicted here, still the author does seem to imply a far-reaching moral issue that is at work. As far as this specific affair is concerned the narrator also implies a worth attached to Sarah, and that she is a woman who is no chattel slave to be passed around and abused by patriarchs or kings.

The flow of the Genesis material is interrupted by the atypical narrative of four eastern kings in chap. 14, but in chap. 15 the motif of childlessness continues. In spite of the promises he had received, it appears that Eliezer of Damascus will be Abraham's last heir. In chap. 16, however, the barrenness of Sarah and the fact that she was over 65 years old convinced her to propose a dramatic solution to the problem.[33] As the subject in 16:1, Sarah

---

her." Phipps, *Assertive Biblical Women*, 9, concludes that, "Sarah's life is largely a saga of suffering, even though one must read between the lines of the patriarchal narrator to discover it. Although she is sometimes denigrated by Abraham, she does not always accept the doormat role." It is worth reading Teubal's arguments on the matter of Sarah as sister and wife, and how she diverges from most scholars on this question. Teubal, *Sarah the Priestess*, 15, says, "In all this it would seem that Sarah was passed back and forth from one man to the other without a word, like the passive patriarchal wife she is supposed to be, with no feelings of her own. We will see, in later chapters, that this was not the case at all." Westermann, *Genesis 12-36*, 165, observes the tragedy, "The ruse appears to have succeeded; both live and all is well with them; but the marriage and the family are destroyed."

[32]The question of justice toward Pharaoh is raised here. See Westermann, *Genesis 12-36*, 165-167. The king's question: "What is this you have done to me?" is called by Westermann "the high point of the narrative" (166).

[33]Westermann, *Genesis 12-36*, 237, comments that for "a married woman to be without children in the patriarchal world is a misfortune of overwhelming proportions."

determines to give her maidservant to Abraham,[34] avowing, "I shall obtain children (אִבָּנֶה; lit., I may be built-up-with-sons) by her" (16:2; see 30:3).[35] It is interesting that Abraham had been married to Sarah for about 30 years, but with no offspring. What might have been the real relationship between the two?[36] There is no indication that

---

[34]In v. 1 her name precedes the verb, a Hebrew construction where emphasis is intended.

[35]Regarding v. 2, Westermann, *Genesis 12-36*, 239, notes "In the patriarchal period there was no other way for a woman to be a member of society." The precise relationship between Sarah and Hagar is unclear. Was she strictly a "slave" or more a "maidservant," in the sense of Leah and Rachel? See Westermann, *Genesis 12-36*, 237-238. Similar marital arrangements were known in the second millennium BC. In the Code of Hammurabi, number 146, the provision is stipulated: "When a seignior married a hierodule and she gave a female slave to her husband and she has then borne children, if later that female slave has claimed equality with her mistress because she bore children, her mistress may not sell her; she may mark her with the slave-mark and count her among the slaves," *ANET*, 172. The adoption of slaves in order to bear children for the family is known from the Nuzi archives: "If Gilimninu bears children, Shennima shall not take another wife. But if Gilimninu fails to bear children, Gilimninu shall get for Shennima a woman from the Lullu country (i.e., a slave girl) as concubine. In that case, Gilimninu herself shall have authority over the offspring." The text was published first in the Harvard Semitic Series (V, 1929). See in Speiser, *Genesis,* 120. There were fairly specific laws in the ancient Near East dealing with relationships between husbands, wives, secondary wives, concubines, and slaves and the special provisions made for slave-wives and their children. These may be examined in the *Lipit-Ishtar Lawcode, ANET*, 160, *The Code of Hammurabi, ANET*, 172-173; the *Hittite Laws, ANET* 190, numbers 31ff.; see H. W. F. Saggs, *The Greatness that was Babylon*, 186-188, 201-203, 205.

[36]Westermann, *Genesis 12-36*, 238, detects a problem—the "tightly packed and laconic exchange in utter frankness catches an excerpt from the shared life of two people which began with betrothal and marriage and led to the express recognition that the union has remained without issue. There is no need to say what suffering, reproach, and bitterness this brought to the couple; it is all compressed into Sarah's opening words, הִנֵּה־נָא." Teubal, *Sarah the Priestess,* 32, notes, "What seems most difficult to accept is that patriarchal men,

Abraham had ever questioned her barrenness and we can assume he had never asked for another woman, a concubine, to bear him children. But because posterity was so important, a surrogate mother was sought finally by Sarah herself, who intervened with the suggestion that Abraham should take her own maidservant Hagar in order to "build up" her lineage. It is stressed that Sarah hoped for her own child, but it would be through her maidservant, Hagar.

Sarah's address to Abraham, "Pray now . . . come in (בֹּא־נָא . . . הִנֵּה־נָא) to my maid" (16:2), implies a demand, showing that Sarah exerted influence. It is she who persuades her husband and who herself possessed the right to give her own maidservant to him. Whatever the social laws might have been, they allowed some authority and control to reside with women in Sarah's social class. On the other hand, as far as Hagar is concerned, this arrangement demonstrates how women might be abused.[37] Sarah charges God with her inability to bear children (עֲצָרַנִי יְהוָה מִלֶּדֶת, see 20:18), which implies a theological perspective that believes God is the cause of everything. Abraham's response is without comment, and it simply says, "So Abram hearkened to Sarai's voice" (16:2b). His quiet obedience conveys the idea of an unassertive, passive patriarch.[38]

---

whose aspirations are generally to have successors and heirs, would have stood by barren wives for decades without replacing them or taking second wives or concubines as was customary in those days."

[37]See Trible, *Texts of Terror*.

[38]*Ibid.*, 11, notes, "No mighty patriarch is Abram, but rather the silent, acquiescent, and minor figure in a drama between two women." Teubal, *Sarah the Priestess*, 31, comments, "In her dealings with her handmaid Hagar, Sarah obviously had the authority to invoke or abide by the legal system applicable in her homeland." Teubal also believes that Sarah wielded this authority because as a priestess she had certain rights under Babylonian laws (31-52). See also S. Teubal, *Hagar the Egyptian, The Lost Tradition of the Matriarchs* (San Francisco: Harper & Row, 1990).

Hagar's discovery that she was pregnant caused her to think differently toward Sarah and she treated her mistress as of "light worth (קָלַל, be small, of little account) in her eyes" (16:4). The sensitivity inherent in such a familial relationship has now become a crisis.[39] Speiser[40] says Sarah hated Hagar over this incident and Abraham did nothing to "intervene in the bitter rivalry between two headstrong women." Teubal,[41] however, says Speiser has distorted Sarah's character and that the entire relationship must be viewed based on Mesopotamian law.[42] It is certain that the passage demonstrates how hostility and jealousy could erupt where even society and law permitted such domestic arrangements. The severity of the rivalry then shifts from Hagar to Sarah's accusation against Abraham. She perceives him as one who should take action. Sarah says to him that "the wrong (חָמָס; treat violently, represents here a severe indictment; see Gen 6:11; Judg 9:24; Job 19:7; Mal 2:16) done to me is upon you!" (16:5). Sarah appeals to the question of justice, an apparent reference to a violation of legal law in Mesopotamia.[43] Her indictment of Abraham took the form of an appeal to God: "May Yahweh see justice (שָׁפַט) done between me and you" (16:5). She appears to charge Abraham with the injustice and assumes that God should settle the dispute. That Sarah can make these judicial statements indicates a level of autonomy for women in her social class who could operate under societal law.[44]

---

[39]Westermann, *Genesis 12-26*, 240. He observes also that "the oppressed when liberated becomes the oppressor" (241).

[40]Speiser, *Genesis*, 157.

[41]Teubal, *Sarah the Priestess*, 40.

[42]*Ibid.*, 31-52.

[43]See n. 35 and The Code of Hammurabi.

[44]See Westermann, *Genesis* 2.240-241. Bruce Vawter, *On Genesis: A New Reading* (Garden City: Doubleday, 1977): 215, concludes, "Legalities aside, however, it must be admitted that at least Sarah does not cut too happy a figure in this episode, neither in her recriminations over a development for which she herself was partly responsible and which was the miscarriage of a plan designed more for her benefit than anyone else's nor in her vengeful treatment of Hagar after the fact."

Westermann[45] suggests that "Sarah's case has three parts: the brief, pregnant accusation . . . , the reason for the accusation, and the demand for a legal decision" and, therefore, that "Sarah demands a legal decision, not in a case between herself and Hagar, but between herself and Abraham." They are apparently following legal procedure and it is from this that Abraham gives Sarah the right to do what she will with Hagar: "Here, your maid is in your hand, deal with her as it seems good in your eyes. So Sarah afflicted her, so she had to flee from her" (16:6). "Afflict" (עָנָה) means "harsh treatment" and is the same term used for the way Israel was treated in Egypt.[46] Westermann notes, "It is striking that Abraham's decision is completely in favor of Sarah."[47] Trible[48] summarizes, "Conflicts between these two women revolve around three males. At the center is Abraham, their common husband." She also notes:

> Hagar is Israel, from exodus to exile, yet with differences. And these differences yield terror. All we who are heirs of Sarah and Abraham, by flesh and spirit, must answer for the terror in Hagar's story. To neglect the theological challenge she presents is to falsify faith" (28-29).[49]

However, Trible tends to sermonize the ancient circumstance for a modern audience.

---

[45]*Ibid.*, 241.

[46]Trible, *Texts of Terror*, 13-18. As the Hebrew had afflicted the Egyptian, so the Egyptians would afflict the Hebrews later. She says also of her mistreatment, "Hagar is a fleeting yet haunting figure in scripture" (27).

[47]Westermann, *Genesis* 2.241.

[48]Trible, *Texts of Terror*, 27-28.

[49]*Ibid.*, 28-29. Trible and others insist that both Sarah and Hagar were "victims" of patriarchy. See also Gale Yee, *ABD*, 5.982. This approach overloads the ancient Near Eastern culture and society, as well as the biblical material, with modern social issues and concepts that often have little, if any, relation to the actual situation of the ancient world. It is just this historical, cultural, and societal environment of the ancient period that remains the problem for the interpreter.

In Gen 17, Sarai's name is changed to Sarah (v. 15), as was Abram's changed to Abraham earlier. No reason is given for the change except that she is promised a son through whom nations would be born (v. 16). The change marks a new beginning. The promise evokes laughter (יִצְחָק) from Abraham (v. 17), and no wonder since Abraham is one hundred and Sarah is ninety. Sarah will also laugh for the same reason when she hears this same news, apparently for the first time later from three strangers (18:12). The promise looks back to the question of Eliezer as heir, which was already raised (15:4). After Ishmael's birth Abraham had thought that he would be the rightful heir, but now he is even told the name of the son that would be born to Sarah (v. 19): "You shall call his name Isaac" (יִצְחָק, he laughs).

The episode in Gen 18 was supernatural, an appearance of God by the terebinths of Mamre (v. 1). The mention of trees likely identifies the place as a known sanctuary.[50] It was a place of antiquity and it became necessary to identify it later as Hebron (see 13:18; 35:27). Abraham and Sarah had been associated with the site since first entering Canaan (see 13:18). Here the couple are depicted as typical nomadic tent-dwellers living at the edge of the wilderness. On a hot, dusty day, three visitors approached, and in true desert hospitality, Abraham ran, greeted them, and requested they refresh themselves. Abraham addressed one of them as "My lord" (אֲדֹנָי; Sir; the men actually represent God; see vv. 1, 13). Abraham summoned Sarah to perform the domestic chore of making bread (18:6), but Abraham as well as the servants were all involved in the entertainment preparations (18:7-8). During the meal, Sarah had apparently withdrawn from the association of the men. We are immediately

---

[50]God had appeared to Abraham when he first entered Canaan at "the place Shechem," and specified here was also a tree called the "terebinth of Moreh." After the event, Abraham built an altar (12:6-7). Trees often were associated with idolatry and other cult activities (see Gen 35:4; Josh 24:26; Judg 9:6, 37). See also Theodor Gaster, *Myth, Legend, and Custom in the Old Testament* (New York: Harper and Row, 1969): 156-57; Y. Arbeitman, *ABD*, 4.492-93; and Westermann, *Genesis 12-36*, 277.

informed of the purpose of the visit. The very first recorded utterance from the visitors after the meal was the question, "Where is Sarah your wife?" (v. 9), and then from v. 10 she is the leading subject. That they knew her name perhaps suggests their divine nature. Sarah, who is eavesdropping from behind the tent-flap, overhears that she will have a son within one year (v. 10). The basic theme of the Abraham and Sarah narratives is then disclosed once again: "And Abraham and Sarah were old, advanced in days. The way of women had ceased for Sarah" (v. 11; see 11:30; 15:1-2; 16:1). The news caused a natural reaction, and "Sarah laughed within herself, saying, 'After I have become worn, is there to be pleasure for me?'" Sarah finds only humor in the idea, which most likely means sexual pleasure, and as an afterthought adds: "And my lord is old!" (v. 12). Her reflection on such a ridiculous presumption by the guests prompts an immediate response from one of them: "But the Lord (יהוה) said to Abraham: 'Why does Sarah laugh (צָחֲקָה) and say: Shall I really give birth, now that I am old?'" (v. 13). The question is a rebuke toward Sarah, and the further question, "Is anything beyond the Lord (יהוה)?" is seemingly addressed toward Sarah and her incredulity.[51] She tries to deny or excuse herself that she had laughed, "No, I did not laugh," but his sharp reply was: "No, indeed you laughed" (v. 15). The motif of laughter runs through the passage, and obviously plays on the name Isaac (יִצְחָק), though the name itself does not appear.

The Abimelech incident in Gen 20 contains the essence but not the kind of detail given in chap. 12. Apparently desirous to solidify his relation with Abraham, who himself was a man of power and influence, Abimelech takes Sarah into his harem. As before, Abraham had made sure Sarah was rumored to be his sister, and again Abraham shows himself to be fearful, using subterfuge to save himself. Abimelech emerges in the story as a better man than

---

[51]Westermann, *Genesis 12-36*, 281-182. There is emphasis on the name יהוה, Yahweh, God's personal name, running through the passage.

Abraham. He considered taking another man's wife a "monstrous guilt" (חֲטָאָה גְדֹלָה; v. 9).

One of the perplexing issues in the text is how unexpected it is to find Abimelech attracted to a woman who is ninety years old. Do we assume this to be sexual attraction? The question is often dealt with from typical critical directions, but Teubal theorizes that if Sarah was a priestess then sexual relations between kings and priestesses was in keeping with ancient Near Eastern customs. She claims this is the background of both Pharaoh and Abimelech wanting Sarah.[52] The reply to Abimelech by Abraham that Sarah "is truly my sister, my father's daughter, but not my mother's daughter" (v. 12) is odd, since she has been identified at first as Terah's daughter-in-law in 11:31, a point already discussed above. The tragedies that came to Abimelech's kingdom were caused, just as in Egypt, "on account of Sarah (עַל־דְּבַר see vv. 11, 18; see also 12:13, 16, 17)." "God had obstructed every womb in Abimelech's household," just as Sarah was obstructed from bearing before (16:2).

Ever since the plaintive note of Sarah's barrenness (11:30) a tension, or contradiction, has echoed behind the promises to Abraham. But here in 21:1 the conclusion is spoken with strong emphasis: "Now the Lord took account of Sarah as he had said; the Lord did for Sarah as he had stated." This introduces the birth of Isaac. In 21:2, the long-awaited, but more often doubted, fulfillment is announced with two verbs: "Sarah became pregnant and bore to Abraham a son in his old age." The conception and birth through unusual circumstances, and also that the child is born to Abraham, is stressed (see vv. 3, 5, 7; 17:15-21).[53] The birth is clearly due to none other than God's action. "Abraham called the name of his son . . . Isaac (יִצְחָק, v. 3)" and Sarah's joy is exclaimed: "God has made

---

[52]Teubal, *Sarah the Priestess*; esp. the chapter on "The Hieros Gamos," 110-122.

[53]See Steinberg, *JSOT* (1991) for the importance given to patrilineal descent.

laughter for me" and that all others who hear of it "will laugh for me (v. 5; see Ps 113:9)." For a ninety-year-old woman to have given birth would certainly become the occasion for talk and banter. The laughter motif is carried through the entire story.

Teubal[54] connects this passage with Sarah's role as priestess and that her "religious office has a direct bearing on the conception of Isaac." She places the stories in remote antiquity, as early as the Jemdet Nasr period (3100-2900 BC). She compares this period to the Canaan of the texts of Genesis and relates the matriarchs' activities to those of women in the ancient religions. By this she thinks the position of biblical women is made more clear. Somewhere in the long period between 3000 BC and 1500 BC was the time of the patriarchs. But Teubal[55] points out that the earlier Sumerian codes were more concerned with the well-being of women than were the later Babylonian or Assyrian laws. Therefore an earlier date is suggested than the more commonly accepted 16th century. She claims that the religious outlook of ancient Mesopotamia provides us with a possible understanding of who Sarah really was and that it was in this period that "religion permeated the lives of the ancient Near Eastern peoples."[56] Teubal's thesis emphasizes that there was a widespread and important function of women in ancient Mesopotamia. She believes that in Genesis many of the archaic customs are implied and "the matriarchs of Genesis could have belonged to the ranks of a religious order."[57] She refers to the goddess Inanna, who was to remain childless, and that priestesses also were to do the same.[58] In the event that a priestess did bear a child it was to be sacrificed. She raises the question that this could have some relation to the long-perplexing sacrifice of Isaac (עֲקֵדָה; the Akedah, to tie up a sacrificial victim, 22:9) in

---

[54]Teubal, *Sarah the Priestess*, 72.
[55]*Ibid.*, 73-75.
[56]*Ibid.*, 77.
[57]*Ibid.*, 82.
[58]*Ibid.*, 82-83.

chap. 22 and to Abraham and Sarah's attempt to comply.⁵⁹ Teubal does indeed provide some intriguing answers to a number of illusive questions raised in the narratives. Her thesis is imaginative, erudite, and well-researched. At the same time, however, it continues in the realm of complete speculation.

The joy that came to Sarah because of Isaac is interrupted when, on the day of Isaac's weaning-feast, Sarah saw Ishmael laughing (מְצַחֵק). This is sometimes translated as playing.⁶⁰ Some have tried to see in this expression Ishmael abusing Isaac, and therefore explaining the following conduct of Sarah, but there is nothing to suggest this.⁶¹ The act of "laughing" and "playing" are derived from the same root. It seems that the idea of children laughing and having a good time is the sense, which continues the laughing theme.⁶²

The joy of Hagar's son Ishmael reminded Sarah of the old rivalry and jealousy. Indignant, she ordered Abraham to drive out the two. Her attitude was based on the fear that even yet her son Isaac could be excluded from the inheritance in preference for Abraham's first-born son. Scholars deal with this material in a variety of ways.⁶³

---

⁵⁹*Ibid.*, 83.

⁶⁰The LXX adds "with her son Isaac."

⁶¹Speiser, *Genesis*, 155; Vawter, *Genesis*, 248-49; Trible, *Texts of Terror*, n. 44.

⁶²Vawter, *Genesis*, 248-249.

⁶³Trible, *Texts of Terror*, 21, says that, "With a disturbing twist, the words of Sarah anticipate vocabulary and themes from the Exodus narrative. When plagues threatened the life of his firstborn son, Pharaoh cast out (גרש) the Hebrew slaves. Like the monarch, Sarah the matriarch wants to protect the life of her own son by casting out (גרש) Hagar the slave. Having once fled from affliction (16:6b), Hagar continues to prefigure Israel's story even as Sarah foreshadows Egypt's role. Irony abounds." J. Cheryl Exum, "The Mothers of Israel: The Patriarchal Narratives from a Feminist Perspective," *BibRev* 2 (1986): 60-67, comments that, "From a feminist perspective, both women suffer: one is cast out, becoming the mother of a great nation excluded

Westermann's[64] summation addresses the situation more accurately:

> What Sarah is providing for is her son's future. To censure Sarah's demand from the point of view of individual ethic or our own religious attitude is to fail to see that Sarah is in a struggle for her own very existence; in later forms of society such struggles are transferred to the social or political sphere, while here they take place within the family circle.

Again, Teubal would insist that by exerting her authority as a priestess Sarah was only following Mesopotamian law and was justly seeking to maintain her own matrilineal descent group. Sarah's feelings of hostility look back to 16:5. It is clear that Sarah herself wields sufficient authority in the incident causing Abraham to comply immediately with her strong demand. Abraham is not shown here controlling his women with absolute authority.

---

from the covenant; the other stays within the patriarchal hearth and almost loses her only child to the father, who is prepared to offer him to God as a sacrifice (Genesis 22)." Phipps, *Assertive Biblical Women*, 12, says, "After bearing her own child, Sarah regains status and becomes determined to evict her adopted son Ishmael. She is so consumed by feelings of superiority that she cannot tolerate seeing her biological son play with the offspring of a slave from the African continent." It is doubtful that superiority is the real reason for casting them out; this reads back upon the text more than can be claimed. Berquist, *Reclaiming Her Story*, 50, adds, "Then Sarah sends Hagar and little Ishmael away, and distance makes the silence permanent. Even if one would speak, they would be too far apart to hear each other. Distance is the strongest silence, but even before the sending, the silence was stronger than the greatest distance. The one crying in the wilderness is never heard, especially when others try not to hear." These are examples of imposing modern standards onto the text. Teubal, on the other hand, strives to view the material from an ancient Near Eastern perspective instead of reading the text from a contemporary sociological or religious bias.

[64]Westermann, *Genesis 12-36*, 339. See Jub 17:4-6.

4. *Sarah's Death*

Sarah was 127 years old when she died (23:1; lit., "100 years and 20 years and 7 years," an extended form). This may emphasize that her life was complete. Is it significant that her death occurs immediately following the taking of Isaac to be sacrificed? Some speculate that just as Abraham had sent Ishmael and Hagar into the desert, with few provisions, and therefore seemingly to die, so the command to take Isaac is a rebuke to Abraham. That he would have provided them with such sparse provisions is disturbing, since this was not Sarah's bidding. She had simply said, "Send them away" (21:10). It is interesting that 22:1 begins, "And it was after these things that God tested Abraham." Also both 21:14, which is about Hagar and her son, and 22:3, which is about Isaac, begin with the statement: "And Abraham arose early in the morning." The literary connection here seems to be more than coincidental. Both are the beginning of an ordeal. It is speculated further that the shock at hearing of the taking of Isaac to be sacrificed caused Sarah's death.[65]

Abraham's effort and negotiations to purchase a burial place for Sarah, as well as the site chosen raises more questions. As Von Rad[66] says of the narrative, "But in the context of these severe traditions which are immovably concentrated on theology it surprises one with narrative graphicness and humorous freshness." There is an emphasis on the place of her death at Kiriath Arba, which is identified as the later city, Hebron (23:2). After negotiations

---

[65]Everett Fox, *In the Beginning, a New English Rendition of the Book of Genesis* (New York: Schocken, 1983): 79, comments that "Structurally, this brief tale foreshadows the next chapter, the ordeal of Yitzhak. It speaks of a journey into the unknown, a child at the point of death, the intervention of God's 'messenger,' the parent's sighting of the way out, and the promise of future blessing. Of course the differences between the two stories are equally important." See Shlomo Riskin, "Abraham Rebuked," *Jerusalem Post* (Week ending Nov. 6, 1993): 23.

[66]Von Rad, *Genesis*, 246

with the Hittite inhabitants, and especially with one known as Ephron, Abraham bought a field and the cave of Machpelah (23:9, 17, 19, 20). There is no clue whether Abraham was seeking a family sepulchre or whether it was a site strictly for Sarah. But that an entire chapter would be devoted to her death and burial, and stressing such detail as it does has been observed by many commentators.[67] Teubal speculates that Mamre was important because of Sarah's religious office. She thinks that Sarah lived here most of her life, yet apart from Abraham who apparently "lived in the land of the Philistines" (Gen 21:34).[68] Because Hebron remained an important religious center for the Hebrews down to the time of David, she says that, "Of all the places associated with the matriarch, Hebron at least should carry the affix 'City of Sarah'."[69] She also discusses the importance of Sarah from the standpoint of the offspring interred later in the cave of Machpelah as all members of her own descent group.[70] Teubal[71] is making the case that the "narrated incidents in the matriarch's life took place on consecrated ground" and that there had been a history of Abraham and Sarah visiting holy places in their initial sojourn into Canaan. She postulates that Abraham visited these sites in order to receive oracles, possibly from Sarah and that, "The sacred grove of Mamre at Hebron and the grave in the field of Machpelah, facing Mamre, should take their hallowed place in history in remembrance of the matriarch Sarah."[72]

It is striking, too, that after Sarah's death there is very little further told us about Abraham. The marriage to Keturah is told in order to mention Abraham's other tribal descendants, but we do not even know where they lived. Teubal observes, "Of the forty-eight years of Abraham's life

---

[67]See the summary given by Westermann, *Genesis 12-36*, 376.
[68]Teubal, *Sarah the Priestess*, 30.
[69]*Ibid.*
[70]*Ibid.*, 95.
[71]*Ibid.*, 88.
[72]*Ibid.*, 95.

after Sarah's death there is no detail whatever. In other words, it is Sarah's role that furthers the story."[73] Also, in the remaining part of Genesis, the text is concerned with her descendants, not Abram's.[74] Those later buried in the sepulchre were Abraham, Isaac, Rebekah, Leah, and Jacob. The text seems to underscore the importance attached to Sarah. In the report about the marriage of Isaac to Rebekah, the MT states that he "brought her into the tent of Sarah his mother" (24:67). There are textual problems here.[75] Teubal believes that the marriage of Isaac and Rebekah took place in his mother's tent, and all because Rebekah was to be the one that would succeed Sarah as priestess. "In other words," she says, "Sarah's tent was a storehouse."[76] Teubal's views seem radical, yet she has tried to view the text of Genesis from the culture and religion of ancient Mesopotamia. She has shown the challenge faced in the narratives when dealing with Sarah's life and death and that there are far more questions raised than are finally answered. Whatever the facts may have been about Sarah must be left for future scholarship. Teubal sounds convincing in the context of her own arguments from silence as she tries to fill in the voids. Because the matriarchs were not passive figures, she assumes they must have been figures of great authority, thus priestesses of an older religion. But the

---

[73]*Ibid.*, xv.

[74]*Ibid.*, 95.

[75]See Speiser, *Genesis*, 185. "Sarah his mother" (שָׂרָה אִמּוֹ) is a possible addition; see Westermann, *Genesis 12-36*, 382, 391. Speiser, *Genesis*, 182, says the MT is "grammatically unmanageable" but that "The words 'his mother Sarah' probably stood originally at the end of the verse and were moved up from there through an old scribal error."

[76]Teubal, *Sarah the Priestess*, 102, also traces the history of the goddesses all the way back to when "Inanna's grandmother, Ninlil, who was a participant in the Sacred Marriage in Nippur, bore the title *sarrat-e-ki-ur*, queen of the reed hut. Indeed, the name Sarah may have originated from a title." Most certainly, Sarah's name was from a title (see n. 3 above), but again, Teubal's efforts to solve the problems of the Genesis text with such reconstructions must be viewed with great caution.

problem remains that the premise is speculative and finally unsustainable.

By emphasizing Sarah's death and burial as it does, the biblical material most likely reflects a theological issue, viz., now for the first time a piece of Canaan became the property of the sojourning Abraham. Machpelah, a grave site, strangely symbolized that the Hebrew family now, in fact, became heirs of the Promised Land. As Von Rad[77] aptly notes, "The complete absence of a religious atmosphere and of pious words which makes our narrative seem so 'worldly' must not hide the fact that here a fact central to Israel's faith is being described."

5. *Later References to Sarah*

Other than in Genesis, Sarah is mentioned once more in the OT, in a section where Isaiah speaks to a disheartened, captive Israel. The prophet encourages the people to, "Look to Abraham your father and to Sarah who bore you" (51:2). The traditional belief of Abraham and Sarah as the parents of the nation of Israel is clearly seen in this later poetic expression.

In post-biblical Judaism, Sarah is spoken of as the first mother of Israel and is commonly presented as an example of piety and of beauty. Numerous legends and midrashes sprang up about her life and demeanor as the ideal person and wife. An Aramaic document containing stories and legends of the Patriarchs tells how the servants of Pharaoh praised Sarah to their lord, describing her hair, eyes, mouth, and other parts of her body, finally declaring her great beauty.[78]

---

[77]Von Rad, *Genesis,* 249.

[78]Known as the *Genesis Apocryphon*, the document was found in Qumran Cave I. Its date is placed from the first century BC to about AD 70. It is also referred to as "Little Genesis." Theodor H. Gaster, *The Dead Sea Scriptures* (Garden City: Doubleday, 1964): 256-267, calls it "Memoirs of the Patriarchs."

> How comely is the shape of her face, how [. . .] and finespun are her tresses! How beautiful her eyes! How delicate is her nose and the whole lustre of her countenance! How fair are her breasts, and how comely withal is her complexion! How comely too are her arms, and how perfect her hands! How [delightful] are her hands to behold, how lovely her palms, how long and slender all her fingers! How comely are her feet! How well-rounded her thighs! No maiden or new-wed bride is fairer than she! Her beauty is greater than all other women's and she excels them all! What is more, along with all this beauty she has great wisdom, and the . . . of her hands is fair indeed.[79]

The language and sentiment is like the Song of Solomon. On the other hand, in the writings of Josephus such language or any explicit description of Sarah's beauty is completely avoided. He is always protective, portraying her as beyond reproach. In the episode with Pharaoh it is the character of the Egyptians which makes both Abraham and Sarah the victims. Josephus writes that Abraham,

> took Sarra with him and fearing the Egyptians' frenzy for women, lest the king should slay him because of his wife's beauty, he devised the following scheme: he pretended to be her brother and, telling her that their interest required it, instructing her to play the part accordingly.[80]

Amaru[81] explores how Josephus pictures the Jewish heroes and heroines and shows that he always presents them as models with exemplary traits, and that "an unreal quality is

---

[79]Gaster, *The Dead Sea Scriptures*, 259-260. He also says, "This stereotyped description of womanly beauty and accomplishment is echoed in the accounts of Mary in some of the apocryphal Infancy gospels" (287).

[80]Josephus, *Jewish Antiquities* 1.162.

[81]Betsy Halpern Amaru, "Portraits of Biblical Women in Josephus' Antiquities," *JJS* 39 (1988): 143-70.

sensed in the characterizations" and the "biblical narratives are distorted, all giving the impression of idealized abstractions."[82] Josephus makes Sarah a lady who has no blemish, is submissive and chaste,[83] and is given no direct speech in his narratives. He also deletes any attributes of initiative given to her in the biblical text.[84] Clearly, Josephus saw the biblical text as unsuitable to repeat in his history, so he sought to mask the real character of Sarah as given in Genesis.[85] Thus there is a variation in the way Sarah is regarded by later authors. From the writer of the Genesis Apocryphon, which is almost an erotic description of Sarah's beauty, to the squeamish Josephus who idealizes the matriarch, there are wide differences.

The NT references to Sarah are very brief when compared to the amount of material on Sarah given in Genesis. In Rom 4:19 her "barrenness" is cited and in 9:9 her "conception" and the "promise." In Heb 11:11, it is Sarah's "faith" that is noted. In Gal 4:21-31, an allegorical contrast between Sarah and Hagar is made, although her name is not mentioned. The above passages present few questions for the application of hermeneutical principles but the passage in 1 Pet 3:6, where Sarah is spoken of as an example of "submissiveness" to her husband, is one which has prime concern for the contemporary Christian. Whatever Peter is doing in this epistle is not a portrayal of

---

[82]*Ibid.*, 143.

[83]Amaru, *ibid.* 145, says, "Sarah, the first of the heroine models, emerges from Josephus' pen as the ideal spouse for a dominant, strong founding father. Beautiful, pious and, like all of his heroines, devoid of character blemish, Sarah is most notable for her submissiveness and her chastity."

[84]Amaru, *ibid.*, also notes, "Whatever her significance to the biblical story line, in every scene shared with her spouse her role is diminished and her presence made unobtrusive, consistently permitting Abraham to hold 'centre stage'."

[85]As far as the biblical material in Gen 12:11-20 is concerned, Amaru, *ibid.*, notes that "Except for Sarah's beauty, none of this fits well with a romantic image of the virtuous, chaste wife, let alone of the heroic husband."

the Sarah known in the Genesis narratives. Peter was not ignorant of the Genesis material, but his brief and definitive formula for behavior is apparently modeled on later Jewish idealizations of holy women. He finds far more kinship with Josephus than with Genesis. His ideal wife perhaps was descriptive of what was thought of as a good and submissive lady in the Hellenistic world, and may have had missionary overtones.[86]

Conclusion

Sarah, like Abraham, was idealized in later writings. Her story, as it is actually presented in the Genesis narratives, has become obscured with time and theology. While Genesis presents a realistic picture of how a woman in the ancient Near Eastern world might have lived, we still do not know much about the actual person, Sarah. Whether she was a priestess, an upper-class citizen of Babylonian

---

[86]See David L. Balch, *Let Wives Be Submissive, The Domestic Code in 1 Peter* (*SBLMS* 26; Atlanta: Scholars Press, 1981): 95-121. See Wayne Grudem, "Wives Like Sarah, and the Husbands Who Honor Them," *Recovering Biblical Manhood and Womanhood, A Response to Evangelical Feminism* (ed. J. Piper & W. Grudem; Wheaton: Crossway, 1991): 194-208, who fails to consider the weight of the total Genesis material. He ignores the tension between the 1 Peter text and the large amount of material on Sarah in Genesis. His appeal to Genesis (196-98) is more to answer others than to grapple with the narratives themselves. If Abraham obeyed Sarah (e.g., Gen 16:2, 6), then he regards this as disobedience to God. He insists that Abraham is an authority figure and when he complies with Sarah's demands he is guilty of sin (197). The final result is that he diminishes the whole complex story of Sarah. Rather than considering Peter's words within a frame conditioned by centuries of literature and theological development about Sarah, as well as the Hellenistic world and its own ideals of the well-demeanored wife, Grudem forces on Genesis a theological construct. He discounts Balch and others as denying divine authority and commands (n. 25). Grudem is an example of reading backwards and judging the ancient setting from an assumed preferable moral interpretation, and in this he is similar to those who address modern social issues and read back into Genesis material concepts and values in order to find biblical meaning for their cause.

society, or most likely, a simple Bedouin wife following her husband from place to place, she is shown to be a real person, with definite rights and special privileges. Though she was the wife of patriarchal Abraham, she is clearly presented in Genesis as independent of her husband in many respects and very much an individual in her own right.[87]

Through the centuries, Sarah has won the hearts of generations of believers. They have understood that she, as the principal matriarch, was unique and crucial in the history of faith, and that with her improbable and laughable conception of a son in her old age, biblical history had its own inception. As this history moved forward, it, like Sarah's own life proved also to be arduous and improbable. Sarah has left a biblical, as well as an extrabiblical, legacy that continues to the present. The stories, legends, writings, and articles that have been written instruct and challenge us, and there is no end in sight. There is no question that Sarah has rightly has won the epithet, "mother of the faithful."

---

[87]Many writers charge that biblical patriarchy was despotic and oppressive, denying to women basic rights; yet the Genesis story of Sarah does not support this inference. Teubal, for instance, finds in Sarah a figure who reflects a time before patriarchy. Because Sarah has rights and authority in Genesis, Teubal reconstructs the narratives around the thesis that Sarah was a forceful and independent person, even an honored priestess. She claims that patriarchy finally prevailed in Canaan during the biblical period. However, there are serious problems with this view. While Teubal has forced a careful approach to the culture and society of the ancient Near East, she has assumed for the patriarchal time a restrictive social order for women and male dominance that is, in fact, overstated and in excess of the facts.

Chapter Three

DEBORAH—JUDGE, PROPHETESS, MILITARY LEADER, AND MOTHER IN ISRAEL

Charme E. Robarts

The life of Deborah, a prophetess and the lone female judge in Israel's history (Judg 4:4), has evoked various images. Calvin[1] argued long ago that God's approval of Deborah's public service was in order to shame the men and "to show them their slothfulness." However, Foh[2] counters that, "All this is pure inference. . . . There is no indication that the men were slothful in Deborah's or Huldah's time." Others stress Deborah's public work, both religious and judicial.[3] Alternatively, Carmody[4] stresses the charismatic personality which exerts influence more "through spiritual force rather than through organizational office."

Such varied emphases raise several important questions. What qualified a person in ancient Israel to be selected by Yahweh to serve as a judge? Who appointed Deborah? How did she fare in a cast of all male judges? Did the writer of Judges give gender-specific role definitions for ancient Israel or for the twentieth-century world?

---

[1]John Calvin, *Letters of John Calvin* (trans. M. R. Gilchrist; Philadelphia: Presbyterian Board of Publications, 1858): 38.

[2]Susan T. Foh, *Women & the Word of God: A Response to Biblical Feminism* (Phillipsburg, NJ: Presbyterian and Reformed Publ. Co., 1979): 84-85.

[3]Dana Nolan Fewell, "Judges," *The Women's Bible Commentary* (ed. Carol A. Newsom and Sharon H. Ringe; Louisville: Westminster, 1992): 68-69.

[4]Denise Lardner Carmody, *Biblical Woman: Contemporary Reflections on Scriptural Texts* (New York: Crossroad, 1992): 27-31.

1. Judges in Recent Scholarship

A. Literary Overview of Judges

Webb has noted that Martin Noth's understanding of Deuteronomy–2 Kings as the work of a single Deuteronomistic historian has impeded serious consideration of Judges as its own literary unit.[5] Also, since Judg 2:6 appears to be a more logical extension of the end of Joshua 23 and gives a rhetorical framework for the main section of the book, Judg 1:1-2:5 and 17-21 are commonly regarded as later additions used by one or more historians who appropriated the main narratives to reflect a religious philosophy which was read back into Israel's history.[6]

However, the final form of the book is not without coherency when read as a whole.[7] Chap. 1 describes the Israelites continued attempts to subdue the promised land after the death of Joshua. There is no national unity. Individual tribes pursue their own territories. Lack of political unity is characterized in theological tones in the latter part of the book, with the refrain "there was no king in Israel" . . . "everyone did what was right in his own eyes" (17:6; 18:1; 19:1; 21:25). This refrain serves as a fitting summary to the events in the main narrative. There was neither a king on the throne, nor was God himself regarded

---

[5] Barry G. Webb, *The Book of Judges: An Integrated Reading* (JSOTSup 46; Sheffield: JSOT, 1987): 207. See also Martin Noth, *Überleiferungsgeschichtliche Studien* (2nd ed.; Tübingen: M. Niemeyer, 1957).

[6] For detailed discussion of the formation of the present book of Judges, see C. F. Burney, *The Book of Judges* (New York: KTAV, 1970 [1903, 1918]): 34-50; G. F. Moore, *Critical and Exegetical Commentary on Judges* (ICC; New York: C. Scribner's Sons, 1895): 13-37; and Robert G. Boling, *Judges* (AB; Garden City, NY: Doubleday, 1975): 29-38.

[7] For discussion of the theological unity of Judges, see Brevard S. Childs, *Old Testament Theology in a Canonical Context* (Philadelphia: Fortress, 1985): 113-115. For discussion of the narrative form, see Lillian R. Klein, *The Triumph of Irony in Judges* (Bible and Literature Series 14; Sheffield: Almond, 1989): 12-21.

as Israel's sovereign. While the question of whether or not Judges is a pro-monarchical document is outside the scope of this essay, failure to regard Yahweh as sovereign is of obvious concern to the editor of Judges, who interpreted Israel's history of oppression in Canaan as a direct result of this failure.

Viewing Judges as a literary unit, I propose the following contracted outline, with theological movements:

1. *Introduction.* Judg 1:1-2:5 emphasizes Yahweh's role in delivering the promised land to the appointed tribes, and their incomplete conquest of Canaan (note parallels in Josh 13-18). Judg 2:1-15 sets forth Yahweh's complaint to all Israel of the broken covenant, and his consequent refusal to drive out the nations. The people weep and sacrifice, but their repentance is short lived.[8] This section shows the need for divine grace and strikes a foreboding chord signaling Israel's perpetual faithlessness.

2. *Exposition.* Judg 2:6-23 is an expositional unit establishing a cause and effect rubric—Israel's sin resulting in Yahweh's handing them over to their oppressors, the subsequent cry for help, and Yahweh's intervention. This exposition is general and reflects the viewpoint of Yahweh.[9] The individual narratives reflect the themes and motifs of the exposition.[10] The total picture is a progression of anti-

---

[8]The closing formula, "the land was at rest for . . . years," which follows in the main narratives should be viewed as intentionally juxtaposed with "again the people did evil . . . and cried to the Lord," exposing Israel's disregard for Yahweh until a time of trouble.

[9]Moore, *Judges,* 63, observes that the author's aim was not purely historical, but moral and religious, noting that "the lesson of history is for him the chief thing of history."

[10]Discussion of the relationship between the exposition, the main narrative and the resolution is a valuable contribution of narrative criticism. See Klein, *Triumph of Irony in Judges,* 193-196; Shimon Bar-Efrat, *Narrative Art in the Bible* (JSOTSup 70, Sheffield: Almond, 1984); Meir Sternberg, *The Poetics of Biblical Narrative: Ideological Literature and the Drama of Reading* (Bloomington: Indiana Univ.

Yahwism. Judg 3:1-6 catalogues the nations which Yahweh left in the promised land to test the fidelity of the Israelites. They, like their forefathers, would know war, since they would eventually invoke Yahweh's wrath by intermarrying with the pagans and becoming idolatrous.

3. *The Individual Judges.* Judg 3:7-16:31 details the individual episodes of the judges. Each episode relates its own stories of sin and grace and work within the larger framework of the book to reveal the extent of Israel's unfaithfulness and the extent of the mercy and longsuffering of Yahweh. Several narratives are introduced with *"again* Israel did evil in the sight of the Lord," indicating the historian's emphasis on Israel's perpetual faithlessness.

4. *Epilogue.* The problem of breaking covenant with Yahweh was presented in the exposition (2:1-5). Chaps. 17-21 function as the predictable resolution. The general cycle of evil, oppression, crying out to Yahweh, deliverance, peace, and then return to evil has been laid out in chaps. 1-16. Now chaps. 17-21 collapse the cycle into final episodes of lawlessness which are punctuated by the refrain, "in those days there was no king in Israel" (17:6; 18:1;19:1; 21:25). The narrator has prepared the reader for the degenerate end to the story by a series of stories which extend from the ideal leader Joshua to the undisciplined Samson. Though the main narratives do not indict all of the judges, the people are always indicted by their return to idolatry after the death of the judge. This final section[11] chronicles the idolatry of the prophet Micah, (17-18), the unseemly behavior of some of the Levites, who should be leaders among the Israelites, and the savagery of the men of Gibeah (19-20) which resulted in civil war and the rape of hundreds of Israelite women (21).

Press, 1987): 268, discussing modes of shaping the narrative future, lists three forms of foreshadowing: analogy, paradigm, and dramatic forecast.

[11]Fewell, "Judges" *Women's Bible Commentary,* 66-67 sees the stories as revealing a "downward spiral for Israel." Chaps. 17-21 provide an appropriate ending to the record of a degenerate community in which women are largely depicted as dispensable, reflective of Israel's attitude toward Yahweh.

B. *The Judges Motif in Judges*

The story of Deborah should be considered in its contextual setting in the book of Judges, for it is a part of the entire drama recorded to describe the pre-monarchical history of Yahweh's covenant people after the initial conquest of Canaan. Men and women alike take their places in this socio-theological history.

1. *Descriptions of the Judges and Their Activities.* The details about the judges are not uniform. In 2:16 the narrator gives a general statement, "the Lord raised up judges who saved them . . . ," but in the individual narratives, the descriptions of the judges and details of the stories are varied. The most common terms used to describe the judges are as follows.

a. *Judges.* The Hebrew title of the book is שׁוֹפְטִים drawn from the expositional formula in 2:16 "And the Lord raised up *judges* who saved them out of the power of those plundering them." The English understanding of "judges" as those who arbitrate disputes is too narrow since the verse above describes a military function. Deborah functions in both capacities as one to whom the Israelites came for judgment (4:4,5), and as one who was, along with Barak, an instrument of Yahweh's military deliverance. The noun שֹׁפֵט (judge) is not used directly to describe any one individual (although in 2:16-17 it is applied to the judges in general). It is applied to Yahweh in 11:27, indicating that Yahweh is the true judge. The verbal form שָׁפַט (judge) is applied to the protagonists, as they are described as judging or delivering Israel.

b. *Saviors.* The noun מוֹשִׁיעַ (savior), or its related verb יָשַׁע (save) is applied to four of the judges: Othniel, Ehud, Shamgar, and Tola. Neither Deborah, Barak, Jephthah nor any of the minor judges are described as "saving," according to Boling.[12] Barak and Gideon are not designated as "judging" or "saving" Israel, but obviously their military

---

[12] Boling, *Judges*, 6-7.

activity includes them among those who delivered, saved, or vindicated Israel, just as Deborah and Jephthah "saved" Israel from going out of existence.[13]

c. *People Empowered by the Spirit of Yahweh.* The Spirit of Yahweh is mentioned in connection with four of the judges: Othniel, Gideon, Jephthah, and Samson. However, there is no stereotypical formula to describe the phenomenon. Boling suggests that the Spirit of Yahweh is an abstraction referring to a force which gives humans the ability to exert great power, but the presence of the spirit does "not make the man an automaton," rather, the Spirit of Yahweh is "one of the many components in the personality."[14] The Spirit of Yahweh is mentioned in close connection with a judge actually going to battle in every case except in reference to Samson, where the text reads "The spirit of the Lord began to stir him in Mahaneh-dan," (13:25). In this case, the presence of the spirit of Yahweh is related to the divine promise made to the parents of Samson that their son would be a deliverer of Israel.

d. *Proclaimers.* In addition to serving as military deliverers, and in Deborah's case, as one arbitrating disputes, the judges also proclaimed the intentions of Yahweh (3:28; and 4:6; 8:3). Deborah is the only judge described as a prophet and, in the tradition of the other biblical prophets, she spoke the word of Yahweh. Her summons to Barak is couched in the "command of Yahweh," and her prophetic competency is proved by the outcome of the battle and the extrication of the enemy at the hand of a woman.[15] In her song, Deborah proclaims the mighty acts of Yahweh.

---

[13]For further discussion on the meaning of שׁפט and the other descriptors of the judges' activities, see Moore, *Commentary on Judges*, 11-12, 71, 88; and Burney, *The Book of Judges*, 85,86.

[14]Boling, *Judges*, 25, 26; Webb, *The Book of Judges*, 61-65; and Arthur E. Cundall and Leon Morris, *Judges and Ruth* (TynC; Downers Grove: InterVarsity Press, 1968): 42-45.

[15]David L. Petersen, *The Roles of Israel's Prophets*, (JSOTSup 17; Sheffield: Sheffield Press, 1981).

e. *People Raised Up by Yahweh.* The formula "Yahweh raised up judges" appears first in the introductory section (2:11-23), emphasizing the initiative of Yahweh in the deliverance of Israel. This phrase underscores the editor's objective to show that Yahweh's will and power are the consuming forces in these narratives of war between Israel and her enemies.[16] Othniel (3:9) and Ehud (3:15) are introduced by this formula.

2. *Conclusions about the Descriptions of the Judges.* The editor of the book of Judges obviously was not concerned to provide a checklist of descriptions by which to distinguish a full-fledged judge from an auxiliary. The survey above shows that the descriptions are not applied consistently to each judge. Philological concerns cannot be pressed too far in regard to the terms "judging" or "saving," as these words seem to be used in a general sense to describe military leadership. Alternating use of descriptions does not distinguish one judge as legitimate and another as illegitimate. As far as the narrative purpose is concerned, the defining quality of each judge was that he/she was one of the ones whom "the Lord raised up to save the Israelites. . ." (2:16).

The details of the individual episodes mitigate against categorically praising the judges as the moral heroes of the story.[17] Jephthah's rash vow (11:30ff.) betrays his skewed understanding of relationship to Yahweh. Samson and Gideon exhibit considerable weakness. The presence of the "spirit of Yahweh" in some of the accounts indicates only that Yahweh empowered the judge and his army, not that the

---

[16]Older commentaries and more recent narrative critics generally agree that the overall theme of the book is to show Yahweh as the real judge and deliverer and conversely to demonstrate Israel's unfaithfulness and gradual anarchy. The refrain, "in those days there was no king in Israel," refers not just to the absence of a human king, but to the fact that Yahweh himself was not regarded as king in Israel.

[17]Klein, *Triumph of Irony in Judges*, 17-18, proposes that each judge "symbolizes an aspect of Israel, a weakness, a quality which leads to the narrative consequences of that episode" and that Yahweh is the antagonist to the political, non–ethical values of Israel.

judge's every action was in perfect harmony with the will of Yahweh. Neither the absence of a "spirit of Yahweh" phrase or the poor behavior of the protagonists deters the author/editor from ascribing to Yahweh the credit for subduing Israel's enemies. Invoking Yahweh's name is not always a true indicator of the moral character of the judge. In Gideon's case, his threats, though in the name of Yahweh (8:4-9), seem to be angry ravings from one who is concerned for self-glory. The fact that he eventually leads the people away from Yahweh (8:22-28) adds to the suspicion. Klein[18] observes correctly that,

> With few (but significant) exceptions, the development of each major judge narrative leads to a decline. . . —even during the judge's lifetime. Typically, after becoming a leader of the people and eliminating the source of oppression, the judge leads the people away from Yahweh. . . . Instead of teaching the people, the judge "learns" from them.

The exception to Klein's rule is Deborah.[19] Among the major judges, she escapes unscathed as a spiritual leader. Gideon eventually leads the people to idolatry, and Jephthah engages the people in civil war. Samson's trust in a Philistine woman leads to his own imprisonment, and one can assume that his capture gives way to Philistine oppression of the Israelites.

3. In summary, a comparison of terms and descriptors applied to the judges places each of them on a level plane as legitimately recognized judges in Israel. Regardless of their social standing, tribe, or gender, they all took their place in the literary and historical scheme of the book of Judges. They were appointed or raised up by Yahweh to deliver Israel, and he is credited with the victory in each case.

---

[18] Klein, *The Triumph of Irony in Judges*, 19-20.

[19] If Ehud is considered a major judge, he too is an exception to Klein's observation.

There is no reason to indiscriminately regard the judges as models for leadership. Some of the judges were responsible leaders, while others began responsibly, but because they were spiritually inept, became poor leaders. Their fitness as leaders was ultimately determined by their allegiance to the way of Yahweh. A primary question for the book of Judges, then, is not *who may be a judge?* but, *Why the continual need for a judge?* The narrative's emphatic answer is *sin*.

The absence of the designation "judge" to refer to any of the individual judges provides the backdrop for understanding the identity of the true judge—Yahweh (11:27). Yahweh as judge or deliverer emerges as a strong emphasis. The theme is first presented in the introduction by the emphasis on Yahweh's initiative and is repeated in the various episodes involving the judges. Amit[20] accurately understands the structure of the Deborah narrative as ultimately expressing the same theme. The reader is led to question the identity of the hero by the introduction of a succession of characters—Deborah, Barak, and Jael— none of whom is the real deliverer. The motif is played out in both prose and poetry in the Deborah story, the poetry especially underscoring the triumph of Yahweh.

2. *Deborah*

We are now in position to consider the story of Deborah in the setting of the "judges" motif in the book of Judges.

A. *Judge*

Deborah's story is told twice, first in chap. 4 in prose; and then in chap. 5 in poetry in the Song of Deborah. The song is traditionally held to be the older of the two accounts.[21] While literature on the discrepancies in the two

---

[20]Y. Amit, "Judges 4: Its Contents and Form," *JSOT* 39 (1987): 89-111.

[21]Most scholars think the song is the oldest piece of literature in the Hebrew Bible, dated between the 12th and 11th centuries. See O.

accounts is vast[22] and will not be the focus of this essay, Freedman's observation that "lyric poetry is not prose narrative, still less journalistic reporting" is astute.[23] Even with the gaps, both accounts advance the theme of Yahweh as deliverer and Deborah, Barak, and Jael as instruments of his deliverance.

Deborah is first mentioned in 4:4 with the formula components: 1) Israel did evil, 2) so the Lord sold them, and 3) they cried to the Lord for help. The usual "so the Lord raised up a judge" is replaced with the introduction of "Deborah a prophetess, wife of Lappidoth[24] who was שֹׁפְטָה (judging) Israel at that time." Scholars have emphasized various elements of the introduction of Deborah, e.g., Moore[25] argues rightly that the term שֹׁפְטָה should be rendered as elsewhere in the book, *she delivered Israel.*

V. 5 describes her judicial activity under the Palm of Deborah.[26] That "the Israelites came to her to have their disputes settled" is reminiscent of Samuel's role as arbitrator (1 Sam 3:20-4:1). Deborah's seat of judgment is between Ramah and Bethel; the same region where Samuel worked (1 Sam 7:15-17).

Eissfeldt, *The Old Testament: An Introduction* (trans. P. R. Ackroyd; New York: Scribner and Sons, 1965): 100-101; D. Harvey, "Deborah," in *IDB*, (ed. G. A. Buttrick; New York: Abingdon, 1962): 1.809; David Noel Freedman, *Pottery, Poetry, and Prophecy* (Winona Lake, IN: Eisenbrauns, 1980): 118-119, 131.

[22] Among the discrepancies are the names of the tribes who participated in the battle, the location of the battle, the identity of the kings/generals of Canaanites, and the description of Sisera's death. See Moore, *Judges,* 107-173; Athalya Brenner, "A Triangle and a Rhombus in Narrative Structure," *VT*, 40 (1990): 129-138; Webb, *Judges: An Integrated Reading*, 133-44; and Burney, *Judges,* 78-83.

[23] Freedman, *Pottery, Poetry and Prophecy*, 153.

[24] "Wife of Lappidoth" could be rendered "fiery woman," as in NEB footnote.

[25] Moore, *Judges,* 113.

[26] Cf. Moore, *Judges,* 113, who views v. 5 as a circumstantial addition by a late editor who took the verb in v. 4 in the sense of giving judicial decisions.

Amit focuses on the deviation from the formulaic pattern, i.e., instead of the usual "the Lord raised up a deliverer," Deborah is introduced as prophetess who was judging Israel at that time. Amit says the substitution may at first prompt the reader to assume that Deborah is the savior, but that assumption is actually foiled by,

> a) avoidance of the formula: "And the Lord raised a savior";
> b) stress on Deborah's sex: she is a 'prophetess' and wife of Lappidoth—which does not connect her with the figure of a soldier like Ehud, or Othniel;
> c) stress on Deborah's judgeship as dealing with personal disputes, not as leading a military force.

For Amit, the narrative structure highlights 1) the question of whether a judge is also a savior and 2) the introduction of Barak and his refusal to accept the appointment as deliverer enhances the riddle of the identity of the savior. His conclusion is that Deborah (eventually sharing the military duties) and Barak are secondary in a heroic hierarchy with God at the top of the structure.[27] Though the narrative does not technically distinguish between the protagonists, whether they are called judges or saviors, Amit correctly understands the strong emphasis in the Deborah story, and throughout the book, that Yahweh holds the power for deliverance.

Fewell and Gunn[28] point to the unexpected gender-role reversal as a controlling perspective in the narrative and argue that Judg 4 and 5 reveal a complex picture of women acting in a patriarchal world. However, Sternberg,[29] emphasizing the "incongruous deliverer" motif, says that Deborah,

---

[27] Amit, *JSOT* (1987): 91ff.

[28] Dana Nolan Fewell and David M. Gunn, "Controlling Perspectives Women, Men and the Authority of Violence in Judges 4 & 5," *JAAR* 58 (1990): 389-411.

[29] Sternberg, *The Poetics of Biblical Narrative*, (Bloomington: Indiana Univ. Press, 1985): 272.

springs at us from nowhere, complete with husband, national role, foreign antagonist, and seat of judgment bearing her name: all expositional features calculated to bring her sex into marked dissonance with her offices past and to come.

Hanselman[30] rightly criticizes Sternberg: 1) his treatment of the narrative as dominated by the supposition that the story is about "how the God of the Fathers could use *"even a woman,"* and 2) his focus on Barak as the central figure with Deborah's actions significant only as they relate to Barak's.

Fewell and Gunn rightly give Deborah full status as a military leader, but their feminist perspective can hardly be the "controlling perspective." Sternberg correctly implies that Deborah is in an unusual place for her gender, and if by "incongruous deliverer motif" he means that the Bible regularly records God using people whom others may regard as unlikely to accomplish his will, then he is accurate. However, the fact that God used people of *his choice* questions the human idea of "incongruous." The OT is replete with characters who for one reason or another seem unlikely candidates for the task they are given or for the honor or recognition they receive, yet are chosen by God. Time and again Yahweh foils the idea of incongrous or unlikely leaders.

Nothing in the narrative suggests that Deborah's gender improved or detracted from her status as judge/deliver, nor is there indication that Yahweh had any reservations about her functioning in this role.

B. *Prophetess*

While Moore is willing to translate שָׁפַט as "delivering" or "vindicating," he diminishes her status as prophetess.

---

[30]Stephen W. Hanselman, "Narrative Theory, Ideology, and Transformation in Judges 4," *Anti Covenant: Counter-reading Women's Lives in the Hebrew Bible* (ed. Mieke Bal; JSOTSup 81; Sheffield: Almond, 1989): 111, n 4.

Referring to Exod 15:20 (Miriam singing the victory song after the crossing of the Red Sea), he comments that prophetess should be taken in the "older sense of the word," meaning "inspired woman."[31] This is an unnecessary distinction. Deborah is pictured as speaking for Yahweh (4:6), prophesying the outcome of the battle (4:7, 9) and encouraging faith and obedience (4:14). These are typical of activities of other biblical characters who are described as prophets. While prophetesses may have been less common than prophets, they served equally in this role. Gender was not an issue. Deborah's prophetic activity was not unlike that of other biblical prophets.

C. *Military Leader*

King Jabin and the Canaanites had oppressed the Israelites for twenty years. The overpowering nature of these enemies is accentuated by the mention of their nine hundred chariots of iron (4:2-3). Deborah, the judge and prophetess from the hill country of Ephraim, summoned Barak to marshal the forces. Deborah's authority was apparently not limited to the hill country of Ephraim, since she sent for Barak, of Kedesh-naphtali, to marshal the forces of Naphtali and Zebulun.[32]

---

[31]Moore, *Judges*, 112. See recently F. LaGard Smith, *Men of Strength For Women of God* (Eugene, OR: Harvest House, 1989): 114-118. Smith attempts to diminish Deborah's role by arguing that her story points to the neglect of the men of Israel in fulfilling their leadership roles, and that Deborah's call was for "a return to *strong male leadership*." Smith's reasoning ignores at least two facts: 1) the text does not indicate that Yahweh was not more displeased with the men than the women (he was displeased with *Israel*), and 2) Yahweh found men to serve as judges in the other narratives.

[32]The Song of Deborah in chap. 5 lists seven other tribes who either joined in the battle or were reprimanded for not participating. Discrepancies in the accounts of the battle in chaps. 4 and 5 have been discussed in terms of literary genre, historical criticism and form criticism by Freedman, *Pottery, Poetry, and Prophecy*, 147-166; and Boling, *Judges*, 101-120. The Song of Deborah has several other tribes participating in the battle, see A. D. H. Mayes, "The Historical Context of the Battle Against Sisera," *VT* 19 (1969): 353-360; W. F.

Barak's reluctance to answer the summons unless Deborah accompanies him in the battle is interesting. Was Barak cowardly? Or did his response indicate his recognition of Deborah's role as spokeswoman for Yahweh, thus one whose presence would assure the victory? One can *wonder* if Barak may have been afraid or even reluctant to follow a woman, but the account *clearly* shows that he submitted himself to Deborah and followed her instructions to gather the troops and later to begin the attack.

Deborah's answer is as difficult to interpret as Barak's reluctance. Was Deborah reprimanding Barak's lack of trust? Did her prophetic statement about the Lord handing Sisera over to a woman reveal that Deborah was engaged in a power struggle with gender as a central issue? The NIV translation of v. 9 suggests a gender conflict :

"Very well," Deborah said, "I will go with you." *But because of the way you are going about this*, the honor will not be yours, for the LORD will hand Sisera over to a woman (italics mine).

The NIV footnote and the RSV translation is a better reading:

And she said, "I will surely go with you; *nevertheless, the road on which you are going* will not lead to your glory for the Lord will sell Sisera into the hand of a woman" (italics mine).

The Hebrew word דֶּרֶךְ may mean "way" or "road." The more natural reading of v. 9 is that Deborah is referring to her earlier command in v. 6 that Barak lead troops to Mount Tabor, while Yahweh would lure Sisera to the Wadi Kishon. It is there that Sisera would be killed by Jael, not on the mountain where Barak would be. Barak would not receive the glory for killing Sisera, but it is conjectural to suggest that the Hebrew text means "it is because of the way you are handling this (situation)."

Albright, "The Song of Deborah in Light of Archeology," *BASOR* 62(1936): 26-31.

Fewell and Gunn interpret Deborah's answer—"it will not be your glorying on the way you are going, for Yahweh will sell Sisera into the hand of a woman" (4:9)—as an insult to Barak and to patriarchy's short-sighted view of women. They also suggest that the narrative further unnerves the patriarchal mindset by bringing another exceptional woman (Jael) into the picture, who takes charge of the story.[33]

While some of their points are well-made and serve to highlight long-overlooked feminine perspectives, Fewell and Gunn read a strongly feminist agenda into the text, incorrectly seeing a proliferation of anti-male attitudes, sexual overtones, and in the Jael section, tones of sexual violence.[34] They take these perspectives to be those of the characters and of the readers of this narrative. While it is true that the Hebrew Bible does not shy away from sex or violence, much of Fewell and Gunn's argument is overstated.

Whatever the situation was with Deborah and Barak, she did accompany him to the battle and actually gave the signal for the attack. Her prophecy of victory and the defeat of the enemy at the hand of a woman were fulfilled by Israel's victory. While female leadership in marshaling the forces and initiating the battle may have been uncommon, the victory was secured with Deborah's leadership. There is no clear indication in the text that her role in this incident was viewed as a gender issue.

D. *A Mother in Israel*

The Song of Deborah and Barak in Judg 5 recapitulates the story. The prose record (chap. 4) has been selective in its reporting, and the poem (chap. 5) celebrates and elaborates the victory. Clearly the song gives accolades to Deborah and Barak for their leadership in the victory over the Canaanites, but the emphasis of the song is that Yahweh is the victor. The opening couplet introduces the song as

---

[33]Fewell and Gunn, *JAAR* (1990): 399.
[34]*Ibid.*, 392-399.

one of praise to Yahweh; v. 3 stresses that Yahweh is the object of the exultation. He is depicted as marching like one leading in battle (v. 4), and is shown to be sovereign over nature, invoking its power by causing a great thunderstorm which flooded the river Kishon and swept away the enemies (vv. 4b, 23). The mountains quake before him and the stars from heaven fight (vv.5, 20) to bring down the enemies of the Lord.[35]

Woven into the fabric of the song are praises for those who joined Yahweh in the battle. Deborah is highlighted as the one who arose to restore the caravans (פְּרָזוֹן v.7),[36] suggesting earlier loss of commerce and other aspects of normal life due to oppression. This way of life "ceased . . . until Deborah, a *mother* in Israel, arose." Whether this is a literal description of Deborah is not indicated in the narrative or the song. Fewell views the designation as suggesting Deborah to be a "nursemaid to politically-incapacitated Israel."[37] Noting Deborah's counsel, inspiration, and leadership, Exum suggests that a "mother in Israel" means that she was one

> who brings liberation from oppression, provides protection, and ensures the well-being and security of her people.[38]

---

[35]Klein, *Triumph of Irony in Judges*, 44, observes that the song has many singers, but that Deborah's verses keep the focus on Yahweh.

[36]For discussion of the difficulty in translation of the word פְּרָזוֹן, see Burney, *Judges*, 114-116; John Gray, "Israel in the Song of Deborah," *Ascribe to the Lord : Biblical and Other Studies in Memory of Peter C. Craigie* (ed. L. Eslinger and G. Taylor; JSOTSup 67; Sheffield: JSOT, 1988): 428. Since the first person singular ending and the more obscure second person singular ending are the same, there is difficulty in determining whether Deborah is the singer (when *I*, Deborah, arose) or if the song is sung antiphonally (when *you*, Deborah, arose). See also, Alexander Globe, "The Literary Structure and Unity of the Song of Deborah," *JBL* 93 (1974): 493-512.

[37]Fewell, "Judges," *Woman's Bible Commentary*, 69.

[38]Cheryl Exum, "Mother in Israel," *Feminist Interpretation of the Bible* (ed. L. M. Russell; Philadelphia: Westminster, 1985): 86.

Obviously, literal motherhood would have no bearing on her part in the military drama, so the appellative is meant as a term of admiration, suggesting that the Israelites saw no conflict between recognized feminine roles and characteristics such as motherhood, and the less conventional role which Deborah played as deliverer. Her "motherhood" did not diminish her spiritual or military leadership.

Conclusion

Deborah functioned as a judge, prophetess and military leader. The text does not minimize any of these roles because Deborah was a woman.[39] She was a woman, the wife of Lappidoth, and she also was regarded with admiration by the phrase "mother in Israel." None of these attributes cast doubt on her spiritual and political functions. Intentional diminishing of roles that are "unconventional" from a patriarchal standpoint reflects a hegemonic masculinity which defines femininity according to its relationship to the accepted definition of masculinity.[40] To suggest that Deborah would not have played the role of military or spiritual leader if the men of Israel had been responsible[41] is to make current gender conflicts apply to the ancient setting rather than allowing the text to apply its meaning to the present situation.

If Deborah's answer to Barak concerning the credit for the victory (4:9) suggests gender conflict, which is no doubt a timeless struggle in the human realm, this struggle does not

---

[39] Donald K. Campbell, *Judges: Leaders in Crisis Times* (Wheaton: Victor Books, 1989): 51, notes, "Though she had a prominent position in her society, she also assumed her proper place at home as wife and homemaker. Today's Christian career woman should seek the same balance." Such a statement diverts attention from Deborah's place as a military and spiritual leader, and does a serious injustice to the point of the text.

[40] See Mary Sewart Van Leeuwen, ed., *After Eden—Facing the Challenge of Gender Reconciliation* (Grand Rapids: Eerdmans, 1993): 225-267.

[41] Smith, *Men of Strength For Women of God*, 114-118.

govern the focus of the narrative, nor does it provide answers to questions about hierarchical order. What is clear is that Yahweh chose Deborah from among his rebellious people to accomplish his will. She responded to her calling and the battle at Megiddo was secured. Barak recognized her authority and obeyed her instructions. The Song of Deborah gives accolades to Yahweh, and to all the human participants who were obedient in that particular episode of Israel's history.

The elements of Deborah's story call for another look at how Scripture presents women. While the biblical text sometimes leaves them in the shadows, obscured by male characters, (but still part of divine purpose, whether bearing children, or letting spies out a window), sometimes it presents them in more obvious roles as instruments of divine purpose as in the case of Deborah. That there are fewer women playing "prominent" roles in Scripture does not detract from their crucial places in the history of faith.

Chapter Four

"WISE WOMEN" IN THE BIBLE: IDENTIFYING A TRAJECTORY

Michael S. Moore

Recently a frustrated student asked me about the Wisdom Woman, the female figure alluded to in Prov 1, 8, and 9. Had I heard, she asked, about a recent conference in Minneapolis where hundreds of Protestant women had "re-imagined" God as the goddess Sophia?[1] Who exactly *was* this Sophia? Did Israel worship her? Was she a mediator between God and humanity? Was she *a* god or was she *the* God? Was it all right to pray to her today?[2]

For weeks, she struggled to understand the biblical text while I struggled to understand this conference. One of the presenters at the conference, listed as the co-founder of a group called CLOUT (Christian Lesbians Out Together), had invited participants to celebrate "the miracle of being lesbian, out, and Christian." Another woman proclaimed that Mary and Martha were not biological sisters, but lesbian "fore-sisters." Still another, a self-avowed lesbian Presbyterian, had boldly issued the following challenge:

---

[1]The now-famous "Re-Imagining" Conference, sponsored by the St. Paul, Minneapolis and Minnesota Councils of Churches and held at the Minneapolis Convention Center in Minneapolis, MN on Nov. 4-7, 1993.

[2]The Wisdom Woman in Prov 1-9 is interpreted in at least four different ways: 1) as an indigenous Hebrew goddess; 2) as a foreign goddess; 3) as an extension, or hypostatization of the one God Yahweh; 4) simply as a literary symbol for the Hebrew wisdom tradition. See M. S. Moore, "Wise Women or Wisdom Woman? A Biblical Study of Women's Roles," *ResQ* 35 (1993): 147-158.

> Sexuality and spirituality have to come together—and Church, we're going to teach you!³

I had always suspected that goddess religion was going on "out there" somewhere, perhaps being practiced by New Age devotees or some other comfortable stereotype. Now one of my own students was presenting me with evidence for seeing it *not* in the dignified halls of academia, or the garish columns of the tabloids, but right in the stately pews of American Protestant churches.⁴

Soon afterwards, she wrote a startling confession:

> I hadn't realized how deeply into fertility worship I was lapsing. The Christian response is, of course, to thank God for the ability to birth and lactate and nurture, etc. These acts, while critical to myself, do not define me as Deity (i.e., womb=goddess)!⁵

To be honest, I have a great deal of difficulty knowing how to interpret this confession, for the pantheistic presuppositions behind it are deeply troubling. To hear someone claiming to wear the name of Christ say that she had once considered herself to be a *divine being* is profoundly disturbing, to say the least. If this example is at all representative, the degree to which goddess religion has penetrated into American Protestantism today is much higher than I had ever imagined.⁶

---

³Dottie Chase, "United Methodist Women Get a Taste of Sophia Worship," *Good News: The Bimonthly Magazine for United Methodists* (Jan-Feb 1994): 36-38.

⁴According to *The Presbyterian Layman* (Jan-Feb 1994): 3, Presbyterian officials had originally planned a series of events to follow this conference throughout the PCUSA. Further, an anonymous donor had given Louisville Seminary a monetary gift for the express purpose of establishing a "re-imagining center" on campus as a permanent training facility.

⁵Personal correspondence. Used by permission.

⁶Gerda Weiler, *Ich verwerfe im Lande die Kriege. Das verborgene Matriarchat im Alten Testament* (Munich: Verlag Frauenoffensive,

This incident vividly illustrates a major issue now affecting Euro-American religious life.[7] Contemporary Christians are caught in the crossfire of a nasty ecclesiastical gender war,[8] a war which, like all wars, has steadily grown from a few isolated skirmishes into a hemispheric conflict, and this for a number of reasons: the prevalence of confusion over gender roles,[9] the physical and emotional

---

1984): 338, advocates that Judeo-Christian women will never be free to worship the Goddess until the negative view of fertility religion embedded in the OT is replaced with a new openness to God as "Grossen Mutter." For Weiler, the Canaanites were just as correct in their approach to deity as were the Israelites. In response to this kind of thinking, Mary Hayter, *The New Eve in Christ—The Use and Abuse of the Bible in the Debate About Women in the Church* (Grand Rapids: Eerdmans, 1987): 18, rightly points out that the "essential dissonance is not between the Old Testament and femininity, but between the Old Testament and nature religion." For Hayter, both "the feminists who venerate a female deity and those who react against this by stressing the maleness of God are revitalizing the unhealthy emphases of the fertility cultus . . ., departing from faith in a transcendent Creator . . . (and) re-magicalizing religion."

[7]For a thorough summary and analysis of contemporary European perspectives, see Notger Slenzka, "Feministiche Theologie," *TRu* 58 (1993): 396-436.

[8]I am in agreement with Rebecca Merrill Groothuis, *Women Caught in the Conflict: The Culture War Between Traditionalism and Feminism* (Grand Rapids: Baker, 1994): 175, that the "debate within evangelicalism is not occurring in isolation from contemporary culture," but that "this in-house evangelical conflict is a smaller-scale replica of the cultural conflict in progress in secular society." Groothuis' analysis is indebted to the anthropology of James D. Hunter, *Culture Wars: The Struggle to Define America* (New York: Basic/Harper Collins, 1991).

[9]For contrasting views on ministry to homosexuals, see Stanton L. Jones, "The Loving Opposition," *Christianity Today* 37, 8 (1993): 18-25; and Thomas W. Strieter, "Theological Reflection on Pastoral Care for Gays and Lesbians," *Currents in Theology and Mission* 20 (1993): 268-277. George Guilder, *Men and Marriage* (Gretna, LA: Pelican, 1992): 179-185, discusses the brave new world of biogenetic engineering in the broader social context of what he calls "the sexual suicide technocracy."

abuse of women,[10] the prevalence and persistence of adultery,[11] the prevalence and acceptability of divorce,[12] the widespread problem of fatherlessness,[13] the fear of failure in meaningful sexual relationships,[14] the growing disdain for biblical morality.[15] Some men, however few, finally seem to be understanding why women are so angry.[16] And some

---

[10]See Rita-Lou Clarke, *Pastoral Care of Battered Women* (Louisville: Westminster/John Knox, 1991); Bill Flatt, "The Misuse of Power and Sex in Helping Relationships," *ResQ* 36 (1994): 101-110.

[11]Annette Lawson, *Adultery* (New York: Basic Books, 1988); M. S. Moore, "David's Inner Conflict," *Reconciliation: A Study of Biblical Families in Conflict* (Joplin, MO: College Press, 1994): 123-137.

[12]Judith Wallerstein and Sandra Blakeslee, *Second Chances: Men, Women and Children a Decade After Divorce* (New York: Ticknor and Fields, 1989), are doing the pioneer longitudinal work.

[13]One of the few biblical theological studies of this problem is John Miller, *Biblical Faith and Fathering: Why We Call God "Father"* (New York: Paulist Press, 1989). See also Michael O'Donnell and Michelle Morris, *Heart of the Warrior: A Battle Plan for Fathers to Reclaim their Families* (Abilene: ACU Press, 1993).

[14]Guilder, *Men and Marriage*, 115, notes, "To the sexual liberal, gender is a cage. Behind cruel bars of custom and tradition, men and women for centuries have looked longingly across forbidden spaces at one another and yearned to be free of sexual roles. The men dream of nurturing and consoling; the women want the right to be tough and child-free. Today it is widely believed that the dream of escape can come true at last."

[15]See Peter Berger's pioneering study *The Sacred Canopy: Elements of a Sociological Theory of Religion* (Garden City, NY: Anchor Books, 1967), esp. "Secularization and the Problem of Legitimation" (155-171). R. Judson Carlberg, in an editorial in *Christianity Today* 38,7 (June 20, 1994): 18-19, is convinced that American intellectuals are moving from a "culture of disbelief" to a "culture of disrespect." Carlberg builds his analysis on that of Stephen L. Carter, *Culture of Disbelief: How American Law and Politics Trivialize Religious Devotion* (New York: Basic, 1993).

[16]Paul K. Jewett, *Man as Male and Female* (Grand Rapids: Eerdmans, 1975), writes from the perspective of Christian dogmatic theology. Carroll D. Osburn, *Women in the Church: Refocusing the Discussion* (Abilene, TX: Restoration Perspectives, 1994), writes from the perspective of a NT theologian trying to serve the church.

women, however few, are beginning to see that not all attempts to speak to their anger are uniformly redemptive.[17]

Investigation of the biblical "wise women" trajectory can add a significant dimension to the current discussion of women. It has long been argued that biblical wisdom literature was generated by a group of "the wise," whose intellectual, social, and theological orientation differed from other such groups, i.e., priests and prophets.[18] Against this, Whybray[19] argues that there is no consistent evidence for the existence of a separate class of "wise men." Rather, such men seem to have combined such roles as soothsayer, counselor, cult official, exorcist, bureaucrat, and even physician. I am inclined to agree with Crenshaw[20] that "a group of professional sages existed in Israel." Israel may or may not have had a separate group that was known as "the wise." Yet enough is now known about "wise women" in Israel and the ancient Near East to suggest that "wise women" should be understood as a general category which encompasses a wide range of conduct in which, I suggest, the common denominator is that of creating order out of chaos, i.e., mediatorial activity.

This essay surveys the biblical wisdom tradition and asks of it pointed questions about gender and gender roles. Among the trajectories in Scripture[21]—including the

---

[17]See the brilliant response to the Minneapolis conference offered by Katherine Kersten, "How the Feminist Establishment Hurts Women," *Christianity Today* 38,7 (June 20, 1994): 20-25.

[18]See J. Lindblom, "Wisdom in the Old Testament Prophets," *Wisdom in Israel and the Ancient Near East* (VTSup 3; ed. M. Noth and D. W. Thomas; Leiden: Brill, 1969 repr. of 1955 ed.): 194-97.

[19]R. N. Whybray, *The Intellectual Tradition in the Old Testament* (BZAW 135; Berlin: W. de Gruyter, 1974): 15-16.

[20]James L. Crenshaw, *Old Testament Wisdom: An Introduction* (Atlanta: John Knox, 1981): 29. For exegesis of the critical passage, Jer 18:18, see M. S. Moore, "Jeremiah's Progressive Paradox," *RB* 93 (1986): 400-10.

[21]See Helmut Koester and James M. Robinson, *Trajectories Through Early Christianity* (Philadelphia: Fortress, 1971). Odil H.

prophetic,[22] the priestly,[23] and the apocalyptic traditions[24] —the wisdom tradition is well-equipped to help Israel address the divine desire and fundamental human need for gender reconciliation.[25] Although some are more enamored with prophets than sages, it must be observed that whenever a domestic, military, or theological conflict arises in Israel, the path to peace is often likely to go through the voice of a wise person rather than a warrior.[26] In Restoration thought, the tendency is to view theological conflict in terms of

---

Steck, "Das Problem theologischer Strömungen in nachexilischer Zeit," *EvT* 28 (1968): 445-458, prefers the metaphor "streams of tradition."

[22]For an example, see Mary Joan Winn Leith, "Verse and Reverse: The Transformation of the Woman, Israel, in Hosea 1-3," *Gender and Difference in Ancient Israel* (ed. P. Day; Minneapolis: Fortress, 1989): 95-108.

[23]For an example, see Mayer I. Gruber, "Women in the Cult According to the Priestly Code," *The Motherhood of God and Other Studies* (South Florida Studies in the History of Judaism 57; Atlanta: Scholars Press, 1992): 62, "P has many . . . positive possibilities to suggest to us about the place of women in biblical thought."

[24]For an example, see M. Bar-Ilan's, "The Attitude Toward Women in Several Non-Canonical Books," *Beth Mikra* 39 (1993): 141-152 (Hebrew), analysis of 1 Enoch and 4 Ezra.

[25]This is not to exclude other tradition-trajectories from discussion, but it is to focus on one which is often overlooked, particularly among Restorationists. John T. Willis, "Women in the Old Testament," *Essays on Women in Earliest Christianity* (ed. C. D. Osburn; Joplin, MO: College Press, 1993): 1.39, is right to insist that "the Old Testament presents several views of women," yet "the biblical interpreter must . . . strive to understand the view of women as it is presented in each Old Testament context." While the present essay focuses on one of these contexts, viz., the wisdom context, it does not attempt to go so far as to posit "friction between heterogeneous perceptions of femininity" in Scripture, as in Ilana Pardes, *Countertraditions in the Bible: A Feminist Approach* (Cambridge: Harvard Univ. Press, 1992): 4.

[26]The wise woman of Tekoa mediates *domestic*, the wise woman of Abel mediates *military* and the medium from Endor mediates *spiritual* conflict in 2 Sam 14:1-20; 20:14-22; and 1 Sam 28:1-25. P. Kyle McCarter, *2 Samuel* (AB 9; Garden City, NY: Doubleday, 1984): 345, thinks that Abigail is, in fact, a wise woman.

prophetic and apocalyptic categories, excluding the category of wisdom.[27] However, wisdom emphasizes a side of God that can be found nowhere else, viz., the patience and maturity to wage peace in the face of war, the restorative desire to create order out of chaos.[28] In spite of its relative unfamiliarity, the biblical wisdom tradition still holds the power to transform the church as it wrestles afresh with the problems confronting it, even its present conflict over gender.

1. *Methodological Considerations*

Granting that wisdom is a relatively self-contained and accessible tradition-trajectory within Scripture as a whole, the decision still has to be made with regard to where one ought to begin within *it*. Do we focus *within wisdom* on the roles "wise women" enact in the diachronic world of history, or do we focus only on overtly synchronic portrayals like the imaginative literary portrait of the Wisdom Woman in Prov 1-9? Should portrayals about "real women" be given precedence over portrayals about "imaginary women?" Is one more important than the other?[29]

---

[27]See Richard T. Hughes and C. Leonard Allen, *Illusions of Innocence: Protestant Primitivism in America* (Chicago: Univ. of Chicago Press, 1988): 58-78. For further study tracing the development of wisdom through both Testaments, see Kathleen O'Connor, *The Wisdom Literature* (Message of Biblical Spirituality 5; Wilmington, DE: Michael Glazier, 1988).

[28]See G. Von Rad, *Wisdom in Israel* (Nashville: Abingdon, 1972): 144-176; H. J. Hermisson, "Observations on Creation Theology in Wisdom," *Israelite Wisdom: Theological and Literary Essays in Honor of Samuel Terrien* (Missoula: Scholars Press, 1978): 43-57; J. Andrew Dearman, "Wisdom and Religion as a Cultural Synthesis," *Religion and Culture in Ancient Israel* (Peabody, MA: Hendrickson, 1992): esp. 210-213.

[29]Unfortunately, this is the skewed impression left by many contemporary biblical studies of gender. I am aware, with Brevard Childs, "The Theological Problem of Old Testament History," *Biblical Theology of the Old and New Testaments* (Minneapolis: Fortress, 1992): 196, that "the problem of how to deal with Old Testament

Literary critics rightly emphasize the importance of allowing the text to speak on its own terms, through its own structures and in its own symbolic languages.[30] Historical critics, on the other hand, rightly emphasize the importance of asking questions about real women in the real world—women mentioned in the biblical text, yet genuine historical personages for whom the text preserves much more than mere literary metaphor or semiotic symbol.[31]

Historical criticism, once universally accepted as necessary and normative, is now dismissed by many as atomistic and wooden.[32] While there are limitations to historical criticism, "the historico-critical method is the indispensable method for scientific study of the meaning of the ancient text."[33] On the other hand, synchronic literary methods are helpful because they keep us close to the text itself.[34]

---

history theologically has been a persistent one throughout the history of the church." Yet I also agree with Baruch Halpern, *The First Historians: The Hebrew Bible and History* (San Francisco: Harper and Row, 1988): xvii, that "text-centered interpretation is meaningless interpretation when applied to historical literature."

[30]See Claudia Camp, *Wisdom and the Feminine in the Book of Proverbs* (Sheffield: Almond, 1985): 71-77; Mieke Bal, ed., *Anti-Covenant: Counter-Reading Women's Lives in the Hebrew Bible* (Sheffield: Almond, 1989): 11-15; Edgar V. McKnight, *The Bible and the Reader: An Introduction to Literary Criticism* (Philadelphia: Fortress, 1985).

[31]See G. Ernest Wright, "Women and Masculine Theological Vocabulary in the Old Testament," *Grace upon Grace: Essays in Honor of Lester J. Kuyper* (ed. J. I. Cook; Grand Rapids: Eerdmans, 1975): 65. See also David Damrosch, *The Narrative Covenant: Transformations of Genre in the Growth of the Biblical Literature* (San Francisco: Harper and Row, 1987).

[32]William E. Phipps, *Assertive Biblical Women* (Westport, CT: Greenwood, 1992), offers rather shallow criticism regarding gender issues.

[33]Commission biblique pontificale, "L'interprétation de la Bible dans l'Église," *Bib* 74 (1993): 454 (translation mine).

[34]*Ibid.*, 464, the Commission biblique pontificale argues correctly that the "synchronic approach to the text demands that it be

Obviously a holistic approach will give attention to both if we are to understand wisdom as a self-contained biblical tradition spanning both Testaments, and to highlight the female roles within this tradition. We need to include the actual roles of wise women in Israelite history[35] as well as the manner in which these roles are later embellished by literary authors reworking and reshaping this material to serve the needs of later audiences.[36]

2. *Wise Women in Israel*

The seeds of this study were planted years ago while doing dissertational research into the roles enacted by selected magico-religious specialists in the ancient Near East. Examining these roles from a comparative anthropological perspective, it became increasingly clear that one of the major roles enacted by many female magico-religious specialists in the ancient Near East was that of *mediator*.[37] Further study uncovered striking recurrences of this same

---

completed by diachronic studies." Further, it is argued, "The Bible is a word to the real world, which God has pronounced in history, and with which he addresses us today by the intermediation of human authors" (466).

[35]Two recent studies of women painstakingly informed by archaeological research are Carol Meyers, *Discovering Eve: Ancient Israelite Women in Context* (New York: Oxford, 1988); and Karel van der Toorn, *From Her Cradle to Her Grave: The Role of Religion in the Life of the Israelite and the Babylonian Woman* (Sheffield: JSOT Press, 1994).

[36]On *static* vs. *dynamic* approaches to biblical studies generally, see Darrell Jodock, *The Church's Bible: Its Contemporary Authority* (Minneapolis: Fortress,1989): 31-67.

[37]Profs. Herbert Huffmon and Paul Riemann supervised this research at Drew University, material which was eventually published as "The Roles Enacted by Selected Ancient Near Eastern Magico-Religious Specialists," *The Balaam Traditions: Their Character and Development* (SBLDS 113; Atlanta: Scholars, 1990): esp. 21-29. Critical reviews appear in *JBL* 110 (1991) 703-706, and *CBQ* 54 (1992) 330 331.

basic role in the wise woman of Tekoa.[38] The conclusions of these earlier studies undergird and inform the present one. Consequently the primary focus of this essay will not be on whether this female societal role has been *historically* preserved, but on whether this historical memory then went on to spawn a literary biblical wisdom *trajectory* about women.[39]

When one begins to examine the historical base of this trajectory, several women can be seen to play important mediatorial roles in the books of *Samuel*, roles which anticipate and foreshadow the mediatorial roles later enacted by Solomon, the highest personification of Israelite wisdom in Scripture.[40] Like their Near Eastern counterparts, each of these women successfully untangles a thorny problem for a royal patron at a critical point in that patron's life. In the process, each addresses a different *kind* of conflict: Abigail and the wise woman of Tekoa mediate violent *domestic* conflicts (1 Sam 25:2-42; 2 Sam 14:1-20); the wise woman of Abel mediates a *military* conflict (2 Sam 20:14-22); the medium of Endor mediates a *spiritual* conflict between Saul and Samuel, even after the latter party to this conflict has already died (1 Sam 28:3-25).[41]

---

[38]See Moore, *ResQ* (1993): 147-58.

[39]Further research might be undertaken to ascertain whether this role trajectory continues through the Judaism of the intertestamental period. On rabbinical Judaism, see Bernadette Brooten, *Women Leaders in the Ancient Synagogue* (Brown Judaic Studies 36; Chico, CA: Scholars, 1982); on Josephus and Ps.-Philo, see Cheryl Anne Brown, *No Longer Be Silent: First Century Jewish Portraits of Biblical Women* (Louisville: Westminster/John Knox, 1992); on Susanna and Judith, see André LaCocque, *The Feminine Unconventional: Four Subversive Figures in Israel's Tradition* (Minneapolis: Fortress, 1990).

[40]Note Solomon's famous mediation of a dispute between two mothers over the same child in 1 Kgs 3:16-28, perhaps *the* paradigmatic example of Solomon's wisdom.

[41]See the predominantly diachronic studies of R. Whybray, *The Succession Narrative* (Napierville, IL: Allenson, 1968): 59; and J. Hoftijzer, "David and the Tekoite Woman," *VT* 20 (1970): 419-444. See also the predominantly synchronic studies of P. Trible, *Texts of*

Further, each one of these mediators approaches the delicate task of conflict resolution by means of a common counseling methodology, a pattern I call *parable + praxis*. This pattern, when practiced by non-Yahwists in ancient Near Eastern ritual texts, appears to have its deepest roots in the primeval mists of sympathetic magic, with its deliberate pairing of myth and ritual.[42] Certainly one does not need to posit a polytheistic origin for the corresponding behavior of female mediators in Israel, yet there still seems to be a deliberate connection between word and work, between parable and praxis in the stories of *Samuel*.[43]

The point is that Hebrew *women*, not men, seem most prone in *Samuel* to approach conflict resolution by means of this pattern. The wise woman of Tekoa makes sure that David is led to make a decision in the imaginary world before she moves him to take action in the real world.[44] Another wise woman engages Joab by means of proverbial and metaphorical speech before finally throwing Sheba's head over the walls of Abel, a city she proudly calls a "mother in Israel."[45] The medium of Endor combines words of power with a royal meal in the service of her patron Saul.[46] Abigail also combines food with word as she feeds David's army, then pleads fervently with him not to degenerate into that which he hates.[47]

Terror (Philadelphia: Fortress, 1984): 37-63; and C. Camp, "The Wise Women of 2 Samuel: A Role Model of Women in Early Israel?" *CBQ* 43 (1981): 14-29.

[42]Moore, *The Balaam Traditions*, 24.

[43]Moore, "Wise Women or Wisdom Woman?," 152-156.

[44]2 Sam 14:13.

[45]The "peace-loving and faithful (אמני, שלמי) wise woman" of Abel functions at a place which is recognized as a site where people customarily "inquired" ("let them inquire [שאל] at Abel," 2 Sam 20:18-19) of the divine world, a probable reference to pre-Yahwistic divinatory activity. On the use of שאל in Deut 18:11, see Joanne K. Kuemmerlin-McLean, "Magic in the Old Testament," *ABD* 4.469.

[46]1 Sam 28:1-25.

[47]1 Sam 25:24-31.

In summary, there were in Israelite religion a number of "wise women" who were recognized and consulted in matters of conflict and who intervened in a variety of ways.

3. The Hebraic Trajectory

Israelite writers go to a great deal of trouble to maintain the pattern of *parable* + *praxis* for a long period of time, artfully embellishing, yet carefully preserving this same basic pattern in several portrayals of Israelite heroines, all of whom share a common role as mediator.

Naomi, for example, resolves one of the most painful conflicts in all of the Bible, the conflict between God's command to be fruitful and multiply and the realities of famine, death, and widowhood which threaten to make compliance to this command impossible.[48] At its core, Naomi's dilemma is very much like Abigail's, or the Tekoite woman's. Each woman finds herself led into a stressful conflict and is forced to resolve it with only minimal resources. Significantly, each instinctively resorts to a pattern of *parable* + *praxis*. Naomi resolves her problem by teaching Ruth how to attract Boaz through a carefully designed ruse, then sends her out to implement it. The narrator of Ruth elaborates and embellishes this pattern to ever-higher planes of artistic genius, but in essence it looks very much like its predecessors in the books of *Samuel*.

The twist in *Esther* is the narrator's decision to highlight this pattern of parable + praxis by comparing it with another one.[49] *Esther* provides a study in conflict resolution in

---

[48]See R.M. Hals, *The Theology of the Book of Ruth* (Philadelphia: Fortress, 1969); A. Brenner, "Naomi and Ruth," *VT* 33 (1983): 385-397; Katheryn Pfisterer Darr, "'More Than Seven Sons': Critical, Rabbinical, and Feminist Perspectives on Ruth," *Far More Precious Than Jewels: Perspectives on Biblical Women* (Louisville: Westminster/John Knox, 1991): 55-84; Moore, "Naomi's Journey," *Reconciliation*, 151-163.

[49]See S. Talmon, "Wisdom in the Book of Esther," *VT* 13 (1963): 419-455; J. A. Loader, "Esther as a Novel with Different Levels

contrast with Mordecai's classically prophetic approach. Esther chooses not to confront Haman directly, but diplomatically manipulates the king by means of a series of dinner parties. Like Abigail and the medium of Endor, Esther uses these meals with a hidden agenda. Only after Haman has been sufficiently lured into the meals does she reveal to the king Haman's sinister plot to kill the Jews. The story of Esther, then, provides an alternative method of conflict resolution to the prophetic method of direct confrontation.

The apocryphal story of Judith takes the elements of this trajectory to baroque extremes.[50] Compared with its predecessors, note the excesses to which this story goes. Judith is a woman who, unlike Esther and the Tekoite woman, never doubts her abilities and is never, ever afraid of the unknown. Judith is more divine than human, more like the Wisdom Woman than the medium of Endor. And unlike the men around Abigail, the men around Judith are not merely obstinate, but are also inept and cowardly. Further, Judith not only cuts off the head of an infidel (like her wise-woman counterpart centuries earlier in Abel), she also combines this bloody deed with a whole series of verbal creations. As Chesnutt[51] has argued, Judith is one of several female characters in the Jewish literary heritage who "assume an active leadership role in political, military, and religious matters and who could be respected for so doing." In dealing with conflict, she delivers an angry diatribe against the fearful elders of Bethuliah, makes a seductive

---

of Meaning," *ZAW* 90 (1978) 417-421; Moore, "Esther's Decision," *Reconciliation*, 87-98.

[50]See M. Delcor, "Le livre de Judith et l'époque grecque," *Klio* 49 (1967): 151-179; T. Craven, *Artistry and Faith in the Book of Judith* (SBLDS 70; Chico: Scholars Press, 1983); A. LaCocque, "Judith," *The Feminine Unconventional*, 31-48.

[51]Randall D. Chesnutt, "Jewish Women in the Greco-Roman Era," *Essays on Women in Earliest Christianity* (ed. C. D. Osburn; Joplin, MO: College Press, 1993): 1.112-114.

speech to entrap her enemy Holofernes, and gives a long wordy psalm to celebrate his untimely death, punctuated by the revealing line, "The Lord Almighty has foiled (our enemies) by the hand of a woman."[52]

It may be suggested, then, that "wise women" sometimes work overtly, sometimes covertly, sometimes publicly, sometimes privately, but, unlike prophetesses, their service does not focus on public proclamation or the interpretation of mysteries. Later authors, determined to keep this role-set before Israel, deliberately and imaginatively elaborate the counseling pattern used by such women as Naomi, Esther, and Judith into a full-blown trajectory within the larger corpus of the wisdom traditions of the OT.

Eventually this trajectory transcends the bounds of reality altogether. The portrayals of the Wisdom Woman in Prov 1-9 and the "worthy woman" in Prov 31,[53] probably composed under some degree of Hellenistic influence,[54] explode the conventional categories of Hebrew history and literary narrative about women. Much like the "virtuous woman" of Victorian America,[55] these women reflect a cultural attempt to lift up and institutionalize an idealized portrayal, a portrayal designed to distill all previous portrayals into one consummate portrait of Israelite femininity.

---

[52]H. L. Jansen, "La composition du chant de Judith," *AcOr* 15 (1936): 63-71.

[53]See D. Garrett, *Proverbs, Ecclesiastes, Song of Songs* (NAC 14; Nashville: Broadman, 1993): 63-116, 245-52. See on "Lady Wisdom," Roland D. Murphy, *The Tree of Life* (New York: Doubleday, 1990): 133-149.

[54]Martin Hengel, *Judaism and Hellenism* (Philadelphia: Fortress, 1974): 153-157, dates Prov 1-9 to the middle of the third century BC, yet late Hellenistic influence is sharply disputed by W. F. Albright, "Canaanite-Phoenician Sources in Hebrew Wisdom," *VTSup* 3 (1955) 9.

[55]See Barbara Welter, "The Cult of True Womanhood, 1820-1860," *Dimity Convictions: The American Woman in the Nineteenth Century* (Athens, OH: Ohio Univ. Press, 1976) 21-41.

Consequently the women at the beginning and end of *Proverbs* are to be understood as idealized characters, a compilation of a variety of characteristics from a variety of ancient biblical women. They exist, not as real Israelite women, but as composite characters in the theological world of the scribes responsible for preserving that trajectory which brought them to birth in the first place.[56] In these literary and symbolic depictions, such Wisdom Women continue the thrust of creating order from chaos in everyday situations.

4. *The Hellenistic Trajectory*

Whether or not the development of female roles in *Proverbs* may be partially influenced by the Hellenization of Judaism generally, the Greek world also has its own gender trajectory. Rooted, again, in the roles enacted by Anatolian wise women and other female magico-religious specialists, this trajectory includes a fascinating variety of heroines, queens, witches, sybils, and goddesses from all over the Greek-speaking world.[57] The question is whether, or how much, these female figures may have influenced portrayals of women in the NT. One searches in vain for most of these roles among women in the NT.

The NT portrays Christian women as serving in various capacities. It is important to remember that "wise women" in the Jewish heritage demonstrate a wide variety of conduct too, yet with a common denominator of working to create order from chaos. Just as Abigail, Esther, and the woman of Tekoa differed slightly in their work, so Prisca[58] enacts a role different from that of Dorcas, Nympha, and Lydia.

---

[56]See Tikva Frymer-Kensky, "Wisdom, the Lover of Man," *In the Wake of the Goddesses: Women, Culture, and the Biblical Transformation of Pagan Myth* (New York: Free Press, 1992): 179-183.

[57]See Barbara Smith, "Greece," *The Feminist Companion to Mythology* (ed. C. Larrington; London: Pandora, 1992): 65-101.

[58]See David E. Aune, *Prophecy in Early Christianity and the Ancient Mediterranean World* (Grand Rapids: Eerdmans, 1983); Ben

This then raises the question, "Why are some female roles emphasized in the NT and not others?" The answer I am suggesting is that the early church was more interested in theology (particularly Hebrew theology) than sociology. Early Christian men and women instinctively turned to their Hebraic roots to formulate their attitudes toward gender and gender roles. The Hebraic wisdom trajectory plays a crucial role in the formulation because it provides such a strong, visible link to their spiritual past. Wisdom is a primary, if not *the* primary source informing and guiding the roles enacted by Christian women in the NT. Certainly there are prophetesses in the NT, but these women are rarely named. Instead, women like Lydia, Phoebe, and Prisca receive more prominence. Why? Highlighting the work of *these* women vs. *those* women does not appear to be an accident. In fact, it serves at least two important purposes.

First, it creates a ready-made hedge around the church with regard to the problem of goddess religion. Why is goddess religion almost never addressed in the NT? Certainly not because it was never practiced in the first century. Goddess religion was very much alive and flourishing in the Hellenistic world of the first century. The answer must be that the worship of Sophia, Isis, Venus, or the Great Mother fails to gain ground among early Christian women to some extent because their Hebraic role models were utterly incompatible with it.[59]

Second, although no evidence exists concerning the continuance of the "wise woman" category into the NT (in terms of mediation, parable + praxis), there is historical precedent in the OT historical/literary heritage for women serving in a number of indirect ways and being respected for so doing. This might explain, to some extent, why Sophia and other goddesses never hold much attraction for Christian

---

Witherington, III, *Women in the Earliest Churches* (Cambridge: Cambridge Univ. Press, 1988).

[59]See L. R. Farnell, *The Cults of the Greek States* (Oxford: Univ. Press, 1907): 3.106-116.

women in the earliest churches.[60] While some serve as prophetesses, other Christian women like Lydia use their homes and their tables to lead others to Christ. Christian women like Phoebe use their civic and political connections to help the church *change* its environment, not assimilate to it.[61] Christian women like Prisca use their minds and their hearts to teach others the gospel of *Christ*, not the mysteries of Sophia. Christian women in the NT are thus freed to rise above the chaotic confusion all around them about gender and go on to spiritual maturity within a well-defined Christian monotheistic faith.

Conclusion

Early Christian men do not discourage this development. Instead, they welcome and encourage these women in order that they might together fulfill a common vocation (see Rom 16). In the NT, both genders seem to realize what their roles are. Both seem to understand that ministry includes, but is much more than, public assemblies, conferences, conventions, and other corporate ritual. Counseling and teaching behind the scenes are equally important, and just as demanding.

Certainly in the OT and in the NT not all service was relegated to priests and prophets, and contemporary discussion is remiss unless it includes the wider range of categories. Wise women served a very important function in ancient Israel, and so did a number of memorable NT women, following closely in their footsteps.

---

[60]See Gregory E. Sterling, "Women in the Hellenistic and Roman Worlds (323 BCE–138 CE)," *Essays on Women in Earliest Christianity*, 1.89.

[61]See James Walters, "'Phoebe' and 'Junia(s)'—Rom 16:1-2, 7," *Essays on Women in Earliest Christianity*, 1.167-190.

Chapter Five

HULDAH AND OTHER BIBLICAL PROPHETESSES

John T. Willis

Huldah and other prophetesses are commended in the Bible for their prophetic work. In view of the divinely approved role of women as God's servants, it is important that these commendations be understood accurately.

1. *The Function of Prophets and Prophetesses*

A. *The Biblical Definition of a Prophet.* A prophet is one who speaks for God to a specific audience. At least five biblical texts contain this definition.

1. According to Exod 7:1, the Lord said to Moses, "See I make you *as God* to Pharaoh; and Aaron your brother shall be *your prophet.*" According to the parallel passage in Exod 4:16, the Lord said to Moses, "He [Aaron] shall *speak for you to the people,* and he shall be *a mouth for you,* and you shall be to him as God." As Moses' "prophet," Aaron "speaks for him" or "is a mouth for him" to a designated audience. In this relationship, Moses is to Aaron what God is to a prophet.[1]

2. According to Amos 7:16, Amaziah the priest of Bethel forbade Amos to proclaim God's message any longer in North Israel, saying, "Do not *prophesy* against Israel, and do not *preach* against the house of Isaac." The synonymous parallelism shows that "to prophesy" is "to preach."

---

[1] See G. V. Smith, "Prophet; Prophecy," *ISBE*, 3.988.

3. Jer 1:5 relates these words of the Lord to Jeremiah, "I appointed you *a prophet to the nations*." Jeremiah tried to evade the Lord's call by saying, "I do not know how *to speak*" (v. 6). But the Lord insisted, saying, "You shall go *to all* to whom I *send* you, and you shall *speak* whatever I command you" (v.7). This passage indicates that a prophet is someone God sends to a specific audience (here, the nations) to speak to that audience whatever God commands.

4. In response to Jeremiah's second recorded complaint, in which he accuses the Lord of forsaking him when his persecutors curse and insult him (Jer 15:10-18), the Lord calls him to repent, and promises that if he will utter what is precious, he will "serve as my [God's] *mouth*" (v. 19). This text shows that a prophet is a "mouth(piece)" for God to a designated audience.

5. In the course of trying to resolve the conflict between the tongue-speakers and the prophets in the church at Corinth in the first century AD, Paul states matter-of-factly that "those who *prophesy speak to* other people for their upbuilding and encouragement and consolation" (1 Cor 14:3). Here again, a "prophet" is defined as one who "speaks to" others in God's behalf.

B. *Biblical Metaphors Indicating a Prophet's Function.* Biblical speakers and writers used metaphors from at least four spheres of life very familiar in their day to portray the function of a "prophet."

1. *From Activities in the Royal Court.* Frequently God is depicted as a "king" who "sits on his throne" "reigning" over his creation, mankind, and his own chosen people (Exod 15:18; 1 Sam 8:7; 2 Kgs 19:15; Pss 47:2, 7-8; 99:1; 1 Tim 6:15; Rev 7:10; etc.). Biblical writers use four terms in reference to a prophet in the context of this metaphor.

a) *A Prophet is a Member of God's Council.* In ancient times, a king gathered a select council of trusted individuals before him at the beginning of each day. He told them their respective responsibilities and sent out each one to accomplish his/her task for that day. This often consisted of taking the king's message to an individual or a group. Thus, the biblical writers spoke of a prophet as a member of God's council whom God sent out to carry his message to a designated audience. God condemns false prophets in the following language:

> I did not *send* the prophets,
>   yet they *ran*;
> I did not speak to them,
>   yet they prophesied.
> But if they had *stood in my council,*
>   they would have *proclaimed my words*
>   *to my people* (Jer 23: 21-22; see v.18).

Again, a prophet is defined as one who *proclaims* God's words to a specified audience.

   b) *A Prophet is a Man of God.* When a king sent a man to do a specific task, that person ceased to be "his own man"; he was "the king's man." For example, Ittai the Gittite refused to leave king David when news came that Absalom was on his way to Jerusalem to usurp the throne from his own father; Ittai had committed himself to David, and he resolved to be faithful to that commitment (2 Sam 15:13-23). Accordingly, a faithful prophet of God did not belong to himself; he belonged to his King, Yahweh; he was a " man of God" (1 Sam 2:27; 9:6-8, 10; 2 Kgs 5:8).

   c) *A Prophet is a Servant of God.* In one sense of the term, every person in a nation was the "servant" of the king of that nation. Still, ancient Near Eastern kings had a special group of individuals as confidants who were always ready to serve. Thus, Saul, was surrounded at Gibeah by "his servants" under the charge of Doeg the Edomite when he learned of the whereabouts of David and his companions (1 Sam 22:6-10). Thus, the "confidants/ confidantes" of Yahweh are his prophets/prophetesses. Accordingly, "my/ his servants the prophets" is a common, stereotyped phrase in Scripture (see Amos 3:7; Jer 7:25; 26:5).

d) *A Prophet is a Messenger of God.* A king in the ancient Near East usually sent out members of his council with a message from that king to a specified audience. Naturally, these individuals are called "the king's messengers" (see 1 Kgs 20:2, 5; 2 Kgs 19:9, 14), which appears interchangeably with "the king's servants" (1 Kgs 20:6). Similarly, the Bible refers to a "prophet" (Hag 1:1) as "the messenger of the Lord" (Hag 1:13), to "prophets" as "the messengers of God" (2 Chron 36:15-16), and to their "message" as "the Lord's message" (Hag 1:13).

It was common in the ancient Near East for a messenger of a king to introduce the king's message with a stereotyped formula, as "Thus says Ben-hadad" (1 Kgs 20:2); "Thus says the great king, the king of Assyria" (2 Kgs 18:19); or "Thus says King Cyrus of Persia" (Ezra 1:2). Naturally, then, a prophet of God, the great king of the universe, routinely introduced the message God had given him with the words, "Thus says the Lord" (1 Kgs 21:19; Isa 10:24).

2. *From the Means of Protecting A Walled City.* In the ancient Near East, peoples of various cultures built towns and cities on high hills and mountains, and erected thick walls around them for protection. They placed individuals at strategic places on these walls in "shifts" to watch all activities taking place outside the city so that the city might not be penetrated by surprise. When one of these individuals saw a sign of danger, he would cry out to the king or a high governmental official nearby (2 Sam 18:24-27; Isa 21:6), or blow a trumpet in a certain manner (Amos 3:6; Jer 6:17) to warn the people in the city. This individual was called a "sentinel" or a "watchman." Metaphorically, a prophet sees beyond the earthly sphere to God's activities encroaching on the present situation, and his/her responsi-bility is to announce what he/she sees. Therefore, the Bible refers to a prophet as a "watchman" or "sentinel" (Ezek 3:16-21; 33:1-9). His task is to "announce" what he "sees" (what God reveals to him) to a specified audience (see Isa 21:6). Thus, he is a proclaimer of God's message.

3. *From Divination.* In his condemnation of the false

prophets of Judah, Micah announced,

> The *seers* shall be disgraced,
> and the *diviners* put to shame (Mic 3:7).

The synonymous parallelism here equates "seers" and "diviners." However, in vv. 5-6, Micah calls these same individuals "prophets." Furthermore, 1 Sam 9:9 explains: "the one who is now called a *prophet* was formerly called a *seer*." Micah 3:7 indicates that one of the terms used for "diviners" was "seers." A diviner was one who had special access to the unseen realm of deities. Since a prophet received divine messages to declare to designated audiences, it was natural for biblical writers to call a prophet a "seer." For example, when the Lord "showed Amos" (literally, caused Amos to see) the visions of the locusts, the drought, and the plumb line, and he proclaimed these visions at Bethel (Amos 7:1-9), Amaziah forbade him to "prophesy" any more there, addressing him as "seer" (v. 12). Again, the responsibility of a prophet was to proclaim what God showed him to a designated audience.

4. *From the Process of Refining Metals.* In the ancient Near East, skilled workers refined metals by putting them in a furnace, and increasing the heat by blowing air into the furnace with a bellows, until the alloys melted off and the pure metal (silver, gold, etc.) remained. The Lord told Jeremiah that he had made him a "tester and a refiner" among the people. Metaphorically, his message was like increasing the heat in the furnace. The desired result was to remove sin from the hearts of the hearers and thus create a pure heart (Jer 6:27-30). Isaiah uses the same metaphor in describing the effect of God's word on the hearts of the hearers (Isa 1:22, 25). Again, the task of the prophet is to proclaim God's message to a specified audience.[2]

---

[2]See H. H. Rowley, "The Nature of Old Testament Prophecy in the Light of Recent Study," *HTR* 38 (1945): 1-38; Idem, *The Servant of the Lord and other Essays on the Old Testament* (2nd ed., rev.; Oxford: Blackwell, 1965): 97-134. R. B. Y. Scott, *The Relevance of the Prophets* (rev. ed.; New York: Macmillan, 1968): 1-17, concludes:

C. *Biblical Portrayals of Prophets' Activities.* A study of the activities of OT prophets in the fifteen prophetic books and elsewhere shows that the basic task of a prophet was to proclaim God's message to a designated audience. In doing this, sometimes he/she spoke of *the past* (Amos 4:6-11; Hos 11: 1-4); sometimes of *the present* (Isa 1:2-17; Jer 5:20-31); and sometimes of *the future* (Amos 3:14-15; Hos 9:2-6). A prophet, then, sometimes *predicted the future*; but this was not his/her basic work. "It is a common misconception of OT prophecy that it means prediction."[3] Furthermore, when he/she predicted the future, that prediction was inseparably related to the needs and circumstances of the audience he/she was presently addressing. Sometimes a prophet had an ecstatic experience (1 Sam 10:9-13; 19:20-24), but this is not what made that person a prophet. "Divine inspiration was what made a person a prophet. . . . The prophet is the one who can speak in the name of God."[4]

2. *Huldah the Prophetess*

2 Kgs 22:1-23:27 and 2 Chron 34:1-35:19 report Josiah's reform of all the pagan religious practices which his grandfather Manasseh (2 Kgs 21:1-18) and his father Amon (2 Kgs 21:19-26) had promoted in Judah. After continuing in the sinful ways of his ancestors for eight years, Josiah began to seek Yahweh, and in the twelfth year of his reign he began to remove some of the sinful practices they had fostered (2 Chron 34:3). In the eighteenth year of his reign, he ordered his people to repair the temple, which Manasseh and Amon had allowed to degenerate badly (2 Kgs 22:3-7).

"The prophets of Israel . . . were spokesmen of a living Word from God" (13). See further Abraham J. Heschel, *The Prophets: An Introduction* (New York: Harper and Row, 1969 [first published in 1962]): 20-22; and Joseph Blenkinsopp, *A History of Prophecy in Israel* (Philadelphia: Westminster, 1983): 35-38.

[3]John L McKenzie, S. J. , "Prophet, Prophecy," *Dictionary of the Bible* (New York: The Bruce Publishing Company, 1965): 698.

[4]John J. Schmitt, "Prophecy (Preexilic Hebrew)," *ABD* 5 (1992): 482.

In the course of this repair work, the priest Hilkiah found a copy of "the book of the law" in the temple, and sent it by Shaphan the secretary to read to Josiah. Josiah was horrified by its message, which announced curses on those who engaged in the very religious practices taking place in Jerusalem at the time; and he sent five of his men to "inquire of the Lord" for him "concerning the words of the book that has been found" (vv. 8-13). These men *naturally and routinely* went to the "prophetess Huldah." She instructed them to tell Josiah that Yahweh would bring disaster on Jerusalem because of the idolatrous practices taking place there; however, Josiah would not experience this disaster because he repented and humbled himself when Shaphan read the book to him and he heard Huldah's message (2 Kgs 22:14-20; 2 Chron 34:22-28).[5]

Huldah fits the biblical definition and description of a prophet. 1) The Bible calls her a "prophetess" (2 Kgs 22:14; 2 Chron 34:22). 2) She introduces her words with a messenger formula: "Thus says the Lord, the God of Israel" (2 Kgs 22:15, 18; 2 Chron 34:22, 26); "Thus says the Lord" (2 Kgs 22:16; 2 Chron 34:22, 26); and "says the Lord" (2 Kgs 22:19; 2 Chron 34:27). 3) Josiah sends his men to her to "inquire of the Lord" (2 Kgs 22:13, 18; 2 Chron 34:21, 26).[6] 1 Sam 28:6 indicates it was a common practice for kings to "inquire of the Lord" by sending to a prophet. 4) Huldah speaks God's message with the same authority and assurance as her male counterparts (2 Kgs 22:16-20; 2 Chron 34:24-28). 5) Her message that Yahweh is going

---

[5]On the structure of Huldah's oracle, see, Simon J. de Vries, "The Forms of Prophetic Address in Chronicles," *HAR* 10 (1986): 22-24.

[6]Appealing to parallels in Esarhaddon's "Black Stone" and Nabonidus' "Cylinder Inscription," Lowell K. Handy, "The Role of Huldah in Josiah's Cult Reform," *ZAW* 106 (1994): 40-53, describes Huldah as a "double-check" for Josiah, who already knew that the book that Hilkiah had found contained the genuine word of God. However, it may be that Josiah was fearful when he realized it *might* be the genuine word of God, and he sent his men to inquire of the Lord to see if this was indeed the case.

to punish Judah for abandoning him to worship other gods (2 Kgs 22:15-16; 2 Chron 34:24-25) is a common theme of OT prophets (see e.g., Hos 2:13; Isa 2:8, 18, 20-21; Ezek 8:1-18). 6) Her assurance that Yahweh will bless the penitent and humble of heart (2 Kgs 22:19; 2 Chron 34:27) agrees with prophetic assurances elsewhere in Scripture (cf. e.g., Isa 57:15; Mic 6:8; Jer 18:7-8). 7) 1-2 Kings and 1-2 Chronicles present Huldah as a true prophetess of Yahweh, whose word was reliable and authoritative for the king and all the people of Judah (2 Kgs 22:13, 19; 2 Chron 34:21, 27).

The biblical text indicates that Huldah had already been established as a well-known spokeswoman of Yahweh some time before Josiah sent to inquire of Yahweh, because the men whom Josiah sent apparently thought of her immediately as the proper "prophet" to approach.[7] Phipps[8] notes:

> The biblical text does not suggest that seeking divine revelation from a woman was in any way unusual. Modern readers might be amazed that a male high priest and a male secretary of state would be part of a group seeking expert knowledge from a woman, but the ancient historian does not express surprise at the situation.

Since the authors of Kings and Chronicles view her as a true prophet of Yahweh, it is very likely that she was one of the prophets who condemned Manasseh for desecrating the temple and bringing all kinds of pagan practices into Judah and Jerusalem (2 Kgs 21:10-15; 2 Chron 33:18). Scholars have identified Huldah as a cult prophet (a prophet who functioned in an official capacity in the Jerusalem temple)[9] or

---

[7]See J. J. Reeve and R. K. Harrison, "Huldah," *ISBE*, 2.774.

[8]William E. Phipps, "A Woman Was the First to Declare Scripture Holy," *BibRev* 6:2 (1990): 14-15, 44. See further Arlene Swidler, "In Search of Huldah," *TBT* 98 (1978): 1783.

[9]Ivan Engnell, "Huldah," *Svenskt Bibliskt Uppslagsverk* (Stockholm: Nordiska Uppslagsböcker, 1962): 1.col. 988; John Priest,

a court prophet (a prophet who was always available to the king and high officials for consultation).[10] Either or both of these is possible, but neither should be taken to mean that Huldah spoke what the worshipers who frequented the temple or the king and royal court wanted to hear. On the contrary, the biblical text relates that she proclaimed a message announcing the fall of Jerusalem and of the temple because of the sins of God's people who lived and worshiped there.[11]

"Huldah's Oracle," *VT* 30 (1980): 366-68.

[10]Pauline A. Viviano, "Huldah," *ABD*, 3.321.

[11]Scholars regard 2 Kgs 22-23 as pivotal chapters for some major critical issues in OT study. The literature on these chapters is immense, and cannot be listed here. Huldah's promise to Josiah that he would be gathered to his grave "in peace" (2 Kgs 22:20) is a vital text in scholarly research, because in fact Josiah was killed in battle at Megiddo by the Egyptians under Pharaoh Neco (2 Kgs 23:29-30; 2 Chron 35:20-25). This has led several scholars to conclude that the Books of Kings (or the Deuteronomistic History, i.e. Deuteronomy-2 Kings) were produced in two editions: 1) the first edition would have been written before Josiah was killed in battle (609 BC) by someone who knew of Huldah's promise but wrote before Josiah died; 2) the second edition would have been written by someone living after the Babylonians destroyed Jerusalem and the temple and carried the Jews into exile (587 BC), and after Evil-merodach, king of Babylon, set Jehoiachin, king of Judah, free from prison in the thirty-seventh year of his exile (561 BC), and even after Jehoiachin's death, since 2 Kings 25 relates these events as already having occurred. However, this does not explain why both Huldah's promise and Josiah's death in battle are in the present text of 2 Kings, apparently without any embarrassment to the writer who preserved the accounts of both. Christopher T. Begg's, *1 and 2 Kings* (NJBC; Englewood Cliffs: Prentiss Hall, 1990): 184, explanation of the phrase "in peace" is compelling: "The expression need not mean that Josiah is to die a natural death, as in fact he does not (see 23:29). Even though he was killed in combat, Josiah can still be said to have died peacefully, since he was spared witnessing the annihilation of his nation." On this complex issue, see F. Horst, "Die Kultusreform des Königs Josias," *ZDMG* 77 (1923): 220-38; Alfred Jepsen, "Die Reform des Josias," *Festschrift für A. Baumgärtel* (Berlin: A Töpelmann, 1959): 97-108; M. Sekine, "Beobachtungen zu der josianischen Reform," *VT* 22 (1972): 361-68; M. Rose, "Bemerkungen zum historischen Fundament des Josia-Bildes in II Reg. 22 ff.," *ZAW*

3. Other Biblical Prophetesses

Huldah is but one of many prophetesses mentioned in Scripture.[12]

A. *Miriam.* Exod 15:19-21 states that after Pharaoh's horses, chariots, and drivers went into the sea, and the Lord brought back the waters of the sea upon them, while the Israelites walked through the sea on dry land, "the prophetess" Miriam took a tambourine and summoned her audience to praise the Lord in song because he had triumphed gloriously over the Egyptians. The sequence of thought is the same as in Exod 14:22-15:18: The Egyptian horses, chariots, and drivers pursued the Israelites into the sea (14: 22-25), the waters of the sea returned and covered them so that none escaped (14:26-28), the Israelites walked on dry ground through the sea (14: 29-31), and Moses and the Israelites praised the Lord in song because he had triumphed gloriously over the Egyptians (15:1-18). Exod 15:1 and 15:21 are identical except that the singer in 15:1 says, " I will sing to the Lord," whereas the singer in 15:21 summons her hearers, " Sing to the Lord."

Several think these are two different songs, probably having come into the present text from two originally

---

89 (1977): 50-63; A. D. H. Mayes, "King and Covenant: A Study of 2 Kings 22-23," *Hermathena* 125 (1978): 34-47; Christopher Levin, "Joschija im deuteronomistischen Geschichtswerk," *ZAW* 96 (1984): 312-43; N. Lohfink, "The Cult Reform of Josiah of Judah: 2 Kings 22-23 as a Source for the History of Israelite Religion," *Ancient Israelite Religion. Essays in Honor of Frank Moore Cross* (ed. P. D. Miller, Jr., P. D. Hanson and S. D. McBride; Philadelphia: Fortress, 1987): 459-75; Pierfelice Tagliacarne, "Keiner war wie er," *Untersuchung zur Struktur von 2 Konige 22-23* (ATAT 31; St. Ottilien: EOS, 1989)· xi. + 473; C. Conroy, "Reflections on the Exegetical Task: Apropos of Recent Studies on 2 Kings 22-23," *Pentateuchal and Deuteronomistic Studies. Papers Read at the XIIIth IOSOT Congress, Leuven 1989* (BETL 94: Leuven: Leuven Univ. Press/Peeters, 1990): 255-68.

[12]For a discussion of Huldah and several of the women mentioned below from a positive point of view, see Maria Eugenia Iriarte, "Mujer y ministerio: Antiguo Testamento," *Biblia y Fe* 16 (1990): 29-50.

different sources. However, Janzen[13] has suggested that 15:19 is a narrative device called "analepsis" (the temporary withholding of vital information in favor of its belated introduction later for one effect or another). "Them" in v. 21 is a masculine pronoun in Hebrew, and therefore does not refer to the women (or, at least, the women alone) in v. 20. The imperative "Sing" in v. 21 is also masculine plural. Janzen suggests that Miriam led the people of Israel through the whole hymn, and that Moses and the Israelites (15:1), led by the dancing women (15:20), responded antiphonally to her lead. The process followed this pattern: Miriam called on Moses and the Israelites to sing to the Lord (15:21); then Moses and the Israelites responded, "I will sing to the Lord" (15:1).

Whether this is the correct interpretation or not, Exod 15:19-21 shows that Miriam was a prophetess, and that she called on her fellows to praise God in song to celebrate his victory over the Egyptians. In harmony with this portrait of Miriam, "the prophet Micah (6:4) regards her as a divinely commissioned leader alongside Moses and Aaron during the wilderness journey."[14] The Lord spoke through her just as he spoke through Moses and Aaron (Num 12:2).

B. *Deborah.* The author of Judges refers to Deborah as "judge" (4:4-5), "mother in Israel" (5:7), and "prophetess" (4:4).[15] As prophetess, Deborah declared to Barak that the Lord commanded him to go to Mount Tabor with warriors from the tribes of Naphtali and Zebulun, and promised that the Lord would give Sisera into his hand (4:6-7). Her actions here are parallel to those of other prophets, like Samuel, when he instructed Saul utterly to destroy the Amalekites (1 Sam 15:2-3); Shemaiah, when he told Rehoboam not to fight against Jeroboam I and the Israelites

---

[13]J. Gerald Janzen, "Song of Moses, Song of Miriam: Who is Seconding Whom?" *CBQ* 54 (1992): 211-20 (quote on 214).

[14]Rita J. Burns, "Miriam," *ABD* 4.870.

[15]Similarly, Samuel was a "priest" (1 Sam 2:18; 7:9-10; 9:11-13, 22-24), a "judge" (1 Sam 7:6, 15-17), and a "prophet" (1 Sam 3:20; 9:6-10; 19:20) at the same time.

as he had planned (1 Kgs 12:21-24); and Micaiah, when he warned Ahab that if he fought against Ben-hadad of Syria at Ramoth-gilead he would be killed (1 Kgs 22:15-28). When Barak refused to go without her, Deborah accompanied him to the battleground (vv. 8-10).[16] Deborah's role as a "mother in Israel" corroborates her role as a prophet. Based on the function of a "mother" depicted throughout Scripture, the meaning here is that Deborah protected (see Gen. 21:14-19; Exod 2:2-4), provided security for (see Prov. 31:15, 21, 27-28), counseled (see Gen 27:42-45), and taught (see Prov 31:26; 2 Tim 1:5; 3:14-15) God's people.[17]

Like Miriam "the prophetess" (Exod 15:20), she (along with Barak) composed and sang a hymn praising Yahweh for giving the Israelites the victory over the Canaanites under Jabin and Sisera (Judg 5:1). The direct addresses to Deborah (vv. 7, 12) and to Barak (v. 12) in this hymn, and the references to Deborah and Barak in the third person (v. 15) suggest that Deborah, Barak, and the Israelites sang this song antiphonally, perhaps like the song of Miriam.[18]

As God's prophetess, Deborah proclaimed God's word to Barak, and went with him to battle. When God gave the Israelites the victory, she composed and sang a song praising him for his power and guidance.

C. *The "Prophetess" Mentioned in Isa 8:3.* In relating the third "sign" which he gave Ahaz to discourage him from sending to Tiglath-pileser III of Assyria for help against the Syro-Ephraimite attack under Rezin and Pekah and to trust in Yahweh,[19] Isaiah says:

---

[16]See Danna Nolan Fewell and David M. Gunn, "Controlling Perspectives: Women, Men and the Authority of Violence in Judges 4 & 5," *JAAR* 58 (1990): 389-411.

[17]See J. Cheryl Exum, "'Mother in Israel': A Familiar Figure Reconsidered," *Feminist Interpretation of the Bible* (ed. Letty Russell; Philadelphia: Westminster, 1985): 73-85.

[18]See Clarence J. Vos, *Woman in Old Testament Worship* (Delft: Judels & Brinkman, 1968): 179-80.

[19]The first "sign" was that of Shear-jashub (Isa 7:3-9), and the

> I went to *the prophetess*, and she conceived and bore a son. Then the Lord said to me, "Call his name Maher-shalal-hash-baz" (Isa 8:3).

"The prophetess" here is clearly Isaiah's wife.[20]

> But it is most unlikely that he uses that title for her just because she is his wife. . . . It is possible that Isaiah's wife, as Huldah at the time of Jeremiah (see 2 Kings 22:14), might have held the position of cultic prophetess at the sanctuary in Jerusalem. Since Isaiah placed high value on the temple, in spite of the hesitations which he expressed about the cultic piety, it is certainly not an impossibility.[21]

There can be little doubt that Isaiah's wife was a prophetess in her own right, and that she performed her God-given role of proclaiming God's message to designated audiences as needs and opportunities presented themselves, just as did Deborah, Huldah, and her own husband.

D. *The False Prophetesses Rebuked by Ezekiel.* Ezek 13 relates Ezekiel's oracles against the prophets (vv. 1-16) and prophetesses (vv. 17-23) of Judah. Ezekiel denounces them for essentially the same sins, i.e., they "prophesy out of

---

second was that of Immanuel (Isa 7:10-17) (compare Isa 8:18, which refers to all three "signs" as being "from Yahweh of hosts who dwells on Mount Zion").

[20] See J. J. M. Roberts, "Isaiah and His Children," *Biblical and Related Studies Presented to Samuel Iwry* (ed. A. Kort and S. Morschauser; Winona Lake: Eisenbrauns, 1985): 198.

[21] Hans Wildberger, *Isaiah 1-12: A Commentary* (trans. T. H. Trapp; Minneapolis: Fortress, 1991 [originally published in German in 1980]): 337. See also I. Hylander, "War Jesaja Nabi?" *Le Monde Oriental* 25 (1931): 53-56; C. B. Reynolds, "Isaiah's Wife," *JTS* 36 (1935): 182-85; A. Jepsen, "Die Nebiah in Jes 8:3," *ZAW* 72 (1960): 267-68; John N. Oswalt, *The Book of Isaiah Chapters 1-39* (NICOT, Grand Rapids: Eerdmans, 1986): 222-23; and Phyllis Bird, "The Place of Women in the Israelite Cultus," *Ancient Israelite Religion. Essays in Honor of Frank Moore Cross* (ed. P. D. Miller, Jr., P. D. Hanson, and S. D. McBride; Philadelphia: Fortress, 1987): 404, 415 n. 29.

their own imagination, 'Hear the word of the Lord!'" (vv. 2, 17), and they practice divination (magic, fortune-telling) and lying (vv. 6-9, 18-23). Therefore, God "is against them" (vv. 8-9, 20) and will punish them (vv. 11-15, 20-21); thus, he says, "you shall know that I am the Lord" (vv. 9, 14, 21, 23).

This text assumes that both prophets and prophetesses were at work among God's people in the days of Ezekiel. Some (undoubtedly the majority) of them were false prophets; they pretended to proclaim God's message, when in reality they were proclaiming what the people wanted to hear so that they could benefit therefrom (see vv. 10, 16, 18-23). The similarity in wording and thought between Ezekiel's denunciation of false prophets and prophetesses, and the denunciation of false prophets by Micah (3:5-8) and Jeremiah (23:9-40), suggests that the term "prophets" in the latter passages is comprehensive, including both men and women.

E. *Noadiah*. Nehemiah reports that one scheme which his enemies Tobiah and Sanballat had contrived against him was to hire the prophet Shemaiah to persuade Nehemiah to barricade himself in the Jerusalem temple to prevent his enemies from killing him, but Nehemiah refused (Neh 6:10-14). Then Nehemiah prays that God will punish Tobiah and Sanballat for doing this, as well as "the prophetess Noadiah and the rest of the prophets" who wanted to make him afraid (v. 14).

Noadiah is a false prophetess. But Nehemiah does not indicate any reservation about women prophesying; in fact, he speaks of Noadiah "and the rest of the prophets." Rather, his concern is that Noadiah proclaimed a message God had not authorized her to proclaim, and her purpose in declaring this message was unbecoming of a true prophet of God, viz., to demoralize Nehemiah.

F. *Anna*. Luke relates that when Joseph and Mary brought Jesus to the Jerusalem temple to present him to the Lord (Luke 2:22), an eighty-four year old "prophetess" named

Anna approached. She was a woman who worshiped at the temple constantly, fasting and participating in the prayers of the people attending the daily sacrifice (v. 37; see Luke 1:10). Upon seeing Joseph, Mary, and Jesus, Anna began to "praise God" and to "*speak* about the child (Jesus) *to* all who were looking for the redemption of Jerusalem" (v. 38). The Greek verb translated "speak" here is in the imperfect, which indicates continual action. Thus, the text means that Anna spoke about the child on this occasion and on numerous later occasions, as opportunities presented themselves.[22]

Anna's actions here provide another example that the Bible understands a prophet(ess) as one who speaks God's message to a designated audience. The inspired author, Luke, clearly commends Anna to his readers for doing this.

G. *The Prophetesses at Pentecost.* After the Holy Spirit came in Jerusalem on the first Pentecost after Jesus' death and resurrection, and there was confusion among the multitudes of Jews who had come to the festival, Peter addressed the people. He began by affirming that the events which were taking place on this occasion were spoken beforehand by the prophet Joel (2:28-32):

> In the last days it will be, God declares,
>   that I will pour out my Spirit upon all flesh,
>   and your sons *and your daughters* shall
>   *prophesy* . . .
> Even upon my slaves, both men *and women*
>   in those days I will pour out my Spirit;
>   and *they* shall *prophesy* (Acts 2:17-18).

One must assume that the Holy Spirit fell on both "men and women" on this occasion and that both men and women "prophesied," i.e., proclaimed God's message to a specified audience.[23]

---

[22]See Joseph A. Fitzmyer, *The Gospel according to Luke I-IX* (AB 28; Garden City: Doubleday, 1981): 431.

[23]See Allen Black, "Women in the Gospel of Luke," *Essays on*

H. *Philip's Four Virgin Daughters.* Luke says that "Philip the evangelist" (see Acts 6:5; 8:4-13, 26-40) had four virgin daughters "who had the gift of prophecy" (Acts 21:8-9 NRSV; lit. "virgin prophesying daughters"). They are evidence that the gift of prophecy was a privilege of women in the early church (see 1 Cor 11:5; Rev 2:20) and that the practice of prophecy among women evident in the OT was again manifested (e.g., 2 Kgs 22:14; Neh 6:14). In Acts, these four prophetesses demonstrate the fulfillment of Joel's prophecy that in the latter days the Spirit of God would be poured out on the daughters of Israel (2:14-21; Joel 2:28).[24]

I. *The Prophetesses at Corinth.* In 1 Cor 11:4-5, Paul refers to both men and women praying (i.e., leading public prayer) and prophesying (i.e., proclaiming God's word to a designated audience) in the assemblies of the church at Corinth (see also v. 13). He expresses no qualms about the divine acceptability of both women and men leading public prayer and proclaiming God's word in the public assembly, but he is concerned that some of the men are doing this with their heads covered, and that some of the women were doing it with their heads uncovered (vv. 4-7, 10, 13-15). Even though it may be impossible for modern readers to appreciate fully why this concerned Paul, the context shows that in the cultural situation at Corinth in the first century, if a man covered his head while praying or prophesying, he dishonored his "head," Christ (vv. 3, 7); whereas if a woman did not cover her head with a veil while praying or prophesying, she dishonored her "head," i.e., her husband (vv. 3, 5).[25]

It is instructive that Paul teaches here that a woman can lead prayer or prophesy (proclaim God's message) in the public assembly of the church *and at the same time* honor

---

Women in Earliest Christianity (ed. C. D. Osburn; Joplin, MO: College Press, 1993): 1.456-68.

[24]JoAnn Ford Watson, "Philip (Person)," *ABD* 5.311-12.

[25]See Hans Conzelmann, *1 Corinthians* (Hermeneia; trans. J. W. Leitch; Philadelphia: Fortress, 1975 [originally published in German in 1969]): 181-91.

and be in subjection to her husband. Orr and Walther[26] sum up Paul's teaching here pointedly and succinctly:

> There is no question that women were engaging in prayer and prophecy in public worship in Corinth... The specific problem that elicits the theological analysis of the relationship between men and women has to do with how women should be attired and particularly how they should wear their hair when taking part in worship leadership. Paul is trying to ensure that the appearance of women in the church concurs with acceptable standards of decency and order.... It is probable that Paul has in mind married women throughout.... The heart of his argument seems to be that just as the man stands before God uncovered because of his spiritual subordination to Christ, so the woman should stand veiled because of her spiritual subordination to her husband. Probably her veiling is an indication of her married state, which reflects her relationship to her husband; and this ought not to be put aside for any reason... because it would be a reflection upon her husband.... A woman who participates in Corinthian worship leadership *ought* to exercise her freedom responsibly.... The wife ought to lead in public worship in such a way (with such traditional decorum) that she will not bring disgrace or dishonor to her husband. Presumably the principle would apply to unmarried women, *mutatis mutandis*.

---

[26]William F. Orr and James Arthur Walter, *I Corinthians* (AB 32; Garden City: Doubleday, 1976); 263-64. See the summary of views in Mark Black, "1 Cor 11:2-16—A Re-investigation," *Essays on Women in Earliest Christianity*, 1.191-218.

4. *Summary*

OT and NT passages which refer to prophetesses agree in a remarkable way. They demonstrate and/or assume that a prophet is an individual who proclaims God's message to a designated audience, and that God used both men and women to perform this function—in Israel and in the church. One should take these texts into consideration, for instance, when interpreting 1 Cor 14:34-35 and 1 Tim 2:8-15, which instruct women to be silent in the church. Concord between the OT and the NT exists when one realizes that in 1 Cor 14:34-35 and 1 Tim 2:8-15 Paul's instructions are not universal for all churches in all ages, but pertain to specific situations that had arisen among the people to whom Paul was writing. Osburn[27] has argued cogently that this is the case in 1 Cor 14: 34-35:

> Far from being intolerant, Paul neither teaches nor suggests in this text anything regarding patriarchalism or female subjection. The real issue is not the *extent* to which a woman may participate in the work and worship of the church, but the *manner*. Paul's corrective does not ban women from speaking in public, but stops the disruptive verbal misconduct of certain wives who are giving free rein to "irresistible impulses" to "pipe up" at will with questions in the assembly. . . .

Similarly, Geer[28] contends correctly that Paul's concern in 1 Tim 2:8-15 is not that women might have authority over men in the church but that certain assertive women in the church who had been influenced by false teachers would teach error. For this reason, he charges them to "be silent."

---

[27]Carroll D. Osburn, "The Interpretation of 1 Cor 14:34-35," *Essays on Women in Earliest Christianity* (ed. C. D. Osburn; Joplin: College Press, 1993): 1.242. For his arguments supporting this, see 219-42.

[28]Thomas C. Geer Jr., "Admonitions to Women in 1 Tim 2:8-15," *Essays on Women in Earliest Christianity* (ed. C. D. Osburn, Joplin: College Press, 1993): 1.281-302.

The contemporary church should take into consideration the examples of Huldah and other biblical prophetesses whose work is analogous to that of prophetesses in the churches of the NT era. Specifically, they spoke God's word to a specific audience. In this connection, they 1) were called "prophets," 2) claimed to speak from God, 3) were recognized among the believers as "prophets," 4) spoke with authority and assurance, and 5) were reliable.

Although the role and function of prophecy in our contemporary churches may differ somewhat from that in the churches of the NT era, there can be no doubt that prophetesses were an important and integral part of the life of the early church.

Chapter Six

MATE, MOTHER, AND METAPHOR: GOMER AND ISRAEL IN HOSEA 1-3

Timothy M. Willis

To borrow an opening line from Volume 1 of these essays, "Hosea 1-3 illustrates for modern Christians as well as anything else in the OT the 'strange world of the Bible'."[1] It refers to practices and ideas in ancient Israel with which modern Christians are no longer familiar or comfortable. This latter fact raises some basic questions about how a modern person is to go about not only interpreting Scripture, but also appropriating biblical teachings.

The opening chapters of Hosea speak of God in a marriage relationship with Israel. In using this metaphor, I see Hosea addressing the modern reader in two respects. First, Hosea reveals some important aspects of the character of God. He speaks both of God's wrath and punishment and of God's love and forgiveness. A more extensive investigation of the complementarity of these divine characteristics would be worthwhile; but, since the main concern of these studies is biblical teachings on women and the relationship between women and men, I will focus most of this investigation on the second aspect of Hosea's teachings, namely that Hosea touches on the institution of marriage by drawing parallels between his own (real) marriage and the (metaphorical) marriage between God and Israel. If Hosea had spoken solely of the metaphor, one might argue that he does not intend to say anything directly about human marriage. But because Hosea's own marriage

---

[1]Thomas C. Geer, Jr., "Admonitions to Women in 1 Tim 2:8-15," *Essays on Women in Earliest Christianity* (ed. C. D. Osburn; Joplin, MO: College Press, 1993): 1.281.

is used for comparisons, and because that marriage is apparently influenced by the "marriage" between God and Israel, it would seem appropriate to consider what the metaphor reveals about God's teachings regarding human marriage generally.

Certainly, the modern reader must be careful about how Hosea's teachings on human marriage are derived from the text. Hosea's use of the marriage metaphor is tailored to his own time and place. There are certain aspects of the metaphor which are emphasized because of the corrupt religious conditions in Israel of the eighth century BC. The metaphor assumes an agrarian, patriarchal mode of marriage. It assumes certain conventions (vows, economic and personal responsibilities, punishments for breach of marriage) which Israel shared with its neighbors, indicating that those are neither exclusively Israelite nor exclusively "biblical." Moreover, the modern reader must keep in mind that the marriage between God and Israel is metaphorical. It is different *a priori* from a human marriage because one partner (the husband) is perfect and pure. God alone exemplifies the ideal in a marriage, and only the ideal. He cannot absolutely represent a real human husband, because the latter is human; thus the metaphor is not perfect, nor should we expect it to be.[2]

1. *Critical Issues Arising from Hosea 1-3*[3]

As in the study of any biblical writing, especially one as "foreign" to us as Hosea, it is essential that we address certain "critical issues" regarding what the text is saying,

---

[2]On the use of metaphor in Hos 1-3, see Helgard Balz-Cochois, "Gomer oder die Macht der Astarte: Versuch einer feministischen Interpretation von Hos 1-4," *EvT* 42 (1982): 37-65; Renita J. Weems, "Gomer: Victim of Violence or Victim of Metaphor?" *Semeia* 47 (1989): 87-90, 101.

[3]Throughout this paper, I will be using the versification found in modern translations, rather than that of the Hebrew Bible. In the latter, Hos 1 ends with v. 9, making 1:10-11 (English) into 2:1-2 (Hebrew), and 2:1-23 (English) into 2:3-25 (Hebrew).

before asking what it means for a modern Christian. The list of critical issues concerning Hos 1-3 which OT scholars have raised seems virtually endless. These run the gamut from the historicity of Hosea's family life to the history of the book's development, from the translation of Hebrew terms to questions about "popular" and "official" religion in ancient Israel. It is impossible in this forum to deal with the volume and the complexity of these issues; yet, one's conclusions about all of these issues might ultimately affect his/her interpretation of any one of them. Therefore, I will survey surfacially some of the more significant questions that have been raised (particularly those concerning Gomer), indicating the general parameters of the discussions and my own conclusions on each.

A. *Diachronic versus Synchronic Approaches*[4]

The first issue which one must resolve is whether to take a diachronic or a synchronic approach to the text of Hos 1-3. A diachronic approach would involve the use of source and/or redaction criticism, at the least. This approach assumes that Hosea's prophecies were first spoken, then written down (by Hosea or one of his "disciples"), and finally edited (arranged, and perhaps even altered in the process) into their present form.[5] The immediate goal in this sort of approach is to isolate what Hosea himself said at one time from what he said at some other time, as well as isolating all of what Hosea said from what some later (reconstructed) editor added, or how he might have nuanced Hosea's words (this assumes, of course, that such editing actually took place). The long-term goal in this sort of

---

[4]A helpful discussion of this issue is provided by Walter Vogels, "Diachronic and Synchronic Studies of Hosea 1-3," *BZ* 28 (1984): 94-98.

[5]This assumption might seem "unscriptural" and a denial of the text's inspiration to some. There is a good biblical example of this basic process provided by Jeremiah (see Jer 36, and then consider the present form of that book), though there is major debate over the extent to which an editor might alter the prophet's words.

approach is to reconstruct the development of theological thought in Israel, as reflected in the book of Hosea.

There have been many studies of Hosea over the past century which have adopted this kind of approach. The following is a sampling of the types of questions raised by this approach which have generated the most discussion: (a) Do the biographical stance of Hos 1, the autobiographical stance of Hos 3, and the non-biographical stance of the remainder of Hosea indicate different authors/editors? (b) Since Hos 1-3 speak almost exclusively within the framework of the husband-wife metaphor, yet the remaining chapters do not, should we conclude that different authors/ editors are responsible for those differences?[6] (c) Why would a northern prophet speak of southern Judah as the exception in the middle of an oracle of condemnation against northern Israel (Hos 1:7)? (d) Were the statements of hope for northern Israel in these chapters (Hos 1:10-2:1; 2:14-23; 3:5) originally spoken at the same time as the announcements of judgment to which they are now attached? (e) Why does the speaker speak *to* the children in Hos 2:2-3, but *about* the children in Hos 2:4ff.? (f) Within the condemnation section of chapter 2 (2:2-13), does the prediction of the wife's repentance (v. 7) mark the end of one prophecy? If not, why does talk of condemnation continue/resume in vv. 8ff.?

Varying answers to these questions have led to several theories about what Hosea himself said and wrote in contrast to what some later editor(s) wrote. A basic criticism of this type of approach, however, is that one must make use of assumptions about what Hosea would or would not have

---

[6]The few who have argued for multiple authorship on these grounds have usually attributed chapters 1-3 to Hosea and 4-14 to a later prophet/editor. A novel idea, suggested by Yehezkel Kaufmann, *The Religion of Israel* (trans. M. Greenberg; Chicago: Univ. of Chicago, 1966): 368-71, is that Hos 1-3 comes to us from the ninth century BC, and was incorporated by Hosea into his book a century later. A majority of studies have concluded that Hosea is equally responsible for both parts of the book. See F. I. Andersen and D. N. Freedman, *Hosea* (AB; Garden City: Doubleday, 1980): 68, 115.

thought and said, and those assumptions are based on very fragmentary information about Israelite life and thought during Hosea's lifetime. So, most studies of Hosea in the past generation have been willing to attribute much more of the book to Hosea himself than did previous scholars.[7]

The present study uses a synchronic approach. This sort of approach does not necessarily assume that Hosea spoke all of Hos 1-3 at the same time or even that he wrote all that is contained in these chapters (although some, like myself, might conclude that after studying the question). Rather, it assumes only that the contents of these three chapters should be considered together, as constitutive of a unified message from the book of Hosea. (After all, it is by the book—not the man—that all subsequent generations of believers have been taught.) Many who use this approach actually incorporate some (diachronic) redaction critical analysis in their own (synchronic) analysis, but they focus primarily on what is taught in this material in its present form. It is this synchronic consideration of the contents of these chapters which has raised most of the critical issues remaining to be described.

B. *The Meaning of* זְנוּנִים *(Wife/Woman of Promiscuity)*

God's earliest command to Hosea is one of the most enigmatic given in Scripture.

> And the Lord said to Hosea, "Go, take to yourself a wife/woman of promiscuity (זְנוּנִים) and children of promiscuity (זְנוּנִים), because the land is surely promiscuous (זָנֹה תִזְנֶה) from after the Lord" (Hos 1:2; my translation).

---

[7]See Andersen and Freedman, *Hosea*, 52-76. For exceptions to this (and for bibliography on previous redactional analyses), see Lothar Ruppert, "Erwägungen zur Kompositions- und Redaktionsgeschichte von Hosea 1-3," *BZ* 26 (1982): 208-23; and William D. Whitt, "The Divorce of Yahweh and Asherah in Hos 2:4-7, 12ff." *SJOT* 1 (1992): 31-67.

The plural noun זְנוּנִים is listed in the lexicons as one of three nouns derived from the root זנה (to fornicate, be promiscuous), which carries a broader meaning than simply "to commit adultery" (נָאַף). In comparison to that term, it seems to add the notions of pre-marital as well as extra-marital offenses, multiplicity of offenses and, less often, the foreign origin of the offender.[8]

The issue raised here is whether the term זְנוּנִים (wife/woman of promiscuity) also carries a connotation of cultic prostitution, that is, that sexual intercourse was part of the obligatory rituals of certain foreign religions practiced in Israel. The traditional description of cultic prostitution as an institution is that male and female cultic personnel (קְדֵשִׁים and קְדֵשׁוֹת, respectively) at the various local sanctuaries (high places) engaged in sexual intercourse with worshipers, as a symbolic way of bringing the divine blessing of fertility to the worshipers' families and farms.[9] References to sexual activity in the cults of other peoples close to Israel lead to the conclusion that the same could have existed in Israel. The principal example of this from the OT is Tamar, daughter-in-law of Judah. She is called זוֹנָה (prostitute; Gen 38:15) by Judah and קְדֵשָׁה (Gen 38:21-22) by Judah's friend. The

---

[8] See Andersen and Freedman, *Hosea*, 116; and, Phyllis Bird, "'To Play the Harlot': An Inquiry Into An Old Testament Metaphor," *Gender and Difference in Ancient Israel* (ed. P. L. Day; Minneapolis: Augsburg Fortress, 1989): 76.

[9] A more radical theory has been proposed by Hans Walter Wolff *Hosea* (trans. G. Stansell; Hermeneia; Philadelphia: Fortress, 1974): 14-15, who describes Gomer as "a young Israelite woman, ready for marriage, who had demonstrably taken part in the Canaanite bridal rite of initiation that had become customary." The "bridal rite of initiation" to which he refers—and in which he believes all women were participating—is having sexual intercourse with a cultic functionary for the purpose of demonstrating one's fertility prior to marriage. The primary evidence for such a practice comes from a description of Babylonian life by the Greek historian Herodotus, whose objectivity is now seriously questioned (see below). Also, the fact that both male and female functionaries of this category are mentioned in the OT undermines Wolff's basic argument; so, many (see succeeding note) concur that cultic prostitution existed, but not as Wolff describes it.

latter term is used to designate certain cultic individuals forbidden under Mosaic law (Deut 23:17; see 1 Kgs 14:23-24; 15:12; 22:46; 2 Kgs 23:7; Hos 4:14; there is a cognate Babylonian term, *qadistu*, which some scholars believe designates cultic personnel who engaged in cultic sexual activity in Babylon; but see below). Later, Tamar is accused of being a prostitute (זָנְתָה) and becoming pregnant by זְנוּנִים; (Gen 38:24). So, in the minds of many scholars, the interchange between the root זנה and the term קְדֵשָׁה indicates that זְנוּנִים (the term used to describe Gomer) denotes a cultic component to the sexual (mis)behavior, as well as promiscuity.[10]

The main point in regard to Hosea and Gomer in this line of interpretation is that God, in Hos 1-3, is mostly concerned with the foreign religious practices that have been introduced into Israel. Gomer, who is called a "wife of promiscuity" (זְנוּנִים), is thought to serve as a perfect illustration of what is wrong in Israel, because not only is she promiscuous, but she engages in her promiscuity as a part of her participation in the rituals of Canaanite religions, which are the target of God's accusation of religious adultery against Israel.[11]

In recent years, however, the whole notion that cultic prostitution as an institution existed in Israel has been brought into serious question. The questioning goes back at least to the criticisms of Rudolph,[12] who held that Wolff's evidence for the existence of cultic prostitution is shaky.

---

[10]For example, H. H. Rowley, "The Marriage of Hosea," *BJRL* 39 (1956): 225; James Luther Mays, *Hosea, a Commentary* (Philadelphia: Westminster, 1969): 23-26; Henry McKeating, *The Books of Amos, Hosea and Micah* (Cambridge: Cambridge Univ. Press, 1971): 71-73; Andersen and Freedman, *Hosea*, 68-69, 125; F. C. Fensham, "The Marriage Metaphor in Hosea for the Covenant Relationship Between the Lord and His People (Hos. 1:2-9)," *JNWSL* 12 (1984): 71-73; Bird, *Gender and Difference*, 87.

[11]Andersen and Freedman, *Hosea*, 125.

[12]Wilhelm Rudolph, "Präparierte Jungfrauen? (Zu Hosea 1)," *ZAW* 75 (1963): 65-73.

This was declared more forcefully several years later, when Fisher[13] argued that too much had been read into the biblical references to קְדֵשִׁים and קְדֵשׁוֹת (male and female cultic personnel). These could simply denote a particular (foreign) class of priestly personnel; thus, it would be a professional term. Fisher's suggestion has now been solidly reinforced in a study by Westenholz,[14] whose research indicates that the Babylonian term *qadistu* refers to a particular class of priestly functionaries. There is no indication that their work included sexual rites of any sort; rather, they seem to have used spells and incantations in functioning as midwives (see, for example, Isa 47:1ff., esp. v. 9). Any sexual connotation seems to have been "supplied" by prejudiced foreign observers, like Herodotus (see n. 9), but without actual basis in history.

More pertinent to the discussion of Gomer, there appears to be no direct correlation between קְדֵשָׁה and זְנוּנִים. The use of the former term in the Tamar story was probably a "polite" way for Judah's friend to search for the prostitute to whom Judah owed a gift.[15] The two terms are not used in the same context anywhere else in the OT. On the other hand, the roots זנה and נאף (to fornicate and to commit adultery) are used together in such a way as to suggest synonymity (see Hos 2:2, 13; Gen 38:24). The nature of the distinctions between these terms has already been

---

[13]Eugene J. Fisher, "Cultic Prostitution in the Ancient Near East? A Reassessment," *BTB* 6 (1976): 225-36.

[14]Joan Goodnick Westenholz, "Tamar, *qedesa, qadistu,* and Sacred Prostitution in Mesopotamia," *HTR* 82 (1989): 245-65 (esp. 254-55, 260, 265); see also Mary Joan Winn Leith, "Verse and Reverse: The Transformation of the Woman, Israel, in Hosea 1-3," *Gender and Difference in Ancient Israel* (ed. P. L. Day; Minneapolis: Augsburg Fortress, 1989): 98; Karel van der Toorn, "Female Prostitution in Payment of Vows in Ancient Israel," *JBL* 108 (1989): 201-205.

[15]"Hirah [Judah's friend] is not trying to change the nature of the affair from one with a common prostitute to one with a sacred prostitute; rather he is denying the affair and pretending to take the kid to the female cultic figure for a sacrifice, as in Hos 4:14." See Westenholz, *HTR* (1989): 248.

mentioned, with זְנוּנִים probably indicating frequency of sexual activity rather than any cultic significance.¹⁶ This does not preclude the possibility that there might have been instances of sexual activity in certain ritual contexts;¹⁷ but at this point, the connection between Gomer's promiscuity (זְנוּנִים) and any ritual activity becomes mere speculation.

This leads to the rather bland conclusion that Gomer was guilty of common (not cultic) sexual promiscuity. Her infidelities are simply analogous to the religious sins of Israel, which are designated as "adulteries" by God; they are not one in the same. This is supported in a couple of ways through other passages in Hosea. In Hos 4:1-2, Hosea accuses Israel of having no "faithfulness or love," terms also used to describe the relationship between spouses. Hosea then proceeds to delineate this unfaithfulness by mentioning "swearing, lying, killing, stealing, and adultery." No reference to cultic impropriety is given, yet the people are accused of being "unfaithful."¹⁸ Similarly, the fact that Hosea calls the worship of idols "fornication" (Hos 4:17-18) does not necessarily imply that those foreign cults included sexual rituals. More likely, Hosea simply has in mind "being joined" to foreigners and their religious beliefs (see Hos 5:13; 12:1; 14:3).

C. *Hosea's Family and Hos. 1:2*

Two other important questions arise from God's command to Hosea in Hos 1:2. These concern the moral status of Gomer and her children.¹⁹

---

[16]Bird, *Gender and Difference*, 80.

[17]For example, there is much evidence of the practice of *hieros gamos*, which usually involved intercourse between a priestess and a king, to symbolize the union between a deity and the king. See also perhaps Amos 2:7-8.

[18]Hosea does mention adultery and (foreign) sacrifices side by side in Hos 4:14, but apparently as separate and distinct offenses (see discussion below).

[19]For previous surveys of the question, see Sydney Lawrence Brown, *The Book of Hosea* (London: Methuen, 1932). 2-3; Robert

The main struggle with God's command to marry a "woman of promiscuity" is that it would seem to be forcing Hosea to participate in sin (see 1 Cor 6:15-20). Also, it could be said that marrying an already sinful Gomer diminishes her appropriateness as an analogy for Israel, which is described elsewhere (Ezek 16) as originally good and later corrupted. These are not major problems for some, because God occasionally required his prophets to engage in activity that normally would be considered improper (for example, Isaiah walking around naked; Isa 20:1-6).[20] Also, portraying Israel as originally sinful could be a reflection of the idolatrous world in which the patriarchs had lived (see Gen 35:2; Josh 24:15).[21] The major problem with this line of reasoning is that Hosea, like Ezekiel, seems to use the Exodus/Mt. Sinai event as his starting-point for talking about Israel's marriage with God. Hos 2:7, in particular, reflects the idea of an originally good marriage (between God and Israel) gone sour.

Another proposed solution which in the past was more popular is that the command—even Hosea's entire marriage—was purely allegorical.[22] This view is hardly found

---

Gordis, "Hosea's Marriage and Message: A New Approach," *HUCA* 27 (1954): 10-14; Mays, *Hosea*, 23.

[20]For this and other examples, see Gordis, *HUCA* (1954): 14 (n. 9); Mays, *Hosea*, 35ff.; McKeating, *The Books of Amos, Hosea and Micah*, 77-78; Dwight H. Small, "The Prophet Hosea: God's Alternative to Divorce for the Reason of Infidelity," *JPsychTh* 7 (1979): 133-40; Andersen and Freedman, *Hosea*, 164-65; H. D. Beeby, *Grace Abounding: A Commentary on the Book of Hosea* (Grand Rapids: Eerdmans, 1989): 14.

[21]Rowley, *BJRL* (1956): 225; David Allan Hubbard, *With Bands of Love: Lessons from the Book of Hosea* (Grand Rapids: Eerdmans, 1968): 52; McKeating, *The Books of Amos, Hosea and Micah*, 75-77; Patricia A. Forseth, "Hosea, Gomer, and Elective Grace: Reflections of an Armchair Theologian," *RefJ* 35, no. 11 (Nov 1985): 15; Beeby, *Grace Abounding*, 14.

[22]See Gordis, *HUCA* (1954): 10 (n. 4) for a list of proponents. See also Fokkelien van Dijk-Hemmes, "The Imagination of Power. An Intertextual Analysis of Two Biblical Love Songs: The Song of Songs and Hosea 2," *JSOT* 44 (1989): 79.

today, because there is no reason to assume that an allegory in which God calls for a prophet to marry a promiscuous woman would be any less scandalous than for that to happen in real life.[23] Yet another way to explain this command is to say that God's reference to Gomer as a "wife of promiscuity" is really a reflection of her citizenship in Israel, rather than her own individual sinfulness. The main argument here is that the rest of the verse (Hos 1:2) indicates that the entire nation is really being condemned here. The children are given the same label as Gomer (see below on this problem), and both labels are explained by the statement, "because the land is surely promiscuous from after the Lord." Thus, the description of Gomer could have been the description for any Israelite woman that Hosea would have married.[24] A variation proposed by those who hold that Gomer is guilty of cultic prositution is that she is here condemned for something that had become acceptable in the land.[25] I have already argued that Gomer is not a cult prositute (see above), so I would reject this variation. Further, the main theory here (that Gomer herself was not guilty of promiscuity) undercuts the "bite" of God's indictment. More important, it solves nothing, because Hosea later must marry a prostitute, whether Gomer or some other woman (see on Hos 3, below).

---

[23]George Adam Smith, *The Book of the Twelve Prophets, Commonly Called the Minor Prophets* (ExpB; London: Hodder and Stoughton, 1898): 1.236; Rowley, *BJRL* (1956): 214-17; Andersen and Freedman, *Hosea*, 68-69; James Burton Coffman, *Commentary on the Minor Prophets. Vol. 2: Hosea, Obadiah, Micah* (Austin: Firm Foundation, 1981): 6; James Montgomery Boice, *The Minor Prophets: An Expositional Commentary* (Grand Rapids: Zondervan, 1983-1986): 15-16.

[24]Gordis, *HUCA* (1954): 14-15; Coffman, *Commentary on the Minor Prophets*, 6; James Limburg, *Hosea-Micah* (Atlanta: John Knox, 1988): 8; Bird, *Gender and Difference*, 80.

[25]Mays, *Hosea*, 3 and 26; Wolff, *Hosea*, 13-16; Fensham, *JNWSL* (1984): 73; Bird, *Gender and Difference*, 87-88; Irene Kerasote Rallis, "Nuptial Imagery in the Book of Hosea: Israel as the Bride of Yahweh," *StVladThQ* 34 (1990): 203-204.

This leads to the most popular interpretation of God's description of Gomer as a "wife of promiscuity," which is that the description is proleptic, a retrospective interpretation of an earlier command. In other words, what God actually did was to tell Hosea to marry Gomer, and later, when Gomer became promiscuous, Hosea interpreted God's command as what amounted to a command to marry a "wife of promiscuity."[26] The major problem with this view is that it makes it difficult to explain why the children are called "children of promiscuity." Since this is the second time that that issue has been raised, let us turn to it briefly.

There are three plausible interpretations of the phrase, "and children of promiscuity." The first is that these are children born by Gomer to previous lovers. This would explain why there is no verb in this phrase.[27] The problem with this interpretation is that it again contradicts the picture of a good marriage which goes sour (Hos 2:7). A second interpretation is that only the first child mentioned in Hosea 1 is Hosea's child. Only in regard to this first child does it explicitly say, "and she [Gomer] bore him [Hosea] a son" (Hos 1:3b). The other two receive names ("Not Loved" and "Not My People") which suggest disinheritance by Hosea, and they are not explicitly said to be born by Gomer for Hosea.[28] This latter point is not all that telling, though. Of the twelve sons of Jacob, only six are explicitly stated as being born for Jacob (see Gen 29:31-30:24; 35:17). The

---

[26]Brown, *The Book of Hosea*, 3; Leroy Waterman, "Hosea, Chapters 1-3, in Retrospect and Prospect," *JNES* 14 (1955): 101-103; Andersen and Freedman, *Hosea*, 46, 116-17, 159-67; Boice, *The Minor Prophets*, 13.

[27]As it stands in the text, the phrase looks like the second half of a compound direct object. Thus, God's command seems to be that Hosea is to "take" Gomer and the children at the same time. See the objection by Fensham, *JNWSL* (1984): 73 (n. 16); likewise Rowley, *BJRL* (1956): 213 (n. 2).

[28]Smith, *The Book of the Twelve Prophets*, 244; Rowley, *BJRL* (1956): 229; H. L. Ellison, "The Message of Hosea in the Light of His Marriage," *EvQ* 41 (1969): 5; Forseth, *RefJ* (1985): 15; Beeby, *Grace Abounding*, 16.

identity of the father of the other six is supplied by the context. The context of Hos 1 suggests that Hosea is the father of the second and third children mentioned.[29] Likewise, the giving of unflattering names to a prophet's children is not without parallel. Isaiah names one of his children, "The Spoil Speeds, the Prey Hastens," meaning that a foreign army is hurrying to ravage Syria and Israel (Isa 8:1-4). This leaves room for either of two other interpretations. If one concludes that the label given to Gomer merely represents her citizenship among a sinful people, then the children would convey the same notion. Likewise, if one concludes that Gomer's designation is proleptic, then the same label for the children is proleptic. They are called "children of promiscuity" simply because their mother eventually comes to promiscuity. This final view is supported by Hos 2:4-5, where the children are said to be "children of promiscuity, because their mother has committed fornication/been promiscuous" (זָנְתָה). The children are given the same label as their mother, but only she is accused of wrongdoing (see Ezra 9-10, esp. 10:3).

Let us now put these observations together with those concerning the moral status of Gomer at the time of her marriage to Hosea. The interpretation of the command in Hos 1:2 with the greatest support seems to be that it is proleptic. Hosea, looking back on the history of his marriage, views God's initial command to marry Gomer as a command to marry a promiscuous woman, with the further implication that their children also would have to be considered "children of promiscuity." For someone who knew his marriage to be divinely ordained, this might have seemed enigmatic and cruel. But Hosea provides an explanation for how to understand this command in its final line (Hos 1:2c). God is using Hosea's family as a metaphor for the religious promiscuity of the entire land.[30] This

---

[29]Mays, *Hosea*, 26; Andersen and Freedman, *Hosea*, 168.

[30]It is easy to be confused by assuming that Gomer's infidelity must have occurred prior to the condemnations expressed in the names of the three children. This is not necessary, though. Those condemnations do not specify why God is disowning his people, only that

interpretation relies in part, however, on conclusions regarding other critical issues, which have not yet been discussed.

D. *Reality or Metaphor in Hosea 2?*

One of the obstacles to an easy reading of Hos 2 is the fact that reality and metaphor have become intermingled. Hosea writes about his own marriage to Gomer, but also about God's marriage to Israel. Distinguishing absolutely between the two is very difficult.[31] It is possible, in fact, to read all of vv. 2-23 as references to God's marriage with Israel, although this seems a bit strained in some of the early verses (see n. 33). It is likely that all of vv. 8-23 are speaking specifically only of God's relationship to Israel. Similarly, vv. 2-5a are most easily understood as describing Hosea's relationship to Gomer.[32] On the other hand, vv. 5b-7 are probably speaking of God and Israel, although one

---

he is (see Rowley, *BJRL* [1956]: 232). Several reasons (besides infidelity) for the punishment of Israel are supplied in the rest of the book. It could be that the oracles of the naming of Hosea's children circulated for several years before Gomer's promiscuous activity began, and that religious infidelity was merely one of several sins so condemned. The present shape of Hos 1, then, could be seen as a secondary recasting (by Hosea) of those oracles, in which the reasons for the condemnations are couched in a more poignant (for Hosea) way.

Some scholars have questioned why Gomer is accused of infidelity in 1:2-3 and then never mentioned again in the chapter (see Wolff, *Hosea*, 9-10). Perhaps the idea that Hosea is here recasting some earlier oracles could explain that fact.

[31] See Andersen and Freedman, *Hosea*, 46-47; Weems, *Semeia* (1989): 88-89. It has become generally accepted, since Wolff, *Hosea*, 32, that the chapter contains an anthology of sayings by Hosea, which share a common setting of the courtroom.

[32] The formula in Hos 2:2 uses "wife" and "husband" rather than "people" and "God," which suggests a real human couple. The description of the adornments and humiliation of the wife in 2:2-3 seems real rather than metaphorical. Further, to speak of Israel becoming "like" a wilderness and a parched land–rather than actually being those things–seems awkward. See Gordis, *HUCA* (1954): 22-23.

could argue (more easily here than in the subsequent verses) that the situation of Hosea and Gomer could also fit.[33]

But determining the more direct object of the discussion in each section does not resolve the issues raised here. Due to the parallels being drawn between Hosea-Gomer and God-Israel, one cannot say that something said about one relationship does not also apply to the other. On the other hand, one cannot assume that everything said about one relationship automatically applies to the other as well. For example, I have twice alluded to the nature of the marriage as described in Hos 2:7 (a good marriage which turns sour). I have also now expressed the opinion that this verse is speaking specifically of God's marriage to Israel. But this does not necessarily mean that Hosea's marriage to Gomer was also an originally good marriage that turned sour. Thus, any conclusions about Hosea's marriage based on one's use of Hos 2:7 must be understood to be tentative.[34]

E. *Does Hos 2:2 Reflect Divorce or Separation?*

Studies of the marriage metaphor in Hosea are fairly evenly divided in their interpretation of Hos 2:2. At first glance, the wording sounds like a reversal of the common biblical formula, "I will be your God, and you will be my people." That formula is taken by some to be a derivative of a wedding vow formula, so the formula here would be

---

[33]Most of the things said in vv. 5b-7 could be applied to either situation. One piece of evidence, however, suggests the God-Israel marriage to me more than the other. This is the list of items given to the wife in v. 5b. These products provided the economic foundation for the nation of Israel, and they are the very things mentioned in vv. 8ff. as the gifts received by the Israelites for which they give thanks to the Baals.

[34]More broadly stated, any conclusions about Hosea's historical marriage to Gomer that are based on any part of Hos 2 should probably be considered partially speculative. It is possible to read even vv. 2-5a as referring to God and Israel, with "the wife" = "the land" and "the children" = "the inhabitants of the land." See Wolff, *Hosea*, 34; Limburg, *Hosea-Micah*, 10; Rallis, *StVladThQ* (1990): 206.

declaring that the wedding is over (i.e., a divorce). So, many commentators conclude that Hosea (and thus Yahweh) here is declaring a divorce from his wife.[35] Others have objected to this conclusion, however, arguing instead that Hosea is merely punishing his wife as an adulteress and acknowledging an estrangement. Divorce supposedly would not have allowed a chance for the reconciliation predicted in Hos 2:14-23, because such reconciliation is said to be strictly forbidden in Mosaic law (Deut 24:1-4).[36] However, Andersen and Freedman[37] have pointed out that the law forbids remarriage only after the wife has married another man. Moreover, Jeremiah builds on Hos 2 for his judgment speech against Judah a century later, and he clearly understands Hosea to be talking about an actual divorce (see Jer 3:6-10). Thus, it seems best to understand Hos 2:2 as a declaration of divorce.[38]

---

[35] Brown, *The Book of Hosea*, 13-25; Fensham, *JNWSL* (1984): 74; Hubbard, *With Bands of Love*, 55-57. There have been some over the years who have questioned whether it is appropriate to understand these formulas as related to weddings/divorces, seeing them instead as *post facto* declarations. A recent study of this question should finally lay these objections to rest. See Gordon Paul Hugenberger, *Marriage as a Covenant: A Study of Biblical Law and Ethics Governing Marriage Developed from the Perspective of Malachi* (VTSup 52; Leiden: Brill, 1994): 216-39. For presentations of the extrabiblical evidence, see Mordechai A. Friedman, "Israel's Response in Hosea 2:17b: 'You Are My Husband'," *JBL* 99 (1980): 202-203 (n. 15); P. A. Kruger, "Israel, the Harlot (Hos. 2:4-9)," *JNWSL* 11 (1985): 111 (n. 21); Whitt, *SJOT* (1992): 35.

[36] Gordis, *HUCA* (1954): 20-21; Rowley, *BJRL* (1956): 227-28; Ellison, *EvQ* (1969): 4; Small, *JPsychTh* (1979): 137-38.

[37] Andersen and Freedman, *Hosea*, 222. They also believe that there is no actual "divorce" in Hosea 2, only a statement of estrangement. On this, see n. 35, above.

[38] The divorce-formula is also used by God in Hos 1:9. The correspondence between 1:9 and 2:2 would seem to support those who see 1:10-2:1 as a secondary intrusion. However, the inclusion of those verses hints at the bigger structure of these three chapters, where three oracles of condemantion and punishment are each answered by promises of restoration.

F. Who is the Woman of Hos 3?

Hos 3 describes how Hosea fulfills another command of God by "buying" a prostituting adulteress and preventing her from seeing any other men (3:1-3). This is explained as a metaphor for Israel, which would exist for several years without anyone or anything to lead it into false worship, until the people returned to worship the Lord and submit to the rulership of his (faithful) Davidic king (3:4-5).

The debated identity of the woman whom Hosea buys here is crucial to the interpretations of many who study Hosea. Some scholars of past generations tended to see this chapter as purely allegorical,[39] but this view is rarely found today. A minority conclude that this is a second wife of Hosea, the primary reason being that the woman in chap. 3 is never named. Purposefully avoiding to name Gomer would not seem necessary, so this unnamed woman must be somebody else. Also, the absence of any reference to the children seems odd to some.[40] In spite of these problems, most have understood Hos 3 to refer again to Hosea's relationship with Gomer. The differences between chap. 3 and the events described or suggested in chaps. 1-2 can be explained by the passage of time. A few have suggested that the events of chap. 3 actually preceded those of chap. 1,[41] or that chap. 3 provides a second (autobiographical) rendition of the story of chap. 1;[42] but these suggestions are almost universally rejected today. It is more likely that chap. 3 provides a sequel to the events of chaps. 1-2.[43] Gomer has become a true prostitute. To win her back, Hosea goes to

---

[39]For a list of proponents, see Gordis, *HUCA* (1954): 27 (n. 40).
[40]See Rowley, *BJRL* (1956): 219-20.
[41]*Ibid.*, 205-6.
[42]Gordis, *HUCA* 1954): 27-30; also, McKeating, *The Books of Amos, Hosea and Micah*, 76-77. For a full refutation of this view, see Rowley, *BJRL* (1956): 222-24.
[43]Smith, *The Book of the Twelve Prophets*, 239; Rowley, *BJRL* (1956): 224ff.; Hubbard, *With Bands of Love*, 52-55; Mays, *Hosea*, 54-56; Andersen and Freedman, *Hosea*, 117-18; Beeby, *Grace Abounding*, 35-36; Rallis, *StVladThQ* (1990): 201-203.

her and "buys her services" permanently (see below). He purchases her sexual fidelity, in the hopes of eventually gaining her absolute fidelity.

The cultural and theological implications of Hosea's action will be discussed shortly. But first, we should consider its significances for one's interpretation of Hos 1-2. One important implication is that Gomer is seen to be involved in "normal" prostitution, not cultic prostitution. The notion that Gomer engaged in cultic prostitution assumes, in part, that the practice of it was not considered immoral and that Hosea was about the business of convincing his audience of its sinfulness. The label given to Gomer at the beginning of Hos 3 blatantly reflects adultery of a sort which would have been considered sinful by anyone in the society. Either Hosea had been successful in a short amount of time in his attempt to convince his audience of the immorality of their cultic practices, or Gomer was guilty of simple marital infidelity.

Also, the fact that Hos 3 serves as a sequel to the story of Hosea's marriage with Gomer does not resolve the question of whether Hos 2:2 is describing a divorce, or is simply an acknowledgment of estrangement. Either interpretation could provide an adequate backdrop for chap. 3.

G. *Did Hosea buy his wife back from slavery?*

A less discussed issue has been the nature of Hosea's "purchase" of Gomer in Hos 3. The meaning of the verb in 3:2 אֶכְּרֶהָ (I bought her) has never been fully explained.[44] It is either to be derived from the root נכר, (to be foreign) or it is the Niphal (passive/reflexive) form from the root כרה (to buy). I would tend to take the latter view, seeing Deut 2:6 as helpful for providing a useful interpretation here. In Deut 2:6, the Lord tells the people of Israel that they are to "buy grain" (תִּשְׁבְּרוּ) and "purchase" (תִּכְרוּ) water from the

---

[44]For discussions, see Gordis, *HUCA* (1954): 25-26; Rowley, *BJRL* (1956): 203; Andersen and Freedman, *Hosea*, 298-300; Walter Vogels, "Hosea's Gift to Gomer (Hos 3,2)," *Bib* 69 (1988): 412-13.

Edomites, the latter verb being derived from the root כרה. The Israelites would not have bought the water itself, however, but the rights to the water from certain wells. By analogy, Hosea could be "buying the (sexual) rights for himself" (using the reflexive sense) to the prostitute/adulteress.

The price that Hosea pays has also been the subject of some speculation. Strangely, the price is paid in currency (fifteen shekels) and in grain (barley). Some have calculated the value of the grain to be fifteen shekels, leading to the conclusion that Hosea was paying the price of a slave (30 shekels) for Gomer. But this is sheer speculation. The price of barley would have fluctuated enough to make any conclusions about its monetary value uncertain. The context merely suggests that the price paid was sufficient to satisfy the woman's financial needs adequately, so that she would not feel it necessary to seek out other lovers.

2. *The Contents of Hos 1-3*

These conclusions regarding the criticial issues related to Hos 1-3 lead to the following reconstruction of the contents of those chapters. Following the superscription to the entire book (Hos 1:1), there is a series of three clumps of oracles—each corresponding to a chapter—with certain important common features in each. Chap. 1 opens with a declaration of Israel's infidelity, illustrated through a parallel situation in Hosea's own marriage (1:2). The names of Hosea's three children are used to communicate the Lord's judgment on Israel and his announcement of divorce (1:3-9; see n. 37). This is then answered by a promise of renewed covenant (1:10-2:1). Chap. 2 comprises a second round of oracles, beginning with talk of divorce and public humiliation of the adulterous wife. Israel's "adultery" is here detailed more precisely as idolatry, with the humiliation and divorce taking the form of agricultural ruin (2:2-13). This is answered by a lengthy promise of courtship (in the form of an exile to the couple's wilderness "honeymoon spot") and renewed marriage between God and Israel (2:14-23). Chap. 3 focuses on Hosea's own situation, describing how the restoration of his marriage involved the purchase of his wife's "services" on a permanent basis. This is then used to illustrate God's intention to isolate Israel from "distractions," in order to win her back.

3. Hos 1-3 and Biblical Teachings on Marriage Relationships

Reflection on what Hos 1-3 has to say to modern readers has yielded mixed results. On a strictly theological level, Hosea illustrates in a poignant way the personal side of God, how his love for his people and his ability to forgive surpass his justified anger and his decisions to punish wrongdoing. Fensham[45] is probably right to compare the teachings of Exod 32-34 to the teachings of Hos 1-3. That section of Exodus describes idolatry and separation from God, followed by restoration of the relationship based on the fact that God's mercy and love outweigh his wrath (see esp. Exod 34:6-7). Some conservative scholars see in Hosea's talk of a future ideal covenant references to the coming of Jesus and the establishment of the Christian covenant (e.g., Paul talks of the church as the bride of Christ; Eph 5:23-33).[46] Such a Christocentric interpretation is clearly not understood by other OT prophets, who speak specifically of the Israelite people being restored to their land in a proper relationship with their God (see Jer 3:15-18; Ezek 37:15-28). So, it is likely that Hosea's teachings also had the restoration of physical Israel in mind. That Christian writers use the metaphor of marriage to describe the Christian covenant merely indicates how appropriate it is to think of such a covenant in terms of a marriage.

The reverse application of this as a metaphor has also been traditionally recognized in Christianity. Since it is helpful to think of the covenant between God and his people as a marriage, it is also helpful to look to God's covenant relationship with his people as a model for human marriage.

---

[45]Fensham, *JNWSL* (1984): 76-77.
[46]Hubbard, *With Bands of Love*, 61-62; Rallis, *StVladThQ* (1990): 217-18.

This "tradition" of appropriation has scriptural precedence, going back at least to Paul in Eph 5.

But the correspondences between a human marriage and the covenant relationship of God with his people should not be pressed too far. It is possible to draw unwarranted conclusions (either consciously or subconsciously) from the use of such metaphors, conclusions which actually yield results in everyday life which are entirely at odds with the original intent of the metaphor.[47] From the writings of women scholars on Hos 1-3 come two concerns about such unwarranted conclusions.[48] First, Laffey[49] comments that:

> From a feminist perspective, one thing is certain: the women and the children [in Hosea 1-3]—the possessions and the powerless—are *used*. The relationship is hierarchical: just as God is superior to humans, men are superior to women. Men are godlike; women are sexually promiscuous and faithless. This symbolism has been one of the most damaging to women in the entire Old Testament. More perhaps than any other, it has served to legitimate sexual discrimination. Its implications continue to permeate much Christian theology.

Secondly, Weems[50] asks:

> ... [How] are we as biblical theologians to come to grips with the prophet's association of God with sexual violence? [referring to the stripping and public

---

[47]The same caution needs to be given for interpreting Jesus' parables. When one tries to discern a significance for every detail of a parable, one often reads more into it than was intended.

[48]I am not saying that the impressions or concerns of these women writers are unwarranted. To the contrary, I believe that their comments reflect to some degree the conclusions of some Christians about marriage relationships.

[49]Alice Laffey, *An Introduction to the Old Testament: A Feminist Perspective* (Philadelphia: Fortress, 1988): 169.

[50]Weems, *Semeia* (1989): 100.

> humiliation of the wife in Hos 2:3, 6, 10] In his sagacious attempt to portray the passionate and compassionate side of YHWH, has the prophet/poet risked those insights when the basic premise of his message evolves around the untenable image of violence against a woman? Does the fact that the marriage metaphor is *"only* a metaphor" and the motif of sexual violence *"only* a theme of the metaphor" insulate them from serious theological scrutiny? . . . a risky metaphor ["risky" because of the possibility of misinterpretation] gives rise to a risky deduction: here, to the extent that God's covenant with Israel is like a marriage between a man and a woman, then a husband's physical punishment against his wife is as warranted as God's punishment of Israel.

The concerns raised by these women are 1) that putting God in the role of faithful husband and Israel in the role of unfaithful wife reflects and promotes a "double standard" in marriages, and 2) that God's use of force to discipline Israel will justify to some the use of force in dealing with wives.

There might be some validity to the first concern, but it is going too far to say that Hosea assumes or intends to promote a double standard.[51] There is no reason to assume that Israel is portrayed as the wife and God as the husband *because* the male Israelite prophet thought of men as good and women as prone to infidelity, nor does Hosea intend to say that husbands are spiritually superior to their wives. Rather, the primary reason for using the metaphor in this way seems to be that it most easily reflects some economic realities of marriage in a patriarchal society. A significant aspect of Hosea's use of this metaphor is that God has provided for Israel's physical needs, but Israel has

---

[51]While one might argue that a "double standard" did exist in the minds of many Israelite men, it is not to be assumed that any of the biblical authors maintained such a view, e.g., the laws of Deuteronomy reflect a sense of mutual culpability in cases of extra-marital sex (see Deut 22:22-27).

responded by expressing her gratitude to other gods (Hos 2:5, 8, 12-13, 15, 21-23).[52] In a patriarchal society, a husband's principal obligation is to provide for the physical needs of his wife and children. If Hosea had placed Israel in the role of the husband, he would also have had to spend time simply explaining why the wife (God) uncharacteristically was the family breadwinner. Such a diversion from the main intent of the metaphor's use would have unnecessarily confused his immediate audience, thereby diminishing the metaphor's usefulness.[53]

Concern regarding violence toward one's wife requires discussion. The call for public stripping and humiliation (Hos 2:3, 10) is not all that surprising, given the cultural context of ancient Israel. Such actions were the custom in cases of adultery in much of the region at the time, including Israel.[54] One must admit that this custom does in some sense reflect a double standard, because there is no evidence of a converse practice against adulterous husbands. It is tempting, as a Christian, to dismiss this problem as a pre-Christian practice which is supplanted by more enlightened ones in Christianity. This would mean that Christ's love demonstrated for the church has also redefined a husband's love for his wife by eliminating any reference to corporal punishment in the use of the marriage metaphor.[55] Then we

---

[52]This aspect of Hosea's use of the metaphor is completely overlooked in F. van Dijk-Hemmes, *JSOT* (1989): 85-86, evaluation of it. She argues that the nature of Israel's sins (viz., that the men were causing their daughters to participate in cultic prostitution; see Hos 4:13-14) would have been better represented by making Israel a male rapist.

[53]See further the comments of John T. Willis, "Women in the Old Testament," *Essays on Women in Earliest Christianity* (ed. C. D. Osburn; Joplin, MO: College Press, 1993): 1.25-29.

[54]See Gordis, *HUCA* (1954) 20-21; Wolff, *Hosea*, 34; Kruger, *JNWSL* (1985): 111; John Huehnergard, "Biblical Notes on Some New Akkadian Texts from Emar (Syria)," *CBQ* 47 (1985): 428-34; Whitt, *SJOT* (1992): 36; Saul M. Olyan, "'In the Sight of Her Lovers': On the Interpretation of *nablût* in Hos 2,12," *BZ* n. s. 36 (1992): 255-61.

[55]One would have to admit, however, that it is still retained in the

could simply ignore Hosea's use of this part of the metaphor as inappropriate for Christian doctrine. But this is moving away from the text too quickly.

One factor which must be considered in studying a document like Hosea is that of perspective, both that of the writer (Hosea) and of his readers—specifically of androcentrism. In other words, we should not ignore or disdain the fact that it is written by someone with a male perspective to readers with a male perspective.[56] This is blatant in a passage like Hos 3, where the Lord is relying on Hosea's perspective as a scorned husband to appreciate fully his reaction to Israel's idolatry; or a passage like Hos 4:13-14, where Hosea specifically addresses the men of Israel.

> If we conclude that the Bible is androcentric, should we completely reject it as sacred scripture . . .? If we hang on to it as sacred scripture, what do we do with its androcentrism? Is the androcentrism, as [David] Clines argues, an unfortunate but not necessarily an insurmountable problem?[57]

I would contend that the androcentrism of Hos 1-3 is not "unfortunate" at all; instead, recognizing that Hosea's prophecies are primarily addressed to men is an aspect of the text which one should not ignore when trying to understand its message.[58]

NT in the references to God disciplining Christians as a father disciplines his children.

[56] I realize I have just stepped on thousands of toes, the toes of people who assume that inspiration gives Scripture a gender-free, divine perspective. I would simply ask such individuals to reconsider the validity—and necessity—of such an assumption.

[57] Danna Nolan Fewell, "Reading the Bible Ideologically: Feminist Criticism," *To Each Its Own Meaning: An Introduction to Biblical Criticisms and Their Application* (ed. S. R. Haynes and S. L. McKenzie; Louisville, KY: Westminster/John Knox, 1993): 248.

[58] Is it "unfortunate" that Hosea is from northern Israel rather than southern Judah, like Amos? Is it "unfortunate" that Hosea is Israelite rather than ancient Greek or British or German or Bantu?

Let us assume the worst of Hosea's audience—that they are men who hold to a double standard about marriage. They believe that their own acts of infidelity against their wives are inconsequential, that "boys will be boys." At the same time, they believe that the greatest offense that a wife can commit against her husband is to be sexually unfaithful, an offense to which a husband is required to respond in the severest manner possible. Assuming that that was the case in Hosea's day, how would his message have been received by those proud, male listeners? They are accused of (collectively) being (1) a woman (2) who does not appreciate the fact that she is married to the ideal husband and (3) who becomes not just an adulteress, but a promiscuous, prostituting adulteress. For such men, this would have been the most humiliating of accusations.

One gets this impression about Hosea's message most clearly from Hos 4:11-14. Hosea's (male) audience is "a people without understanding" (v. 14), because they do not see that their practice of idolatry makes them guilty of two types of adultery. In this passage, Hosea first speaks of the people's idolatry as adultery and harlotry (vv. 12-13a), and then he accuses the men of being more sinful than the women. He says that their "daughters" and "brides" engage in adultery, it is true, but they do so with the men of Israel; thus, the men are just as guilty in these acts of adultery as the women (vv. 13b-14a). But the men are guilty of more wrongdoing, because they also offer sacrifices which are overseen by foreign קְדֵשׁוֹת (priestesses); they are guilty of religious adultery against the Lord.[59]

It is also helpful, in some sense, to consider how a male audience would have received the fact that God (and Hosea) used corporal punishment and public humiliation as a means to reconciliation.[60] Such a response to an adulterous wife

---

[59]Others have concluded that Hosea places greater guilt on the men in Hos 4:14. See Beeby, *Grace Abounding*, 56-57; Bird, *Gender and Difference*, 83-86; Hugenberger, *Marriage as a Covenant*, 334-34; cf. Andersen and Freedman, *Hosea*, 369.

[60]Hubbard, *With Bands of Love*, 58-59; Wolff, *Hosea*, 32;

would have been expected in that culture, but not with the goal of reconciliation in mind. From a male perspective, an adulterous wife was a major embarrassment, a direct attack on her husband's honor in the community (not to mention his ego). A man without honor held no respect in his community, and protecting the sexual virtue of the women of his family was the most important way in which a man maintained his honor.[61] The public humiliation of an unfaithful wife (or daughter) was a man's way of retaining some of his personal honor. He was effectively distancing himself from the guilty party, demonstrating to his community that he does not allow such a woman to live under his roof and that he will provide no support for such a woman.

What is proclaimed in the promises of restoration of Hos 1-3 directly challenges these notions of honor. The acceptance of the humiliated woman probably constituted social suicide in the minds of Hosea's male audience. It called for those Israelite men to look beyond the immediate shame brought on by the woman's adultery; it called for them to love their wives more than themselves, to ignore their own dishonor for the sake of their wives. Such a change in understanding might seem like a small thing to the modern reader. After all, Hosea does not call for the elimination of the practice of humiliating the adulteress; nor does he call for the introduction of a corresponding practice of humiliating adulterous men. Yet, I would suggest that his teachings signalled a significant first step toward a shift in the attitude of Israelite men about their wives and marriage, a shift that placed the needs of the marriage above the needs of one spouse.

Finally, I would submit that God even sets the example for Hosea himself. Several commentators have stated that

---

Weems, *Semeia* (1989): 97-98; Rallis, *StVladThQ* (1990): 203.

[61]See William Robertson Smith, *Kinship and Marriage in Early Arabia* (London, 1885): 125. On the concept of "honor" in Middle Eastern thought, see J. G. Peristiany, *Honour and Shame: The Values of Mediterranean Society* (Chicago: Univ. of Chicago Press, 1966).

Hosea's love for Gomer prompted him to give their marriage a second chance and, consequently, showed him a deeper understanding of God's dealings with Israel.[62] I am inclined to believe that the reverse happened. It seems more likely that Hosea would have looked upon divorce and humiliation as the natural and proper response to Gomer's infidelity, that he—like his fellow male Israelites—would not naturally have looked beyond that to the possibility of reuniting with his unfaithful wife. In fact, it is likely that such an outcome would have seemed absurd to him, unless there was some extraordinary stimulus prompting him to do so. So, I would submit that God first declared his love for Israel to Hosea, his hope for a restored covenant with his people, which then served as inspiration for Hosea himself when he went (by the command of God) to try to restore his own marriage with Gomer.[63]

Conclusion

This investigation reveals the complexity involved in interpreting the prophecies of Hosea and, consequently, the potential complexity in appropriating the message of any biblical text in one's present context. My own conclusions suggest that recent study of Hosea's use of the broken marriage metaphor might be going beyond the evidence available in some respects (particularly regarding cultic sexual activity on the part of Gomer), thereby leading to conclusions and interpretations which are not supported by the text nor intended by Hosea. Conversely, some good questions have recently been raised about the validity of how we apply biblical teachings to modern American society (see Fewell), particularly when the literary vehicle for communicating those teachings includes metaphors (see Weems). There is plenty of room for continued discussion about these matters.

---

[62]Gordis, *HUCA* (1954): 11 (n. 7); Waterman, *JNES* (1955): 104; Rowley, *BJRL* (1956): 230; Ellison, *EvQ* (1969): 3; Rallis, *StVladThQ* (1990): 205, 217.

[63]See Hubbard, *With Bands of Love*, 58-59.

I conclude that Hosea portrays Yahweh as the husband and Israel as the wife because he wishes to emphasize the fact that Yahweh has been a faithful provider and Israel the ungrateful recipient. This in no way should be viewed as a reflection of the approval of a "double standard" regarding extramarital sexual activity. In fact, Hosea's main target is the male population of eighth century Israel. His comments might suggest that a "double standard" was held by his male contemporaries. But his comments are not intended to promote or support that double standard; in fact, they should have the ultimate effect of undermining it.

It appears that the Israelite men of Hosea's day viewed their participation in Baal religious practices and their adoption of Canaanite ethical/moral standards as acceptable, but Hosea sets out to convince them that Yahweh sees these as "harlotry." He assumes that they view harlotry/ prostitution as an institution in which women are the guilty parties. A woman's participation in it is repugnant to her family, potentially bringing the deepest of shame upon her family, and therefore deserving of the harshest punitive measures. However, Hosea's prophecies turn the tables on these men, because he asserts that they are the prostitutes, and guilty of more wrong than the women (Hos 4:13-14). Thus, the impression that Hosea's prophecies promote the idea that "men are godlike; women are sexually promiscuous and faithless" is patently denied.

The conclusion that Hosea promotes (unwittingly) male domination and a husband's use of force against his wife cannot be entirely denied; but Hosea's reference to force still must be understood within its context. The actions described in Hos 2:3, 6, 10 were typically those used by a husband against an unfaithful wife. But their ultimate purpose at the time was to shame the wife while at the same time maintaining the honor of the husband. Hosea presents an ideal counter to that, one in which reconciliation is the ultimate goal. He does this, in spite of the fact that he lives in a "man's world," where a premium is placed on a man's honor, and where such a marriage (and even more so, a remarriage) would destroy a man's honor. Thus, the example of Yahweh's love for his people redefines the Israelite (and the Christian) perception of love and faithfulness in marriage. In a world where it probably had become natural for husbands to demand more love and faithfulness from their wives than they themselves actually gave, Yahweh and Hosea demonstrate how a husband's love and faithfulness toward his wife can and should be the dominant characteristic in a marriage. Thus, the message for the males of Hosea's time would have been radical, as it placed love for wife above personal (male) honor. Finally, it is possible that the ultimate outcome of this change in attitude is supposed to be the termination of inequality in marriage (see 1 Cor 7:4, 10-16; Eph 5:21-33), just as an attitude of brotherhood between master and slave has contributed to the demise of slavery.

Chapter Seven

THE CAPABLE WIFE (Prov 31:10-31)

Jack P. Lewis

Prov 31:10-31, the only section of the book which lacks a heading, is an acrostic poem with a line for each of the twenty-two letters of the Hebrew alphabet in proper sequence[1] and is the only such poem in the book.[2] The acrostic displays the skill of the poet, facilitates memorization, and may also imply comprehensive coverage of the subject.[3] Seventeen of the verses are synthetic parallel. The acrostic form makes the poem skip from subject to subject; but there exists a structure that has not often been noticed.

A chiasm is suggested in the use of "valor" and "husband" (vv. 10, 11) followed by "husband" and "valor" (vv. 28, 29). Two nine-verse units (vv. 10-18 and 21-29) are separated by a two-verse chiastic unit (vv. 19, 20). The chiasm is obliterated when English does not distinguish between two words יָד and כַּף (*yadh* and *kaph*) for hand and when variety (put/reaches) is used in rendering the verb שָׁלַח (extend). The two units balance each other in theme and general language, each sharing 14 terms. These units are then followed by a two-verse unit (vv. 30, 31).[4]

---

[1]The LXX has the letter פ before ע *GKC*, 5h.

[2]Other acrostics are Pss 9, 25, 34, 111, 112, 119, 145; Lam 1-4; Nah 1:2-7; Sir 51:13-30.

[3]W. G. E. Watson, *Classical Hebrew Poetry* (JSOTSup 26; Sheffield: JSOT Press, 1984): 198.

[4]Murray H. Lichtenstein, "Chiasm and Symmetry in Proverbs 31," *CBQ* 44 (1982): 202-11. Watson, *Classical Hebrew Poetry*, 194, has argued that the first half is composed of couplets broken only by the tricolon of v. 15 and the second half by that of v. 30. Watson also sees

The poem,⁵ which describes the woman with verbs rather than adjectives, is not a picture of the Hebrew woman at worship, but of her in activities of daily life where she exercises a great deal of freedom.⁶ The poem gives the most complete example of economic activity reported in the OT.⁷ The wife is praised for home activities, not for intellectual achievement. Yet much is not covered. The romantic love of the Song of Songs (or love as a word at all) is not depicted. The only hint at religious emotions comes at the end where the poet says, "A woman who fears the Lord is to be praised" (Prov 31:30).⁸

1. *The Text of Prov 31:10-31*

The rhetorical question, "Who can find" (מִי יִמְצָא), occurs once more in the OT, there asking, "a faithful man who can find?" (Prov 20:6). The question is an exclamation

---

v. 15 as the mathematical center of the poem. D. A. Garrett, *Proverbs*, (NAC 14; Nashville: Broadman, 1993): 248, suggests a chiastic structure for the total poem with v. 23 as its central point. Claudia V. Camp, *Wisdom and the Feminine in the Book of Proverbs* (Sheffield: JSOT, 1985): 196-91, offers the hypothesis that the female figures of chaps. 1-9 and 31 form an *inclusio*, or envelope, for the content of the rest of the book.

⁵Garrett, *Proverbs*, 247, among others, alludes to the poem as a "wisdom poem," but A. Wolters, "Proverbs XXXI 10-31 as Heroic Hymn: A Form-critical Analysis," *VT* 38 (1988): 446-57, has suggested that it belongs to the hymnic genre, a form he argues is not tied to the praise of God or to the temple liturgy. He also notices that there are parallels to Ps 111. See also A. P. Ross, *Proverbs* (EBC; Grand Rapids: Zondervan, 1991): 5.429.

⁶C. H. Toy, *A Critical and Exegetical Commentary on the Book of Proverbs* (ICC; New York: C. Scribner's Sons, 1908): 549, says, "The woman is regarded by the author as an independent individual, not merely as an appendage of her husband."

⁷John H. Otwell, *And Sarah Laughed* (Philadelphia: Westminster, 1977): 146.

⁸The LXX reads, "It is a wise woman that is blessed, and let her praise the fear of the Lord."

The Capable Wife (Prov 31:10-31)

of praise which contrasts with the sentiment of the wisdom writer who in pessimism said, "One man among a thousand I found, but a woman among all these I have not found" (Eccl 7:28). Note the same sort of question in Gen 41:38; Eccl 7:24; and Job 28:12.

The question "Who can find a capable wife (אֵשֶׁת־חַיִל; γυναῖκα ἀνδρείαν [LXX]; *mulierem fortem* [Vulg.]; valiant [Douay])?" is not primarily concerned with moral excellence as the uninformed might conclude from the current understanding of the KJV's "virtuous woman," a term from *The Geneva Bible* (1560), that had a different connotation in 1611.[9] The Hebrew language described traits by the sort of genitive construction used here. A kindhearted woman is an אֵשֶׁת־חֵן (Prov 11:16); the foolish woman is an אֵשֶׁת־כְּסִילוּת (Prov 9:13).[10] אֵשֶׁת־חַיִל is the female counterpart of אַנְשֵׁי־חַיִל (capable men; Gen 47:6) or of גִּבֹּר־חַיִל, but need not convey military implications.

חַיִל (capable) occurs frequently as the absolute following a construct form of אִישׁ (man; 1 Sam 31:12; 2 Sam 23:20; 24:9; 1 Kgs 1:42; 1 Chron 10:12; 11:22; 26:8), בֶּן (son; 2 Sam 17:10; 1 Kgs 1:52; etc.), גִּבּוֹר (soldier; Judg 6:12; 11:1; 1 Kgs 11:28; 2 Kgs 5:1; etc.), and other masculine nouns.[11] It may describe a man of skill (Gen 47:6; Exod 18:21; 1 Chron 26:31) or one of property like Boaz (Ruth 2:1). It is less frequent with feminine nouns. To do virtuously עָשָׂה חַיִל (Num 24:18; Deut 8:18; Ruth 4:11; Pss 60:[14]12; 108:[14]13; 118:15, 16; Prov 31:29; Ezek 28:4) is an idiom for military prowess, gaining wealth, or admirable action. אֵשֶׁת־חַיִל elsewhere describes Ruth (Ruth 3:11) and the wife of noble character who is the crown of her husband (Prov 12:4). חַיִל also occurs in Prov 31:3, 29 translated "strength" and "excellence" (NRSV).

---

[9]"Virtuous," *OED*, 12.241-42.

[10]N. P. Bratsiotis, "אִישׁ" *TDOT*, 1.224.

[11]H. Eising, "חַיִל," *TDOT*, 4.348-55; C. P. Weber, "חיל," *TWOT*, 1:272.

The woman is neither said to be a wise woman (אִשָּׁה חֲכָמָה) as were the women of Tekoa and Abel (2 Sam 14:2; 20:16) nor a great woman (אִשָּׁה גְדוֹלָה) as was the Shunammite (2 Kgs 4:8), though one should not assume that she has neither of these qualities. "Wisdom of women" (חַכְמוֹת נָשִׁים; Prov 14:1) is not explicitly attributed to her.

The value of the woman, implying her rarity, is stressed. "She is worth מֶכֶר (far more; Num 20:19; Deut 18:8) than rubies," a comparison earlier made in Proverbs for wisdom (Prov 3:15; 8:11; see also 8:19; 16:16; 20:15; Job 28:15-19). A Sumerian proverb stated, "An unseemly wife living in the house is worse than all devils."[12] *Papyrus Insinger* 9.8.8 states, "There is she who fills her house with wealth without there being an income."[13] The wicked wife is contrasted with the good wife in Sir 25:16-26:18.

The modern identity of the stone of comparison (מִפְּנִים; Prov 3:15)[14] is uncertain, e.g., λίθον πολυτελῶν (precious stones [LXX]); rubies [KJV]; jewels [NIV/NRSV]; red coral [REB]; pearls [NJB]. The Vulgate (and Douay) read "far and from the uttermost coasts is the price of her."[15] However, our poem does not raise the question of the woman's fertility. Ben Sira said, "He who acquires a wife gets his best possession, a helper fit for him and a pillar of support" (Sir 36:24).[16]

---

[12]E. I. Gordon, *Sumerian Proverbs: Glimpses of Everyday Life in Ancient Mesopotamia* (Philadelphia: Univ. of Philadelphia Press, 1959; reprint, NY: Greenwood, 1968): 468.

[13]M. Lichtheim, *Ancient Egyptian Literature: A Book of Readings* (Berkeley: Univ. of California Press, 1980): 3.19.

[14]See Job 28:18; Prov 8:11; 20:15; Lam 4:7; Sir. 7:19; 30:15.

[15]The Douay renders the perfects as past tense; the KJV as present. See Paul Joüon, "Les Temps dans Proverbes 31:10-31 (La Femme Forte)," *Bib* 3 (1922): 349-352.

[16]See also B. Gemser, "Instructions of 'Onchsheshongy," *SVT* 7 (1960): 112-13; M. Lichtheim, *Late Egyptian Literature in the International Context: A Study of Demotic Instruction* (OBO 52; Göttingen: Vandenhoeck & Ruprecht, 1983): 49-50.

The capable wife's activities are depicted in relation to her husband and family. Though enjoying much freedom, she is not a liberated woman who has purposely turned her back on family life for an independent career. Her industry contrasts with that of the Samaritan women whom Amos called the "cows of Bashan" (Amos 4:1). She does not oppress the poor, but helps them (v. 20).

"The heart of her husband (בַּעַל) trusts her." Trust (not confined to any specific area of life) here has no reference to marital fidelity or affection. It does not deal with jealousy (see Prov 6:34). Apparently her husband remains the head of the family but leaves household management to his wife. The contrast with the cautions against the wife given by Ptah-Hotep about 2450 BC[17] or with an Egyptian proverb of the fifth century BC are striking: "Let your wife regard your wealth; do not trust her with it. Do not trust her (even) with her provisions for one year."[18] Sir 42:6 also warns against trust of an evil wife and Sir 33:19 against entrusting her with one's property. "Trust is the basis of relationship . . . trust is something we give, while trustworthiness is something we must earn."[19]

Egyptian wisdom at the end of the Empire said,

> Thou shouldst not supervise (too closely) thy wife in her (own) house, when thou knowest that she is efficient. Do not say to her: "Where is it? Fetch (it) for us!" when she has put (it) in the (most) useful place. Let thine eye have regard, while thou art silent, that thou mayest recognize her abilities. How happy it is when thy hand is with her."[20]

---

[17]330; *ANET*^{2}, 413.

[18]Gemser, *SVTP* (1960): 120.

[19]Noella McLees, "In the Gates: Reflections on Christian Womanhood," *Epiphany* 7 (1986): 23.

[20]"Instructions of Ani" 9.1-5; *ANET*^{2}, 421.

"He will have no lack[21] of gain."[22] שָׁלָל is rendered variously: spoils [Douay]; nothing of value [NIV]; profit [NJB]; children are not lacking [REB].[23] Wisdom offers riches to those who seek her (Prov 8:18).

V. 12. "She does him [LXX: her husband] good and not harm (see Prov 3:30) all the days of her life (see Lev 18:18)." A prudent wife is from the Lord (Prov 19:14).

V. 13. "She seeks[24] wool and flax,[25] and works with willing (בְּחֵפֶץ) hands."[26] Clothes making was considered women's work (see 1 Sam 2:19). Prov 31:19, 22, 24 suggests that she herself works and does it with pleasure.[27] The sluggard's hands refuse to labor (Prov 21:25).

---

[21]חֶסֶר; see Ps 34:[11]10.

[22]שָׁלָל; see Ps 119:162; Prov 1:13; 16:19; Isa 9:2; *KB*³, 1419; K. J. Austel, "שָׁלַל," *TWOT*, 2.930.

[23]The suggestion of D. Winton Thomas, "Textual and Philological Notes on Some Passages in the Book of Proverbs," *SVTP* 3 (1955): 291-92; *idem*, "Notes on Some Passages in the Book of Proverbs," *VT* 15 (April 1965): 277-29, from an Arabic proverb with parallels in classical sources, that the phrase should be understood 'wool is not lacking to her,' has not found acceptance in English translations. G. R. Driver's proposal [cited in B. Gemser, *Sprüche Solomos* (HZAT; Tübingen: J. C. B. Mohr, 1963): 108], that שָׁלָל should be "offspring," though reflected in the REB, has not gained general acceptance.

[24]דָּרַשׁ; μερυομένη (gathering [LXX]; *quaesivit* [Vulg.]; selects [NIV]).

[25]See Exod 9:31; Isa 19:9; Deut 22:11; Josh 2:6; Hos 2:5, 9 [7, 11].

[26]*consilio manuum suarum* (Vulg.); counsel of her hands (Douay). For חֵפֶץ, see Job 31:16; Isa 44:28; 58:3; Eccl 3:17. M. Dahood, *Proverbs and Northwest Semitic Philology* (Rome: Pontifical Biblical Institute, 1963): 60-61, proposes, "which her hands turn into a work of beauty." See L. J. Wood, "חָפֵץ," *TWOT*, 1.311.

[27]F. Delitzsch, *Biblical Commentary on the Proverbs of Solomon* (trans. M. G. Easton; (Edinburgh: T. & T. Clark 1874-1875; reprint, Grand Rapids: Eerdmans, 1950): 2.328-29.

The Capable Wife (Prov 31:10-31)

V. 14. "She is like the ships of the merchant, bringing her goods[28] from afar."[29] Further note of her trade is in v. 24. She goes beyond her immediate neighborhood.

V. 15. "She gets up while it is still dark; she provides food (טֶרֶף)[30] for her family and portions (חֹק; Gen 47:22; Prov 30:8)[31] for her servant girls (see Prov 27:27)." The sluggard, on the other hand, sleeps all day (Prov 6:9-10; 20:13). Drawing water (Gen 24:15; 1 Sam 9:11) and meal preparation (Gen 18:6) were customarily done by women, but both men and women tended flocks (Gen 29:9; 27:8).

V. 16. "She considers[32] a field and buys (לָקַח) it."[33] Some might see this as being outside a woman's sphere.[34]

"With the fruit of her hands, she plants (see Isa 5:2, 7) a vineyard." It is the money her hands have earned. Vine culture is significant in Palestine (see Judg 9:27; Neh 5:3; Prov 24:30; Isa 7:23) and women keep vineyards (Cant 1:6).

V. 17. "She girds her loins with strength (עֹז; see Ps 93:1; Prov 31:25a)."[35] Clothing had to be bound up for work (1 Kgs 18:46; 2 Kgs 4:29), giving rise to the metaphor. The NIV paraphrases, "She sets about her work vigorously," and the REB, "resolutely."

---

[28]*panem suum* (Vulg.); her bread (Douay).

[29]מִמֶּרְחָק; Isa 10:3; 30:27; Jer 5:15; Ezek 23:40.

[30]Douay reads "prey"; the *BHS* proposal is טֹרַח (duties). The verse has three stiches where all the others except v. 30 have two.

[31]Victuals [Douay]; but חֹק can also mean daily tasks (Exod 5:14).

[32]זָמְמָה; see Prov 21:27; 30:32.

[33]Dahood, *Proverbs and Northwest Semitic Philology*: 61, has questioned that the use of the verb לָקַח in this sense is a convincing argument for a late date for the Proverb.

[34]See W. O. E. Oesterley, *The Book of Proverbs* (London: Methuen, 1929): 284.

[35]LXX adds "resolutely" (ἰσχυρῶς).

To "and strengthens (אָמֵץ) her arms" (Ps 89:[22]21), LXX adds "for work." REB reads, "tackles her work with vigour."

V. 18. "She perceives (טָעַם; Ps 34:[9]8)³⁶ that her merchandise (סַחַר; see Prov 3:14)³⁷ is profitable."³⁸

"Her lamp does not go out at night."³⁹ "Lamp"⁴⁰ is preferred to "candle" (KJV) as the light source of the period. Extinction of the lamp is a sign of calamity (Job 18:6; Prov 13:9; 20:20). Whybray⁴¹ interpreted the burning of the lamp at night as a sign of prosperity; but here it is an indication of industry comparable to modern "burning midnight oil."

V. 19. "She puts her hands⁴² to the distaff (כִּישׁוֹר)." Women's work in spinning is age old (see Exod 35:26).⁴³ Translators have guessed at the meaning of the term.⁴⁴ LXX has συμφέροντα (needful works). Vulg. reads *ad fortia*, and Douay translates "strong things." Symmachus, Aquila, and Theodotion have ἀνδρείας (strenuously). Jerome guesses *"fortia"* (gallant deeds), which in Douay became "strong things."⁴⁵

---

³⁶Douay reads "tasted."

³⁷Douay reads "traffic."

³⁸כִּי־טוֹב; Gen 1:4, 10; Prov 3:14.

³⁹See Lam 2:19.

⁴⁰נֵר, λύχνος (LXX); *lucerna* (Vulg.).

⁴¹R. N. Whybray, *The Book of Proverbs* (Cambridge: Cambridge Univ. Press, 1972): 185.

⁴²For the idiom שָׁלַח יָדוֹ, see Job 28:9.

⁴³See m. *Ketuboth* 5.5.

⁴⁴כִּישׁוֹר is an *hapax*. KB^3, 451, defines it as a whorl for turning the distaff.

⁴⁵G. R. Driver, "Notes on Hebrew Lexicography," *JTS* 23 (1922): 407, proposed "mending," "darning," or "knitting."

"And her hands hold the spindle." Spinning was a part of everyday life. Women prepared materials for the tabernacle (Exod 35:25-26).

V. 20. "In generosity this woman opens her hands to the poor (עָנִי; Prov 14:21; Amos 2:7)," who here are paralleled to "the needy" (אֶבְיוֹן; Job 31:16-20; Amos 2:6). A third term for the poor, though not occurring here, is דָּל (see Prov 19:17), concern for whom is blessed (see Prov 11:25). The writer uses here the same expression (יָדֶיהָ שִׁלְּחָה) for the wife's charity as in v. 19 for her industry. In Israel, lack of concern for the poor is blameworthy (see Ezek 16:49).

V. 21. "She is not so involved in activities that she has neglected her own house." She is not afraid of snow for her household (Prov 25:13; 26:1) for she has made preparation. Windows of houses had no glass, and the house only had a brazier for heat (see Jer 36:22). One was dependent for warmth on clothing (see Hag 1:6).

"Her household is clothed[46] in scarlet."[47] The Syriac and the Targum have "scarlet," but the LXX (δισσὰς χλαίνας) and Vul. (*duplicibus*) read "double" (שְׁנַיִם) here and were followed by Luther, Coverdale (For all her household folkes are double clothed), the Douay, and the REB. This reading is preferred by the OT Text Project.[48]

V. 22. "She makes herself coverings (מַרְבַדִּים; see Prov 7:16)."[49] A non-biblical occurrence of the word has been identified.[50]

---

[46]See Ezek 9:2, 3 for the form לְבֻשׁ, also written defectively.

[47]שְׁנִים; Gen 38:28. See Dahood, 62, on the Ugaritic term.

[48]*Preliminary and Interim Report on the Hebrew Old Testament Text Project* (Stuttgart: United Bible Societies, 1977): 3.564.

[49]Symmachus reads ἀμφιτάπους (carpets); Theodotion has περιστρώματα; Jerome reads *stragulatam vestem*; Douay has "clothing of tapestry"; and NJB reads "quilts."

[50]Dahood, *Proverbs*, 62.

"Her clothing is fine linen (שֵׁשׁ)[51] and purple (אַרְגָּמָן)." These materials were imports from Egypt and Phoenicia. Purple, linked with kings (Judg 8:26; Cant 3:10; Jer 10:4; Esth 8:15) or the rich, suggests the finest quality.[52]

V. 23. "Her husband (who is mentioned elsewhere only in verses 11 and 28) is known in the gates (Job 29:7; Prov 22:22; 24:7) when he sits among the elders of the land."[53] At the gate of the town all the community's affairs were discussed.[54] An obvious contrast is with the later statement: when the wicked woman's husband "takes his meals among the neighbors, he cannot help sighing bitterly" (Sir 25:18). One should not make an argument from silence and conclude that the husband is inactive or is a shirker.[55]

V. 24. "She makes linen garments (סָדִין; Judg 14:12-13; Isa 3:23; KB^3, 702; underskirt; LXX: σινδόνας; Vulg.: sindon; see Mark 14:51) and sells (מָכַר; Gen 37:27; Exod 21:8) them."[56]

"She delivers girdles (חֲגוֹר; 1 Sam 18:4; 2 Sam 18:11) to the merchant (כְּנַעֲנִי; Job [40:30]41:6)."[57]

---

[51]Luther has *"weisse Seide,"* KJV "silk," and Douay "linen."

[52]W. T. McKane, *Proverbs* (OTL; Philadelphia: Westminster, 1978): 668-69.

[53]Dahood, *Proverbs*, 62-63.

[54]See Gen 19:1; Deut 21:19; 22:15; Job 29:7; Prov 24:7. See also R. de Vaux, *Ancient Israel* (trans. J. McHugh; NY: McGraw-Hill, 1961): 152. Wisdom stands at the side of the gate (Prov 8:3).

[55]One needed leisure to be wise (Sir 38:24). R. Meir said, "Engage not overmuch in business, but occupy thyself with the Torah" (*m. Aboth* 4.10).

[56]S. Talmon, "The Sectarian *Yachadh*—A Biblical Noun," *VT* 3 (1953): 134, observed that the sentence in Hebrew is incomplete in which an element is divided between the two parts of the sentence, and he proposed adding לָכֵן אֲנִי to the first stich. English translations supply the direct object.

[57]Χαναναίοις (LXX); *Chananeos* (Vulg.); Chanaanite (Douay).

The Capable Wife (Prov 31:10-31)   165

V. 25. In LXX, v. 25 follows v. 26 of the MT. "Strength (עֹז; Ps 29:11) and dignity (הָדָר; Ps 104:1; honor [KJV]; dignity [NIV/NRSV]) are her clothing." Compare v. 17. Allusion is to the economic strength of her household. On metaphorical clothing, see Job 29:14; Pss 93:1; 104:1.

"She laughs (see Job 5:22; 39:7, 18, 22; 41:[21]29) at the time to come." With no fear or anxiety, she can laugh at whatever the future holds. She has ample reserves. The idiom is for lack of undue concern, e.g., Job 39:7.

V. 26. "She opens her mouth with wisdom, and the teaching of kindness (תּוֹרַת־חֶסֶד; see Prov 3:3; 11:17; 21:21) is on her tongue."[58] It is the mother's faithful instruction (Prov 1:8; 6:20; see 31:1). However, that the woman educates her children is not mentioned at all; it takes place by example and pattern.[59] The commendation contrasts with the gossip (Prov 20:19), the foolish woman who is noisy (Prov 9:13), and the contentious woman (Prov 25:24).

V. 27. "She looks well (צוֹפִיָּה; see Gen 31:49; Hab 2.1)[60] to the ways[61] of her household and does not eat the bread of idleness." She is tireless in her devotion. Proverbs contrasts the wise (חָכָם) and the idle (lazy; עַצְלָה; see Prov 19:15). The sluggard is described in Prov 6:6, 9.

V. 28. "Her children rise up (see Gen 37:35; Lev 19:32; Job 29:8; Jer 26:17) and call her happy (see Gen 30:13)."[62]

---

[58]Origen: τάξιν ἐστείλατο; Theodotion: νόμος χάριτος; Vulg.: *lex clementiae*; Douay reads "law of clemency"; KJV renders "law of kindness"; and REB has "her teaching is sound."

[59]L. Köhler, *Hebrew Man* (Nashville: Abingdon, 1956): 63.

[60]The feminine participle of צָפָה (watch as a watchman; 2 Sam 18:24; Ps 37:32). GKC 75v (212). LXX: στέγναι διατριβαὶ οἴκων αὐτῆς (the ways of her house are careful); Vulg. has *considerat*.

[61]Douay has "paths."

[62]The verb is a *pi'el* form. The duty of honoring mother with the disgrace for failure is later expounded in Sir 3:4, 11.

"Her husband (בַּעַל) too, and he praises her (Cant 6:9)."[63]

V. 29. "Many women (בָּנוֹת; daughters; Gen 30:13; Cant 2:2; 6:9] have done excellently (חַיִל; see v. 10),[64] but you surpass them all." LXX has a double translation creating the tristich: "have obtained wealth, many have wrought valiantly, but you have exceeded and surpassed all."

V. 30. "Charm (חֵן; see 1:9; 11:16) is deceptive (שֶׁקֶר; Ps 33:17; Prov 6:17, 19; 13:5)." Although Ibn Ezra has the husband continue his praise, it is likely that here the poet approves the praise of the husband.[65]

"Beauty (יֳפִי 6:25) is fleeting (הֶבֶל; see Gen 4:4; Prov 13:11)."[66] The woman "is not described as "attractive" in the modern, largely physical sense."[67] Ahikar said, "The beauty of a woman is her good sense and the word of her mouth is her adornment."[68] See also Sir 26:13-18.

---

[63]"The Instructions of Ani," 9.4 ($ANET^3$, 421), urge the son to recognize the abilities of the wife.

[64]The idiom עָשָׂה חַיִל occurs in Num 24:18; Ruth 4:11; ἐκτήσαντο πλοῦτον (LXX); acquire wealth (Targum); *congregaverant divitias* (Vulg.); gathered together riches (Douay). The rendering is possible (Deut 8:17; Ezek 28:4), but does not fit here. NJB reads, "done admirable things"; REB reads "How gifted she is."

[65]Delitzsch, *Biblical Commentary*, 2.340-41.

[66]Ptah-Hotep warned, "One is made a fool by limbs of fayence, as she stands (there), becomes (all) cornelian" [285] ($ANET^2$, 413). The Syriac "Story of Ahikar," 2.19, in *The Apocrypha and Pseudepigrapha of the Old Testament in English* (ed. R. H. Charles; Oxford: Clarendon, 1913): 2.730, "My son, go not after the beauty of a woman, and lust not after her in thy heart because the beauty of a woman is her good sense, and her adornment is the word of her mouth."

[67]W. G. Plaut, *Book of Proverbs* (New York: Union of American Hebrew Congregations, 1961): 312. See Sir 26.17, 18.

[68]"The Story of Ahikar" 2.19, in Charles, *Apocrypha and Pseudepigrapha*, 2.730.

V. 30b. "A woman who fears the Lord is to be praised" (see Isa 41:16).[69] The LXX reads, "But let her praise the fear of the Lord."[70] That the verse is an insertion of a scribe (popular as the view is)[71] is only a subjective judgment.

Watson has argued that the verse is a tricola and that a line of extra length marks a climax of special emphasis.[72] Earlier in the book the strange woman in forsaking her marriage bond forgot the covenant of her God (Prov 2:17).

The verb "praise" is used in v. 28 for the action of her husband. Only here in fear of the Lord are the woman's traits reachable by all.[73] The book began with "The fear of the Lord is the beginning of knowledge; fools despise wisdom and instruction" (Prov 1:7). Humility and fear of the Lord (Prov 22:4; 23:17) are praised. The LXX has a doublet: "an intelligent woman is praised, and let her praise the fear of the Lord." Ben Sira said, "A pious wife is given to the man who fears the Lord" (Sir 26:23).

V. 31. "Give her the fruit of her hands,[74] and let her works praise her in the gates." Receiving the credit she

---

[69]GKC, 54g. "Fear of the Lord" occurs in Prov 1:29; 8:13.

[70]H. P. Rüger, "Zum Text von Prv. 31, 30," *Die Welt des Orients* 5 (1969-1970): 96-99.

[71]Toy, *A Critical and Exegetical Commentary*, 548-50; R. B. Y. Scott, *Proverbs* (AB 18; Garden City, NY: Doubleday, 1965): 185. For a survey of the influence of one's worldview on the treatment of this issue, see Al Wolters, "Nature and Grace in the Interpretation of Proverbs 31:10-31," *CTJ* 19 (1984): 153-66.

[72]Watson, *Classical Hebrew Poetry*, 183. See also R. N. Whybray, *The Composition of the Book of Proverbs*. JSOTSup 168; Sheffield: JSOT Press, 1994): 155-56, who sees the challenge arising from the mistaken view that in the thought of the ancient world the sacred and the secular were two separate spheres.

[73]D. Kidner, *Proverbs* (TyndOTC; London: Tyndale, 1964): 184.

[74]"Praise her" (REB) and "extol" (NJB) assume the verb form תְּנוּ from תָּנָה (Judg 5:11; 11:40; Ps 8:[2]1) rather than תְּנוּ from נָתַן. See

deserves (see Ps 128:1-2), she will be praised openly. LXX has "Let her husband be praised." That "domestic and womanly virtues would hardly be the subject of discussion in the gates of the town"⁷⁵ is merely a subjective judgment.

It must be remembered that Proverbs (which deals with the behavior of both men and women) depicts in a number of passages the good wife and mother (Prov 11:16; 12:4; 18:22; 19:14), in others the quarrelsome wife (Prov 19:13; 21:9, 19; 25:24; 27:15), and in still others the adulteress (Prov 6:26; 7:10-19). Young men are warned against prostitutes (Prov 9:13; 22:14; 23:27; 29:3). Lemuel's mother warns him against giving his strength to women (Prov 31:3). Unforgettable is the comparison "Like a gold ring in a pig's snout is a beautiful woman without good sense" (Prov 11:22). The wife that brings shame (מְבִישָׁה) is rottenness in a husband's bones (Prov 12:4).

The picture of women, however, is more positive than negative. The wise woman builds her house (Prov 14:1). The good wife is the crown of her husband (Prov 12:4). The one finding a wife finds a good thing and obtains favor from the Lord (Prov 18:22). A prudent wife is from the Lord (Prov 19:14). Marriage is a sacred covenant (בְּרִית אֱלֹהֶיהָ Prov 2:17), and monogamy is praised (Prov 5:15-19; see also Eccl 9:9).

Both father and mother are to be heeded (Prov 1:8, 9; 6:20; see also 4:3 and poetic parallels in 10:1; 15:20; 17:25; 23:22, 25). Both are included in condemnation of abuse by children (Prov 19:26; 20:20; 28:24). Oesterley remarked that Proverbs is the only OT book in which a rational estimate of woman is found.⁷⁶

W. A. van der Weiden, *Le Livre des Proverbes: Notes philologiques* (Rome: Pontifical Biblical Institute, 1970): 155-56.

⁷⁵See Oesterley, *Book of Proverbs*, 287; and C. T. Fritsch, *Proverbs* (IB; Nashville: Abingdon Press, 1955): 4.957.

⁷⁶Oesterley, *Book of Proverbs*, 84.

2. History of Interpretation

A. Greek Interpretation of Prov 31:10-31

The poem undergoes interpretation in the process of translation into Greek, possibly made as early as the middle of the second century BC.[77] In Greek (where the poem appears after Prov 29:27),[78] the woman becomes a woman of heroic deeds (γυναῖκα ἀνδρείαν),[79] and in v. 30, she is a woman of intelligence (γυνὴ συνετή) in contrast with the Hebrew where she fears the Lord (אִשָּׁה יִרְאַת־יְהֹוָה.)

The translators were noncommittal about the woman's price, using λίθων πολυτελῶν (precious stones) for her value. The Latin has "far and from the uttermost coasts is her value." She is made the subject of 11b: "She stands in no need of fine spoils."

In Greek, v. 12 (apart from Codex Alexandrinus) is compressed from "good and not evil" to merely "good all of her life" with the indirect objective pronoun replaced by "the husband"—"She works all her life for her husband's good." V. 13 has "draws out (μηρυομένη) wool and flax" rather than "seeks." The Greek can be very literal, e.g., in v. 18 טָעֲמָה becomes ἐγεύσατο (taste; Vulg. *gustavit*). In v. 21 שָׁנִים (scarlet) is read διοσάς (double) and is carried over into v. 22 in connection with מַרְבַדִּים (χλαίνας; cloak; blanket). In vv. 25-26, the LXX has the stich for the Hebrew letter פ (στόμα; mouth) before that of the letter ע (ἰσχύν; strength), an alphabetic sequence paralleled in Ps 33; Lam 2, 3, and 4. Verse 29 interprets עָשׂוּ חָיִל as ἐκτήσαντο πλοῦτον (have obtained riches) but also as "wrought valiantly."

---

[77]G. Gerleman, *Studies in the Septuagint, III. Proverbs* (Lund: Gleerup, 1956): 60.

[78]Greek has the sequence Prov 30:15-33; 31:1-9; 25-29; and 31:10-31.

[79]See *1 Clem.* 55.3; *BAGD*, 63.

The LXX has a double translation of v. 30: "A wise woman is blessed" and "Let her praise the fear of the Lord." The LXX made the husband much more prominent than he is in the Hebrew text by the insertion of "her/the husband" and by limiting phrases to the woman. She does her husband good (12a); "her husband is not anxious about those at home" (21a); she makes clothes for her husband (22a); "her husband praises her" (28b); a woman's beauty is vain; a wise woman is blessed (31b, c); and "let her husband be praised in the gates" (31b).

B. *Prov 31:10-31 in Jewish and Christian Writers*

Philo of Alexandria in commenting on the Greek word ᾠκοδόμησε (formed; Gen 2:22) observes, "For to man are entrusted the public affairs of state; while to a woman the affairs of home are proper. The lack of her is ruin, but her being near at hand constitutes household management."[80]

Prov 31:10-31 has left little trace in early rabbinic literature. Only vv. 30-31 are cited in the *Mishnah* and that as what the daughters of Jerusalem said on the 15th of Ab and the Day of Atonement as they went forth to dance in the vineyards,[81] calling on young men to consider family rather than beauty. The scholars homilized the phrases as applied to the study of the Torah in various generations.[82]

R. Nehemiah[83] is credited with comparing the Torah to the Woman of Valor, having deduced from Prov 31:14 that where the words of Scripture are poor in one place they are rich in another. R. Yohanan[84] used Prov 31:26 to describe words of Menahem the cake baker. The *Midrash* found the midwives of Egypt who feared the Lord described by Prov

---

[80]Philo, *Questions and Answers on Genesis* 1:26.

[81]*m. Taanit* 4:8; *b. Tannith* 76b; *y. Taanith* 4.7.

[82]*b. Sanhedrin* 20a.

[83]*y. Rosh Hashanah* 3:5.

[84]*y. Sanhedrin* 2:6 [IV J].

31:30.[85] R. Jeremiah[86] is credited with the observation that Solomon concluded both the books of Proverbs and Ecclesiastes with references to fear.

More often noticed across the years is the daily prayer in which a man thanks the Lord that he was not born a woman,[87] repetition of which is a part of the daily morning prayer.[88]

Any Christian consideration of Prov 31:10-31 from the first and second centuries if it ever existed has not survived. The first notice in extant materials is in Clement of Alexandria's *Paedagogus*[89] where in setting forth the wife's duties the writer underscores his list by citation of Prov 31:19-20 from the LXX. Insisting that the woman whose life is framed according to God appears in clothes she has made rather than in those from the market, Clement alludes to the wife who clothes both herself and her husband by her working, and then cites Prov 31:26, 27, 30 from memory according to the LXX.[90]

Gregory Nazianzus in the funeral oration for his father praised his father's marriage as being to a valiant woman,[91] and he found his sister Gorgonia more than worthy of being described by the words of Solomon: "Now to praise my sister in these points would be to praise a statue for its shadow or a lion for its claws, without allusion to its greatest perfections."[92]

---

[85]*Ex. Rab.* 1:15.

[86]*Qoh. Rab.* 3:14.1.

[87]*b. Menachoth* 43b.

[88]*The Standard Prayer Book* (trans., S. Singer; New York: Block, 1952): 6.

[89]Clement of Alexandria, *Paed.* 3.10 (*ANF* 2.283; *GCS*, 264-65).

[90]*Idem*, *Paed.* 3.11 (*ANF* 2.287; *GCS*, 273).

[91]Gregory of Nazianzus, *Or.* 18.7 (*PG* 35.992; $NPNF^2$ 7.256).

[92]*Idem*, *Or.* 8.9 (*PG* 35.797; $NPNF^2$ 7.240).

The entire poem is cited in its Greek form in the early third century *Didascalia Apostolorum*[93] in an admonition to women about behavior and in the slightly later *Apostolic Constitutions*.[94]

Further literal interpretation of the Greek text comes from Paulinus of Nola,[95] in a letter before AD 396, who found Amanda, the wife of Aper, described by phrases from Prov 31. Other phrases were used in consoling Pammachius over the loss of his wife.[96] Basil[97] found in "she has not eaten her bread idle" a proof text in his argument for labor against the evil of idleness.

At the same time, the conviction of the multiple meaning of Scripture (literal, tropological, allegorical, and anagogical)[98] made allegorization of Prov 31:10-31 easy. Beginning with Origen,[99] writers saw in the poem an allegory of the church. Ambrose[100] (AD 333-397) applied the poem to the church, a development of the concept of the church as the bride of Christ. Jerome[101] (AD 347-435) also allegorizes the worthy woman to be the church, the bride

---

[93]Trans. in R. H. Connally, *Didascalia Apostolorum* (Oxford: Clarendon Press, 1929): 22-23.

[94]*Apostolic Constitutions* 1.8 (*ANF* 7.394).

[95]Paulinus of Nola, *Letter* 44.4 (ACW 36.238-40).

[96]*Idem, Letter* 13.5 (ACW 35.122).

[97]Basil, *Ascet.* (*PG* 31.1012); idem, *The Long Rules*, Q. 37 (*F. of C.* 9:307).

[98]James D. Wood, *The Interpretation of the Bible* (London: Duckworth, 1958): 72.

[99]Origen, *Expositio in Proverbia* (*PG* 17.252); J. Obersteiner, "Die Erklärung von Proverbia 31, 10-31, durch Beda den Ehrwürdigen und Bruno von Asti," *Theologische-Praktische Quartalschrift* 102 (1954): 1-13.

[100]Ambrose, *On the Christian Faith*, 2:Intro. (*NPNF*^{2} 10.225); *Expositio Evang. sec. Luc.* VIII.10 (*PL* 15.1768).

[101]Jerome, *Letter 69.5* (*NPNF*^{2} 6.144).

The Capable Wife (Prov 31:10-31)

(see 2 Cor 11:2). John Cassian[102] (AD 360-419) finds Prov 31:21 an addition to the description of the manifold grace of the church, and he applies the passage as a proof against idleness.[103]

Augustine (AD 411) found Prov 31:26 to be descriptive of wisdom,[104] but he further expounded the allegory of the church.[105] The motif can be traced through Bede and found an exponent in Bruno (AD 1045-1123).

A *Midrash* of the Middle Ages, dating about AD 1270, assumes that each verse of the Song represents a different biblical heroine.[106]

In addition to allegorical interpretation which saw Prov 31:10-31 as the church, familiarity with the passage established a stereotype of "womanly virtue" in the Middle Ages. Coletti[107] suggests that Chaucer in the fourteenth century subtly appropriated a cluster of words, images, and ideas from its Latin version in composing his *Shipman's Tale*. His portrait is of a scheming middle-class couple, not portraying people as they should be, but in irony depicting them as they actually are in their business deals, fine clothes, and extramarital affairs.

Martin Luther, rejecting the allegorical interpretation, repeatedly alludes to texts from Prov 31:10-31 for various proofs that have little to do with understanding the passage itself. Discussing the word "substance," for instance, he observes that the husband who trusts in the strong woman has

---

[102]John Cassian, *Conference* 14.8 (*NPNF*^{2} 11.437).

[103]*Idem*, *Institutes* 10.21 (*NPNF*^{2} 11.274).

[104]Augustine, *Second Discourse on Ps. 26*, 21 (ACW 29.280).

[105]*Idem*, *Sermo 37 de proverbiis*, c. 31 (*PL* 38.221-235).

[106]B. L. Visotzky, "Midrash Eishet Chayil," *Conservative Judaism* 38 (1986), 21-25.

[107]Theresa Coletti, "The *Mulier Fortis* and Chaucer's *Shipman's Tale*," *The Chaucer Review* 15 (1981): 236-49.

no need of the spoils of philosophy.[108] He contrasts the energetic housewife whose "hands hold the spindle" with the idle men who make trouble for him.[109] Luther takes "Her lamp does not go out at night" as referring to the time of death,[110] but elsewhere he argues that "light" in Scripture signifies good fortune or success.[111]

Nevertheless, Luther's basic approach to the poem is literal. Luther identifies the gates where the husband sits with "places where public matters are handled."[112] Commenting on Gen 47:7, he writes

> Solomon means a woman who does her duty as a wife and a good worker, an excellent lady of the house, a housewife who takes care of the house, brings up children, and diligently and promptly performs the function of an honorable and godly matron.[113]

He applies "The heart of her husband trusts in her" to his relation to his own wife.[114] Indeed, in considering the word "domestic," he seems to summarize Prov 31:10-31 as a pattern for a wife.[115] At the same time, Luther was aware

---

[108]Martin Luther, "First Lectures on the Psalms," 69:1 (*Luther's Works* [St. Louis: Concordia, 1974], 10.356).

[109]*Idem*, "Notes on Ecclesiastes," 4:6 (*Luther's Works* 15.66).

[110]*Idem*, "First Lectures on the Psalms," 1:32 (*Luther's Works* 10.18).

[111]*Idem*, "Lectures on Nahum," 1:9 (*Luther's Works*, 18.290); "Lectures on Joel," 2:22 (*Luther's Works* 18.90).

[112]*Idem*, "Lectures on the Psalms," 9:13 (*Luther's Works* 10.95); 118:20 (*Luther's Works* 14:91).

[113]*Idem*, "Lectures on Genesis," 47:7 (*Luther's Works* 8.110).

[114]E. M. Plass, *What Luther Says* (St. Louis: Concordia, 1959), 2:888.

[115]Luther, "Lectures on Titus," 2:5 (*Luther's Works* 29:56). See also "Letter to Hans Luther," Nov. 21, 1519 (*Luther's Works* 48.334).

that Augustine had identified the woman with wisdom,[116] and a gloss to his lectures on Romans remarks, "And concerning His wisdom, it is said that it carries law and mercy on its tongue."[117]

In the sixteenth century, Catherine des Roches gave a paraphrase of the poem honoring her mother as the ideal woman with herself as the one praising her—which justified her own literary career.[118] She depicts by paraphrase a relationship in marriage between equals, describes the wife as supervisor of servant girls, and magnifies the public aspects of her activities. The wife spends her days out in the fields. She identifies with the activities permitted in current society to her class.

C. *Modern Interpretation of Prov 31:10-31*

The crucial question in interpretation is how we are to consider this poem which ostensibly praises the capable wife. At the beginning of the nineteenth century, Adam Clarke, considering the poem to be a model for the ideal wife, suggested that the mother of John and Charles Wesley was the equal to the woman described.[119] Gardner Spring in 1825 used Prov 31:20 as a sermon text preached before the New York Female Mission Society. Alluding to Proverbs, which was understood literally but not exegeted in detail, Spring praised the virtues of diligence and economy as woman's true glory. A critic took exception to his statement, "I know of nothing which a woman may not study and acquire to advantage." The reviewer, who obviously

---

[116]*Idem*, "Lectures on Galatians," 3:22 (*Luther's Works* 27.274; *LCC* 15:109n).

[117]*Idem*, "Lectures on Romans," 3:22-24 (*Luther's Works* 25.31).

[118]Anne R. Larsen, "Legitimizing the Daughter's Writing. Catherine des Roches' Proverbial Good Wife," *Sixteenth Century Journal* 21 (1990): 559-74.

[119]Adam Clarke, *The Holy Bible . . . A Commentary and Critical Notes* (New York and Nashville: Abingdon-Cokesbury Press, 1832): 3.794.

allowed women less liberty, felt that a woman should devote her attention to "the faithful performance of those duties connected with her subordinate station." Spring advocated that women should study "moral science" and gave praise to mothers and women who influenced the young.[120]

Around 1860, Rabbi Meir Leibush Malbin, expounded the poem literally and symbolically. The literal exposition found the husband engaged in Torah studies, explained "the day to come" (v. 25) as transition to the other world, and saw the reward (v. 31) to be in the other world. He also expounded a *darash* on the poem. The woman of valor is a pliant soul which the intellect finds. Various actions or deeds are described as wool and flaxen cloths. Factual, worldly education can be acquired by "trading." The soul cries out of the dark night of earthy existence to give the food of Torah to her household which are the faculties of understanding. The vineyard is the field of study and mental growth. Her household is clothed in the manifold garments of Torah and good deeds. The children are the good deeds performed.[121] Such a *darash* can only be considered by the modern mind as a fantasy of the intellect.

Near the end of the century the allegorical interpretation which saw the woman as the bride, the church (see Rev 21:9), and the husband as Christ became common.[122] The allegorical interpretation by which the woman is a personification of Wisdom has been advocated recently by Jacobs.[123]

---

[120]Review of "The Excellence and Influence of the Female Character," a sermon by Gardner Spring, in *Methodist Review* 8 (1825): 196-99; 223-29; 266-69.

[121]Rabbi Meir Leibush Malbim, *Malbim on Mishley* (ed. C. Wengrov; Jerusalem/New York, Feldheim, 1982), 318-27.

[122]E.g., John Miller, *A Commentary on the Proverbs* (Princeton, NJ: Evangelical Reformed Publication Co, 1887): 533-54.

[123]Edmond Jacobs, "Sagesse et Alphabet: A propos de Proverbes 31.10-31," in *Hommages à André Dupont-Sommer* (ed. A. Caquot and M. Philonenko; Paris: Adrien-Maisonneuve, 1971): 287-95. In the patristic period, see Hilary, "*Tractatus in CXXVII Psalmum*" 9 (*PL*

Toy[124] characterized the Song as "the Alphabetic Ode or 'Golden ABC' of the perfect wife." Oesterley[125] said, "We may well believe that the picture presented reflects what was a reality in many a Jewish home." Hamp[126] saw this picture of the ideal woman as a corresponding one to that of the virtuous man depicted in Job 31. Whybray[127] noted that the whole is viewed from the male viewpoint, and that the poem is possibly a handbook for prospective bridegrooms. Others have thought it was intended to describe the sort of bride a young man should seek.[128] Crook's[129] conjecture, (from Egyptian parallels) that the poem is a paradigm (from the first known school of home economics) for the bride-to-be of a man of influence, has not won acceptance. Crook sees the woman as an ideal that never existed.

Lyons[130] argues that the woman is a wise matriarch patterned from the status of women in pre-monarchial Israel, as is depicted by the mother of Micah (Judg 17:1-4). She, however, does not explain how the husband motif in the poem fits with the widow status of Micah's mother. She conjectures that similar conditions existed again in post-exilic Judah as she tries to accommodate her theory to that of a post-exilic date for the Proverbs making earlier material

---

9.708), and Ambrose, *De Joseph Patriarcha* 76 (*PL* 14.702), *De Tobia* 77 (*PL* 14:826).

[124]Toy, *A Critical and Exegetical Commentary*, 542.

[125]Oesterley, *The Book of Proverbs*, 287.

[126]V. Hamp, *Das Buch der Sprüche* (Echter Bibel 4; Würzburg: Echter-Verlag, 1959): 502.

[127]R. N. Whybray, *The Book of Proverbs* (Cambridge: Cambridge Univ. Press, 1972): 184.

[128]Garrett, *Proverbs*, 248.

[129]M. B. Crook, "The Marriageable Maiden of Prov. 31:10-31," *JNES* 12 (1954): 139.

[130]E. L. Lyons, "A Note on Proverbs 31:10-31," *The Listening Heart. Essays in Wisdom and the Psalms in Honor of Roland E. Murphy* (ed. K. G. Hogland, Elizabeth F. Huwiler, J. T. Glass, and R. W. Lee; JSOTSup 58; Sheffield: JSOT Press, 1987): 237-245.

relevant again. Emmerson[131] notes, "The efficient wife of Prov 31:10-31 is no downtrodden creature, but self-confident and outgoing, and this is not merely an individual but an ideal to be followed."

McKane considers that the writer is describing "a recognizable and credible portrait of a particular kind of woman.[132] While K. T. Aitken thinks the poem gives an insight into the place of women in the Israelite family, reference is to the woman of the "upper class," not a blueprint for the ideal Israelite housewife at that time, nor one for the ideal housewife in Western society.[133]

McLees, finding in an Amish woman the contentment of knowing her place in the world, saw in Proverbs and the Amish woman "a wholeness or integrity of life and belief that is a hallmark of Christian womanhood."[134] McLees advocates that one "begin to embody these [Christian] beliefs in the way we live."[135] She sees the woman of Proverbs knowing what she believes in. Willing work in ordinary things ennobles her and them. McLees sees in the modern world the ideal values of housewifery and husbandry replaced by the demands of the consumer economy.[136] She extols the ability to do common things well. The woman of Proverbs knows who she is, a trait McLees found missing in much of modern life.[137]

---

[131]G. I. Emmerson, "Women in Ancient Israel," *The World of Ancient Israel* (ed. R. E. Clements; Cambridge: Cambridge Univ. Press, 1989): 381.

[132]McKane, *Proverbs*, 665-70.

[133]Kenneth T. Aitken, *Proverbs* (Philadelphia: Westminster, 1986): 158.

[134]McLees, *Epiphany* (1986): 22.

[135]*Ibid.*

[136]*Ibid.*, 23.

[137]*Ibid.*, 24.

Metlitzki,[138] annoyed at the traditional interpretation of the poem as depicting "the ideal housewife," asserts that the picture "is much more than an 'ideal housewife.' It is a picture of a human being who exemplifies the meaning of wisdom as the art of life, the art of going about the business of living in this world in the right relation to one's tasks and fellow creatures."

In a quite different tack, because Wisdom in the Proverbs is personified as a human female with many of the traits of the wife (Wis 7:12-22; Sir 1:6-20), some have conjectured that chap. 31 was intended to depict personified Wisdom.[139]

The most extended statement of this case is that of McCreesh, who largely argues from parallels of vocabulary.[140] He considers that the poem is a coda for the whole book summarizing major motifs and ideas. Wisdom is the good wife. McCreesh's case enjoys a vogue at the present with agreement from Farmer[141] and others.[142] Wolters[143] has offered a defense of the case by arguing that the word צוֹפִיָּה (*tsopiyya*; she looks well; v. 27) is intended as a play on σοφία (*sophia*; wisdom).

---

[138]Dorothée Metlitzki, "A Woman of Virtue. A Note on *Eset Hakyil*," *Orim* 1 (1986): 23-26.

[139]Camp, *Wisdom*, 188-90.

[140]Thomas P. McCreesh, "Wisdom as Wife: Proverbs 31:10-31," *RB* 92 (1985): 25-46.

[141]J. A. Farmer, *Proverbs and Ecclesiastes* (ITC; Grand Rapids: Eerdmans, 1991): 124-27.

[142]"She is no less than Woman Wisdom made real," Garrett, *Proverbs*, 252. She "is not simply an ideal portrait of some man's dream but also represents a universal type of wisdom," Camp, *Wisdom*, 92-93. See also J. N. Aletti, "Seduction et Parole in Proverbes i-ix," *VT* 27 (1977): 144.

[143]Al Wolters, "*Sopiyya* (Prov 31:27) as Hymnic Participle and Play on *Sophia*," *JBL* 104 (1985): 577-87.

However, while wisdom builds her house of seven pillars (Prov 9:1-6), the house of the capable woman is not a palace of seven pillars.[144] The book begins and ends with notice of the fear of the Lord (Prov 1:7; 31:30). One feels that the value of occurrences of parallel vocabulary has been stretched beyond its legitimate limits in arguing the case. Furthermore, if the poem is a personification of Lady Wisdom, is it not redundant to say that she (Wisdom) opens her mouth with wisdom (v. 26)? In addition to stressing the similarities, one should also notice the differences. Mother imagery is not applied to wisdom in the book,[145] but the capable woman has children. The love motif of chaps. 1-9 is not present. Rather than being praised in the gates, Wisdom cries out there (Prov 1:21; 8:3).

After all hypotheses are expounded, if the writer described what was completely foreign to his culture and life, he would not have been understood. One may recall Miriam, Deborah, Ruth, Abigail, the Shunammite, and Huldah as Israelite women. While the specific activities of the Capable Wife are time and culturally conditioned, her virtues of trustworthiness, diligence, thrift, resourcefulness, and fear of the Lord are timeless and universally valid.[146]

---

[144]A. Barucq, "Proverbes (Livre des)," *Supplement au Dictionnaire de la Bible*, 8.1466.

[145]Camp, *Wisdom*, 82.

[146]A popular level homiletical treatment of the poem is Darlene Craig, *A Worthy Woman* (Salem, OR: Valor, 1983). The feminist, Patricia Gundry, *The Complete Woman* (Garden City, NY: Doubleday, 1981), has used the phrases of Prov 31:1-31 as headings for expounding her ideas of modern womanhood.

Chapter Eight

A NOTE ON LUKE 18:29-30

John McRay and Carroll D. Osburn

Truly I say to you, there is no man who has left house or wife or brothers or parents or children, for the sake of the kingdom of God, who will not receive manifold more in this time, and in the age to come eternal life (Luke 18:29-30, RSV).

In current discussion of the place of women in the ministry of Christ, Luke 18:29-30 has been largely neglected.[1] However, Heine[2] mentions this text in arguing that, "a striking feature of the Jesus tradition is its marked hostility to the family." Comparing the Jesus group with

---

[1] This text is omitted in such representative works as Carol A. Newsom and Sharon H. Ringe, ed., *The Women's Bible Commentary* (Louisville: Westminster/John Knox, 1992); Elisabeth Schüssler Fiorenza, *In Memory of Her* (New York: Crossroad, 1983); Ben Witherington III, *Women in the Earliest Churches* (SNTSMS 59; Cambridge: Cambridge Univ. Press, 1988); Virginia R. Mollenkott, *Women, Men and the Bible* (New York: Crossroad, 1992); Letha D. Scanzoni and Nancy A. Hardesty, *All We're Meant to Be: Biblical Feminism for Today* (3rd ed.; Grand Rapids: Eerdmans, 1992); Gilbert Bilezikian, *Beyond Sex Roles* (2nd ed.; Grand Rapids: Baker, 1985); Aida Besançon Spencer, *Beyond the Curse: Women Called to Ministry* (Nashville: T. Nelson, 1985); Evelyn and Frank Stagg, *Woman in the World of Jesus* (Philadelphia: Westminster, 1978); James B. Hurley, *Man and Woman in Biblical Perspective* (Grand Rapids: Zondervan, 1981); Werner Neuer, *Man & Woman in Christian Perspective* (trans. G. J. Wenham; Wheaton: Crossway, 1991); and John Piper and Wayne Grudem, ed., *Recovering Biblical Manhood & Womanhood: A Response to Evangelical Feminism* (Wheaton: Crossway, 1991).

[2] Susanne Heine, *Women and Early Christianity: A Reappraisal* (trans. J. Bowden; Minneapolis: Augsburg, 1988): 62-64.

"the life-style of itinerant Cynic philosophers who also went through the land and lived unmarried" provides "basis for supposing that the Jesus group did not marry."[3] "The best evidence," she says, for early Christians "leaving wives is in Luke." This thesis "is confirmed above all by Luke, who, in contrast to Mark (10:29), also mentions wives among those who are abandoned (18:29; 14:26)."[4] She continues, regarding Luke 18:29,

> The history of the text, as in the parallels in Mark and Matthew, shows that at this point there has been a good deal of tinkering around, as if not all the tradents were sure whether the wife should be abandoned along with all the other members of the family.

On the other hand, Marshall[5] notes that Luke has in mind the possible disruption of family relationships which may result from discipleship.

A significant question exists, then, concerning Luke's portrayal of women. Did discipleship, in Jesus' view, demand the abandonment of wives, as Heine suggests?

---

[3]Heine, *Women and Early Christianity*, 64, is reliant upon Gerd Theissen, *The First Followers of Jesus: A Sociological Analysis of the Earliest Christianity* (trans. J. Bowden; London: SCM, 1978).

[4]*Ibid.* The view that Jesus had a negative view toward family relationships is an old one. Ernest Renan, *La Vie de Jésus* (2nd ed.; Paris: Calmann Lévy, 1864): *passim*; [ET *The Life of Jesus* (New York: Random House, 1927)], notes that Jesus rebelled against parental authority as a child and as an adult was harsh to his relatives, thus breaking with his family to form a new support group. The view of Renan was countered by F. D. Maurice, *The Gospel of the Kingdom of Heaven* (London: Macmillan, 1888): 36, et al. Recently, Ferdinand Mount, *The Subversive Family* (London: Unwin, 1982): 3, 15-28, lists Jesus among other nationalistic demagogues whose view toward the family is negative. Cf. the response of Ieuan Ellis, "Jesus and the Subversive Family," *SJT* 38 (1985): 173-88.

[5]I. Howard Marshall, *The Gospel of Luke* (NIGTC; Grand Rapids: Eerdmans, 1978): 459.

1. *The Text of Luke 18:29-30*

These words of Jesus occur at the conclusion of a story about a man who came to him and asked what he needed to do to inherit eternal life (18:18-30). He was a man of wealth who would not leave what he had in order to follow Jesus, a sad fact which prompted Jesus to inform those standing nearby that it is easier for a camel to go through the eye of a needle than for a rich man to enter the kingdom of heaven. The astonished listeners exclaimed, "Who then can be saved?" This prompted Peter to respond that they had left τὰ ἴδια (their own possessions) and followed him. The RSV and NRSV render "homes," but the NIV appropriately reads "all we had." Some manuscripts from each of the three major textual traditions substitute πάντα (all things) for "own possessions." It seems obvious that this reading in ℵ A W Ψ 33 𝔐 it^f vulg syr$^{p.h}$ arose from the influence of the parallels in Matt 19:27 and Mark 10:28.

At this point, Jesus said that those who had left all their possessions would receive many times more in this age, as well as eternal life in the age to come. It is interesting that the parallel stories in Matthew and Mark have Jesus speaking from a seeming masculine perspective:

> And *everyone* (πᾶς ὅστις, masculine gender) who has left houses or brothers or fields, for my name's sake, will receive a hundredfold, and will inherit eternal life (Matt 19:29, NRSV).

> Jesus, said "Truly I tell you, there is *no one* (οὐδείς ἐστιν ὅς, masculine gender) who has left house or brothers or sisters or mother or father or children or fields, for my sake and for the sake of the good news, who will not receive a hundredfold now in this age—houses, brothers and sisters, mothers and children, and fields with persecutions—and in the age to come eternal life (Mark 10:29, NRSV).

However, the masculine gender in the ancient world, as in our modern world, was often inclusive of both genders. And there is nothing in either Matthew or Mark which indicates whether the person who leaves family and possessions to follow Jesus is, in this instance, a male or female. At this point, however, Luke injects into the story the word γυναῖκα (wife) in place of sister, as well as "parents" in the place of "father and mother."[6]

Matthew	Mark	Luke
houses	house	house
or brothers	and brothers	or wife
or sisters	and sisters	or brothers
or father	and mother	or parents
or mother	and father	
or children	and children	or children
or fields	and fields	

The occurrences of γυναῖκα (wife) after "mother" at Matt 19:29 in ℵ C L W Δ Θ f^{13} 𝔐 [incl. E F G H Σ TR KJV] syr$^{(c).p.h}$ cop$^{sa.bo}$ arm eth geo slav Bas GregNyss Cyr Amb Jer, as well as after "father" in Mark 10:29 in A C Ψ f^{13} 𝔐 it^f syr$^{p.h}$ cop$^{bo(mss)}$ [TR KJV], seem to be the result of later scribal assimilation to the Lucan parallel.[7] Similarly, the reading "parents or brothers *or sisters* or wife"

---

[6]See Erich Klostermann, *Das Lukasevangelium* (HNT; 2nd ed.; Tübingen: J. C. B. Mohr, 1929): 182-83.

[7]See *The New Testament in Greek: The Gospel According to St. Luke* (ed. by the International Greek New Testament Project; Oxford: Clarendon, 1984): 2.104-105, for an extensive critical apparatus. Bruce M. Metzger, *A Textual Commentary on the Greek New Testament* (corr. ed.; London: United Bible Societies, 1975): 50, notes that the replacement of "father and mother" by "parents" in ms 1 in Matt 19:29 may reflect similar influence from the same parallel, but could have arisen independently. Metzger also notes that the absence of "father" in several Old Latin witnesses appears to be the result of homoeoteleuton. There is no indication of textual variation at Mark 10:29 in *UBS Greek NT* (4th ed.; Stuttgart: Deutsche Bibelgesellschaft, 1993), nor is there comment on that text in Metzger, *Textual Commentary on the Greek New Testament*, 106.

in D X Δ Ψ *et al.* at Luke 18:29 appears to be the result of scribal assimilation to the Matthaean and/or Markan parallels. The omission of "and children" by Δ at Mark 10:29 and by cop^{sa} at Luke 18:29 seems accidental. While the omission of "and fields" by Ψ at Mark 10:29 could be accidental, there is the possibility of a theologically-motivated alteration to minimize the prospect of material reward. The perspective in Luke, then, is unmistakably that of a husband leaving his wife.

2. *The Interpretation of Luke 18:29-30*

It may be useful to preface the discussion of Luke 18:19-20 with a note regarding Farmer's[8] view, based on the priority of Matthew, that Luke structured the text of Luke 18:29-30 as he did in support of persecuted Christians, explaining that the "sociological ground for the Jewish persecution of Christians in Matthew is religious," but that in Luke "the sociological ground for persecution of Christians is more political than religious."

Farmer stresses that in Matthew the disciples are instructed to admonish the Gentiles to keep the law, even down to the smallest detail (see Matt 5:17-20). In Luke, on the other hand, there is no such dominical command to keep the law. In the diaspora, Christians had no legal standing other than being perceived as Jews. However, Christian claims to be heirs of the promises in the Law and Prophets—and thus to claim privileges of religion in the eyes of Roman authorities—engendered rage and envy among Jews, since most Gentile Christians were not circumcised as a sign of the covenant. So, Farmer contends, in view of the malicious adversaries among the Jews of the diaspora, it was "necessary for Luke to prove that Christian claims to the promises of the Law and the Prophets were just and valid ones" (153). Consequently, as in other texts, such as Luke

---

[8]W. R. Farmer, "The Two-Gospel Hypothesis," *The Interrelations of the Gospels* (BETL 95; Leuven: Leuven Univ. Press, 1990): 152-153.

6:20-23, 12:4-12, and 21:12-19, where participation in the kingdom is stressed in a context of persection, in 18:29-30 "for the sake of the kingdom of God" validates this radical call to discipleship.

Alternatively, Fitzmyer[9] contends that Luke has derived the material for this episode from Mark 10:23-31, with its counterpart being Matt 19:23-30. In addition to several modifications of the Marcan text in vv. 24-27, Luke further alters Peter's comment to Jesus in v. 28, substituting τὰ ἴδια (what we had) for the Marcan πάντα (all things). Luke then alters the list of things to be renounced by substituting the motivation, "for the sake of the kingdom of God," for the Marcan "because of me and because of the gospel." With regard to reward, Luke deletes "with persecutions." "The upshot," Fitzmyer notes (1202), "is that Luke has curtailed the Marcan form of this episode, but he has scarcely 'greatly weakened' it."[10]

A. *Destruction of existing marriage.* Initially, it may be observed that Heine[11] does not argue the existence of "wandering charismatics" in the early church, but merely assumes the thesis of Theissen. Theissen's[12] theory of early

---

[9]Joseph A. Fitzmyer, *The Gospel According to Luke (X-XXIV)* (AB; Garden City, NY: Doubleday, 1985): 1202. See also T. Schramm, *Der Markus-Stoff bei Lukas: Eine literarkritische und redaktionsgeschichtliche Untersuchung* (SNTSMS 14; Cambridge: Cambridge Univ. Press, 1971): 142; and Frederick W. Danker, *Jesus and the New Age: A Commentary on St. Luke's Gospel* (Philadelphia: Fortress, 1988): 301.

[10]Cf. John M. Creed, *The Gospel According to St. Luke* (London: Macmillan, 1953): 226, who detects here, "a greatly weakened version of Mk x.23-27."

[11]Heine, *Women and Early Christianity*, 64-65. Also assuming Theissen's thesis of "wandering charismatics" is Philip Francis Esler, *Community and Gospel in Luke-Acts: The Social and Political Motivations of Lucan Theology* (SNTSMS 57; Cambridge: Cambridge Univ. Press, 1987): 118.

[12]See Gerd Theissen, *The Sociology of Early Palestinian Christianity* (trans. J. Bowden; Philadelphia: Fortress, 1978): 8-16.

Christianity is based on the existence and importance of "wandering charismatics" who are defined by the four characteristics of homelessness, lack of family ties, lack of possessions, and lack of security and protection. While Theissen does not refer to Luke 18:29-30, he does cite Mark 10:29 and Luke 14:26 as meaning that they had left their families. Theissen observes, "Of course the members of the Jesus movement defended themselves against the charge of having a completely negative attitude towards the family," and cites Luke 8:19-21; 22:28ff.; and Mark 10:30 as reflective of their reshaping of the concept of the family.[13] It was simply understood, according to Theissen, that "this sort of thing was part of the tribulations of the last days and therefore was a necessity (Luke 12:52f.; Matt 10:20)."[14]

However, Theissen's theory of *Wanderradikalismus* has been seriously challenged. Harvey[15] argued that while the existence of wandering charismatics may be granted in an instance or two, "there is no evidence that it acquired anything like the importance which is implied by Theissen's theory." Regarding Theissen's triad of "wandering charismatics," the support group behind them, and Jesus as Son of Man (their role model), Malina[16] points out that, "To say that other groups formed similar patterns is no explanation." The same could be said for Schottroff's[17] suggested relationship between the followers of Jesus and wandering Cynics. Further, regarding Theissen's description of factors, Malina notes that Theissen "offers no cross-cultural models to generate heuristic explanations of the factors that he describes." Malina concludes that the sociological models to

---

[13]Theissen, *Sociology of Early Palestinian Christianity*, 12.

[14]*Ibid.*

[15]A. E. Harvey, "Review of Theissen, *The First Followers of Jesus*," *JTS* 30 (1979): 282.

[16]Bruce J. Malina, "Review of Theissen, *Sociology of Early Palestinian Christianity*," *CBQ* 41 (1979): 177-78.

[17]See Luise Schottroff, "Frauen in der Nachfolge Jesu in neutestamentlicher Zeit," *Traditionen der Befreiung: Sozialgeschichtliche Bibelauslegungen* (ed. W. Schottroff and W. Stegemann; Munich: Chr. Kaiser, 1980): 2.91-133, esp. 122.

which Theissen refers "are simply inadequate for the data he seeks to explain." Kraemer[18] observes, "Theissen creates the erroneous impression that he has derived his theoretical models from early Christian sources . . . [but] this is not the case." Heine's uncritical acceptance of the intriguing, but unfounded, "wandering charismatic" thesis proposed by Theissen renders unacceptable her view of Luke 18:29-30 as reflecting hostility to the family.

B. *Disruption of family relationships.* The thought of Luke 18:29-30, according to Marshall,[19] is rather one,

> of the possible disruption of family relationships (12.52f.; 14:26) which may result from discipleship. If so, the idea of material loss and reward is not present in Lk., possibly because he wished to avoid the idea of material reward for disciples.

---

[18]Ross S. Kraemer, "Review of Theissen, *Sociology of Early Palestinian Christianity, JBL* 98 (1979): 437. See also admonitions to caution regarding Theissen's work in Robin Scroggs, "The Sociological Interpretation of the New Testament: The Present State of Research," *NTS* 26 (1980): 164-179.

[19]Marshall, *The Gospel of Luke*, 459. See also Martin Dibelius, *Jesus* (trans. C. Hedrick and F. C. Grant; Philadelphia: Westminster, 1949): 60-61. Alternatively, Marshall, *The Gospel of Luke*, 688, followed by Robert H. Stein, *Luke* (NAC 24; Nashville: Broadman, 1992): 459, proposes that the inclusion of "wife" in the list, as in the list in 14:26, "may be of renouncing the possibility of marriage rather than the breaking up of an existing marriage," as in Matt 19:10-12 (Mark 10:11-12). Heine's, *Women and Early Christianity*, 65, argument, that the prohibition against putting away one's wife cannot "be cited in the case of the praxis of the Jesus group, as this text is not in the context of discipleship," is more than curious, for in this section of Mark the theme of discipleship is actually focused. See among others Morna Hooker, *The Message of Mark* (London: Epworth, 1983): 109-110; Jack Dean Kingsbury, *Conflict in Mark* (Minneapolis: Fortress, 1989): 103-104. See also Martin Hengel, *Studies in the Gospel of Mark* (Philadelphia: Fortress, 1985); Ernest Best, *Following Jesus: Discipleship in the Gospel of Mark* (JSNTSup 4; Sheffield: JSOT Press, 1981); and Frank J. Matera, *What Are They Saying About Mark?* (New York: Paulist Press, 1987).

Now that the apostles had wives who were not abandoned, but shared in their lives seems clear from 1 Cor 9:5.[20] As Evans[21] suggests: "Luke has modified Mark probably because he wishes to avoid the idea that the disciples are motivated to follow Jesus because they hope for a material reward in this life." Manson[22] observed that this lends itself to a spiritual interpretation of the text. Talbert[23] explains,

> The principle is that one gives everything to God and then receives back from him what he wants to give. Luke, unlike Mark 10:30 and Matt 19:29, does not promise wealth but only community ("house" in v. 29 refers to family; "wife, brothers, parents, and children" to various parts of the family). The evangelist does not connect prosperity with piety in any kind of necessary cause and effect relationship. . . . This raises the issue of the larger biblical perspective about wealth and poverty.

Johnson[24] concludes,

> It is just as hard to leave family and friends and boats and tax collector's booth, as it is to leave "great wealth" when it means throwing one's life completely over to God in faith. The words of promise concerning those who have left all such things, therefore, stands as surety for what was told the ruler: giving away possessions makes a "treasure in heaven."

---

[20]See A. R. C. Leaney, *The Gospel According to Luke* (London: A. & C. Black, 1958): 237.

[21]Craig A. Evans, *Luke* (NIBC; Peabody, MA: Hendricksen, 1990): 274.

[22]William Manson, *The Gospel of Luke* (MNTC; London: Hodder and Stoughton, 1930): 207.

[23]Charles Talbert, *Reading Luke: A Literary and Theological Commentary on the Third Gospel* (New York: Crossroad, 1992): 173. See Leon Morris, *Luke* (TNTC; Grand Rapids: Eerdmans, 1989): 294.

[24]Luke Timothy Johnson, *The Gospel of Luke* (SP 3; Collegeville, MN: Liturgical Press, 1991): 281.

Danker[25] correctly notes that, when the materialist (18:18) declines to participate in the kingdom in its present form, he excludes himself from participating in its final phase as well. The parallel with the disciples is that those who sacrifice in the interest of the kingdom receive more "in this time" and "eternal life" is theirs in the future. Thus, in Luke a decision to "follow" Jesus requires "endurance" (8:15), because participation in his mission will cause division in households (12:49-53); however, those who choose to participate fully in the mission will find a new support system (8:21; Acts 2:44-47; 4:32).

3. The Other Lucan "Abandonment" Texts

A. *Luke 12:49-53.* Luke 12:1-53, which begins with an exhortation to courage in the face of tribulation and continues with a warning against greed, is climaxed by a paragraph that explicitly raises the issue of judgment. Whether addressed to the disciples[26] or to the crowds,[27] the prophetic challenge anticipated by Simeon (2:34-35)[28] and John the Baptist (3:16-17)[29] is articulated by Jesus himself—"they will be divided, father against son and son against father, mother against daughter and daughter against mother." This Lucan text, according to Danker,[30] "challenges ideals that

---

[25]Frederick W. Danker, *Luke* (Philadelphia: Fortress, 1987): 21.

[26]Talbert, *Reading Luke*, 144.

[27]Johnson, *The Gospel of Luke*, 209; and Eric Franklin, *Christ the Lord: A Study in the Purpose and Theology of Luke-Acts* (Philadelphia: Westminster, 1975): 151.

[28]On 2:34-35, Earle Ellis, *The Gospel of Luke* (rev. ed.; Greenwood, SC: Attic, 1974): 182, notes, "The call for decision is a call for 'division'."

[29]Ellis, *The Gospel of Luke*, 182, thinks "fire" in v. 49 refers to the outpouring of the Holy Spirit (Acts 2:3) in terms of "tongues of fire," but Evans, *Luke*, 199, appears correct in observing that in this context "fire" refers to judgment, as in 3:16-17.

[30]Danker, *Jesus and the New Age*, 272. See e.g., *idem*, *Benefactor: Epigraphic Study of a Graeco-Roman Semantic Field* (St. Louis: Clayton, 1982): 181, where a devotee of Isis says, "You saw to it that parents were honored by their children."

found expression across Mediterranean culture." As Fitzmyer[31] observes, "The Lucan Jesus has come during the era of Augustan peace, as a sign of peace among human beings. . . . Yet his ministry is now described by him as a source of discord among the very people he came to serve and save." This may allude to Mic 7:6, which reads, "A son treats his father with contempt, a daughter rises up against her mother, a daughter-in-law against her mother-in-law; a man's enemies are those of his own household."[32] In fact, there is a whole series of texts both in the OT and apocalyptic literature which speak of intra-family conflict as a sign of the End. Black[33] cites Jub 23:16, 19,

> and in that generation the sons will convict their fathers and their elders of sin and unrighteousness. . . . and they will strive with one another, the young with the old, and the old with the young,

and *m. Sota* 9, 15, "with the footprints of the Messiah presumption shall increase. . . . Children shall shame the elders and the elders shall rise up before the children, 'for the son dishonoreth . . .'" (Mic 7:6). One might add 1 Enoch 99:5, "in those days . . . they will abandon their children (that are still) sucklings, and not return to them, and shall have no pity on their beloved ones," and 1 Enoch 100:1-2, "in those days . . . a man shall not withhold his hand from slaying his sons and his sons' sons, and the sinner shall not withhold his hand from his honored brother."

---

[31] Fitzmyer, *The Gospel According to Luke (X-XXIV)*, 995.

[32] See I. Ellis, *SJT* (1985): 179, for the view that, when making a special vow as a Nazarite, one is *separated* to the Lord and may not go near a dead body, even that of a close family member (Num 6:7), and that it is in this context that Jesus' warnings of division must be understood.

[33] Matthew Black, "'Not Peace but a Sword': Matt 10:34ff; Luke 12:51ff," *Jesus and the Politics of His Day* (ed. E. Bammel and C. F. D. Moule; Cambridge: Cambridge Univ. Press, 1984): 288.

Such division, according to Johnson,[34] "is created by the diverse decisions made in response to the prophet himself and his message about the kingdom of God." It is important to note, as Marshall[35] observes, that the saying in 12:53 suggests to the disciples that "a time of fulfillment is at hand, the result of which, however, will be persecution; it is in that situation that the summons to faithfulness in the preceding section takes on especial relevance and stringency." When faced with a conflict of loyalty, Jesus' disciples are asked to give priority to requirements of the kingdom, whatever the cost.

B. *Luke 14:26.* In 14:26, Luke includes a statement of Jesus similar to the one in 18:29-30, only more compelling in its demands. "If anyone comes to me and does not hate his father and mother, his wife and children, his brothers and sisters—yes, even his own life—he cannot be my disciple" (NIV). Here, as in the later passage, Luke includes the word "wife," but not "husband," making it clear that Jesus spoke from a masculine perspective on this occasion.

---

[34]Johnson, *The Gospel of Luke*, 209. See also Robert C. Tannehill, *The Narrative Unity of Luke-Acts: A Literary Interpretation* (Philadelphia: Fortress, 1986): 1.252-53. Cf. S. G. F. Brandon, *Jesus and the Zealots* (Manchester: Manchester Univ. Press, 1967): 320-21, who detects in this text lingering traces of Jesus the political zealot that have escaped the modification of Jesus by the successive evangelists into the "pacific Christ." See also idem, "Jesus and the Zealots: A Correction," *NTS* 17 (1971): 453. F. W. Beare, *The Earliest Records of Jesus* (Oxford: Blackwell, 1962): 229, observes, ". . . some astray Zealot phrases have somehow intruded their way into the Gospel record." With a different approach, yet similar result, Rudolf Bultmann, *Die Geschichte der synoptischen Tradition* (5th ed.; Göttingen: Vandenhoeck und Ruprecht, 1961): 166, explains the words as a community saying. Cf. however, Stephen Neill and Tom Wright, *The Interpretation of the New Testament 1861-1986* (2nd ed.; Oxford: Oxford Univ. Press, 1988): 357. Alternatively, Otto Betz, "Jesu heiliger Krieg," *NovT* 2 (1958): 116ff., understands the "zealotic" phrases not to be against Rome, but against Belial, the strong one (Matt 12:29), when the godless will be destroyed in the final holy war of the last days occurs—and even families will be torn apart.

[35]Marshall, *The Gospel of Luke*, 545.

Michel[36] suggests that the requirement in Luke 14:26 is not to hate in the psychological sense, but a warning not to love anyone or anything more.[37] This abnegation, Michel argues, is not to be taken fanatically, but christocentrically. It may well be, as Marshall[38] posits, that lying behind this text is Deut 33:9:

> He said of his father and mother,
>   "I have no regard for them."
> He did not recognize his brothers
>   or acknowledge his own children,
> but he watched over your word
>   and guarded your covenant.

As Luke reads one clause with seven objects, Grundmann[39] thinks that the wording may be a secondary expansion. Regarding the inclusion of "wife," Marshall[40] concludes

---

[36] Otto Michel, "μισέω," *TDNT* 4.690-91. See also M.-J. Lagrange, *Evangile selon Luc* (Paris: Victor Lecoffre, 1921): 408-09.

[37] It may be noted in passing that Leif E. Vaage, "Q¹ and the Historical Jesus: Some Peculiar Sayings (7:33-34; 9:57-58, 59-60; 14:26-27)," *Foundations & Facets Forum* 5,2 (June 1989): 159-176, has not been able to avoid whimsical supposition in deducing from the texts that Jesus' peculiarities include being a "real party animal," "a bit of a hellion," "a bit raucous," "shiftless," and "shameless." He adds, "Luke 9:59-60, 14:26 makes going with Jesus a matter of going against familial bonds," which is not to be unexpected from one noted for such "outrageous behavior." Consequently, Vaage notes, such passages are to be viewed as accurate depictions of the peculiarity of the historical Jesus. Reflecting a Jesus Seminar viewpoint, Vaage notes: "The man emerges here as neither apocalyptical seer nor sapiential sage. He was rather a bit of an imp, in Socrates' terms a social gad-fly, an irritant on the skin of conventional mores and values, a marginal figure in the provincial context of Galilee and Judea whose style of life and appeal to others was to go a different way than the 'normal' one" (175).

[38] Marshall, *The Gospel of Luke*, 592. Stein, *Luke*, 397, posits a love/hate dichotomy from Gen 29:30-31, where Jacob loves Rachel and hates Leah, and mentions also Deut 21:15-17, but is less convincing.

[39] Walter Grundmann, *Das Evangelium nach Lukas* (THKNT; Berlin: Evangelische Verlagsanstalt, 1966): 302.

[40] Marshall, *The Gospel of Luke*, 592.

that, "it is unlikely that we should see a deliberate Lucan theme here, and more probable that he is stressing the link with 14:20." In the parable of the great banquet (14:15-24), all three excuses offered for refusing the invitation involve commercial and family life. Johnson[41] observes that,

> By attaching these sayings to the parable of the banquet, Luke has not only established a literary connection between them; he has again effectively symbolized the pattern of the acceptance and rejection of the Prophet through the language of possessions.

Luke follows a consistent pattern in this section of alternating sayings of rejection, calls to conversion, and teachings on discipleship. In this regard, Johnson[42] notes that having concluded the parable with a sombre verdict on those originally invited, Jesus turns his attention to the crowds in v. 25 and repeats the same warning to those who contemplate following him. Hence, Luke 14:26 is to be taken as hyperbolical, i.e., entanglement with persons and things can, in effect, be a refusal of the invitation to discipleship.[43] Malina and Neyrey[44] observe that "Honor your father and mother" is honorable behavior for most Jews in Jesus' world (Luke 18:20), but in certain circumstances, an offspring might be informed that unless he "hates his father and mother" (14:26) he cannot have honor as a disciple of Jesus. In this instance, honor is valued, but precisely what constitutes honor varies according to the situation, reversing the values, as Luke 18:20 and 14:26 illustrate. The focus is

---

[41]Luke Timothy Johnson, *The Literary Function of Possessions in Luke-Acts* (SBLDS 39; Atlanta: Scholars Press, 1977): 147. See also Robert H. Stein, "Luke 14:26 and the Question of Authenticity," *Foundations and Facets Forum* 5,2 (June 1989): 187-92, esp. 190-91.

[42]Johnson, *The Gospel of Luke*, 232-33.

[43]Evans, *Luke*, 229, sees the text as "forceful exaggeration." See also Johnson, *The Gospel of Luke*, 232-33.

[44]See Bruce Malina and Jerome Neyrey, "Honor and Shame in Luke-Acts: Pivotal Values of the Mediterranean World," *The Social World of Luke-Acts* (ed. J. Neyrey; Peabody, MA: Hendrickson, 1991): 26-27.

on one's preference for Jesus over all relationships (14:26), including one's wife, and all of one's possessions (14:33).

Conclusion

We conclude, then, that Heine's proposal that the Jesus tradition exhibits a marked hostility to the family by mandating an unmarried lifestyle is not supported by Luke 18:29-30, nor is it a necessary conclusion to be drawn from other Lucan passages, such as 12:49-53 and 14:26.[45]

Black[46] has presented a strong case that Luke is seeking neither to enhance nor to suppress the social position of women. Rather, Luke's strong interest in the "Restoration of Israel" theme, as evidenced in the Joel 2 quotation in Peter's Pentecost sermon in Acts 2, makes explicit that both men and women participate in the salvation experience.[47]

As Jesus inaugurates the new movement on his home soil, Dibelius[48] says,

---

[45]Marcion's asceticism appears based upon a disordered sexuality. See E. C. Blackman, *Marcion and His Influence* (London: SPCK, 1948): 104-05; Hendrik F. Stander, "Marcion," *Encyclopedia of Early Christianity* (ed. E. Ferguson; New York: Garland, 1990): 568-569; and James E. Goehring, "Asceticism," *Encyclopedia of Early Christianity*, 104-07.

[46]Allen Black, "Women in the Gospel of Luke," *Essays on Women in Earliest Christianity* (ed. C. Osburn; Joplin, MO: College Press, 1993): 1.445-68. Cf. Leonard Swidler, *Biblical Affirmations of Women* (Philadelphia: Westminster, 1979): 170-71, 280, who argues that both Jesus and Luke wished to liberate women from the oppressive Jewish system. On the other hand, Elisabeth Schüssler Fiorenza, "A Feminist Critical Interpretation for Liberation. Martha and Mary. Luke 10:38-42," *Religion and Intellectual Life* 3 (1986): 21-36; and Elizabeth Tetlow, *Women and Ministry* (New York: Paulist, 1908): 101-108, think Luke attempted to suppress the activities of women in the churches of his time.

[47]Black, "Women in Luke," *Essays on Women in Earliest Christianity*, 1.466-67, stresses the male/female pairings in Isa 40-66 as foundational for the substructure of Luke's thinking.

[48]Dibelius, *Jesus*, 58-60.

he travels from place to place surrounded by his group of disciples. But in the places that he touches he leaves behind a larger circle of adherents—people who remain in their families and at their work, but are nevertheless ready to testify to Jesus' cause. The command of poverty, the watchword to "follow" Jesus on his journeyings, holds good only for the inner group of *disciples*; it states the presuppositions of their existence. . . . The names of the disciples in the Gospels exceed the limit of the figure 12; several women, and perhaps still others (Acts 1:21), belong to the list. . . . For most of the inner circle of followers of Jesus the step from ordinary life to an itinerant one was not attended with such great sacrifices. For what they gave up was the poor and narrow life of fishermen, farmers, craftsmen, or publicans. What they got in exchange was an equally poor but free life of constant journeying. Its poverty was not a practice of asceticism, but was the condition of their participation in this movement inaugurated by Jesus. Its features were preaching in the open air, in houses, in synagogues, the healing of the sick, and constant journeying—then repetition of the same activity in another place, and so on through Galilee and the neighboring regions.

More important than the question of gender in these Lucan passages is the stringent demand of discipleship set forward. Rather than being viewed as either pro- or anti-feminist, Luke is to be seen as involving both men and women in the Restoration. In this connection, Luke 18:29-30 serves, not to denigrate marital or family relationships by a call to celibacy, but to specify the possible disruption of family relationships which may result from the acceptance of the call to join his inner group of itinerant disciples (Luke 9:23).

Chapter Nine

WOMEN IN THE GOSPEL OF JOHN

Frank Wheeler

The Gospel of John portrays women as maintaining their normal societal status.[1] Regarding religious devotion, however, several women are depicted as having an unusually active faith. Their faith in Jesus is not dependent on others, but on a direct encounter with Jesus himself from which they draw their own conclusion regarding his identity. While their role in the story of John is rather minimal, the contribution women make to the message of the Fourth Gospel is disproportionately strong. Some of the most profound statements or demonstrations of faith are made by women or in association with women as the result of their belief in Jesus.

One of the more interesting facets of the story told in the Fourth Gospel is the focus on individuals as they discover who Jesus is and then struggle to know how to respond appropriately. Again and again, people come to recognize Jesus as prophet or Messiah, yet the reaction is mixed. While some stay with him and follow closely, others go and

---

[1] Ross Shephard Kraemer, *Her Share of the Blessings—Women's Religions Among Pagans, Jews, and Christians in the Greco-Roman World* (New York: Oxford Univ. Press, 1992): 93ff., has shown that women's participation in religious activities was directly connected to the social constraints under which they lived, and notes that the situation regarding Jewish women was more complex than previously thought. The evidence suggests Jewish women in the diaspora were more active than were those in Palestine; however, Kraemer also detects that women may have been more active in Palestine than Rabbinic sources indicate. Even so, it appears that religious activities of women were considerably less public than were those of men.

proclaim his identity to friends and even the authorities. Still others are described as rejecting Jesus and the claims made about him. Another group is viewed as recognizing Jesus for who he is, but fearful of the authorities and of being dismissed from the synagogue they refuse to admit their belief in Jesus (7:11-13; 9:18-23; 12:10-11, 42-43; 16:1-4). As one reads through the story, individuals such as John the baptizer, Nathanael, the Samaritan woman, the military official in Capernaum (chap. 4), the crowd in chapter six whom Jesus fed, the blind man (chap. 9), Martha, Mary, and Mary Magdalene all stand out as people who have in fact recognized Jesus as one in whom to believe. At the same time Nicodemus, the paralytic (chap. 5), the "Jews" who are afraid to speak openly about him (7:13), the blind man's parents, and Joseph of Arimathea (19:38) seem to know who Jesus is but do not admit it publicly. Obviously, the "Jews"[2] as a whole react negatively and at times violently.

Much of the impact of the Fourth Gospel is the result of readers identifying with specific individuals and deciding either to follow or not follow their example. Throughout the story of John, the question continually remains, will they recognize who Jesus is and if so, how will they respond?

Women, though "minor characters," play a significant part in this dynamic of John. The first sign is the result of Jesus' mother's concern. The woman of Samaria confesses Jesus to be the Messiah and leads her village to recognize Jesus as the Savior of the world. The last sign is the result of Martha and Mary sending for Jesus. In conversation with Martha, Jesus proclaims, "I am the resurrection and the Life," after which Martha confesses him to be "the Messiah, the son of God, the one coming into the world." Mary Magdalene is the first to see the resurrected Jesus and the first to proclaim that fact, "I have seen the Lord." These incidents and statements alone make the reader aware of the impact women have on the message of John.

---

[2]The identity of "the Jews" in the Fourth Gospel is debated. For further discussion see John Ashton, "The Identity of the ΙΟΥΔΑΙΟΙ in the Fourth Gospel," *NovT* 27 (1985):40-75.

The situation of the Fourth Gospel, which has been extensively debated,[3] sheds even more light on the role of these women in John. Three general categories of theories are: 1) a missionary emphasis directed toward outsiders, diaspora Jews or Samaritans; 2) a corrective document addressing issues within the Christian community, such as anti-docetic and anti-sacramental themes; 3) a sharp dialogue with the synagogue. The approach adopted in this study is the third. Two prominent themes in John support the idea that the community was in conflict/dialogue with the synagogue and its leaders:[4] 1) comparison of Jesus with Jewish festivals and major Jewish figures, and 2) discovery of who Jesus is and acknowledging him as Messiah. Woven together throughout John, these two themes address a timidity of faith precipitated by the struggle the readers are having with their ancestry. Thus, John portrays Jesus as replacing many of the Jewish festivals and concepts and as being greater than Abraham, Jacob, and Moses. Among the things with which Jesus is compared are the Temple (chap.

---

[3] On this discussion, see Robert Kysar, *The Fourth Evangelist and His Gospel, An Examination of Contemporary Scholarship* (Minneapolis: Augsburg, 1975); *idem*, "The Fourth Gospel: A Report on Recent Research," *ANRW* 2.25/3 (New York: Walter De Gruyter, 1985): 2389-2480, esp. 2425-2435.

[4]Though many agree that some sort of struggle with Judaism is behind the Fourth Gospel, the specifics of that struggle are debated. For details of this discussion see J. Louis Martyn, *History and Theology in the Fourth Gospel* (rev. ed.; Nashville: Abingdon, 1979); Raymond E. Brown, *The Gospel According to John* (2 vols; 2nd ed.; New York: Doubleday, 1977); *idem, The Community of the Beloved Disciple, The Life, Loves, and Hates of an Individual Church in New Testament Times* (New York: Paulist Press, 1979); D. Moody Smith, "The Contribution of J. Louis Martyn to the Understanding of the Gospel of John," *Studies in Paul and John, The Conversation Continues, In Honor of J. Louis Martyn* (ed. R. T. Fortna and B. R. Gaventa; Nashville: Abingdon, 1990): 275-294; Rudolf Schnackenburg, *The Gospel According to St. John* (3 vols.; trans. Kevin Smith; New York: Crossroad, 1990); William Horbury, "The Benediction of the *Minim* and Early Jewish-Christian Controversy," *JTS* 33 (1982):19-61; John Ashton, *Understanding the Fourth Gospel* (Oxford: Clarendon, 1991).

2), rites of purification (chap. 2), worship at Jerusalem and Mt. Gerizim (chap. 4), John's baptism of purification (chap. 3), the healing traditions of Israel (chap. 5), the Feast of Tabernacles (7:37, 8:12), and the Feast of Dedication (chap. 10). In this regard, the importance and benefits of confessing Jesus to be the Messiah are clearly emphasized.

The theme of acknowledging Jesus as the Messiah is equally important. Throughout the Fourth Gospel, several individuals publicly identify Jesus as the Messiah or other related terms. These obviously support the purpose statement in 20:31, "These things are written in order that you might believe that Jesus is the Messiah the son of God."

In contrast are those who apparently believe, yet are reluctant to acknowledge their faith openly because of their fear of the consequences. Several statements indicate fear of the Jews or expulsion from the synagogue as a reason for not publicly confessing their faith in Jesus (7:11-13; 9:18-23; 12:10-11, 42-43; 16:1-4). Such statements suggest that there were in fact "secret" disciples of Jesus who continued to remain within the "comfort zone" of their Jewish heritage. Joseph of Arimathea (19:38) was one of these, as was perhaps Nicodemus (19:38-9;12:42).

The themes of Jesus' replacement of Jewish institutions and festivals, Jesus' superiority to Abraham, Jacob, and Moses, the numerous confessions of Jesus' identity, and the specific references to some believing but not openly confessing faith in Jesus strongly support the claim that John was written to encourage secret disciples of Jesus to abandon their fear and confess him to be the Messiah. Evidently, these individuals wanted to function within both worlds. John challenges them to leave the synagogue and find true life in Jesus.[5]

---

[5]Recently, Sarah J. Tanzer, "Salvation is *for* the Jews: Secret Christian Jews in the Gospel of John," *The Future of Early Christianity, Essays in Honor of Helmut Koester* (ed. Birger A. Pearson; Minneapolis: Fortress, 1991): 285-300, has written a convincing essay on this very point. Because her emphasis lies on the

So throughout John readers are challenged to allow Jesus' signs, Jesus' teaching, the reactions to his signs and teachings, and especially the individual characters to lead them to a stronger and more open belief in Jesus. The impact that the women in John have within this purpose will become clearer as our study progresses. Five individuals—Jesus' mother, the Samaritan woman, Martha, Mary, and Mary Magdalene—will be examined with regard to how each contributes to this challenge.[6]

1. *The Mother of Jesus*

Few individuals have received more attention in the Gospel of John than Mary the mother of Jesus.[7] Not mentioned by name, Jesus' mother appears in the Fourth Gospel only two times,[8] each at very significant moments: as Jesus begins his ministry at the wedding feast in Cana (2:1-11) and as his ministry comes to an end at the cross (19:25-27).

Gospel of John as a whole, Tanzer does not deal much with the women in John. The contribution that the women in John make to this theme will become more apparent through the remainder of our study.

[6]The woman in John 7:53-8:11 makes no real contribution to the story of John. No conversation occurs, her level of belief is unclear, perhaps minimal, and she only says one thing. Furthermore, the importance of this to the message of the gospel is diminished by the diverse textual history of this story. For further discussion of the textual data involved in this pericope see Bruce M. Metzger, *A Textual Commentary on the Greek New Testament* (corr. edition; New York: United Bible Societies, 1975): 219-222; and Neil R. Lightfoot, *How We Got the Bible* (2nd ed.; Grand Rapids: Baker, 1988): 70-72.

[7]A vast amount of material is available on Mary the mother of Jesus in the Gospel of John. A few key studies include Raymond F. Collins, "Mary in the Fourth Gospel, A Decade of Johannine Studies," *LS* 3 (1970):99-142; John McHugh, *The Mother of Jesus in the New Testament* (London: Darton, Longman & Todd, 1975): 351-403, 462-66; Raymond E. Brown and K. P. Donfried, et al., ed., *Mary in the New Testament* (Philadelphia: Fortress, 1978): 179-218.

[8]A reference to Jesus' mother is found at 6:42.

A. *The Wedding Feast at Cana 2:1-11*

The role of the wedding feast at Cana in John's story is clear. It presents Jesus' first sign, his "glory" is made known, and his own disciples are said to believe in him (2:11). Jesus' mother, then, is depicted as presenting him and his power to the public.

Moloney[9] has argued that the section of John running from Cana (2:1-11) to Cana (4:46-54) is a single unit constructed to show a journey of faith by several individuals. Within this section different levels of faith are shown: "the Jews," Nicodemus, the Samaritan woman, and the Samaritan villagers. A progression of faith is said to occur among these individuals. Moloney notes that these episodes are framed by the first and second "signs" as well as two examples of "complete" faith: that of Jesus' mother in a Jewish setting and that of the official at Cana in a non-Jewish setting. While the two incidents at Cana do seem to form an *inclusio*, Mary's faith is not so much an example of "complete" faith as it is a faith that is developing. From this perspective Jesus' mother is an example of faith that is to be followed because it leads others to Jesus. Indeed, at the close of the passage the sign is said to result in Jesus' glory being revealed and the disciples' believing in Jesus.

When Jesus' mother realized that the wine had run out she indicated to her son, "They have no wine." Whether she expected a miracle (or not) is not clear, but she does apparently think her son can somehow help. Furthermore, Jesus' response indicates that she did expect him to do something, for Jesus did not appear to be interested in helping at first. Jesus' response, "What (is that) to me and to you, woman?" may seem harsh, but his mother was not in

---

[9]Francis J. Moloney, "From Cana to Cana (John 2:1-4:54) and the Fourth Evangelist's Concept of Correct (and Incorrect) Faith," *Studia Biblica 1978 II. Papers on the Gospels* (Sixth International Congress on Biblical Studies; ed. E. A. Livingstone; Sheffield: JSOT, 1980): 185-213. Moloney has developed this thesis more thoroughly in *Belief in the Word, Reading John 1-4* (Minneapolis: Fortress, 1993).

the least daunted. Ignoring his reluctance to help, as mothers do at times, she proceeded to tell the servants, "Do whatever he says to you." The key to understanding the significance of Jesus' mother in this incident lies with two statements: "Do whatever he tells you" (v. 5) and "he revealed his glory and his disciples believed in him" (v. 11).

As a result of Mary's confidence that her son could help, Jesus' first sign is recorded and his "glory" is revealed. Obviously, they had already believed in Jesus to a certain extent, so the statement that his disciples "believed" in him implies the development of a greater level of belief. Both themes, glory and belief, are significant to the message of John. Since the statement in John 20:31 (". . . these are written that you may believe that Jesus is the Messiah") is an important clue to the purpose of the Gospel, Mary's role in helping Jesus' disciples come to a greater level of belief in him is significant.

The conclusion to the Cana incident clearly indicates the focus to be christological. While Mary is not the center of the story, her confident expectation that her son could help provides an example for others to follow in leading believers to Jesus.

The theme of leading others to Jesus is especially important at the beginning of Jesus' ministry. In chap. 1, John the baptizer points some of his disciples toward Jesus and then both Andrew and Philip bring their brothers to Jesus. Now Jesus' own mother, though evidently not a "disciple" herself, is instrumental in the disciples believing in him to a greater extent. The following two chapters present a contrast between a Jewish leader, Nicodemus, who is not quite ready to acknowledge who Jesus is and a Samaritan woman who not only recognizes him as Messiah, but proclaims it to her entire village. Within this variety of examples of faith, Mary is an example of a developing faith that is yet to be made complete, for she is not described as being one of Jesus' disciples (2:12, "After this he went down to Capernaum with his mother, his brothers, and his disciples.")[10] She does believe that her son can help at the wedding feast, but her trust seems to be from the perspective of a confident mother rather than a disciple with complete[11] faith. Nevertheless, her level of faith is to be viewed as instrumental in helping his own disciples come to a greater level of belief.

B. *At the Cross 19:25-27*

Mary's appearance at the cross differs from her presence at the wedding feast in that she says nothing—her presence alone is important. Several aspects of Mary's appearance at Jesus' execution (19:25-27) indicate that her presence is significant for the readers of the Gospel. First, she is an eyewitness to his suffering and the culmination of his ministry. Second, she is there without her other sons. Third, her presence along with the beloved disciple and Mary Magdalene brings together three individuals very important to John's Gospel.

Jesus' use of the generic "woman" in addressing his mother (as at Cana) and the appearance of the beloved disciple cause many to view Mary's appearance at the cross as primarily symbolic. The proposed symbolism, however, is widely divergent and has little justification from the

---

[10] K. P. Donfried, "The Mother of Jesus in the Gospel of John," *Mary in the New Testament*, 193, observes that Jesus' mother "falls into a general category of those who, despite their good intentions, misunderstand Jesus (e.g., Nicodemus in chap. 3, and the Samaritan woman in chap. 4)." Donfried further suggests that Mary's request for a sign shows a naive trust and a lack of comprehension that ultimately leads to solid faith (for other examples 4:47, 48, 53; 20:30-31). He concludes that "until she appears at the foot of the cross, she is not yet a model for believers and indeed is kept distinct from the disciples who at Cana saw his glory and believed in him."

[11] Moloney's term "authentic" faith may be acceptable as long as it allows for a distinction between different levels such as Mary's faith and that of the Samaritan woman. I do not think Mary's faith is on the same level as the Samaritan woman's. Thus, I prefer the term "developing" faith.

specific context. Suggestions range 1) from interpreting Mary as an intercessor or intermediary, 2) to viewing her typologically as the new Eve, 3) to her representing Jewish Christianity that overcomes the offense of the cross and turns to Jesus, or 4) to her becoming a mother to the beloved disciple as foreshadowing male and female equity within the church.

Such a diversity of interpretation causes some to abandon a symbolic interpretation altogether and prefer the simple explanation of a dying son concerned about the welfare of his mother. Dodd,[12] for instance, does not regard the scene as theologically motivated, and concludes, "Attempts to give a symbolic meaning are in general singularly unconvincing." Now it is important to note that symbolism is an important aspect of the Fourth Gospel,[13] e.g., the contrast between light and darkness, the concept of Logos, the "I am" sayings, some of the signs, and living water, all of which provide some of the main themes of the Fourth Gospel. However, any attempt at identifying symbolism within a given passage must be closely governed by the specific text as well as the context. In contrast to Peter who denied Jesus, we find Jesus' mother, along with other women and the beloved disciple, at the cross as

---

[12]C. H. Dodd, *The Interpretation of the Fourth Gospel* (Cambridge: Cambridge Univ. Press, 1953): 428, n. 2. See also A. M. Hunter, *The Gospel According to John* (Cambridge: Cambridge Univ. Press, 1965): 179.

[13]See the discussion of symbolism in John by C. K. Barrett in *Essays on John* (Philadelphia: Westminster, 1982): 65-79. See also the excellent discussion by R. Alan Culpepper, *Anatomy of the Fourth Gospel, A Study in Literary Design* (Philadelphia: Fortress, 1983): 180-202. For further discussion see C. H. Dodd, *The Interpretation of the Fourth Gospel*, 133-43; Sandra M. Schneiders, "History and Symbolism in the Fourth Gospel," *L'evangile de Jean: sources, redaction, theologie* (ed. M. de Jonge; BETL 44; Gembloux: J. Duculot, 1977): 371-76; Xavier Leon-Dufour, "Towards a Symbolic Reading of the Fourth Gospel," *NTS* 27 (1981): 439-56; John Painter, "Johannine Symbols: A Case Study in Epistemology," *Journal of Theology for Southern Africa* 27 (1979): 26-41.

witnesses of Jesus' death. Nevertheless, while there may be some symbolic elements in the scene, the text itself does not suggest that Jesus' mother herself should be viewed symbolically.

Mary's presence only at the beginning and the end of Jesus' ministry is important. Crucial statements associated with these incidents emphasize this significance:

> Jesus did this, the first of his signs, in Cana of Galilee, and revealed his glory; and his disciples believed in him (2:11).

> After this, when Jesus knew that all was finished . . . (19:28).

Mary's presence at the beginning and end of Jesus' ministry, however, must not be overemphasized. In both scenes the emphasis is clearly christological. What is important for the readers of John to recognize is that Mary is present with Jesus at the cross, at the climax of his ministry. She is not present throughout Jesus' ministry after Cana, so she does not see the other signs, but she is present at the end. Mary's simple faith, though not yet complete at Cana, has brought her to the cross where she now becomes a witness. Since his brothers are not there, Jesus is concerned about his mother's future and he asks the "beloved disciple" to care for her.

Though the implication may not be so obvious, John's readers may find comfort and encouragement from Mary's presence at the cross. Readers are involved in a struggle with their heritage over the identity of Jesus. While the intensity of this struggle is somewhat difficult to ascertain, the emphasis on the theme of "witness" throughout John suggests his readers were not confident in their faith to the point of being witnesses themselves for Jesus. Knowing that Mary had not followed Jesus all along, yet she was a witness at a crucial point in his ministry, might conceivably encourage some readers to show a greater level of faith (to the point of confessing Jesus to be the Messiah). Similarly, though they themselves might not have been very effective witnesses along the way, they could, like Mary, be more effective now that their own situation is becoming more crucial. Comforted by the thought of Jesus taking care of those who are his witnesses,[14] readers may now follow Mary's example with greater commitment. Jesus' mother does not verbally confess her faith in Jesus, but her presence at the cross with those who are known to be his disciples is critical. Those who confess Jesus to be the Messiah will be supported by Jesus' followers. In this manner, Mary may be viewed as an example of faith for John's readers.[15]

2. *The Samaritan Woman*

The contribution of the Samaritan woman to the message of the Fourth Gospel is also significant.[16] The themes of Life, worship, testimony, and Jesus as Messiah suggest this story is central to the Gospel. In their own way, each of these themes has a christological focus. Overcoming significant deterrents and barriers, e.g., male-female, Jew-Samaritan, in order to be an effective witness to Jesus also develops an important concept in John's Gospel. Furthermore, as a result of the woman's witness a Samaritan village confesses Jesus to be the "Savior of the world."

Because of the emphasis upon the Jew-Samaritan

---

[14]E.g., the blind man, Samaritan woman, Jesus' mother.

[15]McHugh, *The Mother of Jesus*, 403, interprets the scene of Mary at the cross, not having seen Jesus' deeds throughout his ministry, as an example of the statement "Blessed are those who have not seen but believe" (John 20:29).

[16]See Martinus de Boer, "John 4:27—Women (and Men) in the Gospel and Community of John," *Women in the Biblical Tradition* (ed. G. J. Brooke; Lewiston: Edwin Mellen, 1992): 208-30; Stephen D. Moore, "Are there Impurities in the Living Water that the Johannine Jesus Dispenses? Deconstruction, Feminism, and the Samaritan Woman," *Biblical Interpretation* 1 (1993): 207-27; Teresa Okure, *The Johannine Approach to Mission, A Contextual Study of John 4:1-42* (Tübingen: J. C. B. Mohr [Paul Siebeck], 1988); Birger Olsson, *Structure and Meaning in the Fourth Gospel, A Text-Linguistic Analysis of John 2:1-11 and 4:1-42* (Lund: CWK Gleerup, 1974).

relationship rather than the male-female relationship in this story, this chapter has been the basis for several proposals suggesting the Gospel to have a missionary purpose toward the Samaritans.[17] A better perspective, however, would be to focus on the Samaritan woman's overcoming several barriers—whether cultural,[18] social, spiritual, or gender related—on her journey from not knowing Jesus to proclaiming him to her entire village.

Initially, the woman of Samaria sees Jesus as a thirsty Jewish traveler who is rather bold in asking for a drink. The woman's misunderstanding of Jesus' reference to living water parallels Nicodemus' difficulty in understanding the concept of being born again. Yet, beyond her failure to comprehend the significance of "living water,"[19] the woman slowly but definitely works through the cultural barriers between her and Jesus.

The request by Jesus that the woman bring her husband leads to her gaining further insight into Jesus' identity: "Sir, I perceive that you are a prophet." Reference to the woman's past[20] focuses more on helping her learn who

---

[17]See further M. Pamment, "Is there Convincing Evidence of Samaritan Influence on the Fourth Gospel?" *ZNW* 73 (1982): 221-30; Kysar, "The Fourth Gospel, A Report on Recent Research," *ANRW* 2.25/3.2429.

[18]The differences between the Jews and the Samaritans are well known and need not be summarized here.

[19]For a good analysis of the irony involved in the two level discussion between Jesus and the woman see Gail R. O'Day, *Revelation in the Fourth Gospel* (Philadelphia: Fortress, 1986): 61-91.

[20]According to Schnackenburg, *The Gospel According to St. John*, 1:433 (citing H. L. Strack and P. Billerbeck, *Kommentar zum Neuen Testament aus Talmud und Midrasch* [Munich: Beck, 1922-55] 2:437), "The Jews held that a woman could only marry twice, or three times at most, and with the strict views of Orientals on morality, the Samaritans must also have considered such frequent re-marriage as dishonourable and illegitimate." Turid Karlsen Seim, "Roles of Women in the Gospel of John," *Aspects on the Johannine Literature, Papers Presented at a Conference of Scandinavian New Testament*

Jesus is than upon her moral status. Her question regarding worship may be seen either as a "sidestep" to avoid the topic of her past or as a genuine attempt to discover more about Jesus as a prophet. In fact, the conversation exhibits a good bit of theological depth on the part of the Samaritan, something quite unexpected in either Samaritan or Jewish cultures.[21] Even as a "sidestep," the question results in the woman's coming to a greater understanding of Jesus.

The discourse on worship contains a parallel to the discussion with Nicodemus concerning that which is spirit. Though neither Nicodemus nor the Samaritan woman seems to perceive Jesus' thought, the woman's openness sustains her to yet another level of belief. This discussion regarding worship in spirit suggests that one must have a certain quality in order to worship God. The woman is getting closer to having that quality; in fact, as she wonders and then hears that Jesus is Messiah, she "moves" into that realm in which God is worshiped. When she realizes who Jesus is, she is anxious to proclaim his identity publicly. Worship of God inevitably involves proclaiming who Jesus is.

In some manner, the phrase "worship the Father in spirit and truth" must be linked with the concept of worship of God "neither on this mountain nor in Jerusalem." Jesus is neither the Savior of the Jews nor of the Samaritans, but as Messiah he is the Savior of the world.[22] Inevitably, true

---

Exegetes at Uppsala (ConBNT 18; ed., L. Hartman and B. Olsson; Uppsala: Almqvist–Wiksell, 1987): 68, observes concerning the negative judgments regarding the woman's moral status: "They do not sufficiently take into account that matters of marriage and divorce were primarily men's privilege, and that the point of Jesus' statement is not to expose her morals but to show his prophetic power through his miraculous knowledge of her special situation."

[21]From a literary perspective Sandra M. Schneiders, *The Revelatory Text, Interpreting the New Testament as Sacred Scripture* (San Francisco: Harper, 1991): 190, observes, "Nowhere in the fourth gospel is there a dialogue of such theological depth and intensity."

[22]Hendirkus Boers, *Neither on this Mountain nor in Jerusalem, A Study of John 4* (SBLMS 35; Atlanta: Scholars Press, 1988): 199.

worship involves proclaiming who Jesus is, but also overcomes all barriers that humanity might construct. At this point the woman's perception of Jesus compels her to run to the village and tell the villagers who she thinks Jesus is.

As she tells her fellow villagers about him she claims that in fact he may well be the Messiah. As a result of her progression in faith, an entire Samaritan village turns out to see who this individual is. Consequently, this woman's testimony results in one of the premiere claims about Jesus in the Gospel of John, "We know that this is truly the Savior of the world" (4:42).

The impact of the woman's testimony to Jesus is especially significant when compared to the conversation between Jesus and his disciples. When Jesus' disciples returned, they were surprised to find Jesus talking with a woman, just as she had been surprised when Jesus asked her for a drink. They appear to hide their astonishment and encourage Jesus to eat the food they had brought. From this point, the conversation continues on two different levels, as with the woman. The disciples, however, never seem to converse on Jesus' level, as the woman finally did. As Jesus continued discussing the situation at hand, he pointed out to them the mission (harvest) ahead—obviously among the Samaritans who would be coming from the village very soon. In contrast, the woman immediately knew her mission without having to be told.

The contrast with Nicodemus in the previous chapter further enhances the importance of the woman's testimony. Nicodemus, a leader of the Jews and member of the Sanhedrin, begins his conversation with Jesus in a simple way, but evidently never progresses beyond that initial level; yet a woman of Samaria progresses in her belief in Jesus to the point of publicly confessing him to be the Messiah. He has so much going for him; she has nothing. Culpepper[23] observes, "He is a male teacher of Israel; she is a woman of Samaria. He has a noble heritage; she has a shameful past.

---

[23]Culpepper, *Anatomy of the Fourth Gospel*, 136.

He has seen signs and knows Jesus is 'from God'; she meets Jesus as a complete stranger." In this striking contrast, a teacher of Israel with so much potential for influence fails to see who Jesus is,[24] yet an apparently insignificant woman of Samaria not only discovers who Jesus is, but tells her entire village about him. Initially, as with Nicodemus, she did not comprehend who Jesus was, but her openness allowed her to consider that there was more to Jesus than her first impression suggested.[25]

That this meeting between Jesus and the woman at the well is central to the overall message of the Gospel of John is clear from the emphasis on the result of her testimony about Jesus. In the closing verses of the pericope, 4:39-42, the term πιστεύειν (to believe) is used three different times (39, 41, 42) in regard to the response of the other villagers. The use of πιστεύειν parallels the statement of purpose for the Gospel in 20:31, "These are written in order that you may believe that Jesus is the Messiah . . ." (ἵνα πιστεύσητε).[26] Even though the term "Messiah" is used only by the woman, it is obvious that the villagers agree he is the Messiah.[27] The phrase "savior of the world" parallels the term "Messiah," at least in this context.[28]

---

[24] The role of Nicodemus in John's Gospel is beyond the scope of this study, but note that whether Nicodemus finally becomes a disciple of Jesus, secret or otherwise, is unclear. See Tanzer, "Salvation is *for* the Jews," *The Future of Early Christianity*, 291-94; Michael Goulder, "Nicodemus," *SJT* 44 (1991):153-68; Culpepper, *Anatomy of the Fourth Gospel*, 134-36; M. de Jonge, "Nicodemus and Jesus: Some Observations on Misunderstanding and Understanding in the Fourth Gospel," *BJRL* 53 (1971): 355.

[25] For further comparison of Nicodemus and the Samaritan woman see Mary Margaret Pazdan, "Nicodemus and the Samaritan Woman: Contrasting Models of Discipleship," *BTB* 17 (1987): 145-48.

[26] W. C. van Unnik, "A Greek Characteristic of Prophecy in the Fourth Gospel," *Text and Interpretation, Studies in the New Testament Presented to Matthew Black* (ed. E. Best and R. McL. Wilson; New York: Cambridge Univ. Press, 1979): 213, makes this observation.

[27] The Samaritans did believe in a coming messianic figure. See further J. Macdonald, *The Theology of the Samaritans* (London: SCM,

The true significance of the Samaritan woman is seen in her testimony. With this woman it is shown that one with apparently little societal status can be very influential with a great many. What makes the difference is the willingness to express openly her commitment to Jesus. Again, in contrast with Nicodemus, about whom the reader is never quite sure regarding his level of faith and commitment,[29] the woman of Samaria compels the reader to recognize and admire her faith and open commitment. Just as the disciples believed as the result of Jesus' mother's actions at Cana (2:11), so now the villagers believe as the result of the Samaritan woman's actions. Though initially she is reluctant to converse with Jesus, she eventually overcomes all the barriers and brings many others to Jesus and then recedes into the background. At the close of the story it is no longer because of the woman that the villagers believe, but because they have heard Jesus themselves. Furthermore, once they hear Jesus, they invite him to "remain" with them a while longer and Jesus remains with them for two days. The impact of the woman's testimony is profound. As the woman recedes into the background the reader is reminded of John the Baptist who gives public testimony bringing others to Jesus and then recedes into the background. John and this woman of Samaria are the only individuals presented in the Gospel of John as bringing many to Jesus.[30]

1964): 362-71; R. J. Coggins, *Samaritans and Jews: The Origins of Samaritanism Reconsidered* (Oxford: Oxford Univ. Press, 1975). See also J.D. Purvis, "The Fourth Gospel and the Samaritans," *NovT* 17 (1975): 161-98.

[28]See further Craig R. Koester, "'The Savior of the World' (John 4:42)," *JBL* 109 (1990): 665-80.

[29]Even at the end Nicodemus is associated with Joseph of Arimathea, a secret disciple of Jesus, in burying the body of Jesus (19:38ff.). At best Nicodemus is only a secret disciple, along with Joseph, who did not publicly proclaim belief in Jesus, due to "fear of the Jews."

[30]Schneiders, *The Revelatory Text*, 193, notes, "This woman is the first and only person (presented) in the public life of Jesus through whose word of witness a group of people is brought to 'come and see' and 'to believe in Jesus'."

Within Jewish culture, women were recognized as competent witnesses only in limited matters. Though they were legally excluded from testifying in many court cases, they were legally competent to make religious vows and oaths and were recognized as prophets.[31] While attitudes toward the value of a woman's testimony varied in Jewish culture, it is clear that the Samaritan villagers valued her testimony enough to listen to what she had to say. Within Samaritan culture the testimony of women appears to have been of more value.[32] Nevertheless, the limited value of a woman's testimony within Jewish culture enhances the impact of the story upon its Jewish readers. Nothing could keep her from sharing her faith openly with others.

While there is definite symbolism within this passage (living water, spirit, food), the woman herself is not symbolic.[33] The practical value of this woman to the readers

---

[31] Robert Gordon Maccini, "A Reassessment of the Woman at the Well in John 4 in Light of the Samaritan Context," *JSNT* 53 (1994): 36.

[32] The differences between Jewish and Samaritan attitudes toward women provide an important element to understanding this story, but the issue is too complex to discuss here. Maccini, *JSNT* (1994): 40, lists several studies along these lines, including Jarl Fossum, "Samaritan Sects and Movements," *The Samaritans* (ed. A. D. Crown; Tübingen: J. C. B. Mohr [Paul Siebeck], 1989): 293-389; Reinhard Pummer, "Samaritan Rituals and Customs," *The Samaritans*, 665-68.

[33] The woman and her husbands have been viewed symbolically. The five husbands plus the sixth man with whom the woman is currently living have been viewed as representing the different gods brought to Samaria by the foreigners brought there from five Mesopotamian and Syrian cities (2 Kgs 17:24). The five husbands are said to represent the deities of the five cities and the sixth man is viewed as representing another god or the true God with whom the Samaritans are illicitly united. For an example of such interpretation see E. C. Hoskyns, *The Fourth Gospel* (ed. F. N. Davey; London: Faber and Faber, 1947): 243. For a view of the Samaritan woman as corporately representing Samaria coming to Jesus as the result of Jesus' attempt to reunite Israel, see Calum M. Carmichael, "Marriage and the Samaritan Woman," *NTS* 26 (1980): 332-46. Koester, *JBL* 109 (1990): 668, also sees the woman as representative of Samaria as a

is tremendous. As noted earlier, the Johannine readers were evidently involved in a struggle or tension with Judaism. Within this context, the community would no doubt exhibit an inward-looking attitude concerned more about survival than evangelizing.[34]

The Fourth Gospel's emphasis on acknowledging Jesus publicly finds powerful expression in the woman of Samaria. The community would no doubt find encouragement in the story of the woman struggling with the numerous barriers facing her and yet advancing to the point of not only publicly professing her faith in Jesus as the Messiah, but in fact influencing many of her fellow villagers to do the same. If this woman of Samaria could openly profess such a commitment to Jesus with little concern as to whether others would agree or not, why could not John's readers do the same? Furthermore, if the villagers confessed their own faith in Jesus rather than relying on what the woman had said, the readers of the Fourth Gospel must openly confess their own faith in Jesus, rather than relying on the faith of others.

3. *Martha and Mary*

With Martha and Mary we again find significant themes in John associated with women. In fact, the story of the raising of Lazarus is pivotal in the narrative of John.[35] Martha is the main character, but soon after this incident Mary is the focus of another important event, the anointing

---

whole. There is no indication within the text itself or any theme within the Fourth Gospel that warrants such an interpretation. See further, Brown, *The Gospel According to John*, 1:171; Schnackenburg, *The Gospel According to St. John*, 1:433; D. A. Carson, *The Gospel According to John* (Grand Rapids: Eerdmans, 1991): 232f.

[34] George R. Beasley-Murray, *John* (Waco: Word, 1987): 66.

[35] Sandra M. Schneiders, "Death in the Community of Eternal Life; History, Theology, and Spirituality in John 11," *Int* 41 (1987): 45-46, argues that, "John 11 is not only the high point of integration of style, composition, and narrative in the Fourth Gospel but also of history, theology, and spirituality."

of Jesus. Lazarus is important only as the object of Jesus' last sign. He in fact never says anything in the story. The location of this story in the Gospel of John is significant. Just as the first sign was initiated by a woman, Jesus' mother, the last sign is initiated by women, Martha and Mary. Jesus' last sign, the raising of Lazarus, incites the Jewish leaders to seek to kill Jesus and thus is the transition to the passion narrative. The focal point of the story is the claim of Jesus to be the Resurrection and the Life and Martha's affirmation of her faith in Jesus.

Martha and Mary send for Jesus when their brother Lazarus is ill. Delaying for a few days,[36] Jesus arrives only after Lazarus has died. When Jesus arrived Martha confronted him with, "If you had been here, my brother would not have died." Evidently, Martha thinks Jesus could have healed Lazarus, an indication of a strong level of faith. Even after Lazarus' death Martha thinks Jesus can help in some way, for she says, "I know that even now God will give you whatever you ask." What Martha thinks Jesus can do now is not clear for she evidently does not think about Jesus' raising Lazarus from the dead. When Jesus mentions resurrection, Martha thinks of the future resurrection "at the last day." In response to Martha, Jesus claims, "I am the resurrection and the life." When asked if she believes this statement of Jesus, Martha makes one of the premiere confessions of faith in the New Testament, "I believe that you are the Messiah, the Son of God, the one coming into the world." The significance of Martha's statement is apparent for several reasons.

The confessional statement by Martha parallels the purpose statement of the Gospel, "These (signs) are written that you may believe that Jesus is the Christ, the Son of God, and that by believing you may have life in his name." Obviously, Martha is in some manner affirming the stated

---

[36]This fits a pattern in John noted by Charles H. Giblin, "Suggestion, Negative Response, and Positive Action in St. John's Portrayal of Jesus (John 2:1-11; 4:46-54; 7:2-14; 11:1-44)," *NTS* 26 (1980): 197-211.

purpose of the book. Her level of faith is significant for she makes this statement *before* Lazarus is raised. While her faith is still incomplete, for she objects when Jesus has the stone rolled away, it is powerful enough to overcome the disappointment Jesus caused her when he failed to come help earlier. This incomplete faith remained effective and was soon confirmed and made complete with the raising of Lazarus.

The confession of Martha is undoubtedly one of the high points of the christology of the Fourth Gospel. It is parallel to the statement made by Peter in chap. 6 after Jesus' discourse in the Capernaum synagogue, "We believe and know that you are the Holy One of God" (6:69). The statement by Peter is a powerful statement as well, but it also is supported by a faith not yet complete. The disciples had not understood the teaching of Jesus regarding the bread of life and the drink Jesus would provide his followers. Nevertheless, both Peter and Martha express the faith they have and remain with Jesus.

The confession by Martha in John 11 may be compared to the confession by Peter in the Synoptic Gospels at Caesarea Philippi. Martha's statement is very close to Matthew's account, "You are the Christ, the Son of the living God" (Matt 16:16). The parallel confessions of Martha and Peter, according to Raymond Brown, are part of the tendency of the Fourth Gospel to give to women roles normally associated with Peter in the other gospels.[37] Two things for which Peter is most remembered are his confession of Jesus at Caesarea Philippi and his being the first witness of the risen Jesus (1 Cor 15:5 and Luke 24:34); however, neither of these is mentioned in the Fourth Gospel. They both appear to be replaced by women, Martha and Mary Magdalene. For Brown, and others, this is a sign that women had a more important status in the Johannine community than in other early Christian communities.[38]

---

[37] Brown, *The Community of the Beloved Disciple*, 190.
[38] See also Sandra M. Schneiders, "Women in the Fourth Gospel

This may very well be the case, but for the moment it is sufficient to note that in the Gospel of John, Martha's confession is as significant as that of the apostle Peter in the Synoptic Gospels.

Martha's statement may also be compared to the confession of Thomas in John 20. When Jesus appeared to him he responded, "My Lord and my God," obviously a profound statement. But Jesus' response to Thomas was, "Have you believed because you have seen me? Blessed are those who have not seen and yet have come to believe" (John 20:29). Actually, Martha's confession is more powerful than Thomas' for she had not yet seen Jesus' or even Lazarus' resurrection. Certainly, Martha would fit into the category of those who have not seen and yet believe.

Martha then tells her sister Mary about Jesus' arrival. Mary approaches Jesus in the same manner as Martha had, "Lord, if you had been here, my brother would not have died." No conversation is mentioned for when Jesus saw the mourning of the group, he was deeply moved and immediately went to the tomb. Mary is not prominent in this scene, but later she anointed Jesus' feet with expensive perfume (John 12:1-8). Within the narrative of John, this action by Mary no doubt points toward Jesus' washing his disciples' feet. Jesus also notes that it is in preparation for his own burial.

The closing statement in the Martha-Mary-Lazarus narrative indicates that because many of the Jews were believing in Jesus due to his raising Lazarus, the Jewish authorities planned "to put Lazarus to death" (12:10-11). John 11:45-53 indicates that the authorities were already planning to put Jesus to death. Thus, Mary's anointing of Jesus is quite appropriate as a conclusion to this section of the Gospel.

Clearly, Jesus was impressed with Mary's actions, but he must have been even more impressed with the fact that

---

and the Role of Women in the Contemporary Church," *BTB* 12 (1982): 41.

Martha, Mary, and Lazarus would allow (or invite) him to stay with them. The authorities were looking for him and had demanded that any one who knew his whereabouts should let them know. As the Gospel of John addresses those whose faith is wavering and are not ready to acknowledge Jesus publicly, this incident must be a challenge. Martha, Mary, and Lazarus were putting their lives in danger by allowing Jesus to be with them. Their courage, no doubt, was strengthened by the raising of Lazarus, but it was their faith, especially Martha's, that sustained her/them in this time of danger.

4. *Mary Magdalene*

Mary Magdalene appears twice in the Gospel of John, at the cross and at the empty tomb.[39] All four Gospels agree that Mary was one of the first to see the empty tomb.[40] Furthermore, similar to Matthew, John records Jesus' appearance to Mary in the garden and his sending her with a message to the apostles.[41] Unique to John is Mary's initial failure to recognize Jesus, her holding on to Jesus, a reference to his ascension, and Mary's report to the disciples, "I have seen the Lord." Obviously, one of the primary factors in this account is the importance of Mary as a witness not only to the crucifixion itself, but to the empty tomb and to the resurrected Jesus.

Two aspects of this record of Mary's encounter with

---

[39] Matthew and Mark mention both as well. For a thorough study of the importance of Mary Magdalene within the early church and Gnosticism, see Susan Haskins, *Mary Magdalene, Myth and Metaphor* (New York: Harcourt Brace & Co., 1993).

[40] Numerous questions exist concerning the relationship between the Fourth Gospel's account of Mary's visit to the empty tomb and the accounts of the Synoptic Gospels and other possible sources of John. The issues which persist, however, do not hinder seeing the importance that the Fourth Gospel places on Mary's witness to the resurrected Jesus.

[41] See Matt 28:9-10. Mark 16:9-10 mentions an appearance to Mary but she is given no commission.

Jesus are important for our purposes. First, according to this account Mary is the first to see the resurrected Jesus. Even though Peter and the beloved disciple had entered the tomb before Mary,[42] she remains at the tomb when the two leave and thus actually sees the Lord before they do. Secondly, Jesus gives Mary a message to relay to the disciples about his ascending to the Father. As she relays the message she tells the disciples, "I have seen the Lord." Thus, she becomes at this point the first to carry the message of the resurrection to others.

Mary's prominence among witnesses to the resurrected Jesus is significant for John's readers.[43] Throughout the Fourth Gospel, importance has been placed on the testimony of seemingly unimportant people: the Samaritan woman, the blind man, Martha, and now Mary Magdalene. Within the context of the struggle that the readers of John were

---

[42] Presumably Mary had not entered the tomb when she first saw the stone rolled away and ran to tell the apostles. The difficulty between the statements in 20:8 (that the "other" disciple believed when he entered the tomb) and in 20:9 (that they still did not understand that Jesus had to rise from the dead) is explained by Paul S. Minear, "We Don't Know Where. . . ," *Int* 30 (1976): 125-39, who suggests (127) that the disciples did not believe in the resurrection at that point, but simply what Mary had told them about Jesus' body being gone from the tomb.

[43] Of the six resurrection appearances of Jesus in the Gospels, five of them include Mary. Furthermore, each time Mary is mentioned, she is listed first. The one time she is not mentioned is in John 21 where Jesus appears to several disciples on the sea shore. In his list of witnesses of the resurrected Jesus in 1 Cor 15, however, Paul does not mention Mary Magdalene. For possible reasons as to why Paul does not mention her, see Gerald O'Collins and Daniel Kendall, "Mary Magdalene as Major Witness to Jesus' Resurrection," *TS* 48 (1987): 631-46, esp. 639ff. Pheme Perkins, "'I Have Seen the Lord' (John 20:18)—Women Witnesses to the Resurrection," *Int* 46 (1992): 41, argues, "Recovering the primitive tradition of Mary as one of the individual witnesses implies that she should have a place alongside other witnesses in creedal formulas. The first-century prejudice against women as public witnesses, probably the reason that she does not appear there in the canon, should not be repeated in today's churches."

experiencing with their Jewish heritage, the importance of every individual's testimony to Jesus is emphasized by these stories. Regardless of how one views oneself, as important or not, every person's testimony is essential. The fact that she is a woman is significant, for although women's testimony was not normally acceptable for those of a Jewish background,[44] Mary's testimony is effective.[45]

Whether Mary is to be viewed as the apostle to the apostles[46] or as having a claim to apostleship as "equal in every respect to both Peter's and Paul's,"[47] it is clear that her testimony is significant within the purpose of the Fourth Gospel. She came to believe in the resurrected Lord on the basis of her own experience. She relied upon no one, but now she becomes the basis upon which others believe until they see Jesus for themselves. Prior to the disciples as a whole, Mary sees Jesus, converses with him, and confesses him to be Lord. Then she is sent to share the message of the resurrection and the ascension with the apostles. In the Fourth Gospel, Mary serves as a capstone to a series of women who come to faith through their own encounter with Jesus.[48]

---

[44] O'Collins and Kendall, *TS* 48 (1987): 640. On the importance of Mary's testimony, see also Francois Bovon, "Le privilege pascal de Marie-Madeleine," *NTS* 30 (1984): 50-62.

[45] Based on Minear's suggestion that the disciples believed Mary's report about the empty tomb (see above note 43), Karen Heidebrecht Thiessen, "Jesus and Women in the Gospel of John," *Direction* 19 (1990): 52-64, suggests that "Since the witness of a woman was not considered credible within that particular cultural context, it is possible that John wanted to highlight the Beloved Disciple's belief in the report of a woman!" (59).

[46] This famous phrase evidently goes back to Hippolytus' commentary on the Canticle of Canticles. Elisabeth Schüssler Fiorenza, *In Memory of Her, A Feminist Theological Reconstruction of Christian Origins* (New York: Crossroad, 1983): 332, emphasizes this aspect of Mary's role in John. See also the article by Fiorenza, "Mary Magdalene: Apostle to the Apostles," *UTS Journal* (1975): 22ff.

[47] Schneiders, *BTB* (1982): 44.

[48] See further Perkins, *Int* (1992): 41.

Another aspect of the message Mary is to carry to the disciples has to do with announcing a new relationship between Jesus and his disciples. Jesus instructs Mary to "Go to my brothers and say to them, 'I am ascending to my Father and your Father, to my God and your God'" (20:17). Formerly, they had been disciples, now they are "brothers" of Jesus. This new relationship is important for the message of the Gospel of John. When believers or disciples become brothers or sisters of Jesus they have a new incentive for their witness. No longer are they giving testimony about someone to whom they are related simply as a disciple, but now they are sharing their belief about someone who is their brother.

By the time the Fourth Gospel had been written, it was obvious that the leaders of the Jewish Christians would not be able to lead effectively in the struggle with Judaism without the help of every member of the community. The more individuals within the community that would confess their belief in Jesus as the Messiah, the stronger would be their collective witness to Jesus. Emphasizing the effectiveness of the testimony of Mary would no doubt encourage others to share their faith in Jesus as the Messiah. That Jesus would entrust the announcement of his resurrection and ascension to one whose testimony would not normally be accepted, that of a woman, agrees with the idea throughout the Gospel that even though an individual may not appear to be important, the message and the effect of the testimony is significant.

Conclusion

The contribution of women to the message of the Fourth Gospel is crucial. As was rather uncommon in their world, they are not dependent on others for their faith in Jesus.[49]

---

[49] Perkins, *Int* (1992): 41, observes "The women in the Fourth Gospel come to faith through their own encounter with Jesus." Schneiders, *BTB* 12 (1982): 44, similarly observes, "They evince remarkable originality in their relationships with Jesus and extraordinary initiative in their activities within the community."

When compared with women in the Synoptic Gospels, these women make much more significant contributions to the ministry of Jesus. In fact, women function more importantly in John than most men do in the Gospels as a whole. In the story of the Fourth Gospel, none of these women has a "major role" in terms of "characterization." In fact, each would be considered a minor character. Yet women make a contribution to the message of the Fourth Gospel that is disproportionate to their role in the story.[50] With each woman the reader discovers something about Jesus that is central to the message of the gospel. With Jesus' mother, the reader sees Jesus' first sign and along with the disciples sees Jesus' glory. No one, male or female, is depicted as bringing as many to Jesus as the woman of Samaria. With the Samaritan Woman, the reader sees Jesus' prophetic powers of insight, his Messiahship, and that relationship with God is not dependent on the Temple but an inward spirituality. With Martha, the reader learns that Jesus is the Resurrection and Life. With Mary, the reader is made aware that Jesus' death and burial are imminent. Then with Mary Magdalene, the reader discovers that Jesus is risen and indeed is Lord. Each encounter with Jesus focuses on his identity—precisely what the Fourth Gospel is all about, viz., recognizing the identity of Jesus and proclaiming who he is.[51]

The Fourth Gospel addresses a crisis of faith. The Jewish Christians in the Johannine community were evidently fearful about publicly confessing their faith in Jesus as the Messiah. Such timidity of faith would endanger the continuing existence of the Christian community as much

---

[50]Culpepper, *Anatomy of the Fourth Gospel*, 106, says that the minor characters in general "have a disproportionately high representational value. They are vital to the fulfillment of the Gospel's purpose."

[51]*Ibid.*, 97, notes that "The plot of the gospel is propelled by conflict between belief and unbelief as responses to Jesus." Furthermore, "Plot development in John . . . is a matter of how Jesus' identity comes to be recognized and how it fails to be recognized" (88).

as—if not more than—any outside threat. Moreover, the attempt to remain secret in their discipleship is a direct contradiction of what the Life brought by the Messiah is all about. In this manner these women provide the readers of this Gospel with a challenge—they have recognized who Jesus is and have proclaimed their faith in him, and thus, they are presented as models to emulate. Will readers of the Fourth Gospel overcome their own timidity of faith and share their faith in Jesus with their Jewish heritage? Each reader is invited to struggle with and to answer this question.

While the focus in John is not to argue for greater recognition of women in terms of discipleship and ministry, that certainly could have been one of the results within the early Christian community. The focus, rather, appears to be on discipleship and giving testimony to Jesus as Messiah. In the Fourth Gospel, women are shown to be capable of fulfilling that role as well as men.

The Fourth Gospel offers several insights for the current discussion regarding women and the church.

1) However unexpected it might have been socially or religiously, women had a profound impact at crucial points in Jesus' ministry.

2) After coming to faith in Jesus on their own, these women were not reluctant to share that faith with others.

3) These women are portrayed as examples to follow.

4) The main concern of these women was discipleship rather than leadership, yet because of their discipleship they are portrayed as leaders.

5) Those who are important and influential within the community are those who are willing to confess and witness to others about their faith in Jesus. Some may appear to be important, but unless they share their faith with others they are not influential.

6) The impact of the message does not rest upon the importance of the messenger but upon the willingness of the messenger and the heart of the receiver.

Much current discussion of women in the church focuses on authority and power. In the Fourth Gospel, the issues of authority and power do not arise, except in regard to Jesus' own authority. Perhaps in the church today there is too much misguided focus on authority and power, when the real issues to be addressed are discipleship and influence. The Fourth Gospel may not have as much to say directly about the public or official roles of women in the church as one might like. Nevertheless, this Gospel does make it clear that the faith, testimony, and discipleship of women is equal to that of men and is equally as important to the Christian community. The value of women's discipleship and influence has been tremendously overlooked.

Just as John's Gospel presents a challenge to recognize and proclaim who Jesus is, it also challenges us to give greater recognition to the value and function of women as disciples of Jesus today.

Chapter Ten

ΥΠΑΝΔΡΟΣ—SUBORDINATION OF WOMEN IN ROM 7:2?

James C. Walters

In Rom 7:2 Paul uses ὕπανδρος to designate a married woman. The adjective is translated "married" in the NIV, TEV, RSV, JB, NEB, *et al.* Because the term can be viewed as the combination of ἀνήρ (male) and ὑπό (under), some have surmised that the word denotes the idea of a woman's subordination to her husband, and that coupled with the analogy to the law, it amounts to a condensed commentary on the Christian view of the relation between a wife and her husband. For instance, Lloyd-Jones[1] writes:

> A woman who is married to a man is under the authority of that man; she is under the power and the control of that man; she is under the power and the control of her husband. . . . And it is absolutely essential to the Apostle's argument because he is comparing this husband with the law. . . . What does marriage mean? The very term the Apostle used, the term that is normally used, is a term which in and of itself suggests a kind of subordination.

This comment assumes answers to four questions which should be carefully investigated. First, is this the term that is "normally" used? Second, what are the possible meanings of ὕπανδρος? Next, to which of these possible meanings does the usage in Rom 7:2 most closely correspond? And finally, what is one to make of Paul's analogy with the Law?

---

[1] D. M. Lloyd-Jones, *Romans* (Grand Rapids: Zondervan, 1973): 18.

1. Normal?

In Greek literature between Homer and the middle ages, I have been able to locate only 78 occurrences of ὕπανδρος, and many of these are in Christian literature citing or alluding to Rom 7:2. Neither Paul nor any other NT writer uses ὕπανδρος outside of Rom 7:2. The word normally used by ancient Greek writers to designate a married woman—both within the NT and outside it—is γυνή (woman or wife). The other times Paul refers to married persons in his letters, he uses attributive participles of the verb form γαμέω (to marry; 1 Cor 7:10, 33, 34). When referring to a married woman, the participle is in the feminine gender (τοῖς γεγαμηκόσιν, 7:10; ἡ γαμήσασα, 7:34); when designating a married man, the participle is masculine (ὁ γαμήσας, 7:33). That ὕπανδρος is a word Paul can use for a married woman is apparent from Rom 7:2; that it is the term "normally" used—by either Paul or other ancient authors who wrote in Greek—is not.

Excursus: Determining the Possible Meanings

Whether or not the idea of subordination is inherent in Paul's usage of ὕπανδρος cannot be determined by root analysis. It is true that ὕπανδρος was formed by the fusion of ἀνήρ with the preposition ὑπό. It is also true that ἀνήρ can mean 'man' or 'husband' and that ὑπό can mean 'under'. It does not follow, however, that the combination of the two necessarily means "one under (the power of) a man or husband." Words have a *current* value that is limited to the time and setting in which they are used (synchronic analysis). The history or etymology of the word—how it came to be as it now appears—is an interesting question in its own right (diachronic analysis).[2] However, a word's

---

[2]For a good introduction to the distinction between synchronic and diachronic approaches, see Moises Silva, *Biblical Words and Their Meaning: An Introduction to Lexical Semantics* (Grand Rapids: Zondervan, 1983): 17-51. This distinction was made by Ferdinand de Saussure, *Course in General Linguistics* (New York: McGraw-Hill,

ΥΠΑΝΔΡΟΣ—Subordination of Women in Rom 7:2?

history is usually irrelevant to the task of ascertaining its current meaning.³ All words—whether Greek, Hebrew or English—have a history.⁴ There are two questions translators/ interpreters must ask before factoring etymological data into decisions regarding the current meaning of a word: Was the speaker or writer aware of the root—and, did this information play any role in his/her mind?⁵

Admittedly, it is more likely that a word was used with the intent of featuring its etymology if the word under consideration is "transparent" (e.g., the English word "submarine" or the Greek word ὕπανδρος).⁶ "Submarine" was obviously formed by the fusion of the prefix "sub-" and the word "marine." However, even a transparent word like "submarine" conjures up the image of a particular navy

---

1966): 79-81. Saussure's book was originally published in French in 1915, but his insights and those of his colleagues in general linguistics were slow to influence biblical studies. Not until James Barr published *The Semantics of Biblical Language* (Oxford: Oxford Univ. Press, 1961), did biblical studies begin to take serious note of this development.

³J. Vendryes, *Language: A Linguistic Introduction to History* (New York: Alfred A. Knopf, 1925): 176. Saussure, *Course in General Linguistics*, 81f., illustrated the irrelevance of diachronic information by comparing linguistics to a chess game: To understand the *state* of the game it is not necessary to know how the chess pieces came to reside in their respective places—in fact how they got there is irrelevant. Obviously etymological information must, by default, play a primary role when synchronic attestations are lacking.

⁴As Anthony Thiselton, "Semantics and New Testament Interpretation," in *New Testament Interpretation: Essays on Principles and Methods* (ed. I. H. Marshall; Grand Rapids: Eerdmans, 1977): 81, points out, *dent de lion* belongs to the etymology of the English word "dandelion." However, "lion's tooth" plays no role in the meaning of the word for modern speakers and writers.

⁵Silva, *Biblical Words*, 48.

⁶English has fewer transparent words than more synthetic languages like Greek and German. On transparency, see Stephen Ullmann, *The Principles of Semantics* (New York: Philosophical Library, 1957): 83ff., or the less technical discussion in Silva, *Biblical Words*, 48f.

vessel more readily for contemporary readers than the idea of "underwater." Few readers or hearers pause to consider even the etymology of a transparent word unless attention is drawn to it by the speaker or writer. Therefore, primacy should be given to synchronic analysis: How was the word used during the time period and in the social and geographical location most closely associated with the speaker or writer? The etymology of the word and the role that its history may have played in a particular usage should be pursued as a second and separate question.

2. Possible Meanings of ὕπανδρος

I have located and reviewed 78 occurrences of ὕπανδρος beginning in the hellenistic period. As I indicated above, many of these texts occur in Christian authors who either cite Rom 7:2 (15 times) or one of the texts from the Greek OT (LXX) where ὕπανδρος is found (Num 5:20, 29; Prov 6:24, 29; Sir 9:9; 41:23). The remaining examples are found in pagan and Christian authors who use the term (apparently) independently of the biblical usages. On the basis of my reading of the texts, I have divided these remaining usages into three groups.

In the first group, ὕπανδρος is used to differentiate a married woman from an unmarried woman (παρθένος) and/or a widow (χήρα). Polybius, describing Philip's abuse of power, tells of the king's sexual exploits, including seducing widows and corrupting married women (γυναῖκας τὰς ὑπάνδρους).[7] Similarly, a marginal note in Homer's *Iliad* mentions the parts of the Homeric house/palace where the αἱ ὕπανδροι may be appropriately found as opposed to αἱ παρθένοι καὶ αἱ χῆραι (unmarried and widows).[8]

---

[7]*Polybius* 10.26.3.

[8]Scholion, Homer's *Iliad* 3.125. See also Amphilochius, *Contra haereticos* 939. Similarly, Aelian uses the word to refer to a mated female bird (Aelianus, *De natura animalium* 3.42.8).

The second category of usage is one where ὕπανδρος designates a woman who is sexually off-limits to men other than her husband. Many of these texts are warnings directed to men who might contemplate sexual relations with a married woman. Notable here are OT texts from the LXX. Prov 6:23-24 says that the correction and guidance of the Law will keep one from a married woman (ἀπὸ γυναικὸς ὑπάνδρου). Prov 6:29 warns that a man who has intercourse with a married woman will not be without guilt (ὁ εἰσελθὼν πρὸς γυναῖκα ὕπανδρον). Sir 9:9 warns against social interaction with another man's wife (ὑπάνδρου γυναικός) because it can lead to destruction, while Sir 41:21 includes gazing upon another man's wife (γυναικὸς ὑπάνδρου) among those things for which a man should be ashamed. In Num 5:20, 29 the word occurs in the context of regulations related to the trial by ordeal of a woman expected by her husband to have had sexual relations with another man. Finally, it is noteworthy that when Aelian uses ὕπανδρος to refer to a female mated bird, he does so in a context where he is discussing the watchful and jealous behavior of the male species. If the male purple coot sees the "mistress of its house to be adulterous, it strangles itself."[9]

The third category corresponds to something like a "mode of life" that is expected of a married woman. A good example of this meaning is in Diodorus Siculus, who recounts a story that is repeated in two of the other texts where ὕπανδρος is found.[10] Diodorus describes in detail the bizarre story of a young woman named Heraïs who is given in marriage to Samiades. After they had been married for a year, Samiades went on a long journey leaving his wife behind. Heraïs became ill with an abdominal tumor which

---

[9]Aelianus, *De natura animalium* 3.42.8.

[10]Diodorus Siculus, *Bibliotheca Historica* 32.10.4, written between 60 and 30 BC. The other texts are Posidonius, *Fragmenta* 85.48, a Stoic philosopher in Rhodes who lived c. 135-50 BC, and Photius, *Bibliotheca*, Codex 244, 377, line 39. Photius was a 9th century patriarch of Byzantium who kept accounts of the books he read.

eventually burst revealing male genitals. Her hermaphroditic condition was concealed with the cooperation of family and servants. Upon recovery, Diodorus says that she "wore feminine attire and continued to conduct herself as a homebody and as one subject to a husband (ὕπανδρος)."[11] Upon his return, Samiades sought the sexual company of his wife, but she resisted. Fearing embarrassment, her father attempted to shield her from Samiades and a quarrel erupted between the father and Samiades. The latter subsequently resorted to a lawsuit to force his wife to fulfill her obligations. When it became apparent that the judge was about to order Heraïs to go home with Samiades, she displayed the male genitals to the judge and protested that "a man should not be required to cohabit with a man."[12]

Here ὕπανδρος involves sexual obligations, as in the examples noted in the second category of usage. However, the association of female apparel and domesticity with this particular usage suggests that broader social assumptions could be included. A "mode of life" expected of wives seems, therefore, to belong to this usage.[13]

Although ὕπανδρος was sometimes used simply to designate a married woman as distinct from an unmarried woman without any apparent emphasis on her social status vis-a-vis her husband, it was also used to refer to a husband's rights, especially regarding sexual expectations. Fitzmyer[14] is correct, then, when he sees in ὕπανδρος a legal connotation: "By OT law a wife was considered the chattel or property of her husband, and he had rights over her that could be violated by her or by another man."

---

[11]*Diodorus Siculus* 32.10.4. The translation is from the Loeb Classical Library. The Greek phrase reads: τὴν δὲ ἀπολυθεῖσαν τῆς νόσου τὴν ἐσθῆτα φορεῖν γυναικείαν, καὶ τὴν ἄλλην ἀγωγὴν οἰκουρὸν καὶ ὕπανδρον διαφυλάττειν.

[12]*Diodorus Siculus* 32.10.6.

[13]See also Eustathius, *Commentarii ad Homeri Odysseam*, 1.260, lines 26f.

[14] Joseph Fitzmyer, *Romans* (AB; New York: Doubleday, 1993): 457.

3. The Meaning of ὕπανδρος in Rom. 7:2

The rhetorical goal of Paul's letter to the Romans was to create as much common ground as possible between Jewish and Gentile Christians. To accomplish this task it was necessary for Paul to avoid depreciating Israel's covenantal status, while at the same time disallowing ethnic barriers that would render supposed common ground meaningless. If successful, the letter would facilitate unity in and among the Roman Christian communities, answer critics of Paul's gospel as the delivery of the Jerusalem contribution approached, and help create a more unified base for Paul's westward mission.[15] The Roman letter was obviously a monumental undertaking, however, the most difficult part of the literary task Paul faced was that of explaining the Christian's relationship to the law.[16] It is this issue that Paul faces squarely in the seventh chapter of the letter.

The law of Moses represented an enormous ethnic barrier which limited the incorporation of Gentiles into Jewish communities—as well as into many Christian communities—in the first century AD. The law, and more particularly the way of life it defined, provided a protective boundary that guarded diaspora Jewish communities from invasion by the pagan world.[17] As long as the law served a function in Christian communities parallel to the one it served in Jewish communities, Christianity could only be an ethnic/nationalistic religion. Paul, in his work among Gentiles, saw this truth clearly. The controversy over circumcision and dietary laws in early Christianity was in

---

[15]For a more detailed treatment of the setting and purpose of the letter, as well as extensive bibliography, see James C. Walters, *Ethnic Issues in Paul's Letter to the Romans* (Valley Forge, PA: Trinity Press International, 1993).

[16]Fitzmyer's, *Romans*, 455, comment regarding the difficulty of Rom 7 would find few scholarly dissenters: "Paul's ideas on the law are complicated, and this chapter becomes the most difficult in the letter to understand."

[17]See discussion of boundary-keeping functions in Wayne Meeks, *The First Urban Christians* (New Haven: Yale Univ. Press, 1983): 97.

fact a debate over this issue.[18]

In Rom 7:1-6 Paul says that because Christians have died to the law, they are free to be united with Christ for the purpose of bearing fruit for God.[19] By mentioning the goals of "bearing fruit for God" in v. 4 and serving in "the new life of the Spirit" in v. 6, Paul seeks to ameliorate the fears of those who might be uncomfortable with the effects of his claim that Christians have been released from the law. In fact, by focusing on the Christian's death to sin in chap. 6 prior to facing the issue of the law in chap. 7, Paul has already framed the discussion in the least alarming fashion. Therefore, the transition to the discussion of the law is already underway in chap. 6 and is becoming obvious by the middle of the chapter. Rom 6:14 claims that "sin shall not rule over you; for you are not under law but under grace" (ὑπὸ νόμον ἀλλὰ ὑπὸ χάριν). That Paul knows his critics wait at the door is indicated by the following verse: "What then? Shall we sin because we are not under law but under grace" (ὑπὸ νόμον ἀλλὰ ὑπὸ χάριν)? "Absolutely not!" Paul's use of ὑπό to indicate a position under the power of

---

[18] Hence Paul's rebuke of Peter in Antioch (Gal 2:14), "If you being a Jew live as a Gentile and not as a Jew, how is it that you require Gentiles to Judaize?!" See James Dunn, "The Theology of Galatians: The Issue of Covenantal Nomism," *Pauline Theology* (ed. Jouette Bassler; Minneapolis: Fortress, 1991): 130.

[19] That Paul means the Jewish law and not Roman law or law in some general sense is indicated by the context and also by the assumption in the analogy that a woman cannot initiate a divorce. In Roman law women could initiate a divorce, in Jewish law they could not. For extensive bibliography reflecting the various positions that have been taken on the meaning of "law" here, see Fitzmyer, *Romans*, 455f. On differences in the social situations of Jewish and non-Jewish women in the period, compare the essays of Gregory Sterling and Randall Chesnutt in *Essays on Women in Earliest Christianity* (ed. C. D. Osburn; Joplin, MO: College Press, 1993): 1.41-92, 93-130. On the Roman legal situation, see Susan Treggiari, *Roman Marriage: Iusti Coniuges from the Time of Cicero to the Time of Ulpian* (Oxford: Clarendon, 1991): 435-82. Jewish practice was based primarily on interpretations of Deut 24:1-4. See Jacob Neusner, *Judaism: The Evidence of the Mishnah* (Chicago: Univ. of Chicago Press, 1981): 59f.

some overlord is indicated by his use of κυριεύσει (have dominion) in v. 14 and the extended slavery analogy in vv. 16-23.[20] His use of κυριεύει (binding) in 7:1 and δουλεύειν (enslave) in 7:6 suggests that Paul still had not abandoned the metaphor in the passage under consideration. Therefore it is very likely that Paul chose ὕπανδρος in Rom 7:2 because the ὑπό prefix tightened his analogy between marriage and the law, an analogy that needed—as we shall see below—all the tightening it could get!

The context of Rom 7:2 contains indications, therefore, that Paul used ὕπανδρος with the intent of emphasizing its etymology.[21] However, as in the examples cited in the second category above, the authority or power of the husband over his wife is focused on sexual obligations. The crucial issue for the analogy in Rom 7:2-3 is that of determining when a married woman can be with another man without being called an adulteress. Therefore, τοῦ νόμου τοῦ ἀνδρός (the law of the husband) should be understood in this context as the law that establishes the husband's right to exclusive sexual access to his wife. Consequently, the husband does not directly represent the law in the analogy; husband and law are not in apposition.[22]

4. *The Analogy to the Law*

At first glance the analogy Paul makes between the Christian's freedom from the law and a woman's freedom from marital obligations seems straightforward. Yet, a

---

[20]On the development of the argument in this section, see James Dunn, *Romans* (WBC; Dallas: Word Books, 1988): 1.333-57.

[21]That an author could use the word with the intent of utilizing aspects of its etymology is indicated by Num 5:19-20 and also a text in Eustatius' commentary on Homer's *Odyssey*, 1.260, line 27. Both works use the adjective ὕπανδρος in close proximity to the prepositional phrases ὑπὸ ἄνδρα and ὑπὸ ἀνδράσιν, respectively.

[22]Here I agree with C. E. B. Cranfield, *A Critical and Exegetical Commentary on the Epistle to the Romans* (Edinburgh: T & T Clark, 1975): 333.

closer look reveals that the comparison is at best awkward. The most fundamental incongruence is that the woman who becomes free upon her husband's death is the one who—by implication—has died (v. 4). Another way of putting it is that neither the wife nor the husband in the analogy in vv. 2-3 corresponds accurately to the "person" in v. 1 or v. 4; this is because the person who dies in the analogy is not the one who becomes free on that basis.[23] When one puts this ambiguity alongside the problem of interpreting the phrase τοῦ νόμου τοῦ ἀνδρός, the difficulties are undeniable.[24] Scholars have admitted the problem almost without exception.[25] Some have moved to limit the problem by

---

[23]Or, as Joyce Little, "Paul's Use of Analogy: A Structural Analysis of Romans 7:1-6," *CBQ* 46 (198)]: 86, puts it:

> No matter how one distributes the roles, there is no way to get around the fact that these roles cannot be consistently applied throughout the first four verses. The analogical approach cannot get around the switch Paul makes in the subject of freedom from the man in v. 1 to the wife in v. 3. The allegorical approach cannot get around the splitting of the role of the man in v. 1 into the two roles of husband and wife in v. 2.

[24]No other scholar has been as negative (and dramatic) as C. H. Dodd, *The Epistle of Paul to the Romans* (New York: Harper & Brothers, 1932): 101, in pointing out the problems with the analogy:

> What, then, is the application of the illustration, or metaphor, or allegory, or whatever it is? Broadly speaking, what seems to be in Paul's mind is the idea that a man was wedded to Law (which means wedded to Sin), but by death he is free to be wedded to Christ. Thus "law" plays a double part. The whole story is an example of the working of a law, and, at the same time, "Law" is a character in the story! To make confusion worse confounded, it is not Law, the first husband, who dies: The Christian, on the other hand, is *dead to the law*. The illustration, therefore, has gone hopelessly astray. The only *tertium comparationis* that remains is the bare fact that, in one way or another, death puts an end to obligation.

[25]In a recently published Evangelical commentary on Romans, James Edwards, *Romans* (NIBC; Peabody, MA: Hendrickson, 1992): 179, wrote:

> The analogy is not exactly appropriate to illustrate the point of verse 1, however, because it fails the test of logic at the end.

restricting the role of the analogy. Fitzmyer's[26] recent judgment, that Paul "uses the illustration for one point only: the law's obligation ceases when death occurs . . .," concurs with that of a number of recent scholars. Others, such as Sanday and Headlam,[27] have discerned an allegory in which the wife represented the true self and the husband stood for the preconversion state, while the law of the husband was the law which condemned the preconversion state and the new marriage was the union of the convert with Christ.

Joyce Little[28] is critical of both the analogical and allegorical approaches that have been offered to explain the verses. She argues that the failure of scholars to make sense of *Rom.* 7:1-4 by interpreting verses 2-3 as an analogy or an allegory stems from the fact that Paul is making not one analogy but two and that the point Paul wishes to arrive at is in verse 6, viz., that we die to the law in order to "serve in the new life of the Spirit." The first marriage (v. 2) is then a straight analogy attempting to cast light on verse one—particularly how death can free someone from law. The second marriage (v. 3) is a stepping stone Paul uses to move

---

In verses 2-3 the husband (=law) dies, whereas in verse 4 it is the believer (=wife) who dies to the law. Obviously, it is not the law which dies but the believer who dies in Christ, as Paul says in verse 4. Because the analogy does not correspond in every respect to the point it illustrates, it is unwise to press it too far.

[26]Joseph Fitzmyer, *Romans*, 455. See also H. M. Gale, *The Use of Analogy in the Letters of Paul* (Philadelphia: Westminster, 1964): 198; Cranfield, *Commentary on the Epistle to the Romans*, 1.335; Ernst Käsemann, *Commentary on Romans* (trans. Geoffrey W. Bromiley; Grand Rapids: Eerdmans, 1980): 187.

[27]William Sanday and Arthur Headlam, *A Critical and Exegetical Commentary on the Epistle to the Romans* (ICC; Edinburgh: T & T Clark, 1895): 172. More recently, J. C. O'Neill, *Paul's Letter to the Romans* (Baltimore: Penguin, 1975): 122, has interpreted the wife as the believer and the husband as the body. For a brief description of other allegorical views, including patristic writers, see Little, *CBQ* 46 (1984): 86.

[28]Little, *CBQ* (1984): 89.

sequentially from the first analogy to the point in v. 6: Fruitfulness in the second marriage is made possible by being freed from the law. The movement to the second analogy would then reflect Paul's desire to affirm the Christian's freedom from the law without leaving himself open to the charge of encouraging sin.[29]

Although Little's approach does resolve some of the difficulties one faces in the text, she ultimately has to admit that the point Paul wishes to illustrate finds no exact human counterpart:

> Paul is trying in this analogy to express the reality of a unique event in the world, an event which makes it possible for a man to die and yet live. There are no parallels for this experience. Nor are there any parallels in law for the process by which this new event makes it possible for a man to die into a new freedom before the law.[30]

This dilemma is one that interpreters often face when they look closely at Pauline analogies, a dilemma that should warn interpreters to proceed with hermeneutical caution. In his study of Pauline analogies, Gale[31] emphasizes that the analogical pictures that Paul presents often include elements that do not correspond accurately to the life situations from which they are drawn. Rom 7:1-6 is one of the eleven

---

[29] In fact, Little, *CBQ* (1984): 90, argues for a threefold use of the double analogy:

> First, Paul is concerned with demonstrating that the law played a necessary role prior to the coming of Christ (hence the validity of the law governing the first marriage). Second, Paul wishes to use vv. 2-3 as an analogy demonstrating that death can change one's relationship to the law. Third, Paul wishes to use the analogy structurally as a means by which to develop his view that our death to the law takes place for a specific purpose, in order that we might "serve in the new life of the Spirit."

[30] *Ibid.*, 87.

[31] Gale, *The Use of Analogy in the Letters of Paul*, 231.

examples of this phenomenon that Gale includes to substantiate his point. The reason for this is not that "Paul lacks the gift for sustained illustration of ideas through concrete images" or that he has a "defect of imagination," as Dodd claims.³² Rather, Paul operates with a fluid approach wherein he exercises considerable freedom to adapt the phenomena on which his analogies are based to the realities he wishes to illustrate.

The hermeneutical implications of the preceding discussion are rather obvious. The interpreter should be extremely cautious when pressing Paul's analogies into the service of a point other than the one on which Paul was focused. Furthermore, Paul's analogies should not be used to uncover what Paul believed or thought about the human situation that provided the basis for the analogy.³³

Conclusion

Whether or not one agrees with the views of marriage expressed by D. M. Lloyd-Jones which I cited at the outset of this essay, it should be apparent that neither Paul's use of ὕπανδρος, nor the argument of Rom 7:1-6, should be used to advance such an interpretation. These verses do not represent a commentary on the Christian view of the relation between a wife and her husband. Ὕπανδρος is not the term normally used by Paul—nor other biblical authors, or even pagan writers—to refer to a married woman. Paul used the word in Rom 7:2 to underscore the husband's exclusive sexual rights, a strategy that strengthened his legal analogy. Moreover, the analogy to the law does not indicate that the Christian husband is the law to his wife because husband and law are not in apposition in the text, and because the use of a Pauline analogy to decipher the Apostle's thought regarding this matter is a hermeneutical mistake from the start.

---

³²Dodd, *Epistle to the Romans*, 120f.

³³This point serves as the climactic conclusion of Gale's, *The Use of Analogy in the Letters of Paul*, 231, study of the Pauline analogies.

Chapter Eleven

1 COR 7:4 —AUTHORITY OVER THE BODY

Robert F. Hull, Jr.

The wife does not have authority over her own body, but the husband; likewise also the husband does not have authority over his own body, but the wife.

Studies on the place of women in early Christianity often refer to Paul's instructions about marriage in 1 Cor 7:3-4 as evidence that he championed an egalitarianism between the sexes without parallel in the Greco-Roman world.[1] These studies take as a given that women were subordinate to men in virtually all relationships in Jewish and Greco-Roman antiquity. Thus, if Paul claims that Christian husbands and wives have equal authority over one another's bodies, this is evidence that he was setting forth a new and revolutionary pattern.[2] In the language of Robin Scroggs, Paul lays the basis for the "eschatological woman,"

---

[1]The classic statement of this position is Robin Scroggs, "Paul and the Eschatological Woman," *JAAR* 40 (1972): 283-303. Scroggs calls attention especially (294-95) to the number and structure of statements expressing reciprocal obligations and rights of men and women in 1 Cor 7. Wayne Meeks, "The Image of the Androgyne: Some Uses of a Symbol in Earliest Christianity," *HR* 13 (1974): 19, also notes the number of "monotonously parallel statements" about the obligations of men and women.

[2]So Ruth A. Tucker and Walter L. Liefeld, *Daughters of the Church* (Grand Rapids: Zondervan, 1987): 74, who, commenting on 1 Cor 7:4, assume that "men in Paul's day may have felt that they 'owned' their wives and could deal with them in any way they chose." Note Scroggs, *JAAR* 40 (1972): 295, that, "It would have been easy, and in keeping with the times, had Paul stopped with the judgment that the woman's body belonged to the man."

liberated by the gospel to take her place alongside the man in every sphere of life.³ In this interpretation, 1 Cor 7:4 provides support for the construction of Paul as a feminist.⁴

On the other hand, some scholars hold that Paul remained a traditionalist with regard to women, but that the gospel he preached did result in a number of women laying hold on new-found freedoms and behaving in ways that threatened to upset the status quo. For these students such passages as 1 Cor 11:2-16 and 1 Cor 14:34-35 show that Paul acted to forestall the upsetting of the social order by putting women back into their customary roles.⁵ A recent study along these lines holds that some of the "liberated" women of Corinth had separated themselves from their families, including husbands, to devote themselves to an ascetic way of life. It is primarily these women who are being addressed in 1 Cor 7:2-5. The neatly-balanced reciprocal rules are only a rhetorical device of Paul's by which he is really requiring these independent women to submit again to the men, who are unwilling to forego the sexual relationship the women have abandoned.⁶

Despite all the attention devoted to 1 Cor 7 as a whole, v. 4 has attracted remarkably little attention either in regard to marital relationships in Jewish and Greco-Roman culture or

---

³See n. 1.

⁴Scholars holding this view typically explain texts in the Pauline epistles that restrict the behavior or demeanor of women (1 Cor 11:2-16; 14:34-35; 1 Tim 2:8-15) as interpolations or compositions by a later writer expressing a conservative reaction to Paul's liberationist tendencies. For references, see the essays on the above passages in vol. 1 of the present study.

⁵See Elisabeth Schüssler Fiorenza, *In Memory of Her* (New York: Crossroad, 1985): 230-33; Bernadette Brooten, "Paul and the Law: How Complete Was the Departure?" *Princeton Seminary Bulletin* Supplementary Issue 1 (1990): 73-80.

⁶Antoinette Clark Wire, *The Corinthian Women Prophets: A reconstruction through Paul's Rhetoric* (Minneapolis: Fortress, 1990): 79-84. See also Gordon Fee, *The First Epistle to the Corinthians* (Grand Rapids: Eerdmans, 1987): 278, 280.

to the specific problems being addressed at Corinth. It is the aim of the present study to mend this neglect.

1. *The Cultural Context of 1 Cor 7:4*

Placing this verse within the context of "women's issues" has the potential to skew the way we approach the passage. The "marriage rules" in 1 Cor 7:2-5 appear surprising to modern readers in the western world precisely because we read them in light of contemporary concerns for male/female equality and we read them against popular generalizations about the roles and relationships of men and women in antiquity.[7] In comparison with what we perceive to have been the universal male-dominated realities of marriage in the Jewish and Greco-Roman worlds, Paul's language sounds distinctly modern.[8] But we must be cautious about constructing broad generalizations about male/female social roles in antiquity and then understanding all male/female interaction as conforming to these generalizations.[9]

---

[7]For good introductions to the place of women in Jewish and Greco-Roman society in the Hellenistic and Roman eras see the essays by Gregory E. Sterling and Randall D. Chesnutt, respectively, in vol. 1 of the present work. To the bibliographies cited there should be added Eva Cantarella, *Pandora's Daughters: The Role and Status of Women in Greek and Roman Antiquity* (trans. M. Fant; Baltimore: Johns Hopkins Univ. Press, 1987) and Pauline Schmitt Pantel, ed., *A History of Women in the West* I. From *Ancient Goddesses to Christian Saints* (trans. A. Goldhammer; Cambridge: Harvard Univ. Press, 1992).

[8]The comment of Brendan Byrne, *Paul and the Christian Woman* (Collegeville, MN: Liturgical Press, 1988): 20, is typical of many in recent studies: "The mutuality expressed here diverges sharply from the ethos of the surrounding culture which tended to see everything solely from the point of view of male rights and convenience."

[9]Randall Chesnutt, "Jewish Women in the Greco-Roman Era," *Essays on Women in Earliest Christianity* (ed. C. D. Osburn; Joplin, MO: College Press, 1994): 1.130, says, "Any study of women in the NT and early Christianity which proceeds on the assumption of a monolithic model of ancient Judaism is misinformed and distorted. Judaism existed in the Greco-Roman world in countless local varieties. Before comparing or contrasting ancient Jewish belief and practice with regard to women and some NT text on the subject, one must specify

Notwithstanding the caution I have just raised, the generally subservient position of women to men from the most ancient times for which we have record through the Roman and Byzantine eras of the Mediterranean world is not in question. The social and political hierarchy Aristotle outlined in his *Politics* remains basic to the discussion of social roles in writings well beyond the NT era, and, for many people, even to the present time. It is here we first find discussed the proper relationships of the constituent pairs in a household, namely master to slaves, husband to wife, father to children.[10] "By nature," writes Aristotle, "the male is related to the female thus: the one is superior, the other inferior; the one ruler, the other ruled."[11] But the significance of 1 Cor 7:4 cannot be ascertained by an appeal to the generally subordinate position of women in relation to men in antiquity. 1 Cor 7:4 has to do not with gender roles in general, but with the *relationship* (not *roles*) of husband and wife as sexual partners in marriage. Our question concerns how the equality of husband and wife within the sexual relationship as Paul stipulates it in this verse relates to the cultural norms of Jewish and Greco-Roman society in Corinth in the first century of the Christian era.

A. *Jewish, Greek, and Roman Marriage*

1. *Marriage in the Legal Traditions in the NT Era.* During the oldest periods for which we have data the woman, whether Jewish, Greek, or Roman, was under the authority of a male. The patriarchal narratives of the OT represent the father as giving his daughter to be betrothed (Gen 29:18-19; 34:12). This picture is confirmed in the legal tradition of the Pentateuch (Exod 22:16-17). At the point of

---

which Jewish text, or *which* group of Jews is meant." What Chesnutt says of women in Judaism can be asserted also, *mutatis mutandis*, of the role of women in pagan society and religion in the Greco-Roman world.

[10] Aristotle, *Pol.* 1259a, b (trans. H. Rackham, LCL: Cambridge: Harvard Univ. Press, 1950): 58-61.

[11] Aristotle, *Pol.* 1254b (LCL, 21).

betrothal, she passed under the authority of her husband, who can be said to have "acquired" (Heb. קנה) a wife (Ruth 4:5, 10). Similarly, under Greek law, a woman's (or girl's) father was her lord (κύριος; *kurios*) until she was transferred by marriage to the power of her new *kurios*, her husband.[12] Roman women lived under the ancient institution of *patria potestas*, that is, the control of the male head of the family (*paterfamilias*), whether grandfather, father, or husband.[13] By custom and law these respective traditions had implications for property rights, divorce, and the legal definition of marriage.

During the Hellenistic and Roman periods, however, marriage laws and practices among Jews, Greeks, and Romans underwent important changes from earlier times.[14] There was a move in all three groups toward marriage as an agreement between husband and wife.[15] Marriage contracts from these times illustrate a concern to stipulate mutual obligations of husband and wife.[16] Thus, even on the legal front, in the first century AD the tendency was toward recognizing more "rights" for women in marriage.

---

[12]See Gregory Sterling, "Women in the Hellenistic and Roman Worlds," *Essays on Women in Earliest Christianity*, 1.59-60.

[13]See Jane F. Gardner, *Women in Roman Law and Society* (Bloomington: Indiana Univ. Press, 1986): 5-14.

[14]By the time of the late Roman republic (mid-2nd century BC), marriage was generally consensual, and the wife retained her status as an heir in her birth family until the death of her father. For the legal and social ramifications of this development, see Suzanne Dixon, *The Roman Family* (Baltimore: Johns Hopkins Univ. Press, 1992): 74-77.

[15]See S. R. Llewelyn, ed. *New Documents Illustrating Early Christianity*, 6 (AHDRC; Sydney: Macquarie Univ., 1992): 12, who notes, "In antiquity different legal systems ran in parallel and each could and did exert an influence on the other." This article discusses (1-18) papyrus documents illustrating some changes in marriage law in Hellenistic and Roman Egypt and their implications for the NT, and also summarizes important developments outside of Egypt.

[16]For specific changes see Llewelyn, *Early Documents Illustrating Early Christianity*, 2, 4, 12.

2. *Marriage in the Moral Tradition in the NT Era.* The legal status of husbands and wives in marriage has no necessary connection with the moral and personal concerns about what marriage means. This was true in ancient times, as it is still in our own times. 1 Cor 7:3 reminds us that there were "obligations" in marriage, but whether Paul had in mind moral obligations or specific legislation regarding sexual intercourse is not clear.[17] In any case, v. 4 is not a reminder of a law, but a statement about how a husband and wife ought to regard each other as partners in the sexual relationship. As such, it invites us to consider whether there are analogues in ancient literature to Paul's statement about reciprocal "authority over the body."

It is difficult for moderns of European ancestry to talk about partnership in a sexual marriage relationship without invoking the emotional language of romance, in which a man and woman freely choose each other (or "fall in love") and seek to attain perfect bliss in bodily self-giving. We should not expect this ideal to be represented in ancient sources, since the concept of romantic love is not a universal construct. Nor should we necessarily expect that references to the marriage relationship will carry the same emotional overtones as modern discourse in the West. Nevertheless,

---

[17]Among rabbinic teachings attributed to pre-AD 70 sages, there is concern with the question of sexual obligations in marriage. In the Judaism of the eras here under concern, marriage (and procreation) was regarded as a commandment (*mitzvah*). Exod 21:10 specifies the obligations of a master who takes a slave as a bride and then marries another woman, including the stipulation that he "not diminish . . . her marital rights." Commenting on this law, the schools of Shammai and Hillel differed on the length of time and the reasons for which a man could legitimately deny to his wife sexual intercourse (*Ketubot* 5.6; *b. Ketubot* 47b, 48a). Eventually a considerable body of rabbinic commentary emerged on the husband's obligation (*mitzvah*) to provide marital intercourse, even for non-procreative purposes. Although the husband's "rights" are sometimes mentioned (*Ketubot* 5.7), the overwhelming concern is with the wife's rights. See David M. Feldman, *Birth Control and Jewish Law* (Westport: Greenwood, 1968): 60-80. In classical Athens, Solon's law required that the husband of an heiress approach her sexually three times a month. (Plutarch, *Solon* 20.3.1).

many Greek and Latin sources, dating all the way to Homeric times, do portray mutual respect and affection as the ideal of marriage.[18]

For attitudes about marriage during the Julio-Claudian era (44 BC-AD 68), Plutarch (AD 50-120) is often quoted. He comments on Solon's prohibition of dowries in most marriages: "For he did not wish marriage to be for profit or price, but that a husband and wife should live together for childbearing, and delight, and affection."[19] Even such control as a husband exercised over a wife ought to be, said Plutarch, "not as the owner has control of a piece of property, but as the soul controls the body, by entering into her feelings and being knit to her through goodwill."[20] In addition to these somewhat stilted expressions, there are the far more emotive letters of Cicero to his absent wife[21] and Pliny to his.[22]

It is the later Stoic moralists who provide the closest ideological analogues to Paul's instructions. Hierokles (AD

---

[18]Homer, *Odyssey*, 6. 182-85 has Odysseus say of his own partnership with Penelope: "For nothing is stronger and better than this: When a man and wife live together in their home, their thoughts of one accord—a great pain to their enemies, but a joy to their friends, as they themselves especially know."

[19]*Solon* 20. 4. Sarah Pomeroy's, *Goddesses, Whores, Wives, and Slaves: Women in Classical Antiquity* (New York: Schocken, 1975): 87, judgment that in classical Athens (time of Solon) "connubial intercourse was devoid of any concept of spiritual union" seems unduly harsh. It is difficult to say for certain what emotions people in the past may have felt, particularly if it was not the literary fashion to speak of such things. Prior to the first century BC most sources focus on the external arrangements and conditions of marriage, not on emotions.

[20]Plutarch, *Advice to Bride and Groom, Moralia* 2.142E (trans. F. Babbitt; LCL; Cambridge: Harvard Univ. Press, 1962): 323.

[21]Cicero, *To His Family* 14.4 in Robert Y. Tyrrell, ed., *Cicero in his Letters* (London: Macmillan, 1922): 12-15.

[22]Pliny, *Epist.* 7. I owe these examples to Dixon, *The Roman Family*, 87, who says "There are probably elements of literary conceit in all of these, but all see it as appropriate to adopt the language and imagery of passionate, romantic love when speaking of married love."

117-138) describes marriage as a koinonia of husband and wife, a "yoking" of the two.[23] He also speaks of the married couple as "having become partners even as far as their bodies and more, even of their souls."[24] Antipater, another of the later Stoics, writes also of this community of possession, noting that husbands and wives have in common "not only their property and the things that are nearest and dearest to all men—namely their children and their souls—but also their bodies."[25] In all of Greco-Roman literature, however, no other writer approaches so closely to Paul as Musonius Rufus, especially in the rhetorical question, "To whom are all things considered to be common, body, soul, and possessions, except man and wife?"[26] These Stoic philosophers thus come very close to Paul's sentiments in understanding marriage to be a full partnership, including a common "ownership" of the body.[27] They give no support to Scroggs's statement that "it would have been in keeping with the times" to assert that "the woman's body belonged to the man."[28]

---

[23]Hierokles, *On Duties* 4. 28. 21. See ET in A. J. Malherbe, *Moral Exhortation: A Graeco-Roman Sourcebook* (Philadelphia: Westminster, 1986): 98.

[24]Hierokles, *Stobaeus* 4.505.12-20.

[25]Antipater, *On Marriage* 15. See ET in Larry Yarbrough, *Not Like the Gentiles—Marriage Rules in the Letters of Paul* (Atlanta: Scholars Press, 1985): 39. I owe the above two examples to Yarbrough's book.

[26]Musonius Rufus, *F* 14. All three essays of Musonius on the topic "of Marriage" should be read; see Cora Lutz, *Musonius Rufus* (Yale Classical Studies 10; New Haven: Yale Univ. Press, 1947): 89-97.

[27]As Malherbe, *Moral Exhortation,* 88-104, points out, the topic "on marriage" was related by various moralists to the ancient ideals of unity in society and/ or reciprocity in all human relationships. Obviously, one must distinguish between relationships and roles. Even the most "enlightened" moralist, Musonius Rufus, supports very traditional notions about the proper social roles of men and women.

[28]See n. 2.

It could perhaps be argued that moralists such as Plutarch and Musonius Rufus could afford to idealize marriage and the sexual relationship with wives because of the well-nigh universal "double standard." Plutarch himself distinguishes sex for pleasure, which might be indulged in with a slave or paramour, from sex for the procreation of proper heirs, which was the main purpose of sex in marriage.[29] Yet there was no monolithic attitude toward sex, sexual propriety, and sexual pleasure even among men in Jewish or Greco-Roman antiquity. Physicians, playwrights and poets expressed both the grosser and purer aspects of sexuality.[30] Some philosophers and moralists in pagan antiquity were as reticent to speak of sex openly, and as abstemious about sex for pleasure only as some of the church fathers of late antiquity.[31] On the one hand the Latin poet, Ovid (1st c. BC – 1st c. AD) celebrates the joys of sexual bliss (to be sure, with a mistress) and emphasizes the full reciprocal nature of the experience;[32] on the other hand, some of the later Stoics condemned sex for pleasure even in marriage.[33] This ambivalence about sex can also be seen in

---

[29]Plutarch, *Advice to Bride and Groom,* 140 B 16, says a wife should not be indignant when her husband gives way to passion with a paramour or maidservant, "but she should reason that it is respect for her which leads him to share his debauchery, licentiousness, and wantonness with another woman" (LCL, 309).

[30]See, on the whole subject, Peter Brown, *The Body and Society* (New York: Columbia Univ. Press, 1988): 5-25. For attitudes to sexual behavior among classical Greeks, see K. J. Dover, "Classical Greek Attitudes to Sexual Behaviour," *Arethusa* 6 (1973): 59-73.

[31]*Ibid.,* 65-121. Brown here traces attitudes toward sex from Hermas and Tertullian through the Encratites and Gnostics.

[32]Ovid, *Art of Love* 2. 683-87, says, "Let both man and woman feel what delights them equally . . . . I hate her who gives because she must, and who, herself unmoved, is thinking of her wool. Pleasure given as a duty has no charms for me; for me let no woman be dutiful." A little farther on (2. 727-28), he emphasizes the importance of mutual sexual fulfilment: "Haste side by side to the goal: Then is pleasure full, when man and woman lie vanquished together."

[33]Musonius Rufus, *F* 12. Lutz, *Musonius Rufus,* 87, says, "Men who are not wantons or immoral are bound to consider sexual

some rabbinic comments which extol the importance of bringing children into the world but are deeply suspicious of the means by which this is accomplished.[34]

It is characteristic of NT authors to portray Gentiles as complete sexual profligates (Rom 1:24-27; Eph 4:17-19; 1 Pet 4:3-4). No doubt the sexual practices of many Greeks and Romans in the NT era were reprehensible, but it was not uncommon for philosophers of the time to exalt sexual chastity as a virtue. Handbooks on marriage by Greek and Latin authors typically celebrate the affection and concord of the couple, rather than counseling either sexual passivity by the wife or an insistence on marital "rights" by the husband.

Jewish sources that may reflect attitudes toward marriage and sexuality during the NT era are difficult to identify, due to problems of dating rabbinic tradition. Of course such phenomena as positive portrayals of marriage within the Hebrew Bible (Book of Ruth, for example) as well as the use of the language of tenderness in God's "wooing" of Israel to be his bride (Hos 2:14) suggest that the ideology of marriage was not dominated by purely selfish male interests. Jewish tradition on this subject usually takes the form of debate and pronouncement directed to men on the legal regulations guarding marriage. Even so, the blessings of the marriage ceremony given in the Talmud do include references to companionship and mutual joy.[35]

---

intercourse justified only when it occurs in marriage and is indulged in for the purpose of begetting children, since that is lawful, but unjust and unlawful when it is mere pleasure-seeking, even in marriage."

[34]See David Biale, *From Intercourse to Discourse: Control of Sexuality in Rabbinic Literature* (Center for Hermeneutical Studies, Protocol of the 62nd Colloquy; San Anselmo, CA: Center for Hermeneutical Studies, 1992): 3-6, 17-23.

[35]See *b. Ketubot* 20a in Feldman, *Birth Control*, 35: "Blessed art Thou, O Lord our King, God of the universe, who has created joy and gladness, bridegroom and bride, mirth and exultation, pleasure and delight, peace and companionship."

1 Cor 7:4—Authority Over the Body

The references above go far to demonstrate that in ancient sources dealing with the moral and emotional relationship in marriage, a concern for mutuality of interests and a true partnership both of body and spirit is a fairly stock ingredient.

The way in which Paul frames his support for mutuality and reciprocity is, however, quite unusual, particularly his use of the phrase "authority over the body." Because of the singularity of this phrase in the context of sexual love, it is necessary to ask about possible literary influences on Paul in his formulation of 1 Cor 7:4.

2. The Literary Context of 1 Cor 7:4

A. *Classical Literature.* I have found only one passage in classical literature with a *verbal* resemblance to 1 Cor 7:4 and its immediate context. In discussing slavery, Aristophanes (c. 445-385 BC) writes, "For a man's body [of the slave], such is fate, belongs (τὸν κύριον κρατεῖν) not to himself, but to who'er has bought it."[36] A scholion attributed to Junt[ilius?] reads ἐξουσιάζειν (have right or authority over) for κρατεῖν (take into possession, hold). What makes the passage intriguing is not only the variant reading, which gives us the rare phrase ἐξουσιάζειν σῶμα (have authority over body), but also the reference to purchasing a slave, which occurs also in the context of 1 Cor 7:4, namely at 6:20 (although 1 Cor has a different word for "purchase"). It is not impossible that Paul knew Aristophanes, who was much quoted in antiquity, but it seems to me highly unlikely that Paul's language has been influenced by this passage.

B. *The Old Testament.* Neh 9:37 (LXX) yields an example of the word combination σῶμα (body) + ἐξουσιάζω (have authority). In a reference to the Babylonian exile, the author

---

[36]Aristophanes, *Plutus* 5 in *Aristophanes* (trans. B. B. Rogers; LCL; Cambridge: Harvard Univ. Press, 1946): 365. The use of the word σῶμα body) as a synonym for "slave" is attested in Greek literature from the 4th c. BC on; See *LSJ*, σῶμα, 1749 (II. 2); see Rev 18:13 for an example in the NT.

observes that the remnant in occupied Judaea are now under kings who "have authority over our bodies" (τὰ σώματα ἡμῶν ἐξουσιάζουσιν). Nothing suggests that Paul had this text in mind when writing 1 Cor 7:4, but there may be here an unconscious verbal allusion.

A more interesting linkage occurs in Sirach 47:18 where the author, in his recounting of Israel's famous heroes, chides Solomon, saying, "You took women to lie at your side and were brought into subjection in your body (ἐνεξουσιάσθης ἐν τῷ σώματί σου)." Again, the resemblance is not close enough to suggest a literary borrowing by Paul, but the connection of the phrase in question with sexual activity makes it worth our notice.

C. *The New Testament.* Only in 1 Cor 7 and 1 Thess 4 does Paul issue specific directives about entering into marriage and the sexual relationship appropriate to marriage. Direct literary connections with 1 Cor 7:4 must be sought, therefore, in its immediate context and in Paul's earlier teaching about marriage in 1 Thessalonians.

1. *1 Cor 7:4 and Paul's Argument.* Although by common consent, 7:1 introduces a major section of 1 Cor, Paul's argument is not unrelated to the discussion immediately preceding. Indeed, the recurring term πορνεία (fornication; 5:1; 6:13, 18; 7:2) and related words (πόρνος [fornicator], 6:9; πόρνη [prostitute], 6:16) show that a concern with sexual misconduct drives much of the argument of chaps. 5-7, even though the specific examples of sexual misconduct differ in the three chaps.[37] In its turn, 5:1-13 is linked to earlier parts of the letter by several key terms including "boasting" (1:29, 31; 3:21; 4:7-5:6); "power" (4:19-20; 5:4) and "being puffed up" (4:6, 18, 19; 5:2).[38]

---

[37]An admirable example of a close reading of the text with attention to literary structure is Charles H. Talbert, *Reading Corinthians* (New York: Crossroad, 1989).

[38]*Ibid.*, 12.

These seemingly disparate themes are all related to what seems to be a misplaced understanding on the part of some at Corinth about what it means to be "spiritual" (2:10-3:1; 12:1-3). Some in Corinth appear to believe that since they are now living in the power of the Spirit of Christ, they have been freed from any strictures on their life in the world, including any limitations on sexual conduct. "All things are lawful" (6:12; 10:23) and "food for the stomach and the stomach for food" (6:13) were their slogans. The sexual desire is to be treated as a bodily appetite only, with no connection to the moral sphere, which concerned the inner, "spiritual" life only. Others, however, seemed to think that life in the Spirit so transcended corporeal concerns that believers should eschew all sexual conduct, even in marriage, and live an ascetic life, as though the resurrection had already occurred (1 Cor 15:12; see also 4:8).[39]

---

[39]The difficulty of identifying the theological problem or problems (traditionally the "opponents") faced by Paul at Corinth is well known. Since Paul alludes to σχίσματα (divisions) in 11:18, it may be that several erroneous ideologies are at work in Corinth. Efforts to account for the problems on the basis of a thoroughgoing Gnosticism, e.g., Walter Schmithals, *Gnosticism in Corinth* (trans. John E. Steely; New York: Abingdon, 1971), have not proved convincing to most. Many scholars agree that some kind of "enthusiasm" involving an overrealized eschatology is a major part of the problem. See Hans Conzelmann, *1 Corinthians* (trans. J. Leitch; Hermeneia; Philadelphia: Fortress, 1975): 15-16; and Gordon D. Fee, *The First Epistle to the Corinthians* (NIC; Grand Rapids: Eerdmans, 1987): 10-12. For a methodological critique of past efforts and a model for identifying opponents in Paul's letters see Jerry L. Sumney, *Identifying Paul's Opponents. The Question of Method in 2 Corinthians* (JSNT Sup 40; Sheffield: Sheffield Academic Press, 1990). Although the abstention from sexual relations is related to a complex of issues at Corinth, it is not necessary to connect it especially with an "overrealized eschatology." In fact, the practice of sexual abstinence in connection with religious cults, particularly those of Egypt (which were well-represented in Paul's Corinth) was widespread. See Richard E. Oster, Jr., "Use, Misuse and Neglect of Archaeological Evidence in Some Modern Works on 1 Corinthians (1 Cor 7,1-5; 8,10; 11,2-17; 12,14-26)," *ZNW* 83 (1992): 58-64.

2. *A Corinthian Maxim and Paul's Response.* The Corinthian "ascetics" expressed their attitude toward sexual conduct in a maxim:[40] "It is good for a man not to touch a woman" (1 Cor 7:1). Although Paul does not reject this maxim, neither does he accept it uncritically. Rather, in keeping with the instructions laid down in handbooks of rhetoric, he adds what Aristotle calls an "epilogue,"[41] that is, explanatory material applying the general statement to a particular situation or rhetorical strategy.[42] It is in Paul's qualification of the maxim that he sets out his distinctive understanding of the sexual relationship within marriage, as well as connected issues. But Paul is not working *ad hoc.* Rather, he adapts to the Corinthian situation "marriage rules" formulated earlier in his pastoral letter to the Thessalonian believers (1 Thess 4:3-8). This passage, therefore, forms part of the literary context of 1 Cor 7:1-7. Specifically, 1 Thess 4:3-4 probably underlies the formulation of 1 Cor 7:1-2, which is foundational for understanding 1 Cor 7:4.

> For this is the will of God, your holiness, that you abstain from fornication; each of you should know how to obtain a wife for himself in holiness and honor (1 Thess 4:3-4; my translation).

---

[40]A classic discussion of the maxim (γνώμη; Lat. *sententia*) in ancient literature is Pseudo-Aristotle, *Rhetoric to Alexander* 11 (trans. H. Rackham; LCL; Cambridge: Harvard Univ. Press, 1957): 335-37. On the use of the maxim in Paul's argumentation in 1 Cor, see Rollin Ramsaran, "More Than an Opinion: Paul's Rhetorical Maxim in 1 Corinthians 7:25-26," *CBQ* (forthcoming 1995). Especially relevant is Ramsaran's discussion of καλόν (good; noble) in the formulation of Greco-Roman maxims.

[41]Aristotle, *The Art of Rhetoric* 1419b-1420a (LCL, 467-71).

[42]Pseudo-Aristotle, *Rhetoric to Alexander* 1430 b (LCL, 337), says, "When you say something that is usually accepted, there is no need to produce reasons because what you say is not unfamiliar and does not meet with incredulity; but when what you say is paradoxical, you must specify the reasons briefly, so as to avoid prolixity and not arouse incredulity. The maxims that you produce should be related to the matter in hand, in order that what you say may not seem clumsy and irrelevant."

1 Thess may well be the earliest of Paul's letters.⁴³ Since the "marriage rules" laid down there are not given in response to any stated problem, they probably summarize the paraenesis Paul delivered as part of his general instructions to new believers.⁴⁴ These precepts validate marriage, in part, as a hedge against sexually immoral behavior. They instruct the Thessalonian congregation that "each should know how to obtain a wife for himself in holiness and honor."⁴⁵ It is made clear that the pattern of behavior Paul enjoins on the Thessalonians is intended to distinguish Christian sexual conduct as not motivated by "passion of desire as the Gentiles who do not know God" (1 Thess 4:5). This statement reflects a characteristically Jewish condemnation of Gentile moral behavior.⁴⁶ As we have seen, some Greco-Roman moralists also condemn promiscuous sexual behavior and sexual self-indulgence,⁴⁷ but where the moralists recommend abstinence and sexual self-control, Paul recommends marriage in order to avoid *porneia* (fornication) a tack more common to Jewish moralists.⁴⁸ Paul also differs from most ancient moralists in his lack of reference to procreation as the supreme end of

---

⁴³See W. G. Kümmel, *Introduction to the New Testament* (rev. and trans. H. C. Kee; Nashville: Abingdon, 1975): 257-60.

⁴⁴So Larry O. Yarbrough, *Not Like the Gentiles: Marriage Rules in the Letters of Paul* (SBLDS; Atlanta: Scholars Press, 1985): 66-67.

⁴⁵The expression τὸ ἑαυτοῦ σκεῦος κτᾶσθαι (to acquire a vessel for himself) is variously translated "to take a wife for himself" (RSV), "to control his own body" (NIV), and "[to guard] his member" (NAB). For a list of commentaries in support of each option refer to Yarbrough, *Not Like the Gentiles*, 68, n. 8. I follow his thorough discussion (68-76) here. Recent support for the option that σκεῦος refers to the male sexual organ is found in Charles A. Wanamaker, *The Epistles to the Thessalonians* (NIGTC; Grand Rapids: Eerdmans, 1990).

⁴⁶See, e.g. *Sib. Or.* 3.591-99 in R. H. Charles, *The Apocrypha and Pseudepigrapha of the Old Testament* (Oxford: Clarendon, 1913): 2.389. See also *Ep. Arist.* 152 in Moses Hadas, ed., *Aristeas to Philocrates* (New York: Harper, 1951): 161.

⁴⁷See above, n. 33.

⁴⁸See references in Biale, *From Intercourse to Discourse*, 23-8.

marriage. Moreover, it is clear that Paul does not understand these guidelines as general moral precepts, but as reflecting the will of God specifically embodied in the new community, the church ("For this is the will of God, your sanctification" 1 Thess 4:3). The sexual purity of the Thessalonians was one proof that they had "turned to God from idols to serve the living and true God" (1 Thess 1:9). That is, Paul offers a *theological,* not an *ethical* basis for marriage and a faithful sexual relationship.

When Paul adapts his general paraenesis to the specific situation at Corinth the result is 1) the application of the teaching to both men *and* women (whereas in 1 Thess only men are addressed); 2) the relating of marriage to the larger question about who should have authority over the body of a person who is united to Christ in the church. In his response to the Corinthian maxim, (7:1) Paul uses catchwords and intertextual echoes that place his teachings about marriage in the larger framework of the purposes of God in creation and redemption as well as the smaller framework of particular problems at Corinth.

3. *The Framework of Paul's Argument.* The problem that called forth Paul's response was the apparent decision of some to refrain from sexual activity, even though they were married. But this decision represents only one side of a bipolar attitude about the body and its activities represented at Corinth. The other pole of the problem is dealt with in 6:12-20, which forms the immediate framework for 7:1-7. Paul's response brings both attitudes under the implicit judgment of the purpose of God in creation by means of catchword "echoes" of Scripture.[49]

In his earlier discussion of sexual intercourse with a prostitute (6:15-16), Paul quotes Gen 2:24 (LXX), writing, "Do you not know that whoever unites himself with the

---

[49]For the explication of the idea that Paul often relies, not on direct quotations, but oblique "echoes" of Scripture in his arguments, see Richard B. Hays, *Echoes of Scripture in the Letters of Paul* (New Haven: Yale Univ. Press, 1989).

prostitute is one body [with her], for 'the two,' it says, 'shall be one flesh'." He challenges the libertine notion that what one does with the body is irrelevant, pointing out that the Christian's body has become a "member" (μέλη) of the body of Christ joined to Christ in resurrection (6:14-15), and therefore cannot be united with a prostitute, thus to become one body with her. Here the word "body" (σῶμα) is clearly an "echo" of the word "flesh" (σάρξ) of Gen 2:24. Paul bases his critique of the Corinthians on the divine intention that legitimate sexual union is between not simply a man and a woman, but a husband and his wife. Thus, his discussion of 7:1-7 is anticipated by 6:12-20. The catchword πορνεία (fornication: 6:13, 15, 16, 18) recurs in 7:2 and the catchword σῶμα (body: 6:13, 15, 16, 18, 19, 20) recurs in 7:4. "Let each have" of 7:2 may echo Gen 2:24.

The contextual nature of Paul's response cautions us against generalizing too broadly about Paul's "marriage rules." Some scholars, for example, understand the phrase "because of instances of sexual misconduct," to express Paul's sole rationale for marriage.[50] Yet, we must remember that Paul was not writing a general treatise on marriage, but countering particular problems and answering specific questions.[51] In view of his rhetorical moves and countermoves in 7:8-40, it is perilous to stop at any point and conclude that we have pinned down Paul.[52]

---

[50]So J. Weiss, *Der erste Korintherbrief* (Göttingen: Vandenhoeck & Ruprecht, 1910): 172, who says that in 1 Cor 7:3-4 marriage is considered "only as the ordinance for a regulated satisfying of the sexual desire and is thought of neither for the producing of children nor for partnership in life."

[51]As Weiss, *ibid.*, goes on to acknowledge.

[52]For a discussion of Paul's rhetorical strategies in 1 Cor 7 see Ramsaran, "More Than An Opinion," *CBQ* (forthcoming). In recent years considerable attention has been given to Paul's use of Greco-Roman rhetoric in 1 Cor. See Wire, *The Corinthian Women Prophets* (n. 6 above); Margaret M. Mitchell, *Paul and the Rhetoric of Reconciliation* (Louisville: Westminster/John Knox, 1993); Stephen M. Pogoloff, *Logos and Sophia. The Rhetorical Situation of 1 Corinthians* (SBLDS, 134; Atlanta: Scholars Press, 1992); Rollin A.

It is important for our purposes to note that against the background of the specific problems at Corinth, Paul is able to draw upon both his own earlier teaching (at Thessalonica) and the theology of creation from Scripture (Gen 2:24) to fashion a statement about marriage that reminds one of some of the Stoic expressions about marriage, yet goes beyond them in the specificity of language as well as the theological grounding of the argument. This mutuality is specifically related here to the reciprocal "obligation" of sexual intercourse, (7:3) but both the foundations and the implications of his statement in 7:4 have to do with far more than sexual relations. The analogues to this concern for mutuality of rights in marriage are striking and important, yet by themselves wholly inadequate to account for the form in which Paul states them or for their place in his argument. Only Paul's theological convictions can account for the principle laid down in 1 Cor 7:4.

3. The Theological Context of 1 Cor 7:4

A. *Paul's "Body" Language.* The "body" language of 1 Cor 7:4 is theologically related to that of 6:12-19. Paul's use of σῶμα (body) in these passages is by no means easy to specify, but it is probably best taken to represent the physical body, rather than the whole person.[53] The logic ("Theo"-logic) of Paul's argument does not, however, depend on the precise meaning given to σῶμα. A paraphrase may help to tie his "body language" together and enable us to appreciate the theological basis of his language.

Ramsaran, "The Function of Greco-Roman Maxims in Paul's Argumentation: A Case Study in 1 Corinthians," (unpublished Ph. D. diss., Boston University, 1994).

[53]Since Rudolf Bultmann's, *Theology of the New Testament* (New York: Harper & Row, 1951): 1.193-203, classic treatment, a kind of consensus has obtained in NT theology that "body" in Paul characteristically denotes the whole person (understood as a Hebraic notion) rather than the physical body (understood as a Greek notion). See E. Schweizer, "σῶμα," *TDNT* 7.1025-1044. Cf., however, Robert Gundry, *Soma in Biblica Theology* (SNTSMS 29; Cambridge: Cambridge Univ. Press, 1976).

1 Cor 7:4—Authority Over the Body

When you Corinthians became believers, you were united with Christ. Your bodies (σώματα) became members (μέλη) of him (6:15). Thus united with Christ, your body (σῶμα; i.e., each of you) became a temple of the Holy Spirit (6:19), and you are not free to do with your bodies anything you wish, just to satisfy your desires. Since your bodies are members of Christ, you cannot "take away" (ἄρας) the members of Christ and "join them" (κολλώμενος, 6:16) to a prostitute so as to become a "member" of her (6:15). Since sexual union is a becoming "one flesh" (6:16; Gen 2:24) and in fact, "one body," and since the body is not "for fornication" (πορνεία) but for the Lord (6:13), union with a prostitute is unthinkable. As those in whom the Holy Spirit lives, you are not "your own" to do with your bodies as you please. To change the metaphor, you were bought (like a slave) for a price (6:19) and set to God's service. Therefore, whatever you do with your body is to bring glory to God (6:20).

All of this has implications for a question you wrote about, namely, whether it is best to have no sexual relations at all (7:1), but to live as the spiritual people of the new age. This is not an option for those who are already married—except for a limited time and with mutual agreement (7:5). The sexual relationship within the bounds of marriage is an appropriate use of the body. Not only does it guard against illicit unions (7:2), but it is an obligation each owes the other (7:3). After all, "you are not your own" even in this relationship. Nothing is to "have authority over" you (6:12)—not the illicit sexual desires leading to fornication (6:13), nor the illicit denial of sex in marriage for the practice of pious acts (7:1). The wife does not even "have authority over" her own body, nor does the husband "have authority over" his own body. Each is obligated to the other sexually in a totally mutual relationship under the authority of Christ.

B. *Pastoral Implications.* Paul is not a marriage counselor. His purpose is not to lay down general precepts for a happy home. Paul is first and foremost a pastoral theologian addressing situational needs of various congregations. Nevertheless, if we can learn first to hear Paul speaking to a cultural context very different from our own, we might also "overhear" in his words a needed word from the Lord concerning the marriage of all those who are first of all in union with Christ and who wish to glorify God in their bodies. Here are some suggestions for how our thinking might be guided:

1. The texts we have been considering are addressed to believers only. They have limited, if any, value if used as general principles applying to any marriage. Their foundation is theological, not psychological or humanistic.

2. With respect to 7:4 specifically, the modern western reader is apt to hear this quite differently than Paul's readers would have done so. In modern marriage, at least in the U.S., sexual intercourse is quite often caricatured as the husband's privilege and the wife's obligation.[54] Given such an understanding, 1 Cor 7:4 might be, and doubtless has been, used by Christian husbands or counselors to constrain a reluctant wife to comply, since this is a "command" of Scripture.[55] This understanding is alien to the bulk of moral teaching of both Jewish and Greco-Roman tradition. On the whole, the Greco-Roman writings on marriage paint an idyllic picture of the sexual relationship, limiting its purpose to procreation and providing little, if any, support to the notion that sex (with his wife) was a man's "right." As for Judaism, rabbinic discussion on sexual intercourse far more

---

[54] Fee, *The First Epistle to the Corinthians*, 280.

[55] Thus Alan Padgett, "Feminism in First Corinthians. A Dialogue with Elisabeth Schüssler Fiorenza," *EvQ* 58 (1986): 126, cautions that a legalistic interpretation of the verse "impl[ies] that a man can demand sex from his wife." It would probably not occur to many moderns in the West that the verse could be used to imply that a woman "can demand sex" from her husband!

often insists on the *husband's* obligations than the wife's. *Her* rights were being protected.⁵⁶

3. Any use of this text to insist on one's "rights" in the marriage bed badly misunderstands Paul. Indeed, it is the willing mutual submission of the marriage partners in a situation of complete parity that makes Paul's teaching so worthy of note. Each freely *gives* control of the body to the other; each *gives* the other "the obligation."⁵⁷ This is not a "natural" view of marriage. Such mutual subordination is nurtured in the school of Christ and learned in subordination to him.

---

⁵⁶See n. 17 above.

⁵⁷See Robert Jewett, *Paul's Anthropological Terms* (Leiden: Brill, 1971), with reference to Else Kähler, *Die Frau in den paulinischen Briefen unter besonderer Berucksichtigung des Begriffes der Unterordnung* (Zürich: Gotthelf-Verlag, 1960): 14ff.

Chapter Twelve

PRISCILLA AND AQUILA— CO-WORKERS IN CHRIST

Wendell Willis

Among Paul's hosts and companions, no couple receives more attention than Prisca (or Priscilla) and Aquila, although these two are only mentioned in four NT writings—Acts, Romans, 1 Corinthians and 2 Timothy.[1] Fundamentally, it is because of Priscilla's mention that these brief passages have evoked so much interest in recent biblical study. In contemporary discussion of the role which women played in primitive Christianity, Priscilla is important both because she is more frequently mentioned than other Christian women of the first century and because these passages have been alleged to show that she had a leadership role in the Pauline mission. However, as there is very little concrete information given about Priscilla in these texts, most conclusions about her remain largely hypothetical, as is the case, of course, with many of the less prominent people in the NT.

1. *Acts 18:1-3, 18-22, 26-28*

Prisca and her husband, Aquila, are first encountered in Corinth (Acts 18:2-3). In this brief mention, we are told that

---

[1] Priscilla is the diminutive form for Prisca. Both are Roman names and it is reasonable to conjecture that both had some connection with a Roman family, either as members or former slaves. This might also explain why they returned to Rome when opportunity permitted. William Ramsay, *St. Paul, the Traveller and the Roman Citizen,* (London: Hodder & Stoughton, 1902): 268f., speculates that Aquila was Jewish and a freedman with the name of his Roman owner, while Priscilla was not Jewish.

Aquila was originally from Pontus,[2] but most recently he and his wife had relocated from Rome to Corinth. The cause of their relocation was a persecution of Jews in Rome by Emperor Claudius, who banished "all Jews" from the Imperial city. The second thing we learn is that by occupation they were "tentmakers" (σκηνοποιοί), just like the apostle Paul. The third piece of information is that their house and shop, perhaps the same place, became a base for Paul, who joined them in work. Each of these three pieces of information must be explored in greater depth.

In the first mention of Priscilla (Acts 18:2), the name of her husband, Aquila, is given first, but in the next reference (Acts 18:18) the textual evidence places Priscilla first (as in Rom 16:3 and 2 Tim 4:19, although there is a textual problem with the latter passage).[3] In Acts 18:26 there is less certainty, for the Western textual tradition (D ψ 0120), the Byzantine texts, and the Syriac and Sahidic versions all place Aquila first.[4] The order of their names has been a prominent concern in contemporary discussion and will be evaluted later in this study. At this point, it is only to be noted that the order of their names and the significance of that order are both problematic.

---

[2]Pontus was known as having a strong Jewish settlement. There another Aquila, a Jewish proselyte, did a Greek translation of the OT during Hadrian's rule (Phil, *Leg. Gaius*, 36). See also R. Schumacher, "Aquila und Priscilla," *Theologie und Glaube* 12 (1920): 87.

[3]Bruce Metzger, *A Textual Commentary on the Greek New Testament* (corr. ed.; New York: United Bible Societies, 1975): 650.

[4]*Ibid.*, 466-67. The editors of the UBS Greek NT detect here a Western revision intended to accentuate the prominence of Priscilla. Jeffery Childers and Curt Niccum, "'Anti-Feminist' Tendency in the 'Western' Text of Acts?" *Essays on Women in Earliest Christianity* (ed. C. D. Osburn; Joplin, MO: College Press, 1993): 1.486-87, chide Ben Witherington III, *Women in the Earliest Churches* (Cambridge: Cambridge Univ. Press, 1988): 153-54, for assuming that the naming of Aquila first could have been motivated only by conscious anti-feminism, and acknowledge only the possibility of theological motivation at this point.

The banishment of Jews from Rome under Claudius is reported by the Roman historian, Suetonius, in his "life of Claudius." In an off-handed remark, he says: "Since the Jews constantly made disturbances at the instigation of Chrestus, he [Claudius] expelled them from Rome."[5] What is uncertain is whether, historically, virtually "all" Jews in Rome were driven from the city or whether only "very many" were expelled. Suetonius' own remark is stated as generally as is Acts 18:2, so no firm answer seems possible. However, as Klauck observes, it is unlikely that the Emperor tried to rid his capital of the total Jewish population, which was quite a large number.[6] It seems more likely that basically those Jews involved in the tumult were expelled from Rome.[7]

One importance of this issue is that it relates to whether or not one should think of Priscilla and Aquila as already being Christians when Paul first met them in Corinth. If Claudius focused upon those Jews who were causing a disturbance over "Chrestus" (surely Christus), then it was most probably Christian Jews who were at issue. Since this couple were exiled because of participating in such disturbances, the possibility increases that they were already Christians before meeting Paul.

Haenchen gives three persuasive reasons for believing that Priscilla and Aquila were already Christians before

---

[5]Suetonius, *The Lives of the Caesars* 5.25, reads "Judaeos impulsore Chresto asidue tumultuantis Roma expulit." See J. C. Rolfe, *Suetonius* (LCL; New York: Macmillan, 1914): 52. Claudius, whose own character is very debated, was emperor from AD 41-54.

[6]Hans-Josef Klauck, *Hausgemeinde und Hauskirche im frühen Christentum* (SBS 103; Stuttgart: Katholisches Bibelwerk, 1981): 22. See also Schumacher, *Theologie und Glaube* (1920): 87, who quotes Hilgenfeld to the same effect. On the Jewish population in Rome, see James F. Jeffers, *Conflict in Rome* (Minneapolis: Fortress, 1991): 10.

[7]Ernst Haenchen, *Acts of Apostles* (Philadelphia: Westminster, 1971): 538, says that Suetonius is perhaps both a simplification and yet an exaggeration, too, as the banishment would have been of the leaders. Similarly, Jeffers, *Conflict in Rome*, 12-13.

meeting Paul. 1) If they were converted by Paul, surely Luke would have mentioned this about his hero apostle to the Gentiles. 2) Luke wants to picture Paul as leading the Christian expansion into Corinth and therefore he fails to mention that his couple were already believers.[8] 3) If Paul converted Priscilla and Aquila, then they and not Stephanus, would be the "first fruits of Achaia" (1 Cor 16:15).[9]

If this couple were already believers, then it is quite understandable that they offered hospitality to Paul for his mission work at Corinth and allowed him to share their workshop.[10]

Thus it does seem probable that Priscilla and Aquila were Christians already in Rome, and even leaders of the church there (the reason for their exile). If so, one further issue arises, viz., what were the characteristics of their Christian faith prior to meeting Paul? Wedderburn[11]

---

[8] Wolf-Henning Ollrog, *Paulus und seine Mitarbeiter* (WMANT 50; Neukirchen-Vluyn: Neukirchener Verlag; 1979): 25, believes that Acts does not mention that Priscilla and Aquila were Christians because it wants to show Paul as the one who brings Christianity to Rome.

[9] Haenchen, *Acts of Apostles*, 533, adds, "That a Jewish couple expelled because of the conflict with Christians in Rome deliberately gave a Christian missionary work and shelter is far more improbable than that Paul found lodging with Christians who had fled from Rome." See also Klauck, *Hausgemeinde und Hauskirche im frühen Christentum*, 22; and Schumacher, *Theologie und Glaube*, (1920): 89. Metzger, *Textual Commentary on the Greek New Testament*, 460, cites textual evidence that Paul and Aquila were both of the tribe of Benjamin.

[10] On tentmaking, see Ron Hock, *The Social Context of Paul's Ministry*, (Philadelphia: Fortress, 1980): 20-21, who observes that "leather worker" is probably a more accurate designation of their trade. Since it was an occupation with low public esteem, that may have encouraged mutual recognition only among its practitioners.

[11] A. J. M. Wedderburn, *Reason for Romans* (Edinburgh: T. & T. Clark, 1988): 56. This would be supported by Acts 2 which suggests that prominent among the hearers of Peter's sermon were Hellenistic Jews, who were pilgrims to Jerusalem. It is notable that in Acts 2:9, 10 among the Jewish pilgrims to Jerusalem who heard Peter's sermon were residents of both Pontus and Rome.

Priscilla and Aquila—Co-Workers in Christ

suggests that in Rome they were taught and themselves did teach a form of Hellenistic Jewish Christianity which was critical of the Jerusalem temple and the Law (similar to that of Stephen, the Hellenist preacher in Acts 6). This type of preaching would quickly create problems with Jewish leaders who would have thought this to be blasphemous.

Later in Acts 18 Priscilla and Aquila appear to have moved to Ephesus and serve as instructors of Apollos. Witherington suggests that since Luke does not mention the content of their teaching, it was the identity of the teachers and pupil that he wishes to highlight.[12] If they were recent converts (by Paul at Corinth), it is hard to imagine that they would be able to instruct the brilliant Apollos in a more complete manner. However, since Apollos is really the focus of the story for Acts, it is doubtful that the teachers or the content of their teaching are as important to Luke as the pupil, an urban, educated man who was humble enough to accept instruction from this "blue collar" couple. He is to serve as a paradigm for other learned and influential people whose understanding needs some correction (to "orthodox Christianity"?).

This passage is a good example of scholarly tendencies to find what one is looking for in texts. In traditional interpretations, Priscilla has been regarded as only incidentally present—perhaps acting as hostess.[13] In more contemporary interpretation this has been reversed—Priscilla is set forth as the pedagogue, and Aquila's status is minimized[14] (although Harnack had earlier described them

---

[12]Ben Witherington III, *Women and the Genesis of Christianity* (Cambridge: University Press, 1990): 220.

[13]Schumacher, *Theologie und Glaube* (1920): 97, citing 1 Tim 2:12, insists that any teaching she did would be unoffical. It is noteworthy that Adolf von Harnack, *The Mission and Expansion of Christianity* (trans. J. Moffatt; London: Williams and Norgate, 1908): 2.79, comparing Phil 4:3 about Clement with Rom 16:3, which also calls Priscilla a συνεργός, claims that she was actually an apostle.

[14]For example Elisabeth Schüssler Fiorenza, "Women in the Pre-Pauline and Pauline Churches" *USQR* 33 (1978): 157, concludes, "The

as "Prisca the missionary, with her husband Aquila.")[15]

It seems that the most natural reading of the text is to say that both husband and wife shared in the work of teaching—nothing being said of one leading and one watching. Perhaps this was something of a team ministry. At the least, one may say that she took part in teaching.[16] While nothing is said specifically on the topic of instruction, the only defect in Apollos' teaching seems to have been in relation to Christian baptism and the Spirit.[17] It is surely noteworthy that Apollos is not just any itinerant Christian, but one "well versed in scripture." This is evidenced in Apollos' own subsequent successful mission work.[18]

Thus it is clear that Luke wants the reader to appreciate that this couple were knowledgeable enough to teach Apollos in a way he would accept, although he was already a well-known disciple, and would become more so. What remains uncertain is why this story is important for Luke. In the larger story of Acts he may intend to show that eccentric views associated with the Christian movement are taken into the larger and orthodox Christian story.

---

text clearly assumes that Prisca was the catechist and teacher of Apollos." Ben Witherington, III, *Women in the Earliest Church* (Cambridge: Cambridge Univ. Press, 1988): 154, comments, "if anyone is indicated by Luke as the primary instructor, it is Priscilla." Schumacher, *Theologie und Glaube* (1920): 97, notes that in Chrysostom's text of Acts Ἀκύλας is missing in 18:26, so that Priscilla alone corrects Apollos.

[15]von Harnack, *Mission and Expansion of Chrisitianity*, 1.79.

[16]J. W. McGarvey, *Acts of the Apostles*, (Cincinnati: Standard, 1892): 2.148 a century ago gave a more balanced interpretation, "It should be observed that Priscilla took part with her husband in giving more perfect instruction to Apollos, and this illustrates the manner in which faithful women were eminent helpers of the apostles and evangelists in the spread of the gospel." Similarly Witherington, *Woman and Genesis*, 220.

[17]Haenchen, *Acts of Apostles*, 551.

[18]*Ibid.*, 219.

2. *1 Corinthians 16:19*

In the benediction of 1 Cor 16:19 in a letter written from Ephesus, Paul adds warm greetings to Aquila and Prisca and "to the church in their house." Aquila and Priscilla (note that here he is named first) send greetings to a church who would value hearing from them, and to learn of their successful work in "missions." They alone are included in the greetings which Paul sends from Ephesus—even though Apollos is in Ephesus, and had great influence in Corinth.[19]

The role of house churches in earliest Christianity has been the subject of several investigations.[20] For the present purposes, the important information gained is that in Ephesus, as earlier in Corinth, and later in Rome, Priscilla and Aquila had leading roles in the Christian community. It is not stated on what basis they had such influence. Theissen suggests that their recurring provision of a house that will accommodate the Christian gathering suggests that they were "scarcely insolvent."[21] However, their itinerancy accompanied with their menial trade of "leather worker" would suggest also they were not wealthy.

---

[19]Ollrog, *Paulus und seine Mitarbeiter,* 27. The question of "factions" at Corinth and the accompanying possibility that Apollos was a focus for one group, might explain his omission in Paul's greetings. However, the existence, composition and views of these factions is very contested, and well beyond the scope of this study.

[20]Most recently, L. Michael White, *Building God's House* (Baltimore: Johns Hopkins, 1990). Although this work stresses the later stage of the development from house churches to government sponsored building post-Constantine, White gives a good description of the social implications of the house church. For the earlier period, see Floyd Filson, "The Significance of the Early House Churches," *JBL* 58 (1939): 105-112, esp. 105-109.

[21]Gerd Theissen, *The Social Setting of Pauline Christianity* (Philadelphia: Fortress, 1982): 90. Much of Theissen's reconstruction is creative supposition. We know really nothing of the size of "modest" houses, nor need we assume that the church in Ephesus was large (what would constitute a "large" church in this day?) The same caveat applies to Jeffers, *Conflict In Rome,* 21 when he makes a similar judgment about their house in Rome.

Of course, the "house church" in the first century was the only real possibility for the Christian movement. If Petersen is correct, the significance of this fact is not one of location, but the aspect of Christian community which the house church represented and embodied.[22] House churches were a decisive factor in the mission work of the Christians because they provided location, support and leadership for the churches. Along with Priscilla (and Aquila), and no doubt others (Acts 17:4, 12), women played a role in founding and sustaining these house churches.[23]

As in Acts 18 one can see that the leadership of this couple in the church continued strong after their move to Ephesus. One may even speculate that they continued to work with Paul (both as artisans and missionaries) in this new field.[24] Ellis argues that the phrase "the brothers" mentioned in 16:20 and apparently including Prisca and Aquila) denotes a smaller circle—which provided leadership—than simply "οἱ ἅγιοι" (the saints) or "αἱ ἐκκλησίαι" (the churches).[25] He mentions specifically Priscilla and Aquila, a suggestion borne out by the couple's prominent position elsewhere in Paul's letters.

---

[22]Joan Petersen, "House Churches in Rome" *Vigilae Christianae* 23 (1969): 264f. See also A. J. Malherbe, *Social Aspects of Early Christianity* (Baton Rouge, LA: Louisiana State University, 1977): 60-91, on the social impact of house churches.

[23]Fiorenza, *USQR* (1978): 56. Jeffers, *Conflict in Rome*, 20, thinks this would be especially true of Rome, where crowding made the cost of square footage at a premium.

[24]Schumacher, *Theologie und Glaube* (1920): 94; Klauck, *Hausgemeinde und Hauskirche im frühen Christentum*, 23. He also notes that the "household" was the inner circle of slaves and dependents. It has been suggested that "Epanetus, the first of Asia" (Rom 16:5) was perhaps also a member of their household and/or guild. Malherbe, *Social Aspects*, 90f., suggests that in Ephesus the household of Priscilla was perhaps a household collegia (he thinks that the "Hall of Tyrannus" was where the guild of leatherworkers met).

[25]E. Earle Ellis, "Paul and his Co-workers," *NTS* 17 (1970/71): 446-47, believes that when used in the plural with the article, "the brothers" refers in Paul's writings to an inner circle of workers who lead in the Christian mission efforts.

3. *Romans 16:3-5*

The next reference to Priscilla and Aquila is found in Paul's closing greetings in Romans 16.[26] From this reference four pieces of information are disclosed. First, that Paul says that they "risked their necks" for him (ὑπὲρ τῆς ψυχῆς μου τὸν ἑαυτῶν τράχηλον ὑπέθηκαν). Second, he classes them in a special group of associates, the "fellow workers" (συνεργούς). Third, that "all the Gentile churches give thanks for them" (εὐχαριστῶ . . . πᾶσαι αἱ ἐκκλησίαι τῶν ἐθνῶν). Finally, their presence in Rome may have great significance for the Pauline mission. "Clearly, they were a major factor in the Gentile mission."[27]

The phrase "to put one's neck on the block" (τράχηλον ὑπέθηκαν) was a metaphor for taking great risks, and probably is used in that sense here.[28] But it also could have a literal meaning, given Paul's troubles in Ephesus and other cities.[29] It may well be that on some occasion Priscilla and Aquila intervened and protected Paul at great personal risk.

---

[26]For discussion of whether chap. 16 was originally part of the Roman letter, see Harry Gamble, *The Textual History of the Letter to the Romans* (Grand Rapids: Eerdmans, 1979). Much of what is said here about the couple is important, regardless of how one decides this issue, but if this chapter was originally part of the Roman letter, it adds to our knowledge of their return to Rome.

[27]Witherington, *Women in the Earliest Church*, 114. Ramsay, *St. Paul the Traveller and the Roman Citizen*, 254f., suggests that perhaps it was their report of Christianity in Rome prior to their exile, and their ongoing interest in the church there, that led Paul to feel the necessity of going to Rome.

[28]Schumacher, *Theologie und Glaube* (1920): 96f., cites Philonides #1044, quoted in Adolph Deissmann, *Light from the Ancient East* (New York: Harper, 1922): 117f.

[29]C. E. B. Cranfield, *The Epistle to the Romans*, (ICC; Edinburgh: T. & T. Clark, 1979): 795, suggests that the events in Ephesus in Acts 19:23-40 are a possible reference, but it could also refer to something which took place on an occasion of which we are not informed. Nevertheless, it seems that the knowledge of this action was widespread in the churches of the Gentile mission.

Paul says that not only does he owe them deep personal thanks, so also do "all the Gentile churches." This probably refers to their ongoing association and help with Paul in Corinth and Ephesus, although its mention in the Roman letter is surely related to Paul's evangelistic plans to go through Rome. It is likely that they are now associated with a house church in Rome, as they had been before in Corinth and Ephesus.[30] If indeed they were Jewish Christians before being exiled from Rome and prior to meeting Paul, one might conjecture that this couple were vital to the Pauline mission in establishing churches among both Jews and Gentiles. This view is supported by Paul's argument that Gentile believers are "indebted" (ὀφειλέται) to the Jews for "spiritual things" (Rom 15:27), perhaps mentioning Priscilla and Aquila as concrete examples of this indebtedness.

Third, Priscilla and Aquila are called "co-workers" (συνεργούς) with Paul, the only ones so named in Romans 16. This term indicates that this Christian pair have a special relationship with Paul.[31] Paul uses it in 1 Cor 3:9 for Apollos and himself, and it seems to be a term that designates a group of people who take leadership in the ministry of the gospel.[32] This special term supports the idea that in 1 Cor 16:20 the designation "the brothers" indicates a special group of believers.[33]

---

[30]Fiorenza, *USQR*, (1978): 156. White, *Building God's House*, 106f., suggests a "house church network from the Aegean" that Paul now calls upon for introduction, hospitality, and support in his mission westward (including Phoebe, his former host in Cenchraea).

[31]Schumacher, *Theologie und Glaube* (1920): 96. Victor P. Furnish, "Fellow Workers in God's Service," *JBL* 80 (1961): 364-70, examines whether the term stresses association among the workers themselves, or their association with God. See also 2 Cor 8:23; Phil 2:25; 4:3; Col 4:1; and Phlm 1, 24.

[32]Thus it is equivalent to διάκονος in 3:5, as in some manuscripts of 1 Thess 3:2. See Georg Bertram, "συνεργέω," *TDNT* 7.874. David M. Scholer, "Paul's Women Co-Workers in the Ministry of the Church," *Daughters of Sara* (1980): 41, notes that Priscilla is so named without any distinction made on the basis of her sex.

[33]See note 25.

4. *2 Timothy 4:19*

The final mention of Prisca and Aquila is in a catalogue of greetings at the end of 2 Timothy. No information is given and little implied, that extends our knowledge of their activity in the gospel. However, if the letter is authentic (which would also imply Paul continued his mission after the Roman imprisonment) this greeting tells us that Priscilla and Aquila have again settled in Ephesus where they had previously conducted a successful ministry.

Conclusion

What, then may be concluded about Priscilla and Aquila and their roles as Paul's associates in the early Christian mission? In brief, they were among Paul's most loyal supporters. As Hort[34] suggests, they seem to have been the "leading edge" of Paul's mission in Rome, and perhaps in Ephesus as well. Their home formed the focus of the churches which Paul established in these cities. They were willing to do this even at personal risk, and therefore Paul was proud to name them (both) as "fellow workers." For the present study, what can one conclude about Priscilla's function in this work? Is it possible to determine what responsibilities she fulfilled or status she occupied in the church?

A. *Priscilla's Primacy*

Many scholars have stated that in references to Priscilla and Aquila, she is most often named first, a practice which would have been uncommon in the first century.[35] This investigation has shown that while this is basically true, it is not consistently so both because in the first reference, in

---

[34]F. J. A. Hort, *Prolegomena to St. Paul's Epistles to the Romans and Ephesians* (New York: Macmillan, 1895): 17-18.

[35]Scholer, *Daughters of Sara* (1980): 4, for example, says, "It should not be missed that, in spite of the general cultural position of women in the first century AD in the Roman Empire and especially married women, Paul names Priscilla first."

Acts 18:1, Aquila is named first (and so in 1 Cor 16:3), and because there are textual problems with the references in Acts 18:26 and 2 Tim 4:19. Nonetheless, apart from settling the textual issues of each mention of Priscilla and Aquila, there have been many far-reaching conclusions drawn from the order of their names, none of which seems certain.

1) Some have suggested that Priscilla was the first convert within their household. 2) Others propose that she was the more important one in the Christian mission effort.[36] 3) Another explanation is that she was of a more noble family.[37] This might find some confirmation in the Roman "Ceometeris Priscillae," a cemetery in Rome possibly linked with Priscilla—if this cemetery is named for Priscilla as a benefactor of the Christians who gave land for their burial, as the Coemetetaris Domitillae had been (it is believed that Domitillae was buried there, and hence the cemetery named for her). There is no reference in Christian history explicitly making the connection, however.[38] Fiorenza goes beyond

---

[36]Ollrog, *Paulus und seine Mitarbeiter*, 25. Klauck, *Hausgemeinde und Hauskirche im frühen Christentum*, 26, comments on Harnack's view that Priscilla was the missionary, and Aquila had importance as her husband. Adolf Harnack, *The Mission and Expansion of Christianity* (trans. J. Moffatt; New York: Putnam's Sons, 1908): 79. Klauck himself believes that it is because of her willingness to have her house used by the church.

[37]Schumacher, *Theologie und Glaube* (1920): 88. Options two and three are combined by Hort, *Proglegomena to St. Paul's Epistles to the Romans and Ephesians*, 13-15, who suggests that her more noble/important family gave her financial resources to be helpful to the Christians. If so, one thinks also of Lydia at Philippi. Jeffers, *Conflict in Rome*, 21 says that Prisca was a common Latin name in Rome, and says "although we cannot know for certain, Prisca may have been a Roman who met and married Aquila in Rome." If she was a Roman, she would possess Roman citizenship and greater social status than her mate.

[38]Hort, *Proglegomena to St. Paul's Epistles to the Romans and Ephesians*, 14. W. Sanday and A. C. Headlam, *The Epistle to the Romans* (ICC; Edinburg: T. & T. Clark, 1902): 419, discuss the association of Priscilla's name with this cemetery and the association of her name and that of Aquila with an old Roman family, the Acilians.

the clear evidence when she concludes it is because Priscilla is the most important member of the family for the church that she is named first.[39]

On the issue of a woman's name preceding a husband's, Marleen Flory suggests from a thorough study of Latin epitaphs that most often when the wife's name precedes her husband's it is due to social status. She is a citizen, he a freed-person or she is a freed-person and he a slave. The goal seems to have been to advance the status of their children. However, in some inscriptions for the grave of a child, the wife is named first because of the high emotional attachment of a grieving mother.[40] However, in regard to the present couple, there is no indication of concern about children or social status, and the sentiments motivating burial inscriptions may not be active in other places.

In summary, the mention of *both* Aquila and Priscilla by name surely suggests *both* were important. However, their relative importance and their respective work in the Gentile mission cannot be determined by the order of their names in the NT, even if such usage were consistent—which it is not.

B. *Leaders Among Gentile Churches.*

It does seem clear that they took a leading role in the church beyond being Paul's hosts and perhaps even

---

They think that their names suggest they had been freedmen in this gens, but they find the evidence associated with St. Prisca church on the Aventine in Rome insufficient to establish a connection of Aquila and Prisca with this site.

[39]Fiorenza, *USQR* (1978): 156, who notes similarly, "Prisca is most frequently mentioned before her husband Aquila because she is not defined by her role as a wife but is recognized because of her own outstanding missionary contribution" (45). The concern about importance tied to gender roles is anachronistic in this literature.

[40]Marleen Flory, "Where Women Precede Men: Factors Influencing the Order of Names in Roman Epitaphs," *Classical Journal* 79 (1984): 216-24.

sponsor.[41] Fiorenza rightly notes these parallels between their life and Paul's. "Like Paul, Priscilla and Aquila were by trade tentmakers and supported their missionary activity through their own work. Like Paul, they were Jewish Christians and financially independent from the churches they served. Like Paul they traveled to spread the gospel and suffered for their missionary activity."[42] They took aside Apollos to further instruct him in the Christian faith. While it is not possible to know exact roles, it does seem implied that Priscilla joined her husband in this instruction.[43]

Klauck makes the interesting suggestion that Priscilla and Aquila were the "quartermasters" for Paul, in Corinth by accident and in Ephesus and Rome by plan.[44] His speculation may be even expanded. Is it possible that they were planners behind Paul's work in Ephesus and then in Rome? In Acts 18 Paul accompanies the couple to Ephesus (18:18), but quickly leaves to tour in Antioch and lower Asia Minor. It is Priscilla and Aquila who stay in Ephesus, working in the synagogues, and teaching others like Apollos. They are leaders in the Ephesian church initially. It is later that Paul returns for a more extended mission effort. The fact that Priscilla and Aquila remain in Ephesus after Paul's departure confirms again their ability in leadership for this Gentile Christian community. That they

---

[41]Theissen, *The Social Setting of Pauline Christianity*, 90, suggests that their ability to take in Paul (as an employee? and even Apollos?) implies that they were "scarcely insolvent."

[42]Fiorenza, *USQR* (1978): 57, neglects to mention that they, also like Paul, were Jewish Christian missionaries to Gentiles. Perhaps that was the most decisive and vital commonalty of their close relationship.

[43]W. J. Coneybeare and J. S. Howsen, *The Life and Epistles of St. Paul* (Grand Rapids: Eerdmans, 1959 reprint): 300, n. 4, suggest that since Prisca was an instructor of Apollos, we might infer that she was a woman of good education. This too is a baseless assumption, since we have no knowledge of the education of either, nor whether their education (or its lack) affected their influence in the Christian communities.

[44]Klauck, *Hausgemeinde und Hauskirche im frühen Christentum*, 24.

were able to correct and instruct Apollos proves that Paul was vindicated in this trust, as does their ongoing value to the Pauline mission.

The next encounter is when Paul writes from Corinth to Rome announcing his planned mission work there, where Priscilla and Aquila have already gone and become church leaders. Are they the "advance party" for the Pauline mission? While their move from Rome to Corinth was not their own choice, that from Corinth to Ephesus was—then from Ephesus back to Rome (where they may have anticipated yet more trouble). The relocating of home and business was because of their desire to be helpful to Paul's mission.[45]

Many scholars have puzzled over Romans 14 and 15 about how Paul could know concretely about tensions between Jewish and Gentile Christians in Rome.[46] Is it not most reasonable to think that probably his associates, Priscilla and Aquila, were his source of information? Indeed, one might even speculate that it was their invitation or encouragement that prompted Paul to finally make concrete arrangements to visit the Roman church.

In fact, because Prisca and Aquila had been the center of house churches in Corinth, Ephesus, and Rome (perhaps twice, including before their exile) shows that their leadership in Christian mission was not limited to assisting Paul. They were certainly strong supporters and benefactors of Paul, but at the same time they were also independent church leaders.[47]

Granting readily that these are all conjectures, the question is whether they are conjectures that the slim explicit information about Priscilla and Aquila in the NT can

---

[45]Ollrog, *Paulus und seine Mitarbeiter*, 27. See Wedderburn's point, noted above, n. 11.

[46]See Karl Donfried, *The Romans Debate* (Peabody, MA: Hendrickson, 1994).

[47]Ollrog, *Paulus und seine Mitarbeiter*, 27.

support. Witherington summarizes well on their importance:

> One gets the impression they were two of Paul's closest and most reliable workers, and it is likely they were involved in a wide range of activities from providing hospitality for Paul to church planting, to teaching and preaching (Rom 16:5; 1 Cor 16:19; and Acts 18:1-3, 26-28). Clearly they were a major factor in the Gentile mission.[48]

To conclude, one can confidently state that this Christian couple had a long and distinguished service in the mission work of the first century. While in many ways their paths, their work, and even their mission activities closely resemble Paul's, there is a notable difference. Apart from which one is named first, the fact is they are always named together. Whereas Paul did his evangelistic work as a single person, they did theirs as married people. In so doing they had the additional benefit to the Christian mission of providing a meeting place through their house (into which they invited Gentiles). In this way also, they provide a cameo glimpse of the work of other Christians who also established and nurtured churches, Christians whose names remain unknown, but to whom, as Priscilla and Aquila, Gentile Christians are indebted even today.

---

[48]Witherington, *Women in the Earliest Church*, 114. Schumacher, *Theologie und Glaube* (1920): 98, insists that Priscilla's teaching was unoffical, private and not ministerial, since women could not teach in public gatherings (1 Cor 14:35 and 1 Tim 2:12). In some ways, this begs the question at issue.

Chapter Thirteen

WOMEN AND PROPHECY IN THE CORINTHIAN CHURCH

Gary Selby

One cannot read very far in the literature dealing with women in the contemporary church without encountering claims based upon the prophesying women mentioned at several points in the NT. For some, these prophetesses are an insignificant, if not an embarrassing, exception to what are otherwise viewed as clear and absolute prohibitions against all forms of public expression by women.[1] At the other extreme are those who view these women as forcing a complete reinterpretation of those very prohibitions and providing biblical evidence for free and unrestricted expression by women in the contemporary church.[2] In between are those who see in the women who prophesied some grounds for public expression, but only within very limited roles and situations.[3]

---

[1] See, for example, George W. Knight, *The New Testament Teaching on the Role Relationship of Men and Women* (Grand Rapids: Baker, 1977).

[2] See John T. Bristow, *What Paul Really Said About Women* (San Francisco: Harper and Row, 1988): 311-58; Letha Scanzoni and Nancy Hardesty, *All We're Meant to Be: A Biblical Approach to Woman's Liberation* (Waco: Word, 1974): 169-81; and Elisabeth Schüssler Fiorenza, *In Memory of Her; A Feminist Theological Reconstruction of Christian Origins* (New York: Crossroad, 1977).

[3] E.g., Susan T. Foh, *Women and the Word of God: A Response to Biblical Feminism* (Grand Rapids: Baker, 1979): 100-28; Wayne A. Grudem, "Prophecy Yes, But Teaching—No: Paul's Consistent Advocacy of Women's Participation Without Governing Authority," *JETS* 30 (1987): 11-23; and H. Wayne House, *The Role of Women in Ministry Today* (Nashville: Thomas Nelson, 1990): 108-140.

This diversity of opinion obviously reflects differences in attitudes toward Scripture as well as the hermeneutical principles by which ancient texts are applied to current situations. However, it may also reflect divergent or incomplete understandings of what prophecy actually was in the ancient world and in the early church. While it is clear that women did prophesy in the Corinthian church, for instance, precisely what they did, how they were perceived, and under what special restrictions they worked must be understood in terms of ancient practice rather than in terms of current issues in today's churches.

1. Backgrounds of Prophecy: An Overview

A. Methodological Matters

In his summary of recent works on prophecy, Aune[4] observes that it is all too common to "regard the contribution of Greco-Roman prophetic and oracular traditions as being of little value in understanding the phenomenon of early Christian prophecy." Such neglect, according to Aune, reflects the implicit notion that whatever is distinctly Greco-Roman is somehow a corruption of the biblical norm, while continuities with the Jewish tradition indicate faithfulness to the biblical norm. The acute Hellenization of Judaism during the three centuries prior to the Christian era should be sufficient reason to avoid premature dismissal of Greco-Roman data. Hill,[5] reflecting this awareness, argues the influence of Greek ecstatic prophecy on the Corinthians.[6]

---

[4]David Aune, *Prophecy in Early Christianity and the Ancient Mediterranean World* (Grand Rapids: Eerdmans, 1983): 1-17.
[5]David Hill, *New Testament Prophecy* (Atlanta: John Knox, 1979): 121.
[6]J. Reiling, *Hermas and Christian Prophecy: A Study of the Eleventh Mandate* (Leiden: Brill, 1973), demonstrates the inroads made by Hellenistic magical divination into the Christian communities in and around Rome from the last decade of the first century to about the middle of the second.

Women and Prophecy in the Corinthian Church

Boring[7] reflects a similar understanding:

> It is too simple to claim that Christian prophecy is "biblical," "Israelite" or "Jewish," in contrast to "Greek" or "Hellenistic," for both these streams were complex realities, as was early Christian prophecy, and the streams did not always flow in separate channels.

B. *Prophecy in the Greco-Roman World*

The phenomenon of prophecy was widely attested in the Greek world, located, as Boring observes, "within the broad spectrum of devices by which information from the gods was transmitted and received."[8] In its earliest usage, the "prophecy" word group carried with it the idea of publicly declaring and making known[9] and to prophesy meant to be a proclaimer or an interpreter.[10] The public declaration of a divinely-received message was closely, though not always exclusively, associated with the institution known as the oracle, of which the one at Delphi was the most famous.[11]

---

[7]M. Eugene Boring, *The Continuing Voice of Jesus* (Louisville: Westminister/Knox, 1991): 58.

[8]*Ibid.*, 49.

[9]E.g., Euripides, *Bacch.*, 211; Plato, *Resp.* 10.619c; *Leg. 9.871c.* See Helmut Krämer, "Προφήτης: A. The Word Group in Profane Greek," *TDNT,* 6.783-784.

[10]E.g., Pindar's, *Frag.* 150, invocation of the Muse: "Be thou mine oracle, and I shall be thine interpreter (προφητεύσω)." See the classic study of E. Fascher, *Προφήτης. Eine sprach- und religions-geschichtliche Untersuchung* (Giessen: A. Töpelmann, 1927, augmented by H. Bacht, "Religionsgeschichtliches zum Inspirations-problem. Die Pythischen Dialoge Plutarchs von Chäronea," *Scholastik* 17 (1942): 50-69; *idem*, "Die prophetische Inspiration in der kirchlichen Reflexion der vormontanistischen Zeit," *Scholastik* 19 (1944): 1-18; and *idem*, "Wahres und falsches Prophetentum," *Bib* 32 (1951): 237-62.

[11]For discussions of oracles in the ancient world, including others at Dodona, Ptoion, Corope, Claros, etc., see Robert Flaciere, *Greek Oracles*, (trans. D. Garman; London: Elek, 1965); H. W. Parke, *Greek Oracles* (London: Hutchinson, 1967).

There the god Apollo was believed to take possession of the priestess, called the "Pythia," inducing a trance-like state[12] in which she spoke the words of the god which were then "interpreted" by a prophet or prophetess for the inquirer.[13] Some earlier NT scholars attempted unsuccessfully to trace Christian prophecy to the oracular phenomena of classical Greek society.[14] However, although Christian prophecy cannot be equated with older forms of Greek prophecy such as the Delphic oracle,[15] the legacy of ancient oracular prophecy was significant in later Hellenistic society. Though the popularity of the Delphic oracle may have waned by the NT era,[16] such prophetesses were still frequently mentioned in writings contemporary with the NT.[17]

Classical times also witnessed wandering prophetesses called Sibyls who uttered spontaneous oracles in hexameter verse. Although the Sibyls practiced their arts centuries before the Christian era, the legends about them and the

---

[12]See Plato, *Phdr.* 244b, where Socrates states that the prophetess at Delphi and the priestess at Dodona "have conferred many splendid benefits upon Greece, both in private and in public affairs, but few or none when they have been in their right minds."

[13]The Pythia herself was commonly called προμάντις and only occasionally προφῆτις (see Herodotus, 6.66; 7.111, 141; Thucydides, 5.16). On this basis, Christopher Forbes, "Early Christian Inspired Speech and Hellenistic Popular Religon," *NovT* 28 (1986): 257-270, argues that the "prophet, at least at Delphi, had a separate function from the Pythia—perhaps that of interpreter or even administrator of the oracle." See also Plato, *Timaeus* 71e-72b.

[14]E.g., Hans Leisegang, *Der Heilige Geist: Das Wesen und Werden der mystisch-intuitiven Erkenntnis in der Philosophie und Religion der Griechen* (Leipzig: B. G. Teubner, 1919).

[15]See C. K. Barrett, *The Holy Spirit and the Gospel Tradition* (London: SPCK, 1947), and Boring, *Continuing Voice of Jesus,* 48-51.

[16]E.g., Plutarch *De Pythiae oraculis* and *De defectu oraculorum,* appear to look back on a time in the past when oracle enjoyed greater prominence. Pausanias, *Phocis, Ozolian Locri* 12.11, also depicts oracles as prominent in the distant past. Martin P. Nilsson, *Greek Folk Religion* (New York: Harper, 1961): 124, asserts that "In the Hellenistic age the old oracles of Greece lost their popularity."

[17]See e.g., Plutarch, *De Pythiae oraculis.*

written oracles they left behind "were immensely popular and enjoyed excellent reputation"—even into NT times.[18] So famous were they, in fact, that even Jewish and Christian writers well into the first and second centuries mentioned the Sibyls and even quoted their prophecies.[19]

Prophecy existed in various forms in the Greco-Roman world of the NT era. 1) During the reign of Tiberius, Germanicus consulted the shrine of the Clarian Apollo,[20] and at a remote station in Britain a Tungrian cohort set up a votive inscription to the voice of the Clarian Apollo.[21] At Mt. Carmel, Vespasian received a prophecy of his coming greatness,[22] and in the shrine of the Paphian Venus Titus had his hopes confirmed.[23] Cicero[24] consulted the Pythia, as did Nero.[25] During the Hellenistic period (mid-fourth to mid-first centuries BC), the great oracle sanctuaries experienced a decline, but "the revival of oracles that began in the first century AD was just one expression of a widespread nostalgia for the past."[26] For example, the new

---

[18]Aune, *Prophecy in Early Christianity and the Ancient Mediterranean World*, 37. The earliest known classical reference is Heraclitus (sixth century BC), recorded in Plutarch, *De Pythiae oraculis* 397-99; 401; see also, Pausanius, *Phocis, Ozolian Locri* 12, and A. S. Pease "Sibylla," *The Oxford Classical Dictionary* (2nd ed.; Oxford: Oxford Univ. Press: 1970): 984.

[19]See for example, Josephus, *AJ* 1.118. References to the Sibyl by Christian authors include Clement of Alexandria, *Exhortation to the Greeks* 2; *Strom.* 1.107.6; Justin Martyr, *First Apol.* 1.20; and later Lactantius *Div. Inst.* 1.6.

[20]Tacitus, *Annals* 2.54.

[21]Ludwig Friedländer, *Darstellungen aus der sittengeschichte Roms in der zeit von August bis zum ausgang der Antonine* (9th ed. by G. Wissowa; Leipzig: S. Hirzel, 1919): 4.469.

[22]Tacitus, *Historiarum* 2.78, who also notes that Vespasian openly kept at court an astrologer named Seleucus, whom he regarded as an oracle.

[23]Suetonius, *De Vita Caesarum, Divus Titus* 5.

[24]Suetonius, *Cicero* 5.

[25]Suetonius, *Nero* 40.

[26]Aune, *Prophecy in Early Christianity*, 51.

oracle of Asclepius in Paphlagonia achieved uncommon acceptance for its primarily medical oracles, in spite of strong criticism in which Epicureans and Christians found themselves in an uncommon alliance against pagan superstition.[27] Too, the oracles of Mopsus and Amphilochus were still flourishing.[28]

2) Independent of shrines was an eschatological prophecy, e.g., Hystaspes' (first century BC/AD) predictions of the destruction of the world followed by an age of bliss,[29] and spontaneous prophecies in Rome in response to crises.[30]

3) In another vein, Plutarch[31] mentions the entrance of a god in the manner of ventriloquists (πύθωνα; pythona) into prophets, prompting their utterances; however, these were not ventriloquists, but mediums speaking in trances with strange voices.[32]

4) In line with ancient usage, there were also prophets who did not so much predict as proclaim.[33] Philosophers

---

[27]Lucian of Samosata, *Alexander* 35.

[28]Plutarch, *De defectu oraculorum* 414b.

[29]See J. Z. Smith, "Wisdom and Apocalyptic," *Religious Syncretism in Antiquity: Essays in Conversation with Geo Widengren* (ed. B. Pearson; Missoula, MT: Scholars Press, 1975): 131-56.

[30]See Dio Cassius, *Roman History* 55.31.2-3, regarding prophetic activity in Rome during a famine in 7 AD. Note also the prophecy of a famine by Agabus in Acts 11:27-30.

[31]Plutarch, *De defectu oraculorum* 414e. See also Josephus, *Ant* 6.329.

[32]See E. R. Dodds, *The Greeks and the Irrational* (Berkeley: Univ. of California Press, 1951): 71-72. Note the involuntary utterances of the slave girl with a πνεῦμα πύθωνα (spirit of divination) in Acts 16:16-18. See Mark 1:24-26; 3:11; 5:7-12, for examples of possession and involuntary speech. Early Christian fathers viewed these as demon possessed, e.g., Origen, *De principiis* 3.4-5; Jerome, *Ep. ad Avitum* 8.

[33]For discussion of "non ecstatic" uses of the term "prophecy," see Terrance Callan, "Prophecy and Ecstasy in Greco-Roman Religion and in 1 Corinthians," *NovT* 27 (1985): 125-40. See also Theodore

whose principal task was teaching were sometimes called "prophets,"[34] e.g., Epicureans were referred to as προφῆται of Epicurus,[35] and Timon is called a prophet of the teaching of Pyrrho.[36] Among these wandering Hellenistic teachers was Apollonius of Tyana (3-97 AD), who principally taught Greek moral and civic virtues and only occasionally foretold the future.[37]

5) Within the mystery cults, still others prophesied in frenzied, ritualistic chants.[38] Polybius[39] mentions certain priests of Cybele who prophesied in ritualistic frenzy, foretelling Manilus Vulso's victory. Interestingly, while the Dionysiac cult at Rome was comprised largely of women, Livy depicts only men as prophesying, stating, "Men, as if insane, with fanatical tossings of their bodies, would utter prophecies."[40]

However, it was not uncommon for women to prophesy. Not only were there prophetesses in the oracular legacy[41] at Delphi, Dodona,[42] Dityma,[43] and Argos,[44] but prophetesses were still active in the later Hellenistic era at

---

Crone, *Early Christian Prophecy: A Study of its Origin and Function* (Baltimore: St. Mary's Univ. Press, 1973): 12, 44-45.

[34]See, among others, Lucian, *Vitarum Auctio* 8, and Dio Chrysostom, *Or.* 12.47.

[35]Plutarch, *De Pythiae oraculis* 7 [397c].

[36]Sextus Empiricus, *Adv. Mathematicos* 1.53

[37]Philostratus, *Vita Apollonii* 3.42; 4.18, 24.

[38]Livy, *Annals* 38.18.9.

[39]Polybius 21.37.5-7.

[40]Livy, *Annals* 39.13.12. See also Apuleius, *Metamorphoses* 8.28, regarding an ecstatic follower of Cybele, whose prophecy is not of the future, but a confession of wrongdoing.

[41]Strabo, *Geography* 9.2.4; Pausanius 3.4.4; 10.12; Lucian, *Hermotimus* 6, all mention prophetesses.

[42]Strabo, *Geography* 9.2.4.

[43]Iamblichus, *De Mysteriis* 3.11.

[44]Pausanius, 2.24.1; Plutarch, *Pyrrhus* 31.

certain shrines. Strabo[45] mentions current prophetesses (τὰς νῦν προφήτιδας). Plutarch[46] discusses differing influences to which such prophetesses were subjected and remarks, "the power of the spirit does not affect all persons nor the same persons always in the same way, but it only supplies an enkindling and an inception." Other prophetesses functioned apart from shrines, e.g., Martha, whose prophetic statements led to her becoming the religious advisor of Marius (second century BC).[47]

While Boring[48] cautions that NT prophecy cannot be identified with Hellenistic prophecy, Aune[49] argues that the influence of Hellenistic revelatory traditions was influential in certain components of post-apostolic Christianity. Whatever distinctions exist between Christian and Hellenistic prophecy in the NT era, it must be noted that for Christian women to be prophesying would hardly have seemed out of place in the Greco-Roman world.

C. *Prophecy in Judaism*

Unlike Greco-Roman prophecy, in which there was a continuum from the ancient period to the NT era, a discontinuity exists between OT canonical prophecy and that of the NT period. Prophecy in Judaism in the NT era seems to be understood either as belonging to the distant past or the

---

[45]Strabo, *Geography* 7.7.12.
[46]Plutarch, *De defectu oraculorum* 437-438.
[47]Plutarch, *Caius Marius* 17.1-3.
[48]Boring, *Continuing Voice of Jesus,* 49-50, however, overstates the case in declaring that the distinctive feature of Christian prophecy was its clarity.
[49]Aune, *Prophecy in Early Christianity*, 17, argues correctly, "what must be compared are not isolated features but features considered within their structural framework," yet he too easily dismisses contrasts between NT and pagan prophecy as a "theologically motivated attempt to make artificial distinctions between the biblical and the non-biblical world of thought in order to focus on the theologically normative character of the former and the illegitimate nature of the latter" (21).

eschatological future.[50] Nevertheless, Christian appropriation of Hebrew Scriptures did have some influence on the understanding of prophecy in the early church,[51] but it cannot be assumed that OT prophecy is *the* direct source for the reconstruction of the characteristics of early Christian prophecy.[52]

While much divination was condemned in ancient Israel,[53] some forms of divination were approved,[54] among which was prophecy—understandable verbal messages from the supernatural world conveyed through an inspired medium. As far back as the eleventh century BC, itinerant prophets such as Samuel, Elijah, and Elisha served as holy men, sages, miracle workers, and soothsayers, and frequently worked in groups.[55] In the post-exilic temple, however, prophetic guilds were no longer active.[56] From an early period, court prophets were prominent consultants to

---

[50]Aune, *Prophecy in Early Christianity*, 81.

[51]Gerhard Dautzenberg, *Urchristliche Prophetie—Ihre Erforschung, ihre Voraussetzungen im Judentum und ihre Struktur im ersten Korintherbrief* (BWANT; Stuttgart: W. Kohlhammer, 1975): 303.

[52]Boring, *The Continuing Voice of Jesus*, 58.

[53]Lev 19:26; Deut 18:10; 1 Sam 15:23; 2 Kgs 17:17; Isa 3:2; Jer 27:7; Ezek 13:6; Mic 3:11. For extensive discussions of prophecy in the OT, see Johannes Lindblom, *Prophecy in Ancient Israel* (Philadelphia: Muhlenberg, 1962); Joseph Blenkinsopp, *A History of Prophecy in Israel* (Philadelphia: Westminister, 1983); and Walter Brueggemann, *The Prophetic Imagination* (Philadelphia: Westminister, 1978). For a broader treatment, see John T. Greene, *The Role of the Messenger and Message in the Ancient Near East* (BJS, 169; Atlanta: Scholars Press, 1989).

[54]Gen 20:3, 6-7; 37:5-11; Lev 16:7-10; Deut 33:8; Josh 7:14-15; 1 Sam 10:20-21; 19:13-16; 23:9-12; Neh 7:65; Ezek 21:21; Dan 2:1-11.

[55]1 Sam 9; 19:20, 24; 1 Kgs 17; 18:17-29; 22:5-10; 2 Kgs 1:2-17; 2:9-15; 6:1-7, 8-10, 22; 13:14-21; 20:1-11.

[56]See D. L. Petersen, *Late Israelite Prophecy: Studies in Deutero-Prophetic Literature and in Chronicles* (Missoula: Scholars Press, 1977): 87.

the rulers.[57] Other prophets such as Amos and Isaiah were sometimes associated with holy places, religious rituals, and priests.[58] However, such prophets often disdained connection with a royal court or the temple, preferring to remain on the periphery of Israelite society and work independently to provoke social and religious reforms, at times conflicting with priests and kings.[59]

Prophecy was understood as the result of the coming of the Spirit of God upon one (1 Sam 19:20; Isa 61:1). That this sometimes produced ecstatic experiences (1 Sam 19:24) has been a matter of some debate, but that it provided the stimulus for the prophetic utterance and endowed it with the quality of divine revelation is unquestioned. This is a hallmark of prophetic activity.

Some ancient Israelite prophecy involved a revelatory trance experience, perhaps by possession[60] or a vision.[61] Common in the ancient Near East, such trances are thought by some to have been artificially induced, perhaps by music (1 Sam 10:5), dancing (1 Kgs 18:21), flagellation (1 Kgs 18:28-29), or group excitement (1 Sam 19:20-24).[62]

---

[57] 1 Sam 28:5-6; 2 Sam 7:4-17; 1 Kgs 20:13-15, 35-42; 22:5-6; 2 Kgs 3:11-20; 6:8-10; 13:14-19; 2 Chr 12:5-8; 15:1-7. See A. Jepsen, *Nabi: Soziologische Studien zur alttestamentlichen Literatur und Religionsgeschichte* (Munich: C. H. Beck, 1934): 94-99, 152-59.

[58] Amos 7:10-13; Isa 6:1-13; Jer 5:30-31. See Roland de Vaux, *Ancient Israel* (trans. J. McHugh; New York: McGraw-Hill, 1961): 2.384-86. Sigmund Mowinckel, *The Psalms in Israel's Worship* (trans. D. R. Ap-Thomas; Nashville: Abingdon, 1962): 2.58-68, holds that many psalms had a prophetic origin.

[59] R. R. Wilson, "Early Israelite Prophecy," *Int* 32 (1978): 9-10. See also R. E. Clements, *Prophecy and Covenant* (Naperville, IL: A. Allenson, 1965): 119-29.

[60] Isa 8:11; Jer 15:17; Ezek 3:14.

[61] 1 Kgs 22:19-23; Amos 1:1; 7:1; Hos 12:11.

[62] See Johannes Pedersen, *Israel: Its Life and Culture* (2nd ed.; London: Oxford Univ. Press, 1926): 1-2.158; Lindblom, *Prophecy in Ancient Israel*, 58-59. Cf. Aune, *Prophecy in Early Christianity*, 86-87.

Aune,[63] among others, argues that "artificially induced ecstasy" is pejorative. Still, such trances, even if artificially induced, were regarded as legitimate by the Israelites—though this behavior was sometimes labeled as drunkenness (Isa 28:7) or madness (1 Sam 16:14-16; 18:10-11).

As Lindblom[64] observes, the OT prophets, whose authority among their people "naturally depended on the fact that they were regarded as bearers of the divine word," had as their primary function to address abandonment of "the way of the Lord." Whereas rulers reinterpreted Israelite traditions in light of changing times, the OT prophets claimed divine authority to call Israel back to the ancient ideals and traditions of the premonarchical period. Prior to the eighth century BC, prophets were basically speakers, but after that time prophetic documents, such as Amos, Hosea, Micah, and Isaiah, emerged alongside prophetic speech. In addressing these concerns, it was not uncommon for a prophet to point out the inevitably tragic results of taking a course of action other than "the way of the Lord." Prophetic predictions of the future emerge from these calls to religious and social renewal.

Though conflicts sometimes arose between prophets, the real conflicts were between independent prophets and prophets in the royal courts (1 Kgs 1)—which raised the problem of "true" and "false" prophets. Criteria for judging the genuineness of a prophet involved, among other things, 1) fulfillment of prediction (Deut 18:22), 2) message of judgment against breaking the covenant with God rather than a message of salvation which ignores the breaking of the covenant (Jer 28:8-9), 3) good moral conduct (Jer 23:14).

The prophetic ministry in Israel, moreover, did not end with the deaths of the canonical prophets Zechariah, Haggai, and Malachi.[65] To the contrary, prophecy continued in

---

[63]Aune, *Prophecy in Early Christianity*, 87.
[64]Lindblom, *Prophecy*, 202.
[65]This assumption is based on a handful of texts that include *1 Macc* 4:46; 9:27; 14:41; *2 Bar* 85:3; *T. Benj.* 9:2; *b. Sanhedrin*

Judaism into the later NT era, but underwent a number of changes in form and function. OT ideas of prophecy cannot be imposed uncritically upon prophecy in the NT. Still, early Christian prophecy is to be seen, in Greenspahn's words as "part of a perfectly normal and continuing religious phenomenon."[66]

Jewish views of prophecy and the Spirit of God in the past and present exhibit considerable variety. A difference is observed between canonical prophecy of the earlier period and later practice.[67] For instance, Tosephta Sotah 13:2 says, "When the last of the prophets—Haggai, Zechariah, and Malachi—died, the holy spirit ceased in Israel. Despite this they were informed by means of oracles [*bat qol*]."[68] However, some rabbis claimed prophetic ability[69] and viewed the activity of the Spirit as continuing.[70] Philo, whose understanding of prophecy most closely resembles that of the Greek world, believed that prophecy was still available to every good Israelite.[71] Some sects, particularly

---

11a-b; *b. Yoma* 9b; *b. Sotah* 48b; *t. Sotah* 13.2. For two cogent presentations demonstrating the fallacy or this belief, see Fredrick E. Greenspahn, "Why Prophecy Ceased," *JBL* 108 (1989): 37-49; and Blenkinsopp, *History of Prophecy,* 226-280.

[66]Greenspahn, *JBL* (1989): 41. See also Aune, *Prophecy in Early Christianity,* 103-106.

[67]See Otto Michel, "Spätjüdisches Prophetentum," *Neutestamentliche Studien für Rudolf Bultmann* (ed. W. Eltester; Göttingen: Vandenhoeck & Ruprecht, 1954): 60-66.

[68]See Greenspahn, *JBL* (1989): 43.

[69]H. L. Strack and Paul Billerbeck, *Kommentar zum Neuen Testament aus Talmud und Midrasch* (Munich: C. H. Beck, 1924): 2.128.

[70]Martin Hengel, *The Zealots* (trans. D. Smith; Edinburgh: T. & T. Clark, 1989): 234-35.

[71]Philo, *Div. Her.* 259. See also R. Meyer's, "Προφήτης," *TDNT,* 6.821-23, discussion of prophecy in light of Alexandrian theology. Showing the influence of Greek revelatory traditions, Philo at times depicted prophecy as an ecstatic phenomenon in which an indiviudal "truly under the control of divine inspiration has no power of apprehension when he speaks but serves as the channel for the insistent

apocalyptic or millenarian, revered the Torah, yet placed premium upon the alternative forms of revelation through both written and oral prophetic activity.[72]

Common to later Jewish prophecy is the general absence of the tendency to imitate OT prophetic formulas and speech forms.[73] Becker[74] suggests four types of prophets active in Judaism of the NT era: 1) the prophet who, continuing the OT role, is endowed with the Spirit and knows God's will apart from the law (1 Macc 4:46), 2) the political-nationalistic prophet, without an eschatological self-understanding (see Josephus, *Ant.* 13.282-83, 311-12; 15.373ff; *Bell.* 2.113),[75] 3) eschatological prophets

---

words of Another's prompting" (*De Spec. Leg.* 1.65). But see 4.192, where he says that "to a prophet nothing is unknown." For other discussions in Philo of prophecy as a frenzied or ecstatic phenomenon, see *Div. Her.* 249-252; 265-66). As Callan, *NovT* (1985): 125-140, esp. 133-34, has pointed out, however, Philo also recognized another type of prophecy in which the prophet spoke the words of God, but without being entranced. See *De Vit. Mos.* 2.188. In fact, Philo's belief that the entire Pentateuch consisted of oracles given through Moses (*De Vit. Mos.* 2.188), in contrast to the eight specific instances of entranced prophecy which he attributes to Moses (*De Vit. Mos.* 2.246-92), leads Callan, *NovT* (1985): 134, to conclude that Philo viewed this non-ecstatic prophecy as the more important.

[72]Jack P. Lewis, "What do we mean by Jabneh?" *JBR* 32 (1964): 125-132, has argued convincingly that the OT canon was not set by the legendary "council" of Jabneh.

[73]Aune, *Prophecy in Early Judaism*, 106, states, "the integrity of the various forms of early Jewish prophecy is revealed most clearly in its independence from OT prototypes."

[74]Jürgen Becker, *Johannes der Täufer und Jesus von Nazareth* (Neukirchen-Vluyn: Neukirchener Verlag, 1972): 44-60. See also Hengel, *Zealots*, 234-36.

[75]In his accounts of Jewish history, Josephus, for whom prophecy is characteristically the ability to foretell future events, mentions numerous prophets and instances of prophetic activity continuing up through the period of the destruction of Jerusalem in AD 70. *Ant* 13.299, which attributes to Hyrcanus the "three greatest privileges, the rule of the nation, the office of high-priest, and the gift of prophecy: for the Deity was with him and enabled him to foresee and

(Theudas [Josephus, *Ant.* 20.97-98; Acts 5:36] and the Egyptian Jew [Josephus, *Bell.* 2.261ff.]; messianic prophets [Josephus, *Ant.* 18.85]); and 4) a charismatic prophet who demands repentance if Israel is to escape judgment, e.g., the Teacher of Righteousness (1*QpHab* 2:2-3; 7:4-7).[76]

Apocalypticism was widespread in Judaism of the NT era. From the early second century BC, several apocalyptic sects and movements arose within Palestinian Judaism and generated apocalypses for sympathizers who shared their eschatological orientation. A response to the insoluble problem of anxiety and helplessness permeating Palestinian Judaism due to the oppressive conditions, apocalyptic eschatology (the idea that God would intervene to bring a catastrophic end to evil) was a form of political and religious

---

foretell the future." Other references to prophetic activity in Josephus appear remarkably similar to that recorded in Acts 21:10-11.

[76] Of the Qumran Hymns, Millar Burrows, *More Light on the Dead Sea Scrolls* (New York: Viking, 1958): 381, observes that "the most distinctive individual element is the consciousness of having received a divine revelation." Further, many scholars believe that this prophetic consciousness expressed itself particularly in the form of an inspired interpretation of Scripture modeled after the example of Daniel 9:2, such as that which characterizes the Commentary on Habakkuk *QpHab*. Thus Ellis, "The Role of the Christian Prophet in Acts," in *Apostolic History and the Gospel* (ed. W. Gasque and R. P. Martin; Grand Rapids: Eerdmans, 1970): 59, argues, "Without identifying themselves as prophets, the teachers at Qumran engage in an interpretation of Scripture that has as its model the activity of Daniel the prophet." See also *idem*, "Prophecy in the Early Church," *Interpreter's Dictionary of the New Testament* (Supp. vol.; ed. K. Crim; Nashville: Abingdon, 1976): 700-701, and Geza Vermes, *The Dead Sea Scrolls: Qumran In Perspective* (Philadelphia: Fortress, 1981): 167-69, 213-214. Ellis, *Prophecy and Hermeneutic in the Early Church* (Grand Rapids: Eerdmans, 1977): 199-219, sees this "inspired interpretation" as an important part of the role of the prophet in the early church. In addition to his works cited above, Aune, *Prophecy in Early Christianity,* 339-46, however, offers a convincing refutation of this position, going so far as to assert that "There is virtually no evidence . . . that this activity was carried out by those who were labeled 'prophets' in early Christianity."

protest. Apocalyptic visions and visionary literature emerged from the legacy of traditional Israelite prophecy.[77] Such pseudonymous documents as 1 Enoch, 2 Baruch, and the Apocalypse of Abraham, present revelatory literature through visions, woes and laments, testaments, hymns, etc. The clear pattern of correspondence between great historical acts of redemption in Israel's past and new acts anticipated in God's eschatological redemption emerged as a pattern of interpretation in apocalyptic literature.

In common with canonical prophecy, apocalypticism evidences concern for principles and values as they should work out in society, as well as concern for God's judgment when those matters are ignored. A major distinction between OT prophecy and apocalyptic is that the former stressed repentance in view of imminent judgment, whereas the latter offered no conditional aspect but only a pre-determined verdict of God.[78] Prophetic leaders, sometimes called "messiahs," who might arise in this connection were thought to have been selected by God and given supernatural powers to bring about the eschatological rule of God.[79]

One aspect of eschatological deliverance is messianic. The Davidic messiah of popular expectation was thought to be a military figure whose task was to defeat the oppressors and to restore Israel. This human, Davidic messiah whose work was principally militaristic and political is not separable from the transcendental, eschatological figure commonly called the "Son of man."[80] Along with this figure, there was

---

[77]Richard A. Horsley with John S. Hanson, *Bandits, Prophets, and Messiahs: Popular Movements in the Time of Jesus* (San Francisco: Harper & Row, 1985): 151.

[78]John J. Collins, *The Apocalyptic Imagination* (New York: Crossroad, 1992): 17, rightly states that concentration on eschatological aspects of apocalyptic distorts important emphases on cosmological concerns.

[79]See Joseph Bonsirven, *Palestinian Judaism in the Time of Christ* (trans. W. Wolf; New York: McGraw-Hill, 1965): 172-225.

[80]The enigmatic "Son of man" has been variously understood. See Matthew Black, "Jesus and the Son of Man," *JSNT* 1 (1978): 4-17;

expected a returning Elijah as an eschatological prophet (Sir 48:1-14, based on Mal 4:5-6 [MT 3:23-24]); see 4 Ezra 6:26) who would be a forerunner of the messiah (1 En 90:31=Enoch). Also expected was an eschatological "prophet like Moses" (based on Deut 18:15; see 1*QS* 9:10-12 and 4*QTestim* 1-20) who would combine the roles of redeemer, prophet, interpreter of Torah, wonder worker, and sufferer.[81] Leaders of revolutionary movements who maintained a close connection with the wilderness yet swayed large crowds with ideas of liberation were often called prophets.[82] Josephus, *Bell* 2:259, even mentions "false prophets" who provoked insurrections among the people.[83] Too, charismatic leaders in Jewish millenarian movements were regarded as prophets (e.g., Bar Kochba). So, various prophetic types, quite unlike the OT prophets, were active and expected in Judaism of the NT era.

In the Jewish prophetic tradition, as in the Greek world, a woman exercising the gift of prophecy would not have been unheard of or out of place. The canonical Scriptures apply the title "prophetess" to five women: Miriam (Exod 15:20); Deborah (Judg 4:4); Huldah (2 Kings 22:14-20; 2 Chron 34:22-28); Noadiah (Neh 6:14); the wife of Isaiah

---

idem, "Aramaic *bar nasha* and the Son of Man," *ET* 95 (1984): 200-06; James H. Charlesworth, "From Jewish Messianology to Christian Christology: Some Caveats and Perspectives," *Judaisms and Their Messiahs at the Turn of the Christian Era* (ed. J. Neusner, W. S. Green, and E. Frerichs; Cambridge: Cambridge Univ. Press, 1987): 237-41; Chrys C. Caragounis, *The Son of Man: Vision and Interpretation* (WUNT, 38; Tübingen: J. C. B. Mohr, 1986). Alternatively, Geza Vermes, "The Present State of the Son of Man Debate," *JJS* 29 (1978): 121-43; Barnabas Lindars, *Jesus, Son of Man* (Grand Rapids: Eerdmans, 1984); and Maurice Casey, "Method in Our Madness, and Madness in Their Methods: Some Approaches to the Son of Man in Recent Scholarship," *JSNT* 42 (1991): 17-43.

[81]With Meyer, "Προφήτης," *TDNT*, 6.826. Cf. Horsley and Hanson, *Bandits, Prophets, and Messiahs*, 149.

[82]P. W. Barnett, "The Jewish Sign Prophets—AD 40-70—Their Intentions and Origin," *NTS* 27 (1981): 679-697.

[83]See also Josephus, *Ant.* 18.85-87; 20.97-98, 169-71.

(Isa 8:3).[84] Though their numbers are not great, each is mentioned without hesitation or further explanation, indicating that their existence and ministries posed no problems for either the biblical writers or their audiences.

Non-canonical Jewish writings mention Jewish women in similar kinds of prophetic activity.[85] The Babylonian Talmud recognizes seven women who prophesied to Israel: Sarah, Miriam, Deborah, Anna, Abigail, Huldah, and Esther.[86] Targum Judg 5:9 likewise records that the prophetess Deborah, under prophetic inspiration, "did not cease to give exposition of the Torah."[87] In the apocryphal book of Judith, Judith clearly assumes a prophetic role.[88] Therefore, we may conclude that in Judaism as in Greek religion, the prophetic task was not exclusively reserved for men, but was open to women as well.

2. *Women Prophets in 1 Cor 11*

While early Christian prophecy must be understood against the background of its complex antecedents in Greco-Roman and Israelite-Jewish prophecy, it was a multifaceted phenomenon that defies simplistic definition. Significantly different opinions exist concerning the identity of the Corinthian women prophets, precisely what they did, how they were perceived, and to what extent restrictions were placed upon them.

---

[84]N. J. Opperwall, "Prophetess," *ISBE* (rev. G. W. Bromily; Grand Rapids: Eerdmans, 1979-88): 3.1004.

[85]See Randall D. Chesnutt, "Revelatory Experiences Attributed to Biblical Women in Early Jewish Literature," *"Women Like This"— New Perspectives on Jewish Women in the Greco-Roman World* (ed. A.-J. Levine; Atlanta: Scholars Press, 1991): 107-125, on revelatory experiences attributed to biblical women in postbiblical expansions in *Jubilees, Joseph and Aseneth*, and the *Testament of Job*.

[86]*b. Meg.* 14a. See Opperwall, "Prophetess," *ISBE*, 3:1004.

[87]Cited in Strack and Billerbeck, *Kommentar zum Neuen Testament aus Talmud und Midrasch*, 4.116.

[88]*Judith* 8:11-36; 9:1-14; 16:1-17.

A. *Early Christian Prophecy.* Tremendous importance was attached to prophecy in the early church, as indicated in Acts 2:16-21, as well as the lists of functionaries in Rom 12:6, 1 Cor 12:28, and Eph 4:11. More than a little speculation exists regarding these Christian prophets.[89] While most seem to view all Christians as potential prophets,[90] some make a distinction between "prophets" as a special "office" and those "ordinary" church members who prophesy."[91] However, such a distinction has not been established and seems to owe its existence to theological motivation. Too, while roles of strengthening, encouraging, and comforting are commonly acknowledged as characteristic,[92] prophecy is also said to include pastoral preaching and teaching, including charismatic exegesis of OT writings.[93] Others, however, emphasize the function of revelations through spontaneous utterance, thus separating it from teaching and preaching.[94] Depictions of early Christian prophecy as either essentially cognitive or charismatic seem influenced by theological predisposition. Likewise, emphasis on the decline of prophetic activity in the post-apostolic period[95] or

---

[89]Wayne Grudem, *The Gift of Prophecy in 1 Corinthians* (New York: University Press of America, 1982): 3.

[90]Aune, *Prophecy in Early Christianity*, 195.

[91]E.g., F. W. Grosheide, *The First Epistle to the Corinthians* (Grand Rapids: Eerdmans, 1953): 298-99. See also A. von Harnack, "Die Lehre der Zwölf Apostel," TU 2 (1884): 93-158. Cf. Gerhard Friedrich, "Προφήτης," *TDNT* 6:848-55.

[92]E. Cothenet, "Prophétisme dans le Nouveau Testament," *DBSupp.* 8. cols. 1297-1301.

[93]E. Earle Ellis, *Prophecy and Hermeneutic in Early Christianity* (Grand Rapids: Eerdmans, 1987): 182-87.

[94]Siegfried Schatzmann, *A Pauline Theology of Charismata* (Peabody, MA: Hendrickson, 1989): 22. See also G. Dautzenberg, *Urchristliche Prophetie: Ihre Forschung, ihre Voraussetzungen im Judentum und ihre Struktur im ersten Korintherbrief* (BWANT, ed. S. Herrmann and K. Rengstorf; Stuttgart: W. Kohlmammer, 1975): 4.301, who suggests utterances of mysteries and enigmatic riddles.

[95]E.g., Cecil M. Robeck, Jr., "Canon, Regulae Fidei, and Continuing Revelation in the Early Church," *Church, Word and Spirit* (ed. J. Bradley and R. Muller; Grand Rapids: Eerdmans, 1987): 72.

Women and Prophecy in the Corinthian Church   295

continuation beyond the early period either in charismatic[96] or liturgical (evangelistic)[97] modes seems often theologically influenced.

The first insight into the nature and function of prophecy in Christian literature is 1 Thess 5:19-22: "Do not quench the Spirit, do not despise prophesying, but test everything; hold fast to what is good, abstain from every form of evil." While the specific situation which occasioned this instruction cannot be determined, it seems clear that some sort of problem has arisen in the Thessalonian congregation, leading some to reject prophecy. In response, Paul advocates the acceptance of prophecy, but allows for its critical evaluation. From this text, it can be concluded that: 1) the Holy Spirit and prophecy are joined together in "a cause and effect relationship"[98]—a relationship which is emphasized in many other places in the NT as well;[99] 2) prophecy is addressed here as a normal congregational activity; and 3) in contrast to the texts which indicate the enormous influence of prophecy in the early church, it appears obvious that prophecy's influence was not unlimited, but rather was subject to testing (δοκιμάζω) by others in the church.[100] If Paul is referring to prophetic activity in his conjecture that the misconceptions distressing the Thessalonian church might have come about "by spirit"

---

[96]E.g., David Reagan, *The Master Plan: Making Sense of the Controversies Surrounding Bible Prophecy Today* (Eugene, OR: Harvest House, 1993); Hal Lindsey, *The Late Great Planet Earth* (Grand Rapids: Zondervan, 1970).

[97]Cothenet, "Prophétisme," *DBSup.* 8: cols. 1222-1337.

[98]Aune, *Prophecy in Early Christianity*, 191.

[99]In addition to the texts in the Gospels and Acts which have already been examined, the connection of prophecy with the Holy Spirit is strongly emphasized in 2 Pet 1:20-21. Athough talking specifically about the prophets of the OT, the view of prophecy which underlies it may be said to hold for what is said of prophecy in the NT as well.

[100]In addition to the insights into early Christian prophecy mentioned here, Aune, *Prophecy in Early Christianity*, 191, assumes from this text that prophecy was somehow a factor in an intramural church conflict.

(2 Thess 2:2), then a similar limiting of prophecy's influence is reflected in that text (see also 1 John 4:1 and 2 Pet 2:1).

In other places, prophets are clearly identified as church leaders, included among such roles in the early church as apostles, evangelists, pastors, and teachers (Eph 4:11-13; 1 Cor 12:28).[101] As further evidence of their importance they are described along with the apostles in Eph 2:20 as being a constituent element in the foundation of the church. Finally, several texts in the epistles provide insight into the prophets' function in the early church. Clearly, their role in general has to do with building up the church (Rom 12:3-8; 1 Cor 14:3-4, 12; Eph 4:11-16). Rom 12:3-8 makes it clear that the Holy Spirit is at work in churches, and that wherever the Spirit is found, prophecy will be manifested. More specifically, in Eph 3:2-6, Christian prophets (along with the apostles) are said to have been given divine insight into the "mystery of God"—and since the prophet's task was fundamentally a task of proclaiming, implied in that insight is the responsibility of publicly announcing that mystery. Further, in a way that calls to mind the "setting apart" of Barnabas and Saul in Acts 13:1-3, Paul reminds Timothy in 1 Tim 4:14 not to neglect his gift "given to you by prophetic utterance when the council of elders laid their hands upon you." Though not clear in details, prophecy was clearly involved in Timothy's call to ministry.

B. *Women Prophets in 1 Cor 11*. Of all the NT epistles, of course, the one which contains the most extensive treatment of prophecy is 1 Corinthians 11-14 where, in a discussion of spiritual gifts and Christian worship, Paul deals with prophecy in several different contexts. First is his discussion of prophecy and head coverings in 11:2-16; second,

---

[101]Prophecy is the only constant in the Pauline lists of "charismata" (1 Cor 12:8-11, 28-30; 13:1-2; Rom 12:6-8). If the order in which they are listed reflects a ranking in order of importance, then prophets are second in importance only to apostles. But see Stephen S. Smalley, "Spiritual Gifts and 1 Corinthians 12-16," *JBL* 87 (1968): 527-33, who argues that the order in which these gifts are listed, at least in 1 Cor 12, in no way reflects any ranking of importance.

Paul's mention of prophecy among the other spiritual gifts in chap. 12; third, there is his treatment of prophecy and tongues in 14:1-25; and finally, his concluding instruction for orderly worship in 14:26-40. Each of these texts, not surprisingly, has been the subject of intense, continuing debate among scholars who seek to understand their historical background, their precise meaning, and their implications for current church practice. While an exhaustive treatment of this section of 1 Corinthians is beyond the scope of this study, it is important to inquire into precisely what the Corinthian women prophets did, how they might have been perceived by those around them, and under what circumstances they worked.

In this connection, Wire[102] has sought to reconstruct the social and theological dimensions of the Corinthian women prophets. She works from three assumptions: 1) Paul is a rhetorician and all argument in 1 Corinthians serves the function of persuasion, 2) it must not be presumed that Paul's view is correct or that the readers' is incorrect, and 3) while reference is made only occasionally in 1 Corinthians to women prophets, much of the letter is actually written in terms of them. Consequently, Wire does not separate the few passages which speak of women from the issues addressed throughout 1 Corinthians, but in her analysis finds Paul speaking consistently to this group of women throughout the letter.

Wire's depiction of these Corinthian women prophets leaves little to the imagination. Acutely aware of their having been created anew in Christ, they revel in the gifts of the Spirit, including wisdom, prophecy, and ecstatic utterances. Many of them, Wire argues, have opted for celibate lives devoted to prayer, yet remaining free to enjoy food with no restrictions in common meals with all people. Further, they do not disdain apparent disorder in worship, but thrive "on

---

[102]Antionette Clark Wire, *The Corinthian Women Prophets: A Reconstruction of Paul's Rhetoric* (Minneapolis: Fortress, 1990): esp. chap. 6, "Women in the Image and Glory of God: 1 Corinthians 11:2-16."

the expression and interaction of many voices" (147). Thus, Paul is seen as arguing throughout the letter that these women prophets must restrain themselves and submit to a more established social order. So, while he appears in chap. 11 to acknowledge a right to pray and prophesy in public worship, he actually prohibits them from doing so in chap. 14.

However, a number of scholars, among them Scroggs,[103] have raised serious questions about Wire's conclusions. Certainly her tendency to view all statements about women in the Corinthian community as references to the women prophets is unwarranted. Her conclusion that chaps. 1-4, and 15, which appear to be directed to the church as a whole, actually represented Paul's refutation of the theology of the women prophets is likewise unnecessary, as is her assumption that virtually everything Paul opposes in the letter is somehow related to the women prophets. Further, while Paul obviously wishes to persuade his audience, Wire's suggestion that his rhetoric is disingenuously manipulative remains to be proved. Finally, it may be questioned whether her conclusion about the relationship between 11:2-16 and 14:33-36 is true, for if Paul disapproves in chap. 14 what he accepts in chap. 11, then his rhetorical ability stands in considerable question.[104] In short, one cannot assume that the Corinthian women prophets are somehow involved in every issue addressed in 1 Corinthians, but only that they posed a problem in the public assemblies of the church—and represented only one aspect of problems associated with corporate worship dealt with in 1 Cor 11-14.

The principal text in 1 Corinthians in which Paul deals with the women prophets is 11:2-16, where he discusses the

---

[103]See the review of Wire by Robin Scroggs, *JBL* 111 (1992): 546-48.

[104]See also the review of Wire by Robert Gundry, *JAAR* 61 (1993): 392-94.

issue of prophecy in relation to head coverings.[105] Most scholars agree that this text concerns a problem with practices that are occurring in a public setting in which the church is gathered for worship.[106] It begins and ends with an appeal to tradition (παράδοσις, v. 2; συνήθεια, v. 16), which, as an *inclusio*, serves to situate Paul's argument within a context of accepted church practice. The main argument begins in v. 3, centering on the word "head" (κεφαλή): the head of every husband is Christ, the head of the wife is the man, and the head of Christ is God.[107] On the basis of this theological assertion, Paul describes the problem in vv. 4-5, which involves the blurring of gender distinctions, and insists that a man who prays or prophesies with his head covered dishonors his "head" (Christ) while a woman who prays or prophesies with her head uncovered dishonors her "head" (husband). Appealing to their sense of social decorum, Paul asserts that a woman who thus participates without a head covering might as well have her head shaved (v. 6), i.e., appealing to her sense of honor rather than shame. Then, in vv. 7-10, Paul appeals to respect for gender distinctions created by God and to the presence of angels,[108] perhaps as guardians of the created

---

[105]For a discussion of the various problems in this passage, see Mark C. Black, "1 Cor. 11:2-16—A Re-investigation," *Essays on Women in Earliest Christianity*, 1.191-218.

[106]This worship setting can be assumed for a number of reasons. If private practices were under consideration, one wonders why the issue would even have been raised and especially, why it would be included in a section of text which clearly is treating other issues related to public worship. From all other indications, moreover, prophecy was a public activity and there is no compelling reason to believe that the prophecy under consideration is any exception. For further discussion, see Osburn's chapter in this volume, as well as Aune, *Prophecy in Early Christianity*, 196, and Stagg and Stagg, *Women in the World of Jesus*, 177.

[107]For discussion of the meaning of the term "head," see Kenneth V. Neller, "'Submission' in Eph. 5:21-33," *Essays on Women in Earliest Christianity*, 1.251-58.

[108]A number of ancient texts describe angels as, in Talbert's, *Reading Corinthians*, 69, words, "entrusted by God to watch over the

order, as further evidence for the relationships he has posited in v. 3, with its implication that she keep a "sign of authority" (i.e., the head covering on her head).[109] As a balance to that assertion, however, Paul includes a parenthetical statement that in the Lord men and women are interdependent (vv. 11-12) and share a certain complementarity. Finally, in vv. 13-16, he appeals 1) to what is commonly accepted as appropriate, 2) to "common sense"— that since "by nature" (custom) women have long hair and men have short, women should keep their heads covered and men should not, and 3) to universal church practice of women wearing veils in public worship.

Of what did the prophetic activity of these Corinthian women consist, which Paul seeks here to regulate?

---

orders of creation." See, for example, *1 Enoch* 60:12, 16-21; 61:10; 72:1; 82:3; *Jub.* 2:2-3; *1QH* 1.10-11. For a slightly different view see Henry J. Cadbury, "A Qumran Parallel to Paul," *HTR* 51 (1958): 1-2; and Joseph A. Fitzmyer, "A Feature of Qumran Angelology and the NT," *Essays on the Semitic Background to the New Testament* (Missoula: Scholars Press, 1974): 187-204. Based on his reading of *1QM* 7:4-6 and *1QSa* 2:3-11, in comparison with Lev 21:17-23, Fitzmyer observes, "We are invited by the evidence of Qumran to understand that the unveiled head of a woman is like bodily defect which should be excluded from such an assembly, because holy angels are present in their congregation" (200).

[109]Traditionally, this was taken to mean a sign of her submission. For discussion of the range of interpretations of ἐξουσία see Fitzmyer, "Qumran Angelology," *Essays on the Semitic Background to the New Testament,* 191-194. However, Morna D. Hooker, "Authority On Her Head: An Examination of 1 Cor. XI.10," *NTS* 10 (1963-64): 410-16, followed by a number of others, has argued that ἐξουσία here denotes a sign of *her* authority to do what, previously, she had been forbidden to do: ". . . [n]ow woman, too speaks to God in prayer and declares his word in prophecy: to do this she needs authority and power from God. The headcovering which symbolizes the effacement of man's glory in the presence of God also serves as the sign of the ἐξουσία which is given to the woman" (415-416). See also Conzelmann, *I Corinthians,* 69, who believes that "the sign of authority refers to the headcovering which serves as a social symbol of the woman's femaleness."

Opinions vary considerably. While Aune[110] has emphasized the influence of Hellenistic revelatory traditions in post-apostolic Christianity, Boring[111] wisely cautions that NT prophecy itself cannot be identified with Hellenistic prophecy. Indeed, nothing suggests that these Corinthian prophetesses functioned in the manner of Hellentistic oracular prophets, wandering Sybils, or frenzied ritualistic chanters of the mystery religions. Just what relationship might exist between these prophetesses and the Hellenistic mediums speaking in trances remains unclear, although there may be some possible relationship with prophetic moral teaching, as among the Epicureans.

On the other hand, while there is some indication of the continuing existence of the OT prophetic role in which one knows the will of God apart from the Law, OT prophecy is not *the* source for NT prophecy either.[112] While various types of prophets were active and expected in Judaism in the NT era, the Corinthian prophetesses do not appear to have shared the political-nationalistic or revolutionary emphasis that characterized the prophetic activity of many of their Jewish contemporaries. However, some relationship may exist with Jewish eschatological prophets, who stressed principles and values as they work out in society and God's judgment when they are ignored. Perhaps the most that can be said with certainty regarding the relationship of early Christian and Jewish prophetic activity is that early Christian prophecy bears a resemblance to prophecy as a continuing religious phenomenon in Judaism.

From the evidence of the NT itself, prophets were considered to be a constituent element in the founding of the church (Eph 2:20). Ellis[113] and Vermes[114] have both suggested that NT prophets were involved in inspired

---

[110]Aune, *Prophecy in Early Christianity*, 17.
[111]Boring, *Continuing Voice of Jesus*, 49-50.
[112]*Ibid.*, 58.
[113]Ellis, "Role of the Christian Prophet in Acts," *Apostolic History and the Gospel*, 59.
[114]Vermes, *Dead Sea Scrolls*, 213-14.

interpretation of the OT text, but Aune[115] has argued that no evidence exists that this is the case. Grosheide[116] posits a distinction between the prophetic "office," and "ordinary" Christians who prophesy. However, such a distinction cannot be maintained. Hill[117] stresses the "pastoral preaching" and "exhortatory teaching" aspects of prophecy, but Boring[118] prefers a definition of NT prophecy based on that of the SBL Seminar on Early Christian Prophecy (1972-77). At the very least, the early Christian prophets—and presumably the Corinthian prophetesses—were engaged in publicly announcing the "mystery" (Eph 3:2-6), as well as in strengthening, encouraging, and comforting. That there were inherent possibilities of failure in the prophetic role seems clear enough from the admonition in 1 Thess 5:20 not to despise prophecy, but to subject prophetic messages to critical examination. Similarly, in 1 Cor 14:29, prophets are to be subject to "discernment."

Most importantly, the evidence of 1 Cor 11 clearly indicates that this prophetic activity was carried out publicly by women in the Christian assemblies at Corinth. The practice itself is not at issue. What is at issue is the manner in which the Corinthian prophetesses were engaged in that

---

[115] Aune, *Prophecy in Early Christianity*, 339-46.

[116] Grosheide, *First Epistle to the Corinthians,* 298-99.

[117] Hill, *New Testament Prophecy*, 105, 126, 129, 138, 143-44. On pp. 8-9, Hill adapts the SBL Seminar on Early Christian Prophecy (1972-77) as follows: "A Christian prophet is a Christian who functions within the church, occasionally or regularly, as a divinely-inspired speaker who receives intelligible and authoritative revelations or messages which he is impelled to deliver publicly, in oral or written form, to Christian individuals and/or the Christian community."

[118] Cf. M. E. Boring's review of Hill, *New Testament Prophecy*, in *JBL* 100 (1981): 300-02, which criticizes Hill for positing a working definition, but actually operating with another definition of Christian prophecy based on content (e.g., pastoral exhortation). Boring, *Continuing Voice of Jesus*, 38, posits: "The early Christian prophet was an immediately inspired spokesperson for the risen Jesus, who received intelligible messages that he or she felt impelled to deliver to the Christian community or, as a representative of the community, to the general public."

practice. They were doing so in a way—with heads uncovered—that threatened what Paul believed to be a proper male-female relationship. To preserve decorum, therefore, Paul insists that men pray or prophesy with heads uncovered, while women do so with heads covered. Certainly women praying or prophesying in the assembly posed no problem for the Corinthians; from his discussion, neither did women praying or prophesying in the assembly cause problems for Paul, provided they did so in a manner consistent with proper male-female relationships.

Finally, this understanding of 1 Cor 11:2-16 supports the interpretation of 1 Cor 14:34-35 which views Paul's command that "women should be silent" as addressed to a specific problem in the Corinthian church, rather than being absolute prohibitions for all women.[119] His use of the present infinitive construction in 14:34-35 to describe the speaking which women are not allowed to do (λαλεῖν; lit., to keep on speaking) probably indicates a continual, disruptive speaking out.[120] Paul's reference to the asking of questions clarifies the sort of expression he seeks to prohibit. Finally, the text's parallel position with the instructions on tongues and prophecy, with the parallel use of σιγάω (be silent, vv. 28, 30), gives the impression that Paul does not intend to enjoin total silence on women any more than he intends absolutely to silence tongues or prophets. Rather, he wishes to limit their expression in the assembly—just as he does tongues and prophecy—so that order and peace will prevail in the Corinthian worship. What he has said earlier in chap. 11, then, is not contradicted in chap. 14. Paul's concern in both texts is not with women speaking in the assembly, but rather, with their doing so in a way that is inappropriate (11) or disruptive (14).

---

[119]For a more detailed discussion, see Carroll D. Osburn, "The Interpretation of 1 Corinthians 14:34-35," *Essays On Women in Earliest Christianity*, 1.219-42.

[120]*Ibid.*, 233-34. For discussion of the durative character of the Greek present infinitve, see F. W. Blass and A. Debrunner, *A Greek Grammar of the New Testament and Other Early Christian Literature* (trans. and rev. R. Funk; Chicago: Univ. of Chicago Press, 1961): 174.

Conclusion

While the evidence is neither exhaustive nor as detailed as one would prefer it to be, the foregoing analysis nevertheless yields a number of conclusions about prophets and prophecy in general, and the role of women in particular. Prophecy is viewed in the NT, first and foremost, as a supernatural gift given by the Holy Spirit. Paul includes prophecy in his lists of "gifts of the Holy Spirit" (Rom 12:6; 1 Cor 12:8-11; Eph 4:7-12), and connects the rejection of prophecy with "quenching the Spirit" (1 Thess 5:19). Possession of the gift of prophecy, not surprisingly, enables persons to know what cannot be known by normal human means, whether that knowledge is of the future (Acts 11:27; 21:10; Rev 1:1-3), or of the will of God for the church in a particular situation (Acts 13:1-3). Prophecy in the NT is also a decidedly public gift, one which involves speaking publicly and intelligibly the message received from God.[121] The prophet's message seems to have been a spontaneous rather than prepared discourse.[122] The prophetic message, moreover is directed

---

[121] For a discussion of the distinction between" prophecy and other gifts involving speech, see Friedrich, "Προφήτης" *TDNT*, 6.851-55. H. Greeven, "Propheten, Lehrer, Vorsteher bei Paulus," *ZNW* 44 (1952-53): 29ff., argued that there is no clear distinction in the NT between prophecy and teaching. Grudem, *JETS* (1987): 11-23, on the other hand, argued that there is indeed a clear distinction between the two and that teaching was far more important in the early church than prophecy. He greatly overstates this distinction between prophecy and teaching, however, and his argument that teaching was more important than prophecy is unconvincing. See also Grudem, *The Gift of Propehcy in 1 Corinthians*. A number of scholars have attempted to reconstruct prophetic mesages on the basis of other texts, both in and outside of the NT. See, for example, W. C. Van Unnik, "A Formula Describing Prophecy," *NTS* 9 (1962-63): 86-94; and Thomas W. Gillespie, "A Pattern of Prophetic Speech in First Corinthians," *JBL* 97 (1978): 74-95.

[122] Boring, *Continuing Voice of Jesus*, 38, emphasizes this characteristic in his definition of a prophet: "The early Christian prophet was an immediately inspired spokesperson for the risen Jesus, who received intelligible messages that he or she felt impelled to deliver

primarily toward the church, whether to individual Christians (Acts 21:10), or to congregations assembled for worship (Acts 13:1-3; 1 Cor 11-14). Most frequently their message was one of comfort and exhortation to the church (Acts 13:1-3; 1 Cor 14:3). Through prophecy, listeners were informed or instructed (1 Cor 14:19), and at times, warned and brought under judgment (1 Cor 14:24—25). Prophets are thus listed among the persons with spiritual gifts whose task is to build up the church (Rom 12:3-8; Eph 4:11-16). At the same time, Paul stressed in 14:32 that, "the spirit of the prophet is subject to the prophet," i.e., prophecy can and should be controlled by the prophet.

Prophets do not seem to have occupied an "office" as such, but were known more informally, through the exercise of their gifts, as persons to whom God had given special revelations and who communicated them to the church.[123] They were often, therefore, persons of great influence in the early church. In response to prophetic messages, for example, the Antioch church took up a collection of gifts for the poor in Jerusalem (Acts 11:27-30) and began a far-reaching mission to the Gentile world (Acts 13:1-3). Perhaps because of their influence, prophets were chosen to accompany the letter of the "Jerusalem Council" to the Gentile believers (Acts 15:22,32). So great in fact, was the influence of prophets in the early church that the NT, in numerous places, warns of false prophets and provides criteria for judging their character and their messages in order to ensure that they are authentically prophets of God.

---

to the Christian community . . . ." For this reason and because of the emphasis on knowledge to the average person, early Christian prophecy resists comparison to contemporary preaching and teaching. For an excellent discussion, see Ernest Best, "Prophets and Preachers," *SJT* 12 (1959): 129-50.

[123]For discussions of prophets as leaders in the early Church, see Greeven, *ZNW* (1952-53): 31ff.; Hill, *New Testament Prophecy*, 90-105. Cf. Aune, *Prophecy in Early Christianity*, 196ff., for a somewhat different view.

The evidence of the NT further indicates that this prophetic role was not exclusively reserved for men, but included women as well. References to women prophesying, though not as numerous as references to men, are distributed throughout the NT in a way that suggests a general acceptance of prophetesses in the early church. While the references to women prophesying do not explicitly describe their ministries, there is nothing to suggest that they functioned in their role differently than their male counterparts. Certainly, they carried on their ministries within a set of prescribed constraints–but so also did the men who prophesied and prayed.[124] In the absence of evidence to the contrary, therefore, it is plausible to assume that in their prophetic ministries women exercised roles of public expression and influence in the early church just as men did. They were viewed by the church as having received inspired messages from God which they proclaimed to the church–at times in the context of Christian worship. Possessing the gift of prophecy, they were undoubtedly persons of influence and would have been instrumental in determining the direction of the church. From the evidence of the women who prophesied we may thus conclude that the early church viewed whatever restrictions were placed upon woman not as absolute prohibitions against all expression, but rather, as parameters within which that expression could freely take place. In this way, the women who prophesied in the first century Christian church enjoyed an equality of expression and influence alongside of their brothers in Christ.

---

[124]See Richard Oster, "When Men Wore Veils to Worship: The Historical Context of 1 Corinthians 14," *NTS* 34 (1988): 481-505.

Chapter Fourteen

1 COR 11:2-16— PUBLIC OR PRIVATE?

Carroll D. Osburn

Certainly 1 Cor 11:2-16 presents several of the most difficult interpretive tasks in the NT, all of which are contingent to some extent on whether Paul is referring to a public or private assembly. A basic problem underlying the interpretation of 11:2-16 involves the relationship of 11:2-16 with 14:33-35. Three basic positions have emerged in scholarship on this matter: 1) 11:2-16 is taken with the preceding material beginning in 8:1 (which treats eating in a domestic setting meat offered to idols), so that the women in chap. 11 pray and prophesy in a private setting, thus reducing conflict with the public assembly in chap. 14[1], 2) 11:2-16 is a public assembly, but Paul actually mandates that women are not to pray or prophesy,[2] which coheres with the prohibition against women speaking in public in chap. 14, and 3) 11:2-16 is taken with chaps. 11-14 which treat the public assembly of the church, meaning that women did pray and prophesy publicly, but with stipulated conditions of cultural propriety.[3] Even so, the relation of 11:2-16 to 14:33-35 is variously understood by those who adopt this view. Consequently, it is instructive to examine and critique each of these views.

---

[1] See e.g., Philipp Bachmann, *Der erste Brief des Paulus an die Korinther* (KNT 7; 3rd ed.; Leipzig: A. Deichert, 1921): 345-62.

[2] See F. C. Synge, "Studies in Texts—1 Cor 11:2-16," *Theology* 56 (1953): 143.

[3] Most commentaries assume 11:2-16 to go with the following section which treats the public assembly and do not argue the issue. Gordon D. Fee, *The First Epistle to the Corinthians* (NIC; Grand Rapids: Eerdmans, 1987): 505, n. 54, does more than most when he relegates the matter to a brief footnote.

1. The View that 1 Cor 11:2-16 Refers to a Private Setting

Bachmann[4] presented four principal arguments in support of his view that 11:2-16 refers to private assemblies. 1) Since 8:1-11:1 discusses domestic problems and 11:2-16 follows immediately without any indication of change of subject, 11:2-16 belongs to the preceding section. 2) V. 17 begins to refer to the public assemblies of the congregation. 3) Prophecy, as it manifested itself not only at Corinth, but at Thessalonica (1 Thess 5:20) and probably in other cities (see Rom 12:6), cannot be ruled out as being practiced in smaller groups, such as domestic worship. 4) Because "girls" are not mentioned in 11:2-16, only wives, emphasis is on a family context rather than the public assembly.

Since 11:2-16 are taken with the previous material which begins in 8:1 and treats eating (in a domestic setting) meat offered to idols, women praying and prophesying in such private settings would pose no conflict with chap. 14, which treats the public assembly.

However, Bachmann's thesis, that women were allowed to prophesy and pray only in gatherings of a more private sort, but not when the entire church was assembled for worship, was disproved convincingly by Tischleder.[5]

---

[4]Bachmann, *Der erste Brief des Paulus an die Korinther*, 345-62. See also Adolf Schlatter, *Paulus der Bote Jesu* (Stuttgart: Calwer, 1969): 390. E. Earle Ellis, "'Spiritual' Gifts in the Pauline Community," *NTS* 20 (1974): 131, suggests, "the instructions in 1 Cor. xi.5 on praying and prophesying probably reflect the procedures used within the prayer sessions of the pneumatics," whom he postulates, on the analogy of Acts 13:1f., were "smaller sessions of pneumatics, who in varying degree were active as a teaching cadre in the Church." See also Johannes Lindblom, *Geschichte und Offenbarungen: Vorstellungen von göttlichen Weisungen und übernatürlichen Erscheinungen im ältesten Christentum* (Lund: Gleerup, 1968): 140f.

[5]P. Tischleder, *Wesen und Stellung der Frau: nach der Lehre des heiligen Paulus—eine ethisch-exegetische Untersuchung* (NTAbh 10.3-4; Münster: Aschendorf, 1923): 170-83. See also Heinz Dietrich Wendland, *Die Briefe an die Korinther* (NTD 7; 10th ed.; Göttingen: Vandenhoeck & Ruprecht, 1964): 80-83.

For one thing, Tischleder argued, it is difficult to suppose that Paul would mandate in such strong terms a mode of head-covering for a man and wife in a private setting. Further, he argued, it would be peculiar for Paul to place restrictions on an action, only a few chapters later to forbid the action entirely. Too, 10:31-11:1 forms the conclusion of the preceding discussion. Also, prophecy is by its textual definition not designed for private use, but public.

2. *Public Assembly, but Women Not to Pray or Prophesy*

Others have argued that while the context is that of a public assembly of the church, Paul's point nevertheless is that women should not speak, including prayer and prophecy, in the public assembly. Synge,[6] for instance, readily acknowledges that this text refers to the public assembly, but argues that women should not pray and prophesy in public. Synge posits (1) that all prophesy must be with the head uncovered, and since for a woman to be uncovered would be "to dishonor her head," a woman must not prophesy. He also argues (2) that if a woman prophesies uncovered, she must be shorn of her hair. Since that is shameful, she must be covered and therefore cannot prophesy. Synge then argues (3) that "a woman, being one stage lower down the scale, must be veiled" and (4) that a "woman's veil indicates that she belongs to the man." With v. 13, Synge argues (5), since a woman should not be shorn, she may not prophesy. He concludes, "Everyone agrees that God has given women long hair for adornment. That proves that God does not wish them to prophesy."

However, Synge's syllogistic "leap-frogging" through the text leaves much to be desired: 1) the crucial assumption that all prophecy was to be done uncovered, whether by male or female, is not substantiated; 2) the assertion that if a woman prophesies uncovered, she must be shorn, is not demonstrable to Paul's point in vv. 5-6; 3) the notion that a woman must wear a veil because she is "one stage lower down the scale" is not established by convincing argument;

---

[6]Synge, *Theology* (1953): 143.

4) and the conclusion that long hair *per se* indicates that a woman may not pray or prophesy in public does not follow from any reasonable analysis of the text. Synge's dictum is a clear example of how not to engage in NT exegesis.

Weeks[7] argues that the text refers to the public assembly. "Certainly," he says (23), "11:17ff. is concerned with public worship and there is the strongest connection between vv. 2 and 17." Further, he argues, there is "no indication in the text itself that some special sort of private gathering of believers is in view." However, Weeks observes, public prayer and prophesying are matters of authority and "for a woman to engage in prayer or prophecy would place her in the same position as the man. That is, she would be forced to exercise headship." Since the argument in chap. 11 "consistently turns upon the created order" (21), all texts are to be interpreted consistently with that understanding. Public praying and prophesying are seen as matters of authority involving headship. So Weeks suggests that, "v. 5 begins the argument that a woman may not pray or prophesy" (in public). He translates ἀκατακαλύπτω (uncovered) as "by means of the unveiling of the head," meaning that if a woman seeks to take a man's place, then she must uncover her head and thus be in the position of being shorn. But since being shorn is shameful, a woman must realize that to pray or prophesy in public is to be put to shame. "Hence," Weeks concludes (27), "she should realize that praying and prophesying in an authoritative position is contrary to her created function and glory."

This view brings 11:2-16 into line with chap. 14, which treats the public assembly in Corinth. However, there are at least three problems which render Weeks' conclusion unsuitable. First, Weeks assumes the "order of creation" argument as the lens through which all texts must be read. Second, Weeks assumes that praying and prophesying are matters of "authority" and "headship," and hence to be done only by men. Third, Weeks' understanding of "uncovered"

---

[7]Noel Weeks, "Of Silence and Head Covering," *WTJ* 35 (1972): 21-27.

1 Cor 11:2-16—Public or Private?

in v. 5 as "by means of uncovering" is purportedly based upon Robertson's[8] discussion of the instrumental/comitative dative, but actually Robertson treats briefly only the grammatical history of the instrumental case and provides no assistance whatsoever in interpreting ἀκατακαλύπτω in v. 5. This view of "uncovered" is grammatically possible, but has not been demonstrated to be contextually probable.

3. *11:2-16 Refers to Public Assembly in which Women Prayed and Prophesied*

1 Cor 11:2-14:40 has long been recognized by most scholars as a coherent argumentative section.[9] Here Paul

---

[8]A. T. Robertson, *A Grammar of the Greek New Testament in the Light of Historical Research* (Nashville: Broadman, 1934): 526.

[9]See, among others, J. B. Lightfoot, *Notes on the Epistles of St. Paul from Unpublished Commentaries* (London: Macmillan, 1895): 141; C. F. G. Heinrici, *Der erste Brief an die Korinther* (MeyerK 7; 8th ed.; Göttingen: Vandenhoeck & Ruprecht, 1896): 321; J. Weiss, *Der erste Korintherbrief* (MeyerK 7; 9th ed.; Göttingen: Vandenhoeck & Ruprecht, 1910): 268; A. Robertson and A. Plummer, *A Critical and Exegetical Commentary on the First Epistle of St. Paul to the Corinthians* (ICC; New York: Scribner's, 1925): 226; H. L. Goudge, *The First Epistle to the Corinthians* (WC; 5th ed.; London: Methuen, 1926): 94-97; E.-B. Allo, *Saint Paul. Première Épître aux Corinthiens* (EBib; 2nd ed.; Paris: LeCoffre, 1956): 253; C. Wolff, *Der erste Brief des Paulus an die Korinther* (THKNT 7; Berlin: Evangelische Verlagsanstalt, 1975): 65; Luke T. Johnson, *The Writings of the New Testament* (Philadelphia: Fortress, 1986): 283-89; and D. Lührmann, "Freundschaftsbrief trotz Spannungen. Zu Gattung und Aufbau der ersten Korintherbriefs," *Studien zum Text und zur Ethik des Neuen Testaments. Festschrift zum 80. Geburtstag von H. Greeven* (ed. W. Schrage; BZNW 47; Berlin: W. de Gruyter, 1986): 305. William O. Walker, "1 Corinthians 11:2-16 and Paul's Views Regarding Women," *JBL* 94 (1975): 94-110, and G. W. Trompf, "On Attitudes Toward Women in Paul and Paulinist Literature: 1 Corinthians 11:3-16 and its Context," *CBQ* 42 (1980): 196-215, view 11:2-16 as a non-Pauline interpolation inserted between 8:1ff. and 11:17-34, a section treating eating and drinking. Cf. critiques of the former by J. Murphy-O'Connor, "The Non-Pauline Character of 1 Corinthians 11:2-16?" *JBL* 95 (1976): 615-21, and of the latter in *idem*, "Interpolations in 1 Corinthians," *CBQ* 48 (1986): 81-84.

turns to specific manifestations of Corinthian factionalism when the church assembles in one place for worship.[10] As Isaksson[11] remarks, while there is no consensus on the interpretation of 1 Cor 11:2-16, on one point there is now a fair degree of unanimity—"only a few scholars still deny that this text is concerned with the appearance of women at public worship." However, not all who see 11:2-16 as referring to the public assembly understand the text alike. Wire,[12] for instance, proposes that while in chap. 11 Paul seems to acknowledge that women have the right to pray and prophesy in public, in chap. 14 he actually forthrightly denies what he seemingly affirms in chap. 11. Grosheide[13] proposes that 11:2-16 permits women praying and prophesying in public, but not in the assembly of the congregation. Most, however, view the passage as referring to women praying and prophesying in the public assembly of the Corinthian congregation.

Perhaps the most thorough compositional analysis of 1 Cor 11:2-16 within the larger context of chaps. 11-14 is that of Mitchell. In 11:2-14:40, a section of deliberative proof urging unity, Paul turns attention to the inevitable

---

[10]See Margaret M. Mitchell, *Paul and the Rhetoric of Reconciliation: An Exegetical Investigation of the Language and Composition of 1 Corinthians* (Louisville: Westminster/John Knox, 1993): 258. James Moffatt, *The First Epistle of Paul to the Corinthians* (London: Hodder and Stoughton, 1938): 149, correctly observes that the statement of Plutarch, *Roman Questions* 14, "usually women cover their heads and men uncover them, when they go outside the house," is not under consideration because Paul's concern is not with how one appears outdoors, but in worship.

[11]Abel Isaksson, *Marriage and Ministry in the New Temple: a Study with Special Reference to Mt. 19:3-12 and 1 Cor. 11.3-16* (Acta Seminarii Neotestamentici Upsaliensis 24; trans. N. Tomkinson; Lund: C. W. K. Gleerup, 1965):

[12]Antoinette Clark Wire, *The Corinthian Women Prophets: A Reconstruction through Paul's Rhetoric* (Minneapolis: Fortress, 1990): 116-134; 135-58. See critical reviews in Robin Scroggs, *JBL* 111 (1992): 546-48; and Robert Gundry, *JAAR* 61 (1993): 392-394.

[13]F. W. Grosheide, *The First Epistle to the Corinthians* (Grand Rapids: Eerdmans, 1953): 251-52.

factionalism which manifests itself when persons who have little genuine concern for other Christians are forced to be together in one place for worship.[14] Throughout 11:2-14:40, Paul appeals to "building" and "body" images, which play large parts in the earlier sections of 1 Corinthians, to appeal for concord.[15] The purpose of chaps. 11-14 is to persuade the Corinthians to be united rather than divided when they assemble for worship.[16]

Beginning with "I praise you" in 11:2, Paul makes a transition to a new section in 1 Corinthians.[17] This praise is in contrast to 11:17, 22, where Paul specifically does not praise divisive conduct at the Lord's Supper.[18] So, the section 11:2-34 is united rhetorically.[19]

The argument in 11:2-16 is introduced with the disclosure formula θέλω δὲ ὑμᾶς εἰδέναι (I wish you to know), and the topic treats appropriate covering of the κεφαλή (head), specifically when praying and prophesying

---

[14]Goudge, *The First Epistle to the Corinthians*, 94; Allo, *Saint Paul. Première Épître aux Corinthiens*, 270-71.

[15]Mitchell, *Paul and the Rhetoric of Reconciliation*, 258, n. 404, detects lexical evidence for the coherence of chaps. 11-14 in the use of συνέρχεσθαι (gather together) in 11:17, 18, 20, 33, 34; 14:23, 26, and only here in the Pauline corpus.

[16]See Weiss, *Der erste Korintherbrief*, 277-78.

[17]See Mitchell, *Paul and the Rhetoric of Reconciliation*, 194-97 and 207-225, for discussion of Paul's use of praise in deliberative argumentation in 1 Corinthians. See also Jean Héring, *The First Epistle of Saint Paul to the Corinthians* (trans. A. W. Heathcote and P. Allcock; London: Epworth, 1962): 101-02.

[18]See Stanley K. Stowers, *Letter Writing in Greco-Roman Antiquity* (Library of Early Christianity 5; Philadelphia: Westminster, 1986): 80; John Ruef, *Paul's First Letter to Corinth* (Philadelphia: Westminster, 1977): 108; and Grosheide, *The First Epistle to the Corinthians*, 248.

[19]See Mitchell, *Paul and the Rhetoric of Reconciliation*, 260, n. 412, for a survey of various partition theories, e.g., W. Schmithals, "Die Korintherbriefe als Briefsammlung," *ZNW* 64 (1973): 263-88.

in the public worship (vv. 4-5).²⁰ From the developing argument, it is clear that disagreement exists in the church in Corinth concerning various customs of head covering in worship. This text has become a notorious *crux interpretum* involving, among other things,²¹ what kind of head covering is under discussion (veils, hairstyles, hair cuts),²² how Paul's argument can be reconciled with chap. 14:33b-36,²³

---

²⁰Hans Lietzmann, *An die Korinther I.II* (HNT 9; 3rd ed; Tübingen: Mohr, 1931): 53; John C. Hurd, *The Origin of I Corinthians* (London: SPCK, 1965): 90-91; F. F. Bruce, *1 and 2 Corinthians* (Grand Rapids: Eerdmans, 1971): 102; and Fee, *The First Epistle to the Corinthians*, 491-92, suppose that head covering was mentioned in the letter from the Corinthians. On the other hand, J. Murphy-O'Connor, "Sex and Logic in 1 Corinthians 11:2-16," *CBQ* 42 (1980): 482-500, held that it was not mentioned in the letter. C. K. Barrett, *The First Epistle to the Corinthians* (New York: Harper and Row, 1968): 245-46, notes that it is impossible to know how Paul learned of the issue.

²¹See Mark C. Black, "1 Cor 11:2-16—A Reinvestigation," *Essays on Women in Earliest Christianity* (ed. C. D. Osburn; Joplin, MO: College Press, 1993): 1.191-218, for a survey of the various questions and answers.

²²E.g., Richard Oster, "When Men Wore Veils to Worship: the Historical Context of 1 Corinthians 11.4," *NTS* 34 (1988): 481-505; Cynthia Thompson, "Hairstyles, Head-coverings, and St. Paul: Portraits from Roman Corinth," *BA* 51 (1988): 99-115; Morna D. Hooker, "Authority on Her Head: An Examination of 1 Cor. xi.10," *NTS* 10 (1964): 410-16; John P. Meier, "On the Veiling of Hermeneutics (1 Cor. 11:2-16)," *CBQ* 40 (1978): 212-26; J. A. Fitzmyer, "Another Look at Kephale in 1 Corinthians 11:3," *NTS* 35 (1989): 503-11; Joël Delobel, "1 Cor 11:2-16: Towards a Coherent Interpretation," *L'Apôtre Paul: Personnalité, Style et Conception du Ministère* (BETL 73; Leuven: Leuven Univ. Press, 1986): 369-89; D. W. J. Gill, "The Importance of Roman-Portraiture for Head Coverings in 1 Corinthians 11:2-16," *TynBul* 41 (1990): 245-60; and Alan Padgett, "Paul on the Women in the Church: the Contradiction of Coiffure in 1 Corinthians 11:2-16," *JSNT* 20 (1984): 69-86.

²³E.g., James B. Hurley, "Did Paul Require Veils or the Silence of Women? A Consideration of 1 Cor. 11:2-16 and 1 Cor. 14:33b-36," *WTJ* 33 (1973): 190-220; R. W. Allison, "Let Women Be Silent in the Churches (1 Cor. 14:33b-36): What Did Paul Really Say, and What Did it Mean?" *JSNT* 32 (1988): 27-60; E. Earle Ellis, "The Silenced Wives of Corinth (1 Cor 14:34-35)," *New Testament Textual*

whether an "order of creation" is involved,[24] and whether men are actually a part of the controversy or are merely introduced here so that Paul can argue proper women's behavior by analogy.[25]

Criticism: Essays in Honour of Bruce M. Metzger (ed. E. Epp & G. D. Fee; Oxford: Clarendon, 1981): 213-220; and Robert J. Karris, "Women in the Pauline Assembly: To Prophesy, But Not To Speak?" *Women Priests* (ed. L. Swidler & A. Swidler; New York: Paulist, 1977): 205-08.

[24]Among others, Margaret Thrall, *The First and Second Letters of Paul to the Corinthians* (Cambridge: Cambridge Univ. Press, 1965): 79, presents a "graded scale of authority":

>God
>Christ
>Man
>Woman

See also Moffatt, *First Epistle to the Corinthians*, 151; Héring, *The First Epistle of St. Paul to the Corinthians*, 102-03; Bruce, *1 and 2 Corinthians*, 103. However, it is not without good reason that Leon Morris, *The First Epistle of Paul to the Corinthians* (2nd ed.; Grand Rapids: Eerdmans, 1985): 150, observes, "The order of creation has consequences for worship, but Paul's precise meaning is not easy to see." In an astute observation long ago, J. W. McGarvey and P. Y. Pendleton, *Thessalonians, Corinthians, Galatians and Romans* (Cincinnati: Standard, 1916): 109, remarked:

> We would expect him to begin with God and descend by the regular steps, thus: God, Christ, man, woman. But the order is thus: Christ, man; man, woman; God, Christ. Subtle distinctions are to be made with caution, but it is not improbable that Paul's order in this case is determined by the delicate nature of the subject which he handles. Dominion is fruitful of tyranny, and so it is well, before giving man dominion, to remind him that he also is a servant. . . . the arrangement makes the headship of the man over the woman parallel to the headship of God over Christ, and suggests that there should be between husband and wife a unity of will and purpose similar to that which exists between the Father and the Son. . . . All Christian husbands and wives should mutually remember this parallel.

[25]See among others, Alan Padgett, "Feminism in First Corinthians: A Dialogue with Elisabeth Schüssler Fiorenza," *EvQ* 58 (1986): 121-32.

While it is not the intent of this essay to examine these questions in detail, it can be concluded 1) that Paul maintained a strong concern for the unity of the church, 2) that in an effort to compromise, Paul stated his own preference for women to remain covered while engaged in prayer and prophecy in the public assembly so that controversy can be avoided, and 3) that this procedure would be in line with universal church custom.[26] That women were praying and prophesying in the public assembly posed no problem for the Corinthians or for Paul himself.[27]

Conclusion

In line with the Joel prophecy cited in Acts 2:17 on the day of Pentecost, "Your sons and your daughters shall prophesy," women in the Corinthian congregation are praying and prophesying in the assembly in 11:2-16. In 14:34-35, some women are speaking in an instruction setting. The commonality shared by the two texts is not "women speaking in public," but women evidencing disrespect for others, decorum, and propriety, and thus contributing to chaos and disruption. The women in chap. 11 are flouting commonly-accepted cultural norms, with resultant disrespect to their husbands; the women in chap. 14 are impeding instruction by incessant questioning. The latter are told in no uncertain terms to "Pipe down!" The former, while praying and/or prophesying in public worship, should do so in a manner that would not disgrace or dishonor their husbands.[28]

---

[26]For the application of the ancient principle to modern situations where different customs prevail, see Morris, *The First Epistle of Paul to the Corinthians*, 154-55.

[27]With William F. Orr and J. A. Walther, *1 Corinthians* (AB 32; Garden City, NY: Doubleday, 1976): 263.

[28]*Ibid.*, 264, infers correctly that such a principle would apply to an unmarried woman, *mutatis mutandis.*

Chapter Fifteen

WAS SARAH A BELIEVER? REFLECTIONS ON HEBREWS 11:11

James Thompson

"The place to start," writes Buechner,[1] "is with a woman laughing . . . she is laughing because she is pushing ninety-one hard and has just been told that she is going to have a baby." Sarah's laughter, according to the Genesis narrative (18:12), was the response of incredulity. Both she and Abraham laugh (see Gen 17:17) at the idea of their having offspring in their old age. They laugh "at the idea of a baby's being born in the geriatric ward and Medicare's picking up the tab."[2] The promise of a son in their old age was greeted, not with faith, but with the laughter of unbelief.

In the Genesis narrative, Abraham's faith is specifically mentioned once. In response to God's promise of a multitude of descendants, "Abraham believed God, and it was reckoned to him as righteousness" (15:6). Later tradition, however, read the entire Abraham story as an account of the faith recorded in Gen 15:6. His departure from Ur, his sojourning, and his offering of Isaac were all interpreted in light of Gen 15:6 as examples of faith.[3] The faith of Sarah, however, is never mentioned. Although she accompanied Abraham from Ur to Canaan and waited with him for an heir, her point of view is never given. She is characterized only by her barrenness (Gen 15:2; 16:1), spitefulness (Gen 16:6; 21:10), and incredulous laughter.

---

[1] Fredrick Buechner, *Telling the Truth: The Gospel as Comedy, Tragedy and Fairy Tale* (San Francisco: Harper, 1977): 50.
[2] *Ibid.*, 50.
[3] Halvor Moxnes, *Theology in Conflict: Studies in Paul's Understanding of God in Romans* (NovTSup 53; Leiden: Brill, 1980): 155-164.

Since Sarah is never a model of faith in Genesis, one may be surprised to note the portrait of her in the brief comment in Heb 11:11 as it appears in most modern language translations. According to the KJV of Heb 11:11, "Through faith Sara herself received strength to conceive seed, and was delivered of a child when she was past age." The ASV, RSV, and the NEB follow this reading with only minor variations. The NIV and the NRSV are minority voices, each having Abraham in 11:11 as the subject of the sentence. According to the NIV, "By faith Abraham, even though he was past the age—and Sarah herself was barren—was enabled to become a father . . . ." Thus, with the exception of the NIV and the NRSV, Sarah is known in Hebrews, not for her incredulity, but for her faith.

The portrayal of Sarah in Heb 11:11 has been one of the most perplexing issues in studies of the epistle to the Hebrews. In this article, I shall address the controversial question: Has the author of Hebrews reclaimed Sarah by adding her to the list of the faithful? Scholarly opinion has been sharply divided on the issue, as the translations indicate. The unusual Greek construction in Heb 11:11 is the source of the exegetical difficulty, which is especially evident in the textual tradition of the passage. The UBS[4] and Nestle[27] texts, relying primarily on $\mathfrak{P}^{46}$, have the reading πίστει καὶ αὐτὴ Σάρρα στεῖρα δύναμιν εἰς καταβολὴν σπέρματος ἔλαβεν.[4] This is rendered by RSV, "by faith Sarah herself received power to conceive." The difficulty of rendering the verse as it appears in the majority of modern language translations is that καταβολὴ σπέρματος is a technical term for the "sowing of seed, for begetting, and thus refers to the masculine role in reproduction,"[5]

---

[4]Στεῖρα is omitted in $\mathfrak{P}^{13\text{vid}}$ A D K 33 181. The UBS committee argued that the reading of $\mathfrak{P}^{46}$ is the most likely, inasmuch as στεῖρα could easily have dropped out throught transcriptional oversight. See Bruce Metzger, *Textual Commentary on the Greek New Testament* (Stuttgart: United Bible Societies, 1971): 673.

[5]Walter Bauer, *A Greek-English Lexicon of the New Testament and Other Early Christian Literature* (trans. W. F. Arndt and F. W. Gingrich: Chicago: Univ. of Chicago Press, 1957): 409.

corresponding to the feminine role, ὑποδοχή (reception).⁶ This usage is commonly attested in Classical and Hellenistic sources.⁷ Thus, according to Bauer, "If this meaning is correct for Hebrews 11:11, there is some error in the text, since this expression could not be used of Sarah, but only of Abraham."⁸

Attempts to resolve this problem began in the ancient church. Copyists in the early church attempted to solve the problem with the addition of the secondary phrase εἰς τὸ τεκνῶσαι (to bear children; D* P 81 etc.) or ἔτεκεν (give birth; ℵ² D² etc). Since that time, interpreters have offered a variety of explanations. The traditional view (that Sarah is the subject of the sentence) can be traced back to the church fathers. This view rests on the argument that the author of Hebrews employed καταβολὴ σπέρματος in an idiosyncratic way. According to the predominant tradition of the ancient church, καταβολὴ σπέρματος is understood as an abbreviation of εἰς σύλληψιν βεβλημένου σπέρματος; i.e., Sarah "received the power to conceive the seed that had been sown." This view is represented in the modern period by Spicq.⁹ An alternative argument for holding that Sarah is the subject of the sentence appeals to ancient views of physiology and to views that women also "emit seed."¹⁰ A third explanation for Sarah as the subject is represented by Hegermann, who also argues that καταβολή is used in an

---

⁶H.-F. Weiss, *Der Brief an die Hebräer* (KEKNT; Göttingen: Vandenhoeck und Ruprecht, 1991): 587.

⁷See Philo, *De Op. Mund.*, 132; *De Eb.*, 211; *De Cher.*, 49; see Epictetus, *Diss.* 1.13.3.

⁸Bauer, *A Greek-English Lexicon of the New Testament*, 410.

⁹Ceslaus Spicq, *L'Épître aux Hébreux* (Paris: Libraire Lecoffre, 1952): 349.

¹⁰See b. Niddah 31a; Lactantius, *De op. Dei* 12. See also H. J. Cadbury, "The Ancient Physiological Notions Underlying Jn. 1:13 and Heb. 11:11," *Expositor* 9 (1924): 430-39; and Pieter van der Horst, "Sarah's Seminal Emission: Hebrews 11:11 in the Light of Ancient Embryology," *Greeks, Romans, Christians* (ed. D. Balch, E. Ferguson, W. Meeks; Philadelphia: Fortress, 1990): 287-302.

unusual way, but that it is used in the same way as it is used elsewhere in Hebrews, to mean "foundation"; σπέρμα is used, not in the literal sense of the seed that is sown, but in the figurative sense of posterity used elsewhere in Hebrews. Thus, according to Hegermann,[11] "Sarah received the power for the foundation of posterity."

A growing number of interpreters have argued that Abraham is the subject of the sentence, pointing out that, in addition to the masculine language of v. 11, Abraham is clearly the subject of the sentence in vv. 8-12. This solution then leaves one to explain the phrase "Sarah herself" in v. 11. Among others, Windisch[12] suggests that the phrase is a gloss introduced by a copyist. A second view, which has been widely held in the past generation, is that "Sarah herself" should be read as a dative (αὐτῇ Σάρρα). Then the translation would be, "Abraham, with Sarah, received the power to conceive."[13] This usage, according to Bauer,[14] is attested in classical sources. According to Braun,[15] it suggests that Sarah is included, along with Abraham, as a witness to faith.

---

[11]H. Hegermann, *Der Brief an die Hebräer* (THKNT; Berlin: Evangelische Verlaganstalt, 1988): 232.

[12]Hans Windisch, *Der Hebräerbrief* (HNT 14; Tübingen: J. C. B. Mohr, 1931).

[13]This view appears in the margin of the Westcott-Hort text. According to Bauer, *A Greek-English Lexicon*, 410, it conforms to classical usage. Cf. Friedrich Blass and A. Debrunner, *A Greek Grammar of the New Testament and Other Early Christian Literature* (trans. & rev. R. Funk; Chicago: Univ. of Chicago Press, 1961): 194, where the phrase is included as an associative dative. Among modern commentators, this view is held by Otto Michel, *Der Brief an die Hebräer* (KEKNT;12th ed.; Göttingen: Vandenhoeck und Ruprecht, 1966) 396; H. Attridge, *Hebrews* (Hermeneia; Philadelphia: Fortress, 1989): 325; H. Braun, *An die Hebräer* (HNT 14; Tübingen: J. C. B. Mohr, 1984): 359.

[14]Bauer, *A Greek-English Lexicon*, 410.

[15]Braun, *An die Hebräer*, 359.

A third view, first suggested by Black[16] and now followed by a significant number of interpreters, is the suggestion that καὶ αὐτὴ Σάρρα στεῖρα is a Hebraic circumstantial clause to be translated, "By faith, even though Sarah was sterile, he (Abraham) received strength for procreation." The phrase καὶ αὐτὴ Σάρρα is understood as a concessive clause, subordinate to the principal clause in which Abraham is the subject of the main verb.[17] Black[18] argues that this Hebraism is common in the LXX and even in other passages in Hebrews (1:5; 3:10). This interpretation is the basis for the rendering in the NIV and NRSV.

These alternative explanations of Heb 11:11, all based on lexical and grammatical considerations, leave the matter of Sarah's role in Hebrews inconclusive. Other considerations have, however, not been pursued, and may illuminate the issue. In this article, I shall address two issues which have not been sufficiently explored in attempts to understand Sarah's role. One issue is the place of Sarah in Jewish literature; i.e., did the author of Hebrews know a wider tendency to reclaim Sarah and count her among the faithful? The second issue is the larger context of Heb 11; i.e., does the author appeal to traditions in an idiosyncratic way or use bold metaphors in retelling OT stories that would provide the context for interpreting his comments about Sarah?

1. Sarah Within the Context of Jewish Literature

The process of reclaiming Sarah can be observed in the NT. According to 1 Pet 3:6 Sarah is the paradigmatic submissive wife who calls her husband "lord" (see Gen 18:12). Jewish interpretations of Genesis often attribute virtues to Sarah that are never explicitly mentioned in the

---

[16]Matthew Black, "Critical and Exegetical Notes on Three New Testament Texts: Hebrews 11:11, Jude 5, James 1:27," *Apophoreta— Festschrift für Ernst Haenchen* (ed. W. Eltester and F. H. Kettler (BZNW 30; Berlin: Töpelmann, 1964): 39-45.

[17]William Lane, *Hebrews 9-13* (WBC; Dallas: Word, 1991): 344.

[18]See Matthew Black, *An Aramaic Approach to the Gospels and Acts* (3rd ed.; Oxford: Clarendon Press, 1967): 86-88.

narrative of Genesis. In the Targumim, for example, the embarrassment with Sarah's laughter is evident. According to the Targum Pseudo-Jonathan, "(Abraham and Sarah) were advanced in age, and Sarah had ceased having the periods of impurity of women. Sarah wondered in her heart, saying, 'After I have grown old shall I become pregnant.... And my master is old? . . . Later Sarah denied her incredulous response and said, "I did not wonder."[19] Sarah's laughter has turned to wonder in this account which minimizes the embarrassment over her incredulity.

A similar treatment is given to Sarah in Targum Neofiti on Genesis, where Sarah plays a much larger role than in Genesis. Here Sarah specifically mentions her own faith.

> And Sarah said to Abraham: My judgment and my humiliation, my insult and the beginning of my affliction, are delivered into your hand. I forsook my country, the house of my birth, and the house of my father and I have come with you in faith. I went in with you before the kings of the earth, before Pharaoh, king of Egypt, and before Abimelech king of Gerar and said: 'He is my brother' so that he might not kill you. And then I saw that I did not bear and gave to you Hagar the Egyptian, my handmaid.[20]

The most remarkable transformation of Sarah appears in Philo, who devotes considerable attention to Abraham and Sarah and treats the two of them as paradigms for his own time. For example, Philo suggests that the laughter of Abraham and Sarah is not the response of unbelief. According to *De Mut. Nom.* 166, Philo says, "Not only did he himself laugh, but his wife also." Nevertheless Abraham responded, in words not found in Genesis, "Yet he that has promised is 'my lord,' and 'older' than all creation, and I

---

[19]Mihal Maher, *Targum Pseudo-Jonathan: Genesis* (Collegeville, MN: Liturgical Press, 1992): 67.

[20]Martin McNamara, *Targum Neofiti 1: Genesis* (Edinburgh: T. & T. Clark, 1992): 98.

must needs believe him." Thus, according to Philo, the doubt suggested by the laughter was shortlived.

Philo also suggests that Sarah had faith. In his *De Abrahamo* 112, Philo recalls the issue of Sarah's laughter, saying,

> So the Scripture says that the wife first laughed and afterwards, when they said, "Is anything impossible with God" was ashamed and denied the laughter, for she knew that all things were possible with God, a truth she had learned a long time ago in the cradle.[21]

Sarah's confession that "all things are possible with God" signifies growth in knowledge of God.[22]

Philo treats the laughter in several instances, and in each case gives it a positive interpretation. In *Questions on Genesis* 3.55, Philo says, "Rightly did he laugh in his joy over the promise, being filled with great hope and expectation that it would be fulfilled, and because he had already received a vision, through which he knew more certainly him who stands firm. . . . Thus Philo interprets Gen 17-18 in light of Gen 15:6. Sarah's laughter is also given a positive interpretation, for her laughter is the response of joy. In *Leg. All.* 3.218, Philo says, "Sarah, who is virtue, laughs also. . . . Moreover, the offspring is laughter and joy." In many references to Sarah, she is interpreted as the virtue (see *De Cher.* 3, 7; *Leg. All.* 2.82; 3.243-44) that gives birth to laughter. Philo says (*Quod Det. Pot.* 123), "According to Sarah's unerring witness God is the maker of laughter."

In Philo's allegorical treatment of Sarah, he concedes that it was physically impossible for a woman of Sarah's age to give birth to a child. Sarah, however, is a metaphorical figure who represents humanity's capacity to rise above the world of passions and vices and then to give birth to virtue

---

[21]Cited in Moxnes, *Theology in Conflict*, 149.
[22]*Ibid.*

(*De Mut. Nom.* 143). In his allegorical interpretation, Philo consistently interprets Sarah as Virtue, synonymous with Sophia, which brings the heavenly learning to Abraham (*Leg. All.* 2.82; *De Cher.* 9; *De Cong.* 22f.). Therefore Philo says of Abraham and Sarah that it is the female, Virtue, who sows the seeds of correct instruction to the wise man, Abraham.[23]

The evidence of Philo and the Targumim indicate that later narrators exhibited greater interest in Sarah than one finds in the Genesis narrative. One discovers here a developing tradition whereby Sarah was reclaimed among the faithful.

2. Sarah Within the Context of Heb 11

In Heb 11 the treatment of Sarah must be placed within the larger context of the epistle. Heb 11 and 12 are the rhetorical climax to an epistle which has focused its readers' attention on the negative consequences of ἀπιστία (unbelief; 3:12, 19; cf. 4:2), epitomized earlier in the negative example of Israel's (see ὑπόδειγμα [example] in 4:11) failure to endure. The positive example of those whose faith was demonstrated in their endurance (cf. Abraham in 6:15-17) has suggested the importance of πίστις (faith) as the alternative conduct. The theological sections of Hebrews have laid the basis for the author's appeal for the community's faith. This πίστις (faith) is equated with endurance in 10:36-39. After laying before his readers two alternative modes of conduct in 10:39, the author begins the climactic and rhetorically-charged section with the definition of faith in 11:1, which is the basis for the description of the OT witnesses who are introduced in 11:2. The list of witnesses in chapter 11 is intended to remind the readers that their alternatives are clear: they may either "shrink back" or continue to exhibit the faith which their cloud of witnesses has already demonstrated (11:39).

---

[23]See S. G. Sowers, *The Hermeneutics of Philo and Hebrews* (Zürich: EVZ, 1965): 135.

An observation of both the macro- and microstructure of Heb 11 may be helpful in interpreting the smaller units, including Heb 11:11. Beginning in 11:4 πίστει (faith) is used 18 times to describe 14 witnesses, most of whom are not specifically associated with faith in the OT. At the beginning (11:4-7) and end (11:30-31) of this section, brief statements are made describing single instances of faith by OT witnesses. In the central section multiple deeds are recorded of Abraham and his co-heirs (11:8-22) and of Moses (11:23-29).[24] The pace of the recitation quickens in 11:32-38 when a new rhetorical pattern is used to introduce both named and unnamed people who acted "through faith" (11:33). Throughout the chapter the author's commentary emerges at regular intervals as he summarizes the meaning of faith (11:6, 13-16, 38-39).

A noteworthy feature of the macrostructure is that Abraham and Moses play the central role. Whereas one deed is listed for the other witnesses, three (or four) deeds are recorded for Abraham and four deeds are recorded for Moses. Thus a symmetry exists between Abraham and Moses in the center of the narrative.

The microstructure reveals a common pattern which is significant for the interpretation of the smaller units, including 11:11. The pattern can be seen in both simple and complex forms. In its simplest form, the pattern consists of the anaphoric πίστει (faith), followed by the description of a deed by one of the OT witnesses. This simple form may be seen in 11:20, 21, 30, 31. In its more complex form the pattern adds to the simple form one or more dependent clauses describing either a) the motivation of the witness or b) the consequence of the witness' faith. The more complex form may be seen, for example, in the account of Abel, which begins with πίστει followed by the main verb (προσήνεγκεν). The consequence of his sacrifice is

---

[24]Cf. Michael R. Cosby, *The Rhetorical Composition and Function of Hebrews 11* (Macon, GA: Mercer, 1988): 42-43. Cf. also C. Roxe, *Die Wolke der Zeugen* (WUNT 60; Tübingen: J. C. B. Mohr, 1994): 229.

indicated by the two clauses introduced by διά, which state the consequences of his faithful deed (11:4).

The same complex pattern is also found in the account of Noah. After the main clause indicating Noah's deed in 11:7, the consequence of his act is indicated with the phrase introduced by δι' ἧς. A similar pattern is seen in 11:16, where the positive consequences of faith are introduced by διό and γάρ.

In other instances, the opening clause is linked with dependent clauses which indicate the factors motivating the witness. The author refers to what the witness saw or thought. One may note, for example, that 11:10, 14, 16, 26, 27 refer to what the witnesses "saw" or "reckoned."

The description may follow the wording of the LXX closely or depart substantially from the LXX language. In several instances the paraphrase incorporates metaphorical language that superimposes the author's metaphysical and eschatological understanding on the event recorded in the LXX. For example, Abel "still speaks" (11:5); Noah built an ark after being told of "things not yet seen" (11:7); Isaac blessed Jacob because of his faith "in things to come" (11:20).

3. Sarah in Heb 11:11

The reference to Sarah is a part of the Abraham cycle which extends from Heb 11:8 to 11:22. The Abraham cycle resumes the earlier memory of Abraham in 6:13-15. Although Abraham's faith is mentioned only in Gen 15:6, the anaphoric πίστει (faith) introduces Abraham's departure from his homeland (11:8; cf. Gen 12:1-5) and his sojourning (11:9; cf. Gen. 23:4; 26:3; 35:12, 27). Vv. 8-9 describe the deeds of Abraham in language that only faintly echoes the LXX. With v. 10, the author completes the more complex pattern identified above with the γάρ clause indicating Abraham's perspective—he looked, not for an earthly city, but for a heavenly one. This pattern conforms to similar ones in 11:26, 27.

The introduction of Sarah in v. 11 continues the Abraham cycle with the familiar pattern of πίστει (faith) followed by the main clause. With the problematic phrase, καταβολὴ σπέρματος, the author departs substantially from the LXX wording while referring to Gen 21:2 (καὶ συλλαβοῦσα ἔτεκεν εἰς τὸ γῆρας εἰς τὸν καιρόν), thus creating the exegetical difficulty. However, in one significant respect, the author departs from the familiar pattern in v. 11. The phrase καὶ Σάρρα, introducing Sarah, is used only here in recalling the list of witnesses. The phrase has an intensifying effect ("even Sarah"),[25] calling attention to the extraordinary birth of Isaac from one who was barren (στεῖρα). Although the intensifying phrase could suggest a reference to Sarah's incredulity ("even Sarah, who had laughed"), the term στεῖρα suggests that the phrase should be understood as a reference to Sarah's barrenness and old age ("even Sarah who was barren").

The question still remains: Is Sarah, according to Heb 11:11, the one who "received power to deposit seed?" Despite the difficult lexical problems involved, several factors suggest that Sarah is the subject of the sentence. The reclamation of Sarah's faith in Jewish midrash indicates a general tendency to overcome the problem of her laughter, and thus to include her among the faithful. The knowledge of traditions associated with Philo by the author of Hebrews is well known, and thus it is likely that he could call on such a tradition in his recollection of Sarah. Moreover, the author's language elsewhere in Heb 11 suggests that he is capable of bold metaphors. His references to OT events have moved between the historical account and a metahistorical recitation of events. Abel "still speaks" (11:5); Noah was warned about "things to come" (11:7);

---

[25] W. Radl, "αὐτός," *TDNT* 1.189; Bauer, *A Greek-English Lexicon*, 122; E. Schwyzer, *Griechische Grammatik* (Munich: Beck, 1950): 2.211.

Moses chose to suffer "the afflictions of the Christ" (11:26). In the same way, Sarah metaphorically "received the power to deposit seed."

This difficult reading occasioned the attempts to overcome its problems, either by additions to the text or by the grammatical explanations which have been offered in the modern period. Matthew Black's suggestion that the phrase καὶ Σάρρα is a Hebraism to be read as a parenthetic expression overcomes the immediate lexical problem, but it does not adequately demonstrate that this excellent Greek stylist would resort to this infelicitous expression. Similarly, although the datival reading can be supported by a few classical parallels, it remains an unusual expression. Furthermore, the fact that the church fathers, despite the lexical difficulties involved, never gave the datival reading, suggests that it was not recognized as the most likely interpretation. Thus Kuss[26] is correct when he says that the datival reading is only a solution created from embarrassment over the wording of the text. The author of Hebrews, who consistently employs a metahistorical paraphrase of the LXX, includes Sarah as the subject of 11:11 and thus lists her among the faithful. Καταβολὴ σπέρματος is used metaphorically of Sarah's role in the "foundation" of a people. Καταβολή is used here, as in 4:3 and 9:26, to mean "foundation." Σπέρματος has the metaphorical sense that it has in 2:17: The people of God are the offspring, or σπέρμα, of Sarah.

The additional phrase, παρὰ καιρὸν ἡλικίας, points to Sarah's advanced age. Although the tradition recalled the advanced age of Abraham as well as that of Sarah (cf. Rom 4:19),[27] the reference to Sarah's age here is to be understood as a paraphrase of Genesis 18:11, according to which "it had

---

[26]O. Kuss, *Der Brief an die Hebräer* (RNT; Regensburg: Friedreich Pustet, 1966): 172.

[27]In the Genesis narrative, Abraham had additional children by Keturah after the death of Sarah (Gen 25:1-2). According to Philo, *De Abrahamo* 111, both Abraham and Sarah were past their prime.

ceased to be with Sarah after the manner of women." One may also compare the language of Gen 21:2, mentioned above. Thus, according to Hebrews, Sarah, along with Abraham and their immediate descendants, exemplified the faith that perseveres despite the absence of the things that can be seen.

The nature of Sarah's faith is suggested by the phrase, ἐπεὶ πιστὸν ἡγήσατο τὸν ἐπαγγειλάμενον. The clause, with its reference to Sarah's point of view (ἡγήσατο) is reminiscent of the common pattern in Hebrews, according to which the perspective of the believer is recalled.[28] Faith, according to the author of Hebrews, is rooted in the conviction that God is πίστος (faithful; see 10:23) in keeping his promise (see 6:13-15). Whereas the Genesis narrative does not mention Sarah's faith, for the author of Hebrews she joins Abraham who also trusted the God who makes promises.

Sarah's role forms only a small interlude within the Abraham cycle, for Abraham is obviously the subject of Heb 11:12. The author apparently knows the Jewish haggadic tradition reflected also in Rom 4:19, according to which Abraham was "as good as dead." Spicq[29] correctly notes that the presence of the story of Sarah within the Abraham cycle of Heb 11:8-12 is not an insuperable difficulty in the interpretation of this passage. One may note, for example, the analogous passage in 1 Tim 3:10, where the instructions for women are inserted within the larger context of instructions for deacons.[30] One may also note that in Heb 11:23 the cycle of stories of Moses includes not only the incidents of Moses' faithfulness, but that of his parents as well. Thus the fact that the author includes accounts involving those who are closely identified with his heroes as examples of faith suggests that Sarah is also included among the ancient believers.

---

[28]Cf. 11:9, λογισάμενος; 11:26, ἀπέβλεπεν.
[29]Against Weiss, *Der Brief an die Hebräer*, 587.
[30]Spicq, *L'Épître aux Hébreux*, 349.

Chapter Sixteen

TERTULLIAN—AGAINST WOMEN?

Earl Lavender

Tertullian has been often identified as the first of the great Christian misogynists.[1] He is often blamed in studies attempting to identify the beginnings of sexism in the church. Heine,[2] in her work *Women and Early Christianity* observes, "Tertullian constantly provokes the most vehement and spontaneous defensive reaction in feminist circles."

His negative treatment in feminist circles is understandable—one needs only to read his most often quoted work directed to women in general:

> Are you not aware that you are each as Eve? The sentence of God on this sex of yours lives on in our own time; the guilt must then, of necessity, live on also. You are the devil's gateway. You first plucked

---

[1]Paul Monceaux, *Histoire littérarire de l'Afrique chrétienne I: Tertullien et les origines* (Brussels: Culture et civilisation, 1963 repr. of 1901 ed.): 387. See George Tavard, *Women in the Christian Tradition* (Notre Dame: Univ. of Notre Dame Press, 1973): 59, who states, "Tertullian is no ordinary misogynist." It seems, however, that however unusual his hatred of women might be, Tertullian is indeed a misogynist. See also Nancy van Vuuren, *The Subversion of Women as Practiced by Churches, Witch-hunters, and Other Sexists* (Philadelphia: Westminster, 1973): 29; and Rosemary Ruether, "Misogynism and Virginal Feminism in the Fathers of the Church," *Religion and Sexism: Images of Woman in the Jewish and Christian Tradition* (ed. Rosemary Ruether; New York: Simon and Schuster, 1974): 157, and others.

[2]Susanne Heine, *Women and Early Christianity* (trans. John Bowden; London: SCM, 1987): 3-4.

the forbidden fruit and first deserted the divine law. You are she who persuaded him whom the devil was not brave enough to attack. It was you who so readily destroyed the image of God, man.[3]

Language such as "sentence of God on this sex of yours" and "you are the devil's gateway" is hardly acceptable in modern times. It is hard to imagine a more stinging accusation! F. Forester Church comments, "Even allowing for more considerable hyperbole, Tertullian's indictment strikes one as exceptionally vicious."[4] Many insist Tertullian's bias against women is clearly seen in his placing the blame of man's fall on woman—whom he identified as the weaker creature.

Many hold this passage as a key to understanding Tertullian's view of women. Paul Monceaux, in his classic work on North African Christianity, summarizes Tertullian's view of women as the devil's readily available tool with which he could destroy man. Tertullian, according to Monceaux, advocated that the only hope for woman was for her to renounce the graces of her sex. Further, if man was to please God, he had to "separate himself as much as possible from woman."[5]

Fiorenza, reflecting on Tertullian's "devil's gateway" passage identifies Tertullian as one who prohibited women from priestly activities because of "a theology that evidences a deep misogynist contempt and fear of women."[6] Fiorenza calls for freeing the Scriptures and historical tradition from

---

[3] Tertullian, *On the Apparel of Women* 1.1.1-2.
[4] F. Forrester Church, "Sex and Salvation in Tertullian," *HTR* 68 (1975): 85.
[5] Monceaux, *Histoire littérarire de l'Afrique chrétienne I*, 388.
[6] Elisabeth Schüssler Fiorenza, *In Memory of Her* (New York: Crossroads, 1983): 55, is not alone in over-generalizing her negative statements concerning Tertullian's attitude toward women. See other examples in Ruth Tucker, *Women in the Maze* (Downers Grove, IL: InterVarsity Press, 1992): 148; and Vern Bullough, *The Subordinate Sex* (Chicago: Univ. of Illinois Press, 1973): 114.

its androcentric perspective. In particular, she is convinced that Tertullian played a significant role in the gradual patriarchalization of the early church, and that Christian history must be liberated from individuals like Tertullian if it is to have any relevant value. Tertullian, for Fiorenza, is just one of many women-haters who used his power and influence to repress them.[7]

Another writer cites the "devil's gateway" passage and remarks, "Though Tertullian was married, he was deeply sorrowful that this was the case. In attempting to dissuade his wife from remarriage if he should predecease her, he felt her only possible motives for wanting to be married was her natural lust or her desire to rule another man's household and to spend her husband's hard earned money."[8] This example is significant because the writer uses Tertullian's negative "devil's gateway" phrase as the key to interpreting the content of a separate treatise.[9]

The objective student of history is driven to ask what might be the intended purpose of using historical references in such studies. Is it merely to find evidence to support one's predetermined conclusions? If so, is the historical record accurately represented? Far too often, historical documents are used rather than studied. This seems to be particularly true in the study of the history of women and their role in the church. Tertullian serves as an interesting example of one often trampled by such subjective approaches to early writers.

---

[7]Fiorenza, *In Memory of Her*, 55, judges all surviving canonical texts and the writings of patristic orthodoxy to be anti-women. She concludes, "They do not give us historically adequate and theologically appropriate information" (56). Rather than evaluating the texts for their value, she calls for hermeneutics of suspicion and a re-inserting of the feminine perspective.

[8]Vern Bullough, *The Subordinate Sex: A History of Attitudes toward Women* (Boston: Beacon, 1974): 114.

[9]Tertullian, *On the Apparel of Women* 1.1. (ANF 4.14).

Heine[10] warns those approaching history from the feminist perspective:

> One of the greatest problems of feminism and feminist theology seems to me to lie in the fact that women form a negative theory out of their hurt and their negative experience and claim universal validity for it. It is then the 'nature' of the male to be destructive, the 'nature' of the Christian tradition to damage people, to eliminate women from history, to demonize the feminine. This absolutizing of the negative experience, even though—it must be acknowledged—it is largely dominant, creates prejudice and weakens ethical claims.

It is interesting that even in denouncing the claim of a universal validity of the negative experience for women, Heine is convinced this negativity *is* largely dominant. By whose standards is one's existence deemed to be negative? Using modern social norms to judge past sociological conditions cannot but skew our view of history. On the question of Tertullian and misogyny, Elizabeth Carnelley, briefly but correctly remarks,

> It is anachronistic to expect Tertullian to be a feminist, and when he is not, to call him a misogynist. In fact he did not hate, or fear, women. Rather Tertullian's writings must be understood in the context of the prejudices and concerns of his time.[11]

The observation that Tertullian's writings are often used for self-serving purposes is not solely directed toward those who attempt to find someone in history to blame for what they perceive to be the repression of women in the church. Tertullian is also misused by those who insist that "women

---

[10]Susanne Heine, *Frauen der früen Christenheit* (Göttingen: Vandenehoek and Ruprecht, 1986): 3, 4.

[11]Elizabeth Carnelley, "Tertullian and Feminism," *Theology* 92 (1989): 31.

are to remain silent" in the church. For them, Tertullian is a key to the proper understanding of women's role in the church, likely because they agree with his conclusions. They advocate that he represents an unbroken continuance of apostolic teachings and customs. William Weinrich, for example, contends there is a broad central tradition and practice in both the Eastern and Western church which allows men alone to be pastors and sacramental ministers. Weinrich states, "Tertullian may be taken as a representative of this central tradition: 'It is not permitted to a woman to speak in church'."[12] Weinrich, however, avoids any discussion of the problematic discussions presented by Tertullian concerning women. In fact, all who view Tertullian's teaching on women as consistent with Scripture either ignore or deny his call to ascetic extremism, which is inextricably intertwined with his view of women. On both issues, Tertullian appeals to Scripture and tradition. If Tertullian represents the authentic teaching of the early church on women, then why is his rigid asceticism rejected as extreme?

How does one approach the question of Tertullian's view of women and react with an objective conclusion? Tertullian's thought on this matter can only be found by allowing Tertullian to be Tertullian. The modern reader must leave personal sensitivities behind, and enter into Tertullian's world doing one's best to experience his passions and concerns.

On the subject of women, it is significant to note that Tertullian refers to them only as examples or illustrations of deeper concerns. Isolating his comments on women without identifying the major object of his passion often produces misrepresentations of his works.

The purpose of this study is to identify the underlying concerns which drove Tertullian to write and to consider

---

[12]William Weinrich, "Women in the History of the Church," *Recovering Biblical Manhood & Womanhood* (J. Piper and W. Grudem, eds; Wheaton, IL: Crossway Books, 1991): 273.

how these concerns influenced his understanding of women. Was he in any sense opposed to them? Were women, for him, the weaker sex—spiritually and physically inferior to man? Did Tertullian treat women differently in matters of spiritual discipline than men? If, indeed, he was a misogynist, one would expect an affirmative answer to each of these questions.

1. *Tertullian's Method*

How did Tertullian interact with Scripture when confronted by issue or question? Identifying his hermeneutical method is not a simple task. There are nearly as many ideas on how Tertullian used the biblical text as articles written concerning him.[13] While there are numerous thoughts concerning his use of the text, most scholars agree that Tertullian was a defender of the content and accurate interpretation of the Scriptures.[14] He was profoundly familiar with the Bible. Quotations and references to the Scriptures saturate his works. For Tertullian, the Christian faith and practice was to be based solely on the teachings of the Scriptures, which he believed to be the inspired work of the Spirit of God.[15]

In his work *On the Prescription Against Heretics* Tertullian stated that the determination of the canon and its proper interpretation belonged to the church alone.[16] The tract was written to confront heretics with the fact that the Scriptures were not theirs to use.[17] But it also gives the modern reader a view of how Tertullian believed Scripture

---

[13]See the excellent summary of studies through 1981 on Tertullian's use of the text in Robert D. Sider, "Approaches to Tertullian: A Study of Recent Scholarship," *SecCent* 2 (1982): 241-247.

[14]See John F. Jansen, "Tertullian and the New Testament," *SecCent* 2 (1982): 191-96.

[15]Tertullian, *On Prayer* 22. (ANF 3, 687.); *Apology* 20; *et al.* (ANF 3, 33).

[16]Tertullian, *On the Prescription Against Heretics* 37.3 ff.

[17]*Ibid.*, 16-20.

was to be used within the church. For him, the proper reading of Scripture led one to affirm the *rule of faith*, which was the teaching of the church handed from God to Christ, from Christ to the apostles, and finally to the churches through an unbroken line of leaders and apostolic descent.[18]

A thorough treatment of *the rule of faith* is not possible here, but suffice to say that it was Tertullian's absolute hermeneutical criterion.[19] Tertullian's writings reflect that the content of the *rule of faith* was more than just the Scriptures themselves, it was the deposit of the accurate interpretation of Scriptures.[20] Tertullian was convinced the *rule of faith* was in his possession. When he demanded the heretics Marcion and Valentinus identify and defend their relationship to the apostles, he then boldly affirmed: "I am the heir of the apostles. Just as they carefully prepared their will and testament, and committed it to a trust, and adjured (the trustees to be faithful to their charge), even so do I hold it."[21]

Thus, the majority of Tertullian's writing is in defense of what he understood to be the orthodox Christian faith. Because he was a polemicist rather than an exegete, his treatment of Scripture was not consistent in terms of rules of exegesis.[22] The basis of his argumentation was his

---

[18]*Ibid.*, 37.

[19]Otto Juss, "Zur Hermeneutick Tertullians," *Neutestamentliche Aufsätze: Festschrift für Joseph Schmid zum 70. Geburtstag* (ed. J. Blinzler, O. Kuss, F. Mussner; Regensburg: Pustet, 1963): 138-60. See also L. W. Countryman, "Tertullian and the Regula Fidei," *SecCent* 2 (1982): 209-227.

[20]Tertullian, *Pres. Against Heretics* 38. It is important to note that Tertullian did not believe this deposit of interpretation was in addition to the Scriptures, it merely provided for its accurate interpretation. Tertullian, *Against Hermog.* 22.5, was convinced that the Scriptures were the complete revelation of God.

[21]*Ibid.*, 37. (ANF 3.261).

[22]J. H. Waszinck, "Tertullian's Principles and Methods of Exegesis," *Early Christian Literature and the Classical Tradition* (ed. R. M. Grant; Paris: Beauchesne, 1979): 9-31, properly points out that an

conviction that he was a guardian of both orthodoxy and orthopraxis. He freely used Scripture as he deemed fit to defend and explain the content of his *rule of faith*. Claude Rambauz makes the interesting observation that Tertullian's understanding of Scripture was guided by his passions, not by an intellectual evaluation of the text.[23] Therefore, one should not expect from Tertullian fresh insights into the biblical text. What one finds instead is innovative and sometimes offensively sharp ways of using Scripture to defend that which he believed to be the truth (rule of faith), as it was handed to him. This aspect of writing also explains apparent contradictions in his use of Scripture. He did not study Scripture in order to form his belief; he searched Scripture for support of what he believed was accurately handed to him. Whatever the current debate needed in terms of scriptural support, Tertullian found.

His defense of "the rule" was not without method. The clearest statement of his argumentation is found in a work dealing directly with an issue concerning women in the church, *On the Veiling of Virgins*. Tertullian wrote:

> The defense of our opinion is as follows, according to Scripture, nature, and discipline. Scripture establishes the law, nature testifies to it, and discipline demands it . . . Therefore, let it be a rule for you, that you will find God's will in Scripture, nature, and discipline . . . .[24]

This statement provides a concise summary of Tertullian's system of thought. He believed Scripture provided the

---

exegetical approach to the text did not fully develop until the fourth century. During the early centuries the Bible was mostly used for proving one's arguments.

[23] See Claude Rambauz, "La composition et l'exégèse dans les deux lettres 'ad uxorem,' le 'de exhortatione castitaits, 'et la 'de monogamia, 'ou la construction de la pensée dans les traités de Tertullien sur le remariage," *REAug* 22 (1976): 1-28, 201-17; 23 (1977): 18-62.

[24] Tertullian, *On the Veiling of Virgins* 16:1-2.

content of the law, that nature was a witness to its truth, and that the believer was not to question it, but to practice it with discipline. If Scripture left any doubt, nature made clear. If any doubt was left by nature, one was to turn to the stricter discipline in order to leave no question about being within the will of God. To do that which was doubtful was to turn from humility and modesty to "men-pleasing," which offended God.[25]

Tertullian's attitude toward women was formed out of his understanding of the content of the Scriptures, its confirmation in nature, and the necessity of its truth being practiced with great discipline. Using these as categories of thought, we will evaluate Tertullian's view of women.

2. *Women and the Rule of Faith in Scriptures*

As mentioned at the beginning of this study, Tertullian is often presented as one who attacked women or insisted on their being relegated to a secondary position to men (hence, misogynistic). Such is not a fair representation of his thought. While it is true that Tertullian wrote against behaviors in which women participated which he considered sinful, his primary concern was Christian behavior—not "women" as a particularly weak and sinful group.

Tertullian wrote under the assumption that all believers accepted what he considered to be the biblical norm concerning women—they were to be in subjection to their husbands and the male leadership of the church. To expect Tertullian to question the traditional teaching of the role of women in terms of historical and cultural relativity is to expect too much of Tertullian.[26] He was wary of any ideas

---

[25]*Ibid.*

[26]Tertullian, *On the Veiling of Virgins* 17, in fact, insisted the content of Scripture was binding even if cultural norms change. Note his summary of the question of the veil, that some of his era deemed a cultural practice: "It is incumbent, then at all times and in every place to walk mindful of the law." See his refutation of customs as a standard in chapter 8 as well.

that hinted of innovation or change. Tertullian did not question the cultural relativity of Scripture. In fact, Tertullian did not question Scripture at all. As Tavard[27] comments:

> We face no more than Tertullian's conviction that the Scripture is the *lex veritatis,* the law of Truth, and that accordingly it teaches the principles of human behavior as revealed and will by God.

Furthermore, Tertullian did not question tradition (unless he considered it to be a departure from "the rule of faith"). In fact, he warned against those who would change church practices:

> But each individual man is not to think that the institution of his predecessor is to be overturned. Many yield up their own judgment, and its consistency, to the custom of others.[28]

Tavard[29] summarizes Tertullian's treatment of the role of women: "in such questions he still claimed to remain what he always wanted to be, namely a faithful interpreter of the Scriptures and of the universal tradition.

Understanding Tertullian as one who desired to defend at all costs the teaching of the church, let us consider the passages of Scripture which most influenced Tertullian concerning women.

A. *Genesis 2, 1 Corinthians 14, and Woman's Purpose*

For Tertullian, the "universal church tradition" concerning women began with the account of creation in Gen 2. He, with Paul (1 Cor 11:9), was convinced that

---

[27]Tavard, *Women in the Christian Tradition,* 58. See also Tertullian, *Against Hermogenese* 22.5, where he states, "I worship the fullness of the Scripture."

[28]Tertullian, *On Prayer* 22.

[29]Tavard, *Women in the Christian Tradition,* 57.

woman was created out of man "according to the Creator's purpose."[30] Tertullian believed woman's purpose in creation was to serve man, as man's purpose was to serve God.[31] For Tertullian this did not make woman less important than man in God's eternal scheme. He believed the end was the same for all faithful Christians. In the concluding paragraph of the famous "devil's gateway" passage, Tertullian reminded his readers that faithful women would receive the same angelic image and advancement to judging as faithful men.[32] Women, therefore, were to accept their God-given roles while in this temporary world by following his will for their lives.[33]

As mentioned above, Tertullian taught throughout his works that God purposed woman to be in subjection to man because he created her out of man. Note Tertullian's comments on 1 Cor 11 concerning virgins and married women:

> If "the man is the head of the woman," of course he is of the virgin too. . . . To her, then to whom it is equally unbecoming to be shaven or shorn, it is equally becoming to be covered. If "the woman is the glory of man," how much more the virgin, who is a glory withal to herself! If "the woman is of the man," and "For the sake of the man," the rib of Adam was first a virgin. If the "woman ought to have power upon the head," all the more justly ought the virgin . . . .[34]

---

[30]Tertullian, *Against Marcion* 8. (ANF 3, 445).
[31]*Ibid.*
[32]Tertullian, *Apparel* 1.2.
[33]His understanding of the spiritual equality of women is also seen in his argumentation against the Valentinian gnostics. Tertullian, *Against Valentinianos* 32. 5, wrote of this post death existence, "After I die I must be returned to that place where no one marries, where I must be clothed rather than stripped, where, even if I am stripped of my sex, I am classed among the angels, not as a male or female one. No one then will make a thing of me, in which they discover masculinity."
[34]Tertullian, *On the Veiling of Virgins* 7.

Here Tertullian was not offering instruction on the subjection of woman to man. Rather, he assumed such subjection was universally accepted as truth and used it to build the case that all women, whether married or virgins, were to be veiled.

Later in the same work Tertullian referred to Paul's phrase (1 Cor 14:34, 35) insisting on women's silence in the church. Tertullian wrote:

> It is not permitted to a woman to speak in the church; but neither (is it permitted her) to teach, nor to baptize, not to offer, not to claim herself a lot in any manly function, not to say in any sacerdotal office.[35]

While this appears to be a strong admonition to limited women's participation in church functions, the next sentence shows this was not the case. Tertullian writes, "Let us inquire whether any of these be lawful to a virgin." His argument was not directed towards women's restrictions in the context of the church—this was assumed to be unquestionably accepted as universal practice. It was rather an argument that women and virgins should be regarded as equal in the matter of wearing veils.

In his attack of Marcion's selective canon (rejection of Hebrew Scriptures), Tertullian used Paul's directive concerning women's silence in the church for another purpose:

> When enjoining on women's silence in the church, that they speak not for the mere sake of learning (although they even have the right of prophesying, he has already shown when he covers the woman that prophesies with a veil), he goes to the law for his sanction that woman should be under obedience.[36]

---

[35]*Ibid.*, 9.
[36]Tertullian, *Against Marcion* 5.8.

Tertullian pointed out in Paul's restriction of women, Paul appealed to the Hebrew Scriptures, namely the Genesis account of Eve being created out of Adam. He wanted Marcion to concede that Paul, whom Marcion accepted, used the Hebrew Scriptures to prove his point. Once again we observe that Tertullian presumed that women's silence in the church was a truth upon which arguments could be built.[37]

Another passage from Tertullian that is often mentioned in the context of Tertullian limiting the role of women in the church is from *On Prescription Against Heretics*, "The very women of these heretics, how wanton they are! For they are bold enough to teach, to dispute, to enact exorcisms, to undertake cures—it may be even to baptize."[38] Reading the passage in context reveals Tertullian's comments were directed toward the frivolous attitude of leaders among the heretics. The sentence following the quotation above speaks of careless ordinations that were in a constant state of change. Tertullian continued by complaining that heretics placed novices in office and allowed laymen to perform priestly functions. Tertullian's mention of the "wanton women" was offered as absolute proof to "the faithful" that the heretics had no understanding of the Scriptural teaching concerning leadership. This was not an attack on women.

B. *Genesis 6, 1 Corinthians 11:10 and Rebellious Angels*

The next passage that profoundly affected Tertullian's attitude toward women is the reference to the daughters of men marrying angels (sons of God) in Genesis 6. Tertullian was convinced this was the reason behind Paul's instruction that women had to be veiled ("because of the angels" 1 Cor

---

[37]Note in the above citation that Tertullian with Paul allowed for women to prophesy, howbeit with their heads covered. We would wish for him to have expounded on this, but he did not. He does mention in *On the Soul* 9, a young woman who experienced visions and spoke to Christ and the angels during worship. However, Tertullian went out of his way to explain that she spoke of such experiences only after the sacred services was concluded.

[38]Tertullian, *On Prescription Against Heretics* 41.

11:19). Their beauty was such that even angels left their proper abode in order to rebel against God and marry them.[39]

The incident of the angels in both Genesis 6 and 1 Corinthians 11 greatly perplexed Tertullian. In fact, his search for an answer led him to a firm conviction based on a puzzling source. His definition of the canon of the Hebrew Scriptures was apparently affected by his desire to clarify the question of angels and their relationship to women. He embraced the explanation given in the apocryphal book of 1 Enoch. He liked it so much, in fact, that he insisted the book of Enoch be accepted as Scripture.[40] In 1 Enoch 6 and 7, the writer explains that the "sons of God" of Gen 6 were rebellious angels, who were enamored by the beauty of women. 1 Enoch continues by teaching that the angels decided to come to this world and marry the women. They then taught humankind forbidden sciences such as weaponry, the production and use of cosmetics and the refinement of precious metals. This expansion of the Gen 6 passage and its corollary relationship to 1 Cor 11 is foundational in Tertullian's harshest treatment of women, *On the Apparel of Women* (book 1, the "devil's gateway" source).

Tertullian must have been deeply disturbed by the secularization of the church, especially as indicated by women's dress and make-up. Tertullian lived during a time of significant transition within the church.[41] For the first time on a large scale, people were being converted to

---

[39]Tertullian, *Against Marcion* 5.8; idem, *On the Apparel of Women* 1.2,3.

[40]Tertullian cites 1 Enoch in *On Idolatry*; and *Resurrection of the Dead.* He defended its canonicity in *On the Apparel of Women* 1.3, suggesting it was rejected by the Jews because it foretold of the coming of Christ. He inverted 2 Timothy 3:16 by stating "every Scripture suitable for edification is divinely inspired." Therefore, because the teaching in Enoch is true, it should be accepted as Scripture.

[41]See D. E. Groh, "Upper Class Christians in Tertullian's Africa: Some Observations," *Studia Patristica* 14 (1976): 41-47.

Christianity from all social levels. Tertullian claimed there were many prominent citizens who were believers.[42] Thus, it was not unusual for individuals of wealth to be in the assembly of the church. The presence of the wealthy women evidently impacted many women in the church. Tertullian's response to such an influence was swift and pointed. He insisted that women were to forsake this world if they were to hope for the next. He conceded that some women must dress in accordance to their "riches, birth, or past dignities," but warned them to "take heed to temper an evil of this kind; lest, under the pretext of necessity, you give the rein without stint to the indulgence of license."[43]

According to Tertullian this indulgence was not only an indication of rampant materialism on the part of the women but it gave Satan an opportunity to use lust, a tool which he had used effectively since Eden, to destroy man. One would guess that Tertullian, along with the rebellious angels, struggled with the attractive appearance of women. Tertullian pointedly asked what motivated a married woman to adorn herself in an attractive way in the public arena since her husband had already chosen her as his wife.[44] If she was trying to make herself beautiful for others, then she was guilty of participating in the sin of concupiscence.[45] Furthermore, Tertullian asked, dare she be so presumptuous as to improve on the natural work of God?

This is the context of "the devil's gateway" passage. The sharpness of Tertullian's comments were not directed toward the female but toward those who were making themselves available to Satan for his work. All the trappings of this world were directly from Satan, and the women of the church were using them just like worldly women, protested Tertullian. After calling women the "devil's

---

[42]Tertullian, *Apol.* 1.7; *Nat.* 1.1.2. For other references in Tertullian of Christians in prominent positions, see J. H. Waszink, ed., *De Anima* (Amsterdam: J. M. Meulenhoff, 1947): 381-2.

[43]Tertullian, *Apparel* 2.9. (ANF, 22-23).

[44]*Ibid.*, 2.4.

[45]*Ibid.*, 1.

gateway," Tertullian identified what he regarded as the many sins in which the women of his time were participating—wearing dyed wool, embroidery, pearls, onyx and gold, and looking in the mirror with a great vanity. He then concluded, "Accordingly all these things are all the baggage of women in her condemned dead state, instituted as if to swell the pomp of her funeral."[46] Tertullian did not believe that all women carried such baggage. In fact, his point was that true believers could not participate in such materialism. His intent was to sternly rebuke those who were so involved in the things of this world. He questioned how they could call themselves Christians.

Tertullian also denounced men who wished to please "by means of voluptuous attraction," making it clear that this was not a sexist attack.[47] He acknowledged that men had the same wicked desire to please women according to the flesh by trimming their beards, attempting to appear younger by dying their hair, and shaving, all this while constantly consulting the mirror. All of this destroyed modesty, and "where God is, there modesty is; there is sobriety, her assistant and ally."[48]

If one removes all the harsh language of the first chapter of *On the Apparel of Women,* (book 1), it could easily be Tertullian's restatement of Paul's teaching concerning women in 1 Tim 2:8-15. The basic teachings are the same. The passionate and acerbic nature of the writing came from Tertullian's contempt for anyone (men or women) who would make themselves available for Satan's schemes instead of God's work.

3. *The Witness of Nature*

The first pillar of Tertullian's view of women came from what he perceived to be the scriptural view—she was to be in submission to man. One would expect for Tertullian

---

[46]*Ibid.*
[47]*Ibid.*, 2.8.
[48]*Ibid.*

to build strongly on the second pillar of his method, the concurrence of nature (picking up on Paul's lead in 1 Tim 2:15, for example). While Tertullian does appeal to nature on this topic on a limited basis, his lack of argumentation on this point—the physical differences of the woman's body, for example—supports the observation that "woman's role" was not an issue of Tertullian's day. Because woman's role was not being questioned, Tertullian did not attempt to build extensive argumentation in support of his belief on the matter. Nonetheless, Tertullian did appeal to the natural order of things in regards to woman.

In his *Apology,* Tertullian reminded the Romans of a time when their women lived in natural modesty and observed faithfulness in marriage.[49] He then joined them in a lament of the conditions of their present, with no distinction between the dress of the matron and the prostitute. He continued by decrying women's passion for jewels and riches and their desire to divorce "as though it were the natural consequence of marriage."[50] According to Tertullian, the pagans had rejected the natural role for women, and had thereby brought their society to ruin.

In his treatise *On Prayer* Tertullian advocated that women's long hair was nature's way of confirming that wearing a veil was woman's duty.[51] He appealed to 1 Corinthians 11:14 for support. Apparently, there were some who had suggested that while women were to be veiled, virgins need not be. Tertullian argued that law, nature, and discipline demanded all women be veiled, regardless of their marital status. It is interesting to note that the purpose of being veiled was not promoted by Tertullian as a sign of submission. His concern, once again, was that woman without a veil was too much for men and angels, possibly leading them into sin because of her beauty.[52]

---

[49]Tertullian, *Apology* 6.
[50]*Ibid.*
[51]Tertullian, *On Prayer* 22.
[52]*Ibid.*

There is another way Tertullian related nature to his understanding of women. He was certain that which was natural was of God, that which was not was of Satan.[53] If God were able to create purple or blue wool but did not, it must have been because he did not want such to exist, Tertullian reasoned.[54] Of cosmetics, Tertullian wrote:

> For they who rub their skin with medicaments, stain their cheeks with rouge, make their eyes prominent with antimony, sin against HIM. To them, I suppose, the plastic skill of God is displeasing! in their own persons, I suppose, they convict, they censure, the Artificer of all things. For censure they do when they amend, when they add to His work, taking these additions, of course, from the adversary artificer. That adversary artificer is the devil.[55]

Tertullian believed nature expressed the will of God for women. Her natural place was in the home, modestly dressed (without make-up!). Tertullian wrote against the dangers of societal gatherings of women: "You (women), however, have no cause of appearing in public, except such is serious."[56] He identified "serious" work as meeting the needs of the sick or sharing the word of God. Tertullian was convinced that the women who lived according to the will of God, as expressed and reinforced by nature, would stand as a powerful testimony of God's wisdom to the pagans. This was especially so if one seriously pursued the discipline of the Christian life.

3. *Christian Discipline*

It was the pursuit of Christian holiness that ignited Tertullian's passion. Gerald Bray understands this as the focus of Tertullian's thought; "The underlying concern, and

---

[53]Tertullian, *On Apparel* 2.5.
[54]*Ibid.*, 1.7.
[55]*Ibid.*, 2.5.
[56]*Ibid.*, 2.11.

the one which gives unity to the whole, is the preoccupation with sanctification."[57] Bray also comments, "the student who would understand Tertullian must understand above all that his life was the pursuit of holiness in the presence of the living God."[58]

Tertullian defined "holiness" as a life of strict discipline manifested particularly by modesty and chastity. The closer one got to living a heavenly life on earth, the greater the assurance of salvation. As Church[59] summarizes Tertullian's understanding of sanctification:

> In practice this means a gradual self perfection in emulation of angelic likeness. Flesh immortal neither marries nor has sex, nor wears jewels; flesh redeemed, stamped with the baptismal seal, must adhere to the same high standards, or squander, with its sanctity, its claim to eternal life.

Tertullian's promotion of chastity has been characterized as a repudiation of women.[60] But his condemnation was not of women, but of behavior which he believed did not reflect the character of Christ and his spiritual kingdom. In fact, Tertullian believed sexual differences would end at the resurrection. He expounded on this thought in his treatise against Valentinian gnostics:

> After I die I must return to that place where no one marries, where I must be clothed rather than stripped, where, even if I am stripped of my sex, I am classed among the angles, not as a male or female one. No one then will make a thing of me, in which they will discover masculinity.[61]

---

[57]Gerald Bray, *Holiness and the Will of God* (Atlanta: John Knox, 1979): 63.

[58]*Ibid.*, 31.

[59]Church, *HTR* (1975): 99.

[60]Katherine M. Rogers, *The Troublesome Helpmate: a History of Misogyny in Literature* (Seattle: Univ. of Washington, 1966): 14.

[61]Tertullian, *Against Valentinianos* 32.

It is significant that for Tertullian women in the life hereafter would not become men, as some early writers believed. The angelic "nature to be assumed" was sexless. There would be no sexual relations in heaven. Sexual intercourse was not spiritual behavior, even in marriage. Tertullian's concern in the matter of sexuality had nothing to do with a disdain of women. His advice on sexual matters was given to men and women alike. He insisted that chastity was the better way, for it was a reflection of the Christian's eternal state of being.

Tertullian's insistence on holy living according to his rigid standard of spiritual discipline was intensified by his belief that the return of Jesus Christ was imminent. He pleaded with believers that because Christ's return was near, it was foolish to give one's life in pursuit of anything having to do with the flesh. This included both marriage and family. Both could be encumbrances to one's spiritual life in the last days. This was the main reason for Tertullian's stern teaching against remarriage. One marriage was enough, not because women were tainted, but because Christ was returning. Tertullian wrote a plea to his wife to not remarry after his death, for those left widowed "have laid hold for themselves of an eternal gift of the Lord; and while on earth, by abstaining from remarriage, are already counted as belonging to the angelic family."[62]

So, Tertullian was not opposed to marriage. Rather, he was obsessed with eschatological concerns. To assume Tertullian did not wish to be married[63] totally ignores the wonderful tribute he paid his wife:

> What kind of yoke is that of two believers, sharing one hope, one desire, one discipline, one and the

---

[62]Tertullian, *To His Wife* 1.4.

[63]As was mentioned at the beginning of this work, Bullough, *The Subordinate Sex*, 114, suggests Tertullian was "deeply sorrowful" that he was married. Others such as Michael Spanneut, *Tertullien et les premiers moralistes africains* (Gembloux: Duculot, 1969): 45, have come to similar conclusions.

same service? Both are brethren, both fellow-servants; there is no difference of spirit or flesh. They truly are two in one flesh, and where the flesh is one, the spirit is one also. Together they pray, together prostrate themselves, together perform their fasts; mutually teaching, mutually exhorting, mutually sustaining. Equally are both in the Church of God; equally at the banquet of God; equally in straits, in persecutions, in refreshments. Neither keeps secrets from the other; neither is troublesome to the other. . . . Between the two echo psalms and hymns; and they mutually challenge each other as to which shall better chant to their Lord. When Christ sees and hears such things, he rejoices. To these he sends his own peace. Where two are, he is also there. Where he is, the evil one is not.[64]

Marriage in Christ was a wonderful blessing. The only time Tertullian reflected negatively on marriage was when he was comparing it to what he perceived to be the higher calling of celibacy. And celibacy was the higher calling because it represented the nature of life eternal, which was about to begin, according to Tertullian.

The higher call of celibacy introduces an interesting aspect to Tertullian's attitude toward women. His call for them to live celibate lives was a liberating call. Leaving a husband freed the woman from the pressures and work of family life. She was not bound to obey a husband or serve children, which were both consequences of the Fall. A celibate woman could be a vehicle for God's Holy Spirit in a special way. It is interesting to note that all individuals Tertullian commends for ecstatic utterances from God were women. While it is true that Tertullian did not allow for women to assume priestly functions (for this was clearly taught in Scripture, he reasoned), he called men and women with equal passion to pattern the eternal in the present through a life of chastity.

---

[64]Tertullian, *To His Wife* 2.8.7-9. ET in Church, *HTR* (1975): 99.

Before concluding Tertullian's concerns on the disciplined life, it needs to be noted that there is more to Tertullian's negative attitude toward sexuality than just eschatological concerns. Along with many of the Church Fathers, he held sexuality in deep suspicion.[65] In his description of the birth of Jesus, Tertullian spoke of Jesus' mother as having not been involved in any form of impurity, for she had never entered into marriage.[66] He was not able to free sexuality from its association to sin. Of the virgin, he wrote, "the virgin's is the principal sanctity, because it is free from affinity with fornication."[67] This distrust of sexuality was not a rejection of women, but it certainly influenced his attitude toward them, especially as they related to men. The result was a number of passages written by Tertullian that, when taken out of context, can be misunderstood as misogynistic.

4. *Other influences concerning Christian discipline*

Before this study can be concluded, two other topics which are directly involved in Tertullian's attitude toward women must be briefly considered—martyrdom and Montanism. Martyrdom was the Christian's highest calling, according to Tertullian. It was the baptism that assured one of eternal life. This topic provides much insight into Tertullian's disdain for the trappings of this life that might lead one to refuse such a noble end to this temporal existence. Possession of the things of this world could only make one desire to remain here, or worse, deny oneself the privilege to be tortured or martyred for the Lord:

> For such delicacies as tend by their softness and effeminacy to unman the manliness of faith are to be discarded. Otherwise, I know not whether the wrist that has been wont to be surrounded with the palm leaf-like bracelet will endure till it grow into the

---

[65] This is the major premise of Carnelley's, *Theology* (1989), article concerning Tertullian's attitude toward women, especially p. 33.

[66] Tertullian, *Apology* 21.

[67] Tertullian, *On Exhortation to Chastity* 9.

numb hardness of its own chain! I know not
whether the leg that has rejoiced in the anklet will
suffer itself to be squeezed into the gyve! I fear the
neck, beset with pearl and emerald nooses, will give
not room to the broadsword! Wherefore, blessed
sisters, let us meditate on hardships, and we shall not
feel them; let us abandon luxuries, and we shall not
regret them. Let us stand ready to endure every
violence, having nothing which we may fear to leave
behind. . . . Let us cast away earthly ornaments if
we desire heavenly.[68]

Tertullian boldly called for women to be strong in the moment of suffering. As Church comments, "To Tertullian, 'weakness' and 'strength' are the respective attributes not of women and men, but of flesh and spirit."[69] Church then cites Tertullian's thoughts offered to a mix of men and women awaiting execution:

Perhaps the flesh will dread the heavy sword, and
the elevated cross, and the beast's mad rage, and the
capital punishment of flames, and all the
executioner's talent for torture. But let the spirit
respond to itself and to the flesh, that these things,
while very painful, have, even so, been received
with equanimity and with acute desire for the sake of
fame and glory, not only by men, but also by
women, that you, O blessed ones, too may be
worthy of your sex.[70]

Tertullian's esteem for women is clearly seen in the fact that half of his illustrations of courage in *To the Martyrs* are women. This same pattern of sexual equality in examples of faith is also present in *To the Nations* and *Apology*. So, in the discussion of martyrdom, the Christian experience that Tertullian held most closely to his heart, that which would

---

[68]Tertullian, *Apparel* 2.13.
[69]Church, *HTR* (1975): 97.
[70]Tertullian, *To the Martyrs* 4. ET in Church, *HTR* (1975): 97.

assure one of eternal life with God, Tertullian treated men and women as equals.

The influence of Montanism on Tertullian has been endlessly debated. Many have insisted that Tertullian was converted to Montanism in the last years of his life, while others deny an actual conversion. The debate is crucial in this discussion because the Montanists heralded two women leaders, Prisca and Maximilla. If Tertullian insisted women were to be silent in the church, how could he embrace a movement led by women?

The full complexity of the question cannot be addressed in this study; however, I will be presumptuous enough to offer my thoughts on the matter. First, it is not necessary to assume Tertullian fully embraced Montanism. It is quite possible that it appealed to him because of its rigid ascetic code of discipline, and to that end he promoted it. In comparison to a church that from Tertullian's perspective was growing alarmingly complacent in its attitude towards materialism, Montanism was the more authentic form of Christianity.

For whatever reason, Tertullian was deeply influenced by Montanism. Carnelley is correct in observing that Tertullian's suspicion of sexuality was exacerbated by its influence.[71] He could embrace Prisca and Maximilla and encourage others to heed their words, not because he had changed his view on women speaking in the church, but because they were great examples of Christian chastity. Tertullian's deepest concerns were not ecclesiological, but eschatological.

Conclusion

How then, do we accurately represent Tertullian's view of women? First, we acknowledge that many of the questions forced on Tertullian on the issue of women by modern students were not addressed by him. His mention

---

[71]Carnelley, *Theology* (1989): 33.

of women in connection with the church was always under the assumption that women were not to lead in formal worship and were to be submissive to men. To interpret this as misogynistic is to disregard the many positive comments Tertullian made about women and their ministry. Concluding he did not like women and did not treat them fairly is not consistent with his belief in the equality of the soul of men and women after this life. In fact, in some ways, Tertullian liberated women from their presumed role in the home. Through chastity, women could be freed from the restrictions of the home, and live eternal life in the present.

Tertullian's comments directed towards women which are the most damaging and most quoted in feminist literature must be understood in their context. Tertullian was obsessed with the evils of materialism and its effect on the life of the Christian, especially in light of Christ's imminent return. Women must not allow themselves to be tools of Satan for man's destruction by using the forbidden arts of the angels to make themselves beautiful and desired. This very sin caused the fall of both men and angels.

Further, according to Tertullian, Christian men and women must not be driven by earthly sexual behaviors. Rather, all must be aspiring for the eternal in the present. As Carnelley[72] concludes:

> Tertullian's theology is fundamentally scriptural. The exaltation of celibacy, the expectation of the Second Coming, the practice of fasting, and insistence on standing firm under persecution, can all be traced back to the Scriptures. The ambivalence of the Scriptures, and the context of the Montanist influence, heightening eschatological awareness, make Tertullian's ambiguity towards women explicable. He was not a misogynist . . . it was a preoccupation with the next life, which seemed immediate and imminent, which shaped his theology.

---

[72]*Ibid.*, 34.

Eschatological values were breaking into, and transforming the present.

Let us briefly revisit the questions at the beginning of this study. Was Tertullian opposed to women in any sense? It does not seem that he was at all negatively inclined toward them as a sex. Did he consider them to be spiritually and physically inferior to man? It does not seem so, if one considers all of his writings. Did Tertullian treat women differently than men in matters of spiritual discipline? Here the answer is clearly "no." Was he, then, against women? The answer must be negative. Tertullian held women in highest regard. How would he respond to the issues concerning women that are being raised today? The best we can do with such questions is to speculate. Tertullian was, as we are, a product of his time. We are enjoined to leave him there and evaluate him accordingly. Understanding him within his historical context provides one with a different perspective than evaluating him in light of modern issues.

Perhaps the best conclusion of this study will be to allow Tertullian to speak once again. He addressed women with one concern, and that concern was their eternal salvation in Christ:

> Handmaids of the living God, my fellow-servants and sisters, by the right which I, the least consequential of persons, enjoy with you, but the right of fellow-servantship and brotherhood, I make bold address to you a discourse, not out of affectation, for the cause of your salvation. That salvation, not only of women, but also of men, consists primarily in the exhibition of modesty.[73]

---

[73] Tertullian, *Apparel* 2.1.

Chapter Seventeen

WOMEN MINISTERS IN CONSTANTINIAN CHRISTIANITY

Fredrick W. Norris

Did women ever serve in the most important leadership roles of early Christianity? We shall examine four separate clusters of information that deal with women in different Christian groups in the fourth and fifth centuries. Together they suggest that women at times held the highest positions of leadership, even in Constantinian Christianity. However, that claim is a contested one. Gryson[1] concludes:

> From the beginnings of Christianity, women assumed an important role and enjoyed a place of choice in the Christian community. Paul praised several women who assisted him in his apostolic works. Women also possessed the charism of prophecy. There is no evidence, however, that they exercised leadership roles in the community. Even though several women followed Jesus from the onset of his ministry in Galilee and figured among the privileged witnesses of his resurrection, no women appeared among the Twelve or even among the other apostles. As Epiphanius of Salamis pointed out, the successors of the Apostles were all men, and in the Catholic Church there have never been women presbyters. The only duty with which women have been invested is the diaconate, but two centuries had to pass before the female diaconate took a distinct shape.

---

[1]Roger Gryson, *The Ministry of Women in the Early Church* (trans. J. Laporte and M. L. Hall; Collegeville, MN: Liturgical Press, 1976): 109.

Gryson, a Roman Catholic scholar, emphasizes the diaconate because by the third century a set of offices had appeared in church leadership, the so-called threefold ministry of deacons, presbyters and bishops, listed in ascending order of importance. Such a division of ministry exists in some places near the beginning of the second century as Ignatius of Antioch's letters indicate. He distinguished deacons, presbyters and bishops as different people.[2] Gryson's point is that women never reached the higher levels of leadership; they never served as presbyters. He assumes that if they did not hold office as presbyters, they certainly did not lead as bishops.

Gryson's argument depends upon defining leadership roles as clergy within the church. Ministry is ordained ministry, at its highest levels celibate men set aside for tasks in the church's mission. The most important work is the sacramental life of worship. Women have not been priests. They have neither officiated at the Eucharist, nor regularly performed baptisms. Deaconess was the only ordained ministry women were ever given.[3]

1. *History: Doubly Partial*

To show that some women did fill other leadership roles, we have to play detective or historian. Most of the evidence we have supports Gryson. Although evidence about Christianity from the fourth and fifth is relatively full in comparison, say, with the third century, we have less information than we wish. We cannot know all we would like to know because so much has been lost.

---

[2]His *Magnesians* 6 and *Trallians* 3 distinguish bishop, presbyters and deacons. Frances Young, "On ἐπίσκοπος and πρεσβύτερος," *JTS* 45 (1994): 142-148, notices that the NT primarily speaks of bishops and deacons. Presbyters as a group of elderly advisors seems to be a later feature. But that group is functioning in Asia Minor by the time of Ignatius.

[3]Gryson, *Ministry of Women in the Early Church*, 110.

Every history ever written is partial in two senses. In this first sense it does not cover all the data because some material no longer exists. For ancient history all we have are various kinds of texts, inscriptions, images or words on coins, art, architecture, artifacts; yet the bulk of that kind of evidence is gone. Furthermore, some areas of society never get their due. For example in the history of every culture the life of the poor is always underrepresented, probably misrepresented, because they do not leave behind lasting evidence. Usually they do not write or read, so there are no records. Their houses, tools, and clothing were often made of perishable materials like mud, wood, or animal hides. Although in most cultures they form a considerable part of the population, little is left to tell their stories.

Second, history is also partial because it is focused by the writer on particular themes and not others. It always reflects the interests of the one doing the research, the one creating the context and the narrative. A modern historian does not treat everything that is available because that would make the picture so blurred it would disappear. There is no way to avoid this by attempting to be fully objective or totally fair. We can check evidence and show that some aspects of a history are incorrect, but in doing that we do not step out of our skins, take up a position outside our communities and merely state the facts. We only become interested in checking the evidence because of certain values we hold dear, ones that are appreciated by communities to which we belong. Gryson sees himself as an objective historian who describes the texts so that questions about the cultural bias of early Christianity may be asked later. He does not think he is partial.[4] I write this article because I belong to a community of Christians which is struggling to understand who women may be and what they may do in the church. I am convinced that women should be and do all that God has given them gifts to be and do. The selection of some women in fourth- and fifth-century Christianity is

---

[4]*Ibid.,* xi & 113-114.

made because of my sense that this story of women in leadership has not been told enough.[5]

Information about women leaders in the early church is slight. That any such information exists at all is remarkable because the Mediterranean cultures of the period were patriarchal, influenced by local conditions but dominated by what we might term Hellenistic or Greco-Roman patterns. Men ruled.

This tendency was strengthened by Constantinian establishment of Christianity as the regnant religion, a set of decisions in the first third of the fourth century which urged the church to organize in some politically and culturally regularized way so that both orthodox faith and practice would become uniform. Christians had suffered persecution from Roman leaders even at the beginning of the fourth century. When Constantine declared a type of religious toleration and later showed his own preference for Christianity, many—perhaps most—Christians were relieved. Yet that favor had a price. Emperors supported councils quite often for the purpose of tightening their own grip on the people. They understood how important religious piety was, but they wanted it to serve the needs of the state. Conformity to the Christian religion meant that the empire would be united against its enemies.

Around the Mediterranean basin public monuments and political history of the period do not tell us a great deal about women of any religious persuasion because those who kept the records and wrote the histories showed little interest in females. For instance, if you read Suetonius' history of the Roman Caesars or his history of important men you discover little about their mothers, sisters, wives, daughters or concubines because he did not think they swayed the events. Women are mentioned as good breeding stock who brought

---

[5]Gertrude Himmelfarb, *On Looking into the Abyss: Untimely Thoughts on Culture and Society* (New York: Alfred A. Knopf, 1994): particularly "On Looking into the Abyss," 3-26, and "Postmodernist History," 131-161, clearly depicts this twofold partiality of all history.

wealth and family connections to their husbands, but there is only slight speculation about their influence.[6] Therefore, when you do find evidence about a particular woman, you may assume that she was remarkably influential or she would not have been mentioned at all.

2. Nuns and Abbesses, Widows and Deaconesses?

Among others two such women appear in fourth-century Roman Christianity in precisely such important slots. Both are rich widows who have inherited the fortunes of their husbands and are being hounded by relatives and friends to turn the money their way. We must recognize that under Roman law widows could command the wealth of their husbands or we would have no such stories. Yet we must also understand that the culture hemmed in even these rich and thus powerful women, not giving them the range of choices they might have wanted to pursue. Paula, an aristocratic woman of Rome, became involved in the circle of Jerome. Her Christian decision was to become celibate as part of her maturing faith. She went to the Holy Land and gave most of her wealth to the foundation of a monastery and a nunnery in Bethlehem. She was quite generous with her assets.[7]

Melania the younger, another wealthy widow, helped found a monastery and nunnery in Jerusalem, institutions run in cooperation with Rufinus.[8] She also found freedom

---

[6]Born in the late first century, Suetonius, *The Lives of the Caesars*, tells the tales from Julius Caesar to Domitian, and in his *The Lives of Illustrious Men* picks those whom he thinks are significant from about the same period. See Suetonius (LCL; 2 vols., ed. by J. C. Rolfe; Cambridge, MA: Harvard Univ. Press, 1913, rpr. 1970). The history of the church often reflects similar concerns for only men as leaders. It is no accident that Jerome's and Gennadius' history of important men in church history bears the title *The Lives of Illustrious Men* which uses Suetonius' pattern.
[7]Jerome, especially *Ep.* 108, tells the tale of Paula.
[8]Elizabeth Clark, ed. *The Life of Melania the Younger* (New York: E. Mellen, 1984).

to serve within the monastic arena. Paula and Melania the younger are two women selected from a number who are now appearing as historians interested in early Christianity turn to the task of finding out how many such elite celibate or widowed women there were.[9]

Gryson would allow that such women are leaders and would probably see them as deaconesses.[10] He shows that widows were appointed for certain tasks, but he does not see them as the order which Bonnie Bowman Thurston describes.[11] Indeed when fourth-century women became administrators of nunneries in these monastic complexes they founded with their wealth, they must be seen as leaders in a double sense. It is not clear that such leaders of monasteries always saw themselves as fitting within the limited roles of deaconesses, and thus as Gryson says, never actually functioned in "leadership roles."[12]

Both Paula and Melania the younger are also honored as saints of the church through their remembrance within lists of holy people and special feast days.[13] Any definition of church leadership which severely limits the ministry of its

---

[9]Elizabeth Clark, "Devil's Gateway and Bride of Christ: Women in the Early Christian World," (the Ransom–Butler Lectures at Wichita State Univ., 1982) in *Ascetic Piety and Women's Faith: Essays on Late Ancient Christianity* (Studies in Women and Religion, 20; Lewiston, NY: E. Mellen, 1986): 23-60.

[10]Gryson, *Ministry of Women in the Early Church*, 88-90, mentions Olympias, Nectaria, the daughters of Count Terentius, the mother of St. Euthymius, Axia, Casiana, Celerina, and other unnamed deaconesses. The same Olympias and Elisanthia, Lampadia, Theodula, Marthana, and Manaris were named deaconesses who ruled monasteries.

[11]Bonnie Bowman Thurston, *The Widows: A Women's Ministry in the Early Church* (Minneapolis: Fortress, 1989), finds the order developing even within NT times. Young, *JTS* (1994): 143, n. 3, cautions that the earliest evidence about widows is ambiguous and thus that Thurston overstates her case.

[12]Gryson, *Ministry of Women in the Early Church*, 109.

[13]Paula's feast day is 26 January. Melania the Younger appears in the Menologion of the Greek Church, one of its most important lists of saints.

saints deserves serious questioning, more probably outright rejection.

Yet we should notice that this avenue of monastic leadership could be outside the range of congregational or regional leadership designated by the titles of presbyter or bishop or under the guidance of either a male presbyter or bishop. It was probably an option chosen because it was a more open one, unlike the more regularly closed options that Gryson recognizes. Women of wealth, influence and spiritual gifts have often been forced to select alternative routes for their service to God and the church. The strongest single line of women's leadership in Western Christianity has been within such institutions. We in Christian Churches and Churches of Christ have sometimes been able to insist that the history of Christianity shows little place for women in authority because we have been convinced that monasticism has been a dreadful mistake. Our selection of what comprises Christian history, our partiality, has led to those conclusions. And some of our most gifted women have been engaged fully in ministry only on a mission field where no men were present or in a struggling church were no qualified men were available.

Although women frequently followed these routes to ministry, there is some evidence that recognition of their abilities did lead them into congregational leadership. In the internal Roman Catholic debate, it is important to recognize that Gryson views deaconesses as properly ordained ministers with specific functions.[14] He also insists that one important task of deaconesses involved baptism.[15] Adult baptisms, which were often performed with the candidate

---

[14]Gryson, *Ministry of Women in the Early Church*, 115-120, argues that the *Apostolic Constitutions* show deaconesses were ordained. On 88-92, he refers to documents and inscriptions that describe the office and name women who occupied it. He chooses, however, not to extend that evidence into the present as a reason the contemporary Roman Catholic Church should have ordained deaconesses.

[15]*Ibid.*, 109.

fully unclothed and included a bodily anointing with oil, demanded for modesty both private services and women church leaders performing at least the anointing rite. For the sake of modesty, men did not anoint women. As infant baptism became the usual practice, the need for women to anoint adult women decreased and deaconesses among western churches decreased.

Yet according to Bradshaw's[16] fourth rule for the study of early Christian worship, "legislation is better evidence for what it proposes to prohibit than for what it seeks to promote." Deaconesses probably continued to function liturgically in various regions throughout the Roman empire. In the west, the French councils held at Orange in 441, Epaone in 517, Orleans in 533 and Tours in 567 prohibit ordaining deaconesses. In the east, deaconesses were ordained and served at baptism as both the Theodotian and Justinian law codes reveal—and those laws were empire wide.[17]

3. *Presbyters?*

Do we have evidence that women were in positions of leadership within early Christianity that came to be viewed as higher and of more authority than those of nuns and abbesses, widows and deaconesses? There are two pieces

---

[16] Paul F. Bradshaw, *The Search for the Origins of Christian Worship* (Oxford: Oxford Univ. Press, 1992): 68.

[17] See H. Leclercq, "Diaconesse," *DACL* 4.1, 728-729, who notes these conciliar decisions but interprets them as a clear sign that the church severely limited the functions of deaconesses. But he also notices that some Asia Minor, North African, Egyptian, Syrian and Persian churches, usually referred to as heretical Montanists, Monophysites or Nestorians, continued to develop the ordained office of deaconesses with certain roles in teaching, baptizing and celebrating the Lord's Supper. A. Kalsbach, "Diakonisse," *RAC* 3.922-924, handles the eastern imperial law well and basically agrees with Leclercq about the western councils. Also see Gillian Cloke, *This Female Man of God: Women and Spiritual Power in the Patristic Age, AD 350-450* (London: Routledge, 1995), who deftly handles materials about virgins, widows, wives, mothers, nuns, and deaconnesses, but goes no further.

Women Ministers in Constantinian Christianity   365

of evidence that can be read as giving evidence that women were presbyters. Canon 11 from the council of Laodicea in Phrygia, held sometime between 343 and 381, says that πρεσβύτιδας ἤτοι προκαθημένας, as Gryson translates it "senior women" or "female presidents," are not to be appointed in the church.[18] Epiphanius of Salamis provides a clue for one interpretation in saying that πρεσβύτιδας (older widows) were never made "elderesses" [presbyteresses] or "priestesses."[19] If he is right, this canon refers only to "older widows."[20]

But even if πρεσβύτιδας means "older widows," the Laodicean canon then speaks of such women who "presided" and had been previously "appointed." Presiding at worship in the fourth century would have meant that these women were the liturgical leaders of particular congregations. At the table celebration of the Lord's Supper, at what they called the Eucharist, they most probably would have offered prayer for both the bread and the wine. The technical term for "preside," προκάθημαι, is used in early Christian literature to describe acts associated with priests and bishops, deeds done by senior leadership within the church.[21] Also by the fourth century the technical Greek term, καθίστημι (appoint) when used of ministers can have the force of "ordain," or place in the seat of authority.[22]

---

[18] Friedrich Lauchert, *Die Kanones der wichtigsten Altkirchlichen Concilien nebst den apostolischen Kanones* (Freiburg im Breisgau: J. C. B. Mohr, 1896): 73. The text reads: περὶ τοῦ μὴ δεῖν τὰς λεγομένας πρεσβύτιδας ἤτοι προκαθημένας ἐν ἐκκλησίᾳ καθίστασθαι. See Gryson, *Ministry of Women in the Early Church*, 53.

[19] Epiphanius *Panarion* 79.4.1; The translation is from Frank Williams, *The Panarion of Epiphanius* (Nag Hammadi and Manichaen Studies 36; Leiden: Brill, 1994): 623.

[20] Gryson, *Ministry of Women in the Early Church*, 54.

[21] G. W. H. Lampe, *A Patristic Greek Lexicon* (Oxford: Clarendon Press, 1961): 1151.

[22] *Ibid.*, 690, lists the meaning "appoint" of clergy, but the references cited concern bishops and presbyters in the sense of their taking office. Gryson, *Ministry of Women in the Early Church*, 53,

The only reason to set up such a law was that women in Phrygia had actually been appointed to preside at worship. It may be that the practice of Montanists in Phrygia, who appointed women presbyters and bishops, had become a part of catholic churches. In the history of early worship, according to Bradshaw's principles, a legislated prohibition is good evidence that what it prohibits must have happened. Surely some of the bishops attending that council would have known women presbyters. From within the Constantinian establishment, then, this Laodicean council was tightening up the requirements, removing women from positions of leadership which they had occupied.

More in line with this immediate and wider context is the translation of πρεσβῦτις as "presbyteress." An epitaph for a woman named Epiktas, buried on the Greek island of Thera and dated to the third or fourth century, designates her as a πρεσβύτιδος. This epitaph has been read at least since 1900 as meaning that she was a "presbyteress," a female presbyter. That interpretation is connected with reading Laodicea's Canon 11 as referring to an order of women presbyters.[23]

Gryson neither deals with the Thera inscription nor mentions the Phrygian Montanist context of the Laodicean canon. He reads that canon in line with other early texts.[24] I

55, 64, 90, notices a distinction between this word and χειροτονέω (to lay hands on) that is clear in much of the literature but not all.

[23] H. Achelis, "Spuren des Urchistentums auf den griech Insel," *ZNW* 1 (1900): 97. Henri Grégoire, *Recueil des inscriptiones grecque-chrétiennes d'Asie mineure* (Amsterdam: Adolf Hakkert, 1968): fasc. 1, #167, p. 58, reads it that way as does Lampe, *Patristic Greek Lexicon*, 1131. Karen Torjesen, *When Women Were Priests: Women's Leadership in the Early Church & the Scandal of their Subordination in the Rise of Christianity* (San Francisco: Harper, 1993): 10, notices the same interpretation in Denis Feissel's "Notes d'Épigraphie chrétiennes (II)," *Bulletin de Correspondence Hellenique* (1977): 210-212, figure 2.

[24] His understandng of the *Testamentum Domini Nostri Jesu Christi* 1.35.1 is that when it speaks of widows and uses the word πρεσβῦτις, it means "senior women" ... "the title given them, which is none other that the feminine form of 'presbyter,' reveals the high

read the evidence as saying that the Asia Minor church stopped ordaining women as presbyters.

4. *Bishops?*

If women were leaders within monastic institutions, if they were widows and deaconesses who offered services to the needy, if they were ordained presbyters who presided within the worship, did they ever carry the title of bishop? There is a remarkable mosaic on the wall of the Church of Saint Praxedis in Rome. It depicts the Virgin Mary in the center flanked on either side by St. Praxedis and St. Pudentiana, two daughters of Pudens. (The church itself is built on land that had belonged to these sisters.) All three women are pictured with circular halos. On the left in this mosaic is a veiled woman with a square halo whose shape meant that she was still alive when the mosaic was put in place. Her name is abbreviated as *Theodo,* probably a contraction of "Theodora." Its feminine ending has been scratched, perhaps to eliminate it. Over the head of this woman is the word ἐπίσκοπα, the feminine form for the word "bishop."

Some have suggested that the word ἐπίσκοπα was a ninth-century addition to the mosaic, one that does not reflect a fifth-century reality. If that be true, it would still indicate that someone in that century wanted to honor a woman who held such an office. In that interpretation the Theodora depicted is probably the mother of a pope. A ninth-century inscription speaks of Pope Paschus' mother as ἐπίσκοπα *Theodora* but we are not certain that this woman is the Theodora represented in the mosaic. Indeed the mosaic tiles that form the section of the mosaic in the word "bishop,"

---

esteem they enjoyed in the community." When he looks at *Short Rules* 110 from Basil of Caesarea, which deals with a nun confessing her sins, he reads the distinction between πρεσβυτέρα and πρεσβύτερος not as the difference between a "presbyteress" and a "presbyter," but as between a "senior woman" and a "senior man." Given the exact contexts of those passages, he is probably correct. See Gryson, *Ministry of Women in the Early Church,* 66 & 52.

ἐπίσκοπα, and the picture of Theodora appear to be among the oldest in the mosaic. They well may date from the fifth century. That date for those tiles and the judgment that they are not part of a later repair suggest that Theodora was recognized as a bishop during the fifth century while she was still alive.

There is no particular reason to expect this reality. We do not know if a fifth-century Theodora was herself one of the many native Italian bishops in Rome, but it is difficult to interpret this mosaic as saying that she was not a bishop. The tragedy is that we do not have any full record of her life and thus we have no secure description of who she was and how she was able to rise to such a position. There is information which mentions a Theodora from Alexandria who made her way to Rome and brought with her the relics of some Egyptian saints. Perhaps the Theodora of the mosaic was first the bishop of an Egyptian community. Perhaps she brought her community with her to Rome. An inscription within the crypt of this church, although not naming Theodora, presents that as a possibility. If it were the case, as it may be, the fifth-century Theodora herself would have been recognized as a bishop in both Egypt and Italy.[25]

5. *How Could They?*

If the patriarchal culture of early Christianity still gives us some information about women in leadership roles including at least one bishop, what kind of theological

---

[25]Joan Morris, *The Lady Was a Bishop: The Hidden History of Women with Clerical Ordination and the Jurisdiction of Bishops* (New York: Macmillan, 1973): 4-8. Dorothy Irvin, "The Ministry of Women in the Early Church: The Archaeological Evidence," *The Duke Divinity School Review* 45 (1980), 76-86, esp. 79-81 believes that the whole mosaic is restored in the ninth century and that the Theodora is Pope Pascha's mother. But she does not deal with the stylistic effect or the dates of the tiles. If she is correct, that means that a pope recognized his mother as a bishop, not only in an inscription, but also in a mosaic.

arguments could have been mounted to suggest such attainments within a culture that so favored men? That kind of information comes to us from a rather strange source, the Montanists, a group that must be viewed with care. They were usually seen by their Constantinian established opponents as heretical, surely with good cause about certain things. If Montanus considered himself to be the Holy Spirit incarnate, few would see that as orthodox, certainly not you or I. They also developed a type of charismatic activity that their detractors rejected as frenetic.

What concerns us here, however, is their defense of prophecy, particularly women prophets. Epiphanius of Salamis, the fourth-century heresy hunter who fought for what he saw as orthodoxy with all his might, is our source. His *Panarion*, the *Treasure Chest*, lists all the important heretical groups and positions known to him. He usually wins no affection because of the way he waged his battles against heretics. Invited by bishop John to preach at Jerusalem, he took the occasion to denounce John as a heretic while he was a guest in John's pulpit. He was often so overcome by his rage against what he saw as wrong that he would attack nearly anyone who was rumored to be unfaithful. At times he reminds one of a blind Doberman in good health, but angry.

Thus we must be careful when we read Epiphanius to watch out for his point of view as well as the strangeness of his opponents. In this section he seems to be reporting the Montanist position with some clarity, partly because he thinks that merely listing these things will indicate how awful they are. He notices that the Montanists defend the place of women in the church by insisting that Eve received grace because she first ate of the tree and brought wisdom into the world (Gen 3:6), that Miriam, Aaron's sister was a prophet (Exod 15:20), that Philip's four daughters prophesied (Acts 21:9) and that women could be presbyters and bishops because there was no distinction according to gender (Gal 3:28). The Montanists supported their position with other scriptural passages, but Epiphanius, without mentioning what they were, rejects them as irrelevant.[26]

Epiphanius was flabbergasted at these pieces of Scripture put together in that way, made to support women's leadership in the church. He replied that the husband is to rule over the wife (Gen 3:16), that Paul did not allow women to speak or have authority over men (1 Tim 2:12), that a man is not from a woman but a woman from man (1 Cor 11:8) and that Adam was not deceived, but Eve was first deceived and transgressed (1 Tim 2:14).

Epiphanius, the heresy hunter, knew what a women's place was in the church. She was to be quiet, without authority, ruled over by her husband because sin entered human life through Eve. In another section of the *Panarion,* where he deals with a different heresy, he clearly states his own views on women.

> Women are unstable, prone to error, and mean-spirited. As in our earlier chapter on Quintilla, Maximilla and Priscilla [Montanist prophetesses], so here the devil has seen fit to disgorge ridiculous teachings from the mouths of women....
>
> Never at any time has a women ever been a priest... But once more, where has this new story [women as priests] come from? The women's pride and female madness? What has nourished the wickedness that— through female, once more!—pours the feminine habit of speculation into our minds [and] by encouraging its characteristic luxury, tries to compel

---

[26]Epiphanius, *Panarion* 49.1-3. ET in Williams, *Epiphanius,* 22, who notes that Cyprian *Ep.* 75.10 speaks of a prophetess in the third century who celebrated the Eucharist, preached and baptized. For the Greek text and another translation of this section of Epiphanius, see Ronald Heine, *The Montanist Oracles and Testimonia* (North American Patristic Society Patristic Monograph Series, 14; Macon, GA: Mercer Univ. Press, 1989): 132-135, no. 94.

the wretched human race to overstep its proper bounds.[27]

The Montanists obviously did not share this jaundiced view of women. They thought that Eve had been forgiven. Her sin could not mark all women as without possibility of Christian leadership because Moses' sister prophesied and so did Philip's daughters. If Paul said there was no distinction between male and female, then women could be presbyters or bishops.

The Montanists also saw women as leaders because they had seen them prophesy. Tradition about their group speaks of second-century prophetesses, Maximilla and Priscilla, mentioned as leaders with Montanus. In the fourth century Montanists may have had an order of virgins who prophesied. According to them these women's gifts and experiences were real; Scripture provided precedents.

In some ways these kinds of biblical arguments take place even today with nearly the same passages involved. Many Pentecostal and Holiness Christians have believed neither that the gifts of the Spirit have ceased nor that women cannot serve in the highest functions of leadership. They take women in leadership quite seriously both on the basis of these scriptural passages which they find most pertinent and on the basis of experiences within their communities.

---

[27]Epiphanius *Panarion* 79.1.6 & 4.1-2. ET in Williams, *Epiphanius*, 621 & 624. Gryson, *Ministry of Women in the Early Church*, 78 & 113, has a softer translation of the first line, but it still means that women are "weak, fickle and only moderately intelligent." He does notice, however, that such comments are "unkind" and may be a basis for rethinking the contemporary ministry of women. John Chrysostom, who supported the deaconess Olympia and often interpreted biblical passages more favorably toward women, evidently found gifted women to be exceptional. In his *Homilies on 1 Corinthians* 37.1 and his *Homilies on Timothy* 9.1, he also referred to women generally as weak, unstable, and giddy. See Gryson, *Ministry of Women in the Early Church*, 83.

John Paul II, the present Roman Catholic Pope, struggles with Epiphanius' sense of things. He wants women to be honored and he does not look to Eve's sin as maiming all women's nature, but he does not think they can be presbyters or bishops because of the Timothy passages, as well as the long history of Roman Catholic insistence that priests represent Christ and thus must be celibate males.[28] Gryson has read the early history in a sense which supports John Paul, but Coyle,[29] also a Roman Catholic, has warned that patristic evidence shows a kind of male prejudice which affects even the pastoral positions it elaborates.

The third-century Roman church took over the more male-dominant aspects of its culture and forgot the OT women prophets and the daughters of Philip. More importantly, they found little reason to view Gal 3:28 as a primary scriptural reference for considering leadership. The Constantinian churches of the fourth through the sixth century, with their need for conformity and with the support of state establishment, hardened this interpretation.

The importance of the Montanist witness is not that these passages are employed by a group which held some heretical views, but that these biblical passages are part of what is clear to many groups who have a strong interest in the Holy Spirit. One of the weakest points in the restoration heritage is the assumption that those who speak about the Holy Spirit are always dangerous, unbiblical charismatics.

---

[28]John Paul II, *On the Dignity and Vocation of Women, Mulieris Dignitatem*, Apostolic Letter, August 15, 1988. On May 30, 1994, he offered another letter which defended male celibate priests as the only ministry of the Eucharist which Roman Catholics can accept. A speech given July 27, 1994, reiterated the same position.

[29]J. Kevin Coyle, "The Fathers on Women and Women's Ordination," *Église et Théologie* 9 (1978): 51-101, reprinted in Everett Ferguson, David M. Scholer, and Paul Corby Finney, ed., *Women in Early Christianity* (Studies in Early Christianity 15; New York: Garland, 1993): 117-167, warns that male prejudice did color ancient Roman Catholic pastoral work in ways that the papacy has not recognized.

Tertullian, however, became a Montanist primarily because he saw problems with the way that the early third-century church was living. He is a remarkable guide, not only to the activity of the Holy Spirit, but also to the need for the church to develop practices which embody its difference from its society.

When the church sees its very life in its relationships, in the virtues that mark it as different from other communities in society, then it looks for the fruit of the Spirit within its life together and within its ministry in but not of the world. When it searches for that, it turns again to that activity of the Spirit: not so much to the spectacular gifts like *glossolalia*, "speaking in tongues," or to a prophecy that foretells the future, but to proclaiming the gospel through the everyday activity of each member of the body. Then the power is in the practice, neither being a male, nor having an education or wealth, nor possessing certain smooth, "cultured" attitudes. Ancient comments from celibate male bishops about women being generally unstable, prone to error, weak-minded and mean-spirited demands that their viewpoints be seriously criticized as unchristian. Why should one follow their restrictions on women when one disagrees strongly with their views of women?

When the Spirit of God is the guarantor of Christian life, when virtues taught in community equip people for ministry, then women not only become possible leaders, they often become most qualified. In societies like ours, they have known pain and suffering, they have borne abuse, they have been the vulnerable who have reached out to others. We commonly view many of them as saints. And now in a more open society like that of North America, they are demonstrating that they can develop and "master" skills of leadership at any level available.

The Christian community testifies to the priesthood of all believers and practices the conversion and baptism of adults. That baptism is a kind of ordination to ministry. Such a tradition should always have women as leaders. Any who insist that women cannot fill leadership roles should take responsibility to look at Scripture and the history of the church. They should explain the meaning of the passages which the Montanists cited as evidence for their position that women could be presbyters and bishops, a position which so many good people of our own era find definitive. They should explain how deeply-rooted cultural views of women as lesser humans have influenced early Christian views of women.

We of Christian Churches and Churches of Christ often claim to be only biblical, but when we insist that women cannot lead, we follow a restrictive tradition rooted in Greco-Roman patriarchal culture and Constantinian-established Christianity. We share much with Roman Catholics, but our sense of the priesthood of all believers which begins at adult baptism does not allow us to share with them a sense of a priesthood limited to celibate males.[30]

This is a reading of both Scripture and church history which is different from Gryson's. It goes beyond the few passages that Epiphanius says the Montanists raised and the few examples of early Christianity mentioned here from Jerusalem, Bethlehem, Rome, Laodicea and other parts of Asia Minor, the island of Thera, Egypt, North Africa, Syria or Persia. Women in church leadership is biblical. Although seldom mentioned in the early centuries and often denied because of a particular cultural reading of Scripture, such leadership appeared in more than one region or in more than one view of the church. Women were important to Jesus and Paul. Later, during Constantinian establishment, they served in ministry as widows, nuns, and abbesses. They were deaconesses and presbyters; at least one was a bishop.

---

[30]In my *The Apostolic Faith: Protestants and Roman Catholics* (Collegeville, MN: Liturgical Press, 1992), I emphasize how much Christian faith we share with Roman Catholicism. That is my main point. But on this matter (see 142-49), I sadly disagree. Now see "Evangelicals & Catholics Together: The Christian Mission in the Third Millennium," *First Things* 43 (May, 1994): 15-22, for a more recent statement of what we share together.

Chapter Eighteen

WOMEN IN THE EUROPEAN MIDDLE AGES

Dale Pauls

Unaware that the world has not always been the way it was the day they were born, many note change and feel a persistent sense of frustration, a recurrent fear that perhaps the very bedrock foundations of life and truth are fracturing. What every historian knows, however, is that while sometimes change can be channeled and often destructive changes may be restricted or redirected, no one can keep change from happening. It is possible for a subculture to isolate itself and withdraw into smaller and smaller circles of conformity, but change sweeps over such groups, around them, and eventually through them. History is change, and the story of change. Nowhere is this more clearly illustrated than in the history of women in the European Middle Ages (AD 500-1500),[1] a period in which the relative status of women in both church and society significantly fluctuated. The dynamic interaction between societal forces and gender roles and expectations during this era is not unimportant to contemporary concerns.

1. *The History of Women as an Academic Discipline*

Gender studies represent the current frontier of historical research. In recent decades, a history of women has emerged that subscribes to rigorous standards of responsible scholarship.[2] Those reconstructing the history

---

[1] The European Middle Ages will be taken to refer to the period between AD 500 and 1500.

[2] For a useful historiographic survey of medieval gender studies, see Susan Mosher Stuard, ed., *Women in Medieval History and Historiography* (Philadelphia: Univ. of Pennsylvania Press, 1987).

of women, however, face special problems and challenges, especially when their focus is on premodern times. The study of history was formerly based primarily (almost exclusively) on political and legal documents, war chronicles, and surviving correspondence—all sources written by men for other men, from a strictly masculine point of view, and largely silent about women.[3] On the other hand, to uncover what was happening to women, scholars have to examine closely an entirely different set of sources. In addition to the reflections of gender expectations that can be found in penitential manuals, sermons, lives of the saints, rules of monastic orders, canon law, and the decrees of church councils, the careful historian must search for clues as to actual behavior in the visitation records of traveling bishops, in titles and deeds, and court records. Also, the cult of the Virgin or the adoration of Jesus as a baby open windows to understanding the experience of women and children in the Middle Ages. Especially helpful are the occasional writings of medieval women themselves that have resurfaced from beneath centuries of male neglect and disinterestedness. In fact, evidence is currently multiplying exponentially and from an increasingly broad range of sources—from gravestones, demographic surveys such as abbey records, archaeology, art, and domestic architecture.

An example of contemporary scholarship illustrates the interdisciplinary nature of gender studies as a growing academic discipline—longevity or life expectancy. Who outlives whom determines inheritance patterns and consequently who controls property and its usage. In AD 800, the sex ratio was 112 men for every 100 women. Men survived women. By the thirteenth century, however, the sex ratio had become approximately 103-105 women for every 100 men. Historians puzzled by this reversal supposed until

---

[3]See Jonathan Culler, "Reading as a Woman," *Feminisms: An Anthology of Literary Theory & Criticism* (ed. R. R. Warhol & D. Price Herndl; New Brunswick, NJ: Rutgers Univ. Press, 1991): 509-524. See also Elaine Showalter, "Feminist Criticism in the Wilderness," *Writing and Sexual Difference* (ed. E. Abel; Chicago: Univ. of Chicago Press, 1982): 9-35.

recently that before AD 1200 women were more likely than men to be the victims of violence, and certainly many died in childbirth. On this supposition, it seemed reasonable that by AD 1200 women were living longer because a more Christianized culture protected the physically weak and because women had a better chance of survival in the growing cities of eleventh- and twelfth-century Europe.[4]

In 1980, however, Bullough and Campbell[5] determined that this reversal in sex ratios could be better explained by dietary improvement. In the early Middle Ages, as in much of antiquity, the average daily diet consisted mainly of bread and an ever-changing broth enriched by whatever was available. It was deficient in iron which women lose in rates disproportionate to men through childbirth, miscarriage, and menstruation. Consequently, women's resistance was lower and they succumbed to disease, epidemic, and infection in rates somewhat higher than men. Beginning in the ninth century, though, daily diets began to include protein-rich peas, beans, and chickpeas and increased meat and fish, with the result that women began to outlive men.

In order to detect what was really happening between men and women during the European Middle Ages, the scholar must move beyond preconceptions and long-standing assumptions and investigate the wider array of data.

2. *How Attitudes Toward Women Were Shaped*

To understand the history of women in the European Middle Ages, it is imperative to understand how medieval attitudes toward women were shaped. It is a common, although erroneous, assumption that all such attitudes can be traced back to an origin in how certain NT texts were interpreted. However, it may be posited that gender attitudes

---

[4]David Herlihy, "Life Expectancies for Women in Medieval Society," *The Role of Women in the Middle Ages* (ed. R. Morewedge; Albany: State Univ. of New York Press, 1975): 1-22.

[5]Vern Bullough and Cameron Campbell, "Female Longevity and Diet in the Middle Ages," *Speculum* 55 (1980): 315-25.

in the Middle Ages arose from several sources and only marginally from Scripture. The accounts of Jesus' life, ministry, and teaching reveal little or no sexism by anyone's standards; by the standards of his own day, Jesus' attitude toward women was almost revolutionary.[6] In the same spirit, the apostle Paul concluded that there is neither male nor female in Christ Jesus (Gal 3:28), and those passages in which he restricts the roles of Christian women in the public assembly—1 Cor 14:26-40 and 1 Tim 2:9-15—are understood by almost all historians to be addressing the specific circumstances of the churches in Corinth and Ephesus respectively in the light of Greco-Roman culture. Certainly in the astonishingly heterogeneous church of the second and early third centuries, several groups (later dismissed as gnostic, but in their time representing a substantial minority in the church) granted Christian women remarkable dignity, even equality, allowing them even to be priests.[7] Women were recognized in various movements and localities as prophets, missionaries, martyrs, and spiritual leaders.

Another significant source for medieval gender expectations was classical Greek thought which, following in the footsteps of Aristotle, pictured woman as the imperfect version of man and argued that 1) authority and subordination are inevitable and necessary and 2) the physically stronger party is always superior. This led in classical Greek and Roman thought to a whole set of medical and scientific assumptions concerning women's inferiority to men.[8] This cultural legacy would be transmitted into the

---

[6]The Vatican's resistance to female ordination on the simplistic basis of Jesus' having selected only men to be his apostles is culturally and historically naive.

[7]Elaine Pagels, *The Gnostic Gospels* (London: Weidenfeld and Nicolson, 1980): 28-69.

[8]Aristotle, *Politics* 1.2.1-22; Vern Bullough, "Medieval Medical and Scientific Views of Women," *Viator* 4 (1973): 485-501. See also Gregory E. Sterling, "Women in the Hellenistic and Roman Worlds (323 BCE-138 CE), *Essays on Women in Earliest Christianity* (ed. C. D. Osburn; Joplin, MO: College Press, 1993): 1.41-92.

Middle Ages through a system of thought known as Neoplatonism in which everything was perceived in Platonic, hierarchical terms. Within this worldview, differences of any kind—whether age, gender, race, or class—were necessarily understood to imply inequality, so that everyone and everything had his, her, or its exact place in one vast rigid hierarchical system, and was either inferior or superior to everyone or everything else. Rights and privileges were preordained on the basis of birth, that is, class, gender, or race. Until well into the thirteenth century, there was in medieval Europe no other way to see things.

A further source for medieval attitudes toward gender, and perhaps the source most widely-cited throughout the Middle Ages, was the Church Fathers of the third and fourth centuries. For some reason still not entirely clear, these male church leaders became very uncomfortable with the physical and the sexual—with the human body, which in accordance with Platonic dualism was considered inferior to the human spirit. Perhaps ancient religious beliefs about ritual purity contributed to their discomfort. Perhaps they were reacting to the great epidemics of gonorrhea and bubonic plague at the time.[9] Certainly their misogyny was typical of the male chauvinism of the Roman aristocratic class from which many of these church leaders came, especially in the Constantinian church of the late fourth century. In any case, men like Jerome and Augustine (whose painful struggle to repress his own sexuality is so evident in his famous *Confessions*) contributed to the prevalent ecclesiastical view that the only good and trustworthy woman was a dead virgin! They transferred their own problem of temptation onto women—they are evil. The writings of these Church Fathers did much to shape attitudes toward women for over a thousand years.[10]

---

[9]Norman F. Cantor, *The Civilization of the Middle Ages* (New York: Harper Collins, 1993): 72-73.
[10]See Peter Brown, *The Body and Society: Men, Women, and Sexual Renunciation in Early Christianity* (New York: Columbia Univ. Press, 1988) and James A. Brundage, *Law, Sex and Christian*

3. *Women in the Early Middle Ages (AD 500-1000)*

Despite the enormous influence of classical Greek thought as transmitted through the writings of the Church Fathers, women frequently did well from AD 500 through AD 1000, especially aristocratic women who exercised considerable power, influence, and control in both church and society as queens, landowners, abbesses, and martyrs. During the seventh and eighth centuries, certain prestigious abbesses in Anglo-Saxon and Frankish lands presided over what are called "double monastaries," i.e., monasteries that included both male and female monks.[11] They heard the confessions and directed religious affairs of both men and women. Since such abbeys were hundreds of miles from Rome and travel was both primitive and hazardous, these women were the spiritual authorities of all that their eyes surveyed.

To understand the origin of this remarkable female power, historians point to inheritance patterns that survived from old Germanic law codes, especially the Visigothic and Burgundian law codes in what is today northern Spain and southern France. Throughout most of medieval Europe until well into the eleventh century, widows frequently inherited most of the family estate and daughters inherited land along with sons. Moreover, under Irish influence, where blood ties mattered most in determining inheritance, it was not unusual for property to be transmitted matrilineally, that is to the sons of daughters rather than the sons of sons[12]—for the very simple reason that one could be more sure that his daughter's son was his blood than his son's son.

Society in Medieval Europe (Chicago: Univ. of Chicago Press, 1987): 1-123.

[11]Suzanne Fonay Wemple, *Women in Frankish Society: Marriage and the Cloister, 500-900* (Philadelphia: Univ. of Pennsylvania Press, 1990 reprint of a 1981 edition): 142, 159-62, 170.

[12]David Herlihy, *Medieval Households* (Cambridge, MA: Harvard Univ. Press, 1985): 30-43.

In any case, those who owned the property were in control. They endowed the monastaries, built the chapels, chose the priests, and selected the abbots or abbesses. Sometimes, in a husband's absence, being a housewife meant managing a kingdom. Consequently, until about AD 1100, economic class overcame gender as a social determinant and many noblewomen held important posts, e.g., Brunhild, Fredegund, Nanthild, and Balthild, queens of Merovingian Francia, Ethelfleda of Mercia, Agnes of Poitou, and Matilda of Tuscany. In tenth-century Rome, two women, a mother and daughter, Theodora and Marozia, exercised control over the papacy for years.[13] Perhaps the most impressive woman in tenth-century Europe was the playwright and poet Hrotswitha of Gandersheim who deserves acclaim as the first Saxon poet, the first Christian dramatist, and the first German historian.[14] The reason these names are unfamiliar to the general reader lies, it seems, in which gender went on to tell the history.[15]

4. *Women and the Gregorian Reform of the Papacy*

The Gregorian Reform of the papacy that began in the eleventh century marks a watershed with regard to the status of women in Western civilization. In AD 1049, Leo IX became pope and with his associates—Cardinal Humbert of Silva Candida, Peter Damian, and the monk Hildebrand—

---

[13]Jo Ann McNamara and Suzanne Wemple, "The Power of Women through the Family in Medieval Europe: 500-1100," *Feminist Studies* 1 (1973): 136.

[14]See Peter Dronke, *Women Writers of the Middle Ages: A Critical Study of Texts from Perpetua (203) to Marguerite Porete (1310)* (Cambridge: Cambridge Univ. Press, 1984): 55-83; Katharina M. Wilson, "The Saxon Canoness: Hrotsvit of Gandersheim," *Medieval Women Writers* (ed. K. M. Wilson; Athens, GA: Univ. of Georgia Press, 1984): 30-63; Elizabeth Alvida Petroff, *Medieval Women's Visionary Literature* (New York: Oxford Univ. Press, 1986): 83-91, 114-135.

[15]The writings of Hrotswitha, for instance, were buried beneath centuries of masculine devaluation of the feminine and casual disregard for the thinking of women, and were rediscovered only at the close of the fifteenth century.

launched a reform movement. In AD 1073, Hildebrand became pope as Gregory VII. The entire reform movement would be named after him.[16]

These reformers championed the view that clergy should be ascetics and they were determined to destroy the aristocratic nobility's stranglehold on the church by eliminating landowner's making the controlling decisions for church affairs and church property. Their two-part strategy included 1) ending lay control of church patronage such as the appointment of abbots, priests, and bishops and 2) achieving complete clerical celibacy, thus eliminating priestly dynasties that sometimes kept church property in their families for generations. Where there was no marriage and therefore no legitimate children, there could be no familial inheritance and the property would revert to the direct control of the institutional church. Until recently, this reform movement was largely perceived as an anti-corruption campaign, and so historians viewed it favorably. However, its negative impact on women was considerable.

A. *The Increasing Militarization of the Church.* The reformers, in the spirit of their age, understood the church as a warrior society, with its clergy and monks as soldiers of Christ. Worship was viewed as the spiritual branch of warfare. Leo IX had been a warrior-bishop, and continued to lead military campaigns as pope. Gregory VII initiated the idea of the Crusades and his letters are filled with military

---

[16]See Norman F. Cantor, *The Civilization of the Middle Ages*, 243-276. For more extensive coverage, see Colin Morris, *The Papal Monarchy: The Western Church from 1050 to 1250* (Oxford: Clarendon, 1991); I. S. Robinson, *The Papacy, 1073-1198: Continuity and Innovation* (Cambridge: Cambridge Univ. Press, 1990); Gerd Tellenbach, *The Church in Western Europe from the Tenth to the Early Twelfth Century* (trans. T. Reuter; Cambridge: Cambridge Univ. Press, 1993); Karl Frederick Morrison, *Tradition and Authority in the Western Church, 300-1140* (Princeton Univ. Press, 1969); Walter Ullmann, *The Growth of Papal Government in the Middle Ages: A Study in the Ideological Relation of Clerical to Lay Power* (3rd ed.; London: Methuen, 1970).

metaphors.[17] Naturally this militarization of the church led to a sacralizing of warrior values and increasing masculinization of the church.

B. *The Insistence on Clerical Celibacy.* The tenth century witnessed the high point of clerical marriage in Europe. Although celibacy decrees and canons existed since the fourth century, in AD 1000 most rural priests were married out of practical necessity, and some urban priests and even bishops were also married. To undermine and destroy clerical marriages, the reformers launched powerful anti-female attacks. Women were equated with uncontrollable sexuality, irrationality, and demonic temptation. For instance, the venerable Peter Damian, who was himself abandoned early by his mother and then exposed to a childhood of frequent batterings,[18] addressed this diatribe to wives of the clergy (though one can be sure his intended audience was male).

> I speak to you, o charmers of the clergy, appetizing flesh of the devil, that castaway from paradise, you, poison of the minds, deaths of souls, venom of wine and of eating, companions of the very stuff of sin, the cause of our ruin . . . you women of the ancient enemy, you bitches, sows, screech-owls, night-owls, she-wolves, blood-suckers . . . hear me, harlots, prostitutes, with your lascivious kisses, you wallowing places for fat pigs, couches for unclean spirits, demi-goddesses, sirens, witches, devotees of Diana. . . the ancient foe pants to invade the summit of the church's chastity through you. . . . You suck the blood of miserable, unwary men, so that you

---

[17]Ephraim Emerton, trans., *The Correspondence of Pope Gregory VII: Selected Letters from the Registrum* (New York: Columbia University Press, 1932).

[18]To explore further this psycho-sexual foundation to Peter Damian's thought, see Mary McLaughlin, "Survivors and Surrogates: Children and Parents from the Ninth to the Thirteenth Centuries," *The History of Childhood* (ed. L. de Mause; New York: Harper, 1974): 103-105.

might inflate into their inmost parts a lethal poison. They should kill you.[19]

Finally twelfth-century legislation put an official end to clerical marriages. The First Lateran Council (AD 1123) annulled existing clerical marriages, and the Second Lateran Council (AD 1139) decreed that ordination automatically invalidated marriage. The consequences were enormous: "a devastating social revolution"[20] across rural Europe with many victims, a trail of broken homes and abandoned wives. They and their children were left destitute, facing starvation, prostitution, slavery, murder, and suicide. Even more astonishingly, none of the hundreds of decrees on celibacy across centuries of debate show any concern for the fate of these women and children.[21] Urban II even recommended that clerical wives be offered as slaves to nobles who cooperated in church reform.[22]

C. *The Impact of the Reform on Inheritance Patterns.* Previously families, including wealthy female heirs, controlled church property. The papal reformers, in a fifty-year struggle with the German Emperor and other nobility, gained full control over church property by the skillful use of excommunications, interdicts, and political power. The landed nobility could no longer depend on a relatively fluid transfer between lay and church property to provide for their heirs. Deprived of easy access to control over church land, they had to devise other means of preserving their estates. The result was a new and narrow emphasis on paternal lineage and primogeniture (inheritance of the entire estate, or

---

[19]Damian, *"Women who seduced clerics,"* PL 145, 410ff. See Anne Llewellyn Barstow, *Married Priests and the Reforming Papacy: The Eleventh-Century Debates* (New York: Edwin Mellen, 1982): 58-60.

[20]C. N. L. Brooke, "Gregorian Reform in Action: Clerical Marriage in England, 1050-1200" (1956), *Change in Medieval Society* (ed. S. L. Thrupp; New York: Appleton-Century-Crofts, 1964): 49.

[21]Bernard Verkamp, "Cultic Purity and the Law of Celibacy," *Review for Religious* 30 (1971): 206-207.

[22]Barstow, *Married Priests and the Reforming Papacy,* 82-83.

the largest portion thereof, by the oldest son), which neglected younger sons and daughters. Thus, fewer and fewer aristocratic women controlled property and its disposal. Consequently, fewer women exercised authority in society and church, and there were fewer and fewer models of female leadership as time went on.

Was this marginalization of women a deliberate papal policy or an unintended consequence? In the sense that it was entirely thoughtless, it can be judged unintended. If, as Damian wrote, women were "wallowing places for fat pigs," obviously men were free to say anything about them that served their purposes. It did not much matter; women did not much matter.

5. *Women and the Invention of Western Romantic Love*

The Gregorian Reform notwithstanding, in the twelfth century things seemed to be looking up for women in Southern France with what has been called "the invention of Western romantic love."[23] It is astonishing to realize that a great deal of our notion of love as romance—what we say about love, what we say to the ones we love, what we expect them to say to us, how we act and how we expect them to act, i.e., the etiquette of romance—did not exist in Judaic tradition or classical Greece or Rome. It was born in the poetic literature of the courts of southern France, in the poems and songs of the troubadours and the Arthurian—and other—romances. It began with the knight in shining armor and the damsel in distress.

Love and women, at least women of a certain bearing, were idealized. The lady was put on a pedestal and imagined to be perfect and untouchable. She was worth dying for. But as one writer notes, "the passion reserved in Christianity for (God) became focused upon a . . . mortal human being."[24] Such misplaced ardor did women no favors.

---

[23] R. Howard Bloch, *Medieval Misogyny and the Invention of Western Romantic Love* (Chicago: Univ. of Chicago Press, 1991).
[24] *Ibid.*, 10.

Women were still abstractions reduced to a category and denied seriousness as real individuals. They were still something to be possessed by a man. There are two ways to keep women out of the mainstream and out of the way: 1) by vilifying them as Jerome or Damian did or 2) by idealizing them as Arthurian legend did.

Upon closer examination, romantic literature had very little to do with women at all[25]—it had a lot more to do with how the woman made the man feel about himself. It was as if the man said to the woman, "I'm not in love with you; I'm in love with an idea that looks like you." On final analysis, romantic literature such as these Arthurian legends present a childish world in which men are so busy playing heroes that women are fundamentally disregarded.

More insidiously, this literature—especially the "shepherdess" songs that celebrated the male-fantasy encounters between a knight and a shepherdess—naturalized and romanticized rape. Both the male aggression and the female suffering are portrayed as erotically appealing. It is even permissible to laugh at rape. Female characters are playful, resilient, and plastic; whatever is done to them, they resume normal behavior afterwards.[26] Even the language used for sexual assault reinforces this male mythology, e.g., notice the confusion created by the Old French *ravir* and *ravissement*, which as a verb (to ravish) suggests male

---

[25]See C. S. Lewis, *The Discarded Image: An Introduction to Medieval and Renaissance Literature* (Cambridge: Cambridge Univ. Press, 1967); Lynette R. Muir, *Literature and Society in Medieval France: The Mirror and the Image, 1100-1500* (New York: St. Martin's Press, 1985); Lee Patterson, *Negotiating the Past: The Historical Understanding of Medieval Literature* (Madison: Univ. of Wisconsin Press, 1987); F. Goldin, trans., *Lyrics of the Troubadours and Trouveres* (Garden City, NY: Anchor, 1973); John Benton, "Clio and Venus: An Historical View of Medieval Love," *The Meaning of Courtly Love* (ed. F.X. Newman; Albany: State Univ. of New York Press, 1968): 19-42.

[26]Kathryn Gravdal, *Ravishing Maidens: Writing Rape in Medieval French Literature and Law* (Philadelphia: Univ. of Pennsylvania Press, 1991): 104-121.

sexual violence, but as an adjective (ravishing) describes female beauty. This is not far from the assumption that whatever is ravishing begs to be ravished. The moving force behind rape is considered to be the beautiful woman, not male sexual violence.[27] Only today are these twelfth-century premises being challenged.

6. Women in the Late Middle Ages

In the thirteenth through fifteenth centuries, women were increasingly marginalized. They were shut out from the growing legal system, from universities, even from literacy—all of which became church or clerical monopolies and were, therefore, after the Gregorian Reform off limits to women. Even the rise of the sacraments and the doctrine of purgatory (with its insatiable demand for masses for the dead) contributed to this process of excluding women from all positions of social status. As the sacraments—an all-male preserve—were deliberately made more elaborate, more awe-inspiring, more mysterious, more heroic, and more untouchable, the gender prohibited from administering them continued to slide downward in terms of relative social prestige. At the same time female monasteries were bankrupted by both the neglect of male bishops and the necessity of hiring male priests to celebrate their essential sacraments (while the members of male monasteries could easily officiate their own).[28]

The result was that, all other channels of influence and authority having been blocked, by the fourteenth and fifteenth centuries many gifted spiritual women retreated into religious mysticism. Some like Angela of Foligno and Julian of Norwich achieved spectacular notoriety, while others, like Margery Kempe, were bizarre. In the fourteenth century the influence of the mystic Catherine of Siena was such that she could convince the papacy to return from

---

[27]*Ibid.*, 5.
[28]Penelope D. Johnson, *Equal in Monastic Profession: Religious Women in Medieval France* (Chicago: Univ. of Chicago Press, 1991): 225-226.

Avignon to Rome. The fate of the most famous of all—Joan of Arc—well illustrates the paradox of gender. Joan of Arc saw visions, became the French heroine that turned the tide of the Hundred Years War against the English, but eventually was burnt to death at an English stake. In the end the charge that convicted her was dressing like a man.[29]

Meanwhile, women were losing economic status by 1) being shut out from the guilds, which in cities replaced the family as the chief economic unit, and 2) by their exclusion from the impersonal machinery of royal government that in these centuries replaced rule by those of "high birth."[30] Out of the legal revolution of the twelfth and thirteenth centuries, powerful structures emerged to enforce societal uniformity: papal and royal bureaucracies, systems of taxation and justice, and the inquisitorial process. There now existed a governmental hierarchy of specialized agencies—judges, police forces, etc.—to enforce the long-standing hierarchy of Neoplatonic imagination.

Women were also adversely affected by the xenophobia (the fear of strangers) that plagued Europe in the 1140s and 1150s after the unexpected failure of the Second Crusade. Increasingly Jews, heretics, women, lepers, and homosexuals—i.e., all who were identifiably different—were viewed as scapegoats, teleological causes for military defeat or plague or economic depression. Historians note that Europe in the twelfth and thirteenth centuries witnessed "the rise of a persecuting society," the traces of which are still visible today.[31]

---

[29]Anne Llewellyn Barstow, "Joan of Arc and Female Mysticism," *Journal of Feminist Studies in Religion* 1 (1985): 29-42.

[30]See Martha Howell, "Citizenship and Gender: Women's Political Status in Northern Medieval Cities," *Women and Power in the Middle Ages* (ed. M. Erler and M. Kowaleski; Athens: Univ. of Georgia Press, 1988): 37-60, who concludes, "The sternly patriarchal society that was to characterize the seventeenth and eighteenth centuries in northern Europe was taking shape."

[31]R. I. Moore, *The Formation of a Persecuting Society: Power and Deviance in Western Europe, 950-1250* (Oxford: Blackwell, 1987).

These medieval patterns of gender and sexuality proved to have tremendous longevity. Many attitudes that persist even until now have their origins in the twelfth and thirteenth centuries. At least two factors account for this. First, these patterns of gender status and expectation were tested, fine-tuned, and consolidated over the seven centuries from AD 1100 until the Industrial Revolution—700 years during which social conditions in Europe remained remarkably stable. Consequently, these patterns became firmly entrenched and perceived as the way things had always been and the way things ought to be—part of what it meant to be Western, European, and Christian. Second, these patterns coincided with the rise of the legal profession in the thirteenth century and became coded into law. Law then became a rigorously conservative force in society, dedicated to the protection and perpetuation of the power already enjoyed by the privileged.[32] Consequently women were excluded, in whole or in part, from social status and power, from economic opportunities and resources, and from civil rights and legal due process. Such exclusion was facilitated by attitudes, stereotypes, beliefs, and ideology—myths of inability and inferiority—that became encoded in institutional structures, legislation, and even language. Thus women experienced self-perpetuating patterns of inequality and underrepresentation. They could exercise little control over either societal directions or their own individual lives and destinies. They were increasingly restricted to performing societal roles and functions men needed, but did not wish to do themselves. They were encouraged to develop those

---

See also *idem*, *The Origins of European Dissent* (Oxford: Blackwell, 1985); John Boswell, *Christianity, Social Tolerance, and Homosexuality: Gay People in Western Europe from the Beginning of the Christian Era to the Fourteenth Century* (Chicago: Univ. of Chicago Press, 1980): 243-302, 333-334; Michel Mollat, *The Poor in the Middle Ages: An Essay in Social History* (trans. A. Goldhammer; New Haven: Yale Univ. Press, 1978): 112, 251-293; and Jeffrey Richards, *Sex, Dissidence and Damnation: Minority Groups in the Middle Ages* (London: Routledge, 1991).

[32]Brundage, *Law, Sex, and Christian Society in Medieval Europe*, 585-95.

personality characteristics that pleased those having power, such as submissiveness, passivity, and dependence. And all along, men generally viewed women as somehow substandard, as not fully human, as objects to be possessed and controlled. Only recently have these patterns been forcefully challenged in Western culture.

7. *Could It Have Been Otherwise?*

One cannot penetrate the history of the Middle Ages without realizing that it was a physical, crude, earthy age given to everyday violence. For the vast majority of its people, existence was reduced to a matter of raw survival—the question of full gender equality would never have occured to them. All of this makes female leadership of double monasteries all the more remarkable, but of course the days for such abbesses were numbered. In an age when survival often depended upon the illusion of invulnerability, the idea, for instance, that the village church should or even could be led by a woman priest was not a thought that would come naturally to most peasants or nobles. Also, the church became fully assimilated into a system of vassalage that was infused with militaristic function and ideology, and the likelihood of women as regular participants in any form of church leadership diminished.

It was not, however, simply a matter of the sheer physicality, the nameless violence, of the age. More importantly, everything was perceived in Platonic terms even well into the thirteenth century. Differences implied gradations in ascending and descending order that stretched even beyond visible society to the heavenly realms. To the medieval mind, differences of any kind—gender or otherwise—inevitably implied inequality, i.e., clear dominance and clear subordination.

It is astonishing that the one-class social structure involving aristocratic control of society and its resources survived from ancient Egypt and Mesopotamia until well into the eighteenth century AD, a scant two hundred years ago. Medieval people inherited and lived within a hierarchical society based on power, domination, and exploitation to which they did not give a second thought. It had always been that way and they could not imagine it being any other way. It was part of the very fabric of nature, part of God's *order*. Stoic philosophy, along with Platonic thought, provided the mental structure for this medieval universe, but for most it was simply a matter of timeless experience. As it was an age deeply devoted to *stabilitas*, it is, in one sense, remarkable that anything ever changed in the Middle Ages. Until at least the twelfth century, medieval people were not even aware that the order of things could be overturned, and even in the late Middle Ages, the medieval mind remained strongly traditional. It did not occur to most people to question what they felt was God's *order* on earth. Such questioning would be blasphemous.[33] It was not an age mentally open to any reconsideration of gender roles and expectations. It was an age that habitually ranked everything and assigned to everyone a status based almost entirely on birth. As such, it was an age devoted to maintaining the *status quo*, not to questioning and restructuring.

Furthermore, the Middle Ages inherited from late antiquity various cultural structures that reinforced such thought, e.g., the Roman educational system, Roman law, and Roman governmental institutions and attitudes. The educational system adopted with some ecclesiastical censorship was tough and aggressive and gave almost no thought to how anyone felt. It was a psychologically-damaging system that encouraged aggression, violence, and hostility to women.[34] And it transmitted to the Middle Ages a classical tradition—Platonic or Aristotelian—that consistently pictured woman as the imperfect version of man and argued that authority and subordination are always inevitable and the physically stronger party (in this case, man) is in the very nature of things superior.

The Roman heritage also bequeathed to the Middle Ages a commitment to and, by the twelfth century, an obsession

---

[33]Cantor, *The Civilization of the Middle Ages*, 3-5, 480-481.
[34]*Ibid.*, 10-11.

with law as society's primary organizational principle. Roman law was believed, in fine Stoic fashion, to be derived from natural law, thereby affirming the traditional assumption that what exists (e.g., masculine domination) is right and always has been right. It is not surprising that the renaissance of Roman law in the eleventh and twelfth centuries, launched by the rediscovery of Justinian's sixth-century *Corpus iuris civilis*, was accompanied by a relative decline in the status of women. The same pattern can be observed earlier in Carolingian times as Roman law began to reshape Frankish society, although the effects then were intermittent and not sustained. The Roman legal tradition consistently favored absolutism and, in certain papal or royal hands, became an ideology of formidable despotism.

Moreover, the Middle Ages, as it had opportunity, absorbed uncritically the institutions of the Roman Empire, and with it a conservative social stance. Early Christianity, as befitting a largely middle-class social movement seeking imperial toleration, or at least seeking to evade imperial notice and persecution, created a legacy of accepting the prevailing order and not forcing change, of remaining largely silent in the face of slavery, or the brutality of the Roman circus, or rampant prostitution.[35]

In the Middle Ages, Charlemagne was praised for massacring "thousands of heathen Saxons in a single day without flinching"[36] yet no one cared that he had many concubines and mistreated his daughters. It was an age when the church was engaged in constant conflict with unruly nobles, when the papacy itself was often vulnerable to the gangster nobility of the city of Rome. It was an age that glorified physical strength and military prowess.[37] Romanesque architecture depicted the church as God's fortress, with Jesus as the head of the feudal hierarchy.[38]

---

[35]*Ibid.*, 37-38.
[36]*Ibid.*, 179.
[37]*Ibid.*, 203-204.
[38]*Ibid.*, 222.

It was an age when itinerant scholars, many of them aspiring churchmen, traveled great distances at considerable physical risk to study at monastic or cathedral schools and later at the emerging universities.[39] It was also an age when monks came to view themselves as the militia of Christ, when eleventh-century Gregorian reformers understood the church as a warrior society, when warrior values were sacralized and the church was consequently masculinized. It was an age when a papally-inspired "people's crusade" degenerated into massacres of the prosperous Jewish communities in the Rhineland. Conquering Christian crusaders in 1099 made the streets of Jerusalem run red with Muslim and Jewish blood. The crusading idea fused together military force and religious devotion and taught future generations that in the service of Christian faith it is right to kill and destroy.[40]

Matters were not greatly improved in the later Middle Ages. The thirteenth-century struggle, literally to the death, between the papacy and the German Hohenstaufens injected into Europe a new openness to unprincipled violence that further poisoned the moral atmosphere.[41] Meanwhile, the growing bourgeois, locked as they were into their own grim and intensely competitive struggle for survival and advancement, had little compassion for the weak and incompetent.[42] They lived in a faction- and class-ridden urban world of constant distrust, hatred, and drunken violence. The fourteenth and fifteenth centuries were centuries of plague, chronic warfare, and increasingly violent agrarian and urban revolts, e.g., the Jacquerie in France, the Peasant's Revolt of 1381 in England, and repeated uprisings of Flemish and Florentine textile workers. The urban nobility of Renaissance Italy still lived inside fortified towers. Outside city walls, marauding mercenaries put in their time between wars plundering the countryside.

---

[39]*Ibid.*, 319.
[40]*Ibid.*, 301.
[41]*Ibid.*, 461.
[42]*Ibid.*, 470.

Medieval Europe was a darkly-enchanted world. Its literature and art were saturated with images of pain and death. It was a world built on fear. There was fear of the mountains, fear of the seas, fear of the forest, fear of the night, fear of famine, fear of winters unusually cold, fear of summers unusually wet, fear of plague and disease, fear of war, fear of peasants and the urban poor rising in revolt, fear of anonymous violence, fear of Satan and his demons, fear of the apocalypse, and fear of Hell itself. God's order of things was paradoxically and astonishingly fragile. It could all unravel so easily. And in a world given shape by Neoplatonic thought which assigns everyone and everything an exact and pre-ordained place in God's order, anything out of place became a reason to fear. There was an eternally-correct order to society —to be preserved at all costs.

So the classical heritage and the practical demands of an age so physical, so crude, so fearful, and so violent conspired against women maintaining or assuming positions of church leadership in the Middle Ages, and had the church insisted on strict gender equality, and forcefully implemented it, it would probably have lost its solid hold on the imagination and hearts of medieval people.

This is not to subscribe to a strictly determinist view of history, however. Christianity, in its origin, presented a real reconsideration of gender roles and responsibilities. In Scripture, there is an egalitarian strain that runs counter to and undermines the centuries-long pattern of domination and exploitation. Jesus himself was remarkably open to women; even "fallen women" were among his devoted followers. And contrary to popular opinion, he was followed in this by Paul who, far from being misogynistic, speaks restrictively of women (1 Cor 11:2-16; 1 Cor 14:33-35; and 1 Tim 2: 9-15) only as a concession to the dominant social realities of his day[43] and clearly challenges hierarchical thinking by

---

[43]On arguments involving slavery and traditional gender roles, see David Edwin Harrell, Jr., *Quest for a Christian America: The Disciples of Christ and American Society to 1866* (Nashville, TN: Disciples of Christ Historical Society, 1966): 91-138; and Forrest G. Wood, *The*

writing, "There is neither Jew nor Greek, slave nor free, male nor female, for you are all one in Christ Jesus" (Gal 3:28).

Too, the openness of certain circles in the second-century church to female leadership raises intriguing questions. Had the Church Fathers grasped this opening, made different decisions, listened more to Jesus than Plato—more to the prophetic tradition of Hebrew faith than to Stoic philosophy, would the history of the church then have been different? If so, the original Christian message of love and forgiveness with its openness to women would not have been buried beneath the layers of mystical, sacramental, hierarchical, Platonized religion that by the fourth century became so attractive to the fine upstanding citizens of the Empire. Could a faith so simple, so unsophisticated, and so unorganized have survived? Would it have appealed to Constantine or any self-respecting emperor? Could it have met the challenges that accompanied the violent upheavals that began in the late fourth century?

If a faith betrays its original genius, does it not eventually betray itself? No longer quite itself, what does one call this thing that now proves so historically effective or successful? By what standards does one measure such success, and at what cost to the human spirit? And who is to say that another course of action based on different decisions, e.g., a commitment to its original idealism, would not have proved in the long run more effective? In a moral universe, can one divorce efficiency from legitimacy? Can what is illegitimate—contrary to the spirit of its founder—be considered effective?

In any case, by the generation of Jerome and Augustine, the Church Fathers had decided for a grimly joyless view of sexuality and the feminine. Why this happened remains a

---

Arrogance of Faith: Christianity and Race in America from the Colonial Era to the Twentieth Century (New York: A. A. Knopf, 1990): 53-78.

patristic puzzle, although the real difficulty is unraveling the many factors that may have contributed to it and assigning each factor appropriate weight. Perhaps male chauvinism of the Roman aristocratic class (from which came Ambrose, Leo the Great, Benedict, and Gregory the Great) simply won out and wrapped itself, consciously or otherwise, in the justification of Platonic dualism. Perhaps ancient religious beliefs about ritual purity cast a chill across the church. No doubt the misogyny of the Fathers was in part a reaction to sex-drenched Roman society[44] and to the biomedical crises of the fourth century—the increase in gonorrhea and the outbreak of the bubonic plague. Did it seem that society was being punished for its violations of God's immutable order? Or was it always primarily a matter of keeping power in the hands of the male clergy by picturing sexuality, and with it the feminine, as something dark, frightening, and dirty?[45] The mystery remains, but the fourth century marked a watershed in the development of Western civilization.[46]

---

[44]It should be noted, however, that by the late fourth century pagans—far from being the libertarians of popular imagination—became just as prudish as Christians. Pagans and Christians alike felt the judgment of God in the plagues and barbarian threats. Certainly Platonic dualism didn't help matters with its exaltation of the spirit and denigration of the body. And dualism reigned supreme, so Christian prudishness—discomfort with the physical, the sexual, and the sensual—is, historically speaking, a pagan construct. To state what really happened, Christians became as prudish as pagans. The church breathed in the sterility of a dying world.

[45]Cantor, *The Civilization of the Middle Ages*, 72-73.

[46]Karen Jo Torjesen, *When Women Were Priests: Women's Leadership in the Early Church and the Scandal of their Subordination in the Rise of Christianity* (San Francisco: Harper, 1993), despite an anachronistic title and the occasional historical slips, persuasively argues that with regard to gender roles, the church in the third and fourth centuries sold out to classical Greco-Roman culture. In the second and early third centuries the church was intimate and private. It was organized around household gatherings and met behind closed doors, seeking safety in secrecy. In such assemblies, women often exercised considerable influence, leadership, and patronage, as they did in the household itself. The household or *oikos* then was the fundamental socioeconomic unit in society, and women often played the central

What might have been possible in the urbanized cosmopolitan Roman society of the second century—a society still largely at peace, a society that had not yet lost its nerve or confidence, moreover, a society not unfamiliar with female leadership in certain religious contexts—would not be possible again for many centuries. Certain doors were firmly shut—one was the door that might have opened church leadership to women.

Conclusion

Concerning the fate of women in the medieval church, the large picture presents an astonishingly clear pattern. The central issue was always authority and the consolidation of and exercise of power. The church was haunted by the glory of Rome, and given opportunity, it always chose power. In the inevitable power struggles, those with the least power tended to lose what little power they had. As a result of the Gregorian Reform in particular, all women were eventually marginalized, and clerical wives were fully degraded.

All this did not happen without a debate. Many contemporaries argued that the papal reformers were concerned not primarily with moral reform but with asserting authority.[47] Some, such as Serlo of Bayeux, condemned the inhuman legislation of the Gregorian party and its compulsive need to control the church through law. They took their stand on the liberating power of grace and

---

managerial role in its operation, as men (acting on the time-honored Greek model of society) turned their attention to the more public affairs of the *polis* or city or state. Women whose houses were large enough to host churches were especially influential, and all the more so if they were wealthy widows. However, as the growing church went public in the third century and began to meet in basilicas, it conformed to the strict gender roles of Greco-Roman society. This meant in the public sphere exclusively male leadership.

[47]Barstow, *Married Priests and the Reforming Papacy*, 122.

dismissed canon law.[48] It was a struggle between two concepts of the church.[49] One was hierarchical; the other was egalitarian. One was obsessed with proving superiority and compelling obedience; the other was dedicated to moral example and extending mercy towards the failures of others. One focused on status, the other on service.

The triumph of the Gregorian Reform was achieved at a cost, and not only to women. Clergy deprived of legitimized heterosexual outlets were forced to look elsewhere for human affection and intimacy. All men, to the extent their thinking was misogynistic, were deprived of true companionship with women. The medieval church would suffer growing anti-clericalism, and it would increasingly be challenged by religious movements that allowed more active and fulfilling roles for women. Society itself paid an enormous price. A priesthood straining so hard for ascetic purity and sexual celibacy could only soothe rather than sensitize societal conscience. Always falling short of its own ideals, it offered no moral authority to challenge others. The result was an age of excessive grossness presided over by theoretical ascetic purity.[50]

Women, however, paid the greatest price. Noble[51] suggests that the Gregorian Reform (starting in AD 1049) launched a Masculine Millennium that differs from the 1000 years before when 1) church leaders were married; 2) some church communities achieved something close to gender equality in the spirit of Gal 3:28; 3) aristocratic women often controlled property and how it was used; and 4) the misogyny of Aristotle was largely unknown. With the Gregorian Reform, women were driven to the sidelines of the clerical culture that gave birth to the Western scientific tradition. The result was—in science, academia, and

---

[48]*Ibid.*, 135, 137-139, 170.

[49]*Ibid.*, 122-123, 193.

[50]Henry C. Lea, *History of Sacerdotal Celibacy in the Christian Church* (London: Williams and Norgate, 1907): 1.430-445.

[51]David F. Noble, *A World Without Women: The Christian Clerical Culture of Western Science* (New York: A. A. Knopf, 1992).

consequently in societal leadership—a "world without women." It did not have to be that way.

Only in relatively recent times have these gender traditions been effectively challenged. During the past few decades accelerating social change has undermined the supposed verities of the Neoplatonic worldview. Until recently, Cartesian rationalism (a collateral line of Neoplatonic thought) still reigned, with its passion for definition and categorization and its need to be logical, exact, and certain with everyone and everything in his, her or its exact place in the way things ought to be. It is only now in the closing decades of what might be called the second Neoplatonic millennium that the paradigm shifts and fractures beneath the weighty imponderables of such matters as democracy, quantum physics, and biomedical ethics are being recognized.[52] Rights and privileges on the basis of birth—or class, gender, race, or religion—no longer seem pre-ordained. Meanwhile women have found their voices and have broken the monopoly once held by men on literacy, education, creative outlets and networks, Bible scholarship, and historiography. They have even discovered the right to think for themselves. Consequently, women are contributing to a collective understanding of the human

---

[52]See Stephen Toulmin, *Cosmopolis: The Hidden Agenda of Modernity* (New York: Macmillan/Free Press, 1990). In the seventeenth-century quest for logical rigor, mathematical exactitude, and intellectual certitude, Christian doctrine was ascribed geometrical certainty. Certainty became the new hermeneutic, even if facts had to be twisted to achieve it. Toulmin observes that this once-dominant Newtonian or Cartesian worldview is now being replaced by a worldview that is both more biblical and more reasonable, a worldview that has proper respect for intellectual limits, an awareness that little in life fits formulas with the tidy certitude of Euclid's geometry or Newton's physics, and a realistic understanding that timeless contextless abstractions always involve significant omissions. Toulmin points back to the wisdom of the sixteenth-century biblical humanists, such as Erasmus, who called for a return to the Christianity of Jesus and his apostles, a return to the beginning when faith was simple, living, and free from subtlety and intellectualism—in short, a return to the freedom and purity of the gospel.

experience that is more holistic and integrative. As our insights become correspondingly more comprehensive, marginalization becomes easier to see, both in the past and in the present, and more difficult to condone.

Chapter Nineteen

THE PROBLEM OF CREDULITY OF WOMEN IN THE HISTORY OF CHRISTIAN THOUGHT

Gerald C. Tiffin

The history of credulity (perceived and misperceived) of women in the history of Christian thought is deeply rooted in the person of Eve. From the early church Fathers to contemporary times, Eve usually has been pictured and interpreted as an archetypal symbol of female incredulity. Only a few[1] have viewed her role in Eden as anything more than temptress or seducer. Most often she has been cast into other terms, such as progenitor of the "feminine principle"[2] referring to passivity, receptiveness, emotionalism, and darkness as key elements of womanhood.

Historically, pre-Christian as well as Christian men have tended to discount women. That discount has usually been "direct" in the form of public descriptors such as inferior, secondary, idiot, or carnal. As such, the credibility of women (credulity) has not been an issue, since by definition their views, thinking, and preferences have been discounted. This attitude and view has prevailed even into the twentieth century, in spite of historical impulses that have empowered some individuals and certain groups of women. To complicate the history of our journey to the present century, in the few moments when women have not been directly discounted, they have been idealized, which we shall see, turns out nevertheless to constitute another more subtle

---

[1]Phyllis Trible, "The Depatriarchalization in Biblical Interpretation," *JAAR* 41 (1973): 30-48.

[2]See Joan Englesman, "Rediscovering the Feminine Principle," in Shirley Nicholson, *The Goddess Reawakening: The Feminine Principle Today* (Wheaton: Theosophical Publishing House, 1989): chap. 7.

form of discount. Until Victorian England and the emergence of American middle class culture, such idealization only flourished in the late Middle Ages, and then for a short while. The credibility of women has consequently suffered not only from explicit and direct discounting, but ironically from sporadic idealization which results in a very deceptive adoration of the female, all the while using that idealization as another means of excluding authentic contribution and validation of women. This historical vacillation between woman as either daughter of Eve or daughter of the Virgin Mary, or more crudely, seductress or angel, has greatly limited even the discussion let alone any amelioration of the credulity issue for women. It is to this history we turn.

This history needs to be previewed in additional categories. Observers have questioned whether or not the woman has a soul,[3] is a person,[4] or is capable of rational thought.[5] For most of Western history, gender has primarily defined women, while class, nation, religion, or other categories have defined men.[6] The daughters of Eve have usually been viewed in terms of their relationships to men, or some man. Beyond this designation, women have more often than not been defined by their bodies (carnality) rather than their minds. Menstruation, the uterus, the ability to give birth, and the theory of the "wandering womb"[7] have

---

[3] Anonymous, *Have Women Immortal Souls? The Popular Belief Disputed* (London: Frederich Farrah, n.d.): 8-9. This pamphlet is housed in the British Library, London.

[4] Elizabeth Clark and Herbert Richardson, ed., *Women and Religion: A Feminist Sourcebook of Christian Thought* (New York: Harper and Row, 1977): 3.

[5] Most writers/observers who raise questions regarding the credibility of women address this issue.

[6] Bonnie S. Anderson and Judith P. Zinsser, *A History of Their Own: Women in Europe from Prehistory to the Present* (New York: Harper and Row, 1988): xv.

[7] See Ilza Veith, *Hysteria: The History of a Disease* (Chicago: University of Chicago Press, 1982), for the enduring history of this idea.

defined and limited the credulity of women. As such, women have been viewed as needing protection at the very least, and in some eras, as downright evil, because of their sexual natures.

Finally, Gen 3:16 has often been proof enough that women are not credible, evidenced by Eve's seduction by the serpent and her "in kind" seduction of Adam. Her lot, as viewed by most, has been the protection and guardianship of a husband or some other male.

This analysis will examine the widely-held view that the surprising validation and certification of women by Jesus was quickly reversed, if not by Paul, then certainly the early Church Fathers. We shall briefly examine the roots of the credulity question in Judaism first, then the Greco-Roman culture before turning the Christian era. Beyond the early Church Fathers, we shall turn to the Middle Ages, then the Renaissance and Reformation before surveying developments in early modern history, concluding with the Victorian and modern period.

To speak of the credulity of women is to refer to their believability or credibility. For women, rarely has credulity been a matter of personal evaluation, but more often a matter of generic designation. For most of the history of gender relationships, a specific or unusual woman might be viewed as credible, but in order to achieve that status, she usually was forced to overcome the female problem of credulity.

1. *The Greeks*

The Greeks, who are rightfully acknowledged as key to the foundations of Western Civilization, also laid a key part of the foundation which has undermined the credulity of women. Sequestering of women in ancient Greece is well known. But that fact[8] sidesteps the issue of credulity.

---

[8]This was more true in Athens than in Sparta. See Sarah B. Pomeroy, *Goddesses, Whores, Wives, and Slaves: Women in Classical Antiquity* (New York: Schocken, 1975): 58-59.

Hesiod (eighth century), early in the history of Greek thought, presented Pandora—as she opened her box releasing the carnal knowledge of women which in turn became a source of evil to men—as counterpart to Eve.[9] This account served as a preview of the prevailing Greek cultural view that male equaled civilization, order and reason, while female stood for nature, emotion and chaos.[10] A woman was not likely to be consulted or included in government or important deliberation. This view reduced Greek women to lives of silence and submission, in effect living as legal children.[11] In this light, it does not surprise us that the Greek practice of "exposure" of unwanted children, usually meant exposure of females.

Aristotle held very negative views of women. He believed that the woman was in effect a defective male, passive, and secondary even in the process of generation of the race.[12] He was echoing Hippocrates of Cos, who contended that the male seed is stronger than the female seed, resulting in men from strong seed and women from weak seed.[13] This polymath of Greece would influence generations for millennia. While generally contending that females are weaker and inferior to males, and even noting they had fewer teeth than males,[14] he also stated that, ". . . the one is the courage of command, and the other that of subordination."[15]

---

[9]Hesiod, *Works and Days* (LCL; Cambridge: Harvard Univ. Press, 1982): 9.

[10]Anderson and Zinsser, *A History of Their Own*, 31.

[11]Pomeroy, *Goddesses, Whores, Wives, and Slaves*, 74.

[12]Aristotle, *On the Generation of Animals*, 1.20. See A. L. Peck, *Aristotle* (LCL 17; Cambridge: Harvard Univ. Press, 1943): 101-11.

[13]Julia O'Faolain and Lauro Martines, *Not In God's Image* (New York: Harper and Row, 1973): 118.

[14]Anderson and Zinsser, *A History of Their Own*, 28.

[15]Aristotle, *The Politics* 1.13 (1260 A). See H. Rackham, *Aristotle* (LCL 27; Cambridge: Harvard Univ. Press, 1932): 63.

Aristotle was not alone in his views. The Furies in Greek mythology represented female guardians of fertility — usually pictured as behaving in irrational and hysterical ways, typical of women.[16] Yet the Olympian gods, mostly male-oriented, were usually pictured as rational. Xenophon, after describing Ischomachus speaking with his wife regarding marriage as a business association, portrays Socrates' assertion that Ischomachus' wife "truly has a masculine mind."[17] Plato, the teacher of Aristotle, in his *Timaeus* stated, "of the men who come into the world, those who were cowards or led unrighteous lives may with reason be supposed to have changed into the nature of woman in the second generation."[18] Even Hesiod earlier had warned against women who twisted matters by deception.[19] The discounting of women was well under way in the western world.

The assignment of women to sequestered incredulity was reinforced by the presumption that the womb and its tendency to wander in search of sexual satisfaction doomed any possibility of credible participation of public life. Unsatisfied sexual appetites then resulted in disease and dissention, amidst other dysfunctions. Plato put it this way:

> and the same is the case with the so-called womb or matrix of women; the animal within them is desirous of procreating children, and when remaining unfruitful long beyond its proper time, gets discontented and angry, and wandering in every direction through the body, closes up the passages of breath, and, by obstructing respiration, drives them to extremity, causing all varieties of disease.[20]

---

[16]Clark and Richardson, ed., *Women and Religion*, 4.

[17]See O'Faolain and Martines, *Not In God's Image*, 22.

[18]Plato, *Timaeus* 91A. See R. G. Bury, *Plato* (LCL 79; Cambridge: Harvard Univ. Press, 1966): 7.246.

[19]See Vern Bullough, *The Subordinate Sex: A History of Attitudes Towards Women* (Urbana: Univ. of Illinois Press, 1973): 57.

[20]Plato, *Timaeus* 91C. See R. G. Bury, *Plato* (LCL 79; Cambridge: Harvard Univ. Press, 1966): 7.251.

Plato's theory of the wandering womb would carry into the thinking of the early Church Fathers—laminated on to the view that women were defined as "body"—thus carnal and captive of fleshly appetites, always seeking to seduce males.

2. *The Jews*

Aside from the fact that the Genesis account contains the story of Eve which forms the historical backdrop for the larger credulity question, the Jewish tradition beyond Genesis (up until the Christian era) formed a very important part of the emerging credulity issue. Several aspects of women's status in intertestamental Jewish history are well known: that women were not allowed to study Torah; that such study was presumed by many Jews to promote licentiousness, since quoting relevant sections of Torah was the only means available to a woman to demonstrate innocence regarding charges of sexual immorality; that women could not be counted as part of the necessary quorum (*minyan*) needed to conduct official synagogue business, when even a male infant could be counted if necessary; that Jewish women could not testify on their own behalf in courts of law, etc. The credibility of women during the Hellenistic pre-Christian era was subsumed under the presumption that daughters of Eve were seducers, and therefore discounted. For every Esther or Deborah, a Delilah could be presented as representative of the real female nature.

While the reality of Jewish views and treatment of women give important perspective to Jesus' validation and treatment of women, those views were not eliminated by Jesus' example and teaching. Philo, a first-century Jew, asserted the following about male and female differences in a discussion about the soul:

> The soul has, as it were, a dwelling, partly men's quarters, partly women's quarters. Now for the men there is a place where properly dwell the masculine thoughts (these are) wise, sound, just, prudent, pious, filled with freedom and boldness, and kin to

wisdom. And the women's quarters are a place where women's opinions go about and dwell being followers of the female sex. And the female sex is irrational and akin to bestial passions, sorrow, pleasure and desire from which ensue incurable weakness and indescribable diseases.[21]

The credulity question was simply not a question in Jewish tradition at this time. In short, Eve was viewed as the source of evil, condemned even more by the fact that she had seduced Adam and consequently all of humanity by her duping of him.[22]

The continuing influence of this view is seen in the Mishnah. Focusing upon a variety of concerns from family and civic law, to agriculture and cultic purity, the Mishnah evidences important attitudes regarding the credulity of women in the context of concern for protection of male purity and prerogative. The Mishnah generally presents the male as norm, and the female as deviation from that norm, always with a concern to protect male property, including wives and daughters. Women were marginalized, thus restricted from public life. They also were barred from communal study of sacred texts, thus denied access to any real pursuit of intellectual life.[23] In this context, hope for the credibility of women augured by the ministry of Jesus among the Jews, had to be tempered.

Both Jewish and Greek views of credulity fed the Christian era. When coupled with the interpretations of the teachings of Jesus and Paul, a more convoluted view of the credulity question emerged.

---

[21] Philo Judaeus, *Questions and Answers on Genesis* 4.15. See R. Marcus, *Philo* (LCL 74; Cambridge: Harvard Univ. Press, 1953): 288.

[22] See Bernard P. Prusak, "Women: Seductive Siren and Source of Sin?" in Ruether, *Religion and Sexism*, 89ff.

[23] See Judith Romney Wegner, *Chattel or Person: The Status of Women in the Mishnah* (New York: Oxford Univ. Press, 1988).

3. *The Romans*

The early development of the Roman Republic (509-31 BC) occurred in isolation from Greece. But as Greek culture and ideals were transmitted first by Alexander the Great (336-323 BC) and then by those who inherited the residue of his empire, Rome came under the influence of many aspects of Greek culture. This was accelerated as the entire Eastern Mediterranean came under Roman influence by war and treaty in the two centuries before Christ. This Hellenistic world, so named because of pervasive Greek cultural influence, had deeply impacted late Republican Roman society by the early Christian era. As Classical Greek culture was diffused into several Hellenistic Kingdoms (ex. Ptolemaic Egypt), those Kingdoms in turn influenced Rome. Hellenistic art, education, medical practice, philosophy, and language were widely adopted by the Romans.

Some Hellenistic societies around the Eastern Mediterranean even placed queens on thrones (Cleopatra), and offered increased privilege to some women in terms of property and legal rights. Yet the credibility of women remained isolated, sporadic, and reserved for the privileged few. As Rome began to interface with and dominate Hellenistic kingdoms, Roman women were beginning to experience increasing opportunity and status, especially in legal, commercial, and political arenas. Mostly confined to women of the Patrician class and aristocratic and commercial families, this embryonic "liberation" movement was quite limited in theory and scope. Nevertheless, it constituted a certain contrast to the continuing discounting faced by their Jewish counterparts at the dawn of the Christian era.

The docile and virtuous woman remained the ideal Roman woman from early Republican times. Under the power of the "paterfamilias" and the "manus" of a father or husband, the credibility of Roman women during the Republic was rarely an issue, given their dependent status. Only after significant numbers of Roman men left to fight against Carthage (Punic Wars c. 200 BC), did some Roman women gain the opportunity to participate in the civic life of

Rome. By the time of Christ, Roman matrons had achieved some credibility, and Roman girls could achieve some education beyond household functions. Certain Roman women had achieved high political status, often by marriage. Even so, most Roman women in Rome still suffered a credibility gap.[24]

In the first century BC, Cicero reported that, "because of the weakness of woman's intellect and judgment," earlier Romans desired that women should remain under the power of a male guardian. The first century AD historian Tacitus referred to women as "frail by nature."[25] Ulpian in the third century (AD) averred that guardians were (still) necessary for women due to "weakness of their sex . . . ."[26] Galen, the leading medical expert of the time stated that, "The female is more imperfect than the male. The first reason is that she is colder. If, among animals, the warmer ones are more active, it follows that the colder ones are more imperfect."[27] Again, the Jewish author Philo in this same early Empire era not only referred to the irrationality of women,[28] but interpreted Gen 2 as the basis for his negative view of woman's nature. He relegated the lower parts of the soul to the female, linking her nature to the irrational and sensual. Philo blamed this sensuality/sexuality as the basis of Adam's seduction away from God and into sin. For Philo, the only hope for woman was to abandon her sensual nature and focus upon God, in

---

[24]See Pomeroy, *Goddesses, Whores, Wives, and Slaves*, 170-189, for a fuller description of women in Rome.

[25]Tacitus, *Annals*, 3.34. See Clifford H. Moore, *Tacitus* (LCL 76; Cambridge: Harvard Univ. Press, 1962): 2.579.

[26]N. Lewis and M. Reinhold, *Roman Civilization: Sourcebook II: The Empire* (New York: Harper and Row, 1966): 543-44.

[27]*Oeuvres de Galen* (ed. and trans. C. Daremberg; Paris: Bailliere, 1856): 2.99.

[28]Philo, *On the Special Laws*. See F. H. Colson, *Philo* (LCL; London: Heinemann, 1958): 3.113. See also Vern Bullough, *The Subordinate Sex: A History of Attitudes Towards Women* (Urbana: Univ. of Illinois Press, 1973): 109.

effect, becoming a man.[29] Philo's views anticipate the later writings of the Church Fathers who would elaborate upon themes of virginity and celibacy as the main solution to the woman's credulity problem.

Even as the Western Roman Empire (past AD 300) declined, themes which undermined the credulity of women played on quite apart from the writings of the Church Fathers of the first four centuries of the Christian era. A recently published book by Gillian Clark paints a continuing picture of Roman women still under the guardianship of men, unable to adopt outside that relationship; still defined as inherently weak of mind and intellect due to weakness of body and soul; still disadvantaged in most realms of life. So even in the late Roman Western Empire, the status of female was still a disadvantage because she was viewed as physically and constitutionally weaker, intellectually inferior, unable to control bodily desires, and victimized by emotion.[30]

4. Ante-Nicene Church Fathers

Whatever empowering elements Jesus' ministry and gospel offered women in the sense of authentic personhood and validity likely carried into the second century. Yet they were soon challenged by church leaders who interpreted the credibility of women in terms of their inheritance from Eve more than their inheritance as new daughters of the gospel of Jesus.

As the infant church sought separate identity from its Jewish origins and struggled to justify itself to a suspicious and hesitant Roman imperial authority, early second century Christian writings did not address the issue of women in general, let alone issues of credulity. We do catch a glimpse

---

[29]Maryanne Cline Horowitz, "The Image of God in Man—Is Woman Included?" *HTR* 72 (1979): 190-92.

[30]Gillian Clark, *Women in Late Antiquity: Pagan and Christian Lifestyles* (Oxford: Clarendon, 1993): 120 ff.

of growing discounting of women's testimony in the second century *Epistula Apostolorum*, an apocryphal writing. In contradistinction to Jesus' face value confidence in the veracity of women (John 4, woman at well, and Mark 14, woman anointing Jesus with oil), this document presents Mary Magdalene and Sarah reporting the resurrection of Jesus to the apostles. The apostles (male) do not believe them, reminiscent of Luke 24:11. The testimony of women appears to be perceived as nonsense, lacking any credibility.[31] In this same time period, Hippolytus in reference to the appointing of widows, makes it quite clear that wives who have recently been widowed should not be appointed quickly, because they cannot be trusted.[32]

By the third century, church leaders such as Tertullian became quite pointed regarding the credulity issue. His famous "gateway" passage, as he addresses women in his treatise "On the Apparel of Women," reads:

> And do you not know that you are (each) an Eve? The sentence of God on this sex of yours lives in this age: the guilt must of necessity live too. You are the Devil's gateway: you are the unsealer of that (forbidden) tree: you are the first deserter of the divine law: you are she who persuaded him whom the devil was not valiant enough to attack. On account of your desert—that is, death—even the Son of God had to die.[33]

---

[31]Elisabeth Schüssler Fiorenza, "Word, Spirit and Power: Women in Early Christian Communities" in R. Ruether and M. McLaughlin, *Women of the Spirit: Female Leadership in the Jewish and Christian Traditions* (New York: Simon and Schuster, 1979): 52.

[32]Gregory Dix, *The Apostolic Tradition of St. Hippolytus* (London: SPCK, 1968): 20. Presumably Hippolytus feared for the enduring impact of the sexual influence of the marriage state which might contaminate the judgment of the new widow, because its power would wane quite slowly. See O. C. Edwards, Jr., "The Failure of the Ante-Nicene Church to Ordain Women and its Significance for Today," *Nashotah Review* 15 (1975): 325-51.

[33]Tertullian, *On the Apparel of Women*, 1.1. See *ANF* 4. 14.

This statement has come to symbolize the most negative view of women in early Christianity.

Nevertheless, this view played out in a variety of forms in the writings of other Church Fathers. The first sin of disobedience as pictured in Gen 3 was increasingly overlaid with the view that the act of sexual union was actually the first sin. Anderson and Zinsser[34] state it well: "Increasingly, Adam was seen as relatively innocent and as the embodiment of mind, who had been corrupted by Eve, the temptress and embodiment of flesh." In effect, as it was usually interpreted, when Adam saw Eve naked, he (mind and spirit) lost control and gave into fleshly temptation, thus degrading spirit to the level of lust and flesh. All Eve's fault, of course! The Fathers then tended to express fear of male sexual arousal in terms of rejection of sexuality, sometimes, as with Tertullian, accompanied by denunciation of women in general.

Within this line of thinking came medieval glorification of celibacy, virginity, and the monastic focus upon spiritual discipline, which usually meant denial of all appetites. Marriage would become inferior to virginity, and virginity would eventually constitute a basic denial of femaleness as the means of becoming an acceptable person before God.

Another North African, Origen, like many Church Fathers, was deeply influenced by Greek categories of thought which tended to deny the possibility of material expressions of divinity. He continued to play the theme of incredulity into the third century. Whereas Clement of Alexandria (Origen's teacher) believed that Eve seduced Adam into sexual relations before God's timetable of marriage,[35] Origen on the other hand opined that the formation of male and female did not actually occur until

---

[34]Anderson and Zinsser, *History of Their Own*, 79.
[35]Prusak, "Woman: Seductive Siren and Source of Sin?" *Religion and Sexism*, 101.

mankind sinned.³⁶ This of course allowed Origen to designate man as spirit and female as a contravailing negative force which in turn allowed Origen to praise spiritual masculinity and condemn spiritual femininity.³⁷ The stage was then set for a long history of discounting female credibility.

5. Post-Nicene Church Fathers

Beyond the Council of Nicea (AD 325) and the apparent Christianization of the Roman Empire by the end of the fourth century during the reign of Theodosius, church leaders turned their attention to consolidation of church polity and concern for a disintegrating Roman political situation, given the growing threat of Barbarian invasions and interior threats of heresy. The stinging condemning attitudes of Tertullian, and to a lesser extent, other Fathers, temporarily waned in the face of responsibilities of a newly acquired cultural hegemony and the necessity to administer both church and civic affairs in the face of a disintegrating empire.

But the discounting of female credulity reappeared in a statement by the Cappadocian Father and leading Christian thinker, John Chrysostom (ca. AD 400). He concluded that:

> The woman taught once, and ruined all. On this account ... let her not teach. But what is it to other women that she suffered this? It certainly concerns them; for the sex is weak and fickle .... the whole female race transgressed .... Let her not, however, grieve. God hath given her no small consolation, that of childbearing .... By these means they will have no small reward on their account, because they have trained up wrestlers for the service of Christ.³⁸

---

³⁶Horowitz, "The Image of God in Man: Is Woman Included?" *HTR* 72 (1979): 193.

³⁷*Ibid.*

³⁸Chrysostom, *Homilies on Timothy* 9 in *PNF* (ser. 1) 13.436. Anderson and Zinsser, *A History of Their Own*, 79.

Jerome, the surly monk of Rome, stated in the mid-fourth century that "as long as woman is for birth and children, she is different from man as body is from soul. But if she wishes to serve Christ more than the world, then she will cease to be a woman and will be called man."[39] In this view, femaleness cannot exist apart from maleness. It is not only defined by maleness, but essentially subsumed by it. Jerome was known to keep company of virgin women, but still reflected the growing consensus that the feminine nature could not be trusted.

The choices for women then, were not attractive. Either give up your femininity (sexuality) and become as it were, male, or find solace in the very nature (sexuality) that *ipso facto* condemns you.

Another Cappadocian, Gregory Nyssa, reinforced this growing focus upon virginity in his salutory biography of Macrina, his sister. As a virgin teacher, Gregory accorded Macrina status usually reserved for males only, even comparing her to Socrates.[40] This status would not have likely been proffered to Macrina if she had not been a virgin. Her credulity was achieved by denying her femininity.

6. *The Middle Ages*

The transition from the end of the Western Roman Empire (5th century) to the so-called Middle Ages also ushered in the full participation of the church in the political, economic, and social affairs of the larger world. As Barbarian Kingdoms displaced Roman political hegemony, the structure and organization of the church became an important vehicle for continuity of life for many. The missionary activity of the church toward Barbarians extended the influence of Christianity over most of Europe, even into Britain. At the same time, the growing "worldly"

---

[39] Vern Bullough, "Medieval Medical and Scientific Views of Women," *Viator* 4 (1973): 499.

[40] Patricia Wilson Kastcher, "Macrina: Virgin and Teacher," *Union Seminary Studies* 17 (1979): 105-117.

involvement of the church, in the absence of any central western government, contributed to the growing monastic movement. In its earliest forms, monasticism was a movement of individuals outside the church. It took on permanent communal form after the work and life of Benedict of Nursia, who founded his famous monastery at Monte Cassino in 529. Monasticism eventually provided a unique setting which allowed new solutions to deal with the credulity issue for women. It became their hope as well as their bane.

In AD 800, Charlemagne became Holy Roman Emperor. As a Christian, a Frank (Barbarian) and the continuing embodiment of Roman Law and Government, he represented the culminating synthesis of these three traditions as the basis for Western culture in the High Middle Ages. While the Roman Empire continued to flourish in the East in the Byzantine Empire centered at Constantinople; as Islam arose in the East and advanced toward the West in the seventh and eighth centuries; and as Emperors and Popes contended over the delicate balance between church and state, life for most women remained predictable.

The views of the Church Fathers continued to dominate, unaffected by the influence of Barbarian custom and sporadic contact with the Byzantine Empire. Even though Mohammed certainly improved the lot of Arabian women in the early period of Islam, the encroachment of Moslem expansion and continuous threat of invasion did not ameliorate women's status in the West.

Monastic life did provide unusual opportunity for women to study, think, reflect, and theologize. There was a price. Nuns gave up all normal roles which traditionally defined womanhood, e.g., wife, mother, daughter, etc. While women founded and led monastic communities as abbesses, (often administering religious and secular powers, usually afforded males), only a minority of women were involved, at least until the twelfth century. Even though missionaries such as Columban empowered some women (e.g., Hrotsvit at Gandersheim) for monastic leadership, most still presumed that the abbess was functioning out of masculine temperament. It should be noted that in the case of "double" monasteries, wherein males and females co-operated together, nuns usually played the traditional female roles of housekeeping, cooking, and domestic duties.

While some women could find new empowerment through monastic leadership, this development did not necessarily enhance their credibility, at least as women. We have already noted the thinking of Church Fathers (Jerome) who suggested that women abandon their feminine nature, to become as males in order to focus upon God. Increased credibility for some female leaders in the monastic movement was then achieved only by the denial of their distinctive femaleness. Having already noted that women were sometimes viewed as "males turned inside out" sexually speaking and that the uterus needed continual activity to prevent a whole range of diseases and maladies[41] many medieval thinkers urged that women simply renounce their sexual nature through vows of virginity. Augustine himself believed that only the male carried the image of God, therefore woman should abandon sexual activity and focus on God through the Spirit.[42]

7. *The Twelfth Century*

After surviving the tenth-century invasions of the Saracens, Vikings, and Magyars, Western Europe began to transform toward the apex of the medieval Christian Commonwealth in the twelfth century. This was the age of classic and mature Feudalism, renewal in the church through papal and monastic reform, a revived economy of flourishing trade and towns, the growth of centralized governments, especially in England and France, and the feminization of theology evidenced in the cult of the Virgin Mary and dozens of Gothic Cathedrals built in her honor. The heavenly power of the Virgin Mary was matched only

---

[41]Aristotle and the Roman medical sage Galen both held this view.
[42]Bullough, *Viator* (1973): 500.

by the earthly power of such women as Eleanor of Acquitaine, Queen of both France and England in her lifetime, and the best example of the advances and limitations of credulity for women in the high Middle Ages.

But there were others, too. Anna Comnena, historian and daughter of Alexius I, Byzantine Emperor during the first Crusade (1097) illustrated the continuing self-deprecation of women into the twelfth century as she wrote about her mother, Empress Irene. Stating that women best serve as mourners, where their propensity to tears and emotion can be viewed as a positive influence, she also admired her mother for her "manly" mind and ability to hide her cowardice and other "womanly" feelings.[43]

These views about women were echoed and reinforced by Thomas Aquinas, professor-theologian at the University of Paris. As author of the seminal scholastic work, *Summa Theologica*, this Dominican's views would influence generations to come. Since his life's work revolved around the reconciliation of Aristotelian thought to Christianity, the similarity of his views to Aristotle does not surprise us. While he believed woman was also created in God's image, he believed she must remain subject to man, for afterall, ". . . woman is defective and misbegotten, for the active power in the male seed tends to the production of a perfect likeness in the masculine sex, while production of woman comes from defect in the active force . . . ."[44] Aquinas does admit that woman is misbegotten in the individual sense, but not in regards to universal human nature, since she can contribute to human generation.[45] Aquinas certainly urges celibacy for the woman, since her body not only seduced Adam, but remains her main source of inferiority. In fact, Aquinas states that the serpent approached Eve, rather than

---

[43]Bullough, *The Subordinate Sex*, 127-8.

[44]See Thomas Aquinas, *Summa Theologiae* (Matriti: Biblioteca de Autores Cristianos, 1955): 1.680-85, for his 1.q.92.a1-4 discussion. See ET in St. Thomas Aquinas, *Summa Theologiae* (trans. E. Hill; New York: McGraw-Hill, 1964): 37.

[45]*Ibid.*

Adam, because she was more credulous, thus more seduceable and more able to seduce Adam.[46] So Aquinas struggles to present woman as "somewhat useful" in the economy of God, since her reason is simply inferior to man's. Therefore she is subject to man, for "incredible" reasons.

Just a short time earlier, Gratian of Bologna, the jurist who organized canon law in the twelfth century, gave further evidence of this continuing tradition when he wrote:

> Women should be subject to their men. The natural order for mankind is that women should serve men and children their parents, for it is just that the lesser serve the greater. . . .
>
> The image of God is in man and it is one. Women were drawn from man, who has God's jurisdiction as if he were God's vicar, because he has the image of the one God. Therefore woman is not made in God's image. . . .
>
> Adam was deceived by Eve, not Eve by Adam. The woman led him to sin. It is just that he must take on himself her governance, lest the woman slip again with ease.[47]

Woman's presumed handicap continued to limit her activity and privilege.

Medieval historian G. G. Coulton has published some general sayings about women collected by Salimbene, a thirteenth-century Fransiscan, as representative of attitudes toward women among clerics of the time:

---

[46] Ruether, *Religion and Sexism*, 244. Also see Clark and Richardson, *Women and Religion*, 81-2.

[47] Gratian, *The Decretum* in *Corpus Iuris Canonici* (ed. A. Friedberg; Leipzig: B. Tauchnitz, 1879): 1, pt. 2, caus. 33, quest.5, can. 12, 13, 17, 18.

Where women are with men, there shall be no lack of the Devil's birdlime.

Woman was evil from the beginnings, a gate of death, a disciple of the servant, the devil's accomplice, a fount of deception, a dogstart to godly labours, rust corrupting the saints; whose perilous face hath overthrown such as had already become almost angels.

Lo, woman is the head of sin, a weapon of the devil, expulsion from Paradise, mother of guilt, corruption of the ancient law.[48]

While painful to read, if Coulton is correct, the accomplishments and contributions of Christian women of this period are all the more remarkable.

There were advances. New monastic reform movements, beginning with Cluny (910), provided promising avenues for female leadership and intellectual respectability. Hildegard of Bingen (1098-1179) is most notable among such women. She preached, prophesied, established a monastery, and wrote about science, music, and prophecy. The Cistercian, Augustinian, and Dominican movements nurtured others of slightly less achievement, who nevertheless challenged traditional clerical attitudes.

The mystic movement of this time, emphasizing prayer and meditation, also yielded significant women whose presumed female openness and receptivity to God offered some power and influence within the authority and structure of the church, usually not possible any other way. Several lived at the Helfta Convent in Germany.[49] St. Teresa of Avila, St. Bridget of Sweden, and Catherine of Sienna also

---

[48]G. G. Coulton, *From St. Francis to Dante: A Translation of All That is of Primary Interest in the Chronicle of the Franciscan Salimbene (1221-1288)* (London: D. Nutt, 1906): 91-92.

[49]Anderson and Zinsser, *A History of Their Own*, 205-7, esp. story of Christine of Markyate, c. 1123.

followed this tradition, reminding us that some selective women did overcome serious cultural and theological obstacles to their credibility. Even Heloise, that bright young novitiate, engulfed into personal tragedy because of her relationship with the theologian-philosopher Abelard, found more than just notoriety for her sexual misconduct, as she (with insistence from Abelard) accepted banishment to a life of celibacy until her death. From the haven of the convent she redeemed herself with new credibility.

Nothing modified the credibility of women as the Cult of the Virgin Mary which flowered in the twelfth century. This movement resulted in a temporary redefinition of women's credulity. Preached by Bernard of Clairvaux, among others, this cult resulted in modifying medieval theology to include a feminine side to theology. Male characteristics such as judgment, vengeance, condemnation, and dominance were modified with mercy, forgiveness, and nurturing in the figure of the Virgin Mary. The veneration of Mary brought inspiration and hope to mothers and women who sought validation in vows of obedience and chastity outside the cloister.

The impact of the Virgin went further. While not extraordinarily religious herself, Eleanor of Acquitaine, heiress to most of south-central France (the Acquitaine/ Guienne), took advantage of the moment, and used contemporary adoration of the Heavenly queen, Mary to her own advantage.

Married at age fifteen to the future Louis VII, she disappointed him by bearing only daughters. Increasingly disinterested in Louis (she found him more a monk than a king), she was drawn to the future King Henry II of England. After receiving a divorce from Louis in 1152, she married Henry, twelve years her junior. After reigning as Queen of France for fifteen years, she became Queen of England for the next thirty-five. Eleanor had grown up and inherited her traditional lands around Poitiers, where secular courts and new traditions of love and romance had developed. Her grandfather was likely the first troubadour

—setting the stage for a new genre of literature and music, symbolized by lyric poetry. The context for the songs of love by troubadours, and the courts of love were likely developed by Eleanor's daughter and granddaughter. In this setting of powerful women, Eleanor was able to adapt if not transfer the new adoration for the Virgin Mary, who after all was female, to earthly counterparts such as herself.

A powerful, tough, learned, promiscuous, and very influential woman, Eleanor became the symbol for the tradition of courtly love and the idealization of women that tradition represented. Disenfranchised and landless men were instructed in the rules of love, and as such, idealized unattainable married women. Those same women were actually as incredulous as if they were traditional objects of pity or domination. Women idealized as so wondrously fair, virtuous, and "incredible" could ultimately be dismissed and avoided as authentic human beings as easily as those who had been directly discounted for centuries. The discounting was indirect and implicit, not explicit.

Eleanor lays buried in France alongside husband Henry II and son Richard I at the Fontrevaud Abbey she first endowed, and where she lived her last few years after Richard died in 1199. Here we see that Eleanor's painted effigy includes a book in her hands, symbolic of this change in the status of women during her lifetime.[50] It was a temporary change.

8. *Renaissance-Reformation Era*

This period of cultural and artistic advancement likely provided a more civilized world for women of nobility and upper class, but this world of "advance" brought little actual change for women's believability. This is the era when Queens made their political marks in Spain (Isabella), England (Elizabeth), France (Catherine de Medici), Austria (Margaret), and Savoy (Louise). Yet the very word

---

[50]Even Eleanor was imprisoned for more than ten years by Henry, after she led an unsuccessful rebellion against him.

Renaissance, literally and conceptually, signaled continuing difficulty for women. The rebirth and renewal that lay at the heart of the definition of the word, Renaissance, was anchored in classical Greek and Roman civilization which harbored the foundations for many of the roots of the credulity problem for women. To simply recover the beliefs and ideals of the Classical Era could not have altered the credulity issue. The mere renewal of the literature and art of the era, which was so widely sought by humanists and scholars, could not displace old views.

The Renaissance of the fifteenth and sixteenth centuries (which included the Reformation of the sixteenth) surely elevated the dignity and credibility of humankind, with a veritable explosion of new art, and architectural and literary achievements. But woman was not easily helped. After all, this was the era when the burning of witches (almost always women) stood as a denial of the credibility of women; when Joan d'Arc was silenced and then burned for her incredible "voices"; and it was not uncommon to hear that Elizabeth I surely must be a man in drag, because no woman could rule so wisely and effectively.

The latter part of the Renaissance Era included the Protestant Reformation. Most of its leaders left statements which at best were ambivalent toward the credibility of women, usually reinforcing centuries of aspersions. The Lutheran doctrine of the priesthood of all believers might offer theological hope for both genders, but this "spiritual" truth was usually traded for "earthly" subordination and intellectual distrust, in reference to females. If the early rush of freedom and liberation from the Catholic Church included positive results for women, they were withdrawn and limited as the sixteenth century wore on.

Martin Luther thought women to be less "intelligent" than men and "disposed of two gross prejudices that had shaped the clerical image of women," 1) that women were sexually insatiable and a constant danger to men and to society, and 2) that women were of value only for procreation of the human race and the reproduction of the male.[51] Still, in 1524 Luther wrote a letter to the three nuns offering two reasons why a nun might leave the cloister, one of which had to do with having been forced into it against her will. As for the second reason he stated:

> The other reason has to do with the flesh. Women are ashamed to admit this, but Scripture and life reveal that only one woman in thousands has been endowed with God-given aptitude to live in chastity and virginity. A woman is not fully the master of herself. God fashioned her body so that she should be with a man, to have and to rear children. . . . No woman should be ashamed of that for which God made and intended her.[52]

While Luther urged respect for women and eventually married Katherine Von Bora, his actual teachings never quite fulfilled the promise of his theology in regards to the credulity of women.[53]

Like Luther, John Calvin continued the centuries old tradition of defining the potential and roles of women by theological-historical precedent. His reading of the Genesis account allowed him to easily conclude that woman is under man's authority and subjection, condemned by her disobedience and subsequent seduction of Adam into the same.[54] He did acknowledge the positive and contributory role of women to family and domestic life. He did not even object to the ascension of Elizabeth to the throne of England. Calvinist John Knox viewed the prospect of a female

---

[51]H. A. Oberman, *Luther: Man between God and the Devil* (trans. E. Walliser-Schwarzbart; New Haven: Yale Univ. Press, 1989): 277.

[52]*Dr. Martin Luthers Werke: Kritische Gesamtausgabe, Briefwechsel* (ed. O. Clemen; Weimar: H. Böhlaus Nachfolger, 1933): 3.327.

[53]Anderson and Zinsser, *A History of Their Own*, 259.

[54]William DeBoer, "Calvin on the Role of Women," in *Exploring the Heritage of John Calvin* (ed. D. E. Hadwerder; Grand Rapids: Baker, 1976): 242-46.

monarch differently. Writing from Calvin's Geneva while in exile, he complained:

> and such be al women, compared unto man in bearing of authoritie. For their sight in civile regiment is but blindness; their strength, weaknes; their counsel, foolishnes; and judgement, phresie, if it be rightlie considered.[55]

As John Aylmer attempted to defend the right of a woman to rule, in response to Knox's *First Blast* (the planned second and third were never issued), he demonstrated the truth of the dictum, "who needs enemies when we have friends like this?" when he described women as:

> Fond, foolish, wanton, fibbergibbaes, tatlers, triflers, wavering, witless, without counsell, feable, careless, rashe, proude, deintie, nise, talebearers, eavaesdroppers, rumor raisers, evell tongued, worse minded, and in every wise doltified with the dregges of the Devil's dounge hill.[56]

Ironically, he spared Elizabeth these epitaphs, since he hoped for a bishopric, an office he waited a long time to achieve (understandably, assuming Elizabeth read his writings). Most other Anglican leaders of the sixteenth century shared Aylmer's views of the capabilities of women. They concluded that men possessed superior understanding and reasoning, while women required guidance, control, and protection.[57]

Luis Vives, the Spaniard retained by Catherine of Aragon to tutor the future Queen Mary illustrates how dependent major humanist literators of the Renaissance were

---

[55] John Knox, "The First Blast of the Trumpet Against the Monstrous Regiment of Women." See D. Laing, ed., *The Works of John Knox* (Edinburgh: Bennatyne Club, 1855): 373.

[56] Bullough, *The Subordinate Sex,* 202.

[57] *Ibid.*, 203.

upon Classical thinking regarding the capability of women. In regards to the education of women he asserted:

> Therefore, because a woman is a frail thing, and of weak discretion, and may lightly be deceived, which thing our first mother Eve showeth whom the Devil caught with a light argument.[58]

Against the backdrop of the promise of a more noble view of humanity proffered by Renaissance literary and artistic leaders, and the new expectations of a democratized Christianity vaguely promised by some Reformation leaders, the development of witchcraft and the craze to eradicate these sisters of Eve, marked a backward step of any real progress for the credibility of women. Two Dominican inquisitors, Kramer and Sprenger, published their view of witchcraft and why women were more likely than men to be witches (by 1520, their tract had been republished at least fourteen times). The following excerpts speak for themselves:

> As for the question, why a greater number of witches is found in the fragile feminine sex than among men, it is indeed a fact that it were idle to contradict, since it is accredited by actual experience, apart from the verbal testimony of credible witnesses.

As to reasons why women are more superstitious than men, they contend that:

> the first [reason] is, that they are more credulous . . . The second reason is, that women are naturally more impressionable . . . since they are feebler both in mind and body, it is not surprising that they should come under the spell of witchcraft.

They continue on to relate this disposition to Genesis:

---

[58]As cited in Antonia Fraser, *The Wives of Henry VIII* (New York: Random House, 1992): 100.

> But the natural reason is that she is more carnal than a man, as is clear from her many carnal abominations. And it should be noted that there was a defect in the formation of the first woman, since she was formed from a bent rib, that is, a rib of the breast, which is bent as it were in contrary direction of a man. And since through this defect she is an imperfect animal, she always deceives....[59]

Beyond Kramer and Sprenger, learned men such as the French jurist and political theorist Jean Bodin (late sixteenth century) contended that wisdom never came from women, since she is a seducer and given authority over only the least worthy of creatures such as snakes, flies, and other animals of the like estate.[60] These views, with such a long history, have never really died, but began to fade as history moved into the modern era.

9. *Early Modern Europe*

In the Western tradition, the early modern era constitutes primarily the seventeenth and eighteenth centuries, transitioning to the modern world via the French Revolution and the era of Napoleon. This was the period of absolute monarchs (Louis XIV, Peter the Great, etc.), empire building, scientific revolution (seventeenth century), colonization of the "new" world, and growing world awareness—yet old ideas hung on. Even the long and successful reign of Elizabeth I in England during the last half of the sixteenth century raised questions relevant to the credulity issue. Since it was presumed by many that no woman could rule so competently, it was held, in some circles, that Elizabeth was really a male in drag. According to this theory, an "equivalent" male had been substituted at Elizabeth's untimely death to maintain political stability.

---

[59]Heinrich Kramer and James Sprenger, *Malleus Maleficarum* (New York: Dover, 1971): 41-44.

[60]Jean Bodin, *De la demonomanie des corciers* (Paris: 1850), as cited in O'Faolain & Martines, *Not in God's Image*, 210, viewed women as a vehicle of Satan's entrapment of man.

After all, "she" never married, portrayed masculine features, tended toward baldness in later life, and displayed cogent administrative skills not likely from a woman.[61]

A sixteenth century Frenchman referred to women as "vile, inconstant, cowardly, fragile, obstinate, venomous . . . imprudent . . . cunning . . . incorrigible, easily upset, full of hatred, always talking, incapable of keeping a secret, insincere, frivolous, and sexually insatiable."[62] In the late-seventeenth century, the continuing discounting of the credulity of women was displayed by Francois de Salignac de la Mothe-Fenelon in the context of comments regarding the education of females:

> A woman's intellect is normally more feeble and her curiosity greater than those of a man; also it is undesirable to set her to studies which may turn her head. Women should not govern the state or make war or enter the sacred ministry. Thus they can dispense with some of the more difficult branches of knowledge which deal with politics, the military art, jurisprudence, philosophy and theology. Even the majority of the mechanical arts are not suitable to them. They are made for exercise in moderation. Their bodies as well as their minds are less strong and robust than those of men.[63]

Others reinforced this notion that the physiognomy of the woman was her major deficit. This deficit centered in a weak body which created the need for constant vigilance to guard against sickness, fatigue, and overexertion. This view became the basis for the Victorian discounting of women in the nineteenth century, under the guise of idealization.

---

[61]Bullough, *The Subordinate Sex*, 221.
[62]Anderson and Zinsser, *A History of Their Own*, 93.
[63]Francois de Salignac de la Mothe-Fenelon, *Education des Filles* (Paris: E. Flammarion, 1937 reprint): 6, cited in Bullough, *The Subordinate Sex*, 272.

Yet Western Europe was fast approaching major economic, social, and political change, centered in the events and ideas of the French Revolution (1789-99) and the Era of Napoleon (1799-1815). The eighteenth century Age of Reason and Enlightenment which preceded the events of the Revolution emphasized reason over superstition, idealized progress, and replaced tradition with nature as the locus of ultimate reality. Christian English thinkers, such as Newton, Locke, and Smith, each in their own way contributed to a new cosmology which would overturn centuries of hierarchical social theory, including subordinate roles for women.

French philosophers such as Diderot, Voltaire, and Rousseau pressed the new thinking towards actual equality. The philosophes were hosted by wealthy women whose domestic salons became the breeding ground for this emerging egalitarian thinking. These hostesses, with all their "liberated" ideas about sexuality, still could not easily erase the lingering views of incredulity which sometimes even blocked their own personal progress. Yet even enlightenment thinkers failed to press the issue as might have been expected. While championing the rights of slaves, Jews, children, and Indians, they often failed to carry the same torch for women in their writings. This surprising inconsistency is best illustrated by Rousseau in his *Emile* (1762) when he stated:

> Men and women are made for each other, but their mutual dependence is not equal . . . . We could survive without them better than they could without us. In order for them to have what they need . . . we must give it to them, we must want to give it to them, we must consider them deserving of it. They are dependent on our feelings, on the price we put on their merits, on the value we set on their attractions and on their virtues . . . Thus women's entire education should be planned in relation to men. To please men, to be useful to them, to win their love and respect, to raise them as children, care for them as adults, counsel and console them, make their lives

sweet and pleasant: these are women's duties in all ages and these are what they should be taught from childhood.[64]

In short, there was no real Scientific revolution or Enlightenment for women in the seventeenth and eighteenth centuries.

10. *The Victorians*

While women enjoy a greater measure of credibility today than ever before in history, it has been achieved in spite of cultural and religious resistance. In this century, it has been usually begrudgingly recognized, against the long history which has been overviewed already in this essay. Twentieth- century American culture gives lip service to the credulity of women, but still struggles with the legacy of idealization inherited from the Victorian Era. That experience and the values which continue from it are worth reviewing.

The Victorian Era in England centered in the reign of Queen Victoria, the longest reigning monarch in European history (1837-1901). At the moment of English industrial and colonial expansion in mid-nineteenth century, the Victorians effectively dismissed women from the centers of cultural, political, and intellectual power. This occurred not by direct discount, but by the idealization of women, a "device" so subtle and sinister that it is still largely unrecognized to this day, with the continuing effect of undermining the credibility of women. Idealization works to publicly adore and uplift women, but in a way that undermines their credibility; resulting in a discount more insidious and cruel than the traditional direct discount, examples of which have been cited throughout this essay. Here is how idealization originated and functioned.

---

[64]Jean Jacques Rousseau, *Emile* (trans. Barbara Foxley; London: J. M. Dent, 1961): 328.

Industrialization, which came first to Britain in the late eighteenth century, in effect, created the modern separate nuclear family. Before the advent of the British industrial revolution, extended families of two or more generations lived together and engaged in agricultural and sometimes home production. Many children and all the kinfolk were usually needed to survive. With the coming of industrialism, families moved to cities and towns to find work in factories. The extended family was increasingly replaced by the private nuclear family, particularly among middle class families. It was the newly emergent middle class which developed new ideals about the family, which in turn led to new views of womanhood and childbearing.

On the farm, women had played an essential economic role. When they were not aiding directly in the productive work of agriculture, they labored in the home at small goods production (candles, cloth, etc.) which could be sold or traded. Before the nineteenth century, many English women worked closely with husbands as part-time producers and sellers. But women lost their role as producer and manager when families worked in factories. Among the more affluent middle and upper-middle classes, men held the significant positions in the managerial roles and work force. So as business was divorced from the home, the wife ceased as a business partner. She often was locked out of the factory on humanitarian grounds. There was no functioning place for women in this new economic world.

Eventually, the woman was relegated to the home as her proper domain. Her new and exclusive role in the family was now most important. It was her main contribution. She was now to protect her innocent children from the fallen world about them. The burdens of homecare were relieved, at least in the homes of the upper and upper-middle classes, by domestic servants such as a cooks, housekeepers, and governesses who took care of the most basic household tasks in these homes.[65] While these middle class women

---

[65]We are talking about a generalized view of women in mid-Victorian society (1850-1890). This standard view of the impact of

have traditionally been portrayed as inactive and unproductive, in actuality, many of them operated as managers and organizers, and should be acknowledged for their considerable skills in that arena. Nevertheless, different beliefs about the middle class woman developed. This set of beliefs may have been partly myth, but they were accepted. Men came to idealize these women on the basis of these beliefs. This idealization is best understood against the backdrop of actual attitudes toward women.

Women in nineteenth-century England were forbidden access to college and university education because, as one male writer put it, "It is an ascertained physiological fact that the actual capacity of the average male brain is considerably greater than that of the female . . . ."[66] Others in that same time period argued that a woman's intellectual abilities served to hinder her intended destiny, which was to give birth to a son.[67] Women were often reminded that their intellectual abilities were unfit for education; that to enter the arena of education would lead to ruin. Besides, the type of education which really mattered to the middle class female of

---

industrialism upon middle class families and women of England has been seriously questioned by Patricia Branca, *Silent Sisterhood: Middle Class Woman in the Victorian House* (London: Croom Helm, 1975). She argues that the traditionally accepted view of the idle Victorian woman is too general and uncomplimentary to English women of that period. Likely, Branca is correct, especially in her estimation that few middle class families could afford servants, boarding school education for daughters, or the amenities which supposedly distinguished the middle class. Most middle class families had neither the money nor opportunity to hire the kind of help upon which idleness would depend. Branca suggests most of these women (from among 750,000 middle class families) shopped, washed, dealt with crying children, cooked, and managed budgets as do modern housewives. Nevertheless, the images, attitudes, and beliefs which surrounded this newly industrialized rising middle class are of interest to us no matter what the actual circumstances. Image rarely fits reality in these matters.

[66]M. Burrows, "Female Education," *Quarterly Review*, 126 (1869): 144-45.

[67]Patricia Hollis, *Women in Public: Women's Movement: 1850-1900* (London: George Allen and Unwin, 1979): 23.

that era provided her with the abilities to "catch" a husband. If she failed, such an education (music, dance, language, etc.) would not serve a spinster in any practical way. Yet an education which might lead to productive employment was considered unladylike and sure to drive prospective husbands away. A quotation from Burrows summarizes the general male viewpoint regarding women in the nineteenth century:

> The duties of women do not to any great extent lie in the intellectual direction. Their sprightly intuition is often, in practical matters, worth far more than the reasoning faculty which a laborious education has developed in man. . . . The sphere of women is home. Such a cultivation as will make a really good wife, sister, or daughter, to educated men, is the thing to be aimed at, and this must be something which recognizes woman . . . as the complement of man, perfect in herself, and intended to hold an entirely different place in the world . . . the health of women cannot stand much evening reading . . . while the relief from the constant strain upon minds ill prepared for hard and regular study as most of them will be, may make the whole difference in the bill of health . . . for one woman who will beat the man out of the sphere he now occupies there will be two who will frighten him out of matrimony.[68]

The last sentence says it well: marriage was considered the most important goal for the woman.

Throughout most of the nineteenth century, the English medical profession purposely banned women from medical schools for several reasons, some of which are illustrated in this quotation from *Lancet*, Britain's major medical publication between 1850 and 1890:

---

[68]Burrows, "Female Education," *Quarterly Review* (1869): 144-45.

> . . . equal advent of both sexes to intellectual culture is simply impossible on the grounds of organic differences by which the sexes are distinguished. . . .

The article contends that women cannot become physicians because the art of healing

> requires the largest range of personal sympathy. . . however uninteresting or poor, or squalid or repulsive [the case might be] . . . their sympathies are contracted within a narrow circle. They bestow them freely upon a few persons; they cannot bestow them, and would be practically unsexed if they could, upon a wide range of patients.[69]

Eventually, women were admitted to medical schools in Britain, as in America, partly because the male discount so long endured was direct, which ironically made it possible to confront, deny, and overcome it. Therein lies the charity of the direct discount, a kindness rarely, if ever, intended.

At the same time women were excluded from education on the basis of mental and physical inferiority, some men were even questioning whether or not women could claim an immortal soul. In a remarkable nineteenth-century booklet, an anonymous "clerk in holy orders" openly attacked female physical, mental, and social skills. He asserted, "I am only trying to prove that woman is an inferior animal to man."[70] He stated that "women have no creative power, inventive genius, or originality. Rather, a creature of instinct and imitation, beautifully adapted to what nature intended."[71] The author claimed that "monkeys and parrots possess more inquisitiveness than women."[72] Finally, the cleric asserted that "respectable women do not try to use logic or reason;

---

[69]n.a., "Mr. Mill on Female Education," *Lancet* 1 (1869): 136.
[70]Anonymous, *Have Women Immortal Souls? The Popular Belief Disputed* (London: Frederich Farrah, n.d.): 5.
[71]*Ibid.*
[72]*Ibid.*, 6.

they merely seek to learn the duty circumstances require of them, and perform it."⁷³ After repeating his arguments that women are here only to serve men, that they possess no higher faculties, and lack the ability to create and invent, he then marshaled these arguments together to argue that women do not possess immortal souls.⁷⁴ Nevertheless, she had been given enough intellect to perform the duties required of her, he claimed. Astonishingly, he also wrote that:

> Whenever we see a man of weak intellect, a helpless, harmless object, who parts his hair in the middle of his head, and who never does or says anything but what he has been taught, we see a man with a feminine mind.⁷⁵

This attack upon women was often echoed in nineteenth-century England, albeit more mildly, by women themselves. An authoress who called herself "a womanly woman" contended that women are inferior to men as created by God, that their nature requires and enables only certain specific roles and duties, that women are frail and delicate physically, and "in constitution" compared to men.⁷⁶ Her general point of view is best summarized by this statement:

> It is quite in harmony with the infinite wisdom of Him who appointed woman as man's companion, that she should be nearly his equal in this respect; it is also in accordance both with His wisdom and justice, that he to whom she is required to submit should be in some degree her superior, and notwithstanding modern teaching, woman has been placed in a position subordinate to man.⁷⁷

---

⁷³*Ibid.*, 7.

⁷⁴*Ibid.*, 8-11.

⁷⁵*Ibid.*, 12.

⁷⁶A Womanly Woman, *Woman's Rights and the Wife at Home* (London: Robert Hardwicke, 1872): 27-30.

⁷⁷*Ibid.*, 14.

Such reflections upon biblical passages continued and reinforced traditional views of incredulity of women.

The idealization of the middle class Victorian woman rendered her as half angel and half idiot, and functioned as follows: Victorian husbands regarded their wives as fragile, delicate, and naive. Her basic role was to tend the home and raise children. The home was no longer a basic unit of production, but rather an isolated garden of beauty, virtue, and sexual innocence, in which to raise children in extended innocence. This was the environment to which the husband could retreat daily from the sordid world of worldly work. Yes, the father led family and servants in worship and prayer daily as master over his little kingdom, but mother was continuously responsible for the nurture and maintenance of this island of virtue. As a cultivator of moral virtue, the Victorian wife was ignorant of her own sexuality, and thereby qualified to raise her children in a state of innocence, protected from the outside world. This idealization of the wife (she is perfect, innocent, delicate, wonderful) and her role allowed the husband the right to seek sexual pleasure elsewhere. In the final analysis, these women were considered too good (idealization) to venture into the world of manufacturing and business, a sordid and dirty world (the indirect discount). This apparent adoration in effect functioned as a discounting of woman's worth outside of the qualities themselves. Such an idealization made it impossible for them to compete with men, and in turn, gave them something to "do" in the meantime. It disabled women psychologically and physically. It also disabled them legally, for outside the home, women suffered the same legal status as lunatics and children.[78]

At home, the Victorian woman was in effect consigned to indolence and inactivity. She had no purposeful activity. She was made to feel useless and disabled. Therefore, she

---

[78]Ronald Fletcher, *The Family and Marriage in Britain* (New York: Pelican, 1980): 103.

welcomed the protective care of her husband.[79] The idle wife became a symbol of the affluence of the Victorian family. With servants to care for the chores, reading, needlepoint, and visiting constituted the activities of the cultured lady. Clothing became an object of considerable attention and expense. She now made her mark in the drawing room, not the factory. To this end, a woman could only be fulfilled through her marriage, since spinsterhood or employment (as in the case of many lower class women) was viewed as sin, or a social error at best, by the middle class. Women were continually reminded that theirs was a higher, nobler, and more sacred mission than employment, work, or political life. This approach, of course, effectively eliminated women from competition with men. If this idealization of women functioned as a gentle, subtle, and effective discounting of the credibility of women, the methods used seem less gracious.

The medical profession consciously or unconsciously participated. Almost without exception, the medical profession viewed middle class women as inherently sick, weak, and prone to illness and disease. This view functioned like a self-fulfilling prophecy, since the very role to which the middle class woman found herself consigned, played into this interpretation. The confinement and boredom of such an existence itself, fostered invalidism and hypochondria, which in turn was confirmed by physicians.[80]

Additionally, her typical clothing brought on actual invalidism, with dresses laced and constricted at the waist (ideally the span of a man's two hands), holding several pounds (up to twenty) of draped material. Sickness then became the major activity of middle class women. In spite of all her reading of health magazines, she was kept ignorant of her real state.

---

[79]Lorna Duffin, "The Conspicuous Consumptive: Woman as an Invalid" in Sara Delamont and Lorna Duffin, *The Nineteenth Century Woman: Her Cultural and Physical World* (London: Barnes and Noble, 1978): 26.

[80]*Ibid.*, 2.

It was not at all uncommon for doctors to trace female sickness to "femininity,"[81] which referred to the female reproductive system, or the attempt of the woman to try anything beyond the clearly defined limits of the female role. Others were also quick to remind women that if they ventured beyond the preordained roles of nature, biology, or tradition, they would come to no good.[82] So whether the woman played the female role in the socially acceptable sense, or tried to escape, she was trapped. Very few women were willing to risk their health by seeking employment or demanding their rights.

Feminine sickness related to the reproductive cycle was treated as pathological by physicians.[83] Menstruation was treated as an affliction to be endured for life, although some Victorians hoped a cure could be discovered. A pregnant woman was viewed as ill and confined to bed. In effect, the womb created diseases in women not suffered by men— hence their different status. The reproductive process was linked to invalidism and used effectively to discount women. Neurasthenia, characterized by depression, irritability, and inability to resist pain, was believed to be due to reproductive strain. Chlorosis, a disease of young single women, characterized by anemia and loss of energy, is now believed to have been the result of lack of activity among girls who were not allowed or encouraged to engage in productive activity. Poor diet, constricted clothing and lack of exercise

---

[81]Ann Douglas-Wood, "The Fashionable Diseases: Women's Complaints and Their Treatment in Nineteenth Century America" in Mary Hartman and Lois Banner, *Clio's Consciousness Raised* (New York: Harper and Row, 1974): 3-4, also reports that American women were also viewed as sick, (in nineteenth-century America) due to the feminine condition.

[82]Hollis, *Women in Public*, 23. Also see Anonymous, *Have Women Immortal Souls?* 14-16, as earlier cited.

[83]Douglas-Wood, "The Fashionable Diseases," *Clio's Consciousness Raised*, 24, cites extensive evidence that in nineteenth century America, a woman's uterus was both the cause and cure of a host of symptoms. It was widely believed that reproductive organs determined physiology which in turn controlled emotions.

could have been correlated with these symptoms, which is most interesting in the light of the fact that both diseases were eliminated or at least redefined by the 1920s when women's roles and status had significantly changed.[84] For these and other ailments, passivity, quiet rest, cessation of mental activity (including reading), and solitude were often prescribed, all of which in turn demonstrated the prevailing male view of women.[85]

Victorian women were kept ignorant generally, but especially of sexuality, specifically their own. Concerning the Victorian woman, Delamont and Duffin report:

> She might visit the poor with tracts and soup, but not know anything of the structure of society which made them poor; she might minister to the sick, but not receive any medical training . . . . She might bear children, but never speak of the rude facts of life.[86]

Women were presumed unable to enjoy sexual arousal and were cautioned if such occurred. Sexual arousal in women was claimed to cause epilepsy, hysteria, and even insanity. To this end, doctors were known to remove the clitoris.[87] Ovaries were also removed for alleged medical reasons. Women were barred from entering the medical profession, partly because it was considered improper for them to study anatomy in male company. Since the idealized woman was considered pure, she was at the same time acclaimed for her

---

[84]Delamont and Duffin, *Nineteenth-Century Woman*, 37-39.

[85]All this reminds us of the American term, the "feminine mystique" popularized by Betty Freidan in the 1963 book by that same title. That mystique encourages women to believe that they will only be fulfilled as housewives and mothers. Many observers have noted the passivity and boredom which so many women experience in these roles, when restrictively defined. So it is said that some housewives get more sleep than they need because they are bored. Or the time required to do housework for any given woman varies inversely with the challenge and other work to which she is committed.

[86]Delamont and Duffin, *Nineteenth Century Woman*, 136.

[87]*Ibid.*, p. 41.

superior moral and spiritual influence. Chastity was her badge of superiority. Dress, speech, and decorum had to conform to the image of chastity. Husbands could keep a mistress or frequent a prostitute for sexual pleasure, something the idealized mother and lady, confined to idleness and inactivity amidst invalidism, by definition could not provide.[88]

It was the task of the Victorian mother to "reproduce" the race, something which did not require sexual pleasure. Queen Victoria herself (who reigned from 1837-1901) set the example, bearing nine children in two decades. While she, by virtue of her royalty and personality, did not exactly fit the image of the idealized Victorian woman, she did allow herself to be dominated by her husband, Albert. Victorian male writers often openly preached to mothers concerning their obligation to England and future generations, as Allen[89] put it, by producing four children. Allen went on to say that if most women did not produce at least four children, "the race must cease to exist."[90] Many shared this view that the woman's glory was her femininity, which meant child-bearing and domestic duties. Civilization depended upon her. She must produce good male stock. Sacrifice of self was the crown of woman's destiny. Allen continues:

> We ought always to bear in mind—men and women alike—that to all time the vast majority of women must be wives and mothers; that on those women who become wives and mothers depends the future of the race; and if either class must be sacrificed to the other, it is the spinsters whose type perishes with them that should be sacrificed to the matrons who carry on the life and qualities of the species . . . . Whatever modification we make must not interfere with that prime necessity. We will not aid or abet

---

[88]*Ibid.*, Chapter Two.

[89]G. Allen, "Plain Words on the Woman Question," *Fortnightly Review* (Oct., 1889), reprinted in *The Popular Science Monthly* (Dec. 1889): 170-81.

[90]*Ibid.*, 178.

women as a sex in rebelling against maternity, or in quarreling with the constitution of the solar system.[91]

So even the stars were used to reinforce the higher calling of motherhood. This was not lost on young middle class Victorian girls who were taught and trained in domestic duties by governesses from an early age. Later, their mothers further trained them to play their ordained role in society by emphasizing music, especially keyboard, languages, the arts (embroidery, varnish work, working with crepe or chenille, making artificial flowers, etc.), and other activities which would express the ideals of Victorian femininity, and which would never threaten the male world.

Conclusion

The Victorian experience just outlined offers ample illustration of the enduring power of the steady and discernible stream of the credulity problem over the centuries. They added the technique of idealization which, in effect, led to the same conclusions and impact as the direct discounts so often seen in pre-Christian Judaism and continued by Tertullian and other Church Fathers.

The continual references to Eve as archetype and presumed progenitor of the credulity problem of women points to the need to critically reexamine the Genesis text. No passage in Scripture is more important than Genesis 1-3 with regards to this issue. For example, every scholar and exegete must decide whether Genesis 3:16 constitutes a God intended pattern, or is it simply a predictable consequence of sin. In short, Eve has suffered at the hands of "male" exegesis which in turn has significantly and negatively transferred to the lives of women over the centuries.

In this light, the resiliency and actual historical and "credible" achievements of women are indeed significant and worth noting. While the task of this chapter has been to identify and trace the origins and development of the

---

[91]*Ibid.*, 181.

credulity issue, the extensive achievement and counter-activity of women does balance the story and should be noted. Men as well as women resisted this trend to discount women in most every era. While the history of the problem is grim, it can be balanced by the contributions of those who believe in and worked for the credibility of women.

Some will conclude that the current trend among some Christian scholars toward a more egalitarian view of women represents an accommodation to the spirit of the times. That could be. Such an accusation can only be seriously entertained if those who truly believe it are willing to admit that their "incredible" view of women can be dismissed by the same argument, i.e., the incredibility of women has endured within the church because of Christian accommodation to the prevailing "worldly" negative cultural view of women.

On balance, it is easy to conclude that men have exercised a self-serving belief that women are incredible (in more than one way) and thus have justified the self-evident and convenient presumption of their own superiority. This issue wears a more subtle and less transparent face in our own time, but it does endure and deserves to be challenged.

Chapter Twenty

GENDER ROLES AND CONSERVATIVE CHURCHES: 1870-1930

Kathy J. Pulley

In the current discussion about women in conservative churches[1] much of the focus has been exegetical and theological, evolving out of an effort to answer the pressing question "What does the Bible say about the role of women?" A growing number of American religious historians and sociologists are also discussing gender issues in conservative churches.

This study makes an inquiry into the roles of women and men in society and in conservative churches from 1870-1930. It will also suggest and demonstrate ways in which societal and religious role expectations were reflected in the Stone-Campbell churches in particular.[2] Finally the study

---

[1] "Conservative churches," as used in this paper, include those churches that are commonly referred to as "Evangelical," "Pentecostal" and "Fundamentalist," as well as such diverse groups as Churches of Christ, Christian Churches-Independent, Mennonites, and Brethren Churches. Although less is known about the separatist traditions, their basic beliefs about gender roles seem so similar to the more mainstream Evangelicals and the Fundamentalists that the group merits inclusion. George Marsden believes that Evangelicals divided into two groups between 1870 and 1920: the theological liberals and conservatives. By the early 1920s a new branch of conservatives had emerged: the militant Fundamentalists. For a full explanation of "Evangelical" and "Fundamentalist," see George M. Marsden, *Understanding Fundamentalism and Evangelicalism* (Grand Rapids: Eerdmans, 1991): 1-61.

[2] The Stone-Campbell churches refer to the religious groups that originated primarily with Alexander Campbell and Barton Stone. Today the Stone-Campbell churches are represented by three different branches:

will explore the close relationship between social changes and theological shifts. Because humans use cultural expressions to communicate meanings, it is necessary to recognize that a given set of theological beliefs cannot be isolated from their cultural environment.

This is a preliminary investigative study. There are limitations to be recognized before beginning. The first is that there is need for greater inclusion of primary sources. Second, most of the data presented reflect a representative sample of the broad-based middle-class perspective. Therefore, what may be true of this sample may not be true of the elite, poor, and minorities; furthermore, regional differences as well as urban and rural differences might also alter the conclusions. Third, a given text reflects the values of that particular author, not necessarily the values of those to whom she/he wrote. That is, some authors may be attempting to *prescribe* roles for women and men more than *describing* them as they were at the time. Fourth, there are few primary sources from women included. Much more needs to be done to recover diaries, journals, and other literature that reflect what women themselves were thinking about gender issues. Fifth, when one is dealing with a

---

the Christian Church, Disciples of Christ; the Christian Church, Independent; and the Churches of Christ. In the nineteenth century, it would appear that most members of this movement referred to themselves as disciples or Christians. Officially the first division in the movement occurred in 1906, when the Churches of Christ separated from the disciples or Christians. Most historians date the second split around 1926-1927, when the more conservative Christian churches separated from the more liberal Christian churches. Therefore when I present information about the movement before 1906, I will refer to them as "Stone-Campbell" churches, in order to represent the entire movement. However, post-1906 information that is known to represent a specific wing of the movement will be so indicated. It should also be noted that there is difficulty in fixing the actual dates of divisions. Therefore, it would not be unusual for there to be individual churches that conformed to one branch in a majority of beliefs, but dissented in some ways. Further studies may reveal that this was very much the case in regard to women's roles.

controversial issue it is difficult not to let one's own values affect the analysis. To a certain extent, it is impossible for any author not to do this; however, an effort must be made to keep such value judgments appropriately balanced.

Why is the period from approximately 1870-1930 so important? American society was experiencing much change and social upheaval. Urbanization, immigration, industrialization, and technological advances were all changing the American landscape. It has been characterized as a time when the masses began to experience "modernity" or the blossoming of the secularization process. An intellectual crisis was also apparent. Darwin's *Origin of the Species* and German higher criticism challenged long-held views about the Bible. Gender roles were affected by the social transitions and were also going through a period of great flux and confusion.

1. *The Victorian Era: Mixed Ideals*

Before delving into the specifics of the period under consideration, it should be recognized that as Tavard[3] has pointed out, Protestantism was never a movement that developed a clear and consistent understanding of what it meant by "Christian womanhood." However, societies do establish gender-specific expectations, and throughout most of the nineteenth century America experienced a period of stability in regard to gender-specific expectations because the Victorian model of womanhood and manhood became a strong influence.

A. *True Womanhood*

In the nineteenth century the public sector was dominated by the man. He was the primary breadwinner. As business and industry boomed he was in the midst of the economic growth and expansion, often working long hours away from home. The Victorian era ascribed the home to the

---

[3]George Tavard, *Woman in Christian Tradition* (Notre Dame: Notre Dame Univ. Press, 1973): 185.

private sector and therefore a part of the feminine domain. Undoubtedly, the woman deserved the title "queen of the home." It was her responsibility to "shape the character of the children, make the home a haven of peace and order, and exert a moral and uplifting influence on men."[4] This was in stark contrast to the predominant classical Christian, as well as the eighteenth-century, view that women were devious, sexually voracious, emotionally unstable, and physically and intellectually inferior.[5] The true woman who was emerging in the nineteenth century was the exemplar of not only the virtue of domesticity but also piety, purity, and submissiveness.[6]

In regard to sexuality the true woman was perceived to be passive with little sexual appetite. Because she was thought to have moral superiority she was instructed to teach sexual morality to her children, especially her sons.[7] In contrast to this was the Victorian man, known for uncontrollable lust. Real manhood included rugged individualism, the ability to drink a lot of alcohol, and a healthy sexual appetite. Both the alcohol and the sex were perceived to be destructive to the home and to woman's trust and innocence. In fact, historians have noted that the Victorian era experienced a rise in prostitution because of the sexual suppression of the period.[8]

---

[4]Steven Mintz and Susan Kellogg, *Domestic Revolutions: A Social History of American Family Life* (New York: Free Press, 1988): xix.

[5]*Ibid.*, 55. For further discussion of gender roles in eighteenth-century America, see Patricia M. Alexander, "The Creation of the American Eve: The Cultural Dialogue on the Nature and Role of Women in Late Eighteenth Century America," *Early American Literature* 9 (1975): 252-266; Ruth H. Block, "American Feminine Ideals in Transition: The Rise of the Moral Mother, 1785-1815," *Feminist Studies* 4 (1978): 101-26.

[6]Barbara Welter, "The Cult of True Womanhood: 1820-1860," *American Quarterly* 18 (1966): 152.

[7]Carroll Smith-Rosenberg, *Disorderly Conduct: Visions of Gender in Victorian America* (New York: Knopf, 1985): 119, 122.

[8]See Steven Marcus, *The Other Victorians: A Study of Sexuality*

Despite the woman's increasing responsibilities in the home, in all her activities the woman was still to act in submission to the man. He was the superior one and her compliance was expected in all situations. One woman's magazine of the day required that "if he is abusive, never retort."[9] In much Victorian literature this True Woman of the middle class was portrayed as not only submissive, domestic, pure and pious, but also a woman with leisure time. Cogan[10] has said of this woman that she ". . . practices devotions at the shrine of fashion and beauty, the former in whose service she distorts her rib cage and internal organs with corsets, the latter for which she becomes a 'delicate flower' and a passive parasite."

B. *Real Womanhood*

The True Woman was not the only image of ideal womanhood that emerged in the nineteenth century. Cogan[11] theorizes that "real womanhood" was very popular and not all women were as mindless and frail as they have been portrayed to be. Specifically, she argues that the literature between 1840 and 1880 points to the existence of the Real Woman ideal. This ideal appealed to some middle-class as well as working-class women. The Real Woman ideal stressed the survival ethic and encouraged such things as the importance of women being physically fit, receiving a well-rounded education, and working outside the home as it was necessary for the family's economic well-being.

Perhaps the Real Woman ideal emerged, at least partially, as an outgrowth of both the ideals of the Revolutionary War era and the Second Great Awakening.

---

and Pornography in Nineteenth Century England (New York: Basic Books, 1975).
 [9]Welter, *American Quarterly* (1966):161.
 [10]Frances B. Cogan, *All American Girl: The Ideal of Real Womanhood in Mid-Nineteenth-Century America* (Athens: Univ. of Georgia, 1989): 3.
 [11]*Ibid.*, 3-26.

As American writers envisioned the republic they desired, they often compared it to marriage. The social union entered into by marriage represented a "loving partnership" as opposed to "patriarchal dominion"; marriage served as a model for how government should relate to its citizens.[12] The Revolutionary War years had also given women opportunities to deal with financial matters, run farms, and get an education (four-fifths were literate by the 1800s, whereas in 1700 four-fifths could not write their names).[13] The women of the 1800s were acknowledged as being capable of shaping their children's values as well as running their own households.

The Second Great Awakening also created new roles for women and led to the development of some new attitudes. The revivals promoted the notion that everyone was equal before God. Charles Finney's "New Measures" encouraged the public participation of women in both churches and in social reform efforts. In Balmer's[14] assessment of this period he comments, "This idea of women as spiritual titans was new in the nineteenth century and peculiar to America."

The evidence in support of Cogan's premise is strong. Despite the obvious differences between the two ideals, they managed to coexist well during the middle years of the nineteenth century. However, by the 1870s the Real Woman was beginning to blend with an even stronger and more independent image of womanhood, that of the New Woman. This shift, along with other social factors, tended to threaten the True Woman ideal. Thus, the advocates of true womanhood, including many religious leaders, tended to idealize if not mythologize the True Woman ideal even more.

---

[12]Jan Lewis, "The Republican Wife: Virtue and Seduction in the Early Republic," *William and Mary Quarterly* 44 (October 1987): 689.

[13]Mintz and Kellogg, *Domestic Revolutions,* 55-6.

[14]Randall Balmer, "American Fundamentalism: The Ideal of Femininity," *Fundamentalism and Gender* (ed. J. S. Hawley; New York: Oxford Univ. Press, 1994): 51.

In many ways the True Woman came to represent everything that society was not; man was still master, Judeo-Christian doctrinal and moral absolutes were held intact, and in the home, feelings were permitted—all this despite the "unfeeling, technological rationality" experienced by the man when he moved and worked in the real (public) world.[15] Out of this nostalgic clinging to a worldview that was passing and giving way to secularization, women and the home were romanticized—some might even say, "placed on a pedestal." These transitions left their mark on religious institutions.

2. Women Modeling Leadership in the Churches

By the second half of the nineteenth century women had taken on significant roles in the leadership of their churches. This is not all that surprising considering that "religion" was part of the work relegated to the private domestic sphere, which belonged to women. The middle-class white male, busy in the competitive public world of business, politics and labor, had little time or interest in religious and moral issues. Barbara Welter[16] has called this phenomenon "the feminization of American religion," and Ann Douglas has given it considerable attention in her book *The Feminization of American Culture*.[17] Such feminization did not fit well

---

[15]Rosemary Radford Ruether, "Home and Work: Women's Roles and the Transformation of Values," *Perspectives on Marriage* (ed. K. Scott and M. Warren; New York: Oxford Univ. Press, 1993): 290; reprint from *Theological Studies* 36 (1975): 647-659.

[16]Barbara Welter, "The Feminization of American Religion: 1800-1860," *Clio's Consciousness Raised: New Perspectives on the History of Women* (ed. M. S. Hartman and L. Banner; New York: Harper and Row, 1974): 137-57.

[17]See Ann Douglas, *The Feminization of American Culture* (New York: Alfred A. Knopf, 1977): 17-117. Douglas asserts that between 1820-75 Protestant institutions went from being an influential power in the development of American culture to an "influential *ad hoc* organization that was dependent upon other cultural institutions for any power that they did maintain" (24). In 1833, Massachusetts churches were denied state support, thus officially ending established religion in America. Disestablishment seemed to be one more indicator of the

with how men defined themselves. Consequently, it was the women who filled the pews, organized and taught the Sunday School classes, and organized and successfully garnered support for foreign and domestic missions. In addition, many held official leadership positions and preached.

A. *The Positive Contributions of Revivalism*

As mentioned earlier, the Second Great Awakening brought many opportunities for women to lead in their respective religious traditions. In fact Dayton[18] has suggested that next to Quakerism "Evangelicalism . . . has given the greatest role to women in the life of the church." He suggests a number of factors that aided women specifically during this period. For instance, in addition to Finney, John Wesley also accepted women as preachers near the end of his life. Two other factors were abolition and the growth of frontier religions.[19] The same arguments used to end slavery could also be used to support women's equal rights, and Gal 3:28 could be used to promote the freedom of both slaves and women. Religion on the frontier was new and varieties of experimentation existed; therefore, experimenting with women in the pulpit suited the new circumstances.

The holiness churches that were founded and grew during this period made extensive use of women—justifying the practice primarily on the NT account of Pentecost. The Spirit had descended on both males and females. Since the

---

victory of competitiveness and individualism on the American scene. Voluntary organizations had to compete for members and each individual could decide for himself or herself whether to belong to a church. Douglas claims that one consequence of this was that the clergymen who stayed in the profession were "cut off from their masculine heritage" and pushed into a feminine position, which was primarily in the private sphere (17-43).

[18]Donald W. Dayton, *Discovering Our Evangelical Heritage* (New York: Harper and Row, 1976): 86.

[19]*Ibid.*, 87, 90.

holiness churches placed such a high value on Christian experiences, women were already well-trained to provide guidance and leadership.

The mid-nineteenth century was also a time in which many conservative religious groups emphasized their strong conviction that the end of the world was near. One practical consequence of this belief was that there was an urgency to convert the whole world to Christ, and whether it was done by a man or a woman was not of primary importance.[20]

B. *Women Who Made a Difference*

Out of the mid-nineteenth century came such prominent women leaders as Frances Willard and Phoebe Palmer from the Methodist tradition, who are as well known today for their social activism as their work within Methodism. Willard fought for temperance among other things. Dayton[21] comments, "It was perhaps Frances Willard rather than more radical feminists who made suffrage palatable to the masses by tying the issue into 'temperance' and 'home protection'." Both Willard and Palmer published books defending women's preaching.[22] In addition, Palmer established a Protestant welfare institution in New York's Five Points district and spent four years in Great Britain in evangelism efforts.

In the Stone-Campbell churches it seems clear that women were involved in a diversity of ministries including serving as deacons as well as preachers.[23] The earliest

---

[20] See Janette Hassey, *No Time For Silence* (Grand Rapids: Zondervan, 1986): 123-43, regarding reasons for leadership positions for women opening up during the nineteenth century.

[21] Dayton, *Discovering an Evangelical Heritage,* 95.

[22] See Frances Willard, *Woman in the Pulpit* (Boston: D. Lothrop, 1888), and Phoebe Palmer, *Promise of the Father* (Boston: H. V. Degan, 1859).

[23] See Tolbert Fanning, "The Church of Christ," *The Religious Historian* 2.12 (1873): 353-61, who acknowledged a concern about the role of women in this article about "The Deaconship." However, the

women known to be ordained, or to serve as official preachers, in the Stone-Campbell churches were Clara Hale Babcock (ordained in 1888) and Sadie McCoy Crank (ordained in 1892). Both were ordained in Illinois and Babcock served churches there and in North Dakota. Crank served churches in Illinois, Arkansas, and Missouri. *The Christian Standard* published both their obituaries revealing the extent of their involvement in the preaching ministry.[24] Babcock's was submitted by her son:

> Clara Celestia Hale was born in Fitchville, O., May 31, 1850, and passed away at her home in Erie, Ill., Dec. 12, 1924. Her life has been one of service to her Master and to her fellow-men. She was ordained to the ministry in 1888, and took up her work in Erie, serving as minister for fifteen years. She worked in Thomson for nine years; LeClaire, twelve years; organized a church at Rapid City; served at Dixon, Ia., nine years, and Ellendale, N.D., three years. She was married to Israel R. Babcock, Aug. 9, 1865. To this union six children were born, five boys and one girl—of which only one son (Ernest) remains. She was taken sick in January, and obliged to give up her work in Dixon. Regaining her strength, she wished once more to be about her Father's business, and the church at Savanna, Ill., called her. She took up the work in July, and was taken sick at the Sunday evening services after administering baptism to two candidates, making

---

theme of Fanning's article was that "deacon" was not to be an official title given to anyone in the church. He gave examples of women acting as deacons in the NT and concluded that women were as legitimately deacons as men. See also C. Leonard Allen, *Distant Voices: Discovering a Forgotten Past for a Changing Church* (Abilene: ACU Press, 1993), for a short summary of differing perspectives on female deacons held by Stone-Campbell leaders.

[24]Mary Ellen Lantzer, "An Examination of the 1892-93 *Christian Standard* Controversy Concerning Women's Preaching." Masters thesis, Emmanuel School of Religion, 1990: 17-26.

1,502 she had buried in baptism. . . . She was the first lady that we can learn of to be ordained by our brethren. Clinton, Ia. Ernest R. Babcock[25]

Crank lived until 1948, and her obituary testifies to her productivity as a minister:

> *Crank, Sarah McCoy*, died Monday, September 20, with funeral services being held at the Greenfield (Mo.) Christian Church, September 23. Officiating ministers were Earl T. Sechler and Virgil Walker. Place of interment was Pennsboro Cemetery. She was born on a farm near Breckenridge, Ill., Aug. 15, 1863, one of twelve children. At the age of 16 she became sole provider for her family, and supported them by teaching. Unable to accept the religious views of her environment she, through much study, accepted the New Testament position. This acceptance led her into Bible school evangelism and finally the Christian ministry. Her early work was done in Adams and Hancock counties, Ill. In 1902 she moved to southwest Missouri and continued her labors. She organized or reorganized 50 Christian churches, led in the building of 18 houses of worship, baptized approximately 7,000 persons, and conducted 1,000 funerals. . . . Her husband preceded her in death in November, 1940.[26]

The outstanding women in these traditions certainly model the Real Woman ideal more than the True Woman. They were committed to the domestic sphere, but they were far from being delicate flowers. They serve as good examples of both the blending and coexisting of the two different ideals in the mid-nineteenth century.

---

[25]*Ibid.*, 21. From Ernest R. Babcock, "Fallen Asleep," *Christian Standard* 61 (July 25, 1925): 1045.

[26]*Ibid.*, 26. From "Fallen Asleep," *Christian Standard* 84 (November 6, 1948): 737.

C. *Missionary Societies*

The pulpit was not the only arena in which women's voices were being heard in conservative churches and the Stone-Campbell churches. Many women took an interest in missions. In 1874 the women in the Stone-Campbell Movement formed their own missionary society and called it the Christian Women's Board of Missions (C.W.B.M.). It was and continues to be a highly successful group; however, from its beginnings it supported the ideal of true womanhood. Nonetheless, by the end of the nineteenth century some women received encouragement to preach from the C.W.B.M.; thus the society did support, both directly and indirectly, greater participation of women in the public sphere.[27]

3. *The Evolution of the New Woman*

In the last part of the nineteenth century America faced increasing challenges, but the period has taken on the name "Progressive Era" because of the nation's commitment to massive reforms aimed at improving social ills, politics, and economic life. More and more women began to move beyond the private realms of the home and church and into the public realms of men. Women's interest and involvement increased in politics, social reform movements, education, business, and all the professions. The rhetoric about woman's changing role and the family also began to increase. The interest in the ideal of the True Woman began to diminish and what emerged was a strong interest in the New Woman, who was at least partially a continuation of Cogan's representation of the Real Woman. Welter[28] suggests that the reason for the demise of true womanhood was that if women were so perfect then it would inevitably follow that they should take more control of the events in the world, because the men were not managing them well. The True

---

[27]Fred A. Bailey, "The Status of Women in the Disciples of Christ Movement, 1865-1900" (Ph.D. diss., Univ. of Tennessee, 1979): 79-121.

[28]Welter, *The Cult of True Womanhood,* 174.

Woman was replaced with the New Woman in many sectors of society.

A. *Characteristics of the New Woman*

Magazine writers of the 1890s characterized the New Woman as one who "rode a bicycle, played tennis or golf, showed six inches of stocking beneath her skirts, and loosened her corsets. She expected to marry and have children, but she wanted a life beyond her home—perhaps even a career."[29] Typically college educated, the New Woman often participated in such reform areas as suffrage and temperance. She exhibited an independence that was new to the public sphere. Another major change was in her attitude toward work outside the home. Many women had worked in the public sector, but such work was defended by the Real Woman on the basis that it was necessary for the family to survive. The New Woman's attitude was that work was personally satisfying and she had a right to pursue a career. It was estimated that 4 million women worked outside the home in 1890, 5.3 million in 1900, and 7.4 million by 1910.[30]

The New Woman's entrance into the public sphere was a model for other women. She defended her right to the public sphere by claiming that it was personally fulfilling. She also believed that she could more effectively influence the culture by direct involvement instead of the indirect involvement she had at home.

B. *Women's Suffrage*

The evolution of the women's suffrage movement is but one example of women's and society's changing attitudes. Mary Wollstonecraft published her now famous treatise *A*

---

[29]Rosalind Rosenberg, *Beyond Separate Spheres: Intellectual Roots of Modern Feminism* (New Haven: Yale Univ. Press, 1982): 54.

[30]James A. Doyle and Michele A. Paludi, *Sex and Gender: The Human Experience* (Dubuque, IA: Wm. C. Brown, 1991): 51.

Vindication of the Rights of Women in 1833; however, few noticed and many who did notice disagreed with her premises. Women like the Grimke sisters, who were actively involved in the abolitionist campaign, attempted to rally male abolitionists around the women's cause, but there was little success. The first Women's Rights Convention in the United Sates was held in 1848, but the Civil War and slavery successfully moved any thought of women's rights to the back burner. In the late 1860s women's organizations began to form—the most nationally prominent was the National Woman Suffrage Association (NWSA) founded by Susan B. Anthony and Elizabeth Cady Stanton. From 1868 forward there was a women's suffrage amendment introduced into Congress every year; however, the right to vote did not come until 1919.

As large numbers of women were in the work force, members of trade unions, active in politics and social reforms, the support for women's right to vote was finally successful. In addition to arguments that women deserved the right to vote, it was also argued that through the power of the vote women could more effectively reform and give moral order to society. The underlying assumption that continued to prevail in certain sectors was that women were morally superior to men; therefore they should vote.

C. *Temperance*

The Temperance Movement was another move into the public arena that served two purposes: women were influencing the public world directly, but many reasoned that they needed to be involved in order to protect their family. The Women's Christian Temperance Union (WCTU) became the largest women's organization in America in the 1890s.[31] It was closely linked to several Protestant denominations, and Frances Willard served as the President from 1879-1898. She was an articulate spokesperson for

---

[31] Glenda Riley, *Inventing the American Woman: A Perspective on Women's History* (Arlington Heights, IL: Harlan Davidson, 1987): 155.

the group and believed that women must do everything they could, whether publicly or privately, to rid society of the evils of alcohol. Although the movement ultimately failed to take alcohol out of the culture, it did succeed in bringing women from diverse backgrounds and ideologies out of the home and into public discourse.

The social changes occurring in society as well as the women's social reform movements raised the consciousness of America's white middle-class women. The Victorian ideal that had stressed women's natural inferiority, frailty and mental weaknesses was severely challenged by the events and shifting assumptions of the era. The domestic scene itself was also being altered. Women were exploring artificial means of birth control, and they were marrying later and having fewer children.

D. *The Battle of the True Woman Versus the New Woman*

The two ideals of womanhood that emerged in the latter part of the century did not share many similarities. Unlike the peaceful coexistence that the True Woman and the Real Woman had maintained in earlier years, the True Woman and the New Woman represented two different perspectives, and as different sectors of society took sides, it was not possible to blend the two. Perhaps an article that appeared in the *Atlantic Monthly* in 1891 best exemplifies the dichotomous positions. The article, entitled "The Steel-Engraving Lady and the Gibson Girl," was a fictional account of the Gibson Girl interviewing the Steel-Engraving Lady. A few excerpts point out the extreme differences between the two images of women:

> Gibson Girl: "When a man approaches, we do not tremble and droop our eyelids, or gaze adoringly while he lays down the law."
> Steel-Engraving Lady: "And does he like this method?"
> Gibson Girl: "Whether he *likes* it or not makes little difference; he is no longer the one whose

pleasure is to be consulted. . . . You see, I've had a liberal education. I can do everything my brothers do; and do it rather better I fancy. I am an athlete and a college graduate, with a wide universal outlook."

Steel-Engraving Lady: " . . . my training merely taught me to make my brother's home a place which he should find a source of pleasure and inspiration. I was taught grace of motion, drilled in a school of manners, made to enter a room properly, and told how to sit gracefully, to modulate my voice, to preside at the table with fitting dignity."

Gibson Girl: "She surely is an extinct type!"[32]

The Gibson Girl was the New Woman and the Steel-Engraving Lady represented the resurrected True Woman. In narrative form, Ticknor suggested that the Gibson Girl was not necessarily a better example of womanhood than the Steel-Engraving Lady. The article reflected doubt about the alleged progress of the era. If the home had been perceived as the last bastion of goodness and morality against the immorality and evils of society and it was on the demise, what was to become of the nation? Overall, growing numbers were uneasy about the social ills facing the country and since women had been the designated keepers of the domestic private sphere what would happen to the virtues associated with that sphere if women abandoned it—such important virtues as beauty, piety, humility and gentleness? Women struggled and found themselves caught in the middle. Some believed that in fact the Women's Movement at the turn of the century was a result of women being forced to live in two irreconcilable worlds: the private woman's world of aesthetics and nurturance, and as a consequence of their increasing education, the man's world of rationalism and personal achievement.[33]

---

[32]Caroline Ticknor, "The Steel-Engraving Lady and the Gibson Girl," *Atlantic Monthly* 88 (July, 1901): 106-8. The Gibson Girl made her first appearances depicting the New Woman in *Life* in the 1890s.

[33]Rosenberg, *Beyond Separate Spheres*, xix.

4. Reactions of Conservative Churches to the New Woman

Despite gains in education, increased interest in careers, the right to vote, greater participation in the leadership of many churches and other freedoms, there was always some resistance to freeing women from their Victorian-based obligations to remain in the private sphere. As in other sectors of society, there was fear about what would happen to the country if the nation's symbol of virtue was altered. One of the most effective resisters to the New Woman, in all her expressions, was conservative Protestantism. In the midst of the social upheaval and the decline of Victorian values, the Fundamentalist Movement was born.

DeBerg[34] develops the thesis that in order to understand the prominence of Fundamentalism as not just intellectual or theological but a *popular* movement, one must recognize that gender and family issues dominated much of the rhetoric of the day, and popular Fundamentalist speakers and Fundamentalist presses contributed to the nationwide discussions about the ills of America. DeBerg argues that although scholars have looked at Fundamentalism from religious and cultural perspectives, there has been little research done on what made the Movement thrive throughout the general population. Its intellectual and theological foundation may have been the authority of the Bible, opposition to evolutionary theory, and social scientific methodology, but what drove its popularity among the masses of Americans? She believes that it was the gender issue. Fundamentalists, in their rhetoric, placed God's stamp of approval on the Victorian True Woman ideal. Thus, they became major spokespersons for the preservation of that particular cultural norm and important resisters to the values of the New Woman. That is, they specifically and strongly resisted the concept that a woman had value in the public life of the community or the society itself. They opposed women's getting the right to vote, getting a higher education, and

---

[34]Betty A. DeBerg, *Ungodly Women: Gender and the First Wave of American Fundamentalism* (Minneapolis: Fortress, 1990): 7.

working outside the home if it were for any other reason than because of family demands. At least in their rhetoric they eliminated the Real Woman ideal as a viable alternative. Basically, they reversed what their evangelical foreparents and the Second Great Awakening had seemed to secure for women.

However, the Fundamentalists were not the first or only religious group who resisted women's movement into the public sphere. In 1869 the northeastern Congregational minister and scholar Horace Bushnell published *Women's Suffrage: Reform Against Nature,* which by its very title suggested his stance on the issue. Bushnell[35] insisted that if women started voting it would lead to them developing heavier brains which would cause the loss of their uniquely feminine purity and morality. In 1920 the Catholic Bishops of Massachusetts voiced their disagreement with women's suffrage by declaring that a woman entering the political sphere was equivalent to becoming a "fallen woman."[36] The motivation of all the groups was to preserve the domestic sphere and the virtues believed to be concentrated there.

A. *Glorification of the Domestic Sphere*

Fundamentalist periodicals loudly proclaimed the continuation of separate spheres for women; the private sphere of home and family was to be the woman's domain and the public sphere was to be the man's. There was little space for any strain of the New Woman. A common theme used to promote the domestic sphere for women was the glorification of motherhood, and the importance of self-sacrifice and suffering. John Milton Williams said:

---

[35]Horace Bushnell, *Women's Suffrage: A Reform Against Nature* (New York: Scribner's Sons, 1869): 136.

[36]Rosemary Radford Ruether, *New Woman New Earth: Sexist Ideologies and Human Liberation* (San Francisco: Harper and Row, 1975): 22, quoting, "Cardinal Gibbons Says Women Should Keep from the Polls," Documents of the Catholic Bishops of Massachusetts against Women Suffrage, 1916-1920, Sophia Smith Collection, Smith College, Northampton, Massachusetts.

> Woman has no call to the ballot-box, but she has a sphere of her own, of amazing responsibility and importance. She is the divinely appointed guardian of the home . . . . She should more fully realize that her position . . . is the holiest, most responsible, and queenlike assigned to mortals; and dismiss all ambition for anything higher, as there is nothing else here so high for mortals.[37]

Regarding self-sacrifice, the woman was encouraged to set aside her own interests in order to aid in the successes of her husband, father, and brothers. Dwight L. Moody[38] offered praise to a woman who had wanted to finish her college education at Wellesley, but opted to drop out and help her brothers go to college after her father had died.

Women were also discouraged from working outside the home. Although they had often worked outside of the home in the nineteenth century, the common view was that such work was economically necessary for the welfare of the family. As the New Woman pushed forward the principle of the inherent value of work for all persons, the Fundamentalist wave balked. In response to the increased number of women in the work force during World War I, the *Watchman-Examiner* proclaimed that The Great War:

> got women involved in . . . industry, and industrialists found them good workers. . . . At the same time it is true that the distinctive function and the supreme mission of woman is home-making. . . . And homes are fundamental, where the home breaks down the Nation breaks down. . . . We shall purchase our shops and our factories at too high a cost if we give our homes for them.[39]

---

[37]DeBerg, *Ungodly Women*, 45. From John Milton Williams, "Woman Suffrage," *BSac* 50 (April 1893): 343.

[38]*Ibid.*, 48. From Dwight L. Moody, "Mary and Martha," *Northfield Echoes* 6, no. 3 (1899): 237.

[39]*Ibid.*, 57. From "Women and the Industrial Situation," *Watchman-Examiner* 8, no. 9 (February 26, 1920): 271-2.

The suffering of Jesus was closely associated with the necessary suffering of the True Woman, because it was assumed that in her suffering the woman was more like Jesus, and she would be especially rewarded for such behavior in the life to come. Talmage[40] commented:

> Some of you will have no rest in this world. . . . But God has a crown for you . . . and whenever you weep a tear He sets another gem in that crown; . . . until . . . God will say, . . . "The crown is done; let her up, that she may wear it." . . . Angel will cry to angel, "Who is she?" and Christ will say, ". . . She is the one that came up out of great tribulation. . . . She suffered with Me on earth, and now we are going to be glorified together."

B. *Remasculinization of the Churches*

Clearly the intention of this rhetoric was to help the nation restore the Victorian mores. But the Fundamentalist Movement wanted more than a return of women to the home. They also wanted the churches, which had been somewhat relegated to the private sphere of society and to women's supervision, to be returned to the men. What was the rhetoric the Fundamentalists used to achieve their goals of returning women to the home and returning the churches to men? Primarily they hammered home two recurring themes: questioning the biblical legitimacy of women speaking and holding leadership positions and/or any positions of authority in churches, and remasculinizing the churches by replacing feminized language and images with language that conveyed athleticism, militarism, and business-like conduct.

Select Scripture (e.g., 1 Cor 14:34-35 and 1 Tim 2:11-15) was used repeatedly to mandate that women had no authority and to require their silence in the public assembly.

---

[40]*Ibid.* From T. DeWitt Talmage, "The Queens of the Home," *Christian Herald and Signs of Our Times* 10 (September 8, 1887): 565.

These biblical injunctions were interpreted to be universal mandates that generally carried precedence over the talents of a given woman or the needs of a given church. Scripture also dealt with "why" women needed to be silent and in subordination to men: one reason was the order of creation and the other was her responsibility in the fall.[41]

Many conservative churches also developed a strong commitment to dispensational premillennialism. Dispensationalists argued in great detail that female subordination was a part of salvation history, and since the end was near social reform efforts were unnecessary, including suffrage.[42]

For the sake of expediency, and because there was a shortage of male preachers, women preachers continued to be tolerated in some fundamentalist churches until money and men were available to replace them. However, in some sermons the rhetoric against women preachers could be quite harsh. One fundamentalist leader in Seattle said of women preachers, "a 'female pulpiteeress' was an 'unscriptural monstrosity' that belongs to 'the zone of ecclesiastical freaks'."[43]

The battle to reclaim the churches for men went far beyond looking at the biblical issues about authority. Another example of efforts to remasculinize the churces is seen in the preaching of Billy Sunday. One of his oft-repeated sermons, "The Fighting Saint," strongly urged the following of a militant and masculine Christianity:

> Jesus Christ intended his church to be militant as well as persuasive. It must fight as well as pray. . . . The prophets all carried the Big Stick. . . . Strong men resist, weaklings compromise. . . . Lord save

---

[41] Barbara Brown Zikmund, "Biblical Arguments and Women's Place in the Church," *The Bible and Social Reform* (ed. E. R. Sandeen; Philadelphia: Fortress, 1982): 97.

[42] Margaret Lamberts Bendroth, *Fundamentalism and Gender: 1875 to the Present* (New Haven: Yale Univ. Press, 1993): 41-53.

[43] DeBerg, *Ungodly Women*, 79.

us from off-handed, flabby-cheeked, brittle-boned, weak-kneed, thin-skinned, pliable, plastic, spineless, effeminate, sissified, three-caret [sic] Christianity.[44]

Another major indicator of the seriousness of the remasculinization efforts was the large number of individuals and churches that took part in the "Men and Religion Forward Movement" of 1911-1912. It is estimated that over one million people attended events involving seventy-six major cities and 1,093 small towns.[45] The Movement was interdenominational and primarily white and middle class. Its purpose was to bring more male members into the churches. It was believed that women had dominated the churches for too long. The churches were too feminized for men. Fred Smith, one of the leaders of the Movement, was once asked by a reporter why he didn't leave church work to the women, and he replied "When a man is drowning, you don't send a lady out to rescue him. You send a great, big, he-man."[46]

The Movement emphasized that manly church work was reforming the urban environment, dealing with social service issues, and applying business methodologies to the church.[47] Although the Movement never achieved its goal of bringing in three million missing men, the rhetoric of the Movement demonstrates well that gender roles were undergoing change and the issue was an extremely important one. The Men and Religion Forward Movement cannot be blamed or credited fully with the remasculinization of the Protestant churches; however, the influence of the Movement did carry on. By the 1920s the interest in identifying churches with

---

[44]*Ibid.*, 89. From Billy Sunday, in "The Fighting Saint," *Trenton (New Jersey) Evening Times* (January 6, 1916): n.p.

[45]Gail Bederman, "'The Women Have Had Charge of the Church Work Long Enough': The Men and Religion Forward Movement of 1911-1912 and the Masculinization of Middle-Class Protestantism," *American Quarterly* 41 (1989): 432.

[46]*Ibid.*, 440. From Arthur H. Gleason, "Going After Souls on a Business Basis," *Collier's* (23 Dec. 1911): 14.

[47]*Ibid.*, 447-453.

Wall Street and the corporate world had succeeded.[48]

The image of Jesus also underwent change during this period. The Jesus portrayed from the Renaissance through the Victorian era was a meek and kind man, with a soft face and hands. The Jesus who emerged in the 1924 best seller *The Man Nobody Knows,* by Bruce Barton, was a modern and powerful man, with muscular arms and a mind for organization and business.[49]

Another subtle way in which the image of Jesus was altered can be seen in the Fundamentalist theme of dispensationalism. Whether consciously or not, Fundamentalists articulated the Christ who returns in glory as a warrior who would conquer and destroy his enemies.

Popular hymns during this period often reflected militant images and expectations as well. "Onward Christian Soldiers" and "The Fight Is On" are just two of many examples. Fundamentalism tended to thrive in its battles against liberalism by using militant metaphors that conveyed that the Fundamentalists were doing battle for the very fundamentals of the Christian faith. Using masculine language, reclaiming the church for men, and returning women to the home were all part of the overall Fundamentalist cause. In order to overcome the social upheavals and to save Christianity, gender roles had to be altered.

5. *The Stance of Stone-Campbell Churches*

A. *Women in Society*

The Stone-Campbell churches represent but one example of a specific tradition that struggled with feminine and masculine roles; however, it should be noted that the overriding issue behind the gender roles in all the conservative churches seemed to be the paradigmatic shift

---

[48]*Ibid.*, 456.
[49]*Ibid.*

that was taking place over the nature and role of the Bible in modern Protestantism.[50] As with other conservative religious groups mentioned above much of the theological debate about women's role revolved around the interpretation and application of the Bible. It is evident from the literature that the Stone-Campbell churches raised many of the same issues that were being raised in other traditions as well as in American society itself. These churches also produced a number of women who became prominent leaders. Many did so through foreign missions, service as deacons, participation in the social reform movements like temperance and suffrage, and others became pulpit ministers. Babcock and Crank are better known than others but in the *1907 Yearbook of the Disciples of Christ* thirty-nine other women preachers were listed.[51]

Like the prominent Fundamentalists of the period, Stone-Campbell leaders expressed high praise for motherhood. Amanda Bostick[52] wrote in the *Gospel Advocate* in 1889 that "it is the one great desire of every good woman to become a mother." Bruner,[53] blaming the

---

[50]Concerning this Movement see Richard T. Hughes, forthcoming volume from Greenwood Press detailing theological and historical developments in the Churches of Christ, James B. North, *Union in Truth: An Interpretive History of the Restoration Movement* (Cincinnati: Standard Publishing, 1994), and D. Newell Williams, *A Case Study of Mainstream Protestantism: The Disciples' Relation to American Culture, 1880-1989* (ed., Grand Rapids: Eerdmans, 1991).

[51]David A. Jones, "The Ordination of Women in the Christian Church: An Examination of the Debate, 1880-1893," *Encounter* 50 (1989): 201, 214, citing *American Home Missionary, Containing the Year Book of the Disciples of Christ, 1907* 13 (Cincinnati: American Christian Missionary Society, 1907): 602. Jones also notes that the female ministers were listed as being from the following states, with the number from each state noted in parentheses: Missouri (10); Illinois (9); Ohio (5); Iowa (5); Oregon (3); Kansas (2); and Colorado, Idaho, Louisiana, North Dakota, Oklahoma, and Texas (1).

[52]Bailey, "Status of Women," 153. From Amanda Bostick, "Eve," *Gospel Advocate* 31 (March 20, 1889): 181.

[53]*Ibid.*, 166. From F. M. Bruner, "Woman's Work in the Church," *Christian-Evangelist* 20 (July 19, 1883): 4.

lack of good preachers on women, said "many women would rather . . . gratify [their] ambitions and vanities than . . . be mothers of [the church's] most worthy and gifted preachers." Barnes[54] articulated the True Woman ideal concisely for the rural woman with his statement that the "most contented little queen of the earth [was] the mistress of a true husband, a cosy [sic] cottage, a hen-coop, a cooking stove, a gentle cow, a good sewing machine, and a baby."

Alexander Campbell himself had valued higher education for both men and women. Bethany College, which he had founded in 1840, had become co-educational in 1880. The initial importance of women's education lay in the belief that it would leave women better equipped to be good mothers, thereby insuring a purer society for the future. Hymn-writer Jessie H. Brown[55] wrote in the *Christian Standard* that women needed an education in order to be good wives and mothers just as much as men needed an education for banking and other professions. "Surely it takes less power of mind and discipline of character to count money than it takes to make a home and to develop souls." Education was endorsed as long as it was for the sake of children and for the betterment of tomorrow's society. This rationale was very much in keeping with the blending of values from both true womanhood and real womanhood.

The reaction of Stone-Campbell churches to temperance and suffrage was somewhat mixed, depending upon what year it was, who was speaking, and from where they were speaking. However, the mixed reaction was also true of other conservative traditions and to some extent the majority of the middle class in society. Suffrage was not promoted in Stone-Campbell churches in the early years of the Movement, and in later years it was seldom promoted if the justification presented for suffrage was that each woman had the right to the ballot. Despite the efforts of Wollstonecraft,

---

[54]*Ibid.*, 171. From Justus M. Barnes, "Woman Her Mission, and Her Education," *Gospel Advocate* 28 (July 21, 1886): 451.

[55]*Ibid.*, 181. From Jessie H. Brown, "The New Womanhood," *Christian Standard* 28 (May 6, 1893): 354.

Anthony, and others, the promotion of the idea of women's equality had not proven to be successful in the middle years of the nineteenth century. However, near the end of the century, the ballot and temperance began to be linked, and a woman's vote was not only a means of defeating alcohol but also a means of protecting the home.[56] Thus, it became expeditious for many to join in support of both suffrage and temperance, and that included many in the Stone-Campbell churches. Both inside and outside of religious circles a woman's getting the right to vote appeared to guarantee that a multitude of social sins associated with drinking would end.

The campaign against alcohol reached a climactic point in the early part of 1874. Women collectively protested and marched against intemperance in front of saloons, hotels, and other public gathering spots. The campaign was especially vigorous in the Ohio River Valley, and in that area female members of Stone-Campbell churches joined with women from other denominations to abolish saloons.[57] From this point forward the Stone-Campbell churches in this region continued to support temperance and the women's right to vote; however, the farther one went away from the Ohio River Valley the less enthusiasm there was.[58]

Neither J. W. McGarvey (Lexington, KY) nor David Lipscomb (Nashville, TN) showed much support for temperance; consequently, temperance did not become an incentive for supporting suffrage. Therefore, the leadership of the Lipscomb branch supported neither cause in spite of the increasing strength of each after the Women's Crusade of 1874.[59] In 1888 the editor of the *Christian Quarterly Review* and a friend of Lipscomb's, E. W. Herndon, commented that "voting women violated the scriptural principle of wives

---

[56]Aileen S. Kraditor, *Ideas of the Woman's Suffrage Movement: 1890-1920* (New York: Columbia Univ. Press, 1965): 43-75.

[57]Bailey, "Status of Women," 217-8.

[58]*Ibid.*, 220.

[59]*Ibid.*, 222.

submitting to their husbands."⁶⁰ However, Zerelda Wallace,⁶¹ prominent in the C.W.B.M., made a comment at the 14th annual Women's Christian Temperance Union convention that seemed to characterize the sentiment of the Stone-Campbell churches that were not directly linked to Lipscomb:

> You intrust your dearest interests to women . . . why fear to trust her with the ballot . . . ? You call her the queen of the home . . . but without the ballot she is an uncrowned queen, and her sceptre but a broken reed.

The differing responses to temperance and suffrage point to at least two underlying presuppositional differences. The first addresses the question of what means should be used to best guard and protect the home. Some advocated an active and public role for women. Others supported a passive, private role. Thus, those who believed that the best approach to securing the home was having women publicly fight for it also supported women's involvement in temperance and suffrage. Many of those individuals were also moving toward a "New Woman" understanding of the feminine ideal. There is little evidence that Stone-Campbell churches were ever among the radical advocates of women's rights; however, there is evidence that when women began to pursue public life, one unintended consequence was that they believed not only that their involvement would help the family but that it also contributed to a more complete democratization of America.

The Lipscomb wing as well as some other groups within the Stone-Campbell churches criticized any movement of women into the public sphere. They ardently supported the more passive approach to preserving the home. They

---

⁶⁰*Ibid.*, 229-30. From E. W. Herndon, "Woman's Suffrage," *Christian Quarterly Review* 7 (October, 1888): 608.

⁶¹*Ibid.*, 237. From Zerelda Wallace, "Fourteenth Annual Convention of the National W. C. T. U.," *The Union Signal* 13 (December 1, 1887): 22.

believed a women could best serve by staying out of public, remaining in the home and nurturing her husband and children in the ways identified with the True Woman ideal.

The second presuppositional difference that the debates over temperance and suffrage pointed to was the question of institutionalizing the church. Members like David Lipscomb opposed all forms of associations with national organizations. Even though he opposed alcohol, he believed that each church should deal with it on its own. He did not believe members should align themselves with institutions or organizations that were humanmade. [62] Many agreed with Lipscomb; consequently, the fact that it was women who organized against alcohol may have made little difference—the problem was organizing any group outside of the local church regardless of whether it was men, women, or both. Unfortunately, an unintended consequence of anti-institutionalism was that it was another blow against women's involvement in the public life of society. Others who shared Lipscomb's conviction were also against the formation of the missionary societies in the preceding years. Therefore, in the Lipscomb branch there were no opportunities for women to organize themselves nationally in support of foreign missions.

B. *Woman's Role in the Church*

Considering that a religious institution was just one institution among several and recognizing that it had been relegated to the private sphere by many anyway, churches were somewhat limited in their control of the direction of societal reforms. However, each religious body could control what happened within its own ecclesiastical borders. The Stone-Campbell churches struggled over women's official responsibilities—whether they should be called deacons, whether they should teach or be missionaries, and a variety of other specific questions. However, the issue that brought home the seriousness of the gender question was that of a woman's preaching and/or being ordained as a

---

[62]Bailey, "Status of Women," 221.

minister. Clearly, this role was and is the most visible and public role a church leader could fulfill. Several church journals carried articles about the roles of women at various times; however, one of the most concentrated and extensive efforts to discuss the female preaching question in the literature of the Stone-Campbell churches was in the *Christian Standard* between the years 1892 and 1893.[63] The following discussion of those articles provides valuable insights into many of the concerns of both clergy and laity.

C. *The Christian Standard Debate*

The rhetoric of the theological differences discussed in these articles focused around three areas: the interpretation of Scripture that directly spoke of women, the perceived biblical status of women in relation to men, and the authority of those in the preaching ministry.

Those who opposed women in the pulpit interpreted 1 Cor 14:34-35 and 1 Tim 2:8-15 as direct universal commands; therefore, they were as applicable to the church of the 1890s as to the church of the first century. John Briney[64] began the two-year discussion by suggesting that the preaching of women could be settled by rational exegesis. He recognized that the practice was "merely in the bud" in 1892, and it needed to be stopped, concluding that "exegesis ought always to lead practice." He went on to argue that 1 Cor 14:34-35 forbade the speaking of women, not only in Corinth but in all other churches.

---

[63]See Lantzer, "*Christian Standard* Controversy Concerning Women's Preaching." I am indebted to Mary Ellen Lantzer for the work that she has done to pull together all the articles that appeared in the *Christian Standard* during the years 1892-1893. Her master's thesis not only provided an excellent overview of the subject and the individuals involved, but it also contains a copy of each article that appeared in its entirety. References to the articles in the *Christian Standard* are excerpted from Lantzer's compilation.

[64]J. B. Briney, "Paul and Women," *Christian Standard* 28 (February 13, 1892): 136.

Morgan P. Hayden, a midwestern minister, agreed with Briney but serves as an example of one who made his defense around the biblical status of women and their authority. He opposed women's being either elders or ministers.[65] In a series of three articles he proposed that to understand the issue, one needed to understand two underlying questions: what is the true relationship of the sexes to each other and what are the biblical principles which apply to these offices of elder and preacher?[66] Based on his brief explanation of Gen 1-2 he concluded much about the nature of women. In regard to their physical being he said, "Generally, women are smaller and weaker than men; . . . for this reason; . . . woman is less able than man to endure the strain of public life. . . ."[67] Morally, women were more vulnerable than men. She was "capable of refinement of wickedness which men never attain."[68] From his understanding of Paul's and Peter's writings, Hayden advocated that women must remain subordinate to men for the welfare of both the society and the church.

In Hayden's second article, he addressed the question of the authority of different offices in the church. Since apostles and prophets were no longer living, the recognized officers were evangelists, pastors, and teachers.[69] After going through a list of the responsibilities of each, he concluded that women did not have a right to any of these offices. Regarding preaching he said that historically female preachers had existed primarily among heretics and in modern times were found in those groups that had,

> erroneous views of the work of the Holy Spirit . . . or which have defective views of the authority of the inspired writing, as the Unitarians. In the one case

---

[65]Lantzer, "*Christian Standard* Controversy," 56.

[66]M. P. Hayden, "Women Pastors and Evangelists," *Christian Standard* 29 (June 10, 1893): 450-1.

[67]*Ibid.*

[68]*Ibid.*

[69]*Ibid.*, 29 (June 17, 1893): 470.

the practice is the result of fanatical delusion . . . in the other, it is the result of rationalistic presumption.[70]

Hayden was incorrect: female preachers existed in far more communities than he suggested, including his own.

Briney and Hayden provide examples of what the opposition argued and how they argued. In the entire series of articles that appeared in the *Christian Standard* in 1892-3, more supported women than not. Over sixty articles altogether were written, by both men and women. They included at least twenty-nine different authors, and twenty-one clearly endorsed women in the pulpit while six were clearly opposed to it.[71]

Two formidable male supporters who advocated greater leadership roles for women were Thomas T. Holton, an Illinois preacher, and George T. Smith, a pioneer missionary to Japan, who wrote from Steubenville, Ohio. Holton began with a look at Scriptures that had women in public roles. In the NT his list included the speaking of Anna (Luke 2:36), the prophesying of Philip's four daughters (Acts 21:9), and Priscilla's teaching (Acts 18:26).[72] He spoke strongly to the fact that descriptive passages that include women in leadership roles must be kept at the front of one's mind when investigating more difficult texts such as 1 Cor 14:34-35 and 1 Tim 2:8-15. He argued that customs regarding female modesty in the first century were what Paul was addressing in the difficult texts noted above. Finally, he argued that in his day it was no longer shameful for a wife to speak, and it implied neither scandal nor insubordination to her husband.[73]

---

[70]*Ibid.*

[71]Lantzer, "*Christian Standard* Controversy," 29, 70. Some articles were submitted under pseudonyms and a few writers did not indicate a position.

[72]T. T. Holton, "The Subjection of Woman," *Christian Standard* 29 (March 11, 1893): 198-9.

[73]*Ibid.*

George T. Smith entered four articles into the debate, all of which appeared in the last half of 1893. In the first article he simply observed that in his lifetime women in churches were not silent; they prayed, taught Sunday school, read Scripture, spoke in the preacher's absence, and participated in other public speaking roles.[74] His second article was concerned with following the principles of Christ instead of being so bound by the letter of the law. He said,

> The letter kills. . . . If he [a preacher] thinks that a woman can keep silence while she sings it only shows that consistency is not one of his mental attributes. . . . Miss Sickler so spoke that one Chinese woman believed and she baptized her. Was this right or was it wrong? If wrong, would that woman be saved? . . . Do you rejoice to know that a dozen of our sisters are doing as Miss Sickler did? If not, would you prefer to let Chinese, Japanese, and Hindoo [sic] women perish without the gospel? Which do you prefer to save—your theory or souls?[75]

In the last articles, he argued that custom had prevailed in Paul's teachings in 1 Cor 14:34-35, the same kind of "customs" that prevailed in various countries, where missionaries were working. However, NT principles should prevail, not the letter of the NT.[76]

One of the more interesting positive perspectives presented that year was that of Clara Babcock herself. How did she defend her own successful preaching ministry? In her article she said that Paul had commended women to teach, that 1 Corinthians and 1 Timothy had been misinterpreted, and that it was only after the Fall that women

---

[74]George T. Smith, "Does Woman Keep Silence in the Churches?" *Christian Standard* 29 (August 12, 1893): 638.

[75]George T. Smith, "No Man Wishes Woman to Keep Silence in the Churches," *Christian Standard* (October 7, 1893): 798-9.

[76]George T. Smith, "Condition of Woman in Paul's Day," (December 2, 1893): 958.

had lost their equal status with men, but in Christ the equal status had been restored. She also took on those who would degrade women by claiming them to be inferior to men or too weak by nature to carry out the responsibilities of a preacher. In response to a Baptist scholar's comment that suggested a woman's brain was smaller than a man's, thus she was inferior, Babcock[77] said, "It never dawned upon my mind that it was *quantity*, but *quality* that was needed. If this is true reasoning, then we should expect great things from the elephant." In another paragraph, addressed to those who doubted women's physical strength to minister, and doubted her own commitment to her home and family she said,

> I have stood in ice water, and baptized many at once, in and out, any time the occasion demanded, mid summer's heat and winter's cold . . . have never taken cold or been hoarse in work; am forty-three years old, the mother of six children, and every living relative of mine has been brought to faith and obedience.[78]

The articles in the *Christian Standard* did not represent everyone and all perspectives, nor were they exegetically or theologically substantive (and they were never intended to be); however, they do provide the reader with an inside look at the seriousness of the issue and the difficulty of resolving it, even within the ecclesiastical walls. In the midst of the precarious social changes occurring in society regarding gender roles this particular group was not isolated from either society or the rhetoric of the Fundamentalist Movement.

The Stone-Campbell churches remained divided over the issue into the twentieth century. The more liberal Christian Churches, Disciples of Christ, continued to

---

[77]Clara C. Babcock, "Woman in the Pulpit," *Christian Standard* 28 (June 4, 1892): 482.
[78]*Ibid.*

support women in leadership positions. As mentioned earlier, the *1907 Yearbook of the Disciples of Christ* listed forty-one female preachers and in 1911 the women were no longer listed separate from the male preachers.[79] There is also evidence that some among the more liberal members advocated women preachers as a women's rights issue. Persis Christian, a president of the Christian Woman's Board of Mission, is one such example. In an article in the *Christian Standard* during the ordination debate she thought America lagged behind other societies in practicing human rights, and she backed up her argument with a quotation from the Swede E. G. Geiger:[80] "political rights can not be denied woman, even if she voluntarily resigns them for higher duties." As the twentieth century progressed the more liberal Disciples tended to blend their ideas with the ideas of mainstream Protestantism.

The more conservative churches, (known as the Christian Churches, Independent, after a split from the Disciples in 1927) and those who were closely connected to the Lipscomb branch (Churches of Christ) supported the notion that women needed to remain silent. Lipscomb himself thought that "women must teach their own children; must visit the sick, the afflicted, the needy, and, in these quiet ministrations, teach the word of the truth."[81] Further investigation is needed, but there seems to be little evidence to support the idea that women participated in preaching, or in any public leadership roles in this branch, after they split from the larger group and officially became the Churches of Christ in 1906. The conservative Christian Churches and the Churches of Christ seemed to parallel the ideas of the Fundamentalist Movement in regard to women's roles in both society and the church. In both secular and sacred matters the True Woman seemed to be the dominate ideal.

---

[79]Jones, *Encounter* (1989): 201.

[80]Persis L. Christian, "Woman's Interest," *Christian Standard* 28 (April 9, 1892): 324.

[81]Fred Bailey, "Woman's Superiority in Disciple Thought, 1865-1900," *ResQ* 23 (1980): 156-7. From David Lipscomb, "Woman's Work," *Gospel Advocate* 34 (December 1, 1892): 756-7.

6. The Withdrawal of Women from the Public Sphere

By the 1920s the more liberal Disciples churches continued to approve public roles for women, including preaching. The more conservative Christian churches and Churches of Christ aligned with the Fundamentalist position and continued to exclude women from leadership and the public domain.

A. Religious Factors

In Fundamentalist churches there were many factors that could explain the decline of women in leadership positions. Hassey suggests that as the Fundamentalists' interest in reform movements and social action declined so did their support of women in public ministry.[82] This shift occurred in secular society as well. Once women were granted the right to vote, interest in other women's issues diminished.

The 1920s was the decade of the Modernist-Fundamentalist controversy, and the Fundamentalists adamantly and passionately defended inerrancy and a literal interpretation of the Bible. Hassey points out that a by-product of the greater emphasis on inerrancy was the rejection of women in public ministry and leadership.[83] Whereas earlier conservatives had promoted women in leadership because the end was near, there was less urgency about the end times by the 1920s; consequently, Fundamentalists thought there was less need for all church members to be involved in public roles. However, there remained a strong contingent of dispensational premillennialists and many among them became even more opposed to women in public roles in the 1920s. For this group the social liberation of women meant that the "brazen" actions they witnessed in society were just one more sign that the last days were near.[84]

---

[82]Hassey, *No Time for Silence*, 138.
[83]*Ibid.*, 143.
[84]Bendroth, *Fundamentalism and Gender*, 51.

Additional church-related factors are noted by J. R. Flora. In his study of the Brethren Church he found that between 1890 and 1920 forty women had been ordained, after 1920 the figures declined, and by the 1950s there were not any women listed.[85] He suggests that men's taking greater leadership in the church was one factor. He also notes that as churches grew after World War I many small churches merged into large churches and women were not promoted into the pulpits of the larger organized churches.[86] Flora suggests that this same pattern is true of several other free church groups. Whether looking at Fundamentalism generally or in the context of a specific Fundamentalist-type denomination (or sect), the conclusion seems to be the same: women who had been in leadership positions were relegated to the private sphere.

B. *Cultural Factors*

1. *Institutional Influences.* However, Fundamentalists did not make these moves toward greater restriction of women's public roles in a vacuum. Once again they were mirroring similar trends in some important sectors of the culture. For example, such cultural strongholds as medicine, education, and sports also wanted to keep out women. Medical schools began to limit the numbers of women they would allow, higher education often encouraged women to go into home economics tracks in order to be better equipped to run their homes, and competitive male sports sprang up all over the country—"providing 'warrior' activities for even refined, educated men."[87]

2. *The Radical Ideals of Womanhood.* Socially, the New Woman who had emerged gave birth to a variety of liberating possibilities for women. The most radical images to emerge were those of the flapper and the mannish lesbian.

---

[85] J. R. Flora, "Ordination of Women in the Brethren Church: A Case Study from the Anabaptist-Pietist Tradition," *JETS* 30 (1987): 432.

[86] *Ibid.*, 439.

[87] *Ibid.*, 150-51.

The flapper with her modern ways of smoking, drinking, dancing, bobbed hair and short skirts came to symbolize the New Woman for the new age. Often, the New Woman, whether flapper or not, was blamed for the social upheaval and moral decay of this tumultuous period.[88] The mannish lesbian image was one in which a woman valued female friendships more than heterosexual relations. She demanded all the rights and powers of a man and wanted to live and act as if she were a man. Smith-Rosenberg comments that:

> To male physicians, politicians, even modernist writers, the New Woman/Mannish Lesbian symbolized disorder in a world gone mad. To feminists she underscored the irrationality and 'unnaturalness' of a world ordered around male definitions of gender and sexuality.[89]

Neither the flapper nor the mannish lesbian typified American womanhood, but they did draw attention. Consequently, the New Woman ideal was suspect, and this became one more factor that drove many women back into the mythologized True Woman sphere.

By the end of the 1920s women's influence had been greatly reduced in public leadership roles in both fundamentalist churches and in certain sectors of the culture itself. In fact, the Fundamentalist rhetoric of the 1920s focused negatively on the intellectual weakness and psychological vulnerability of women.[90]

However, one could argue that not all was lost during this period. All women got the right to vote, even in the midst of strong conservative church opposition, and the ballot has continued to affect their status in society. Women continued to receive higher education, even if there were barriers in some schools and in some fields. Doors of

---

[88]DeBerg, *Ungodly Women,* 99-117.

[89]Smith-Rosenberg, *Disorderly Conduct,* 40-1, whose essays treat how men and women broke away from sex roles of the Victorian era.

[90]Bendroth, *Fundamentalism and Gender,* 63.

opportunity might have opened slowly, but those in society who had wanted to close such doors altogether were not successful. Despite the efforts of Fundamentalist churches to hang on to what had become a mythical, or exaggerated image of the virtues of the True Woman, they controlled only the ecclesiastical realm. In the public world of politics, education, employment and social reform, they had lost their leverage to argue logically that women, from creation, were inherently inferior and weaker than men. Women's success in the public arena had simply proven that not to be the case.

7. *Social Change and Theological Shifts*

A. *Reassessing the Landscape*

Clearly, society's struggle with gender issues was shared by America's Protestant churches. The Second Great Awakening and the drive toward greater equality for all in the New Republic combined to provide the nation with a powerful impetus for more public participation by women in both church and state affairs. The popular culture and evangelical theology seemed to be mutually guiding, legitimating and supporting each other. Even though the ideals of the True Woman and the Real Woman were very different they lived together somewhat harmoniously.

The period from 1870-1930 represents struggle. Conservative churches began to have second thoughts about the "progress" of the era. Had modern science, industrialization, the politics of human rights, and higher criticism brought the good that was hoped for? If these changes in the public sphere were doubted as being in men's best interest, what would happen to the nation if women entered that public sphere as well? Certainly the fears and anxieties produced by the uncertainties of the period help to explain the interest in keeping women in the domestic sphere.

Again, churches were not alone in this desire. By the end of the 1920s certain sectors of society also had succeeded in keeping women less involved and out of public leadership positions. But the forces for greater equality for women and greater inclusion in public life were also strong. Great numbers of Protestant churches, including Evangelical churches, supported the moves toward greater equality for women. Even if they did not have increasing leadership roles and authority, they were increasingly "in public."

What seems apparent is that there was no longer one Protestant position that seemed to represent both the churches and the populus, as there had been during the years of nineteenth-century revivalism. On one end of the Protestant continuum were the denominations that accommodated their theology to meet the modern cultural demands. On the other end were the Fundamentalists who were hostile to the culture—certainly different from their revivalist foreparents. From the perspective of the greater society, what had emerged was a conflict between secularizing forces and counter-secularizing forces. Fundamentalists were correct to fight the loss of religious language and symbols in the public sphere. But, were Fundamentalists right when they claimed that they were standing above culture and that their views about women represented God's views? Or, were they attempting to be the major spokespersons for the preservation of the Victorian True Woman, who had become idealized far beyond her potential for purity, piety, submissiveness, and domesticity? Who was God's woman: the True, the Real, the New, or a combination? If the question about women's role had not become a part of the bigger concern about the ills of the nation, the Modernist-Fundamentalist controversy, and the battle for the Bible, how might the theological arguments have been different?

B. *Culture and Theology: Is a Separation Possible?*

Cultural factors were always a part of theological developments. Throughout the period 1870-1930, religious attitudes toward women were affected by changing cultural values. The theology of women's role in either the society or the church was never driven by theology alone; religious groups who resisted the cultural changes in women's roles were always supported in their resistance by other important sectors of society.

The debates about how much culture influences theology have been extensive. Part of the difficulty of separating culture and theology is that all theology has been written within a specific cultural context. Therefore, it is easy to say that the Bible is authoritative, but it is much more difficult to peel away the cultural trappings of both ancient and modern times in order to discern universal biblical truth. Even hermeneutics have their own culture-based histories. To use such methods as a literal interpretation of certain texts, or to follow the mandate of "speaking where the Bible speaks and being silent where the Bible is silent," may or may not lead one to the clearest understanding of biblical principles. They also are culturally conditioned.

Throughout the history of Western civilization most of the literature portrays women in less than positive ways. They are almost always presented as seductive, unclean, inferior, and unequal. Consequently, one has to ask whether these characteristics are inherent to the female sex or whether they have tended to be promoted for cultural reasons? Schmidt[91] provides numerous examples of how cultural issues have influenced theological reasoning about the character of women.

One example that is especially relevant is that of women's silence in the public sphere. Schmidt raises the question of why it is easier to keep women silent than to keep them in a veil. He argues that the wearing of a veil would be too much of a cultural anachronism in the modern western world. It has not been practiced for hundreds of years. However, he suggests that the public speaking of women to a mixed audience is a relatively new development.[92] In the United States the practice seems to have started in the mid-1800s. Before Susan B. Anthony spoke at the New York State Teacher's Convention in 1853, the male directors of the convention had to deliberate the matter.

---

[91]Alvin John Schmidt, *Veiled and Silenced: How Culture Shaped Sexist Theology* (Macon, GA: Mercer Univ. Press, 1990).
[92]*Ibid.*, 37.

Approval was finally granted, but following her speech Anthony overheard women commenting, "'Did you ever see such a disgraceful performance?' 'I was never so ashamed of my sex'."[93]

There is no well-defined course for stripping away cultural influences in any given period of human history. Perhaps the most significant means of getting to a "pure" and "Holy" perspective on women's role, is for the Christian to ask "How did Jesus visualize womanhood?"

---

[93]Una Stannard, *Mrs Man* (San Francisco: Germain Books, 1977): 58.

Chapter Twenty-one

THE CULT OF TRUE WOMANHOOD AND THE DISCIPLE PATH TO FEMALE PREACHING

Fred Arthur Bailey

In 1888, Clara C. Babcock quietly began her ministry as the first female evangelist among the Disciples of Christ, preaching for several small Illinois congregations. Four years later, she announced her accomplishment in the *Christian Standard* boasting that she had personally baptized 300 converts in all types of weather from winter's icy winds to summer's oppressive heat. To those brethren who deemed such activities inappropriate for her sex, she retorted that woman's unique characteristics gave her the right to preach. "For centuries," she argued, "woman with her magnetic influence, her tender pleadings, as well as her intuitive powers" had been denied the "rostrum and pulpit." Woman's natural vocation was motherhood, she acknowledged, pointing with pride to her six children who lived in a "happy home [where] each member [was] willing to sacrifice some . . . for the salvation of souls and the glory to God." Babcock, who eventually baptized over 1500 individuals, was no feminist.[1] She, along with other Disciples favorable to women preaching, defined woman's role within the traditional nineteenth century images of the home and the church.

---

[1]Clara C. Babcock, "From the Field," *Christian Standard* 28 (January 2, 1892): 21; Clara C. Babcock, "Woman in the Pulpit," *Christian Standard* 28 (June 4, 1892): 482; Ernest R. Babcock, "Babcock," *Christian Standard* 60 (July 25, 1925): 1045; B. H. Cleaver, "Mrs. C. C. Babcock," *Christian-Evangelist* 62 (December 31, 1925): 1703.

Babcock's acceptance by liberal elements of the Disciples of Christ marked the culmination of a debate which spanned the century's last quarter and fueled their schism with more conservative brethren. While both pro- and anti-women preaching Disciples quoted Scriptures appropriate to their positions, in large measure they drew their lines based upon their cultural perception of woman's role in society.[2] Both sides rejected the concept of feminism—the belief that men and women are socially and politically equal—seeing in this the seeds of society's destruction. In fact, virtually all Disciples were social conservatives who looked upon the female sex as the natural preservers of tradition, a concept embodied in the nineteenth century idea of the "cult of true womanhood." This image grew out of the social ferment of early nineteenth century America and reached its greatest acceptance in the decades following the Civil War. As men engaged in the process of nation and economy building, they abandoned to women the tradition-maintaining institutions of the home and the church. Men became the doers, the builders, and, all too often, the destroyers; women were instructed to preserve, to uplift, and to heal. Religious literature, ladies' magazines, and popular gift books combined to assure woman that when properly submissive to her father, her husband or her clergyman, her influence would transcend society and create a better world. By remaining passively in her domestic sphere and there pleasing her spouse and training her children, woman preserved the moral virtues of society. The essential elements of the cult of true womanhood emphasized the female sex's status in terms of purity, piety, and submissiveness.[3]

In the closing decades of the nineteenth century, comfortable middle class women employed the logic of home-protecting to justify their participation in temperance

---

[2]Fred Arthur Bailey, "The Status of Women in the Disciples of Christ Movement, 1865-1900," (Ph.D. Dissertation, The Univ. of Tennessee, 1979): 35-78.

[3]Barbara Welter, "The Cult of True Womanhood," *American Quarterly* 18 (1966): 151-54.

reforms and extra-congregational missionary societies. If by the reasoning of true womanhood women were by nature home-preservers, then they should have the power— often defined as the ballot—to protect their homes from the saloons, the gambling den, and the bordello. By the same logic, if women were naturally more moral and more religious than men, then they should have the right to express their piety in the pulpit. Liberal Disciples gradually accepted this thinking, allowed their sisters to participate in missionary societies, and through this means eventually saw the logic of women preaching.

Founded in 1874, the Christian Woman's Board of Missions (CWBM) became the vehicle by which the Disciples of Christ accepted a larger church and social role for their sisters. By participating in this society, women learned to organize missions, gained the courage to speak out on church issues, and eventually secured the right of pulpit preaching. At century's end, a number of prominent male and female church leaders were praising the CWBM for its educational influence upon women. In her discussion of the "new womanhood," Ella M. Huffman insisted that "the greatest spiritual development and extension of the sphere of woman's work in the [Christian] church began with the organization of our beloved C.W.B.M."[4] James H. Garrison rejoiced that through this society Disciple women had gained much greater insight as to their capabilities. Addressing a class of young women studying to be "pastoral helpers," he proclaimed that the CWBM's tremendous missionary success was "eclipsed by the greater reflex good which has come to our sisterhood, to our homes, and to our churches."[5]

Jessie H. Brown, a popular CWBM official, stated most clearly its influence upon woman's status. She believed that

---

[4]Ella M. Huffman, "The Higher Conquest," *Christian Oricle* 10 (November 9, 1893): 708.

[5]James H. Garrison, Annual Address to Graduates of the School of Pastoral Helpers [ca. 1900], typescript, Garrison Papers, Disciples of Christ Historical Society.

a wise observer would not look to the schools, churches, and missions created by the organization as its most important achievement. Instead, she averred, "he would point . . . to what it has done as an educator . . . for the individual women whom it has enlisted in its work." She went on to observe that the CWBM uplifted the social nature of women by teaching them how to organize to accomplish specific projects; it uplifted the intellectual side of women by encouragaing them to learn about the world; and it uplifted the spiritual side of women by enabling them to engage in mission work. Jessie Brown concluded her remarks by declaring that "whatever educates women thus, educates the entire church."[6]

This assessment was not shared by church conservatives. For essentially theological reasons, a minority voice within the Disciples movement questioned all missionary societies. To them, a female-dominated missionary society simply compounded the heresy. Speaking the mind of this element, David Lipscomb propounded: "Every man who encourages [the Christian Woman's Board of Missions] works against God, the church, true manhood itself."[7] A vast intellectual chasm separated the *Gospel Advocate* editor from his more liberal brethren. Their radically divergent points of view evolved out of church problems indigenous to the Disciples of Christ and as well as out of the larger cultural question of woman's social status.

The CWBM and its importance to woman's changing position in society must be viewed against the background of the missionary controversy within the Disciple movement. Until the end of the 1830s, Alexander Campbell's restoration plea called for a rejection of all man-made religious creeds and extra-congregational organizations. He and his followers affirmed that the first century church practiced radical congregational autonomy. However, by 1842

---

[6]Jessie H. Brown, "The CWBM as an Educator," *Missionary Tidings* 10 (December 1892): 28.

[7]David Lipscomb, "Woman and Her Work," *Gospel Advocate* 34 (October 13, 1892): 644.

Campbell's theology had evolved to the point that he was willing to accept limited cooperation between individual churches, which eventually led to the creation of the American Christian Missionary Society (ACMS) in 1849. Although it sponsored a few overseas evangelists, the remonstrance of church conservatives kept it from prospering until well after the Civil War. [8]

Prior to 1860, conservative Disciples objected to extra-congregational societies for essentially three reasons: 1) the conviction that human ecclesiastical organizations were unauthorized in the Scriptures; 2) the potential danger that societies might infringe upon local congregational independence; and 3) the anxiety that such an organization might inject politics into this religious movement. The last argument was of particular importance to southern Disciples who feared abolitionist sympathies among their northern brethren. Antebellum conservatives developed sufficient strength to cripple but never to kill the ACMS. In fact, some of those who would most strongly oppose the society after the Civil War supported it prior to 1861.[9] A youthful David Lipscomb, for example, served as the corresponding secretary for a small district convention in Tennessee.[10]

Events associated with the Civil War changed conservative fears of the missionary society into adamant opposition. During the years of conflict, anti-slavery Disciples urged the annual convention of the American Christian Missionary Society to pass a resolution supporting the northern war effort. Emboldened by their pleas, the society in 1863 championed the Union cause in its conflict with "armed traitors [attempting] to overthrow our

---

[8] Bill J. Humble, "The Missionary Society Controversy in the Restoration Movement (1823-1875)," (Ph.D. dissertation, State Univ. of Iowa, 1964): *passim*.

[9] Humble, "The Missionary Society Controversy," 162-64, 177-89. James D. Murch, *Christians Only: A History of the Restoration Movement* (Cincinnati: Standard, 1962): 186.

[10] Earl I. West, *The Life and Times of David Lipscomb* (Henderson, TN: Religious Book Service, 1954): 60-61.

government." The passage of this political resolution gave conservatives from Ohio to Tennessee an issue with which to attack the society. When the war ended, southern Disciples followed the lead of the church's conservatives in not supporting the ACMS.[11]

The decade from 1865 to 1874 was particularly grim for the organization. Faced with widespread church apathy toward its work, the society was unable to adequately support foreign missions. In 1869, the ACMS reorganized around what was called the "Louisville Plan" in hopes of raising funds more efficiently. It was a dismal failure. In the decade prior to this, the society had raised an average of $10,000 annually. For the next ten years it received only about $4,000 per year.[12] Given this bleak situation, pro-society Disciples began to look to their sisters with the hope that they might revitalize the church's lagging missionary spirit.

As early as 1869, these Disciples were impressed with the success of the female missionary organizations among the Baptists, Presbyterians, and Methodists. That year, Isaac Errett published one of the earliest pleas for an expanded role for Disciple women. "An immense proportion of the church's power for good is lost," he suggested, "by the false public sentiment which forbids the active employment of woman's gift in the service of God." He then reprinted a lengthy article demonstrating the good work of Methodist church women in Philadelphia.[13]

Although Errett was one of the more forceful supporters of the ACMS, the initial push to secure a woman's missionary society was primarily the work of Thomas Munnell (1823-1898). An Ohio Disciple, he was the

---

[11]Humble, "Missionary Society Controversy," 211-18.

[12]Humble, "Missionary Society Controversy," 281-94; Grant K. Lewis, *The American Christian Missionary Society and the Disciples of Christ* (St. Louis: Christian Board of Missions, 1937): 204.

[13]Isaac Errett, "Woman's Work," *Christian Standard* 4 (March 6, 1869): 76.

corresponding secretary for the American Christian Missionary Society from 1869 to 1877. He placed the question of woman's missionary opportunities before the society and his spade work prepared the Disciples to accept the creation of the Christian Woman's Board of Missions in 1874. Nonetheless, Munnell's efforts demonstrate the limited concept that he and other leaders of the Christian Church had concerning woman's ability and social status in the early 1870s.

In October, 1869, Munnell published his perception of woman's work in the church, an idea colored by the rationale of true womanhood. He believed strongly that mankind was divided into hemispheres and that the half occupied by women mandated modesty and deference. In his mind, the church, the government, and "any man fit to be a husband" had little use for any "strong-minded woman" clamoring for masculine rights and privileges. The "distinction marked out, both by nature and revelation," Munnell pontificated, "involves distinctive duties for each [sex], among which voting, holding political and military offices, public preaching, and baptizing certainly do not belong to women." Nonetheless, this Disciple envisioned a positive church posture for his sisters. Woman could make her influence felt in "Sunday schools, social meetings, Bible class," and, in a forthright manner, she could go from door to door, "raising money for missionary and other benevolent objects."[14]

Munnell expounded upon the missionary opportunities open to the female sex. He suggested that "if we desire modern [examples] of what woman can do in the Gospel of Christ, look at the missionary women in the Orient." Oriental custom prevented strange males from entering their homes, but women were not prohibited. The result was a productive work among the natives. Munnell pointed out that Protestant women taught religion to eastern families, read the Scriptures to them, distributed tracts, and instructed

---

[14]Thomas Munnell, "Woman's Work in the Church," *Christian Quarterly* 1 (October, 1869): 521 22.

"the heathen women in the knowledge of God." Believing that women out numbered men two to one in this mission effort, he finished his discourse by asking when the Christian Church would discover woman's innate power and invite her "into these many fields of usefulness."[15]

At the urging of Munnell, a "Committee on the Cooperation of Women in the Missionary Work" presented a favorable resolution at the ACMS convention in Indianapolis in October, 1870.[16] Noting that the "Woman's Board of Missions in certain denominations" had "set a noble example to our sisters," the committee admonished that they "become missionaries at home and abroad." Furthermore, the resolution suggested that Disciple women ought to dispense with "costly apparel, release themselves from the slavery of fashion," and use their financial resources for the expansion of the gospel." The memorial closed with a panegyric to true womanhood: "If men rule the world, the women rule the men; and if both shall feel their own personal responsibility to Christ, the desert will blossom the rose, and all flesh will see the salvation of God." The resolution was adopted by a unanimous vote.[17] Nonetheless, the novelty of this proposal was evident. The Indianapolis *Daily Sentinel* reported that the "document provoked considerable merriment and many humorous remarks from Thomas Munnell, of Ohio; George Campbell of Illinois; [and] James Smiley of Indiana."[18] Munnell and his fellow male Disciples could only accept a female missionary society if they indicated a man's superiority over woman through a satire of woman's church role.

Despite the levity associated with the memorial, Munnell made a good faith effort to develop a woman's missionary

---

[15]*Ibid.*, 520, 523.

[16]Thomas Munnell, "Those Women Who Labor With Me in the Gospel," *Christian Standard* 5 (October 8, 1870): 322.

[17]*Proceedings of the Twenty-Second Anniversary Meeting of the American Christian Missionary Society, Held in Indianapolis, Indiana, October 18, 19 and 20, 1870* (Cincinnati: Basworth, Chase, 1870): 23.

[18]Indianapolis *Daily Sentinel*, October 21, 1870.

organization. In December, he published an appeal to the sisters encouraging them to establish congregational societies and suggesting how district and state conventions could be created. In January, 1871, he corresponded with Miss Z. E. Wood imploring her to work as a paid organizer in this project. However, little came of either effort.[19]

The question of beginning a woman's missionary society came before the ACMS convention again the following year. Although this meeting failed to come any closer to establishing such a society for the sisters, the speeches favoring it give some insight to woman's image among the liberal members of this religious movement. Without exception each paid tribute to true womanhood. James Challen believed woman's "peculiarly fitting place was in the church." W. C. Dawson expressed thanks for the "pure, sweet devoted spirits, the representatives of angels here on earth who had worked with him." With faith that woman possessed "more fervor of spirit and deeper devotion of piety than man," J. J. Moss insisted "that she might wake up the dull souls of the brethren." He personally believed that women could preach, but he condemned the concept that they ought to be in politics. Moss regarded female suffrage "as infidelity to God and to the Bible." J. B. New urged young preachers to select a good missionary woman for a wife, but also to "not forget that she should be a good housekeeper." Inevitably, the discussion closed with a male evangelist eulogizing his mother. B.U. Watkins recalled that his father's powerful prayers never moved him. But when he knelt beside his mother's chair and she prayed over him, it was as if a plow had lacerated "his heart, making him feel how wicked a man he had been."[20]

---

[19]Thomas Munnell, "Christian Missions—Woman's Work," *American Christian Review* 13 (December 13, 1870): 397; *idem*, "Christian Missions—Woman's Work," *Evangelist 5* (December 23, 1870): 10; *idem*, "Christian Missions—Woman's Work," *Christian Standard* 6 (January 21, 1871): 19; *idem*, "The Tap-root of the CWBM," *Christian-Evangelist* 25 (June 23, 1898): 397.

[20]*Report on the Proceedings of the Twenty-Third Anniversary Meeting of the General Missionary Convention Held in Cincinnati,*

Pro-society, ecumenical Disciples were on record favoring a woman's missionary organization. Doubtless had they known in the early 1870s the changes which the Christian Woman's Board of Missions would bring for their sisters, these males would have dampened their ardor. However, the altering of woman's status through the agency of the CWBM was an evolutionary process. By the time the Disciple sisters emerged out of the passive role of remaining in the home to the active role of preaching the gospel, most of their liberal brethren accepted as natural the transformation. With rare exception, only the anti-society, evangelistic churchmen bewailed this modification of woman's cultural position.

Whatever desire Isaac Errett and Thomas Munnell had for the establishment of a woman's missionary board, the overwhelming problems of the ACMS occupied their full attention. It remained for a dedicated Disciple sister to instigate the formation of such a society. Caroline Nevill Pearre (1831-1910) was the catalyst for the establishment of the Christian Woman's Board of Missions. A woman of learning and piety, in the late 1860s she taught at the Madison Female Institute, a Disciple college in Kentucky where she accepted the proposal of disciple minister, Dr. S. E. Pearre, and married in 1869.[21] Following their move to Iowa City, Iowa, she became increasingly distressed at the lack of missionary spirit among Christian Church women. Mrs. Pearre's friendship with Mary Thacher, the spouse of the president of the University of Iowa, heightened her desire to engage in mission work. As an officer in the recently formed Congregationalist Woman's Board of Missions, Mrs. Thacher shared with the minister's wife letters she received from her church's missionaries from Mexico and Persia. Mrs. Pearre later recalled the profound sadness she felt because her church had no part in these

---

October 19, 20, 21 and 23, 1871 (Cincinnati: Basworth, Chase, & Hall, 1871): 60-65.

[21]Lorraine Lollis, *The Shape of Adam's Rib: A Lively History of Woman's Work in the Christian Church* (St. Louis: Bethany, 1970): 30.

works. In her words: "My heart began to stir: I wanted to be in it." On the morning of April 10, 1874, Caroline Pearre finished her daily devotional and then determined to lead Disciple women into the mission work.[22]

She wrote immediately to Thomas Munnell, who responded with enthusiasm that "this is a flame of the Lord's kindling, and no man can extinguish it." Munnell provided both encouragement and a list of important individuals to contact. Among these were the editors Isaac Errett and James H. Garrison, and several interested women in Illinois, Indiana, Kentucky, and Ohio.[23] Of particular importance was her correspondence with the ladies aid society of the Central Christian Church in Indianapolis. That active group included in its membership both Marcia Goodwin and Zeralda Wallace, the former a publisher of *The Christian Monitor*, a Disciple woman's magazine, and the latter the widow of a former Indiana governor and the stepmother of Lew Wallace, author of *Ben Hur*. By means of their influence, Indianapolis became the national headquarters of the Christian Woman's Board of Missions.[24]

Because of the friendship between the Pearres and the Thachers, Isaac Errett was invited to address the June graduates of the University of Iowa. While in Iowa City, he stayed at the Pearre home and became increasingly enthusiastic about Caroline Pearre's ideas. Before he left, Errett mailed to the *Christian Standard* an editorial urging the sisters to convene in Cincinnati when the ACMS held its annual meeting in October. This article's title, "Help Those

---

[22]Caroline N. Pearre, "Our Beginning," *Missionary Tidings* 17 (August, 1899): 102-3.

[23]Ida W. Harrison, *Forty Years of Service: A History of the Christian Woman's Board of Missions, 1874-1914* (n.p., [1914]): 21.

[24]Commodore W. Cauble, *Disciples of Christ in Indiana: Achievements of a Century* (Indianapolis: Meigs, 1930): 223, 230. The monthly meetings of the CWBM executive committee were frequently held in the homes of Zeralda Wallace and Marcia Goodwin. Minutes of the executive board of the CWBM 1875-1878, *passim*, typescripts, CWBM Papers, Disciples of Christ Historical Society.

Women," became the rallying cry for the first women's convention among the Disciples of Christ.[25] Errett conveyed his "perfect sympathy with the objects of this movement." He professed to "see in it the dawn of a new era of activity and spiritual growth for Christian women," who he believed possessed "an immense wealth of resources hitherto largely neglected." This effort would not only benefit foreign missions, but also uplift the spirit of womankind. Stating his distaste for those who attacked "female vanity, frivolity, pride and extravagance," he expressed his desire to see this missionary agency bring about " a [grander] development of womanly grace, dignity and strength."[26]

For the next several months additional articles of support were written by Errett in the *Christian Standard,* Garrison in the *Christian,* Munnell in the *Christian Record,* and Marcia Goodwin in the *Christian Monitor.*[27] In September, Mrs. Goodwin enthused: "Dear sisters, while the brethren are talking about women's work in the church, show them that you know what it is by doing it."[28] With such encouragement seventy-five Disciple women gathered in the basement of the Richmond Street Christian Church on October 21, 1874.

---

[25]Lois A. White, "Reformation of the Nineteenth Century, Nine Decades of History," *Christian-Evangelist* 36 (December 7, 1899): 144-45.

[26]Isaac Errett, "Help Those Women," *Christian Standard* 9 (July 11, 1874): 220.

[27]Isaac Errett, "Woman's Work," *Christian Standard* 9 (September 19, 1874): 301; Thomas Munnell, "The General Convention," *Christian Quarterly Review* 5th ser., 1 (September, 1874): 424; Marcia M. B. Goodwin, "Talks to Monitor People," *Christian Monitor* 13 (September, 1874): 428; *Christian Monitor* 12 (October, 1874): 477; Lillis, *The Shape of Adam's Rib,* 31. The *Christian* for 1874 is no longer extant.

[28]Marcia M. B. Goodwin, "Talks to Monitor People," *Christian Monitor* 12 (September, 1874): 428.

Under the guidance of Mrs. Pearre, the convention drew up a constitution modeled on the woman's missionary society of the Congregational Church, and within hours, the American Christian Missionary Society extended recognition to the Christian Woman's Board of Missions. Assembled in joint session, the delegates then listened to addresses given by Caroline Pearre and Marcia Goodwin.[29] Significantly, both women used the rhetoric of true womanhood.

Caroline Pearre looked upon the creation of the woman's missionary board as a "joyous hour." Not only did she believe that the organization of "thousands of Christian women's hearts" would result in the propagation of the gospel, but she also saw it as improving woman's status in the home and in the church. "Let our women be vitalized by this work," she proclaimed, "and deeper earnestness and devotion will be manifested" in the churches. Moments later she again emphasized "Let women be vitalized by this work, and there will be a deeper and broader Christian influence in the home circle."[30] To this Disciple sister woman's traditional position in the religious and domestic spheres would be enhanced by the new movement.

Marcia Goodwin's speech justified woman's role in the CWBM as a natural outgrowth of her character. "while the peace and loveliness of the home-circle . . . must remain uncontaminated," she declared, "the element of love, which underlies and sustains it, is the germ from which shall spring . . . our responsibility to our fellow men." Referring to motherhood, she condemned the man who scorned woman's church work because in doing so he uttered "maledictions upon the hand that supported his feebleness." The entire talk emphasized woman's positive possibilities within the church. According to Mrs. Goodwin, woman, who "imbued her mind with Bible truths," and who had "her heart . . . filled with longings for the world's salvation," had every right to express her emotions. Still, she assured her

---

[29]Lollis, *The Shape of Adam's Rib,* 38.
[30]Caroline N. Pearre, "Woman's Mission Work," *Christian Standard* 9 (November 21, 1874): 369.

brothers that few sisters desired to stand behind the "sacred desk" and to preach. Instead, mission women would set pious examples for their husbands their children, and their neighbors.[31] The convention closed and the CWBM quickly began a program that would in the next twenty-five years raise over three-quarters of a million dollars for mission work.[32]

Initially there was little opposition to the "sister's movement" in the Disciple press. Possibly anti-society churchmen were so opposed to extra-congregational organizations that they deemed their attacks upon the ACMS sufficient to cover the new creation. In addition, the early thrust of the CWBM did not threaten woman's traditional roles as wife and mother. By 1887, the conservative evangelist John T. Poe repented of his early support of the CWBM and became a fervent opponent. He insisted that he had been "misled in the belief that it was an innocent and harmless 'society' of sisters working through the church only."[33] In 1874, however, the only substantial criticism came in the form of an otherwise favorable editorial in the *Apostolic Times.* It praised the creation of the CWBM and complimented the speeches of both Caroline Pearre and Marcia Goodwin. Nonetheless, the paper noted that "Sister Goodwin came very near treading on forbidden ground in regards to female preachers, but she spared the Apostle Paul." The editorialist trusted that "her gifted pen [would] never be found in conflict with "the prohibition of woman's sermonizing.[34] Here was a harbinger of future problems.

For almost the next decade the CWBM escaped effective criticism because it emphasized the conventional concepts of

---

[31] Marcia M. B. Goodwin, "An Address Read Before the Christian Missionary Convention at Cincinnati, Ohio, October 22, 1874," *Christian Monitor* 13 (December 1874): 542-43.

[32] Lollis, *The Shape of Adam's Rib,* 38.

[33] John T. Poe, "The CWBM," *The Gospel Advocate* 29 (September 28, 1887): 617.

[34] "The General Missionary Convention," *Apostolic Times* 6 (October 29, 1874): 4.

true womanhood. Speaking before a Kentucky society in 1876, Mrs. M. K. C. Clay complained that a few male critics had accused her sisters of supporting "Woman's Rights." How could these men, she inquired, believe that in "Kentucky there were any Christian women committed to that doctrine that displaces woman from her God-given sphere, or would degrade her to the accidents that belong to the ballot box."[35] After attending a CWBM meeting in 1877, another Disciple sister observed that "women in quiet, womanly ways in very many churches . . . are doing a great work [teaching] in the families . . . how to give and do for others."[36]

Even as late as 1883, the generally conservative *American Christian Review* praised this work of the sisters. Noting that women's emotional natures often made them "better workers for the salvation of sinners than men," it found in the CWBM "no extravagance, nothing revolutionary or radical." The paper continued: "A higher sense of the duties and responsibilities of wifehood and motherhood must prevail with every woman that thus labors in Christian work."[37] Only when it became clear that the CWBM was leading women out of the home and into the pulpit did the anti-society Disciples severely censure this "sister's movement."

The Christian Woman's Board of Missions provided for Disciple women an avenue by which they could make an active contribution to society at large. As such it became an agency through which the passive virtues of true womanhood evolved into the active contributions of the "new" woman. By means of this organization, numerous Christian Church women gained the experience of

---

[35]Mrs. M. K. C. Clay, "Address Before the Woman's Christian Missionary Society of Kentucky by its President," *Apostolic Times* 8 (September 21, 1876): 596.

[36]Marie E. Cole, "Minutes of the W. B. Missions," *Christian Monitor* 16 (September, 1877): 418.

[37]"Christian Women," *American Christian Review* 26 (May 3, 1883): 139.

participating in church polity, speaking before audiences, and in a few cases even laboring in foreign and domestic missions fields. As a result these women gained greater self-confidence and developed a higher image of their own self-worth. As for male Disciples, the sight of modest Christian women using their special virtues outside of the home circle was most impressive.

Liberal Disciples allowed their missionary sisters to "lecture" before mixed audiences. Evidently a distinction was made between a woman's exhorting the brethren on missionary responsibility from the lecture platform and her standing behind the Sunday pulpit and preaching about the "Great Commission." Conservative, anti-society churchmen do not seem to have readily grasped the subtlety involved in this activity, and none raised a voice against it until after 1885.[38] Even Mrs. Alexander Campbell, who feared the CWBM might lead to women preaching, asked "not to be understood to say, that it would be wrong for women to lecture, or make an address, under all circumstances."[39] Nonetheless, early in the 1880s there were clear signs that through the agency of the CWBM, women could eventually obtain clerical privileges. Most notable of those pointing the way was the editor of the *Christian Monitor*.

Marcia Goodwin marched in the *avant-garde* of the CWBM leadership. In 1881, she published in the *Christian Standard*, a series of articles strongly advocating woman's right to the pulpit. The first took the form of an anthropomorphic parable centering around the misadventures of a "gentle, lady-like" Bantam hen.

Thrilled by the beauty of a spring day, she crowed!
Profound shock and consternation reigned in the

---

[38]For example, John W. McGarvey remained a foe of woman's ordination throughout his life, but he praised the addresses given by the sisters at missionary conventions. See McGarvey, "The General Convention," *Apostolic Times* 9 (November 9, 1877): 680.

[39]Mrs. Alexander Campbell to Mrs. J. M. Mathes, *Christian Monitor* 18 (May 1879): 150.

chicken coop. Immediately the roosters bemoaned this departure from female decorum: "'Hen's haven't any right to crow! Hens are made to take care of the chickens! Their eggs will be ruined while they forsake home duties! . . . she'll put revolutionary notions into the heads of the young pullets, and make them 'un-henly.' A mass rally was quickly organized in which the basic tenets of a true hen's behavior were detailed. 'Hens,' one rooster affirmed, 'should be made to understand that they must stick to their proper sphere! If they want to know anything, let them ask their husbands at home.' There followed a series of resolutions mandating the proper behavior of model 'henhood.' Chastised by this experience, the modest Bantam never again crowed for the joy of a lovely day.[40]

Marcia Goodwin's message was perfectly clear and it elicited several bitter replies from her brethren. In one of these a farmer from Sullivan, Indiana, quoted to her the ancient couplet:

> A whistling girl and a crowing hen
> Always come to the same bad end.[41]

Infuriated, she promptly wrote two additional articles for the *Christian Standard*. "A woman may live an idle, useless life, or devote her days to fashion and folly," she observed, "and she will be applauded for having kept her proper sphere." But let the same woman study the Bible and "publicly proclaim its truth . . . and sneers and calumny are her portions." Referring to the "sacred desk" of preaching, she believed that women sought it for "the most pure and conscientious motives." She condemned those males who spoke of the "immodesty of woman's preaching," because it belittled "not only the sex, but Christianity itself" and thus

---

[40]Marcia M. B. Goodwin, "From My Standpoint," *Christian Standard* 16 (April 2, 1881): 107.

[41]Joseph W. Wolfe, "Olla Podria (Not Editorial) for Mrs. M. M. B. Goodwin," *Christian Standard* 16 (April 23, 1881): 130.

struck "a blow at the foundation of all purity." She believed that women, who were "able . . . to stand before the world as preachers of the gospel," deserved the highest admiration.[42] Marcia Goodwin's ideas were ten years in advance of the disciple movement. Shortly after the appearance of these articles, both her health and the health of her husband deteriorated significantly and her voice was muted.[43]

Although Marcia Goodwin argued with passion for woman's right to the pulpit, none successfully stepped forward to claim the honor.[44] For those few Disciple women who desired publicly to proclaim the gospel, the lecture platform provided an effective substitute. Persis L. Christian (ca. 1840-1918) of Chicago, and later Eureka Springs, Arkansas, emerged as one of the Disciples' most popular female speakers. Although a charter member of the national CWBM, her greatest period of activity for the society was between 1884 and 1893.[45] Her life and philosophy demonstrated the evolution of Disciple sisters from the cult of true womanhood to the "new" woman.

The daughter of a village physician in Illinois, Persis Lemon married George C. Christian in 1866. Shortly

---

[42]Marcia M. B. Goodwin, "From My Standpoint," *Christian Standard* 16 (June 4, 1881): 178; Marcia M. B. Goodwin, "From My Standpoint," *Christian Standard* 16 (June 11, 1881): 186.

[43]"The Death of Mrs. M. M. B. Goodwin," *Christian Companion* 24 (April, 1885): 157; Sarah E. Shortridge, "Death of Sister Goodwin," *Missionary Tidings* 2 (April, 1885): 2.

[44]In 1880, Mary B. Carney claimed in the *American Christian Review* to be holding a pulpit with her husband in Lewis County, Kentucky. The newspaper took a negative view of her activities and she was never recognized in any of the other Disciple papers. J. A. Meng, "A New Sensation," *American Christian Review* 23 (January 13, 1880): 9; Mary B. Carney, "Woman's Question, by a Woman," *American Christian Review* 22 (February 3, 1880): 34; Mary B. Carney, "Letter from Sister Carney," *American Christian Review* 22 (March 23, 1880): 91.

[45]"Mrs. Persis L. Christian," *Christian-Evangelist* 55 (September 19, 1918): 991.

thereafter they moved to Chicago where he became active in the Prohibition Party. In the 1880s he served as its state chairman and in 1884, he was placed in nomination as its presidential candidate. In addition, George Christian was a pillar in the local congregation of the Disciples of Christ.[46] Persis Christian shared with her husband a passion for both temperance and the church. By the late 1880s, she was concentrating most of her energy on developing the Illinois CWBM. As state president, she diligently sought to start new local chapters and to strengthen existing societies.[47] Nonetheless, her articles in the *Christian Standard* made it clear that the prohibition cause was always close to her heart.[48] In 1889, however, her husband's failing health forced them to seek the more temperate environment of the Ozark community of Eureka Springs. Cut off from her former base of activity in Chicago, she agreed to become a national lecturer for the CWBM.[49]

In August, 1890, Christian lectured before the missionary society's state convention in Iowa. Using the flowery language of Victorian sentimentality, one of the participants proclaimed that her success and popularity as a speaker resulted from her womanly demeanor. Persis Christian "opens her mouth with wisdom, and in her tongue is the law of kindness," the writer gushed. "As a woman that feareth the Lord, she shall be praised."[50]

---

[46]D. W. Moore, "George C. Christian," *Christian Standard* 36 (June 22, 1901): 795.

[47]Persis L. Christian, "C. W. B. M., Duties of District and County Managers," *Christian Standard* 23 (February 2, 1889): 68.

[48]Persis L. Christian, "Temperance Movement," *Christian Standard* 17 (November 25, 1882): 375; Persis L. Christian, "Christian Missions and the Liquor Traffic," *Christian Standard* 22 (September 17, 1887): 298, 304.

[49]"Editorial Odds and Ends," *Christian Oricle* 7 (November 6, 1890): 716; Mrs. Otis A. Burgess, untitled notice, *Missionary Tidings* 8 (December, 1890): 19.

[50]"Iowa CWBM Convention at Des Moines, August 20, 1890," *Missionary Tidings* 8 (December 1890): 21.

During the following two years, Persis Christian traveled throughout the region from Missouri to Pennsylvania and from Illinois to Tennessee. Although her lectures expounded upon the importance of church missions, she also encouraged temperance, advocated woman suffrage, and even hinted that women ought to occupy the pulpit. Like most proponents of the "new" woman, however, she retained a faith in her sex's domestic felicity. "Women," she insisted, "have no more important duty than preparation for the management of the home."[51]

Church liberals responded positively to Persis Christian. As early as 1888, an Ohio Disciple believed her power as a speaker was due to her "womanly and refined manner which [wins] the hearts of her auditors."[52] In 1891, others of her religious fellowship echoed that view. Shortly after her four-day series of lectures in Liberty, Missouri, a male Disciple praised his sister in the *Christian Evangelist*. "Several distinguished ladies, such as Susan B. Anthony and Phoebe Cousins" had lectured in this small city, but to him "none of them left such a favorable impression on the public mind as Persis L. Christian."[53] Similar compliments were expressed by liberal Disciples after her visits to Bloomington, Illinois, and Pittsburgh, Pennsylvania.[54]

Persis Christian's view of woman's active role in society through voting and preaching would have been largely unacceptable to her liberal brethren twenty years earlier. However, the reality of a modest, "womanly" sister

---

[51]Persis L. Christian, "The Ethics of Housekeeping," *Christian Standard* 28 (June 16, 1888): 374.

[52]Jessie H. Brown, "The Work of the CWBM in Ohio," *Christian Standard* 23 (June 16, 1888): 374.

[53]A. B. Jones, "Persis L. Christian," *Christian-Evangelist* 28 (February 12, 1891): 105; A. B. Jones, "Persis L. Christian," *Missionary Tidings* 8 (March 1891): 5.

[54]M. M. C., "Mrs. Christian's Lectures and the CWBM Institute at Bloomington, Illinois," *Christian-Evangelist* 28 (April 19, 1891): 236; idem, "Our General Conventions," *Christian Oricle* 8 (October 29, 1891): 690.

advocating the ballot and the pulpit for her sex made these ideas seem less radical. Both by example and advocacy, Persis Christian, and a few others like her, called for the expansion of woman's domain by using logic derived from the cult of true womanhood.

For a handful of Disciple women, service in the mission field provided an opportunity actively to aid humanity. A few women were employed by the CWBM to work among the freedmen in Mississippi, to teach school in Jamaica, and to convert the pagans in Japan and India. The CWBM mission to India was of special interest to them. The society's leaders looked upon it as a unique woman's work among oriental women.

The CWBM saw in India a chance not only to spread the gospel, but also to improve the status of eastern womanhood. As early as 1877, a plea was published in the *Christian Monitor* calling for Disciple women to go to the Orient. The article suggested that there "customs have shut women, as thinking beings away from men: so if we their sisters, go not to them, they perish in their idolatry."[55] Caroline Pearre took up this theme. Speaking before a Kentucky CWBM convention, she observed with disdain: "If we were oriental women, we might recline on our cushions and tinkle our ornaments, and sip our coffee and drowse away our inane lives." She insisted that since American women were products of a higher culture, however, they were responsible for developing the interest of civilization throughout the world.[56] Continuing that theme, several Christian Church women contrasted the rights of their sex in a "free and enlightened America" to the tragic circumstances of Indian women. CWBM speakers pictured the subcontinent a woman's purgatory where daughters were "drowned in innocent babyhood," where young girls were sold into prostitution, and where wives were trapped in the

---

[55]Mrs. N. E. Atkinson, "A Plea for the C. W. Board of Missions," *Christian Monitor* 16 (April, 1877): 173.

[56]Caroline N. Pearre, "Woman's Mission Work," *Christian Standard* 17 (October 7, 1882): 313.

"zenana or harem."[57] Persis Christian was especially concerned. Addressing a CWBM convention in Illinois, she proclaimed that "to us, as women, the condition of the women particularly appeals." She could hardly imagine the degraded condition of such women who from mother to daughter had "been only a beast of burden," and who had "no knowledge of freedom of will or action." Christian women, she averred, must enter "the gates of [their] prison, carrying hope and salvation."[58]

Given this interest, several young women volunteered to undertake the Asian work. By 1887, a girl's school had been established in Bialspur, India, and other Disciple women were organizing mission stations in the same region. One of these attracted attention in the American press.[59] In the summer of 1889, *Harper's Bazar* praised the accomplishments of Miss Mary Graybiel, "a missionary sent out by the Church of the Disciples." Without the help of a white male, this young missionary supervised the construction of a sizable church building. The periodical noted that she served as her own architect, her own purchasing agent, and her own contractor. She hired "a hundred natives" and taught some "to make brick [and] others to quarry stone." When the building was completed, she had proven "herself a person equal to emergencies that would appal [sic] some men." *Harper's Bazar* concluded:

---

[57]Mrs. W. C. Weedon, "Woman's Work in Missions," *Christian Standard* 13 (June 15, 1878): 189; idem, "Woman's Opportunity," *Christian Companion* 24 (November, 1885): 350; Ella B. Myles, "Christian Woman's Mission," *Christian Companion* 26 (February, 1887): 77; Jennie L. Ogg, "Woman—Her Relation to Mission," *Missionary Tidings* 9 (February, 1892): 13.

[58]Persis L. Christian, "Christian Missions," *Christian Standard* 19 (September 20, 1884): 297. CWBM activities in India parallel the action of Protestant missionary women who were trying to gain the right of suffrage for women in China. Jerry Israel, "'For God, for China and for Yale'—The Open Door in Action," *American Historical Review* 75 (February, 1970): 805-6.

[59]Zoe L. Tedrowe, "CWBM," *Christian Monitor* 21 (March, 1882): 125; editorial, *Christian Companion* 26 (May, 1887): 177.

"We are proud of [Miss Graybiel,] as a woman of thrift, tact and great executive ability and glad that she calls our land her home.[60]

Given the efforts of missionary women to improve the status of their sex in other lands, American Disciples began to question woman's limited rights in their own country. In 1888, Mrs. Julia Bosworth asked in the *Christian-Evangelist* why it was wrong for a woman to preach in her native land . . . and yet it is alright for her to cross an ocean . . . to teach and preach the same gospel." Like others in the CWBM Julia Bosworth concluded that women ought "to preach or do 'whatsoever their hands find to do' in America."[61]

By the 1890s, liberal Disciples had become accustomed to seeing missionary women take an active role in church affairs. Thus when Clara Babcock became their first ordained minister, a majority within the Christian Church was prepared to accept her. Almost alone among the liberals, John B. Briney of Knoxville protested Babcock's "innovation." Writing in February, 1892, in the *Christian Standard,* he condemned the heresy of women's preaching and called for its end while "the practice [was] merely in the bud."[62] The intensity of negative response to his articles must have surprised this powerful preacher.

Within a week after Briney's articles were published, the *Christian Standard* editors reported receiving "a small battalion" of replies challenging him and more "reinforcements" were arriving daily. "The ladies," warned the paper, "are on the warpath."[63] Throughout the remainder of 1892

---

[60]*Harper's Bazar,* June 29, 1889, reprinted in *Missionary Tidings* 7 (August, 1889): 8.

[61]Julia M. Bosworth, "The Other Side," *Christian-Evangelist* 25 (August 30, 1888): 542.

[62]John B. Briney, "Paul and Women," *Christian Standard* 28 (February 13, 1892): 136; *idem,* "Paul and Women," *Christian Standard* 28 (February 13, 1892): 136; *idem,* "Paul and Women," *Christian Standard* 28 (February 27, 1892): 182.

[63]Editorial comment, *Christian Standard* 28 (March 5, 1892):

and for most of 1893, Briney found himself overwhelmed in both the *Christian Standard* and in the *Christian-Evangelist* by scores of women's preaching advocates.[64] Only one other liberal Disciple defended his position.[65] Most of Briney's critics affirmed that the church needed the special attributes which womankind possessed. A church majority agreed with H. Milner Black, a minister who wrote for the *Christian-Evangelist*, that the Disciples of Christ could do without "feminine men and masculine women," but it desperately needed "the tender and pathetic womanly presentation of the gospel, to reach some hearts which were well nigh putrefied."[66]

Womanly virtues exemplified by the CWBM convinced liberal Disciples that their sisters deserved a more positive church and social posture. Their conservative brethren, however, failed to support the missionary society and as

---

211. Taking note of this warning, Briney suggested "that probably the prayer path would be the softer one to travel in each of the true solution of the question in hand." As would be expected, his critics assured him of their fidelity to the "prayer path." See John B. Briney, "'Paul and Women' and 'Jairus'," *Christian Standard* 28 (March 26, 1892): 277; Jairus [pseud.], "'Paul and Women'—and Briney," *Christian Standard* 28 (April 16, 1892): 383; M. B. L., "Open Letter to Bros. Hayden and Briney," *Christian Standard* 28 (October 8, 1892): 855.

[64]See both the *Christian Standard* and the *Christian-Evangelist* for 1892-1893 *passim*. Forty two articles in the *Christian Standard* and sixteen articles in the *Christian-Evangelist* expressed solidarity with women preachers.

[65]M. P. Hayden, "Have Women a Right to be Preachers," *Christian Standard* 28 (April 9, 1892): 316; *idem*, "Women Pastors and Evangelists," *Christian Standard* 28 (June 4, 17, 24, 1892): 450, 470, 490; *idem*, "Rejoinder to the Girls," *Christian Standard* 28 (July 8, 1892): 545; *idem*, "Reply to G. T. Smith," *Christian Standard* 29 (July 29, November 4, 1893): 591, 879; *idem*, "Women in Ministry," *Christian Standard* 29 (September 9, 1893): 718; *idem*, "Reply to John Kline," *Christian Standard* 29 (September 23, 1893): 758; *idem*, "Condition of Woman in Paul's Day," *Christian Standard* 29 (December 23, 1893): 1020.

[66]H. Milner Black, "How to Win the Men," *Christian-Evangelist* 31 (April 19, 1893): 246.

would be expected did not significantly modify their concept of woman's role either in religion or in the world at large. Strangely, the conservative press virtually ignored the progress of this woman's missionary organization. Although a few negative remarks appeared as early as 1885, there was no consistent attack upon the CWBM until it directly threatened David Lipscomb's sphere of influence in the early 1890s.

While anti-society Disciples failed to mount a sustained assault upon the CWBM, a few scattered remarks in their religious journals suggested the tenor of their thoughts. Without exception the published comments of conservatives censored the active "new" woman. Writing in the *Firm Foundation* for 1886, "Sarai" criticized those women who desired to "leave home and children and lecture on temperance and preach, etc." To those who believed such women achieved "much good by their public efforts," she replied that "infinitely much more good would [be accomplished] by staying at home and making happiness for husband and children."[67] Three years later, she condemned thoroughly those missionary women who were "deeply absorbed in the heathen of Borrioboola-gha, while their own children roam the streets at will and their husbands seek in the club room the company and comfort denied them at home."[68] Amanda Bostick, a frequent contributor to the *Gospel Advocate*, held a similar position. She was highly critical of missionary societies which demand "all the time and thoughts of mothers, to the neglect of the spiritual training of the children." To her, women's organizations were the source of rising juvenile delinquency.[69] Neither of these women had faith in the concept of "organized mother love."

---

[67]Sarai, "Talks with the Sisters," *Firm Foundation* 2 (August, 1886): 4.

[68]*Ibid.*, *Firm Foundation* 5 (January 15, 1889): 1.

[69]Amanda Bostick, "Lois and Eunice," *Gospel Advocate* 32 (February 19, 1890): 120.

Other attacks on the CWBM, and women's missionary societies, can only be described as occasional sniping. In 1885, an unidentified conservative accused such women of hypocrisy because they espoused love for foreign missions while ignoring those without the gospel at home.[70] Both Sarai and John T. Poe believed that sewing circles and Dorcas societies denied an income to poor women who desperately needed the money which the society sisters obtained from quilt and bonnet making.[71] And at least one conservative critic hinted that missionary women took on masculine characteristics. At an Arkansas CWBM convention, he listened to the speeches of a husband-wife team just returned from India. "Sister M.," he suggested, "was the best man (?) of the two."[72] If these attacks seem petty, the intensity of anti-CWBM feeling would become evident when the society held its national convention in Nashville in October, 1892.

Largely due to the influence of David Lipscomb, Tennessee Disciples only weakly supported missionary societies. Throughout the 1880s, Christian Church mission projects received only a few hundred dollars annually from the entire state. The CWBM had no support at all. Given that situation, Mrs. Alexander Campbell suggested in 1886 that the *Gospel Advocate* of Nashville [should] let its loving voice . . . be heard" supporting missions in "that section over which it holds great sway."[73] Lipscomb ignored her.

The events leading to Lipscomb's strong denunciation of the CWBM in 1892 had begun five years before. In

---

[70]C., "Woman as Missionary," *Gospel Advocate* 27 (July 15, 1885): 442.

[71]Sarai, "Talks with the Sisters," *Firm Foundation* 1 (May, 1885): 13; John T. Poe, "Woman's Aid Societies and the Church," *Gospel Advocate* 36 (October 25, 1894): 680.

[72]J. G. Conner, "The CWBM, ACMS, and ACSSC," *Firm Foundation* 8 (July 5, 1892): 3.

[73]Mrs. Alexander Campbell, "Letter from Sister Campbell," *Missionary Tidings* 3 (February, 1886): 3.

October, 1887, a pro-society evangelist held a meeting at Nashville's Woodland Street Christian Church and shortly afterwards its women organized a missionary auxiliary. With the blessing of three of the congregation's four elders, the women sent out fifty letters to Tennessee churches calling for a cooperative effort by the sisters. Elisha G. Sewell, the dissenting elder, was the co-editor of the *Gospel Advocate*. Only the Christian Church in Chattanooga responded positively to the sisters' request. After two years, the women of both congregations raised sufficient funds to hire Andrew Myhr as a state evangelist to organize additional societies. A few months later in October, 1890, Sewell and nineteen others left the Woodland Street church to found the Tenth Street Church of Christ.[74]

Opposed by the powerful voice of the *Gospel Advocate*, Myhr's work achieved at best modest success. In the fall of 1891, he invited James H. Garrison to speak before the Tennessee missionary convention held at the Woodland church. At its conclusion, Garrison noted tersely in his diary: "Tennessee is yet to rank with our best missionary States."[75] To remedy this situation, the leaders of both the CWBM and the General Christian Missionary Society (formerly the ACMS) agreed to hold their next national convention in Nashville.

Shortly after plans for the convention were announced, Lipscomb registered his extreme displeasure. He considered the chief factor motivating the missionary Disciples was a "desire to triumph over us." As far as he was concerned, the church membership of Nashville opposed the convention. At most, he insisted, only a small number "from Woodland Street and a few from [the] Vine [Street congregation] wish it."[76]

---

[74]Elisha G. Sewell, *Gospels Lessons and Life History* (Nashville: McQuiddy, 1908): 285-300.

[75]Garrison Diary, October 15, 1891, Garrison Papers, Disciples of Christ Historical Society.

[76]David Lipscomb, "The General Convention at Nashville," *Octographic Review* 35 (January 19, 1892): 1.

On the eve of the convention's assembling, Lipscomb published a strongly worded condemnation of them, which made it plain that the thrust of his wrath was aimed at the CWBM. He reminded his pro-missionary society brethren how frequently they quoted Galatians 3:28, "'there is neither male nor female,' . . . yet [they divided] the Christians into male and female societies." The editor declared that the Scriptures commanded woman's silence and submission to man. But the CWBM put women forth "to speak, to manage the society, to employ and send out preachers, and to boss their affairs as the men do theirs." With utter disdain, he quoted a brother who justified such actions because the sisters did "it so deliciously."[77] This last phrase became an epithet which he would use repeatedly in the months to come.

When the convention ended, Lipscomb castigated them both as a disgrace to the "disciples in Tennessee." He was appalled that at a religious meeting "so little reference was made to the Bible." Instead the speeches were of the "old Fourth-of-July spread-eagle variety, praising the Anglo-Saxon prowess . . . and glorifying . . . country."[78] He ridiculed the decorum of these assemblies. " I do not think," the editor complained, "delicious speeches [by the sisters] or animal enthusiasm manifested by constant cheering and hand-clapping . . . compensate in any way for the violated law of God."[79]

From October through December, Lipscomb leveled his aim at the CWBM with the indignation of a man who had witnessed the virtues of true womanhood prostituted. In his mind, the women of the CWBM not only disobeyed the word of God, but they also trespassed "against womanly modesty and position, against motherhood, against the

---

[77]David Lipscomb, "Card of Invitation," *Gospel Advocate* 34 (October 6, 1892): 628-29.

[78]David Lipscomb, "Convention Items," *Gospel Advocate* 34 (October 27, 1892): 676.

[79]David Lipscomb, "Convention Thoughts," *Gospel Advocate* 34 (November 10, 1892): 709.

sanctity of the marriage relationship." Furthermore, "in usurping the function especially committed to men," these women sinned against and drove men "from the church and from God."[80] He held in contempt those sisters who occupied the pulpit of the Vine Street church and made their "'most delicious' speeches."[81] One of these was a "mere girl" who presented a "rambling talk on missions" to Charles Loos, John W. McGarvey, and "other wise men." It "could not profit them," and it "injured her and lowered the standard of womanly modestly."[82]

The attitude of Lipscomb and James H. Garrison toward the sisters' speeches illustrated the wide gulf between pro and anti-society Disciples as they looked upon woman's status. Major lectures were given by Mrs. Otis A. Burgess, Persis L. Christian, and Mrs. Alice Williams of Cameron, Missouri. After returning to St. Louis, Garrison wrote that "the addresses of sister Burgess, . . . Christian and Williams, and the tender, tearful, heart-felt talks" of many other consecrated women impresssed the brotherhood. He affirmed that anyone who sought to "'silence' them with a passage of Scripture, would be guilty of trying to 'stop' the rotation of the earth with a Bible text." The publisher of the *Christian Evangelist* was pleased that these woman manifested "a modesty, a womanliness and self-forgetfulness" that had conquered the prejudices of conservatives.[83]

Lipscomb was far from conquered. He admitted that he was impressed with the arrangement and delivery of Alice Williams' speech, but added with sarcasm: "it was done 'deliciously.'" Lipscomb then condemned her and all other preaching sisters for violating the commandments of the

---

[80]David Lipscomb, "Woman and Her Work," *Gospel Advocate* (1892): 644.

[81]David Lipscomb, "Convention Items," *Gospel Advocate* (1892): 676.

[82]David Lipscomb, "Convention Thoughts," *Gospel Advocate* (1892): 709.

[83][James H. Garrison], "The Nashville, Convention," *Christian-Evangelist* 39 (October 26, 1892): 676.

Apostle Paul. He asked: "will some of these [brethren] who said 'amen' and clapped their hands so heartily, please explain how 'keep silence' could be changed 'to speaking in the churches.'"[84]

The entire Nashville affair ended with a brief, but bitter exchange between the *Christian Evangelist* and the *Gospel Advocate*. Garrison's paper praised "our good women of the C. W. B. M." who resisted without bitterness "the inexpressibly unjust, ungallant, and unchristian attacks of the Gospel Advocate [sic]."[85] Lipscomb responded quickly. Gallantry, he explained was the deference shown by the stronger male sex to the weaker female sex. He suggested that "woman in pants, on the rostrum or managing conventions rejected the offices of gallantry." Professing to "love woman with a true love," he warned his sisters that to disobey Paul's command of silence would lead to "eternal death, despite all [of woman's] 'tender, tearful, heartfelt talks.'"[86]

Little good was accomplished for the CWBM at the Nashville convention. Lipscomb, and those Disciples who accepted his lead, remained unconverted to missionary societies. They believed the CWBM represented both a repudiation of their religious plea and a desecration of the values of true womanhood.

Following the convention, Persis Christian toured Middle and East Tennessee hoping to establish new CWBM auxiliaries and to raise money for missions. Her success was meager. In Murfreesboro she received a collection of only one dollar. The Chattanooga woman's auxiliary which was "once strong and active" had fallen into a "debilitated condition." She had some modest success at the small East

---

[84][David Lispcomb], "Paul's Words and 'Woman's Opportunity,'" *Gospel Advocate* 34 (October 20, 1892): 661.

[85]"Our Budget," *Christian-Evangelist* 29 (November 17, 1892): 724.

[86]David Lipscomb, "An Unjust Charge," *Gospel Advocate* 34 (December 1, 1892): 756.

Tennessee community of Sherman Heights where she created a society of eight members. At Knoxville, her audience was small despite the endorsement of "Bro. Briney." Arriving in Johnson City, the local minister assured her that "there was little or no prejudice. . . against the work" of the CWBM, but no collection was taken. Not until she reached Bristol in upper East Tennessee did she find welcome. There she established a strong chapter containing twenty new CWBM members.[87]

After 1892, Lipscomb felt increasingly alienated from the fellowship of the Disciples of Christ. In August, 1897, he published a series of three articles in the *Gospel Advocate* proclaiming that he no longer considered himself in communion with the Christian Church. He listed a number of theological and philosophical heresies practiced by the liberal Disciples. Among these was the tendency to go beyond the NT example by building "a foreign society, a home society, a woman's society, a church building society," and so on.[88] While no firm date can be readily agreed upon for the actual separation of the Churches of Christ from the Christian Church, these articles are of symbolic importance.

Just two weeks before this event, Elisha G. Sewell published in the *Gospel Advocate* a savage attack upon missionary society women. It provides excellent insight as to the status of women among anti-society Disciples at the point of the movement's division. He began his article by defining woman's proper role in terms of domesticity. The factor which made a home lovely, he affirmed, was the cheerful activity of "a modest and devoted Christian wife and mother." Religious women were to be "home builders" and as such they would become "the queens of the home." By

---

[87]Persis L. Christian, "Work in Tennessee," *Missionary Tidings* 10 (January, 1892): 12.

[88]David Lipscomb, "From the Papers," *Gospel Advocate* 39 (August 19, 1897): 513. See Lipscomb, "From the Papers," *Gospel Advocate* 39 (August 5, 1897): 481; and *idem*, "The Vital Point," *Gospel Advocate* 39 (August 19, 1897): 514-16.

contrast, "women who get up societies, and become presidents and secretaries . . . cast shadow . . . upon those home-working, patient, and plodding women who are seldom known beyond [their] neighborhood." To Sewell, "these president and secretary women and pulpit women" were violating God's law, "while faithful home-keeping and home building women" were honoring God and blessing humanity." Near the end of the article, he reminisced that his mother was not active in a missionary society or any "human organization." She was emphatically a keeper at home, a home builder, working continually . . . for the well-being of her husband and children." In the lesson's conclusion, he praised "the Lord for such wives and mothers, and . . . for their lovely examples in the home and in the assembly of the saints and in the community!"[89] At century's end, evangelistic Disciples were still faithful to the cult of true womanhood.

On the other hand, church liberals had adjusted their perception of woman's status to allow the female sex a role beyond the domestic sphere. The example of modest, Christian women working through the CWBM convinced these churchmen that they had little to fear from an expanded role of women in the church. At the turn of the century, James H. Garrison spoke to the young women graduates of the School of Pastoral Helpers. He was pleased that women were preparing to assist their brethren in the guidance of the church and he praised the "rapid multiplication of callings" allowed women in "our modern life." Nonetheless, he believed that women were not fit for all professions. At some point, a line had to be drawn between those occupations for which she was "preeminently adapted, and others which she would do well to avoid." Since by nature the female sex possessed "finer and higher qualities" of character than the male, she should enter only those careers

---

[89]Elisha G. Sewell, "Woman's Real Position in the Church," *Gospel Advocate* 39 (July 29, 1897): 469. The words "home" and "homes" appeared 38 times in this article of slightly less than one page.

which do not violate the "essential qualities of womanhood."[90]

Neither Lipscomb, Sewell, nor Garrison could divorce their concept of the female sex from the belief that womankind possessed special moral traits superior to those of men. Whether they supported or rejected the CWBM and women preaching, male Disciples defined the status of women in terms of true womanhood. In their collective thought women were to be more moral than men, most were to marry, and all proper women were to be mothers. Members of this religious fellowship almost never perceived of the individual woman as anything other than a sister, a wife or a mother.

---

[90]Garrison, Address to the Graduates of the School of Pastoral Helpers, Garrison Papers, Disciples of Christ Historical Society.

Chapter Twenty-two

THE ROLE OF WOMEN IN THE NEW TESTAMENT DOCTRINE OF MINISTRY

Allan J. McNicol

This essay operates with two basic assumptions. First, it assumes that we can know enough about ministry in the churches of the NT era to enable us to discern its basic *raison d'être* and structure. The issue has been an object of lively discussion for several generations.[1] Most NT scholars in this generation have stressed that there is no master blueprint for the organization of "the ministry" in the NT era.[2] Rather, leadership embodied itself in various forms and manifestations so that it is almost impossible to subsume it under the framework of a common scheme. In this essay we will be a little more adventuresome. We will attempt to provide a brief sketch of the nature of ministry and its function in the churches associated with the Pauline mission. This will serve as a cross-section of the NT teaching on the subject.

Second, this chapter assumes that we have sufficient

---

[1] The debate goes back to the end of the last century when certain theologians in Germany (R. Sohm, A. Harnack) claimed that ministry in the early Gentile churches founded by Paul consisted of the free emergence of the Spirit's gifts and stood in fundamental tension with any concept of the existence of normative church structures. In recent years this view has been reinvigorated by the essay of Ernest Käsemann, "Ministry and Community in the New Testament," *Essays on New Testament Themes* (Philadelphia: Fortress, 1982, ET 1964): 63-94; idem, "Paul and Early Catholicism," *New Testament Questions of Today* (Philadelphia: Fortress, 1969): 236-251.

[2] Eduard Schweizer, *Church Order in the New Testament* (SBT 32; London: SCM, 1961); 13.

information about the activities of women within these structures of ministry that we can identify with some clarity a basic outline of the level of their participation and contribution.[3] We will attempt to delineate not only something about the level of participation of women in ministry in the Pauline churches, but its underlying theological rationale.

1. *Contemporary Debate*

A complicating factor in the whole discussion is that these issues have become heavily politicized. Few in America operate untouched by the cultural and philosophical impact of Western secular liberalism with its foundational view that the full political and judicial effort of the state should be directed towards increasing personal freedoms, individual rights, and tolerance for a wide range of cultures and lifestyles. This belief presumes that everyone has fundamental rights for total equality of opportunity for service in all aspects of our society—including one of its most important institutions: the church.

The momentum of this movement has had such an impact in America that it has affected even such remote areas as historical studies and the interpretation of ancient texts. On the one hand, there are those who look at the world of the first century in the Eastern Mediterranean (definitely not a society based on Western liberalism) as a culture of patriarchy. From this perspective, texts that discuss the role of women in society or ministry are often dismissed either as the artifacts of an ancient culture or, it is said, that they need to be radically reinterpreted on the basis of another cultural ideology.[4]

---

[3]The difficulties of research in this area, in part, have precipitated the publication of this book. Entire journals are devoted to the general subject. A good example is the journal *Daughters of Sarah* which states that it is a "forum for varying views within Christian feminism," and as of 1993, was in its twenty-first volume.

[4]Elisabeth Schüssler Fiorenza, *In Memory of Her: A Feminist*

On the other hand many cultural conservatives, deeply concerned by the moral breakdown of communities, the modern family and, in particular, the growing tendency to separate sexuality from any religious framework, have set the blame for this state of affairs squarely at the door of the movement for the liberation of women. These conservatives call for a re-emphasis on the importance of the submissive role of the woman in family as the cornerstone of society. They tend to utilize the Bible, a classic of our culture, with the subtext of invoking its authority to keep women in their place.

While this heated debate continues it is difficult to examine the biblical materials in total objectivity. Nevertheless, in order for the church to avoid the dangers of either obscurantism or capitulation to the dominant culture, careful historical and theological analysis of the biblical material must continue so that our judgments may be well informed. On the basis of such presuppositions, this essay is offered as a contribution to the discussion.

2. *A Proposal*

Because of the fragmentary nature of the sources, we will not to be able to survey the NT comprehensively. We know very little about either the subject of the ministry or the role of women in the earliest churches among the Jewish Christians. We will focus our study on the early Gentile churches associated with Paul for which we have the considerable evidence of much of Acts and the Pauline letters.

We will argue that this body of teaching operated in a theological framework which presumed that a new era of redemption had arrived in Christ, and that God gave gifts

---

Reconstruction of Christian Origins (New York: Crossroad, 1983); idem, *Bread not Stone: The Challenge of Feminist Biblical Interpretation* (Boston: Beacon, 1984); idem (ed.), *Searching the Scriptures I: A Feminist Introduction* (New York: Crossroad, 1993).

both to women and men to enable them to exercise ministries for the benefit of the body; but, at the same time, the exercise of these ministries should always function in such a way *that their display would not frustrate but enhance the intent of the Creator to recover, within the medium of the new redemptive life, the basic structure of the relationship between male and female (family) which was built into the creation.* The essential paradigm for this structured relationship, recovered in the new redemptive life, is that the husband should love the wife as Christ loved the church, and the wife should submit to the husband as the church submits to Christ. Contemporary discussions on the role of women in ministry should be viewed through this prism.

Procedurally, we will set forth this proposal in four stages. First, we will give a brief sketch of ministry in the Pauline churches. This will be followed by another sketch of the role of women in the ministry of these churches. Third, attention will be drawn to the cautionary comments made by Paul with respect to the activities of women in the assembly. Fourth, we will attempt to describe the theological rationale that informs this discussion. Finally, we will conclude with some comments on the viability of this rationale for the contemporary church.

3. *The Doctrine of Ministry in the NT Era*

Today, when we think of a minister, more than likely we think of one who carries out certain tasks such as preaching the gospel, visiting the sick, and assisting in ritualizing marriages and other rites of passage within the faith community. Theoretically, the minister fulfills these tasks in some way as an extension of the ministry of Christ; but in reality the minister functions under the supervision of the leaders of a religious community from which one also receives compensation. In other words, we tend to think of "the ministry" as a profession. We have come to accept the idea that this profession is filled by people who pursue ministry as a vocation that formally is not markedly different from any other occupation.

A. *The Church as an Eschatological Community: The Basis for Ministry*

When we turn to the NT era we find that the operative concept of ministry emerged within a more defined theological matrix where the church was set apart from the wider society. In the early church, ministry had its origin in certain conclusions that the earliest community of believers drew from the belief that Jesus had died as a ransom for their sins and was raised for their justification. Since Jesus was now at God's right hand, he was the heavenly king (Rom 1:3-4; Acts 2:34-36; 1 Cor 15:24; Eph 1:20-22). As a result of his atoning death, proleptically, through his once-and-for-all sacrifice, Jesus offered the obedience of all those who would be united to him. Consequently, as heavenly high priest, he created a new priesthood comprised of the total complement of believers in him. As the new priesthood, the church is an eschatological community. It is the vanguard of the new creation. J. A. T. Robinson has pointed out that the church stands dynamically between two great moments of the establishment of Christ's sovereignty over the world: the work on Calvary which initiated his triumph over the powers and the final acknowledgment of this triumph.[5] Between these times the church, in imitation of the way followed by Jesus, seeks through its communal life to lead the world to recognize his victory and to live a life in keeping with this reality.

In order to maintain itself and carry out its sacred mission the church needs gifted people in leadership. These people are charged with the responsibility of carrying out the διακονία (support or ministries) of the church. The διάκονος (one commissioned) can be described as the person who performs these services. While in the eyes of the Greeks such an orientation could be considered

---

[5] J. A. T. Robinson, "Kingdom, Church and Ministry," *The Historic Episcopate in the Fullness of the Church* (ed. K. M. Carey; London: Dacre, 1954): 15-18.

undignified and demeaning,[6] hallowed by the action of Christ (Luke 22:27), ministry became a cherished term in the Christian community to describe the work of those who exercised special responsibilities in building up the body.[7]

As a way of life ministry was a work that was highly commended among the early Christians. The Lord called his disciples to ministry (Matt 20:25-27; 23:8-11; 25:40; John 12:26; 13:14). And such service was characteristic of a number of the early churches (1 Cor 16:15; Acts 6:4; 2 Cor 4:1; 8:4; 11:8; Rev 2:19). Ministry enables the church to accomplish its task of setting forth the glory of the Savior throughout the world. The intended result is that the church empowered through ministry would lead the creation to the praise of God for his wisdom and goodness (Eph 3:8-10).

B. *Ministry as Charisma*

It should be stressed that ministry is a dynamic process. The NT writers tend to think of the growth of the community of faith as analogous to the development of a great edifice or temple (1 Cor 3:16-17; Eph 2:21-22; 4:12; 1 Pet 2:5-6).

---

[6]Plato, *Gorgias* 518A. We are indebted to C. E. B. Cranfield, "Diakonia in the New Testament," *Service in Christ: Essays presented to Karl Barth on his 80th Birthday* (ed. J. I. McCord and T. H. L. Parker; London: Epworth, 1966): 36-38, for the reference.

[7]A study by John N. Collins, *Diakonia: Re-interpreting the Ancient Sources* (New York: Oxford Univ. Press, 1990), yields a more specific delineation of ministry. Christian ministry is not associated with worldly power and rule, but it is not strictly the service of slaves either. Rather, in the NT it is the mandate or commission of duly appointed believers to carry out special tasks of spiritual service for the development of the church. Collins understands the NT to teach that ministry is only for a select number set aside by the church in some form of office for special service. It is not done by every Christian. See John N. Collins, *Are All Christians Ministers?* (Collegeville, MN: Liturgical Press, 1992): 2; and Roy A. Harrisville, "Ministry in the New Testament," *Called and Ordained: Lutheran Perspectives on the Office of Ministry* (ed. T. Nichol and M. Kolden; Philadelphia: Fortress, 1990): 3-23.

What is important for our purposes is to note that the heavenly Christ graciously bestows *charismata* (gifts) to enable certain ones to assist his dynamic structure (the church) to grow by the agency of the Spirit. The Spirit provides the empowerment to do the work of ministry.

The lists of gifts found in the Pauline writings (1 Cor 12:4-11, 28-30; Rom 12:6-8; Eph 4:11) are neither exhaustive nor do they serve as a blueprint for the entire history of the church. Rather, the gifts are given in freedom by a Sovereign Lord for the benefit of the development of the οἰκοδομή (new edifice founded by Christ) which is in the process of growing into an integrated whole in keeping with the will of its chief builder (Eph 4:12, 16; 1 Cor 3:9). Just as the human body needs different food and a regimen throughout its life-cycle to remain healthy, so the Spirit will provide appropriate means to bring to perfection the church in its own unique way.

Among the gifts contributing to the growth and development of the church are the various διαιρέσεις (divisions of ministries) noted by Paul in 1 Cor 12:5. Ministries in the early churches materialized in many different manifestations such as the work of the apostles, prophets, evangelists, shepherds, and teachers (Eph 4:11-12). Clearly, this reflects a concern to show that among Christ's gifts to the church there are those individuals to whom the capacity is granted to exhort, guide, and carry out special tasks for the good of the body. As these gifts are exercised the community grows in its understanding that God has not abandoned his community to chaos (1 Cor 12:28; 14:40; Rom 12:6-8; Eph 4:11-12, 16).

C. *Spirit and Structure*

Such observations raise the very important but often misunderstood question of the relationship between spirit and structure. Does the Spirit choose individuals (male and female) who freely and mysteriously respond to personal calls to positions of leadership in the church? Or does the

Spirit work through a framework of roles and structures (offices) always present within the community to carry out his purpose of building up the body of Christ?

We take the position that, for the NT, spirit and structure cannot be separated but fit together. Despite Käsemann's view that charism and office stand in fundamental opposition with each other we believe that the text indicates that they are interdependent.[8] This can be seen in the emergence of the apostles, fellow laborers or ministers, and elders or overseers in the Gentile churches.

As an apostle, Paul considered that a function of his ministry was to exercise a disciplined, authoritative leadership over the churches which he founded. He made himself present to the churches that he founded through the medium of his letters.[9] He did not hesitate to command, admonish, and give sundry instructions (1 Thess 4:10-11; 5:11,12; 2 Thess 3:4, 6, 9-10, 12; 1 Cor 5:3-5; 2 Cor 13:10). Here gift and office were collapsed together. Paul considered his apostleship as a gift (1 Cor 12:28-31). But he had no hesitation in using it as an office.

Working alongside Paul in the performance of his ministry in the Gentile churches were a group of believers who frequently were called the συνεργοί (co-workers) or διάκονοι (ministers). While all Christians were active in the Christian life, these ones were set aside for special commissioned tasks in the life of the church. Interestingly enough, none within this group was called a prophet, pastor, or overseer.[10] But a number who labored with Paul were repeatedly called co-workers or ministers.

---

[8]Käsemann, "Ministry and Community," *Essays on New Testament Themes*, 78, 83.

[9]Abraham Malherbe, *Paul and the Thessalonians: The Philosophic Tradition of Pastoral Care* (Philadelphia: Fortress, 1987): 68-78.

[10]E. Earle Ellis, *Prophecy and Hermeneutic in Early Christianity* (Grand Rapids: Eerdmans, 1980) 5-6.

Timothy was a συνεργός (co-worker) and so was Apollos (1 Thess 3:2; 1 Cor 3:9). The Corinthians were both exhorted to be subject to the oversight of the household of Stephanas which was renowned for διακονία, and to any other co-worker or laborer like them (1 Cor 16:15-16). It would seem that the latter types fulfilled similar tasks to those who in Thessalonica were at work in labor, help, and admonishment (1 Thess 5:12: see Rom 12:8; 1 Tim 5:17). Paul refers to his own ministry of the word as the work of a διάκονος (Col 1:23, 25; Eph 3:7). But it was Timothy who was especially singled out as one who is a true διάκονος (minister). He was called a minister at the outset of Paul's ministry (in a number of well attested manuscripts of 1 Thess 3:2), and at the end (1 Tim 4:6). Thus, we see in the Pauline churches that those who received the gifts for ministry exercised them within the existing structures and offices in the church to facilitate the teaching of the word and growth of the body.

Finally, it is worthy of note that among the ministries in the Pauline churches (1 Cor 12:28) there existed those who had a special gift for κυβέρνησις (administration). As the Pauline churches grew these people became known as the πρεσβύτεροι (elders) or ἐπίσκοποι (overseers or superintendents). It is generally agreed that the former term was used to describe those who filled a role in the early Christian communities similar to the wise and mature Jewish leaders who had oversight over the synagogue (Acts 14:23; 15:1-23; 21:18; 1 Tim 4:14; Titus 1:5). This oversight included maintaining the apostolic tradition and directing the spiritual nourishment of teaching in the church (Acts 20:17-35; 1 Tim 5:17-19).

Likewise, this capacity to oversee the teaching in the church was characteristic of the ministry of the ἐπίσκοπος (overseer). The overseer could both supervise the work and teach (1 Tim 3:1-7; Titus 1:7-9). Yet, even here, the connection between gift and office was maintained. The office of elder or overseer soon became a regular structure in the ancient church. Still, at the time of the Pastoral epistles the office was directly connected with gift and the work of the Holy Spirit (1 Tim 4:14; 2 Tim 1:6).

D. *Preliminary Summary*

The characteristic word for ministry in the NT is διακονία. This word can be understood in two major senses. In a general sense, hallowed by the obedient action of Jesus, it provides an orientation for the church: the priesthood comprised of all believers. In the language of Ephesians, it is the ministry or service for the whole church to extol in praise God's glory before the whole creation. Second, in order to insure growth and maturity in the body of Christ, the Spirit provided a gifted leadership (ministry) that was the instrument for proclamation of the word, teaching, performance of special tasks, and ordering of the body.

This ministry was structured. Structures did not emerge in the early church under any master blueprint. Neither did they just mysteriously appear. They paralleled, in significant ways, certain structures operative in the ancient communities, especially the household or the synagogue. Besides the importance of the apostles and prophets for the early Pauline churches, ministers or co-workers, and elders, or overseers, played prominent roles. After the initial decades the latter (ministers and elders/overseers) became central for "the ministry" of the early church.

What is most significant is that the NT does not arrange these offices into ascending levels of significance. No office is superior to another. Often the least "prominent" role in the church is most vital to the life of the body (1 Cor 12:12-26).

The later threefold hierarchical offices of the bishop, πρεσβύτεροι (priests), and deacons, that emerged in the church in subsequent centuries, and even after being restructured in the Reformation and the nineteenth-century Restoration of Campbell-Stone, still abides in some form, was a fundamental distortion of the NT view of ministry.

All of the structures of leadership, "the offices," operated dynamically for the benefit of the body. It is impossible to rate one as more important than the other.

There is no question that women and men worked together in common service in the early church. But what do we know specifically about the roles women played in the ministries of teaching, assisting, and administration of word and deed in the churches? This issue will be the area of investigation in the next section of this paper.

4. *Participation by Women in the Ministry of the Early Church*

We now proceed to give a synoptic overview of how women went about the work of ministry in the early Gentile churches associated with Paul. Then, in the next section we follow this analysis with an attempt to delineate the reasons why cautionary comments were made about the appropriateness of women functioning in certain areas of ministry.

We have already observed that the offices of ministry in the Pauline churches were multifaceted. We will now observe that in a number of areas women served in ministry; but there is also an area of calling where there is a conspicuous absence of women. Our attention is now directed to these respective areas.

A. *Apostles and Prophets*

Jesus did not choose a woman as one of the Twelve. Neither is there a reference to a woman being called to the revitalized apostolate in Acts (the Twelve), or to a position of apostolic authority, in the sense that Paul received his special call to be the missionary to the nations.

Nevertheless, besides Paul and the Twelve, there were a number of special ambassadors or missionaries in the early church who were also known as apostles. Barnabas and

Silas, who often accompanied Paul on his missions, were called apostles and seemed to share some authority with him (Acts 14:4, 14; see 1 Thess 2:7; 1 Cor 4:9; 9:5-6). There were others who had gained recognition among some by this designation as well (2 Cor 11:5, 13).

Among those called apostles were a husband and wife, Andronicus and Junia, whom Paul considered as notable (Rom 16:7).[11] The use of συγγενεῖς (fellow countrymen) indicates they were Jews (Rom 16:7). They seem to have operated independent of Paul, but their work was known to him (Rom 16:7). A conjecture that may not be that far off the mark is that they were converted before Paul and played a role in founding the church at Rome.[12] In the modern church we are well aware of husbands and wives who work as teams in mission work and are recognized by the church as such. Something similar seems to be the case here. But, in any case, here is evidence that a woman was designated as an apostle.

In the closely related area of prophetic activity there is also evidence that women participated actively (Acts 21:9; 1 Cor 11:5; Rev 2:20).[13] In the listings of gifts there is no indication that the gift of prophecy was restricted to men (1 Cor 12:29; Eph 4:11). The central role of the early Christian prophet was to speak a word from the risen Lord to the church (1 Cor 14:1-40). Since women did function as prophets, the presumption is that women did convey "a word from the Lord" to the assembly (1 Cor 11:5).

---

[11]Ben Witherington III, *Women in the Earliest Churches* (SNTSMS 59; Cambridge: Cambridge Univ. Press, 1988): 115-116, gives a salient summary of the textual and linguistic problems associated with this verse. We accept the view has been substantiated that the correct name is Junia (not Junias) and that these are husband and wife.

[12]C. H. Dodd, *Epistle to the Romans* (London: Collins Fontana, 1959): 241.

[13]In the case of Rev 2:20, the prophetess was condemned not because she was a woman, but for her false teaching.

Indeed, many of the early Christian assemblies convened in homes. By definition, even in traditional societies, homes are places where significant latitude is given to women in carrying out the daily conduct of the household. Both the evidence for women prophets and the actual assemblies taking place in homes raises directly the issue of the range of feminine participation in the actual assemblies of the church (Rom 16:5; 1 Cor 16:19; Col 4:15; Phlm 2).

B. *Women as Teachers, Co-Workers, and Ministers*

Here we focus particularly on those women who worked within the circles of Paul's mission. First there is the work of Prisca. Prisca and her husband Aquila not only provided Paul a place to stay in several cities but were active in the work of evangelistic ministry. They were called συνεργοί (co-workers) of Paul (Rom 16:3). Elsewhere we learn that the co-workers were Paul's close associates in teaching and establishing new churches (see 2 Cor 8:23; Phil 2:25; 4:3; Col 4:11; Phlm 1, 24). This is congruent with the activity of Prisca and her husband as described in Acts 18:1-3, 18, 24-26. There they gave instructions in the important matter of baptism to Apollos. In most texts mentioning the couple, Prisca's name is first. This is usually thought to be an indication of her prominence. A reasonable inference is that this household was a place where the gospel was actively taught and that Prisca was at the forefront of this activity. Prisca was not only an outstanding co-worker but an important teacher in the church.

In the early churches founded by Paul the members of several households would gather in a large room. Praying and prophesying, an early form of the service of the Word, would take place in this setting (1 Cor 14:4-5). During the assembly a meal would be served, and the bread and the cup would be taken in memory of Christ. All members of the household would be present. Since it is anachronistic to talk about the ordered liturgies that developed in the church from the second century onwards, it is reasonable to conclude that in this more informal atmosphere, women like Prisca and

Junia were very active participants in what happened at these meetings.

Indeed, the references to other women who are listed in the Pauline churches as co-workers, ministers, or their equivalents, are quite impressive. At Philippi we note that Euodia and Syntyche struggled together in the gospel with Clemens and other co-workers (συνεργοί) of Paul (Phil 4:3). In Rom 16:1-2 Phoebe, a διάκονος (commissioned minister) of the church in Cenchreae, was commended to the churches in Rome. As a co-minister with Paul she was also called a προστάτις (helper/patron) in the church. The latter term was as significant as the former. It was used in a participial form in Rom 12:8 to describe the process of supervising charitable work in the congregation (see 1 Thess 5:12). Phoebe is a good example to illustrate the claim that women in the Pauline churches were active in similar kinds of ministry.

In addition, there were Mary, Tryphena and Tryphosa, who perhaps were sisters and were called co-laborers with Paul, Persis the mother of Rufus, and Nympha[14] (Rom 16:6, 12-13, 15; Col 4:15). There can be little doubt that these women, some of considerable social stature, played a prominent role in the spread of the gospel and in the process of nurturing the early churches.[15] Titus is told by Paul to instruct the older women to teach the younger women appropriate Christian conduct (Titus 2:3-5). But the evidence seems to indicate that the ministry of women in the churches founded by Paul went well beyond working with other women and children.

C. *The Absence of Women as Elders*

There is no evidence that a woman functioned as an elder or overseer in the early church. However, there is a

---

[14]Witherington, *Women in the Earliest Churches*, 116, 262.

[15]Wayne Meeks, *The First Urban Christians: The Social World of the Apostle Paul* (New Haven: Yale Univ. Press, 1983): 53-63.

question as to the precise meaning of the instruction to the γυναῖκας ("wives" or "women") in 1 Tim 3:11. The lack of a personal pronoun governing γυναῖκας, the similar construction to 3:8 with the repetition of ὡσαύτως (likewise) and other structural and verbal features similar to those that describe the male διάκονοι themselves, do count against understanding this verse as referring only to the wives of the male ministers or "deacons" (1 Tim 3:8-9, 12).[16] The most reasonable alternative position is that these instructions were given to the female διάκονοι (see 1 Tim 5:9-10).[17] Perhaps the reference to the women in 1 Tim 3:11 vis-à-vis the "male deacons" in 3:8, 12 means nothing more than the acknowledgment of the fact that men were normally thought to be the ministers but women did carry out similar duties as well. In any case, the important datum to consider is that, from beginning to end, in the Pauline churches there is no evidence that women functioned as overseers.

Thus, a basic outline of the role of women in the ministries of the Pauline house churches begins to emerge. Women served as missionaries, prophets, teachers, delegates, givers of aid, and doubtless in numerous other ways. The only place where they are not mentioned is in the ministry of public teaching of the word and administration of the churches. This omission may not be accidental. We must investigate more closely because here we are brought to the passages where Paul made some cautionary comments on the ministries of women.

5. *Some Cautionary Comments on Women in Ministry in the Pauline Churches*

Given the previous discussion it comes as a point of interest to find several texts wherein the participation of women in the assembly is curtailed (1 Cor 11:3-16; 14:33-

---

[16] James B. Hurley, *Man and Woman in Biblical Perspective* (Grand Rapids: Zondervan, 1981): 231.

[17] See E. Earle Ellis, *Pauline Theology: Ministry and Society* (Grand Rapids: Ecrdmans, 1989): 76.

36; 1 Tim 2:9-15). What leads Paul to call for women "to be silent," or "not to teach or exercise control" over the men (1 Cor 14:34; 1 Tim 2:12)? What is the range of these prescriptive statements? What theological principle informs them?

In order to answer these questions we will give a brief synopsis of Paul's point in these texts, and then we will discuss the theological rationale that seems to undergird his position. Due to space limitations only the results of our exegesis can be stated here.

1 Cor 11:3-16 constitutes a Pauline regulation on certain features of the dress of both men and women during the time of prayer and prophetic discussion in the assembly. The key issue seems to be whether the women being spiritually free in the Lord should, in the assembly (1 Cor 11:3-5), discard the appropriate head coverings worn by modest women in both Jewish and Gentile cultures. Paul states that there is a tradition in the churches about the rules on these matters. This tradition is anchored in an understanding of the appropriate roles of male and female that were set forth in the creation narrative. By appealing to that tradition Paul argues that the women should maintain the covering. The men may not. The Corinthians should abide by this tradition.

The issue about appropriate conduct and decorum in the assembly also surfaces in 1 Cor 14:34-35. Earlier, because of a chaotic situation in the assembly, Paul gave instructions about the speaking in tongues in 14:27-28. Only two or three were to exercise the gift and if there were no interpreter the one with the gift should be silent. With respect to the activity of the prophets similar instructions, including the appropriate time to be silent and to exercise restraint was given (14:29-32). Paul then turns to give instructions to the wives (14:33b-36).[18] During those occasions when the gifts

---

[18] The word γυναῖκας can be translated either "women" or "wives" depending on the context. The context clearly entails that the translation should be "wives" because of what is said in 14:35. See E.

were being exercised in order to promote good order, likewise, they were not to get involved in the discussions. This was congruent with the law—a probable reference to Gen 2-3, where Adam was created first. If the women intend to make an intervention they should wait and discuss this matter with their husbands at home (14:35). Paul claims that this interpretation of the commandment (laws) of the Lord will be vindicated by the prophets (1 Cor 14:37).

Finally, in remarkably similar terminology to that found in 1 Cor 14:33b-36, again the issue of decorum and conduct of the women in the assembly surfaces in 1 Tim 2:9-15. Earlier in the chapter there was a discussion about the role of prayer in the assembly. This concluded with some instructions as to how the men should pray. This word is followed by a twofold demand placed upon the women. First, while the women are in the assembly, they are to dress modestly and appropriately for a community at prayer. Second, the women are to act like other ancient students. They should learn correct information quietly in full submission to the teacher (1 Thess 4:11; 2 Thess 3:12; 1 Tim 2:2).[19] In the assembly they are not permitted to teach or dictate to the man who is functioning in a capacity of leadership.[20]

Earle Ellis, "The Silenced Wives of Corinth," *New Testament Textual Criticism* (ed. E. J. Epp and G. D. Fee; Oxford: Clarendon, 1981): 213-220. In Ellis' view, the call to be silent (σιγᾶν) is a call not to engage in the discussions about the interpretations of the tongues or the activity of the prophets (see 1 Cor 14:28, 30). This is a different word to the one used in 1 Tim 2:11 (ἡσυχία) where one is called to be quiet out of respect for a teacher.

[19] Paul W. Barnett, "Wives and Women's Ministry," *EvQ* 61 (1989): 229-230.

[20] It is unclear in this passage whether Paul has in mind the "wives" in the house-church or the women in general. Ann L. Bowman, "Women in Ministry: An Exegetical Study of 1 Timothy 2:11-15," *BSac* 149 (1992): 197, gives solid reasons why it may be the latter. We would understand Paul's comments here are prescriptive for all women in the church.

In all three passages the cautionary comments amount to a call for appropriate submissive demeanor on the part of the women in the assembly. They are not to flaunt the tradition of the community on the matter of wearing appropriate head covering in the assembly. The women were not to intervene and disrupt the assembly in the matter of testing the words of the speakers who give utterance under the Spirit. And they were to listen submissively in the assembly to the teacher who was, most likely, the overseer of the church.

All three of these cautionary comments involve an appeal, in some fashion, to the creation narrative. We would assert that this point is not accidental. Paul was well versed in Jewish interpretation of the law about the appropriate role of women in the life of the community of faith.[21] Now, based on the reality of the emergence of a new era after the coming of the Messiah, and with the traditional teaching of the synagogue echoing in the background, Paul gives instructions for these special situations that had come to light among God's people. These instructions represent Paul's understanding of the recovery of the intent of the Creator in establishing the male-female relationship in the beginning.

Although these instructions obviously arise out of unrepeatable situations they should not be dismissed arbitrarily as peculiar *ad hoc* comments that have no relevance beyond the time of first century.[22] The fact is that these instructions stem from a deep-seated theological reflection on the nature of the male-female relationship in light of the renewed redemptive order within the creation that

---

[21] Elisabeth Schüssler Fiorenza, "Women in the Pre-Pauline and Pauline Churches," *USQR* 33 (1978): 161.

[22] Contra Gordon D. Fee, "Issues in Evangelical Hermeneutics, Part III: The Great Watershed-Intentionality and Particularity/Eternality: I Timothy 2:8-15 as a Test Case," *Crux* 26 (1990): 31-37. Our position is in essential agreement on this point with D. Moo, "What Does it Mean Not to Teach or Have Authority Over Men?: 1 Timothy 2:11-15," *Recovering Biblical Manhood and Womanhood: A Response to Evangelical Feminism* (ed. J. Piper and W. Grudem; Wheaton, IL: Crossway, 1991): 179-80, 192-193.

Women in the New Testament Doctrine of Ministry 537

has come to light in Christ. Although the individual situations which precipitated these teachings are only matters of historical interest, the theological understanding which informed these teachings is crucial. Paul's understanding of the claim of the Creator, as stated in Genesis, upon the reign of the Messiah in the interim period before the end, is part of the warp and woof of his theology. Among those who accept the Pauline writings as the norm for theology, this theological rationale must be taken with utmost seriousness.

As such, we will now reflect on this theological rationale in the final section of the paper.

6. *Female and Male in the Medium of the Renewed Redemptive Life*

A clue to finding Paul's underlying theological rationale for the role of male and female in the renewed creation can be seen in Rom 7:2. There he describes the wife as ὕπανδρος (one who lives as subject to her husband). The husband is the head of the household; and in a similar way, for Paul and his heirs, the overseer of the church functions as the leader of the household of God (1 Cor 11:3; Col 3:18; Eph 5:21-23; 1 Tim 3:1-7). This structure is considered foundational for both the natural family and the family of God. All of this Paul took from his understanding of the order of creation that God established in Gen 2:5-25 (especially 2:18) *before* the Fall. For Paul it is axiomatic that the chronological creation of Adam before Eve carries with it the understanding that in the zone of the family the husband is to function as the leader. This normative structure was later distorted by sin. East of Eden headship became an excuse for abuse; but in the new redemptive order in Christ, the normative structure given in creation is being restored along lines in keeping with Paul's understanding of Christology.[23]

---

[23]N. Dahl, "Christ, Creation, and the Church," *Jesus in the Memory of the Early Church: Essays by Nils Alstrup Dahl* (Minneapolis: Augsburg, 1976): 135-137, who is regarded as one of the

Thus, in the new creation, wives are to show faithfulness and devotion to their husbands just as Christ kept his commitments toward the church. But, at the same time, the husband's headship in the home is not an order or status that functions through the instrumentality of coercive power or domination. Rather the husband, also informed by the example of Christ, is to undertake freely a similar commitment toward his wife as the Lord showed toward the church. This is why Paul can appeal for both husbands and wives to be subject to one another in Christ (1 Cor 7:4; Col 3:18; Eph 5:21-24).

Based on his eschatology and Christology, this theological model was the source of Paul's view of the role of women and men in the household of God. Especially, since the created order has come to proleptic fulfillment in Christ, Paul fights strongly to see that this perspective clearly informs what takes place in the assembly. Paul has this in mind when in 1 Cor 11:2 he asserts that the instruction he is about to give on the appropriate decorum of male and female has its origins in the authoritative tradition handed down in the churches (1 Cor 11:2; see 11:16). In essence, the principle inherent in early Christian tradition is that in the restored new creation wives are to be in submission to their husbands. A similar principle is at work in 1 Cor 14:33-35. Here this principle is reinforced by the specific appeal to the law and the interpretation of early

---

foremost authorities on Ephesians has made some very pertinent comments on Eph 5:21-33. Noting that the theme of this pericope is the relationship between husband and wife, Dahl observed that Paul bases his discussion on Gen 2:24 (Eph 5:31). Paul argues that in Gen 2:24 there is embedded not only the ideal order for husband and wife— but the creation account is also a foreshadowing of the ideal order of the new creation that comes about with the exaltation of Christ. Thus, "the man," in Gen 2:24, corresponds to Christ in the new creation and the church to his wife. For Dahl, this deepened reality which has come about in the new creation enhances and elevates Christian marriage which continues in the time of the church. A marriage that is in keeping with the will of the Creator reflects the relationship between Christ and the church.

Christian prophets. And the same point is made in 1 Tim 2:11-15 where, by extension, this prescriptive principle is also applicable for the women in their relationships to the overseers in the ancient house-churches.

With respect to the latter text, the use of the Creation narrative is noteworthy. In 1 Tim 2:13, the grounds given for the command to the woman "not to teach and exercise control" over the man are because Adam ἐπλάσθη (was created) first. This connects directly with the Genesis account, not only because of the reference to Adam and Eve, but because the same verb πλάσσειν (to create) was found in the Greek Bible (LXX) in Gen 2:7, 8, 15, 19. For the author of 1 Timothy, the narratological priority of the male in the foundational story of God's people (Gen 2-3) warranted a position of first importance for the male in decision making both in the natural family and the people of God.

Operating within such a tradition of reading this foundational story, the writer of 1 Timothy, perhaps in light of Gen 3:17 (because you have *heeded* the voice of your wife), holds Adam responsible for the transgression because he did not fulfill his role as leader but allowed himself to be co-opted into the consequences of her being deceived.[24] It is precisely such a situation that the writer of 1 Timothy does not wish to see repeated in the community of the new creation (1 Tim 2:14-15).

So we come to the bottom line for Paul. Women have many gifts for ministry; but caution should be shown in the exercise of these gifts so that the male and female relationship in family, established in creation, and now re-affirmed and enhanced by life both in the household and in the new eschatological community of the church, is in no sense compromised, but elevated and affirmed in the activities of the assembly.

---

[24] Bowman, *B Sac* 149 (1992): 206.

Conclusion

At the outset of this study we proposed to give an overview of a major area of NT teaching on ministry and to determine what role women played therein. Our study has produced several major findings.

With respect to the development of early Gentile Christianity we discovered that, although the ministries were diverse, spirit and structure were intermingled from the beginning, with the result that through appropriate offices God has always provided an ordered way for teaching and discipline in the church.

Second, we found that women were called to a number of ministries in the early church. Women were especially active as co-workers or διάκονοι (ministers) in the Pauline churches. These included widespread responsibilities in giving of aid and teaching.

Third, there was one area of ministry where women were not active. Women did not function as overseers either in the capacity as teachers in the assembly or in the direct exercising of control over the NT churches. We found that theological reasons underscored this state of affairs. In the new creation the basic structure of relationships between male and female, which was established in the first creation (the male created first and the woman made to complement him), has been recovered and should be enhanced in the messianic era. For the early Christians, this entailed a functional headship for the male both in the Christian household and the church. This appeal to the ideal order of creation is substantive and normative. For Paul, evidence of the operation of this relationship must be visible both in the family and the conduct of the household of God.

A proper recovery of these principles would be fortuitous for the modern church. Yet, as the church seeks to understand Scripture, under the guidance of the Spirit, it must not only be aware of the dangers of certain contemporary feminist ideologies, but also should be prepared to affirm the importance of the ministries of women. Contrary to the understanding of many, women did play an active and important role in the ministries of the early church. Today, there are innumerable avenues and opportunities for women to continue and expand these ministries. Furthermore, the results of this study also suggest that the whole area of women's participation in the assembly should be reexamined in the light of a common-sense reading of what were the actual practices in the early Gentile churches. If this is done, it may be found that many of the restrictions placed upon the service of women in the contemporary churches of Christ have no valid biblical or theological basis.

Nevertheless, it should be recognized that the popular contemporary egalitarian view that there is no essential difference between the sexes is simply not endorsed by the NT. The early Christian understanding of the creation account in Genesis is crucial on this point. In the first creation humans were made as male and female. Both had capacities that were able to complement each other beneficially. In the new creation these capacities are enhanced. As part of the process of enhancement the male is to fulfill a role as leader in both the family and the assembly. To the degree that this leadership reflects the model of Christ, the godly woman responds by exercising her gifts for ministry in submission to this leadership. Thus we can affirm that responsibility for oversight in the early church was not necessarily a direct reflection of an ancient patriarchal society, but a working out of a profound picture, based on revelation, of what it means for male and female to live together and be truly human.

Unfortunately, a failure to appreciate these theological principles, ultimately informed by the life of the crucified Messiah, has led to many difficulties. Some have understood the ministries of the elders or of the pulpit-minister to be the highest positions in a hierarchy of power rather than necessary expressions of God's gifts to the church. Such a distorted view, when heard in the context of a widespread acceptance of the liberal secularist emphasis on "rights," leads many to the erroneous position that the biblical recognition of gender distinctions in the natural family and household of God cannot complement the male-female relationship, but instead permits and warrants males to exercise abusive domination.

Just as we need to hear the biblical teaching on the role of husband/wife in God's new world, both in home and the church, we all need also to hear again the word that the true minister is one who excels in service. The most significant ministry or office in the church may be the most inconspicuous whether that be rendered by a woman or a man. That is the basic lesson to be learned by anyone who would be a disciple of the crucified Messiah.

Chapter Twenty-three

WOMEN IN THE CHURCH: THE HERMENEUTICAL PROBLEM

Thomas H. Olbricht

In older materials, written when the role of women in the church was an unchallenged consensus, little attention was paid to hermeneutical strategies. The approach was straightforward and uncomplicated. Paul wrote, ". . . women should be silent in the churches" (1 Cor 14:33). No further comment seemed needed. Whatever the role of women when the church gathered, it was not a speaking one. If organization rather than speaking was at stake, then the matter was settled through the denial of female authority. "I permit no woman to teach or to have authority over a man; she is to keep silent" (1 Tim 2:12).

An example may be found in J. W. Shepherd's remarks in David Lipscomb's commentary on 1 Corinthians:

> No instruction in the New Testament is more positive than this; it is positive, explicit, and universal; and however plausible may be the reasons which are urged for disregarding it, and for suffering women to take an active part in conducting public worship, yet the authority of the inspired apostle remains positive and his meaning cannot be misunderstood. He looks at it from every viewpoint, forbids it altogether, and shows that from every consideration it was to be regarded as improper for them to take any active part in conducting the public service.[1]

---

[1]David Lipscomb, *A Commentary on the New Testament Epistles* (ed. with additional Notes by J. W. Shepherd; Nashville: Gospel Advocate, 1935): 216. Lipscomb last worked on this material

Now, however, the consensus with respect to women has broken down in society, in other confessional groups, and in the restorationist churches. The result is that the interpretation of Scriptures regarding the role of women has become increasingly problematic. We seem to be back to ground zero as far as hermeneutics is concerned.

This essay sets out to assess the manner in which we have interpreted texts in actual practice, then and now.

1. *Restoration Hermeneutics*

In the current climate among Churches of Christ, the impression prevails that hermeneutics revolves totally around commands, examples, and necessary inferences.[2] Our own history, however, reveals at least three major aspects of hermeneutics: 1) the command, example, and necessary inference formula, 2) the dispensations, and 3) the grammatico-historical aspects. It was in this order that the three surfaced in the Thomas and Alexander Campbell movement. It is interesting that the same hermeneutical concerns were not so evident in the early days of the O'Kelly, Jones-Smith, and Stone movements,[3] all of which were molded in the awakening traditions and less influenced by the rational rigors of British empiricism. These leaders were also less interested in detailed ecclesiastical blueprints. The experience of conversion and emotional worship took priority over reason.

---

in 1909. In the Romans commentary produced under the same arrangements (1933) Lipscomb on 16:1, wrote, "Some think she was a publicly recognized deaconess, but we find no recognition in the Scriptures of any such class" (264).

[2] See Thomas Olbricht, "Hermeneutics in the Churches of Christ," *ResQ* 37 (1995): 1-24.

[3] See the "Witnesses' Address" of the "Last Will and Testament" in Charles A. Young, *Historical Documents Advocating Christian Union* (Chicago: Christian Century, 1904): 24, "neither precept nor example."

A. *The command, example, and necessary inference formula*

The first instance of commands, examples and inferences joined together for ascertaining primitive patterns seems to be that of Edward Dering as early as 1572.[4] It appears that this formula was developed in those churches especially interested in patterns of polity, e.g., the Zwinglian reform, Scottish Presbyterians, English Puritans, and the various British independent groups.

The formula appears, as if already widely accepted, in the earliest printed document of the Campbell movement, that is, the "Declaration and Address" of 1809. "Express terms and approved precedents" were granted without question, but inferences were suspect. Thomas Campbell conceded that inferences may be useful, but rejected their ecclesiastical role on the ground that they divide believers.[5]

The tripartite formula has had a checkered career in its five-hundred year history. It has largely been employed by churches intent on restoring overt ecclesiological patterns, but less so by those restoring lifestyle (e.g., such Anabaptists as the Amish) and the charismatic gifts (e.g., Pentecostals. In churches where it once was important, e.g., the Congregationalists (originally Puritans) and the Presbyterians, churchmen have lost even a memory of the formula—but then they are no longer committed to restoring the ordinances of the primitive church.

Over the past twenty years, various writers in Churches of Christ have pointed out the inconsistent manner in which the tripartite formula has been applied.[6] The tripartite formula

---

[4]Edward Dering, *The Praelections . . . upon . . . Hebrews* in *Workes*, 447-448, quoted by Theodore Dwight Bozeman, *To Live Ancient Lives* (Chapel Hill: Univ. of North Carolina Press, 1988): 70. This document was probably published in 1572.

[5]"Declaration and Address," in Young, *Historical Documents*, 110.

[6]Michael W. Casey, "The Development of Necessary Inference in the Hermeneutics of the Disciples of Christ/Churches of Christ," Ph.D.

was useful in our movement as long as restoring the NT church was our driving dynamic. But more recently we have been inspired by discipleship, servanthood, family, and praise. Obvious manifestations of this sea of change are concretized in workshops, films, and electronically reproduced song collections. Critics of changes away from the older driving mission of our churches have attacked revisions in hermeneutics under the appellation "The New Hermeneutic." The "new hermeneutic" in the Churches of Christ, as I have argued elsewhere, is basically a paradigm shift in our driving force.[7]

B. *The Dispensations*

Our tripartite dispensationalism has likewise played a decisive role in the manner in which we have interpreted the Scriptures.[8] This formula was first explicit in our literature in Alexander Campbell's famous 1816 "Sermon on the Law" presented to the Redstone Baptist Association.[9] Even before that, however, the authority of the NT over against the OT

---

diss. Univ. of Pittsburgh, 1986; Milo Hadwin, *The Role of New Testament Examples as Related to Biblical Authority* (Austin: Firm Foundation, 1974); Robert E. Woodrow, "The Nature of Biblical Authority and the Restoration Movement," M.A. thesis, Abilene Christian University, 1983, and Earl D. Edwards, *Gender and Ministry*, (Henderson: Freed-Hardeman University, 1990). See in the latter especially the comments of Lynn Mitchell.

[7]Thomas H. Olbricht, "Hermeneutics: The Beginning Point," *Image* (September-October, 1989).

[8]In the past half century we have obviously made this distinction in sermons on rightly dividing the word, but in the intramural battles of the 1950s this formulation dropped out of our explicit hermeneutic since it was assumed by all the controversialists. J. D. Thomas does not mention the matter in *We Be Brethren* (Abilene: Biblical Research Press, 1958), though in *Heaven's Window* (Abilene: Biblical Research Press, 1974): 93, he made an effort at total hermeneutics, but not systematically.

[9]Alexander Campbell, "Sermon on the Law" in Young, *Historical Documents*, 252.

Women in the Church: The Hermeneutical Problem

for reestablishing the primitive church was implicit. In the "Declaration and Address" Thomas Campbell wrote:

> The New Testament is as perfect a constitution for the worship, discipline, and government of the New Testament Church, and as perfect a rule for the particular duties of its members, as the Old Testament was for the worship, discipline, and government of the Old Testament Church, and the particular duties of its members.[10]

In our movement ever since, we have been adamant against employing the OT to support any Christian practice.

Campbell's perspective on the three dispensations was indebted to the federal or covenantal theology of the Dutch scholars, especially Grotius (1583-1645) and Cocceius (1603-1669).[11] Cocceius held that with the failure of the covenant of works with Adam, God instituted the covenant of grace in three dispensations, the patriarchal, the Mosaic, and the Christian.[12] This dispensationalism not only established a groundwork for what is authoritative in each dispensation, it also provided a means of relating the dispensations. In effect, it became a biblical theology, featuring promise and fulfillment. An example of a "biblical theology" so organized in the restoration movement was Robert Milligan's often reprinted, *An Exposition and Defence of the Scheme of Redemption*.[13]

---

[10] Young, *Historical Documents*, 109.

[11] See especially Robert Frederick West, *Alexander Campbell and Natural Religion* (New Haven: Yale Univ. Press, 1948). See also in regard to the role of these scholars in Biblical criticism, Simon J. De Vries, *Bible and Theology in the Netherlands* (New York: Peter Lang, 1989): 5ff.

[12] "Johannes Cocceius," John McClintock and James Strong, *Cyclopaedia of Biblical, Theological, and Ecclesiastical Literature* (New York: Harper and Brothers, 1895).

[13] Robert Milligan, *An Exposition and Defence of the Scheme of Redemption* (Cincinnati: Carroll Publishing, 1868).

In the past twenty years, the OT has been rediscovered in our movement, in part because of certain influential OT scholars such as John Willis, J. J. M. Roberts, and Rick Marrs. While we have rethought the significance of the OT for Christian faith and life, the inappropriateness of the OT for determining the structures and worship of the church remains essentially intact. We share rediscovery of the OT with other traditions, e.g., Lutherans, who in the past assigned a negligible, if not negative role to the OT.[14]

C. *The Grammatico-Historical Aspects*

Of the three aspects of hermeneutics, Alexander Campbell addressed in detail the traditional principles of biblical interpretation last. He set these forth in *Millennial Harbinger* extras in the early 1830s and published them together in a book titled *Christianity Restored* in 1835. He set out as his purpose "the principles by which the Christian institution may be certainly and satisfactorily ascertained."[15]

Campbell believed that the "scientific," that is, systematic interpretation of the Scripture should proceed according to the same rules for understanding any other document. In that regard, though his "Principles" were sketchy, they were abreast of the best hermeneutic and exegetical principles of the time, especially in the tradition of Ernesti as mediated through Moses Stuart, the foremost American biblical scholar of the first half of the nineteenth century.[16] He was knowledgeable regarding the best grammatico-historical approaches in the early nineteenth century, especially British-American but also German.[17]

---

[14]For such scholars, see Hemchand Gossai, "The Old Testament Among Christian Theologians," *Bible Review* 6 (1990): 22-25, 36.

[15]Campbell, *Christianity Restored* (Reprint, Rosemead: Old Paths Book Club, 1959): 13.

[16]*Ibid.*, 26, 53, 95, 96.

[17]In addition to Boring, see Thomas H. Olbricht, "Alexander Campbell in the Context of American Biblical Scholarship," *ResQ* 33 (1991): 13-28, which sets him in his contemporary context.

It is interesting that Campbell's 1835 "Principles" were not carefully coordinated with dispensationalism, but especially not with the command, example and necessary inference formula. The latter is not even mentioned in the "Principles of Interpretation" or the seven general rules at the end, though the dispensational aspect receives passing mention.[18] The same obtains in later books on hermeneutics in our movement, notably those of Lamar, Dungan, and J. D. Thomas.[19] A student at Freed-Hardeman University raised a perceptive question when he asked me what the "new hermeneutic" controversy regarding command, example, and necessary inference was all about since virtually all the classic books on hermeneutics in our movement did not even discuss this tripartite formula.

Since the time of Campbell, the grammatico-historical interpretation of the Scripture has developed dramatically, first in Germany, then early in this century in Great Britain and in the United States. Collier has identified the manner in which scholars in the Churches of Christ have entered contemporary international biblical scholarship, with a few even receiving widespread acclaim. Viewing these scholars in "The Historical/Contextual School,"[20] Collier bemoans the fact that they have only cursorily addressed the manner in which their work relates to our old hermeneutic or to the interpretation of the Scriptures in the churches.

---

[18]Campbell, "Principles," *Christianity Restored*, 96-98.

[19]J. S. Lamar, *The Organon of Scripture* (Philadelphia: J. B. Lippincott, reprint 1960); D. R. Dungan, *Hermeneutics* (Cincinnati: Standard, n. d.); Thomas, *We Be Brethren*. Thomas, *Heaven's Window*, pp. 81-85, mentions the dispensations, and grammatico-historical approaches in passing.

[20]Gary Collier, "Bringing the Word to Life: An Assessment of the Hermeneutical Impasse in Churches of Christ; Part I: The Rationalist/Inductive School; Part II The Historical/ Contextual School." These papers have not as yet been printed in this form, but are available in electronically procured copy from the Religion Division, Pepperdine University, Malibu, CA 90263. A truncated version is Gary D. Collier, "Bringing the Word to Life: Biblical Hermeneutics in Churches of Christ," *Christian Studies* 11 (1990): 18-40.

2. Application of Hermeneutics in Regard to Music

We have clearly embraced a layered hermeneutic. We have not always fully coordinated the various layers, in part, I suspect, because we have discovered that to do so is complicated in light of various aspects of Scripture. Sometimes practice does not fully reflect theory. In order to discern how we have applied our hermeneutic, I will set forth its benchmark use in regard to the music employed in church worship. While many articles are available I have limited my search to some of the classic and standard books which focus on controversies within the restoration tradition.

The most widely recognized book on the subject before World War II was Kurfees, *Instrumental Music in the Worship*.[21] After the war, Brewer published a small work titled, *A Medley on the Music Question or A potpourri of Philology*.[22] However, the person who has more than anyone else examined the original sources upon which various claims have been made is Ferguson, *A Cappella Music in the Public Worship of the Church*.[23] The most recent book of note is that of Rubel Shelly, *Sing His Praise! A Case for A Cappella Music as Worship Today*.[24]

The telltale signs of the categories of our hermeneutic show up in these materials, but never in any systematic manner. The arguments on instrumental music tend to take the following pattern:

---

[21]M. C. Kurfees, *Instrumental Music in the Worship or the Greek Verb Psallo Philologically and Historically Examined* (Nashville: Gospel Advocate, 1922). Earlier O. E. Payne, *Instrumental Music is Scriptural* (Cincinnati: Standard, 1920), had taken the opposite view.

[22]G. C. Brewer, *A Medley on the Music Question or A Potpourri of Philology* (Nashville: Gospel Advocate, 1948).

[23]Everett Ferguson, *A Cappella Music in the Public Worship of the Church* (Abilene: Biblical Research Press, 1972).

[24]Rubel Shelly, *Sing His Praise! A Case for A Cappella Music as Worship Today* (Nashville: 20th Century Christian, 1987).

Women in the Church: The Hermeneutical Problem

1. Vocal music is authorized in the NT.
2. The NT is silent on instrumental music.
3. No compelling reasons may be advanced from the NT for the employment of instrumental music.
4. The Greek word *Psallo*, found in the NT, translated "sing," does not include instrumental music.
5. The reasons are extra-biblical, based on the work of lexicographers in the original documents.
6. Documents and historians attest to the absence of the use of instrumental music in the earliest churches.
7. The music employed in the NT church serves the function of teaching and edification. Vocal music is the means of attaining these ends.

The matter of authorization is therefore in part a matter of commands, examples, and necessary inferences found in Scripture. In addition, it includes the differences between authorization from the OT and the NT, the witness of ancient grammatical usage, and the historical practices of early Christians and Jews. It has interested me for some time that although we have believed that interpretation involves only the Scriptures themselves, we have always felt free to borrow from whatever materials or authorities exterior to the Scripture may help us in our cause.

A. *Vocal music is authorized in the New Testament*

Shelly has made this point the most pointedly:

> New Testament authority is for *singing* as the means of musical praise to God in the Christian Age. Such passages as Eph 5:19 and Col 3:16 call for "speaking," "teaching," "admonishing," "singing," and "making music in your heart." Each of these actions is related to verbal activity, and not one of them can be performed by a mechanical instrument of music.[25]

---

[25]*Ibid.*, 47.

B. *The NT is silent on instrumental music*

Several of the authors stated the silent argument succinctly. According to Kurfees, "There is not a solitary mention of instrumental music in the worship of any New Testament Church, nor in any instance of Christian worship throughout the Apostolic age."[26] Brewer put it forcefully, "We do not use instrumental music in worship because there is no authority for it in the New Testament."[27]

C. *No compelling reasons may be advanced from the NT for the employment of instrumental music*

The absence of justification for instrumental music was supported on the grounds that nothing is expressly stated in regard to instrumental music in the NT, nor are there examples, or any necessary reasons to employ it. Brewer set forth the case in this manner:

> When we show that we do not use instrumental music in our worship, because there is no scriptural authority, either by precept or example, for such music in Christian worship, we necessarily indict those who use the instruments. Our defense of our own nonuse, nonconformity, charges others by implication or by necessary inference, if not by direct statement, with practicing something for which they have no scriptural authority.[28]

Brewer's statement is the most clear and direct expression of our tripartite hermeneutic formula discovered in these works. However, neither Brewer nor any of the other authors set out systematically to employ these three items as an organizing feature.

---

[26]Kurfees, *Instrumental Music in the Worship*, 2.
[27]Brewer, *A Medley on the Music Question*, 12.
[28]*Ibid.*, 6.

D. *The Greek word Psallo, translated in the NT "sing," does not include instrumental music*

Certain authors from the Christian Church argued that the word ψάλλω (*psallo*; sing) in the NT means play an instrument as well as sing, therefore the use of instrumental music is commanded by the NT. Payne argued at length, citing many ancient texts, that ψάλλω in ancient usage always included instrumentation.[29] Ferguson and Shelly both argued that though in classical works before, during, and after the NT period ψάλλω included playing an instrument, in the NT itself the appropriate understanding is "sing" since the earliest Christians did not play instruments in their worship. Ferguson wrote,

> Historical evidence makes it most unlikely that an instrument can be found in *psallo* in the New Testament and shows that the absence of any clear reference to instrumental music in the church's worship in early day was not accidental. It was not mentioned because it was not there.[30]

E. *The reasons are extra-biblical, based on the work of lexicographers in the original documents*

The major proofs as to the use or non-use of instrumental music, beginning with Kurfees, revolved about statements made by scholars in the lexicons. It is clear therefore that the tripartite formula was left behind and the burden of proof rested with grammatico-historical matters. In our time from certain quarters in our churches there is a tendency to discount the importance of scholarly grammatico-historical hermeneutical dimensions. Alexander Campbell, however, prized them highly, both in his articles on interpretation and in practice, especially in his debates on baptism. Kurfees depended almost entirely on the lexicographers to make his case that ψάλλω in the NT was

---

[29]O. E. Payne, *Instrumental Music is Scriptural*, 41-103.
[30]Ferguson, *A Cappella Music*, 81.

limited to singing. While the testimonies of the lexicographers are important, more so are the original data upon which their conclusions are based. Ferguson in his book appropriately spent most of his time consulting the ancient classical texts to show the basis for the decisions of the lexicographers.

F. *Documents and historians attest to the absence of the use of instrumental music in the earliest churches*

The statements from the historians as to the use of instrumental music by the early Christians was also considered highly important by all these authors. Campbell, in his writings on interpretation, did not detail the employment of historical data, but in regard to baptism, he, in practice, utilized whatever citations supported the case for immersion. It is interesting that we have argued that nothing beyond the period of the NT has any bearing on what we do as New Testament Christians, yet we find it very useful to offer later historical references in support of what we believe to be correct interpretations.

G. *The music employed in the NT church serves the function of teaching and edification. Vocal music is the means of attaining these ends*

It was particularly Ferguson who argued that instrumental music is ruled out on the grounds that it fails to contribute to edification. His argument is therefore inference, but not of the kind traditionally employed in Restoration circles. It is theological reflection upon the ramifications of the centrality of Christ to the NT.

Edification for Paul in 1 Cor 14 meant intelligible, verbal instruction, in contrast to speaking in unintelligible (to those present) tongues. No one is edified by mere sound. It is in this context that he makes disparaging reference to instruments of music (vv. 7, 8; see 13:1). The foreign language would be comparable to instruments. By way of contrast, rational, spiritual, vocal music corresponds to Paul's criterion. "Each one has a hymn, a lesson, a revelation, a tongue, or an interpretation. Let all things be done for edification" (1 Cor 14:26). The synagogue emphasized teaching and did not have instrumental music. The temple emphasized ritual, and it did have instrumental music. Further, in Christian history, where edification has been central, instrumental music has been in the background, but where ritual has been in the forefront, then the instrument has been prominent. An obvious contrast is between the Calvinist churches of the Reformation and the Catholic Church of the late Middle Ages.[31]

The authority of the OT was not discussed to any extent in these books. The chief reason was that the opponents to which these remarks were addressed normally agreed, as Restorationists, that authorization comes from the NT, not the OT. It was mainly Brewer who set forth the perspective that though instrumental music was authorized in the OT, that did not in turn justify its employment by Christians. Brewer wrote regarding a tract favoring instrumental music, "The uninformed reader would be convinced by this tract that the Bible authorizes the use of instrumental music in the praise of God, for it was used in the Old Testament age."[32] As a counter he contended,

> . . . that the whole Jewish economy was abolished, and a new covenant was given. . . . We practice some things that they practiced under the law, but it is because the same things are inculcated in the gospel, and not because they were in the old covenant.[33]

I conclude therefore that in practice we have devoted much more time to grammatico-historical interpretation than current proponents of the tripartite formula have led us to believe. It therefore seems in keeping with our two-hundred year history that our biblical scholars today identify with

---

[31]*Ibid.*, 91.
[32]Brewer, *A Medley on the Music Question*, 45.
[33]*Ibid.*, 50.

what Collier has designated, the historical/contextual school.³⁴ He is correct, however, that our scholars in this camp have not addressed too often the matters that trouble the church. They are inclined to be more interested in the battles of the community of fellow scholars than of the communities of faith. It is important, then, that Carroll Osburn in *Essays on Women in Earliest Christianity* seeks to refocus the expertise of our scholars in such a way that they contribute to the struggles within our communities of faith.

3. *The Application of Hermeneutics to the Role of Women in the Church*

We turn now to the manner in which the role of women has been approached hermeneutically. First, we notice that the biblical mandate is reversed. Whereas the church is to sing because of the absence of any charge to play an instrument, in the case of women, they are to be silent because of an explicit edict. On the surface, therefore, the hermeneutical demands in regard to women's roles seem less complicated. In practice, however they have accumulated various complexities.

A case in point is the responses of Leslie G. Thomas in "Queries and Answers" in the *Firm Foundation*.³⁵ In regard to 1 Cor 14:33, 34, Thomas responded, "The reference is to the public meetings of the church, in which meetings women are not permitted to take a leading part. Teaching a class is not under consideration in this passage."³⁶ The hermeneutical approach is essentially, "it says what it means,

---

³⁴Collier, *Christian Studies*, 11 (1990): 18-40.

³⁵Thomas spent most of his career in Tennessee, but was minister of the Fifth Avenue Church of Christ in Corsicana, Texas, 1935-1939. He was an editorial writer for the *Gospel Advocate*. *Preachers of Today*, (ed. Batsell Barrett Baxter and M. Norvel Young; Nashville: Gospel Advocate, 1959): 2.434. The "Queries and Answers" appeared in the *Firm Foundation* in late 1930s and early 1940s.

³⁶Leslie G. Thomas, *What the Bible Teaches—The Answers To Your Questions*, (ed. J. R. McGill; Austin: Firm Foundation, 1962): 2.195.

Women in the Church: The Hermeneutical Problem

and means what it says." However, the application becomes more complicated since Thomas has set aside a special meaning for "public meeting," and "teaching a class." Teaching a class, it turns out, has a different set of rules.

Thomas set forth two guiding principles, "1) She is not permitted to take a public part when the church assembles for worship (1 Cor 14:33, 34); 2) She is not permitted to teach nor to have dominion over men (1 Tim 2:12)."[37] Concerning classes, he wrote, "If people would only realize that the Bible classes are not the worship which the Lord ordained for the first day of the week, it would help solve many such problems."[38] Thomas did not offer a means of distinguishing between worship and classes, such as, worship always includes the five acts of worship, nor did he advance biblical justification for such a distinction. But he declared, "There is a vast difference in meeting an hour before the time for the regular Lord's day assembly for Bible study, and the assembly itself."[39] In his view the Lord has not legislated on what happens in the Bible study. He therefore concluded,

> It is not wrong for women to teach classes in the Lord's Bible school, provided they are fitted for such teaching and do it under the supervision of the elders of the church. Those who object to such work are guilty of legislating where God has not made a law, and that is a serious matter in his sight.[40]

Furthermore, a woman may teach a class with young men present who are more than twenty-one years of age if she is "authorized by the elders to teach such a class."[41] He thinks a male teacher is preferable, but it would not be wrong for a woman to teach.

---

[37] L. G. Thomas, *What the Bible Teaches*, 195.
[38] *Ibid.*, 201.
[39] *Ibid.*, 197.
[40] *Ibid.*, 195.
[41] *Ibid.*, 196.

C. R. Nichol[42] in a widely circulated book argued much the same as Thomas. He thought that 1 Cor 14 was directed to that church in that time. He argued that when the spirit prompted either a male or female to speak in the public assembly, then both men and women were to keep silent. Since, however, Spirit-filled persons no longer are found in the churches, this verse has no application in the twentieth century. In contrast 1 Tim 2:8-14 was not addressing the matter of Spirit-prompted utterances. The application is "Without regard to time, circumstances or place."[43] Throughout the book, Nichol emphasized subjection. Women may speak as long as they are in subjection. He therefore also held that they may teach men anywhere and also in Bible classes as long as the auspices under which they do it shows their subjection.

> If a woman teaches a Sunday School class, at the solicitation of the elders in the church of Christ, she does not usurp authority over man. . . . In her teaching the Sunday School class in the church of Christ she does so under the oversight of the elders of the church and in subjection to the elders of the congregation.[44]

Thomas believed that women may serve in many other roles. In classes they may read and be involved in the discussion. They may wait on the Lord's table if no man is present, but if men are present, "it would probably be more in keeping with the Lord's will for such public duties to be performed by men."[45] He declared that it was appropriate for an elder to ask a woman to lead singing in case no capable man was present, but he thought she should do it seated.[46] A woman may serve as treasurer of a

---

[42]C. R. Nichol, *God's Woman* (Grand Rapids: Eerdmans, 1938): 124.
[43]*Ibid.*, 146.
[44]*Ibid.*, 154.
[45]Thomas, *What the Bible Teaches*, 203.
[46]*Ibid.*, 170.

Women in the Church: The Hermeneutical Problem   559

congregation, but he thought that though women should be consulted about the business of the church it was better that they not attend business meetings since only men may serve as elders. In all these cases, except for the latter, the reason it was permissible for women to so do was the silence of the Scriptures.[47]

We therefore conclude that Thomas, as well as Nichol, based these decisions upon express statements in Scriptures, the delineation of worship from classes, and the silence of the Scriptures. These were hermeneutical tasks for which the command, example, necessary inference formula seemed not fully adequate.

It is interesting that B. W. Johnson (1833-1894) of the nineteenth century, whose work at one time was frequently carried to Bible classes by church members, complicated the hermeneutics even more. He held the same view as Leslie G. Thomas that the charge to silence was only apropos when "the whole assembly met." "Paul's prohibition of speaking to the women is, *in the churches*"; that is, in the church assemblies when "the whole church is come together into one place (verse 23)."[48] He, however, also believed that the context should be considered because of the prospect that the declaration was only to the churches in Greece, not to all the churches.

> It may be that even this prohibition was due to circumstances that existed in Ephesus, where Timothy was, and in Corinth, and would not apply everywhere. If so, it applies wherever similar circumstances exist, but not elsewhere. . . . Among the Greeks public women were disreputable. For a woman to speak in public would cause the remark that she was shameless. . . . It is noteworthy that

---

[47]*Ibid.*, 170.

[48]B. W. Johnson, *The People's New Testament* (Delight, AR: Gospel Light, n.d.): 2.119.

there is no hint of such a prohibition to any churches except Grecian.[49]

Johnson has therefore placed the matter in the hands of those who are involved in grammatico-historical criticism, especially the task of understanding the text in the light of the location, the ethnic mores, and the time. The task is similar to that of determining the meaning of ψάλλω (*psallo*; sing) in the NT period both within and without Christianity.

Neil Lightfoot[50] likewise felt strongly that a failure to approach these texts without historical or grammatical insight often distorted their meaning and application. But like Nichol, he regarded the utterances of women in the Corinthian church as Spirit-filled, and therefore, no longer possible. To him this explains an apparent contradiction between 1 Cor 11 and 14.

> . . . the conflict between 1 Corinthians 14 and 1 Corinthians 11 is to be explained by reference to two different activities. Chapter 14 is forbidding women, on their own initiative, to speak or teach. Chapter 11 allows exceptions when women are supernaturally controlled and motivated by the Spirit.[51]

In a recent book, Smith[52] has developed a different strategy for establishing the respective gender roles from the Scriptures. His chief argument is that God assigned males the task of spiritual leadership. It is his conviction that both the characteristics of the church and of the home deteriorate when men abandon their God-given responsibility. What is

---

[49] Johnson, *The People's New Testament* 2.119.

[50] Neil R. Lightfoot, *The Role of Women: New Testament Perspectives* (Memphis: Student Association Press, 1978): 9-16.

[51] Lightfoot, *Ibid.*, 35.

[52] F. LaGard Smith, *Men of Strength for Women of God: Has the Time Come for Shared Spiritual Leadership?* (Eugene, OR: Harvest House, 1989): 7-155, develops the case largely from the OT, but imprecisely.

Women in the Church: The Hermeneutical Problem

interesting about his argument hermeneutically is that he established his case first and foremost from the OT. Such a move runs counter to our hermeneutical rule that authorization is derived from the NT. We have never followed the rule, however, when it was to our advantage to do otherwise, for example, in respect to anti-evolution polemic. In my own judgment the rule is wrong. The OT is still God's word for the church, not in respect to institutions, but in respect to theology, for example, the theology of creation.

4. *Hermeneutics as the Presupposition of Exegesis*

Some view hermeneutics as the presuppositions which inform exegesis. That definition is helpful regarding the manner in which decisions are made in Churches of Christ. Exegesis is viewed as imperative, but the manner in which the exegesis relates to what Christians or churches do is further filtered through prior hermeneutical commitments, i.e., even though the exegesis of Deborah's leadership of Israel may be accurate, the implications for Christian governance are minimal since Deborah lived in the time of the OT. In the current climate, it seems that a number of leaders in the churches are open to reexamining the role of women based upon careful exegesis of biblical texts. Upon the perusing of responsible historical and exegetical scholarship, various persons have concluded that the manner of perceiving critical texts on women's roles in the past has been skewed so as to limit unnecessarily the ways in which women may contribute to church life. Even so, confusion persists as to the extent to which these new insights are to be incorporated and translated into the life of the church.

In view of the new exegetical conclusions, we are no longer confident of past agreements regarding the exclusion of the OT, the inflexible delineation of worship from teaching, or of distinguishing spiritual gifts from ordinary Christian gifts in the NT. The crucial question is therefore reopened, i.e., once we have achieved adequate exegetical insight, what are we to do with the results? Careful exegetical work, as such and by itself, does not always furnish clear guidelines to the answer of this question.

At this point, it is useful to assess what has happened to grammatico-historical-literary criticism since Campbell published his "Principles of Interpretation," briefly comparing and contrasting Campbell's work with that of the authors in the two volumes of *Essays on Women in Earliest Christianity* edited by Osburn.

Campbell summed up his hermeneutics with seven rules of interpretation, which may be abbreviated as follows:[53]

1. Consider the historical circumstances of the text.
2. Observe who speaks in what dispensation.
3. The rules for the meaning of words are the same as with the language in any other work.
4. The scope, context and parallel passages must help decide the meaning of a word.
5. In tropical (analogical) language, ascertain the point of resemblance.
6. The point must be determined in symbols, types, allegories, and parables.
7. One must be within an understanding distance of the text through responsiveness and humility.

The majority of Campbell's one hundred pages of comments focus on items 2 through 6. Campbell mentions the need to ascertain subject matter, context, and scope, as well as history, but provides little or no detailed instructions.

In Campbell's time, biblical exegetes had quarried considerable background materials from classical works, the church fathers, and rabbinic materials. For example, Adam Clarke (1762-1832), widely read by early leaders in the Churches of Christ, employed material from all these sources in his eight-volume commentary on the Bible (1810-

---

[53] Campbell, "Principles," *Christianity Restored*, 96-99.

1826), but materials had not as yet been sorted and sifted, especially regarding the situation of women.[54]

Since Campbell's time, much more has become known about the positions and roles of women in the ancient world.[55] While books and articles have been available for the past few decades on the situation of women in biblical times, these insights have not been filtered to any extent in literature among Churches of Christ until collected in the articles in *Essays on Women in Earliest Christianity*. With the appearance of these essays, we have been carried far beyond our ancestors both with regard to cultural backgrounds and to what specific texts mean in their literary and historical settings. The articles by Sterling and Chesnutt on women in Greco-Roman and Jewish settings are splendid contributions to our understanding of women in antiquity. With careful attention to responsible methodology, specific passages have been addressed in terms of their literary and historical contexts: Gal 3:28 (Hailey); Rom 7:2; 16:1-2, 7 (Walters); 1 Cor 7:4 (Hull); 1 Cor 11:2-16 (Black; Osburn); 1 Cor 14:34-35 (Osburn); Eph 5:21-33 (Neller); Acts 16:13-15; Phil 4:2-3 (Pollard); 1 Tim 2:8-15 (Geer); 1 Tim 3:11 (Blackburn); 1 Tim 5:3-16 (Moore); Titus 2:5 (Helton); Heb 11:11 (Thompson). Several essays approach major NT works as a unit: 1 Peter (Thompson); Mark (Aquino and McLemore); Matthew (Chouinard); Luke (Black); Acts (Childers and Niccum). Significantly, women and texts in the OT receive careful attention: Gen 1-3 (Marrs); Sarah (Vancil); Deborah (Robarts); Huldah (J. Willis); Hos 1-3 (T. Willis); Prov 31:10-31 (Lewis). Additionally, chapters are included on women in the early history of Christianity: the post-Apostolic church (Ferguson); Tertullian (Lavender); the Constantinian era (Norris); the European Middle Ages (Pauls). These two volumes exhibit extended linguistic,

---

[54]See W. Neil, "The Criticism and Theological Use of the Bible, 1700-1950," *The Cambridge History of the Bible: The West from the Reformation to the Present Day* (ed. S. Greenslade; Cambridge: Cambridge Univ. Press, 1963): 238-293.

[55]The essays by Rick Marrs (chap. 1) and Timothy Willis (chap. 6) of this volume utilize and employ such material.

literary, and historical analysis. They have placed before us in a significant way the results of sound exegetical and historical work, an approach to which the leaders of our movement have been committed from the beginning.

At the same time, because of the new insights into texts on women provided in *Essays of Women in Earliest Christianity*, a hermeneutical crisis has arisen since we are without adequate hermeneutical guidelines by which to adjudicate seriously these new directions. Helpful to understanding the dilemma are studies of women in Restoration history by Pulley (chap. 20) and Bailey (chap. 21), but the current hermeneutical quandary is well-illustrated by McNicol (chap. 22). Contra Marrs (chap. 1), McNicol accepts the "order of creation" argument, but in distinction from the complementarian perspective argues that women can and should be involved in all aspects of church life, including praying and teaching, except for administrative roles, such as preacher and elder.[56] McNicol's view does open the doors to women significantly wider than is the case in the rather narrow traditional view. Much of McNicol's argument for restricting leadership roles to males, however, is predicated upon biblical understandings other than are argued in *Essays on Women in Earliest Christianity*, especially 1 Cor 11; 14; and 1 Tim 2, and from my understanding of these texts that renders his theological analysis questionable.

Assuming the exegetical thrust of *Essays on Women in Earlist Christianity* to reflect a general consensus among scholars in Churches of Christ, certain observations of Osburn in his *Women in the Church: Refocusing the Discussion*[57] are fundamental to this discussion. First, to

---

[56]McNicol rejects much of the complementarian thinking advocated by John Piper and Wayne Grudem, ed., *Recovering Biblical Manhood & Womanhood* (Wheaton: Crossway, 1991), but the lingering "order of creation" argument is certainly not compatible with evangelical feminism.

[57]Carroll D. Osburn, *Women in the Church: Refocusing the Discussion* (Abilene, TX: Restoration Perspectives, 1994).

narrow down the categories of theological presuppositions of interpreters, Osburn located on the two extremes paternalism and radical feminism, both of which he rejects. Two other positions, complementarianism and evangelical feminism, he identifies as viable options among Churches of Christ.[58] Persons from these two perspectives share, according to Osburn, ten different common presuppositions in which the biblical faith is regarded as historical, Scripture is revealed by a transcendent God, every text must be scrutinized historically and literarily, and decisions made as to how these conclusions may be carried out in responsible ways.[59]

Persons located in these two perspectives are committed to the historical-critical method.[60] Several issues arise as to how these historical-critical results are to be applied—a major one is that certain injunctions in Scripture, once thought to be universally applicable, are now understood to have been specific to a given context and not universally applicable. The question arises, "Is anything in Scripture universally applicable?" Osburn[61] sets out eight principles posed by Scholer[62] as the way to ascertain the universal normativity of any given text:

1. Distinguish between the central core of the biblical message and what is dependent upon and/or what is peripheral to it (contrast resurrection and holy kiss).
2. Determine the relative emphasis given to a topic (compare baptism and footwashing).
3. Distinguish between normative teachings and descriptive narratives (compare Lk 12:33 and 19:8-9 on material wealth).

---

[58]Osburn, *Women in the Church*, 57.
[59]*Ibid.*, 69-70.
[60]*Ibid.*, 72-73.
[61]*Ibid.*, 74-75.
[62]David M. Scholer, "Issues in Biblical Interpretation," *EvQ* 88 (1988): 8-9.

4. Note when a point receives uniform witness and when there are differences (compare prohibitions against homosexuality and women teaching).
5. Distinguish between principles and applications (note 1 Pet 2:18-21 on slavery).
6. Diversity is an indicator of relativity (see Matt 10:5-6 and 28:16-20).
7. Only one option indicates cultural relativity (note more than one option available on homosexuality and resurrection, but basically one option on slavery).
8. Compare and contrast biblical cultural situations with the current situation (contrast attitudes then and now to democracy [Rom 13:1-7]).

These guidelines are very helpful and Osburn is correct to pinpoint the Christological matrix in which the discussion is to be conducted.[63]

Despite these excellent hermeneutical suggestions, however, a conundrum still persists regarding limits, e.g., the question lingers as to whether women can serve as preachers and elders. On one hand, Stendahl[64] argued that the eventual equality of men and women in the church is anticipated in Gal 3:28.

> . . . the first of the three pairs—Jews/Greeks—is clearly implemented in the actual life and structure of the New Testament church. When it comes to the second pair—slave/free—there are slight and indecisive signs of the implications involved. What about the third pair, the one with which we are particularly concerned in this study, "Not *male and Female*"? It is our contention that all three of these pairs have the same potential for implementation in the life and structure of the church, and that we

---

[63]Osburn, *Women in the Church*, 86.
[64]Krister Stendahl, *The Bible and the Role of Women* (Philadelphia: Fortress, 1966).

> cannot dispose of the third by confining it to the realm *coram deo*.⁶⁵

If so, then the grounds for increased roles for women is not simply a matter of what culture dictates, but secured upon the foundations of what has already been announced in the advent of the Lord of Scripture. For Stendahl, that meant the ordaining of women as ministers and church officers.

On the other hand, Hailey⁶⁶ argued that for Paul equality of value is at stake, not equality of roles. She comments,

> It does not follow that there are no unequal roles in the community of faith. Paul himself is claiming an authoritative role as an apostle. Nor would one suggest that the unequal roles of parent-child relationships be considered illegitimate in Christ.⁶⁷

So the question remains as to whether a hermeneutic can be hammered out which makes a distinction between equality of value and equality of roles with respect to men and women. If, however, the various *Essays on Women in Earliest Christianity* does reflect a general consensus among scholars in Churches of Christ, the "order of creation" argument is not accepted and those texts previously used to mandate silence of women, such as 1 Cor 11:2-16; 14:34-35; and 1 Tim 2:11-15, are understood as having been directed to specific situations involving aberrant behavior and do not necessitate universal silence. This does focus the question, then, as to what textual basis remains to forbid women from serving in any capacity, especially since on occasion women such as Deborah did so with divine approval.

---

⁶⁵*Ibid.*, 34.

⁶⁶Jan Hailey, "Neither Male and Female (Gal 3:28)," *Essays on Women in Earliest Christianity* (ed. C. Osburn; Joplin, MO: College Press, 1993): 1.131-166.

⁶⁷*Ibid.*, 1.165.

Conclusion

Though we have had a stated hermeneutic, it has not played a key role in determining what the Scripture meant, or what it means. The tripartite formula of command, example, and necessary inference has been little in evidence in our major issue discussions, including now the role of women. Our more serious interpretations have drawn upon traditional biblical criticism with respect to language and context, as well as to earlier and later contexts. The grammatico-historical contribution is obvious in *Essays on Women in Earliest Christianity*.[68]

I think in keeping with hermeneutical strategies within the Scriptures themselves that the hermeneutical problem is best solved through noticing differences then and now and coming to the conclusion as to what should be done now by working from the theology at stake. Ferguson ended with this approach to instrumental music, as did James Thompson in his chapter on "Submission of Wives in I Peter."[69] In a forthcoming book on hermeneutics, I discuss and defend as biblical the merits of this latter hermeneutical approach.[70]

---

[68] Kenneth V. Neller, "'Submission' in Eph. 5:21-33," *Essays on Women in Earliest Christianity*, 1.243-260, is a good example of what the text meant then and now.

[69] James W. Thompson, "Submission of Wives in 1 Peter," *Essays on Women in Earliest Christianity*, 1.392.

[70] Thomas H. Olbricht, *Hermeneutics: Autobiographical Reflections*.

Appendix One

PRACTICAL IMPLICATIONS OF A CHANGE IN THE ROLE OF WOMEN

Bill Love

Since we at the Bering Drive congregation in Houston began asking our sisters to help lead in worship we have had numerous calls, letters and visits from elders, ministers, and other church members asking about our experience. With a few exceptions these have been friendly inquiries expressing curiosity and asking counsel about the promises and pitfalls of change. Unlike the scholarly essays in these two volumes, this is one minister's personal view of how one church changed, what that experience has meant to the faith community, and the lessons he learned.

1. *Bering Drive's History*

In order for the reader to understand the transition in our thinking and practice regarding the role of women at Bering Drive a brief historical perspective is provided. Our story will make apparent the fact that, while certain principles may apply in all situations, the experience of each church family is unique in some ways.

This congregation was sponsored by the Central Church of Christ in Houston. The Central elders early in the 1960s were perceptive enough to know that the city would grow westward and that a high concentration of business and professional people would live and work in that section of town. They purchased land, hand picked a group of elders and gave a fledgling group their blessing for the new beginning. The church's first minister, Pat Harrell, had a Th.D. from Boston University. Harrell was quite conservative in his understanding of the Scripture and in his theology. However, from the beginning he introduced the worshiping community to a different kind of hermeneutic. Instead of the "face value," flat understanding of Scripture, Harrell showed how the language, literary forms, contexts, and life situations of texts give important clues to their meaning. This was not a "new hermeneutic"—these principles of interpretation are found, for example, in Campbell's *The Christian System*. Harrell was certainly not the only minister in the Churches of Christ who studied the Bible in that way. Nevertheless, this view of the Bible constituted an approach different from that which many Churches of Christ used in 1962. Consequently, decisions about church life based on Bering's reading of Scripture would sometimes differ markedly from decisions other congregations made from their understanding of the Bible.

From the first the church which began meeting on Bering Drive in 1964 pledged itself to the Church of Christ tradition. In explicit written statements they embraced the Restoration tradition of going back to Scripture, of following what they found prescribed there even to their own personal discomfort and the chagrin of others. While being a part of the Church of Christ tradition was important to them, it was not of first importance. Like the early Restorationists, they were determined not to follow church tradition when they felt that Scripture and the lordship of Christ led elsewhere.

Accordingly, over the years Bering Drive has been like most other Churches of Christ in many ways, and different in some ways. It has maintained congregational autonomy, believer baptism by immersion, plurality of elders, non-instrumental music in worship, and weekly communion. On the other hand, it has rejected the notion that all of God's people meet in buildings with "Church of Christ" on the sign out front. As was true with Israel's worship, this congregation enjoys responsive readings and prayers in unison. Finding no instructions in the NT about the tenure of elders, the elders adopted a system of rotation. Each elder serves a limited term, rotates out and another is chosen to take his place. After a year's absence the church may return a former elder to the eldership. Following the lead of

Scriptures, as the years passed the elders focused more on their pastoral roles and less on their organizational and fiscal responsibilities. They attempted to emphasize pastoral care over authority and control, the nurture of spiritual gifts over demands for conformity.

2. *The Role of Women At Bering Drive*

Almost from the first the Bering church, encouraged by the examples of Scripture, recognized the gifts of women in the faith community. Women were asked to fill roles of responsibility in various ministries, and were encouraged to lead ministries when that was the will of the ministry involved. The question of deacons and deaconesses was sidestepped by a decision not to debate the anglicized Greek term but to substitute the English equivalents of "ministries" and "servants."

The Bering elders and ministers first discussed the question of women leading worship in 1975. The arguments I heard for change were prompted more by the equality issues in the larger American culture than by Scriptural considerations. A few women and their husbands issued a strong call for equal rights in worship leadership. The church registered mixed feelings and the elders were divided. For a year the elders and ministers read and studied everything they could find on the subject. For the enlightenment of the leadership, each elder and minister was assigned Scriptures to study and papers to write presenting their findings. At the end of that process the leadership was divided. Some eagerly endorsed the leadership of women in worship, others were convinced that it was unscriptural and unwise. Agreement was reached that the issue should be set aside until the Holy Spirit gave further leading and a statement to that effect was made to the church.

For twelve years the topic was not debated in public as a church-wide concern. In 1988, due to further study and elder rotation, the elders were all of one mind that the role of women in worship should be expanded. This time the leaders themselves initiated the discussion and advocated the change. After careful thought and prayer the elders prepared a statement for the church and I preached four sermons on the topic. In the year that followed, the leaders visited homes for discussion of the questions involved, Sunday School classes were sometimes devoted to the topic, open question-and-answer sessions were conducted for the whole church, and scholarly and popular writings were made available to the church.

At the end of that process we announced that, on a certain Sunday, we would begin asking women to help us lead in worship. At first, we scheduled women to participate the first Sunday of each month. Months later we increased the frequency to the first and third Sundays. Four years later we lifted the frequency restrictions and invitations were issued to women at the discretion of the Worship Ministry members planning the services.

These changes were announced well in advance so that our members had no surprises. They came on those Sundays when women were leading only because they chose to come. They went elsewhere on those Sundays if they were offended at the change, had family visiting who would be offended, or simply needed more time to adjust. The leaders felt that absolute candor before the fact was required in responsible pastoring. We also printed a brief explanation to be included in the Orders of Worship on those Sundays for our visitors. After six months we discontinued the inserts. Since that time we have had a small display in the foyer entitled: "Visitors' Information on the Role of Women." It contains a booklet which includes the elders' statement and the four sermons on the topic. Ushers attempt to engage anyone in conversation who leaves upset during a service. In these six years there have been fewer than half a dozen incidents when people left services due to the leadership of women.

From the first we explained that we believed women should participate at least as much as they did in the first century church. The biblical and theological bases of our thinking are outlined in the four sermons in the booklet. We

Implications of a Change in the Role of Women 573

believed that such leadership would include: the call to worship, leading prayer, reading Scripture, waiting on the Lord's Table, and leading singing.

As with the frequency of women leading, the *kinds* of participation were also planned and phased in. We discovered that women serving at the Table and leading singing were the most difficult role adjustments for some of our members. Not until six years after our initial decision were women invited to lead singing. A third guideline the elders prescribed set out criteria by which women would be selected to lead. Those leading should be women who showed the qualities of spiritual devotion, discretion, modesty, and competence.

Almost every Sunday, women now help lead worship, depending on the worship planner. As Chairman of the Worship Ministry, I suggest that the worship planners include no more than three women to lead in any single service. This suggestion is not a matter of right or wrong, but simply a call to preserve the focus of worship on God and not on our gender concerns. This policy will change as women's participation becomes less an issue.

During this process we lost 15 members out of a membership of 300. Most who left were in their late fifties and upward. Several were long-time members at Bering. On a personal level this exodus was quite painful for me. I still remain on good terms with all of these people. We embrace when we meet at various church functions in the city. My wife and I are especially close to a senior couple who left during the discussion of women's role in the church. Our sister who left is the daughter and niece of four Church of Christ preachers. For her our change felt like a condemnation of her family's faith and their understanding of Scripture, and a jettisoning of our tradition in general.

The issue is rarely discussed now at Bering. A few, probably twenty or so, are still uncomfortable with the participation of women. Most members indicate that they can concentrate on worship again, not on who is leading.

Since the elders introduced the change in 1988 we have been blessed with 179 new members who have come to be a part of our church family. Some have come by baptism, most by placing membership. For some of these new members the role of women is not a significant issue. Others have expressed their joy in seeing what they believe to be an implication of the gospel carried out in church life.

3. *What I Have Learned*

This is a personal statement. Our current elders agree with my observations, but these views are mine personally. The lessons I learned from our experience and for our life here are several.

First, the leadership of the church (elders and staff) must be 100% in agreement that the changes are necessary as a gospel issue. The transition will be rough enough without mixed signals from the leaders.

Second, the leaders should expect to do little else but deal with this change for at least a year. Many hours of pastoral work will be required if the real issues are to be clearly understood and a church split is to be avoided.

Third, a gradual phasing in of the change is the only responsible pastoral procedure. Even those most convinced about an increased role for women will have an adjustment when it actually takes place. Since that is the case, the leaders should consider the feelings of those opposed, of those who are uncomfortable with the change and of those who have family visiting. The gradual phasing in says: "We care about you. We respect your feelings and your thoughts. We do not want to run over you."

Fourth, this is by far the most emotional issue I have dealt with in my thirty-two years of ministry. Gender role discussions touch on a variety of personal issues: family of origin matters, vocational experiences, personal identity questions, the meaning of Scripture in our lives, male/female relations in the church, our political views, and a variety of

Implications of a Change in the Role of Women

other issues I have not identified. Emotionally, this is a 220-volt matter. I was repeatedly surprised at balanced, grace-oriented, committed Christians who became almost irrational on both sides of this issue. In this regard, we discovered that the leaders had the responsibility of taking the brunt of the criticism for their decision. Sometimes that meant defending members, especially women who advocated change, from unwarranted stricture.

Fifth, Scripture is supremely important, and how we read the Bible is a central concern. One of the reasons for the emotion is our deep devotion and attachment to the Scripture. One who is advocating change may discover that he is talking with someone who, for all the changes from legalism to grace, is still operating with a flat, face value hermeneutic. Few challenges are more difficult than trying to discuss a complex topic like hermeneutics in the middle of a heated emotional conversation. Despite the fact that since Pat Harrell began preaching in 1962 this church has consistently been taught from a more adequate hermeneutic, some could not see a text as conditioned by context and intent. It was upsetting to hear: "Bill, the Bible says for women to be silent. Do you believe the Bible or not?" "We have, as a movement, been studying the Bible for over 150 years. Are you telling me that now, all of a sudden, this generation of scholars is the first one smart enough to understand what the Bible is really saying?"

Sixth, there are other sources of strong feelings besides disagreement over biblical texts. Old battles are not forgotten. A church like Bering has made other changes. In terms of personal feelings, someone "won" and someone "lost" those battles. For example, one long-time member and elder felt he had lost on a building program, on a conflict about a Youth Minister and now the women's role. While he had sincere objections to the interpretations of Scripture which allowed women to lead in worship, for him there were other issues involved. This insight has come to me slowly; we preachers are prone to see everything in terms of texts and expositions.

Seventh, we should be careful not to play games with the church or with our own minds during the process. For example, our statement read at the beginning of our discussions was, in fact, a decision of the elders. We invited the church to discuss and decide the issue together, but we had already decided it. Perhaps some of the elders were concerned that a church-wide discussion would sidetrack the change. For whatever reasons, we decided to issue the position paper at the beginning—and we paid the price. Legitimately, irate members objected that we had pretended to be open on the subject when a firm decision had been made at the outset. In retrospect, I believe we should have had an open discussion without any written elders' statement or that we should have set the discussion in other terms: "What are our feelings about what the elders have decided?"

Eighth, and most important of all, the church must be secure enough in the Lord to tackle such a topic. Some in our tradition seem to believe that God loves them because of their flawless understanding of and perfect compliance with the NT as a book of detailed patterns for church life. When that is the case, they cannot afford spiritually and emotionally to think about any significant change. Disagreement among believers on such matters causes major problems in relationships. Discussions of change raise questions of whether we can fellowship with others who do not share our understandings in every detail.

On the other hand, if Christians know that their relationship with God rests on his redemptive love at Golgotha, received at baptism and celebrated at the Lord's Table, they can have confidence and security to consider controversial issues like the role of women in worship. While we made mistakes along the way at Bering, I think we came near to setting this vital spiritual and theological atmosphere. My own view is that we avoided a church split and alienation from those who left because we all know we are sinners, we all confess that we "see in part and prophecy in part," and we all know that our salvation is secure only because of Golgotha.

Appendix Two

FAITH AND GENDER: REFLECTIONS ON DISCUSSIONS AT THE STAMFORD CHURCH OF CHRIST

Dale Pauls

Traditionally Churches of Christ have held, as most churches have until recently, to an understanding of 1 Cor 14:33-35 and 1 Tim 2:11-15 that does not examine context and even sometimes denies the relevance of context, and on that basis have prohibited women from exercising "leadership" roles in public worship. This prohibition has amounted to an almost complete silencing of women in our worship services.

This traditional position has always carried with it certain anomalies. In what way is one then to understand the Pentecost announcement that God's Spirit would be poured out on both men and women and that both would prophesy (Acts 2:17-21)? In what sense did women pray and prophesy in the early church (1 Cor 11:5)? What did Paul mean by there being no male and female in Christ (Gal 3:26-28)?

These first-century anomalies are paralleled by current ones. We sing songs women compose. We read articles women write. We benefit from women's comments as we study together. For the first time in history, women in our culture are generally as educated as men, and as trained for responsible leadership in society. This marks a monumental cultural shift—what no culture expected of women before this shift, it is probable that all (at least all developed Western cultures) will come to expect hereafter. Increasingly, traditional churches are coming to be viewed as among the last bastions of exclusively male leadership.

Matters of faith and gender are being widely discussed throughout the Churches of Christ. The topic has been featured prominently at lectureships at Abilene Christian University and Pepperdine University in recent years, as well as at various workshops and seminars and in various religious publications. Just this past year saw the publication of the first volume of *Essays on Women in Earliest Christianity*, a landmark collection of studies by some of the finest biblical scholars in the Churches of Christ.

While in many places congregations are studying issues related to women, in other places elders and other church leaders have attempted to restrict all discussion. Others see themselves as change agents in terms that are almost messianic. With such extremism, the result is all too often division and substantial attrition.

The church family that assembles at 1264 High Ridge Road in Stamford, Connecticut, has opted to study the topic. At a congregational retreat in 1987, the elders agreed that it would be important for the ministers to lead them, and possibly later the congregation, in a study of women's roles in the church. Exploratory studies were conducted with the elders by myself and Ken Durham that winter, and again in 1991. Meanwhile, on their own initiative, the Tuesday morning Ladies Class, led by Kathryn Koczanskiy, devoted the spring of 1989 to the study of this topic. The same material was repeated during the fall and winter of 1992-93 at a Friday evening study group for the benefit of those unable to attend the morning sessions.

In December 1989 and January 1990, I made a five-week presentation on "Women in the Church at First" to a combined Sunday morning adult Bible class. My approach was textually oriented, with primary focus on ascertaining from the literary and historical contexts the original intent of the text, with concentration on 1 Cor 11:2-16; 14:26-40; Gal 3:26-29; and 1 Tim 2:9-15. It was clear that there is a circumstantial aspect to Paul's specific instructions to churches in Corinth and Ephesus.

In the spring of 1993 this material was repeated for an adult Bible class, but this time was preceded by a three-week study of "Slavery in the Church at First," so as to provide a better understanding of how the early church approached another dominant social convention of its time. It was noted that a century and a half ago in America the debates within Christian circles over slavery parallel almost exactly the discussions now being held over gender matters. The same kinds of arguments were made, based on the same approaches to biblical interpretation. Perhaps no issue illustrates better than slavery how imperative it is to distinguish between what the NT says about new life in Christ (e.g., Gal 3:28) and the actual degree of implementation possible in the first-century church (e.g., 1 Cor 7:17-24; Eph 6:5-9; Col 3:22-4:1; Titus 2:9-10; Phlmn).

These studies of "Slavery in the Church at First" and "Women in the Church at First" were followed by four Sunday mornings of unrestricted and free-ranging discussion of the issues. Those who spoke, both men and women, distinguished themselves by their honesty, maturity, fairness, and mental vigor, but above all by their love and respect for others. As a result it became obvious that there was 1) a deep passion for standing justified before God; 2) a respect for our religious heritage; 3) a refusal to polarize and reduce complex matters to simple either/ors; 4) impressive interpretive skills among us; 5) a sense of awe in examining sacred matters on gender; 6) patience with differing and maturing viewpoints; 7) modesty, vulnerability, and the kind of discipline it takes to surrender personal rights lovingly to the consciences of others; and 8) the courage it takes to state convictions when others disagree. There were many remarkable moments: disclosures that were astonishingly frank, wounds that began to heal and be healed, and powerful insights into Scripture, God, and gender. Perhaps most commendable was the way almost everyone brought the discussion back to Scripture. It was apparent that everyone respected truth, trusted truth, and knew that, in open and free exchange of ideas, truth triumphs.

These discussions ended in May of 1993 with a charge from the elders for the congregation to take personal responsibility for searching Scripture and working toward the creation of a responsible Christian consensus. The topic of faith and gender was addressed in an October retreat by Dr. Paul Watson, both in his presentations and in a small-group discussion.

My studies have led me to conclude that historical evidence suggests that there has always been a dynamic interaction between societal forces and gender roles and expectations. In its time, the NT teaching on gender was revolutionary. The second-century church experienced remarkable diversity in its understanding of gender and church structures. The most influential church leaders in the fourth and fifth centuries became misogynistic for a variety of reasons. As long as the church remained private, organized around household gatherings, and meeting behind closed doors, women often exercised considerable influence, leadership, and patronage—as they did in the household itself. The household was the fundamental socio-economic unit in society and women often played major roles in its operations. This was especially true of women whose houses were large enough to host churches, and all the more so if they were wealthy widows. However, as the church went public in the third century and began to meet in basilicas, it conformed to the stricter gender role expectations of Greco-Roman society—and this meant in the public sphere exclusively male leadership. Historical evidence also suggests that women suffered a further decline in relative status during the Middle Ages.

Long-forgotten societal forces and cultural premises that operated centuries ago have colored the ways we see God and Scripture, and faith and gender. Until quite recently, in fact, traditional gender restrictions were based upon and reinforced by archaic philosophical premises of inequality that almost no one today would admit to holding. It was assumed rather strongly, for instance, that differences of any kind (e.g., gender, race, class) must necessarily imply inequality, so that everyone and everything has his, her, or its exact place in one vast, rigid hierarchical system and is either superior or inferior to everyone or everything else. It was on the basis of such a view that gender roles have been traditionally understood. Consequently, we might say today, reasoning "after the fact," that gender-restrictive roles do not imply inequality, but this was certainly not the traditional understanding that gave shape to such roles. Gender-restrictive roles emphatically did imply gender inequality. Meanwhile, we have rejected these premises of inequality, but consciously or otherwise still attempt all too often to sustain a system built upon these same premises.

Consequently, my ministerial experience with questions of faith and gender suggests the following:

1. *Read the Bible.* We need more who study Scripture and exhibit a genuine willingness to discern truth and be led by it. Gender issues do not just turn on 1 Cor 14 and 1 Tim 2; they turn on an understanding of the entirety of Scripture. Gender issues are informed as much by 1 and 2 Chronicles as by 1 and 2 Timothy. The interpretation of isolated NT texts depends upon acquaintance with the rest of Scripture.

2. *Concentrate on the gospel.* In sharing the redemptive work of God in Christ with others, one receives in return a sharpened, clearer and more compelling understanding of the gospel. Today, the issue of gender affects how many respond to the gospel. Increasing numbers must be persuaded that on matters of faith and gender what we are saying and practicing is, in fact, truly in the spirit of Jesus.

3. *Pay attention to how women are still treated (and thought about) in our world.* Some of us have opportunities to work with Domestic Violence Services or Rape Crisis Centers or similar agencies and we see the dark side of gender issues in our society. Many others do not have such opportunities, but need to stay alert, sensitize themselves to, and inform themselves about these issues. When you see a good article, read it. When you hear of a good show on television, watch it. Something is seriously wrong with the view of women in our society. It needs healing.

4. *Consensus on matters of faith and gender depend upon resolution of these matters:*

a. *To what extent the author's intent and the context determine the meaning of a text.* It will not do to rely upon establishing original intent regarding foot washing, speaking in tongues, the holy kiss, and female adornment, but to disregard literary and historical context for such texts as 1 Cor 14:33-35 and 1 Tim 2:11-15 and claim a mere "face value" understanding. On tongue-speaking, 1 Cor 14:5 reads, "I would like every one of you to speak in tongues," but we point quickly to historical context and original intent, noting that Paul was addressing the specific circumstances of his day. What principle of selectivity is at work when one justifies not washing another's feet, not laying on hands, women not wearing veils, women disregarding injunctions against braided hair or expensive clothes, but dismisses original intent at 1 Cor 14:33-35 and 1 Tim 2:11-15?

b. *The parallel of slavery with women's issues.* The NT teaching on slavery provides a clear example of how the early church dealt with another dominant cultural convention of those times. If the church had pressed Gal 3:28 and Philemon to their full conclusions, it would have challenged the very economic foundation of the Roman world. Slavery was a constant—a given—in the ancient world. If the church had pressed this matter, it would have been perceived as enormously disruptive and threatening to the very fabric of society, and it would have inevitably distracted almost everyone from the primary message of the gospel.

Today, with regard to those passages urging slaves to obey their masters, we again appeal to original intent and original context in counterpoint to those who in the nineteenth century used those very passages to defend slavery as a permanent, God-ordained institution. Today, we see in the biblical teaching on slavery an example of the distinction between the ideal and the actual degree of implementation possible in a given cultural context. Might not the same also be true of gender issues?

c. *What is meant by "leadership."* Does "participation" mean "leadership"? To what extent would a woman's public participation in Sunday worship be a leadership role? Is it in fact a "leadership" role for women to pass collection or communion trays, or lead a prayer or a song, or make an announcement, or read Scripture? Are these not better viewed as "service" roles?

d. *Is it really possible in matters of faith and gender to hold a guaranteed "safe position"?* Some hold that if one stays with traditional positions, one is at least doing the "safe" thing in the eyes of God. However, if one for the sake of tradition holds to a position that hinders the gospel (1 Cor 9:12, 19-23), would one not then be answerable to God for doing what is considered the "safe" thing? If we hold to traditional positions and ask this generation of women to accept restrictive and subordinate roles even though they now have education and training equivalent to men's, might we not be held accountable for that? Is following tradition really a "safe position" sociologically, spiritually, or biblically?

e. *Abuse of women is sinful.* Why is it that women still suffer from wrongs such as rape, domestic violence, verbal abuse, and various forms of gender condescension and disrespect? The church must assume responsibility for the alleviation of these problems—and make certain that it does not contribute to the problem.

f. *Gender identity.* What does it mean to be a man or to be a woman? To the extent that gender distinctiveness exists, can the case be made for at least certain gender-distinctive roles that either males or females more naturally fill? If this case could be made, would it not follow that society suffers when it ignores this distinctiveness? Before we dismantle the gender expectations of the past, have we considered what constructive social functions they once performed and how those functions will be managed in the future? Even so, if gender distinctiveness argues for certain gender-distinctive roles, are those roles not best understood as norms still subject to individual aptitude and immediate context rather than as rigid restrictions that allow no exceptions?

g. *Spiritual leadership.* Concerning the matter of spiritual leadership, what is it in any of these considerations that detracts from training men to lead, to take initiative, and to define agendas and courageously struggle for their fulfillment? Does it really require women to assume or play subordinate roles (roles that are often artificial to them and to our culture) in order for men to succeed at leadership?

Finally, as we work together for answers that are beneficial and constructive, it is important to remember: 1) the sense of loving brotherhood we enjoy with other Churches of Christ and the spiritual safe haven we have traditionally provided for their members transferred into our area; 2) the sanctity of Christian conscience, which is not simply a matter of "comfort zone"; and 3) the recognition that society itself is still struggling to define what is appropriately male and female.

Perhaps sooner than we might imagine, churches will have come to understandings and solutions on matters of faith and gender with which we all can live. The spiritual challenge is to arrive at that point with a minimum of agony. It is wise to remember that in matters this complex we must be cautious on one hand, yet not so caught up in ruminations on the subject that we fail to take whatever action we should as disciples of Jesus in our time. Each of us must take read the Bible, be involved in its interpretation, and work toward a consensus built on honesty, courage, the surrendering of rights, and commitment to the centrality of the gospel.

Our last discussions ended May 16, 1993. We want to stay current with the finest biblical and historical scholarship on faith and gender. We also seek to keep up with the most responsible contemporary social thought on the topic. And we are interested in the experience of other churches that are considering these matters as we work together toward the creation of a loving Christian consensus here and elsewhere.

Appendix Three

REFLECTIONS ON THE "WOMEN'S ISSUE" AT MEADOWBROOK CHURCH, JACKSON, MS

David B. Jackson

The question of the role of women in the church is one of the strongest challenges faced by contemporary heirs of the Restoration Movement. To the extent that it is accepted as an invitation to reexamination of the church's practice in light of Scripture, discussion of the question should be welcomed. There is a danger, however, that such renewed study will be forestalled due to pressures of tradition and fears of conflict in the church.

What follows is intended to describe the situation at the Meadowbrook Church of Christ in Jackson, Mississippi, in very practical, everyday terms by describing real situations. Perhaps thinking about the implications of concrete examples will serve to distill some principles that will help further the struggle for appropriate ways to respond to the threat that change always brings to the church.

1. *Some Typical Situations*

A) A young pre-med student, not a member of the church, accompanied our medical missions team to the jungles of Guatemala. His father-in-law, a physician, is active in our medical-missions efforts. He was so impressed by what he experienced that he began attending more of our services than at his own church. He expressed appreciation for the spiritual emphasis in worship, as well as the biblical content in the preaching and teaching. As a result of his continued interest, his wife and infant daughter visited with him several times. His wife grew up at Meadowbrook, but never became a member.

While visiting in their home one evening, I was asked some penetrating questions. Since their marriage, they had visited several different churches in our community. He was certainly impressed with our involvement in medical missions, which he knew firsthand. He had also learned of other programs in which we are attempting to improve our community. He had even discussed with his wife the implications of becoming members with us. In our discussion at their home, the one point of deepest concern was not at all what might have been expected. As this young mother held her infant daughter in her arms, she expressed deep reservations about the message which her daughter would receive as she grew up in a church that placed restrictions on women that were not exercised toward men. It was evident to her that certain decisions had been made concerning the role of women in the public activities of the church and she found that disturbing.

Her questions did not spring from a cavalier disregard for the expressed will of God. She was not speaking from ignorance of the relevant passages in the NT. Her concern was based in the perception of women being treated as "second class citizens." She was speaking from a cultural background that has accorded women equal access to education, voting, training, and occupations in every field. As a parent, responsible in large part for the impressions made on her daughter from the environment in which she is placed, this mother could not conscientiously consent to restrictions she felt unwarranted either biblically or culturally.

They have not been in worship with us nearly as often as they had been before the "women's issue" surfaced.

B) An adult Sunday school class was planned under the title, "Finding Our Place: the Role of Men and Women in the Church." During one quarter it was presented in a discussion class of mostly middle and older adults. As the teacher, I attempted to provide an honest and thorough examination of the key biblical passages, as well as historical and cultural precedents for current practices.

While stressing the faithfulness to God's will as revealed in Scripture, I suggested that in some areas there may be room for change in our understanding and practice concerning the role of women in the church. The attitude displayed by class participants was that of exploration, interest, and willingness to consider alternatives to past practice in view of our changing culture, insofar as those changes would not contradict the Lord's will for his church.

In the following quarter the same material was taught in the "Young Adult" class. The participants were both single and married, ranging in age from early twenties to mid-thirties. Many of them showed the same enthusiasm for exploration as their older counterparts. Surprisingly, however, some voiced strong, emotion-filled opposition. The objections were not raised to specific conclusions that were at odds with previously-held positions. The pleading question was, "Why bring up this subject at all? Why risk splitting the church?"

One young woman was especially concerned about the impact on her mother who lives five hours away, if she knew the subject was merely under discussion. "She had rather I would become a Pentecostal," was her complaint to a friend, "than to change views on the role of women." She was emotionally overwhelmed by the thought of even investigating the subject. Another was heard to say, "I have turmoil in every other area of my life. Why can't we just leave the church alone? Don't change anything. All of this was settled a long time ago. Now just leave it alone."

C) One of our families is made up of a husband and wife who are both attorneys. He grew up in a traditional congregation of Churches of Christ in a small town. She grew up in a Baptist Church in the same town. His church was perceived in the community to be exclusivistic toward all who did not agree with them and caustic in its treatment of outsiders. He is very active, directing the adult department in our Bible School program. It is doubtful that she will ever become a member because of the impression of his church from "back home." As an educated, highly intelligent woman, she is also deeply concerned about the role of women in the church.

Her interest in the way women are viewed and treated is more than theoretical. She has two daughters who are regularly involved in classes and activities in our church. She is fully adequate to deal with questions of culture and command. "When do you stop just discussing and considering it, and begin to make some appropriate changes?" is her question.

2. Some Observations

There are two distinct reasons why the people of God should welcome this opportunity to engage in a new look at the topic of women in the church. First, any time Christ's people are driven to his Word for guidance, they are demonstrating a real-life dependence on the Bible to do what it was intended to do. Scripture points us to the mind of Christ. As we learn about his will for us and as we attempt to put that will into practice, we are able to take on the characteristics of the one we serve.

Second, to the extent that we base our actions on the leading of the Spirit through the words of inspired writers, rather than on the approval of past practice, we show ourselves to be genuine heirs of the Restoration Movement in America. Only in so doing are we worthy of the legacy of the Campbells, Stone and other heroes among our spiritual ancestors. We stand in a courageous heritage of refusing the approval of mere tradition, no matter how hallowed by years of practice, no matter how emotionally defended by supporters of old conclusions.

In this present discussion on the role of women, these very fundamental aspirations are being denied to those who would advocate change. If anyone should dare to suggest that the honest reevaluation of Scripture might lead to different conclusions than those reached years ago, they will be vigorously attacked as wanting nothing more than to justify previously-reached conclusions by a twisting of the text to suit their own culturally-based ends.

Such an attitude may masquerade as loyalty to "the Old Paths," but in reality it is nothing but blind loyalty to the "safe" position of the tradition of previous generations. This view is sanctified, not by the stamp of God's Spirit, but merely by the earthly authority of historical priority which is the opposite of restorationist ideals. By this spirit neither is God honored, nor is the goal of restoring the church based on the study of his Word.

Perhaps *nothing* should change in the church's present understanding of the role of women in the church—but such a conclusion should be based on a free examination of the relevant passages, based on solid principles of exegesis, with commitment to following God's word wherever it may lead. And if it leads in such a way as to challenge previously held convictions, we must submit in faith to those changes. To do otherwise is to deny by action the principles we claim to uphold with our words.

Perhaps in every age the issues facing the church appear to be more complex than in the preceding one. Each generation feels the weight of the questions facing it with the intensity that comes from urgently seeking needed answers. While few of the questions being debated are new, they have never been faced by *this* church in *this* time before now.

The role of women in the church—including worship, teaching, and serving—is one of the "live" subjects of our time. It has been thrust upon us because our culture has changed. Unlike women in all previous centuries, American women have gained unprecedented status in the twentieth century. Women are full citizens, with the right to vote, to own property, to receive an education, and to find employment in every way that men are.

The question is, how will the church of Jesus, following his will as closely as is humanly possible, under the leadership of the Holy Spirit, and in faithfulness to the words of Scripture, respond to the issue at hand? Ignoring the discussion will not make it sooner disappear. Asserting the conclusions reached in past discussions will not simplify matters for today's questioners. Changing just for the sake of appearing "in step" with the times is to desert both the Lord and the ideal of Restoration.

The church is called on to maintain unity with all its might (Eph 4:1-3). When discussing the role of women, we seem to face a monumental task. Genuine convictions on both sides must be honored, while insistence on personal opinion must not be. Patience and persistence are key components in any strategy for dealing with the subject. As important as this issue is, it is not the heart of the gospel. The message of Jesus must always be our central concern. One casualty in the battle for souls that occurs because of bitterness over how the church responds to the question of the role of women is one too many. For one who is submitted to the will of God, this matter is not essential to salvation. Therefore, let us be careful about whom we drive away from the church due to differing opinions.

In the discussion of any controversial topic, a vital task is to separate the issue from the strong feelings of those who hold deeply to opposing points of view. Whether the arena of discussion is marital discord, a political campaign, or a matter of biblical interpretation, heightened emotions tend to override effective reasoning. The threat of change brings with it feelings of anxiety which are often intense enough to short-circuit effective discussion. In our Restoration heritage, "issues" have forced us into non-fellowshipping sectarian parties, each claiming to be more faithful than the next to the call to follow Jesus as Lord.

When people care deeply about a matter, they are capable of feeling deeply about it. We should feel deeply about whatever concerns the church, and the question of the role of women in the church certainly does, and will, affect the fellowship of Churches of Christ. The task is to attempt, with God's help, to channel the deep convictions in avenues that glorify, rather than shame, the name of Christ.

The founders of the Restoration Movement in America never shied away from honest investigation. In fact, they challenged entrenched traditions in the religious world by appealing to a fresh examination of the biblical text in all matters. Would they not be horrified at those among their spiritual heirs who prefer to avoid the suggestion of open, honest exploration of this perplexing problem?

When God's people are called to study the Bible, that is not to be understood as an invitation merely to confirm the conclusions of the past. The scholars and leaders of previous generations were not less intelligent or diligent than those in the present, and no less honest in their quest for the will of God for his church. Surely, however, we recognize room for new insights concerning the texts of Scripture as tools and information become available which were not known in a previous age. To refuse to modify a position when new evidence warrants such a change is to be guilty of the most blatant form of pharisaic traditionalism.

3. A Suggested Approach

The first step is a call to return to the Bible. Church Leaders must have the courage to lead congregations in honest, searching studies of issues, including the role of women in the church. Such a call must include the commitment to follow wherever the conclusions may lead. To begin with the intent of reaffirming previously-held convictions, whether for the traditional understanding or for change, is to engage in a mockery of the ideal of biblical authority.

Two things are required. The first is, unquestionably difficult, objectivity. The second is to maintain a cautious distinction between challenging previous positions through careful exegesis and discussion, and the implementation of change if and when we come to new conclusions. For too many, merely raising the issue is equivalent to instituting radical change. As soon as someone suggests that a prominent text on the role of women may be culture-specific, rather than a universal principle, the alarm is raised that "they want women preachers in the pulpit."

Having firmly based the study of women in the church on the will of God as revealed in Scripture, a congregation may become involved in a discussion of what changes might reasonably be considered. Such discussion is still months away from initiation of change. A cautious approach such as this takes longer than a rush to institute change, but patience is still a virtue and is a small price to pay.

If the discussions can be based on a genuine concern for searching to find truth, the congregation may be able to negotiate the stormy waters without a boatload of spiritual casualties. When we remember that the role of women is not the heart of the gospel, and when immediate change is not the goal, perhaps we can promote an atmosphere in which genuine differences of opinion can be discussed in a conscientious search for the truth. Such tolerance in non-essentials is required so that the quest will not drive us apart.

At the Meadowbrook congregation, we have engaged in serious discussions, but no significant changes have yet been introduced. The present leadership is not of one mind on the matter, which precludes any major behavioral change within the congregation. I have addressed the topic only rarely from the pulpit, for reasons that are evident. We have had two series of Sunday School lessons for different segments of the congregation. Each lasted for thirteen weeks and focused on careful analyses of key biblical texts. As indicated above, and much to my surprise, older members seemed more comfortable than younger ones with wrestling with the text of Scripture from a new perspective. At least one home Bible study group has discussed the matter at some length.

If change is to come, we must base the decision on confident understanding of Scripture. Patience is required because we are at different levels of understanding. No divided congregation and not one lost soul is worth the price of change in a non-essential issue that comes too quickly, even if it is sanctioned by Scripture. Now is not the time to desert the quest for seeking truth; it is a time for wisdom.

Indexes

Scripture

Genesis
1: *1-6, 8-13, 16, 17, 19, 27, 36*
1-2: *3*
1-3: *1, 4, 36*
1-11: *1-3, 10*
1-50: *1*
1.1-2: *4*
1.1-11.9: *47*
1.2-7: *5*
1.4: *162*
1.5: *27*
1.8: *27*
1.10: *27, 162*
1.22: *9*
1.26: *1, 7*
1.26-28: *1, 8, 9*
1.26-30: *3, 6*
1.27: *6, 7*
1.28: *9*
1.28-30: *8*
2: *14, 16, 17, 19, 21-23, 28, 29, 31*
2-3: *3, 4, 11-14, 20, 33, 36, 535, 539*
2.1-3: *4*
2.3: *9*
2.4-9: *14*
2.5-25: *537*
2.7: *17, 35, 539*
2.7-24: *28, 32*
2.7-25: *14*
2.8: *539*
2.8-13: *28*
2.8-14: *16*
2.8-17: *14*
2.14: *29*
2.15: *14, 16, 539*
2.16: *16*
2.17: *16, 29*
2.18: *27, 537*
2.19: *17, 539*
2.21-24: *18*
2.21-25: *18, 20*
2.22: *170*
2.23: *18, 21, 34*
2.23-24: *21, 22*
2.23-25: *36*
2.24: *18, 22, 31, 254-257, 538*
2.25: *22, 26, 34*
3: *14, 16, 22, 23, 31, 36, 412*
3-11: *3*
3.1: *28*
3.4: *28*
3.1-7: *14, 22, 31*
3.1-24: *14*
3.6: *25, 369*
3.7: *22, 26, 35*
3.8-13: *27*
3.8-24: *14, 28, 32*
3.9: *27*
3.10: *26, 34*
3.12: *22, 24, 34*
3.13: *29*
3.14-19: *27, 28, 29*
3.15: *29*
3.16: *22, 29-34, 370*
3.17: *34, 539*
3.17-19: *16, 31*
3.19: *35*
3.20: *34*
3.20-24: *28, 34*
3.21: *35*
3.22-24: *14*
3.23: *16*
4.4: *166*
4.6: *27*
4.7: *30*
4.10: *27*
5: *47*
5.3: *7*
6: *343, 344*
6.11: *53*
9.1-7: *3*
9.6: *7*
11.7: *6*
11.9: *326*
11.10-26: *47*
11.27-36.43: *44*
11.29: *37, 42, 43, 47*
11.30: *47, 56, 57*
11.31: *41, 46, 57*
12: *47, 56*
12-50: *1, 2*
12.1-3: *1, 48*

Genesis (cont.)
12.1-5: *326*
12.4,5: *47*
12.7: *48*
12.10-20: *48*
12.11: *48*
12.11-20: *66*
12.13: *48-50, 57*
12.14-15: *49*
12.15,19: *47*
12.16: *49, 50, 57*
12.17: *50, 57*
13.14-17: *48*
13.18: *55*
14: *50*
15: *48, 50*
15.1-2: *56*
15.2: *317*
15.4: *55*
15.6: *317, 323, 326*
16: *50*
16-17: *323*
16.1: *50, 56, 317*
16.2: *51, 52, 57*
16.4: *53*
16.5: *53, 60*
16.6: *54, 317*
17: *48*
17.15: *38, 55*
17.15-21: *57*
17.16: *55*
17.17: *55, 317*
17.19: *55*
18: *48*
18.1: *55*
18.6: *55, 161*
18.7,8: *55*
18.9: *56*
18.10: *56*
18.11: *56, 328*
18.12: *55, 56, 317, 320*
18.13: *55, 56*
18.15: *56*
19.1: *164*
20: *49*
20.3: *285*
20.6-7: *285*
20.9: *57*
20.11: *57*
20.12: *41, 43, 44, 46, 57*
20.18: *52, 57*
21.1: *57*
21.2: *57, 327, 329*
21.3: *57*
21.5: *57, 58*
21.7: *57*
21.10: *61, 317*
21.12: *48*
21.14: *61*
21.14-19: *116*
21.34: *62*
22: *59, 60*
22.1: *61*
22.3: *61*
22.9: *58*
22.16-18: *48*
23.1: *61*
23.2: *61*
23.4: *326*
23.9: *62*
23.17: *62*
23.19: *62*
23.20: *62*
24: *39*
24.15: *161*
24.67: *63*
25.1-2: *328*
26.3: *326*
27.8: *161*
27.42-45: *116*
29.9: *161*
29.14: *22*
29:18-19: *242*
29.30, 31: *193*
29.31-30.24: *136*
30.3: *51*
30.13: *165, 166*
31.49: *165*
32.28: *38*
34.12: *242*
35.2: *134*
35.4: *55*
35.12: *326*
35.17: *136*
35.27: *55*
37.5-11: *285*
37.27: *164, 326*
37.35: *165*

Genesis (cont.)
38.15: *130*
38.21, 22: *130*
38.24: *131, 132*
38.28: *163*
41.38: *157*
47.6: *157*
47.7: *174*
47.22: *161*

Exodus
2.2-4: *116*
4.16: *105*
5.14: *161*
7.1: *105*
9.31: *160*
14.22-25: *114*
14.22-15.18: *114*
14.26-28: *114*
14.29-31: *114*
15.1: *114, 115*
15.1-18: *114*
15.18: *106*
15.19: *115*
15.19-21: *114, 115*
15.20: *81, 115, 116, 292, 369*
15.21: *114, 115*
18.4: *20*
18.21: *157*
21.8: *164*
21.10: *244*
22.16-17: *242*
32-34: *144*
34.6, 7: *144*
35.25, 26: *163*
35.26: *162*

Leviticus
16.7-10: *285*
18: *42*
18.6: *43*
18.9: *43*
18.18: *160*
19.26: *285*
19.32: *165*
21.17-23: *300*

Numbers
5:19-20: *233*

5.20: *228, 229*
5.29: *228, 229*
6.7: *191*
12.2: *115*
20.19: *158*
24.18: *157, 166*
33.52: *7*

Deuteronomy
2.6: *142*
4.12-18: *8*
8.17: *166*
8.18: *157*
10.20: *22, 31*
11.22: *22, 31*
13.4: *22, 31*
18.8: *158*
18.10: *285*
18.11: *97*
18.15: *292*
18.22: *287*
21.15-17: *193*
21.19: *164*
22-27: *146*
22.11: *160*
22.15: *164*
23.17: *131*
24.1-4: *140, 232*
33.7: *20*
33.8: *285*
33.9: *193*
33.26: *20*

Joshua
2.6: *160*
7.14-15: *285*
13-18: *71*
22.5: *22, 31*
23: *70*
23.8: *22, 31*
24.2: *38*
24.15: *134*
24.26: *55*

Judges
1-16: *72*
1.1-2.5: *70, 71*
2.1-5: *72*
2.1-15: *71*

Judges (cont.)
 2.6: *70*
 2.6-23: *71*
 2.11-23: *75*
 2.16: *73, 75*
 2.16, 17: *73*
 3.1-6: *72*
 3.7-16.31: *72*
 3.9: *75*
 3.15: *75*
 3.28: *74*
 4: *77, 79, 81, 83*
 4.2, 3: *81*
 4.4: *69, 115, 292*
 4.4, 5: *73, 115*
 4.6: *74, 81, 82*
 4.6, 7: *115*
 4.7: *81*
 4.8-10: *116*
 4.9: *81-83, 85*
 4.14: *81*
 5: *77, 79, 81, 83*
 5.1: *116*
 5.3: *84*
 5.4: *84*
 5.5: *84*
 5.7: *115, 116*
 5.11: *167*
 5.12: *116*
 5.15: *116*
 5.20: *84*
 5.23: *84*
 5.29: *38*
 6.12: *157*
 8.3: *74*
 8.4-9: *76*
 8.22-28: *76*
 8.26: *164*
 9.2-3: *22*
 9.6: *55*
 9.9: *109*
 9.22: *38*
 9.24: *53*
 9.27: *161*
 9.37: *55*
 11.1: *157*
 11.27: *73, 77*
 11.30: *75*
 11.40: *167*

 13.25: *74*
 14.12, 13: *164*
 17-18: *72*
 17-21: *70, 72*
 17.6: *70, 72*
 18.1: *70, 72*
 19-20: *72*
 19.1: *70, 72*
 21: *72*
 21.25: *70, 72*

Ruth
 2.1: *157*
 3.11: *157*
 4.5: *243*
 4.10: *243*
 4.11: *157, 166*

1 Samuel
 2.18: *115*
 2.19: *160*
 2.27: *107*
 3.20: *115*
 6.5: *7*
 7.6: *115*
 7.9, 10: *115*
 7.15-17: *115*
 8.7: *106*
 9: *285*
 9.6-8: *107*
 9.6-10: *115*
 9.10: *107*
 9.11: *161*
 9.11-13: *115*
 9.22-24: *115*
 10.5: *286*
 10.9-13: *110*
 10.20-21: *285*
 15.2, 3: *115*
 15.23: *285*
 16.14-16: *287*
 18.4: *164*
 18.10-11: *287*
 19.13-16: *285*
 19.20: *115, 286*
 19.20-24: *110, 285, 286*
 19.24: *286*
 22.6-10: *107*
 23.9-12: *285*

Indexes

1 Samuel (cont.)
25.2-42: *96*
25.24-31: *97*
28.1-25: *92, 97*
28.3-25: *96*
28.5-6: *286*
28.6: *111*
31.12: *157*

2 Samuel
5.1: *22*
7.4-17: *286*
13.13: *43*
14.1-20: *92, 96*
14.2: *158*
14.13: *97*
15.13-23: *107*
17.10: *157*
18.11: *164*
18.24: *165*
18.24-27: *108*
19.13: *22*
20.3: *22*
20.14-22: *92, 96*
20.16: *158*
20.18-19: *97*
23.20: *157*
24.9: *157*
24.14: *6*

1 Kings
1: *287*
1.42: *157*
1.52: *157*
3.16-28: *96*
11.3: *38*
11.28: *157*
12.21-24: *116*
14.23, 24: *131*
15.12: *131*
17: *285*
18.17-29: *285*
18.21: *286*
18.28-29: *286*
18.46: *161*
19.9: *27*
20.2: *108*
20.5: *108*
20.6: *108*
20.13-15: *286*
20.35-42: *286*
21.19: *108*
22.5-6: *286*
22.5-10: *285*
22.15-28: *116*
22.19-22: *6*
22.19-23: *286*
22.46: *131*

2 Kings
1.2-17: *285*
2.9-15: *285*
3.11-20: *286*
4.8: *158*
4.29: *161*
5.1: *157*
5.8: *107*
6.1-7: *285*
6.8-10: *285, 286*
6.22: *285*
11.18: *7*
13.14-19: *286*
13.14-21: *285*
16.10: *7*
17.17: *285*
17.24: *213*
18.6: *22*
18.19: *108*
19.9: *108*
19.14: *108*
19.15: *106*
20.1-11: *285*
21.1-18: *110*
21.10-15: *112*
21.19-26: *110*
22, 23: *113*
22.1-23.27: *110*
22.3-7: *110*
22.8-13: *111*
22.13: *111, 112*
22.14: *111, 117, 120*
22.14-20: *111, 292*
22.15: *111, 112*
22.16: *111, 112*
22.16-20: *111*
22.18: *111*
22.19: *111, 112*
22.20: *113*

2 Kings (cont.)
  23.7: *131*
  23.29, 30: *113*
  25: *113*

1 Chronicles
  10.12: *157*
  11.22: *157*
  26.8: *157*
  26.31: *157*

2 Chronicles
  12.5-8: *286*
  15.1-7: *286*
  33.18: *112*
  34.1-35.19: *110*
  34.3: *110*
  34.21: *111*, *112*
  34.22: *111*
  34.22-28: *111*, *292*
  34.24, 25: *112*
  34.24-28: *111*
  34.26: *111*
  34.27: *111*, *112*
  35.20-25: *113*
  36.15, 16: *108*

Ezra
  1.2: *108*
  9, 10: *137*
  10.3: *137*

Nehemiah
  5.3: *161*
  6.10-14: *118*
  6.14: *118*, *120*, *292*
  7.65: *285*
  9.37: *249*

Esther
  1.18: *38*
  1.22: *38*
  8.15: *164*

Job
  1.6-7: *6*
  2.1-2: *6*
  2.5: *22*
  5.22: *165*

18.6: *162*
19.7: *53*
28.9: *162*
28.12: *157*
28.18: *158*
28.15-19: *158*
29.7: *164*
29.8: *165*
29.14: *165*
31.16: *160*
31.16-20: *163*
38.2: *27*
38.7: *6*
39.7: *165*
39.18: *165*
39.22: *165*
41.6: *164*
41.29: *165*

Psalms
  8.1: *167*
  8.3-9: *10*
  9: *155*
  20.3: *20*
  25: *155*
  29.11: *165*
  33: *169*
  33.17: *166*
  33.20: *20*
  34: *155*
  34.8: *162*
  34.10: *160*
  37.32: *165*
  47.2: *106*
  47.7, 8: *106*
  60.12: *157*
  70.5: *20*
  82.1: *6*
  89.21: *162*
  93.1: *161*, *165*
  99.1: *106*
  102.5: *22*
  104.1: *165*
  108.13: *157*
  111: *155*, *156*
  112: *155*
  113.9: *58*
  115.9-11: *20*
  118.15, 16: *157*

Psalms (cont.)
119: *155*
119.162: *160*
121.1: *20*
128.1, 2: *168*
145: *155*
146.5: *20*

Proverbs
1: *87*
1-9: *87, 93, 100, 156, 180*
1.7: *167, 180*
1.8: *165*
1.8, 9: *168*
1.9: *166*
1.13: *160*
1.21: *180*
1.29: *167*
2.17: *167, 168*
3.3: *165*
3.14: *162*
3.15: *158*
3.30: *160*
4.3: *168*
5.15-19: *168*
6.6: *165*
6.9: *165*
6.9, 10: *161*
6.17: *166*
6.19: *166*
6.20: *165, 168*
6.23, 24: *229*
6.24: *228*
6.25: *166*
6.26: *168*
6.29: *228, 229*
6.34: *159*
7.10-19: *168*
7.16: *163*
8: *87*
8.3: *164, 180*
8.11: *158*
8.13: *167*
8.16: *38*
8.18: *160*
8.19: *158*
9: *87*
9.1-6: *180*
9.13: *157, 165, 168*

10.1: *168*
11.16: *157, 166, 168*
11.17: *165*
11.22: *166, 168*
11.25: *163*
12.4: *157, 167, 168*
13.5: *166*
13.9: *162*
13.11: *166*
14.1: *158, 168*
14.21: *163*
15.20: *168*
16.16: *158*
16.19: *160*
17.25: *168*
18.22: *168*
19.13: *168*
19.14: *160, 168*
19.15: *165*
19.17: *163*
19.26: *168*
20.6: *156*
20.13: *161*
20.15: *158*
20.19: *165*
20.20: *162, 168*
21.9: *168*
21.19: *168*
21.21: *165*
21.25: *160*
21.27: *161*
22.4: *167*
22.14: *168*
22.22: *164*
23.17: *167*
23.22: *168*
23.25: *168*
23.27: *168*
24.7: *164*
24.30: *161*
25-29: *169*
25.13: *163*
25.24: *165, 168*
26.1: *163*
27.15: *168*
27.27: *161*
28.24: *168*
29.3: *168*
29.27: *169*

Proverbs (cont.)
  30.8: *161*
  30.15-33: *169*
  30.32: *161*
  31: *100, 156, 167, 172, 179*
  31.1: *165*
  31.1-9: *169*
  31.1-31: *180*
  31.3: *157, 168*
  31.10: *166*
  31.10, 11: *155*
  31.10-18: *155*
  31.10-31: *155, 156, 169-175, 178*
  31.11: *164, 169*
  31.12: *160, 169, 170*
  31.13: *160, 169*
  31.14: *161, 170*
  31.15: *116, 155, 156, 161*
  31.16: *161*
  31.17: *161, 165*
  31.18: *162, 169*
  31.19: *160, 162, 163*
  31.19, 20: *155, 171*
  31.20: *159, 163, 175*
  31.21: *116, 163, 169, 170, 173*
  31.21-29: *155*
  31.22: *160, 163, 169, 170*
  31.23: *156, 164*
  31.24: *160, 161, 164*
  31.25: *161, 165, 176*
  31.25, 26: *169*
  31.26: *116, 165, 170, 173, 180*
  31.27: *165, 171, 179*
  31.27, 28: *116*
  31.28: *165, 167, 170*
  31.28, 29: *155, 164*
  31.29: *157, 166, 169*
  31.30: *155, 156, 161, 166, 169-171, 180*
  31.30, 31: *155, 170*
  31.31: *167, 170, 176*

Ecclesiastes
  1.2: *166*
  3.17: *160*
  7.24: *157*
  7.28: *157*
  9.9: *168*

Canticles
  1.6: *161*
  2.2: *166*
  3.10: *164*
  6.9: *166*
  6.10: *39*
  7.10: *30*

Isaiah
  1.2-17: *110*
  1.22: *109*
  1.25: *109*
  2.8: *112*
  2.18: *112*
  2.20, 21: *112*
  3.2: *285*
  3.23: *164*
  5.2: *161*
  5.7: *161*
  6.1-13: *286*
  6.8: *6*
  7.3-9: *116*
  7.10-17: *117*
  7.23: *161*
  8.1-4: *137*
  8.3: *116, 117, 293*
  8.11: *286*
  8.18: *117*
  9.2: *160*
  10.3: *161*
  10.24: *108*
  11.1-9: *9*
  19.9: *160*
  20.1-6: *134*
  21.6: *108*
  24.23: *39*
  28.7: *287*
  30.5: *20*
  30.26: *39*
  30.27: *161*
  32.1: *38*
  41.16: *167*
  44.28: *160*
  47.1: *132*
  47.9: *132*
  49.4: *166*
  49.23: *38*
  51.2: *64*
  57.15: *112*

Isaiah (cont.)
  58.3: *160*
  61.1: *286*

Jeremiah
  1.5: *106*
  1.6: *106*
  1.7: *106*
  3.6-10: *140*
  3.15-18: *144*
  5.15: *161*
  5.20-31: *110*
  5.30-31: *286*
  6.17: *108*
  6.27-30: *109*
  7.25: *107*
  10.4: *164*
  15.10-18: *106*
  15.17: *286*
  15.19: *106*
  18.7, 8: *112*
  18.18: *91*
  23.9-40: *118*
  23.14: *287*
  23.18: *107*
  23.21, 22: *107*
  26.5: *107*
  26.17: *165*
  27.7: *285*
  28:8-9: *287*
  36: *127*
  36.22: *163*

Lamentations
  1-4: *155*
  1.1: *38*
  2: *169*
  2.19: *162*
  3: *169*
  4: *169*
  4.7: *158*

Ezekiel
  1.5: *7*
  1.10: *7*
  1.26: *7*
  1.28: *7*
  3.14: *286*
  3.16-21: *108*
  8.1-18: *112*
  9.2, 3: *163*
  13: *117*
  13.1-16: *117*
  13.2: *118*
  13.6: *285*
  13.6-9: *118*
  13.8, 9: *118*
  13.9: *118*
  13.10: *118*
  13.11-15: *118*
  13.14: *118*
  13.16: *118*
  13.17: *117*
  13.17-23: *117*
  13.18-23: *118*
  13.20: *118*
  13.20, 21: *118*
  13.21: *118*
  13.23: *118*
  16: *134*
  16.49: *163*
  21.21: *285*
  23.14: *7*
  23.40: *161*
  28.4: *157, 166*
  33.1-9: *108*
  37.15-28: *144*

Daniel
  2.1-11: *285*
  9.2: *290*

Hosea
  1: *128, 137, 138, 141, 143*
  1, 2: *141, 142*
  1-3: *125-129, 131, 143-145, 148, 150*
  1.1: *143*
  1.2: *129, 133, 135, 137, 143*
  1.2, 3: *138*
  1.3: *136*
  1.3-9: *143*
  1.7: *128*
  1.9: *126, 140*
  1.10, 11: *126*
  1.10-2.1: *128, 140, 143*
  2: *138-140, 143*
  2.1, 2: *126*

Hosea (cont.)
  2.1-23: *126*
  2.2: *132, 138-140, 142*
  2.2-5: *138, 139*
  2.2-13: *143*
  2.2-23: *138*
  2.2, 3: *128, 138*
  2.2-13: *128*
  2.3: *146, 147, 152*
  2.3-23: *126*
  2.4: *128*
  2.4, 5: *137*
  2.5: *139, 147, 160*
  2.5-7: *139*
  2.6: *146, 152*
  2.7: *128, 134, 136, 139*
  2.8: *128, 139, 147*
  2.8-23: *138*
  2.9: *160*
  2.10: *146, 147, 152*
  2.12, 13: *147*
  2.13: *112*
  2.14: *248*
  2.14-23: *128, 140, 143*
  2.15: *147*
  2.21-23: *147*
  3: *128, 135, 141, 142, 143, 148*
  3.1-3: *141*
  3.2: *142*
  3.4, 5: *141*
  3.5: *128*
  4-14: *128*
  4.1, 2: *133*
  4.11-14: *149*
  4.12, 13: *149*
  4.13, 14: *147-149, 152*
  4.14: *131-133, 149*
  4.17, 18: *133*
  5.13: *133*
  9.2-6: *110*
  11.1-4: *110*
  12.1: *133*
  12.4: *38*
  12.11: *286*
  13.9: *20*
  14.3: *133*

Joel
  2: *195*

  2.28: *120*
  2.28-32: *119*

Amos
  1.1: *286*
  2.6: *163*
  2.7: *163*
  2.7, 8: *133*
  3.6: *108*
  3.7: *107*
  3.14, 15: *110*
  4.1: *159*
  4.6-11: *110*
  7.1-9: *109*
  7.10-13: *286*
  7.12: *109*
  7.16: *105*

Micah
  3.5-8: *118*
  3.7: *109*
  3.5, 6: *109*
  3.11: *285*
  6.4: *115*
  6.8: *112*
  7.6: *191*

Nahum
  1.2-7: *155*

Habakkuk
  2.1: *165*

Haggai
  1.1: *108*
  1.6: *163*
  1.13: *108*

Malachi
  2.16: *53*
  4.5-6 (3:23-24): *292*

Matthew
  5.17-20: *185*
  10.5-6: *566*
  10.20: *187*
  12.29: *192*
  16.16: *216*
  19.10-12: *188*

Matthew (cont.)
  19.23-30: *186*
  19.27: *183*
  19.29: *183, 184, 189*
  20.25-27: *524*
  23.8-11: *524*
  25.40: *524*
  28.9, 10: *218*
  28.16-20: *566*

Mark
  1.24-26: *282*
  3.11: *282*
  5.7-12: *282*
  10.11, 12: *188*
  10.23-31: *186*
  10.24-27: *186*
  10.28: *183, 186*
  10.29: *182-185, 187*
  10.30: *187, 189*
  10.43-44: *9*
  14: *411*
  14.51: *164*
  16.9, 10: *218*

Luke
  1.10: *119*
  2.22: *118*
  2.34, 35: *190*
  2.37: *119*
  2.38: *119*
  3.16, 17: *190*
  6.20-23: *186*
  8.15: *190*
  8.19-21: *187*
  8.21: *190*
  9.23: *196*
  12.1-53: *190*
  12.4-12: *186*
  12.33: *565*
  12.49: *190*
  12.49-53: *190, 195*
  12.52: *187, 188*
  12.53: *192*
  14.15-24: *194*
  14.20: *194*
  14.25: *194*
  14.26: *182, 187, 188, 192-195*
  14.33: *195*

18.18: *190*
18.18-30: *183*
18.20: *194*
18.29: *182, 185, 189*
18.29, 30: *181, 183, 185-188, 192, 195, 196*
19.8-9: *565*
21.12-19: *186*
22.27: *524*
22.28: *187*
24.11: *411*
24.34: *216*

John
  1: *203*
  2: *200*
  2.1-11: *201, 202*
  2.5: *203*
  2.11: *202, 203, 206, 212*
  2.12: *203*
  3: *200, 204*
  4: *198, 200, 204, 411*
  4.39: *211*
  4.39-42: *211*
  4.41: *211*
  4.42: *210, 211*
  4.46-54: *202*
  4.47, 48: *204*
  4.53: *204*
  5: *198, 200*
  6: *216*
  6.42: *201*
  6.69: *216*
  7.11-13: *198, 200*
  7.13: *198*
  7.37: *200*
  7.53-8.11: *201*
  8.12: *200*
  9: *198*
  9.18-23: *198, 200*
  10: *200*
  11: *214, 216*
  11.45-53: *217*
  12.1-8: *217*
  12.10, 11: *198, 200, 217*
  12.26: *524*
  12.42: *200*
  12.42, 43: *198, 200*
  13.14: *524*

John (cont.)
  16.1-4: *198, 200*
  19.25-27: *201, 204*
  19.28: *206*
  19.38: *198, 200, 212*
  19.38, 39: *200*
  20: *217*
  20.8: *219*
  20.9: *219*
  20.17: *221*
  20.29: *207, 217*
  20.30, 31: *204*
  20.31: *200, 203, 211*
  21: *219*

Acts
  1.21: *196*
  2: *195, 264*
  2.3: *190*
  2.9-10: *264*
  2.14-21: *120*
  2.16-21: *294*
  2.17: *316*
  2.17, 18: *119*
  2.34-36: *523*
  2.44-47: *190*
  4.32: *190*
  5.36: *290*
  6: *265*
  6.4: *524*
  6.5: *120*
  8.4-13: *120*
  8.26-40: *120*
  11.27: *304*
  11.27-30: *282, 305*
  13.1-3: *296, 304, 305, 308*
  14.4: *530*
  14.14: *530*
  14.23: *527*
  15.1-23: *527*
  15:22: *305*
  15.32: *305*
  16:16-18: *282*
  16.20: *268*
  17.4: *268*
  17.12: *268*
  18: *265, 268, 274*
  18.1: *271*
  18.1-3: *261, 276, 531*
  18.2: *262, 263*
  18.18: *262, 274, 531*
  18.18-22: *261*
  18.24-26: *531*
  18.26: *262, 272*
  18.26-28: *261, 276*
  19.23-40: *269*
  20.17-35: *527*
  21.8, 9: *120*
  21.9: *370, 530*
  21.18: *527*
  21.10: *304, 305*
  21:10-11: *290*

Romans
  1.3-4: *523*
  1.24-27: *248*
  4.19: *66, 328, 329*
  5.12-21: *33*
  6.14: *233*
  7.1: *233, 234*
  7.1-4: *235*
  7.1-6: *232, 234, 237*
  7.2: *225-227, 231, 233, 235, 237, 537*
  7.2-3: *233-235*
  7.3: *235, 236*
  7.4: *234*
  7.14: *232*
  7.16-23: *232*
  9.9: *66*
  12.3-8: *296, 305*
  12.6: *294, 304, 308*
  12.6-8: *296, 525*
  12.8: *527, 532*
  13.1-7: *566*
  14: *275*
  15: *275*
  15.27: *270*
  16: *269, 270*
  16.1-2: *532*
  16.3: *262, 265, 531*
  16.3-5: *269*
  16.5: *276, 531*
  16.6: *532*
  16.7: *530*
  16.12-13: *532*
  16.15: *532*

1 Corinthians
  1.29: *250*
  1.31: *250*
  2.10-3:1: *251*
  3.5: *270*
  3.9: *270, 525, 527*
  3.16-17: *524*
  3.21: *250*
  4.6: *250*
  4.7-5.6: *250*
  4.8: *251*
  4.9: *530*
  4.18-19: *250*
  4.19-20: *250*
  5.1: *250*
  5.1-13: *250*
  5.2: *250*
  5.3-5: *526*
  5.4: *250*
  6.9: *250*
  6.12: *251, 257*
  6.12-19: *256*
  6.12-20: *254, 255*
  6.13: *250, 251, 255, 257*
  6.14-15: *255*
  6.15: *257*
  6.15-16: *254, 255*
  6.15-20: *134*
  6.16: *250, 257*
  6.18: *250, 255*
  6.19: *255, 257*
  6.20: *249, 255*
  7.1: *250, 252, 254, 257*
  7.1-2: *252*
  7.1-5: *251*
  7.1-7: *252, 254, 255*
  7.2: *250, 255*
  7.2-5: *240, 241*
  7.3: *244, 256, 257*
  7.3-4: *239, 255*
  7.4: *153, 239-242, 244, 249, 250, 252, 255, 256, 258, 538*
  7.5: *257*
  7.8-40: *255*
  7.10: *226*
  7.10-16: *153*
  7.33, 34: *226*
  8.1: *307, 311*
  8.1-11.1: *308*
  8.10: *251*
  9.5: *189*
  9.5-6: *530*
  10.23: *251*
  10.31-11.1: *309*
  11: *293, 297, 302, 303, 310, 312, 316, 341, 344, 560, 564*
  11-14: *296, 297, 305, 312, 313*
  11.2: *299, 310, 313, 538*
  11:2-16: *240, 296, 297, 303, 307, 308, 310, 311, 312, 316, 567*
  11.2-17: *251*
  11.2-34: *313*
  11.2-14.40: *311, 312, 313*
  11.3: *120, 299, 300, 537*
  11.3-5: *534*
  11.3-16: *533, 534*
  11.4- 5: *120, 299, 314*
  11.4-7: *120*
  11.5: *120, 308, 310, 311, 530*
  11.6: *299*
  11.7: *120*
  11.7-10: *299*
  11.8: *370*
  11.9: *340*
  11.10: *120*
  11.11-12: *300*
  11.13: *120, 309*
  11.13-15: *120*
  11.13-16: *300*
  11.14: *347*
  11.16: *299, 538*
  11.17: *308, 310, 313*
  11.17-34: *311*
  11.18: *251, 313*
  11.19: *344*
  11.20: *313*
  11.22: *313*
  11.33: *313*
  11.34: *313*
  12.1-3: *251*
  12.4-11: *525*
  12.5: *525*
  12.8-11: *296, 304*
  12.12-26: *528*
  12.14-26: *251*
  12.28: *294, 296, 525, 527*
  12.28-30: *296, 525*
  12.28-31: *526*

1 Corinthians (cont.)
  12.29: *530*
  13.1: *554*
  13.1-2: *296*
  14: *297, 303, 307, 308, 312, 316, 530, 554, 560, 564*
  14.1-25: *297*
  14.3: *106, 305*
  14.3-4: *296*
  14.4-5: *531*
  14.7-8: *554*
  14.19: *305*
  14.23: *313*
  14.24-25: *305*
  14.26: *313, 555*
  14.26-40: *297, 378*
  14.28: *303, 535*
  14.29: *302*
  14.29-32: *534*
  14.30: *303, 535*
  14.32: *305*
  14.33: *543*
  14.33-34: *556, 557*
  14.33-35: *307, 538*
  14.33-36: *297, 314, 533, 534*
  14.34: *534*
  14.34-35: *122, 240, 303, 316, 534, 567*
  14.35: *276, 534, 535*
  14.37: *535*
  14.40: *525*
  15: *219, 297*
  15.5: *216*
  15.12: *251*
  15.24: *523*
  16.3: *271*
  16.15: *264, 524*
  16.15-16: *527*
  16.19: *267, 276, 531*
  16.20: *270*

2 Corinthians
  4.1: *524*
  8.3: *270*
  8.4: *524*
  8.23: *531*
  11.2: *173*
  11.5: *530*
  11.13: *530*
  11.8: *524*
  13.10: *526*

Galatians
  2.14: *232*
  3.28: *370, 372, 378, 395, 566*
  4.21-31: *66*

Ephesians
  1.20-22: *523*
  2.20: *296, 301*
  2.21-22: *524*
  3.2-6: *296, 302*
  3.7: *527*
  4.7-12: *304*
  4.11: *294, 525, 530*
  4.11-12: *525*
  4.11-13: *296*
  4.11-16: *296, 305*
  4.12: *524, 525*
  4.16: *525*
  4.17-19: *248*
  5: *145*
  5.19: *551*
  5.21-23: *537*
  5.21-24: *538*
  5.21-33: *153, 538*
  5.23-33: *144*
  5.31: *538*

Philippians
  2.25: *270, 531*
  4.3: *265, 270, 531*

Colossians
  1.23: *527*
  1.25: *527*
  3.16: *553*
  3.18: *537, 538*
  4.1: *270*
  4.11: *531*
  4.15: *531, 532*

1 Thessalonians
  1.9: *254*
  2.7: *530*
  3.2: *270, 527*
  4: *250*
  4.3: *254*

1 Thessalonians (cont.)
  4.3-4: *252*
  4.3-8: *252*
  4.5: *253*
  4.10-11: *526*
  4.11: *535*
  5.11-12: *526*
  5.12: *527, 532*
  5.19: *304*
  5.19-22: *295*
  5.20: *302, 308*

2 Thessalonians
  2.2: *296*
  3.4: *526*
  3.6: *526*
  3.9-10: *526*
  3.12: *526, 535*

1 Timothy
  2: *566*
  2.2: *535*
  2.8-14: *560*
  2.8-15: *122, 240, 346*
  2.9-15: *378, 534, 535*
  2.11-15: *535, 539, 567*
  2.12: *276, 370, 534, 543, 557*
  2.13: *539*
  2.14: *370*
  2.14-15: *539*
  2.15: *347*
  3.1-7: *527, 537*
  3.8: *533*
  3.8-9: *533*
  3.10: *329*
  3.11: *533*
  3.12: *533*
  4.6: *527*
  4.14: *296, 527, 528*
  5.9-10: *533*
  5.17: *527*
  5.17-19: *527*
  6.15: *106*

2 Timothy
  1.5: *116*
  1.6: *528*
  3.14, 15: *116*
  3.16: *344*

  4.19: *262, 271, 272*

Titus
  1.5: *527*
  1.7-9: *527*
  2.3-5: *532*

Philemon
  1: *270, 531*
  2: *531*
  24: *270, 531*

Hebrews
  1.5: *320*
  2.17: *328*
  3.10: *320*
  3.12: *324*
  3.19: *324*
  4.2: *324*
  4.3: *328*
  4.11: *324*
  6.13-15: *326, 329*
  6.15-17: *324*
  9.26: *328*
  10.23: *329*
  10.36-39: *324*
  10.39: *324*
  11: *325, 327*
  11.1: *324*
  11.2: *324*
  11.4: *325, 326*
  11.4-7: *325*
  11.5: *326*
  11.6: *325*
  11.7: *326*
  11.8: *326*
  11.8-9: *326*
  11.9: *329*
  11.10: *326*
  11.8-12: *320, 329*
  11.8-22: *325*
  11.10: *326*
  11.11: *66, 318, 320, 324-328*
  11.12: *329*
  11.13-16: *325*
  11.14: *326*
  11.16: *326*
  11.20: *325, 326*
  11.21: *325*

Hebrews (cont.)
  11.22: *326*
  11.23: *329*
  11.23-29: *325*
  11.26: *326, 328, 329*
  11.27: *326*
  11.30-31: *325*
  11.32-38: *325*
  11.33: *325*
  11.38-39: *325*
  11.39: *324*
  12: *324*

1 Peter
  2.5-6: *524*
  2.18-21: *566*
  3.6: *66, 320*
  4.3-4: *248*

2 Peter
  1.20-21: *295*
  2.1: *296*

1 John
  4.1: *296*

Revelation
  1.1-3: *304*
  2.19: *524*
  2.20: *120, 530*
  7.10: *106*
  18.13: *249*
  21.9: *176*

Classical Sources

Aelianus
  De natura animalium
    3.42.8: *228, 229*

Amphilochius
  Contra haereticos
    939: *228*

Antipater
  On Marriage
    15: *246*

Apuleius
  Metamorphoses
    8.28: *283*

Aristophanes
  Plutus
    5: *249*

Aristotle
  On the Generation of Animals
    1.20: *404*

  Politics
    1.2.1-22: *378*
    1.13 (1260a): *404*
    1254b: *242*
    1259a,b: *242*

  The Art of Rhetoric
    1419b-1420a: *252*

Cicero
  To His Family
    14.4: *245*

Dio Cassius
  Roman History
    55.31.2-3: *282*

Dio Chrysostom
  Or.
    12.47: *283*

Diodorus Siculus
  Bibliotheca Historica
    32.10.4: *229, 230*
    32.10.6: *230*

Epictetus
  Diss.
    1.13.3: *319*

Euripides
Bacchae
211: *279*

Eustathius
Commentarii ad Homeri Odysseam
1.260: *230, 233*

Galen
Oeuvres
2.99: *409*

Herodotus
6.66: *280*
7.111, 141: *280*

Hesiod
Works and Days
9: *404*

Hierokles
On Duties
4.28.21: *246*

Stobaeus
4.505.12-20: *246*

Homer
Iliad
3.125: *228*
Odyssey
6.182-85: *245*

Iamblichus
De mysteriis
3.11: *283*

Livy
Annals
38.18.9: *283*
39.13.12: *283*

Lucian
Hermotimus
6: *283*

Vitarum Auctio
8: *283*

Lucian of Samosata
Alexander
35: *282*

Musonius Rufus
F 12: *247*
F 14: *246*

Ovid
Art of Love
1.683-87: *247*
2.727-28: *247*

Pausanius
2.24.1: *283*
3.4.4: *283*
12: *281*
12.11: *280*

Philostratus
Vita Apollonii
3.42: *283*
4.18, 24: *283*

Photius
Bibliotheca
Codex 244, 377: *229*

Pindar
Fragmenta
150: *279*

Plato
Gorgias
518A: *524*
Leges
9.871c: *279*

Phaedra
244b: *280*

Respublica
10.619c: *279*

Timaeus
7.246: *405*
7.251: *405*
71e-72b: *280*

Plato (cont.)
Timaeus (cont.)
91a: *405*
91c: *405*

Pliny
Epistle
7: *245*

Plutarch
Advice to Bride and Groom
2.140B: *247*
2.142E: *245*

Caius Marius
17.1-3: *284*

De defectu oraculorum: *280*
414b: *282*
414e: *282*
437-438: *284*

De Pythiae oraculis: *280*
287-99: *281*
397c: *283*

Pyrrhus
31: 283

Solon
20.3.1: *244*
20.4: *245*

Polybius
10.26.3: *228*
21.37.5-7: *283*

Posidonius
Fragmenta
85.48: *229*

Pseudo-Aristotle
Rhetoric to Alexander
1.21.3-10: *252*
1430b: *252*

Sextus Empiricus
Adv. Mathematicos
1.53: *283*

Strabo
Geography
7.7.12: *284*
9.2.4: *283*

Suetonius
Lives of the Caesars
5.25: *263*
Cicero 5: *281*
Nero 40: *281*
Titus 5: *281*

Tacitus
Annals
2.54: *281*
3.34: *409*

Historiarum
2.78: *281*

Thucydides
5.16: *280*

Jewish Sources

Ahikar
2.19: *166*

Aristeas, Epistle to
152: *253*

Babylonian Talmud
Ketubot
20a: *248*
47b: *244*
48a: *244*

Indexes

Megillah
  14a: *43, 293*

Menachoth
  43b: *171*

Niddah
  31a: *319*

Sanhedrin
  11a-b: *288*
  20a: *170*
  69b: *43*

Tannith
  76b: *170*

Yoma
  9b: *288*

2 Baruch
  85.3: *287*

Ben Sirach
  1.6-20: *179*
  3.4: *165*
  3.11: *165*
  7.19: *158*
  9.9: *228, 229*
  25.16-26.18: *158*
  25.18: *164*
  26.13-18: *166*
  26.17, 18: *166*
  26.23: *167*
  30.15: *158*
  33.19: *159*
  36.24: *158*
  38.24: *164*
  41.21: *229*
  41.23: *228*
  42.6: *159*
  47.18: *250*
  48.1-14: *292*
  51.13-30: *155*

Dead Sea Scrolls
  Genesis Apocryphon: *64, 66*

1QH
  1.10-11: *300*

1QpHab: 290
  2.2-3: *290*
  7.4-7: *290*

1QM
  7.4-6: *300*

1QS
  9.10-12: *292*

1QSa
  2.3-11: *300*

4QTest.
  1-20: *292*

1 Enoch
  60.12: *300*
  60.16-21: *300*
  61.10: *300*
  72.1: *300*
  90.31: *292*
  99.5: *191*
  100.1, 2. *191*

Exodus Rabbah
  1.15: *171*

Ibn Ezra *43*

4 Ezra
  6.26: *292*

Jerusalem Talmud
  Megillah
    14a: *43*

  Rosh Hashanah
    3.5: *170*

  Sanhedrin
    2.6: *170*
    69b: *43*

  Taanith
    4.7: *170*

Josephus
  Antiquities
    1.118: *281*
    1.162: *65, 66*
    6.329: *282*
    13.282-83: *289*
    13.299: *289*
    15.373: *289*
    18:85: *290*
    18.85-87: *292*
    20.97-98: *290, 292*
    20.169-71: *292*

  War
    2.259: *292*
    2.261: *290*
    2.113: *289*

Jubilees
  2.2-3: *300*
  23.16: *191*
  23.19: *191*

Judith
  8.11-36: *293*
  9.1-14: *293*
  16.1-17: *293*

1 Maccabees
  4.46: *287, 289*
  14.41: *287*

Mishna
  Aboth
    4.10: *164*

  Ketubot
    5.6-7: *244*

  Sota
    9: *191*
    15: *191*

  Taanit
    4.8: *170*

Philo
  De Abrahamo
    111: *328*
    112: *323*

De Cherubim
  3: *323*
  7: *323*
  9: *324*
  49: *319*

De Congressu Eruditionis gratia
  22: *324*

De Ebrietate
  211: *319*

De Mutatione Nominum
  166: *322*

De Opficio Mundi
  132: *319*

De Specialibus Legibus
  1.65: *289*
  3.113: *409*
  4.192: *289*

De Vita Mosis
  2.188: *289*
  2.246-92: *289*

Legatio ad Gaium
  36: *262*

Legum Allegoria
  2.82: *323, 324*
  3.218: *323*

Quaestiones et Solutiones in Genesin
  1.26: *170*
  3.55: *323*
  3.243-44: *323*
  4.15: *407*

Quis Rerum Divinarum Heres
  249-252: *289*
  259: *288*
  265-66: *289*

Quod Deterius Potior insidiari soleat
  123: *323*

Indexes

Qoheleth Rabbah
  3.14.1: *171*

Rashi *43*

Syballine Oracles
  3.591-99: *253*

Symmachus *163*

Testament of the XII Patriarchs
  Benjamin
    9.2: *287*

Theodotion *163, 165*

Wisdom of Solomon
  7.12-22: *179*

Christian Sources

Aquinas, Thomas
  Summa Theologiae
    1.680-85: *417*

Ambrose
  De Joseph Patriarcha
    76: *177*

  De Tobia
    77: *177*

  Expositio Evangelii secundem Lucam
    8.10: *172*

  On the Christian Faith
    2.Intro: *172*

Apostolic Constitutions
  1.8: *172*

Augustine
  Second Discourse on Ps. 26
    21: *173*

  Sermo 37 de proverbiis
    31: *173*

Basil
  Sermones ascetici *172*

  The Long Rules
    Q.37: *172*

  The Short Rules
    110: *367*

Cassian, J.
  Conference
    14.8: *173*

  Institutes
    10.21: *173*

Chrysostom, John
  Homilies on 1 Corinthians
    37.1: *371*

  Homilies on Timothy
    9: *413*
    9.1: *371*

Clement of Alexandria
  Exhortation to the Greeks
    2: *281*

  Paedagogus
    3.10: *171*
    3.11: *171*

  Stromata
    1.107.6: *281*

Clement of Rome
  1 Clement
    55.3: *169*

Damian, Peter
  Women who seduced clerics: *384*

Didascalia Apostolorum: *172*

Epiphanius
Panarion
    4.1-2: *371*
    49.1-3: *370*
    79.1.6: *371*
    79.4.1: *365*

Gratian
The Decretum: *418*

Gregory of Nazianzus
Oration
    8.9: *171*
    18.7: *171*

Hilary
Tractatus in CXXVII Psalmum
    9: *176*

Ignatius of Antioch
Magnesians
    6: *358*

Trallians
    3: *358*

Jerome
Ep. ad Avitum
    8: *282*

Letter
    69.5: *172*
    108: *361*

Justin Martyr
First Apology
    1.20: *281*

Knox, John
The First Blast of the Trumpet Against the Monstrous Regiment of Women: *424*

Lactantius
Divine Institutes
    1.6: *281*

De opficio Dei
    12: *319*

Luther, Martin
Briefwechsel: *423*
First Lectures on the Psalms
    1.32: *174*
    69.1: *173*

Lectures on Genesis
    47.7: *174*

Lectures on Galatians
    3.22: *175*

Lectures on Joel
    2.22: *174*

Lectures on Nahum
    1.9: *174*

Lectures on the Psalms
    9.13: *174*

Lectures on Romans
    3.22-24: *175*

Lectures on Titus
    2.5: *174*

Letter to Hans Luther *174*

Notes on Ecclesiastes
    4.6: *174*

Origen
De principiis
    3.4-5: *282*

Expositio in Proverbia *172*

Paulinus of Nola
Letter
    13.5: *172*
    44.4: *172*

Tertullian
Against Hermogenes
    22.5: *337, 340*
    37: *337*
    38: *337*

Indexes   615

Tertullian (cont.)
  Against Marcion
    5.8: *342, 344*
    8: *341*

Tertullian
  Against Valintianos
    32: *349*
    32.5: *341*

  Apology
    1.7: *345*
    6: *347*
    20: *336*
    21: *352*

  On the Apparel of Women
    1: *345, 346*
    1.1: *333, 411*
    1.1.1-2: *332*
    1.2: *341*
    1.2-3: *344*
    1.3: *344*
    1.7: *348*
    2.1: *356*
    2.4: *345*
    2.5: *348*
    2.8: *346*
    2.9: *345*
    2.11: *348*
    2.13: *353*

  On Exhortation to Chastity
    9: *352*

  To the Martyrs
    4: *353*

  On Prayer
    22: *336, 340, 347*

  On the Prescription Against Heretics
    37.3: *336*
    38: *337*
    41: *343*

  On the Veiling of Virgins
    7: *341*
    9: *342*
    16.1-2: *338*
    17: *339*

  To His Wife
    1.4: *350*
    2.8.7-9: *351*

Modern Authors

Achelis, H.: *366*
Aitken, K.: *178*
Albright, W.: *81, 82, 100*
Aletti, J.: *179*
Allen, C.: *93*
Allen, C. L.: *452*
Allen, G.: *439. 440*
Alexander, P. M.: *446*
Allison, R. W.: *314*
Allo, E.-B.: *311, 313*
Amaru, B.: *65, 66*
Amit, Y.: *77, 79*

Andersen, F.: *128-131, 134,-138, 140, 141, 149*
Anderson, B.: *3, 11*
Anderson, B. S.: *402, 404, 412, 413, 419, 423, 427*
Anonymous: *402, 433, 434, 437, 453, 461*
Aquino, F.: *563*
Aschliman, S.: *47*
Ashton, J.: *198-99*
Atkinson, N. E.: *505*
Attridge, H.: *320*

Aune, D.: *101, 278, 281, 284-290, 294, 295, 299, 301, 302, 305*
Austel, J.: *160*
Babcock, C. C.: *475, 485*
Babcock, E. R.: *453, 485*
Bachmann, P.: *307, 308*
Bacht, H.: *279*
Bailey, F. A.: *454, 466, 468-470, 476, 486, 564*
Balch, D.: *67*
Balmer, R.: *448*
Balz-Cochois, H.: *126*
Banner, L.: *437*
Bar-Efrat, S.: *71*
Bar-Ilan, M.: *92*
Barnes, J. M.: *467*
Barnett, P. W.: *292, 535*
Barr, J.: *227*
Barrett, C. K.: *205, 280, 314*
Barstow, A. L.: *384, 388, 397, 398*
Barucq, A.: *180*
Batto, B.: *10*
Bauer, W.: *318-20, 327*
Beare, F.: *192*
Beasley-Murray, G.: *214*
Becker, J.: *289*
Bederman, G.: *464, 465*
Beeby, H.: *134, 136, 141, 149*
Beggs, C.: *113*
Bendroth, M. L.: *463, 477, 479*
Benton, J.: *386*
Berger, P.: *90*
Berquist, J.: *49, 60*
Bertram, G.: *270*
Best, E.: *188, 305*
Betz, O.: *192*
Biale, D.: *248, 253*
Billerbeck, P.: *288*
Bilezikian, G.: *181*
Bird, P.: *12, 117, 130, 131, 133, 135, 149*
Black, A.: *119, 195, 565*
Black, H. M.: *508*
Black, M.: *291, 321*
Black, M. C.: *121, 191, 299, 314, 563*
Blackburn, B.: *563*
Blackman, E.: *195*
Blakeslee, S.: *90*

Blass, F.: *303, 320*
Blenkinsopp, J.: *110, 285*
Bloch, R. H.: *385*
Block, R. H.: *446*
Bodin, J.: *426*
Boers, H.: *209*
Boice, J.: *135, 136*
Boling, R.: *70, 73, 74, 81*
Bonsirven, J.: *291*
Boring, M. E.: *279, 280, 284, 285, 301, 302, 304*
Bostick, A.: *466, 509*
Boswell, J.: *389*
Bosworth, J. M.: *507*
Bowman, A.: *535, 539*
Bovon, F.: *220*
Boyd, J.: *38, 40*
Bozeman, T. D.: *545*
Bradshaw, P. F.: *364*
Branca, P.: *431*
Brandon, S.: *192*
Bratsiotis, N.: *157*
Braun, H.: *320*
Bray, G.: *349*
Brenner, A.: *78, 98*
Brewer, G. C.: *550, 552, 555*
Briney, J. B.: *471, 507, 508*
Bristow, J. T.: *277*
Brodrueil, P.: *10*
Brook, G.: *207*
Brooke, C. N. L.: *384*
Brooten, B.: *96, 240*
Brown, C.: *96*
Brown, J. H.: *467, 488, 504*
Brown, P.: *247*
Brown, R.: *199, 201, 214, 216*
Brown, S.: *133, 136, 140*
Bruce, F. F.: *314, 315*
Brueggemann, W. *6, 9, 13, 16, 22, 285*
Brundage, J. A.: *379, 389*
Bruner, F. M.: *466, 467*
Buechner, F.: *317*
Bullough, V.: *332, 333, 350, 377, 378, 405, 414, 416, 417, 424, 427*
Bultmann, R.: *192, 256*
Burgess, O. A.: *503*
Burrows, M.: *290*

Burrows, M.: *431, 432*
Burney, C.: *70, 74, 78, 84*
Burns, R.: *115*
Bury, R. G.: *405*
Busenitz, I.: *29, 32*
Bushnell, H.: *460*
Byrne, B.: *241*
Cadbury, H. J.: *300, 319*
Callan, T.: *282, 289*
Calvin, J.: *69*
Camp, C.: *94, 97, 156, 179, 180*
Campbell, A.: *546, 548, 549, 562*
Campbell, Mrs. A.: *500, 510*
Campbell, C.: *377*
Campbell, D.: *85*
Campbell, T.: *549*
Cantarella, E.: *241*
Cantor, N. F.: *379, 382, 391-393, 396*
Caragounis, C. C.: *292*
Carlberg, R.: *90*
Carmichael, C.: *213*
Carmody, D.: *69*
Carnelley, E.: *334, 352, 354, 355*
Carney, M. B.: *502*
Carson, D. A.: *214*
Carter, S.: *90*
Casey, M.: *292, 547*
Cassuto, U.: *38, 39, 48*
Cauble, W.: *495*
Charles, R. H.: *253*
Charlesworth, J. H.: *292*
Chase, D.: *88*
Chesnutt, R.: *99, 232, 241, 293*
Childers, J.: *262, 565*
Childs, B.: *70, 93*
Chouinard, L.: *563*
Christian, P. L.: *476, 502-504, 506, 515*
Church, F. F.: *332, 349, 351, 353*
Clark, E.: *361, 362, 402, 405, 418*
Clark, G.: *410*
Clark, R.: *90*
Clark, S.: *18*
Clark, W.: *27*
Clarke, A.: *175*
Clay, M. K. C.: *499*
Cleaver, B. H.: *485*
Clements, R.: *286*

Clifford, R.: *2*
Clines, D.: *7*
Cloke, G.: *364*
Coats, G.: *3, 24, 28*
Coffman, J.: *135*
Cogan, F. B.: *447*
Coggins, R.: *212*
Cole, M. E.: *499*
Coletti, T.: *173*
Collier, G.: *549, 556*
Collins, J. J.: *291*
Collins, J. N.: *524*
Collins, R.: *201*
Coneybeare, W.: *274*
Conner, J. G.: *510*
Conroy, C.: *114*
Conzelmann, H.: *120, 251, 300*
Cosby, M. R.: *325*
Cothenet, E.: *294, 295*
Coulton, G. G.: *419*
Countryman, L. W.: *337*
Coyle, J. K.: *372*
Craig, D.: *180*
Cranfield, C. E. B.: *233, 235, 269, 524*
Craven, T.: *99*
Creed, J.: *186*
Crenshaw, J.: *91*
Crone, T.: *283*
Crook, M.: *177*
Culler, J.: *376*
Culpepper, R.: *205, 210, 211, 222*
Cundall, A.: *74*
Dahl, N. A.: *537, 538*
Dahood, M.: *160, 161, 163, 164*
Damrosch, D.: *94*
Danker, F.: *186, 190*
Darr, K.: *41, 98*
Dautzenberg, G.: *285, 294*
Davidson, R.: *15, 19, 32*
Dayton, D. W.: *450, 451*
Dearman, J.: *93*
DeBerg, B. A.: *459, 461-64, 479*
de Boer, M.: *207*
DeBoer, W.: *423*
Debrunner, A.: *303, 320*
Deissmann, A.: *269*
de Jonge, M.: *211*
Delamont, S.: *436, 438, 439*

Delcor, M.: *99*
Delitzsch, F.: *160, 166*
Delobel, J.: *314*
Dering, E.: *545*
de Salignac de la Mothe-Fenelon, F.: *427*
de Saussure, F.: *226, 227*
de Vaux, R.: *164, 286*
DeVries, S.: *38, 111, 547*
Dibelius, M.: *188, 195*
Dix, G.: *411*
Dixon, S.: *243, 245*
Dodd, C. H.: *205, 234, 237, 530*
Dodds, E. R.: *282*
Donfried, K.: *201, 204, 275*
Douglas, A.: *449*
Douglas-Wood, A.: *437*
Dover, K.: *247*
Doyle, J. A.: *455*
Driver, G.: *160, 162*
Dromke, P.: *381*
Duffin, L.: *436, 438, 439*
Dungan, D. R.: *549*
Dunn, J.: *232, 233*
Edwards, E.: *548*
Edwards, J.: *234*
Edwards, O. C.: *411*
Eising, H.: *157*
Eissfeldt, O.: *77, 78*
Ellis, E. E.: *190, 268, 290, 294, 301, 308, 526, 533-535*
Ellis, I.: *182, 191*
Ellison, H.: *136, 140, 151*
Emerton, E.: *383*
Emmerson, G.: *178*
Englesman, J.: *401*
Engnell, I.: *112*
Errett, I.: *490, 496*
Esler, P.: *186*
Evans, C.: *189, 190, 194*
Exum, J.: *47, 59, 84, 116*
Fanning, T.: *451*
Farmer, J.: *179*
Farmer, W.: *185*
Farnell, L.: *102*
Fascher, E.: *279*
Fee, G. D.: *240, 251, 258, 307, 314, 536*
Feissel, D.: *366*

Feldman, D.: *244, 248*
Fensham, F.: *131, 135, 136, 140, 144*
Ferguson, E.: *372, 550, 553, 555, 563*
Fewell, D.: *69, 72, 79, 80, 83, 84, 116, 148, 151*
Filson, F.: *267*
Finney, P. C.: *372*
Fiorenza, E.: *181, 195, 217, 220, 240, 265, 268, 270, 273, 274, 277, 332, 333, 411, 520, 521, 536*
Firestone, R.: *42*
Fisher, E.: *132*
Fitzmyer, J.: *119, 186, 191, 230-232, 235, 314*
Flaciere, R.: *279*
Flatt, B.: *90*
Fletcher, R.: *435*
Flora, J. R.: *478*
Flory, M.: *273*
Foh, S.: *18, 30-32, 69, 277*
Forbes, C.: *280*
Forseth, P.: *134, 136*
Fossum, J.: *213*
Fox, E.: *61*
Frankfort, H.: *44*
Franklin, E.: *190*
Fraser, A.: *425*
Freedman, D.: *78, 81, 128-131, 134-138, 140, 141, 149*
Freedman, R.: *20*
Frerichs, E.: *292*
Friedländer, L.: *281*
Friedman, M.: *140*
Friedrich, G.: *294, 304*
Fritsch, C.: *168*
Frymer-Kensky, T.: *40, 101*
Furnish, V. P.: *270*
Gale, H. M.: *235-237*
Gamble, H.: *269*
Gardner, J.: *243*
Garrett, D.: *100, 156, 177, 179*
Garrison, J. H.: *487, 513, 517*
Gaster, T.: *55, 64, 65*
Geer, T.: *122, 125, 563*
Gemser, B.: *158-160*
Gerleman, G.: *169*

Giblin, C.: *215*
Gill, D. W. J.: *314*
Gillespie, T.: *304*
Gleason, A. H.: *464*
Globe, A.: *84*
Goehring, J.: *195*
Goodwin, M.: *496, 498, 501, 502*
Gordis, R.: *133-135, 138-142, 147, 151*
Gordon, E.: *158*
Gossai, H.: *550*
Goudge, H. L.: *311, 313*
Goulder, M.: *211*
Gravdal, K.: *386*
Gray, J.: *84*
Greene, J. T.: *285*
Greenspahn, F. E.: *288*
Greeven, H.: *304, 305*
Grégoire, H.: *366*
Groh, D. E.: *344*
Groothius, R.: *89*
Grosheide, F. W.: *294, 302, 312, 313*
Gruber, M.: *92*
Grudem, W.: *67, 181, 277, 294, 304*
Grundmann, W.: *193*
Gryson, R.: *357-359, 362, 363, 365, 367, 371*
Guilder, G.: *89, 90*
Gundry, P.: *180*
Gundry, R.: *256, 297, 312*
Gunn, D.: *79, 80, 83, 116*
Hadas, M.: *253*
Hadwin, M.: *548*
Haenchen, E.: *263, 264, 266*
Hailey, J.: *563, 567*
Halpern, B.: *94*
Hals, R.: *98*
Hamp, V.: *177*
Handy, L.: *111*
Hanselman, S.: *80*
Hanson, J.: *291, 292*
Hardesty, N.: *181, 277*
Harrell, D. E.: *394*
Harrison, I. W.: *495*
Harrison, R.: *112*
Harrisville, R. A.: *524*
Hartman, M.: *437*

Harvey, A.: *187*
Harvey, D.: *78*
Hasell, G.: *5*
Haskins, S.: *218*
Hassey, J.: *451, 477*
Hayden, M. P.: *472, 473, 508*
Hays, R.: *254*
Hayter, M.: *89*
Headlam, A.: *235, 272*
Hegermann, H.: *320*
Heine, R.: *370*
Heine, S.: *181, 182, 186, 188, 195, 331, 334*
Heinrici, C. F. G.: *311*
Helton, S.: *563*
Hengel, M.: *100, 188, 288, 289*
Héring, J.: *313, 315*
Herlihy, D.: *377, 380*
Hermisson, H.: *93*
Herndon, E. W.: *468, 469*
Heschel, A.: *110*
Hess, R.: *25, 31*
Higgins, J.: *26*
Hill, D.: *278, 302, 305*
Himmelfarb, G.: *360*
Hock, R.: *264*
Hoftijzer, J.: *96*
Hollis, P.: *431, 437*
Holton, T. T.: *473*
Hooker, M.: *188, 300, 314*
Horbury, W.: *199*
Horowitz, M. C.: *410, 413*
Horsley, R.: *291, 292*
Horst, F.: *113*
Hort, F. J. A.: *271, 272*
Hoskyns, E.: *213*
House, H. W.: *277*
Howell, M.: *388*
Howson, J.: *274*
Hubbard, D.: *134, 140, 141, 144, 149, 151*
Huehnergard, J.: *147*
Huffman, E. M.: *487*
Hugenberger, G.: *140, 149*
Hughes, R.: *93, 466*
Hull, R. F.: *565*
Humble, B. J.: *489, 490*
Hunter, A.: *205*
Hunter, J.: *89*

Hurd, J. C.: *314*
Hurley, J.: *181, 314, 533*
Hylander, I.: *117*
Isaksson, A.: *312*
Israel, J.: *506*
Iriarte, M.: *114*
Irvin, D.: *368*
Jacobs, E.: *176*
Jacobsen, T.: *39*
Jansen, H.: *100*
Jansen, J. F.: *336*
Janzen, J.: *115*
Jeffers, J.: *263, 267, 272*
Jepsen, A.: *113, 117, 286*
Jewett, P.: *90*
Jewett, R.: *259*
Jodock, D.: *95*
John Paul II: *372*
Johnson, B. W.: *559, 560*
Johnson, L. T.: *189, 190, 192, 194, 311*
Johnson, P. D.: *387*
Joines, K.: *23*
Jones, A. B.: *504*
Jones, D. A.: *466, 476*
Jones, S.: *89*
Joüon, P.: *158*
Juss, O.: *337*
Kähler, E.: *259*
Kalsbach, A.: *364*
Karris, R. J.: *315*
Käsemann, E.: *235, 519, 526*
Kastcher, P. W.: *414*
Kaufmann, Y.: *128*
Kellogg, S.: *446, 448*
Kendall, D.: *219, 220*
Kersten, K.: *91*
Kidner, D.: *167*
Kingsbury, J.: *188*
Klauck, H.-J.: *263, 264, 268, 272, 274*
Klein, L.: *70, 71, 75, 76, 84*
Klostermann, E.: *184*
Knight, G.: *277*
Koester, C.: *212, 213*
Koester, H.: *91*
Köhler, L.: *165*
Kraditor, A. S.: *468*
Kramer, H.: *426*

Krämer, H.: *279*
Kraemer, R.: *188, 197*
Kruger, P.: *140, 147*
Kuemmerlin-McLean, J.: *97*
Kümmel, W. G.: *253*
Kurfees, M. C.: *550, 552*
Kuss, O.: *328*
Kysar, R.: *199, 208*
LaCocque, A.: *96, 99*
Laffey, A.: *145*
Lagrange, M.: *193*
Laing, D.: *424*
Lamar, J. S.: *551*
Lampe, G. W. H.: *365, 366*
Lane, W.: *321*
Lantzer, M. E.: *452, 453, 471-473*
Larsen, A.: *175*
Lauchert, F.: *365*
Lavender, E.: *563*
Lawson, A.: *90*
Lawton, R.: *22*
Lea, H. C.: *398*
Leaney, A.: *189*
Leclercq, H.: *364*
Leith, M.: *92, 132*
Leon-Dufour, X.: *205*
Levin, C.: *114*
Lewis, C. S.: *386*
Lewis, J.: *448*
Lewis, J. P.: *29, 289, 563*
Lewis, N.: *409*
Lichtenstein, M.: *155*
Lichtheim, M.: *158*
Liefeld, W.: *239*
Liesegang, H.: *280*
Lietzmann, H.: *314*
Lightfoot, J. B.: *311*
Lightfoot, N.: *201, 560*
Limburg, J.: *135, 139*
Lindars, B.: *292*
Lindblom, J.: *91, 285-287, 308*
Lindsey, H.: *295*
Lipscomb, D.: *476, 488, 511-515, 543, 544*
Little, J.: *234-236*
Livingstone, E.: *202*
Llewelyn, S. R.: *243*
Lloyd-Jones, D.: *225*
Loader, J.: *98*

Lohfink, N.: *114*
Lollis, L.: *494, 497, 498*
Lührmann, D.: *311*
Lutz, C.: *246, 247*
Lyons, E.: *177*
Maccini, R.: *213*
MacDonald, J.: *211*
Maher, M.: *322*
Malbim, M.: *176*
Malherbe, A.: *246, 268, 526*
Malina, B.: *187, 194*
Manson, W.: *189*
Marcus, R.: *407*
Marcus, S.: *446*
Marrs, R.: *2, 548, 563, 564*
Marsden, G. M.: *443*
Marshall, I.: *182, 188, 192, 193*
Martines, L.: *404, 405, 426*
Martyn, J. L.: *199*
Matera, F.: *188*
Maurice, F.: *182*
Mayes, A.: *81, 113*
Mays, J.: *131, 134, 135, 137, 141*
McCance, D.: *39*
McCarter, K.: *92*
McClintock, J.: *547*
McCreesh, T.: *179*
McGarvey, J. W.: *266, 315, 500*
McHugh, J.: *201, 207*
McKane, W.: *164, 178*
McKeating, H.: *131, 134, 141*
McKenzie, J.: *110*
McKnight, E.: *94*
McLaughlin, M.: *383, 411*
McLees, N.: *159, 178*
McLemore, B.: *563*
McNamara, J. A.: *381*
McNamara, M.: *322*
McNicol, A.: *566*
Meeks, W.: *231, 239, 532*
Meng, J. A.: *502*
Metlitzski, D.: *179*
Metzger, B.: *184, 201, 262, 264, 318*
Meier, J. P.: *314*
Meyer, R.: *288, 292*
Meyers, C.: *95*
Michel, O.: *193, 288, 320*
Millard, A.: *10*

Miller, J.: *90, 176*
Milligan, R.: *547*
Minear, P.: *219, 220*
Mintz, S.: *446, 448*
Mitchell, M.: *255, 312, 313*
Moffatt, J.: *312, 315*
Mollat, M.: *389*
Mollenkott, V.: *181*
Moloney, F.: *202, 204*
Moo, D.: *536*
Monceaux, P.: *331, 332*
Moody, D. L.: *461*
Moore, C. H.: *409*
Moore, D. W.: *503*
Moore, G.: *70, 71, 74, 78, 81*
Moore, M.: *87, 90, 91, 95-99, 563*
Moore, R. I.: *388, 389*
Moore, S.: *207*
Morris, C.: *382*
Morris, J.: *368*
Morris, L.: *74, 189, 315, 316*
Morris, M.: *90*
Morrison, K. F.: *382*
Mount, F.: *182*
Mowinckel, S.: *286*
Moxnes, H.: *317, 323*
Muir, L. R.: *386*
Munnell, T.: *491-493*
Murphy, R.: *108*
Murphy-O'Connor, J.: *311, 314*
Myles, E. B.: *506*
Neil, W.: *563*
Neill, S.: *192*
Neller, K.: *299, 563, 568*
Neuer, W.: *181*
Neusner, J.: *232*
Neyrey, J.: *194*
Niccum, C.: *262, 563*
Nichol, C. R.: *558*
Niditch, S.: *3*
Nilsson, M.: *280*
Noble, D. F.: *398*
Norris, F. W.: *374, 563*
North, J. B.: *466*
Noth, M.: *70*
Oberman, H. A.: *423*
Obersteiner, J.: *172*
O'Collins, G.: *219, 220*
O'Conner, K.: *93*

O'Day, G.: *208*
O'Donnell, M.: *90*
Oesterley, W.: *161, 168, 177*
O'Faolain, J.: *404, 405, 426*
Ogg, J. L.: *506*
Okure, T.: *207*
Olbricht, T.: *546, 548, 568*
Ollrog, W.-H.: *264, 267, 272, 275*
Olsson, B.: *207*
Olyan, S.: *147*
O'Neill, J. C.: *235*
Opperwall, N. J.: *293*
Orr, W. F.: *121, 316*
Osburn, C.: *90, 122, 299, 303, 556, 562-566*
Oster, R.: *251, 306, 314*
Oswalt, J.: *117*
Otwell, J.: *156*
Padgett, A.: *258, 314, 315*
Pagels, E.: *378*
Painter, J.: *205*
Palmer, P.: *451*
Paludi, M. A.: *455*
Pamment, M.: *208*
Pantel, P. S.: *241*
Pardes, I.: *92*
Parke, H. W.: *279*
Patterson, L.: *386*
Pauls, D.: *563*
Payne, O. E.: *550, 553*
Pazdan, M.: *211*
Pearre, C. N.: *494, 495, 497, 505*
Pease, A. S.: *281*
Peck, A. L.: *404*
Pedersen, J.: *286*
Pendelton, P. Y.: *315*
Peristiany, J.: *150*
Perkins, P.: *47, 219, 220, 221*
Petersen, D. L.: *74, 285*
Petersen, J.: *268*
Petroff, E. A.: *381*
Phipps, W.: *49 , 50, 60, 94, 112*
Piper, J.: *181*
Plass, E.: *174*
Plaut, W.: *166*
Plummer, A.: *311*
Poe, J. T.: *498, 510*
Pogoloff, S.: *255*
Pollard, J. P.: *563*

Pomeroy, S.: *245, 403, 404, 409*
Priest, J.: *112*
Prusak, B. P.: *407, 412*
Pulley, K.: *564*
Pummer, R.: *213*
Purvis, J.: *212*
Rackham, H.: *404*
Radl, W.: *327*
Rallis, I.: *135, 139, 141, 144, 150, 151*
Rambuaz, C.: *338*
Ramsaran, R.: *255-256*
Ramsay, W.: *261, 269*
Ramsey, G.: *21*
Reagan, D.: *295*
Reeve, J.: *112*
Reiling, J.: *278*
Reinhold, M.: *409*
Renan, E.: *182*
Rendsburg, G: *3*
Reuf, J.: *313, 315*
Reynolds, C.: *117*
Richards, J.: *389*
Richardson, H.: *402, 405, 418*
Riley, G.: *456*
Riskin, S.: *61*
Robarts, C.: *563*
Robeck, C.: *294*
Roberts, J. J. M.: *117, 548*
Robertson, A.: *311*
Robertson, A. T.: *311*
Robinson, I. S.: *382*
Robinson, J.: *91*
Robinson, J. A. T.: *523*
Rogers, K. M.: *349*
Rolfe, J. C.: *263*
Rose, M.: *113*
Rosenberg, R.: *455, 458*
Ross, A.: *156*
Rousseau, J. J.: *429*
Rowley, H.: *109, 131, 134-136, 138, 140-142, 151*
Roxe, C.: *325*
Rudolph, W.: *131*
Ruether, R.: *331, 411, 418, 449, 460*
Rüger, H.: *167*
Ruppert, L.: *129*
Saggs, H.: *39, 51*

Sanday, W.: *235, 272*
Sarna, N.: *9, 10, 14, 21, 25, 31, 34, 35*
Scanzoni, L.: *181, 277*
Schatzmann, S.: *294*
Schlatter, A.: *308*
Schmidt, A. J.: *482*
Schmidt, W.: *7*
Schmithals, W.: *251, 313*
Schmitt, J.: *110*
Schnackenburg, R.: *199, 208, 214*
Schneiders, S.: *205, 209, 212, 214, 216, 220, 221*
Scholer, D.: *270, 271, 372, 567*
Schramm, T.: *186*
Schumacher, R.: *262-266, 268-270, 272*
Schweizer, E.: *256, 519*
Schwyzer, E.: *327*
Scott, R.: *109, 167*
Scroggs, R.: *188, 239, 297, 312*
Segal, E.: *43*
Seim, T.: *208*
Sekine, M.: *113*
Sewell, E. G.: *511, 516*
Shelly, R.: *550, 551*
Shortridge, S. E.: *502*
Showalter, E.: *376*
Sider, R. D.: *336*
Silva, M.: *226, 227*
Slenzka, N.: *89*
Small, D.: *134, 140*
Smalley, S.: *296*
Smith, B.: *101*
Smith, D. M.: *199*
Smith, F. L.: *81, 85, 560*
Smith, G. A.: *135, 136, 141*
Smith, G. T.: *474*
Smith, G. V.: *105*
Smith, J. Z.: *282*
Smith, W.: *150*
Smith-Rosenberg, C.: *446, 479*
Spanneut, M.: *350*
Speiser, E.: *45, 46, 51, 53, 59, 63*
Spencer, A.: *181*
Spicq, C.: *319, 329*
Sprenger, J.: *426*
Spring, G.: *175, 176*
Stagg, E.: *181, 299*

Stagg, F.: *181, 299*
Stander, H.: *195*
Stannard, U.: *483*
Steck, O.: *91, 92*
Stein, R.: *188, 193, 194*
Steinburg, N.: *44-46, 57*
Stendahl, K.: *566, 567*
Sterling, G.: *103, 232, 241, 243, 378*
Stern, H.: *27*
Sternberg, M.: *71, 79, 80*
Stitzinger, M.: *18*
Stowers, S. *313, 324*
Strack, H. L.: *288*
Strieter, T.: *89*
Strong, J.: *547*
Stuard, S. M.: *375*
Stuart, M.: *548*
Stuhlmueller, C.: *49*
Sumney, J.: *251*
Sunday, B.: *464*
Swidler, A.: *112*
Swidler, L.: *195*
Synge, F. C.: *307, 309*
Tagliacarne, P.: *114*
Talbert, C.: *189, 190, 250, 299*
Talmage, T. D.: *462*
Talmon, S.: *98, 164*
Tannehill, R.: *192*
Tanzer, S.: *200, 201, 211*
Tavard, G.: *331, 340, 445*
Tedrowe, Z. L.: *506*
Tellenbach, G.: *382*
Tetlow, E.: *195*
Teubal, S.: *39-42, 45, 46, 49-53, 57-60, 62, 63, 68*
Theissen, G.: *182, 186-188, 267, 274*
Theissen, K.: *220*
Thiselton, A.: *227*
Thomas, D.: *160*
Thomas, J. D.: *546, 549*
Thomas, L. G.: *556-559*
Thompson, C.: *314*
Thompson, J.: *563, 568*
Thrall, M.: *315*
Thurston, B. B.: *362*
Ticknor, C.: *458*
Tischleder, P.: *308, 309*

Torjesen, K.: *366, 396*
Toulmin, S.: *399*
Townsend, J.: *39*
Toy, C.: *156, 167, 177*
Treggiari, S.: *232*
Trible, P.: *8, 13-16, 18, 21-24, 26, 28, 29, 32, 35, 49, 52, 54, 59, 96, 401*
Trompf, G. W.: *311*
Tucker, R.: *239, 332*
Ullmann, S.: *227*
Ullmann, W.: *382*
Vaage, L.: *193*
Vancil, J.: *565*
van der Horst, P.: *319*
van der Toorn, K.: *95, 132*
van der Weiden, W.: *168*
van Dijk-Hemmes, F.: *134, 147*
Van Leeuwen, M.: *85*
Van Unnik, W.: *211, 304*
Van Vuuren, N.: *331*
Vawter, B.: *53, 59*
Veith, I.: *402*
Vendryes, J.: *227*
Verkamp, B.: *384*
Vermes, G.: *290, 292, 301*
Visotzky, B.: *173*
Vivano, P.: *113*
Vogels, W.: *127, 142*
von Gall, A.: *40*
von Harnack, A.: *265, 266, 272, 294*
Von Rad, G.: *23, 24, 27, 48, 61, 64, 93*
Vos, C.: *116*
Wallace, H.: *27*
Wallace, Z.: *469*
Wallerstein, J.: *90*
Walker, W. O.: *311*
Walter, J.: *121*
Walters, J.: *103, 231, 563*
Walther, J. A.: *316*
Wanamaker, C.: *253*
Waszinck, J. H.: *337, 345*
Waterman, L.: *136, 151*
Watson, J.: *120*
Watson, W.: *155, 167*
Webb, B.: *70, 74, 78*
Weber, C.: *157*

Wedderburn, A. J. M.: *264*
Weedon, W. C.: *506*
Weeks, N.: *310*
Weems, R.: *126, 138, 145, 149, 151*
Wegner, J. R.: *407*
Weiler, G.: *88, 89*
Weiss, H.-F.: *319, 329*
Weiss, J.: *255, 311, 313*
Welter, B.: *100, 446, 447, 449, 454, 486*
Weinrich, W.: *335*
Wemple, S. F.: *380, 381*
Wendland, H. D.: *308*
West, E. I.: *489*
West, R. F.: *547*
Westenholz, J.: *132*
Westermann, C.: *5, 7, 17, 22-24, 26, 27, 29, 37, 48, 50, 51, 53-56, 60, 62, 63*
White, H.: *49*
White, L. A.: *496*
White, L. M.: *267*
Whitt, W.: *129, 140, 147*
Whybray, R.: *91, 96, 162, 167, 177*
Wildberger, H.: *7, 117*
Willard, F.: *451*
Williams, D. N.: *466*
Willis, J.: *7, 19, 23, 30, 92, 147, 548, 563*
Willis, T.: *563*
Wilson, K. M.: *381*
Wilson, R. R.: *286*
Windisch, H.: *320*
Wire, A. C.: *240, 255, 297, 312*
Witherington, B.: *101, 102, 181, 262, 265, 266, 269, 276, 530, 532*
Wolfe, J. W.: *501*
Wolff, C.: *311*
Wolff, H.: *130, 131, 135, 138, 139, 147, 149*
Wolters, A.: *156, 167, 179*
Wood, F.: *394, 395*
Wood, J.: *172*
Wood, L.: *160*
Woodrow, R. E.: *546*
Wright, G.: *94*

Wright, T.: *192*
Yarbrough, L.: *246, 253*
Yee, G.: *47, 54*
Young, C. A.: *544, 545, 547*
Young, E.: *30*
Young, F.: *358, 362*
Zickmund, B. B.: *463*
Zinsser, J. P.: *402, 404, 412, 413, 419, 423, 427*